SIGLA AND SYMBOLS
IN THE TEXTUAL NOTES

The following list will help to identify editors and to locate sigla in their chronological sequence. Sigla in parentheses refer to works only occasionally consulted; they are listed on the opposite page below the list of editions collated. For full descriptions of the works, see pp. xii ff.

ALEX	Alexander, 1951	KTLY	Keightley, 1864
ARD	ARD1 & ARD2	MAL	Malone, 1790
ARD1	Hart, 1905	(mF2FL)	Anon., –1733
ARD2	Lever, 1965	(mSTAU)	Staunton, –1874
(BLAIR)	Blair, 1753	(mTHEO)	Theobald, 1723–33
BUL	Bullen, 1904	(mTBY1, 2, 3)	Thirlby, 1723–33,
CAM	CAM1, CAM2, & CAM3		1733–47, 1747–53
CAM1	Clark, Glover, & Wright,	(N&H)	Neilson-Hill, 1942
	1863	NLSN	Neilson, 1906
CAM2	Wright, 1891	(OXF1)	Craig, [1891]
CAM3	Wilson, 1922	PEL1	Bald, 1956
CAP	Capell, 1767	PEN2	Nosworthy, 1969
(CAPN)	Capell, 1779–83	POPE	POPE1 & POPE2
(CLN2)	Houghton, 1970	POPE1, 2	Pope, 1723, 1728
COL	COL1, (COL2), COL3, &	RANN	Rann, 1786
	COL4	(RID)	Ridley, 1935
COL1, (2), 3,	Collier, 1842, 1853, 1858,	(RLF1)	Rolfe, 1882
4	1875	(RLTR)	Chambers, 1906
(COLNE)	Collier, 1853	ROWE	ROWE1, ROWE2, &
(COT)	Cotgrave, 1655		ROWE3
(DAV)	Davenant, 1673	ROWE1, 2, 3	Rowe, 1709, 1709, 1714
DEL4	Delius, 1872	SING	SING1 & SING2
DYCE	DYCE1, DYCE2, & DYCE3	SING1, 2	Singer, 1826, 1856
DYCE1, 2, 3	Dyce, 1857, 1864, 1875	SIS	Sisson, 1954
(EV1)	Herford, 1899	STAU	Staunton, 1859
EVNS	Evans, 1974	THEO	THEO1, THEO2, & THEO4
Ff	F1, F2, F3, & F4	THEO1, 2, 4	Theobald, 1733, 1740,
F1, 2, 3, 4	Folios, 1623, 1632,		1757
	1663–4, 1685	(TIECK)	Tieck, 1831
(GIL)	Gildon, 1700	v1773,	Johnson & Steevens,
GLO	Clark & Wright, 1864	v1778	1773, 1778
HAL	Halliwell, 1854	v1785	Johnson, Steevens, &
HAN1, (2)	Hanmer, 1743, 1745		Reed, 1785
(HARN)	Harness, 1825	v1793	Steevens & Reed, 1793
(HENL)	Henley, 1901	v1803,	Reed, 1803, 1813
HUD(1), 2	Hudson, 1851, 1880	v1813	
IRV	Irving & Marshall, 1889	v1821	Boswell, 1821
JOHN	JOHN1 & JOHN2	(VERP)	Verplanck, 1847
JOHN1, 2	Johnson, 1765, 1765	WARB	Warburton, 1747
KIT1	Kittredge, 1936	WH	WH1 & WH2
KNT	KNT1, KNT2, & KNT3	WH1, 2	White, 1857, 1883
KNT1, 2, 3	Knight, 1840, 1842, 1867		

Symbols used in the textual notes:

^	punctuation missing or omitted
~	verbal form of lemma unchanged (while punctuation varies)
-	(between sigla) all fully collated eds. between and including those indicated by the two sigla
+	(after a siglum) and all succeeding fully collated eds.
(−)	all sigla following the minus sign within parentheses indicate eds. that agree, not with the variant, but with the Variorum text (i.e., with F1)

822.33
P2e

124723

DATE DUE			

A New Variorum Edition of Shakespeare

Founded by Horace Howard Furness (1833–1912),
continued by Horace Howard Furness, Jr. (1865–1930),
and now issued under the sponsorship of
The Modern Language Association of America.

James G. McManaway, General Editor Emeritus
Richard Knowles and Robert K. Turner, Jr.,
General Editors

A New Variorum Edition of Shakespeare

MEASURE FOR MEASURE

Edited by

MARK ECCLES

The Modern Language Association of America

Library of Congress Catalog Card No. 4-13966
ISBN 0-87352-284-2

Published by The Modern Language Association of America
62 Fifth Avenue, New York, New York 10011

ACKNOWLEDGMENTS

Atheneum Publishers for passages from *The Life of the Drama* by Eric Bentley.

The Athlone Press for passages from *Shakespeare's* Measure for Measure by Mary Lascelles.

Muriel C. Bradbrook for passages from "Authority, Truth, and Justice in *Measure for Measure*" in *Review of English Studies*, 17 (1941), 385–99.

The British Academy for passages from "The Mythical Sorrows of Shakespeare" by Charles J. Sisson in *Proceedings of the British Academy*, 20 (1934), 45–70.

The British Council for passages from *William Shakespeare: The Problem Plays* by Peter Ure.

Cambridge University Press for passages from: "The Ambiguity of *Measure for Measure*" by Lionel C. Knights in *Scrutiny*, 10 (1942), 222–33; Introduction by Arthur Quiller-Couch in *Measure for Measure*; *Shakespeare's Imagery and What It Tells Us* by Caroline F. E. Spurgeon; *Shakespeare's Stagecraft* by John L. Styan; *Measure for Measure* by John Dover Wilson and Arthur Quiller-Couch.

Jonathan Cape Ltd. and the Executors of the R. W. Chambers Estate for passages from *"Measure for Measure"* by Raymond W. Chambers in *Man's Unconquerable Mind*.

Chatto and Windus Ltd., Mrs. Q. D. Leavis, and New York University Press for passages from *"Measure for Measure"* by Frank R. Leavis in *The Common Pursuit*.

Chatto and Windus Ltd. and New Directions Publishing Corp. for passages from "Sense in *Measure for Measure*" by William Empson in *The Structure of Complex Words*. All rights reserved.

Cornell University Press for passages from *The Achievement of Shakespeare's* Measure for Measure by David L. Stevenson. Copyright © 1966 by Cornell University. Used by permission of the publisher, Cornell University Press.

Curtis Brown Ltd., for passages from *Comedy* by John Leslie Palmer.

Doubleday & Company, Inc., for excerpts from *An Approach To Shakespeare* by Derek A. Traversi. Copyright © 1960, 1969 by Derek A. Traversi. Copyright © 1956 by Doubleday & Company, Inc.

Francis Fergusson for passages from *"Measure for Measure"* in *The Human Image in Dramatic Literature*.

Harper & Row, Publishers, Inc., for passages from *Measure for Measure*, "First Folio Edition" edited by Charlotte Porter and Helen A. Clarke. Copyright 1909. By permission of Harper & Row, Publishers, Inc.

Harvard University Press for passages from *Shakespeare and the Natural Condition* by Geoffrey Bush. Copyright © 1956 by the President and Fellows of Harvard College. Reprinted by permission of Harvard University Press.

Holt, Rinehart & Winston for passages from *William Shakespeare* by John Masefield.

Hope Leresche & Sayle for passages from *The Shakespearean Ethic* by John Vyvyan.

Mark Hunter for passages from "Act- and Scene-Division in the Plays of Shakespeare" in *Review of English Studies*, 2 (1926), 295–310.

Journal of English and Germanic Philology for passages from "Scenic Design in *Measure for Measure*" by Anthony Caputi in *Journal of English and Germanic Philology*, 60 (1961), 423–34.

Longman Group Limited for passages from: "The Problem Plays" by Arthur P. Rossiter in *Angel with Horns and Other Shakespeare Lectures*; *Shakespeare* by Henri Fluchere.

The Macmillan Company of Canada Limited for excerpts from "A Shakespearean Experiment: The Dramaturgy of *Measure for Measure*" by Bernard Beckerman in *The Elizabethan Theatre II* edited by David Galloway. Reprinted by permission of the Macmillan Company of Canada Limited.

Macmillan, London and Basingstoke, for passages from *The Living Shakespeare* edited by Oscar James Campbell. By permission of Macmillan, London and Basingstoke.

James C. Maxwell for passages from "Creon and Angelo: A Parallel Study" in *Greece and Rome*, 18 (1949), 32–6.

Methuen & Company Ltd. for passages from: *The Jacobean Drama: An Interpretation* by Una M. Ellis-Fermor; *The Language of Shakespeare's Plays* by Benjamin Ifor Evans; *"Measure for Measure"* in *The New Arden Shakespeare*, edited by J. W. Lever; *Shakespeare's Wordplay* by Molly M. Mahood; *"Measure for Measure* and the Gospels" by George Wilson Knight in *The Wheel of Fire*; *Shakespeare and the Confines of Art* by Philip Edwards; "The Dark Comedies" by Henry B. Charlton in *Shakespearean Comedy*; music for *Measure for Measure* edited by Frederick W. Sternfeld in *The New Arden Shakespeare*, edited by J. W. Lever.

CONTENTS

PREFACE

This is the first edition of *Measure for Measure* to appear in the New Variorum Shakespeare. The text is a modified diplomatic reprint of the First Folio text of 1623, correcting only obvious typographical errors which do not result in forming a word. The lines of the text are numbered consecutively in accordance with the Through Line numbering proposed by R. B. McKerrow in 1939 (*Prolegomena,* pp. 60–2) and adopted in the Norton facsimile of F1 and in the *Oxford Shakespeare Concordances.* With the permission of W. W. Norton & Company, this numbering is used in all references to this play and is supplied, in addition to conventional act-scene-line numbers, in all citations of Shakespeare's other plays. The Globe act-scene-line numbers for the lines of this play are indicated in the running head for each page.

Variorum editions have given me great pleasure ever since my boyhood, when I first discovered Furness at the Washington Public Library. Later Hyder Rollins, then General Editor, let me choose my play and I began to edit it in 1949. Most of the next thirty years was spent in teaching, with intervals to write *Shakespeare in Warwickshire* and to edit *Richard III* and *The Macro Plays,* but editing went on with the aid of generous grants from the Graduate School of the University of Wisconsin and the rich resources of the Memorial Library of the University of Wisconsin at Madison and the Folger Shakespeare Library in Washington.

My warmest thanks for help and advice go to Fredson Bowers, Davy Carozza, Madeleine Doran, Gwynne Blakemore Evans, Margaret Ferguson, Vivian Foss, George Geckle, Richard Hosley, Trevor Howard-Hill, Susan McLeod, James G. McManaway, Andrew J. Sabol, S. Schoenbaum, Charles Shattuck, John Hazel Smith, and especially to Robert K. Turner, Jr., and Richard Knowles, General Editors.

This book is for the great variety of readers, but first of all it is for Elisabeth Norris Eccles.

M. E.

Madison
March 1978

ix

PLAN OF THE WORK

The four main parts of this edition are (1) the text of *Measure for Measure* reprinted from the First Folio edition of 1623, (2) textual notes indicating all significant departures from that text in important editions of the play, (3) a commentary on the text designed to help in explaining its language and to sum up all notes of any value for understanding particular words or lines, and (4) an appendix discussing the text, date of composition, sources, analogues, influences, and music, reprinting sources and critical opinions selected to illustrate the history of criticism of the play, and providing a calendar of stage performances.

The text is a modified diplomatic reprint of that in the Norton facsimile of F1, prepared by Charlton Hinman from copies in the Folger Shakespeare Library. The reprint does not reproduce typographical features such as the long *s*, display and swash letters, and ornaments; abbreviations printed as one letter above another are reproduced as two consecutive letters, the second one superscript. Minor typographical blemishes such as irregular spacing, printing space-types, and wrong-font, damaged, turned, transposed, misprinted, or clearly erroneous or missing letters or punctuation marks have been corrected. If, however, the anomaly is likely to have any bibliographical significance, its correction is recorded in the appendix. Where the error is not clearly typographical, the text has been left unaltered and emendations have been recorded in the textual notes. The F1 lineation of both verse and prose has been preserved, except that a few turned-over lines have been printed continuously; such alteration has been recorded in the appendix. When a verse line occupies two lines of type, it is printed as one, a vertical stroke indicating the end of the first type line. In general, the attempt has been made to omit and ignore all insignificant typographical peculiarities, but to retain or at least record the alteration of any accidental details of possible textual significance.

Through Line Numbers (TLNs) are printed by fives in the right margin; these numbers are used for all notes and cross-references in the edition. Inclusive Globe act-scene-line numbers as determined by the 1891 edition are supplied in arabic numerals in the headline of each page of text, and

Globe act-and-scene division is indicated by boldface arabic numerals in the right margin. The beginning of each Folio column is marked in the right margin by signature-and-column indicators in parentheses.

The textual notes are based on a collation of the following editions. Each entry below is preceded by the siglum which represents that edition in the textual notes. All these editions have been fully collated. The place of publication is not mentioned when it is London.

F2	THE SECOND FOLIO. M^r. *William Shakespeares Comedies, Histories, and Tragedies. . . . The second Impression.*	1632
F3	THE THIRD FOLIO. M^r. *William Shakespear's Comedies, Histories, and Tragedies. . . . The third Impression.*	1663–4
F4	THE FOURTH FOLIO. M^r. *William Shakespear's Comedies, Histories, and Tragedies. . . . The Fourth Edition.*	1685
ROWE1	NICHOLAS ROWE. *Works.* 6 vols. 1709. Vol. 1.	1709
ROWE2	NICHOLAS ROWE. *Works.* 6 vols. 1709. Vol. 1.	1709
ROWE3	NICHOLAS ROWE. *Works.* 8 vols. 1714. Vol. 1.	1714
POPE1	ALEXANDER POPE. *Works.* 6 vols. 1723–5. Vol. 1.	1723
POPE2	ALEXANDER POPE. *Works.* 2nd ed. 8 vols. 1728. Vol. 1.	1728
THEO1	LEWIS THEOBALD. *Works.* 7 vols. 1733. Vol. 1.	1733
THEO2	LEWIS THEOBALD. *Works.* 2nd ed. 8 vols. 1740. Vol. 1.	1740
HAN1	THOMAS HANMER. *Works.* 6 vols. Oxford, 1743–4. Vol. 1.	1743
WARB	WILLIAM WARBURTON. *Works.* 8 vols. 1747. Vol. 1.	1747
THEO4	LEWIS THEOBALD. *Works.* 8 vols. 1757. Vol. 1.	1757
JOHN1	SAMUEL JOHNSON. *Plays.* 8 vols. Printed for J. and R. Tonson, C. Corbet . . . , 1765. Vol. 1.	1765
JOHN2	SAMUEL JOHNSON. *Plays.* 8 vols. Printed for J. and R. Tonson, H. Woodfall . . . , 1765. Vol. 1.	1765
CAP	EDWARD CAPELL. *Comedies, Histories, & Tragedies.* 10 vols. [1767–8.] Vol. 2.	1767
v1773	SAMUEL JOHNSON & GEORGE STEEVENS. *Plays.* 10 vols. 1773. Vol. 2.	1773
v1778	SAMUEL JOHNSON & GEORGE STEEVENS. *Plays.* 10 vols. 1778. Vol. 2.	1778
v1785	SAMUEL JOHNSON, GEORGE STEEVENS, & ISAAC REED. *Plays.* 10 vols. 1785. Vol. 2.	1785
RANN	JOSEPH RANN. *Dramatic Works.* 6 vols. Oxford, 1786–[94]. Vol. 1.	1786
MAL	EDMOND MALONE. *Plays & Poems.* 10 vols. 1790. Vol. 2.	1790

v1793	GEORGE STEEVENS & ISAAC REED. *Plays.* 15 vols. 1793. Vol. 4.	1793
v1803	ISAAC REED. *Plays.* 21 vols. 1803. Vol. 6.	1803
v1813	ISAAC REED. *Plays.* 21 vols. 1813. Vol. 6.	1813
v1821	JAMES BOSWELL. *Plays & Poems.* 21 vols. 1821. Vol. 9.	1821
SING1	SAMUEL W. SINGER. *Dramatic Works.* 10 vols. Chiswick, 1826. Vol. 2.	1826
KNT1	CHARLES KNIGHT. *Comedies, Histories, Tragedies, & Poems.* Pictorial Ed. 55 parts. [1838–43.] Reissued in 8 vols. Part 29 (vol. 2).	1840
KNT2	CHARLES KNIGHT. *Comedies, Histories, Tragedies, & Poems.* 2nd ed. 12 vols. 1842–4. Vol. 3.	1842
COL1	JOHN PAYNE COLLIER. *Works.* 8 vols. 1842–4. Vol. 2.	1842
HAL	JAMES O. HALLIWELL. *Works.* 16 vols. 1853–65. Vol. 3.	1854
SING2	SAMUEL W. SINGER. *Dramatic Works.* 10 vols. 1856. Vol. 1.	1856
DYCE1	ALEXANDER DYCE. *Works.* 6 vols. 1857. Vol. 1.	1857
WH1	RICHARD GRANT WHITE. *Works.* 12 vols. Boston, 1857–66. Vol. 3.	1857
COL3	JOHN PAYNE COLLIER. *Comedies, Histories, Tragedies, & Poems.* "The Second Edition." 6 vols. 1858. Vol. 1.	1858
STAU	HOWARD STAUNTON. *Plays.* 3 vols. 1858–60. Vol. 2.	1859
CAM1	WILLIAM GEORGE CLARK, JOHN GLOVER, & WILLIAM ALDIS WRIGHT. *Works.* Cambridge Sh. 9 vols. Cambridge & London, 1863–6. Vol. 1.	1863
GLO	WILLIAM GEORGE CLARK & WILLIAM ALDIS WRIGHT. *Works.* Globe Ed. Cambridge & London.	1864
KTLY	THOMAS KEIGHTLEY. *Plays.* 6 vols. 1864. Vol. 2.	1864
DYCE2	ALEXANDER DYCE. *Works.* 2nd ed. 9 vols. 1864–7. Vol. 1.	1864
KNT3	CHARLES KNIGHT. *Works.* Pictorial Ed. "The Second Edition, Revised." 8 vols. 1867. Vol. 2.	1867
DEL4	NICOLAUS DELIUS. *Werke.* "Dritte, Revidirte Auflage." 2 vols. Elberfeld, 1872. Vol. 1.	1872
DYCE3	ALEXANDER DYCE. *Works.* 3rd ed. 9 vols. 1875–6. Vol. 1.	1875
COL4	JOHN PAYNE COLLIER. *Plays & Poems.* 8 vols. 1875–8. Vol. 1.	1875
HUD2	HENRY N. HUDSON. *Works.* Harvard Ed. 20 vols. Boston, 1880–1. Vol. 6.	1880

WH2	RICHARD GRANT WHITE. *Comedies, Histories, Tragedies, & Poems.* Riverside Sh. 6 vols. Boston, 1883. Vol. 1.	1883
IRV	HENRY IRVING & FRANK MARSHALL. *Works.* Henry Irving Sh. 8 vols. New York, 1888–90. Vol. 5.	1889
CAM2	WILLIAM ALDIS WRIGHT. *Works.* Cambridge Sh., 2nd ed. 9 vols. 1891–3. Vol. 1.	1891
BUL	A. H. BULLEN. *Works.* Stratford Town Ed. 10 vols. Stratford-on-Avon, 1904–7. Vol. 1.	1904
ARD1	H. C. HART. *MM.* Arden Sh.	1905
NLSN	WILLIAM ALLAN NEILSON. *Works.* Cambridge Ed. Boston.	1906
CAM3	ARTHUR QUILLER-COUCH & JOHN DOVER WILSON. *MM.* New Cambridge Sh. Cambridge.	1922
KIT1	GEORGE LYMAN KITTREDGE. *Works.* Boston.	1936
ALEX	PETER ALEXANDER. *Works.*	1951
SIS	CHARLES JASPER SISSON. *Works.*	1954
PEL1	R. C. BALD. *MM.* Pelican Sh. Baltimore.	1956
ARD2	J. W. LEVER. *MM.* New Arden Sh.	1965
PEN2	J. M. NOSWORTHY. *MM.* New Penguin Sh.	1969
EVNS	G. BLAKEMORE EVANS et al. *Works.* Riverside Sh. Boston.	1974

The following editions, books, and manuscripts are occasionally quoted in the textual notes, and some of them in the commentary or appendix:

COT	JOHN COTGRAVE. *The English Treasury of Wit and Language.*	1655
DAV	WILLIAM DAVENANT. *The Law against Lovers.* In *Works,* Part 2.	1673
GIL	CHARLES GILDON. *Measure for Measure.*	1700
mF2FL	MS notes in F2, Copy 21, Folger Library.	–1733
mTHEO	LEWIS THEOBALD. MS notes in F2, Copy 20, Folger Library.	1723–33
mTBY1	STYAN THIRLBY. MS notes in Pope's 1723 ed., Yale Library.	1723–33
mTBY2	STYAN THIRLBY. MS notes in Theobald's 1733 ed., Folger Library.	1733–47
HAN2	THOMAS HANMER. *Works.* 6 vols. 1745. Vol. 1.	1745
mTBY3	STYAN THIRLBY. MS notes in Warburton's 1747 ed., Folger Library.	1747–53
BLAIR	[HUGH BLAIR.] *Works.* 8 vols. Edinburgh, 1753. Vol. 1.	1753
CAPN	EDWARD CAPELL. *Notes and Various Readings to Shakespeare.* 3 vols.	1779–83

HARN	WILLIAM HARNESS. *Dramatic Works.* 8 vols. 1825–30. Vol. 2.	1825
TIECK	LUDWIG TIECK. *Dramatische Werke.* Tr. A. W. von Schlegel. 9 vols. Berlin, 1825–33. Vol. 5.	1831
VERP	GULIAN C. VERPLANCK. *Plays.* Illustrated Sh. 3 vols. New York, 1847. Vol. 2.	1847
HUD1	HENRY N. HUDSON. *Works.* 11 vols. Boston & Cambridge, Mass., 1851–6. Vol. 2.	1851
COLNE	JOHN PAYNE COLLIER. *Notes and Emendations.* 2nd ed., rev. & enl. 1853. (1st ed. 1852.)	1853
COL2	JOHN PAYNE COLLIER. *Plays.*	1853
mSTAU	HOWARD STAUNTON. MS notes, copied by P. A. Daniel, in Staunton's 1864 ed., vol. 3, Folger Library.	–1874
RLF1	WILLIAM J. ROLFE. *MM.* New York.	1882
OXF1	W. J. CRAIG. *Works.* Oxford Sh.	[1891]
EV1	C. H. HERFORD. *Works.* Eversley Ed. 10 vols. 1899. Vol. 3.	1899
HENL	W. E. HENLEY. *Works.* Edinburgh Folio Ed. 10 vols. Edinburgh, 1901–4. Vol. 1.	1901
RLTR	E. K. CHAMBERS. *MM.* Red Letter Sh.	1906
RID	M. R. RIDLEY. *MM.* New Temple Sh.	1935
N&H	WILLIAM ALLAN NEILSON & CHARLES J. HILL. *Plays & Poems.* Cambridge, Mass.	1942
CLN2	R. E. C. HOUGHTON. *MM.* New Clarendon Sh. Oxford.	1970

The following editions are occasionally quoted in the commentary and the appendix only, and hence are not assigned sigla:

FRANCIS GENTLEMAN. *Plays.* Bell's Ed. 9 vols. [1773–4.] Vol. 3.	1773
MRS. [ELIZABETH] INCHBALD. *MM.* British Theatre.	1808
THOMAS BOWDLER. *The Family Shakespeare.* 2nd ed. 10 vols. 1820. Vol. 2.	1820
P. P. *MM.* Oxberry's New Eng. Drama.	1822
GEORGE DANIEL. *MM.* Cumberland's Brit. Theatre.	1826
R. H. H[ORNE]. *MM.* In *The Illustrated Shakspere, from designs by Kenny Meadows.* 3 vols. 1840–3. Vol. 1.	1840
CHARLES KNIGHT. *The Stratford Shakspere.* 20 vols. 1854–6. Vol. 2.	1854
NICOLAUS DELIUS. *Werke.* 7 vols. Elberfeld, 1854–[61]. Vol. 6.	1860
FRANÇOIS-VICTOR HUGO. *Œuvres.* 18 vols. Paris, 1859–66. Vol. 10.	1862

CHARLES & MARY COWDEN CLARKE. *Plays.* Cassell's
    Illustrated Sh. 3 vols. [1864–8.] Vol. 1.   [1864]
JOHN HUNTER. *MM.* Longmans Sh.   1873
F. J. FURNIVALL. *Works.* Leopold Sh.   1877
WILHELM WAGNER. *Works.* 12 vols. (3–12 with L.
    Proescholdt). Hamburg, 1879–91. Vol. 1.   1880
HENRY MORLEY. *MM.* Cassell's National Library.   1889
ISRAEL GOLLANCZ. *MM.* Temple Ed.   1894
WILLIAM J. ROLFE. *MM.* New York.   1905
SIDNEY LEE. *MM.* Renaissance Sh.   1907
CHARLOTTE PORTER & HELEN A. CLARKE. *MM.* First
    Folio Ed. New York.   1909
EDGAR C. MORRIS. *MM.* Tudor Sh. New York.   1912
WILLARD HIGLEY DURHAM. *MM.* Yale Sh. New Haven.   1926
THOMAS MARC PARROTT. *Twenty-three Plays and the Sonnets.*
    New York.   1938
MARIO PRAZ. *Misura per misura.* Firenze.   1939
G. B. HARRISON. *23 Plays and the Sonnets.* New York.   1948
OSCAR JAMES CAMPBELL. *The Living Shakespeare.* New York.   1949
HARDIN CRAIG. *Works.* Chicago.   1951
DAVIS HARDING. *MM.* New Yale Sh. New Haven.   1954
G. B. HARRISON. *MM.* Penguin Sh.   1954
MICHEL GRIVELET. *Mesure pour mesure.* Collection bilingue
    des classiques étrangers. Paris.   1957
JOHN MUNRO. *Works.* London Sh. 6 vols. 1957. Vol. 2.   1957
JAMES WINNY. *MM.* Hutchinson Eng. Texts.   1959
HAROLD HOBSON. *MM.* Folio Society Ed.   1964
ERNST LEISI. *MM: An Old-Spelling and Old-Meaning Edition.*
    Heidelberg.   1964
DIETER MEHL. In *Mass für Mass.* Ed. L. L. Schücking.
    München.   1964
S. NAGARAJAN. *MM.* Signet Classic Sh. New York.   1964
J. G. SAUNDERS. *MM.* London Eng. Lit. Ser.   1971

A conjectural emendation is recorded in the textual notes only if an
editor subsequently printed such a reading in his text. A few unadopted
conjectures of special interest are discussed in the commentary notes; all
other unadopted conjectures are listed in the appendix.

    The textual notes record substantive or semisubstantive variants from
the Variorum text in the editions collated—that is, either substitutions, omissions, additions, or reorderings of words or passages, or else such changes
of details of spelling, typography, spacing, and lineation as significantly affect
meaning or meter. Misprints go unnoticed unless they create a word in the
English vocabulary or unless they appear to have been taken for a legitimate
word by being repeated in one or more of the four Shakespeare folios.

Variant or modernized spellings are ignored. Variant punctuation is recorded only when meaning is affected. Thus the fact that in various editions an independent clause ends with a comma, semicolon, colon, dash, or period is ignored if the meaning of the sentence or speech is unchanged thereby except in minor degrees of pace or emphasis, whereas a change from comma to semicolon that alters modification is recorded. Similarly, it is not recorded that an obvious rhetorical question is marked with a period in some texts, but a period that distinguishes between a declarative and an interrogative sentence is recorded. Lining which affects meter—i.e., the relining of verse as prose, or of prose as verse, or of verse as different verse—is recorded; the elision or expansion of syllables for metrical purposes, or the addition of diacritical marks to locate accent, is recorded only if the alteration displaces the accent from one syllable to another or changes the number of metrical feet in a line—i.e., if it significantly affects the meter rather than merely making the metrical pattern more obvious.

Variants in the accessories are recorded somewhat more selectively than those in the text proper. Added stage directions which describe action clearly implied by the text are ignored, as are directions for insignificant bits of stage business or those intended merely as props to a reader's imagination. Variants which affect only secondary details of a stage direction are also ignored; in some cases the abbreviation *subst.* is employed to indicate substantial agreement among editions despite differences of detail. All differences about who enters or exits or when he does so, or about stage business that affects the interpretation of a speech or scene, are recorded. Only those variant speech-prefixes which imply disagreement as to the identity of the speaker are recorded; variants of the form or spelling of the prefix are ignored. Variant scene divisions and numberings are recorded, but not alternative ways of indicating these differences. Added and variant indications of locale are recorded, but not the different ways of indicating and particularizing the same place.

A variant reading in the textual notes appears in the form printed in the first edition to adopt that reading; insignificant variations in the spelling, punctuation, typography, spacing, and lineation of the reading in later editions are not recorded. Thus a variant given as "I, F3 +" does not imply that all editions from F3 onwards print "I," in precisely that form: later renditions of the reading may be spelled "Ay" or punctuated "Ay;" or "Ay.", but as these variations do not affect the meaning they are not recorded. When a variant is only a matter of the punctuation after a word, the word in the lemma is not repeated in the note but is replaced by the lemma sign (—), and the absence of punctuation in either lemma or variant is indicated by a caret (ʌ). Thus "(if you be)] ʌ — ~ — ʌ POPE; ʌ — ~ — ! KTLY" indicates that Pope differs significantly from F1 at this point only in omitting parentheses, and Keightley only in omitting parentheses and adding an exclamation mark.

Four kinds of formulae are used in the textual notes as space-saving devices to avoid listing a long series of sigla for editions that agree on a reading:

1) When all editions after a certain one agree with that edition, the agreement is shown by a plus sign after its siglum. Thus ROWE1 + means that all editions collated from Rowe's first edition of 1709 through Evans's edition of 1974 agree substantially with Rowe's text at this point.

2) The abbreviation *etc.* after a siglum for an edition means that all editions collated that are not otherwise accounted for in the note agree with that edition. Thus "againe] F1, SIS, ARD2, EVNS; in again CAM3; backe againe F2 *etc.*" means that every edition but F1 and the editions of Sisson, Lever, Evans, and Wilson agrees substantially with F2.

3) The agreement of three or more editions in chronological succession is indicated by a hyphen between the sigla of the first and last editions in the series. Thus "POPE1-CAP" indicates the agreement of all collated editions from Pope's first edition through Capell's edition.

4) The agreement of a "family" of related editions—i.e., editions by the same editor or bearing the same name—is indicated by the siglum root for that family. Thus THEO indicates the agreement of all editions by Theobald that were collated (THEO1, THEO2, THEO4), CAM the agreement of all "Cambridge" editions collated.

A siglum printed in parentheses and with a minus sign after any of the first three of the above kinds of formulae indicates an exceptional edition in the succession whose text agrees with F1 rather than with the variant in question. Thus "ROWE1 + (−CAP, EVNS)" indicates the agreement of all editions from ROWE1 onwards except for those of Capell and Evans, which agree with F1.

To facilitate the interpretation of the formulae—e.g., to enable the reader to see quickly which fully collated editions are included in such a formula as "ROWE1-SIS"—a chronological list of sigla is provided inside the front and back covers of this edition. An alphabetical list of sigla on the facing pages both identifies the editors and gives the date by which any siglum may be located in the chronological list.

The commentary seeks not only to elucidate the text but also at times to trace the history of the interpretation of the word or passage. Since the commentary can include only a selection from all that has been written about this play, the responsibility for the selection is the editor's. All quotations are enclosed in quotation marks (to set them off from paraphrase or from the present editor's comments) and are reproduced as in the source, except that titles of plays or books are printed in italic and obvious typographical errors are corrected. Omissions within quotations are indicated by points of suspension; when such omissions remove the beginning or end of a sentence but still leave a sentence complete in itself, that remaining sentence is silently given an initial capital or a final period. Quotations made by the commentators have been verified and, where necessary, corrected within square brackets. The commentators' references to passages in this play by act, scene, and line have been replaced by Through Line Numbers within brackets, and quotations of more than a few words from this play have generally been omitted and replaced by a cross-reference, of Through Line Numbers within brackets, to the appropriate passage in this edition. In references to Shakespeare's other plays, Globe act-scene-line numbers are followed by Through Line Numbers within parentheses or square brackets. Quotations from Shakespeare's Poems or Sonnets are made to conform to the texts of the New Variorum edition, and those from the plays, to the most authoritative folio or quarto text; specifically, the following plays are quoted from the best quarto rather than from F1: *Ado, 1H4, 2H4, Ham., LLL, MND, MV, Oth., Per., R2* (+F1), *Rom., Tit., TNK,* and *Tro.* All biblical quotations are printed in the language of the Geneva Bible (ed. 1583) unless some other version is specified.

The notes printed in the commentary are as a rule identified only by the commentator's last name and the date of his book or article; further information is given only when two works of the same date are drawn upon. Full identification will be found in the bibliography at p. 483 or in the lists of editions printed above. Since arabic numerals are used in preference to roman numerals wherever possible, volume-and-page citations appear in the form 9:14 instead of IX, 14. All statements in the commentary not otherwise assigned and all information within square brackets [ ] are the contribution of the editor. When square brackets appear in the work quoted, they have been changed to pointed brackets < >. When the note gives a main entry for Johnson (1755 or 1773), Schmidt, *OED,* or any other dictionary, the dictionary quotes or cites the word from this play. When it does not cite this play, a possible meaning (not necessarily the only one, since a word may suggest more than one sense) is indicated in such a form as "see *OED* (*v.* 1)," "cf. *OED* (*a.* 2)," or "(*OED, sb.* 3a)."

The commentary quotes from and cites the following standard editions unless a different edition is specified:

FRANCIS BEAUMONT & JOHN FLETCHER. *Dramatic Works in the Beaumont and Fletcher Canon.* Gen. ed. Fredson Bowers. Vols. 1–3. Cambridge, 1966–76.

GEORGE CHAPMAN. *Plays and Poems.* Ed. Thomas Marc Parrott. Vols. 1–2. 1910–14.

THOMAS DEKKER. *Dramatic Works.* Ed. Fredson Bowers. 4 vols. Cambridge, 1953–61.

Ben Jonson. Ed. C. H. Herford & Percy & Evelyn Simpson. 11 vols. Oxford, 1925–52.

JOHN LYLY. *Complete Works.* Ed. R. Warwick Bond. 3 vols. Oxford, 1902.

CHRISTOPHER MARLOWE. *Complete Works.* Ed. Fredson Bowers. 2 vols. Cambridge, 1973.

JOHN MARSTON. *Works.* Ed. A. H. Bullen. 3 vols. 1887.

THOMAS MIDDLETON. *Works.* Ed. A. H. Bullen. 8 vols. 1885–6.
THOMAS NASHE. *Works.* Ed. R. B. McKerrow. 5 vols. 1904–10.
The Shakespeare Apocrypha. Ed. C. F. Tucker Brooke. Oxford, 1908.
JOHN WEBSTER. *Complete Works.* Ed. F. L. Lucas. 4 vols. 1927.

    The style of quotation and citation used in the commentary is used also in the appendix.

    The following list of abbreviations and symbols used in this edition does not include many which are in common use or whose full form should be immediately apparent:

a	(in a signature, superscript) left-hand column
a(dj).	adjective, -al
ad.	(in a textual note) added
Add(l).	Addition(al)
Ado	*Much Ado about Nothing*
adv(b).	adverb, -ial
ALEX	P. Alexander's ed., 1951
Ant.	*Antony and Cleopatra*
app.	appendix
Archiv	*Archiv für das Studium der Neueren Sprachen und Literaturen*
ARD	ARD1 and ARD2
ARD1	Arden Sh., ed. H. C. Hart, 1905
ARD2	Arden Sh., ed. J. W. Lever, 1965
A.V.	Authorized Version
AWW	*All's Well that Ends Well*
AYL	*As You Like It*
b	(in a signature, superscript) right-hand column
BLAIR	H. Blair's ed., 1753
BUL	A. H. Bullen's ed., 1904–7
c.	century; circa
CAM	CAM1, CAM2, and CAM3
CAM1	Cambridge Sh., ed. W. G. Clark, J. Glover, & W. A. Wright, 1863–6
CAM2	Cambridge Sh., 2nd ed., ed. W. A. Wright, 1891–3
CAM3	New Cambridge Sh., ed. A. Quiller-Couch & J. D. Wilson, 1922
CAP	E. Capell's ed., [1767–8]
CAPN	E. Capell's *Notes and Various Readings,* 1779–83
ch(s).	chapter(s)
CLN2	New Clarendon Sh., ed. R. E. C. Houghton, 1970
COL	COL1, COL3, and COL4
COL1	J. P. Collier's ed., 1842–4
COL2	J. P. Collier's ed., 1853

COL3	J. P. Collier's ed., 1858
COL4	J. P. Collier's ed., 1875–8
col(s).	column(s)
COLNE	J. P. Collier's *Notes and Emendations,* 2nd ed., 1853
Comp.	Comparative
CompD	*Comparative Drama*
conj.	conjecture; conjunction
conj. in	conjecture published in
Cor.	*Coriolanus*
COT	J. Cotgrave, *The English Treasury of Wit and Language,* 1655
CritQ	*Critical Quarterly*
C.T.	*Canterbury Tales*
Cym.	*Cymbeline*
DA(I)	*Dissertation Abstracts (International)*
DAV	W. Davenant, *The Law against Lovers,* 1673
DEL4	N. Delius's ed., 1872
dem.	demonstrative
dial.	dialect
diss.	dissertation
DYCE	DYCE1, DYCE2, and DYCE3
DYCE1	A. Dyce's ed., 1857
DYCE2	A. Dyce's ed., 1864–7
DYCE3	A. Dyce's ed., 1875–6
EA	*Etudes Anglaises*
E&S	*Essays and Studies by Members of the English Association*
ed.	edited by, edition, editor
EIC	*Essays in Criticism*
ELH	*Journal of English Literary History*
ELN	*English Language Notes*
ELR	*English Literary Renaissance*
Eng.	English
EngRev	*English Review*
enl.	enlarged
Err.	*The Comedy of Errors*
ESA	*English Studies in Africa*
ESn	*Englische Studien*
etc.	*et cetera,* and others, and so forth; (in a textual note) all other fully collated editions
EV1	C. H. Herford's Eversley ed., 1899
EVNS	Riverside Sh., textual ed. G. B. Evans, 1974
Expl	*Explicator*
F, F., F1	First Folio (1623)
F2	Second Folio (1632)
F3	Third Folio (1663–4)

F4	Fourth Folio (1685)
facs.	facsimile
Ff	F1, F2, F3, and F4
fig.	figurative, -ly
fol(s).	folio(s), leaf (leaves)
F.Q.	*Faerie Queene*
Fr.	French
Ger.	German
GIL	C. Gildon, *Measure for Measure,* 1700
GLO	Globe Sh., ed. W. G. Clark & W. A. Wright, 1864
GR	*Germanic Review*
1H4	*1 Henry IV*
2H4	*2 Henry IV*
H5	*Henry V*
1H6	*1 Henry VI*
2H6	*2 Henry VI*
3H6	*3 Henry VI*
H8	*Henry VIII*
HAL	J. O. Halliwell's ed., 1853–65
Ham.	*Hamlet*
HAN1	T. Hanmer's ed., 1743–4
HAN2	T. Hanmer's ed., 1745
HARN	W. Harness's ed., 1825–30
HENL	W. E. Henley's ed., 1901–4
HUD1	H. N. Hudson's ed., 1851–6
HUD2	H. N. Hudson's ed., 1880–1
impers.	impersonal
indic.	indicative
inf.	infinitive
int(erj).	interjection, -al
intr.	intransitive
IRV	Henry Irving Sh., ed. H. Irving & F. Marshall, 1888–90
It.	Italian
JC	*Julius Caesar*
JEGP	*Journal of English and Germanic Philology*
Jn.	*King John*
JOHN	JOHN1 and JOHN2
JOHN1	S. Johnson's 1st ed., 1765
JOHN2	S. Johnson's 2nd ed., 1765
KIT1	G. L. Kittredge's ed., 1936
KNT	KNT1, KNT2, and KNT3
KNT1	C. Knight's ed., [1838–43]
KNT2	C. Knight's ed., 1842–4
KNT3	C. Knight's ed., 1867

KTLY	T. Keightley's ed., 1864
Lang.	Language
lib.	book, library
Lit.	Literature
LLL	*Love's Labour's Lost*
Lr.	*King Lear*
Luc.	*The Rape of Lucrece*
Mac.	*Macbeth*
MAL	E. Malone's ed., 1790
ME	Middle English
mF2FL	MS notes (–1733) in F2, Copy 21, Folger Library
MLN	*Modern Language Notes*
MLQ	*Modern Language Quarterly*
MLR	*Modern Language Review*
MM	*Measure for Measure*
MND	*A Midsummer Night's Dream*
MP	*Modern Philology*
MSC	Malone Society Collections
MSR	Malone Society Reprint
mSTAU	H. Staunton's MS notes (–1874) in his 1864 ed.
mTHEO	L. Theobald's MS notes (1723–33) in F2, Copy 20, Folger Library
mTBY1	S. Thirlby's MS notes in POPE1, 1723–33
mTBY2	S. Thirlby's MS notes in THEO1, 1733–47
mTBY3	S. Thirlby's MS notes in WARB, 1747–53
MV	*The Merchant of Venice*
n(n).	note(s)
N&H	W. A. Neilson ed., rev. C. J. Hill, 1942
N&Q	*Notes and Queries*
N.C.S.	New Cambridge Sh. (CAM3)
N.E.D.	*See OED*
n.F.	*neue Folge,* new series
NLSN	W. A. Neilson's Cambridge ed., 1906
NS	new series
NS	*Die Neueren Sprachen*
N.S.S.	*New Shakspere Society*
N.T.	New Testament
NYT	*New York Times*
NYTCR	*New York Theatre Critics' Reviews*
obs.	obsolete
occas.	occasionally
OE	Old English
OED	*Oxford English Dictionary,* originally published as *A New English Dictionary* and abbreviated *N.E.D.*
om.	omitted

Oth.	*Othello*
OUP	Oxford University Press
OXF1	Oxford Sh., ed. W. J. Craig, [1891]
pa.	past
PBA	*Proceedings of the British Academy*
PBSA	*Papers of the Bibliographical Society of America*
PEL1	Pelican Sh., ed. R. C. Bald, 1956
PEN2	Penguin Sh., ed. J. M. Nosworthy, 1969
Per.	*Pericles*
pers.	person, -al
phr.	phrase
P.L.	*Paradise Lost*
PMLA	*Publications of the Modern Language Association of America*
poet.	poetical
POPE	POPE1 and POPE2
POPE1	A. Pope's ed., 1723–5
POPE2	A. Pope's ed., 1728
poss.	possessive
PP	*Plays and Players*
ppl. a.	participial adjective
pple.	participle
PQ	*Philological Quarterly*
prep.	preposition
prob.	probably
Proc.	*Proceedings*
Prol.	Prologue
pron.	pronoun
pt(s).	part(s)
pub.	public, publication, published
Q	Quarto
r	(in a signature or folio, superscript) recto
R2	*Richard II*
R3	*Richard III*
RAA	*Revue Anglo-Américaine*
RANN	J. Rann's ed., 1786–[94]
RCC	*Revue des Cours et Conférences*
refl.	reflexive
Ren.	Renaissance
RES	*Review of English Studies*
rev.	revised
RID	M. R. Ridley's New Temple Sh., 1935
RLC	*Revue de Littérature Comparée*
RLF1	W. J. Rolfe's ed., 1882
RLTR	E. K. Chambers's Red Letter ed., 1906
Rom.	*Romeo and Juliet*

ROWE	ROWE1, ROWE2, and ROWE3
ROWE1	N. Rowe's 1st ed., 1709
ROWE2	N. Rowe's 2nd ed., 1709
ROWE3	N. Rowe's ed., 1714
rpt.	reprint, -ed
RR	*Romanic Review*
SB	*Studies in Bibliography*
sb.	substantive
SD(s)	stage direction(s)
ser.	series
Sh(n).	Shakespeare(an) (any spelling)
ShAB	*Shakespeare Association Bulletin*
ShakS	*Shakespeare Studies*
Sh. Apoc.	*Shakespeare Apocrypha*
ShN	*Shakespeare Newsletter*
Shr.	*The Taming of the Shrew*
ShS	*Shakespeare Survey*
sig(s).	signature(s)
SING	SING1 and SING2
SING1	S. W. Singer's ed., 1826
SING2	S. W. Singer's ed., 1856
SIS	C. J. Sisson's ed., 1954
SJ	*Shakespeare-Jahrbuch*
SJH	*Shakespeare-Jahrbuch* (Heidelberg)
SJW	*Shakespeare-Jahrbuch* (Weimar)
Son.	*Sonnets*
SP	*Studies in Philology*
SP(s)	speech-prefix(es)
SQ	*Shakespeare Quarterly*
SR	*Sewanee Review*
STAU	H. Staunton's ed., 1858–60
STC	*Short-title Catalogue* (by A. W. Pollard & G. R. Redgrave)
Stud.	Studies
subst.	substantially
t.	tense
TGV	*The Two Gentlemen of Verona*
Th.	Theater, Theatre
THEO	THEO1, THEO2, and THEO4
THEO1	L. Theobald's ed., 1733
THEO2	L. Theobald's ed., 1740
THEO4	L. Theobald's ed., 1757
ThN	*Theatre Notebook*
ThW	*Theatre World* (London, American ed.)
ThWN	*Theatre World* (New York)

TIECK	L. Tieck's revision of A. W. von Schlegel's tr., 1825–33
Tim.	*Timon of Athens*
Tit.	*Titus Andronicus*
TLN	Through Line Number, numbering
TLS	London *Times Literary Supplement*
Tmp.	*The Tempest*
TN	*Twelfth Night*
tr.	translated by, translation, translator
Trans.	*Transactions*
trans.	transitive
transf.	transferred sense
Tro.	*Troilus and Cressida*
(u)	(in citing press-variants) uncorrected
UTQ	*University of Toronto Quarterly*
v	(in a signature or folio, superscript) verso
v.	verb; verse; vide
v1773	S. Johnson & G. Steevens's ed., 1773
v1778	S. Johnson & G. Steevens's ed., 1778
v1785	S. Johnson, G. Steevens, & I. Reed's ed., 1785
v1793	G. Steevens & I. Reed's ed., 1793
v1803	I. Reed's ed., 1803
v1813	I. Reed's ed., 1813
v1821	J. Boswell's ed., 1821
Var.	Variorum
vbl. sb.	verbal substantive
Ven.	*Venus and Adonis*
VERP	G. C. Verplanck's ed., 1847
VLit	*Vierteljahrschrift für Litteraturgeschichte*
V. R.	*Various Readings* in E. Capell's *Notes and Various Readings,* 1779–83
WARB	W. Warburton's ed., 1747
WH	WH1 and WH2
WH1	R. G. White's ed., 1857–66
WH2	R. G. White's ed., 1883
Wiv.	*The Merry Wives of Windsor*
WT	*The Winter's Tale*
ZVL	*Zeitschrift für vergleichende Litteraturgeschichte*

Symbols used in the textual notes:

^   punctuation missing or omitted

~   verbal form of the lemma unchanged (while punctuation varies)

\-   (between two sigla) all fully collated eds. between and including those indicated by the two sigla

\+   (after a siglum) and all succeeding fully collated eds.

(−)   all sigla following the minus sign within parentheses indicate eds. that agree, not with the variant, but with the Variorum text (i.e., with F1)

MEASURE FOR MEASURE

The Scene Vienna.

The names of all the Actors.   2940

Vincentio: the Duke.
Angelo, the Deputie.
Escalus, an ancient Lord.
Claudio, a yong Gentleman.
Lucio, a fantastique.   2945
2. Other like Gentlemen.
Prouost.
Thomas. ⎫
Peter. ⎬ *2. Friers.*

Elbow, a simple Constable.   2950
Froth, a foolish Gentleman.
Clowne.
Abhorson, an Executioner.
Barnardine, a dissolute prisoner.
Isabella, sister to Claudio.   2955
Mariana, betrothed to Angelo.
Iuliet, beloued of Claudio.
Francisca, a Nun.
Mistris Ouer-don, a Bawd.

2939 *The Scene Vienna*] F1 specifies "The Scene" only for *Tmp.* and *MM,* two of the plays Ralph Crane transcribed (see p. 294). Sh. mentions Vienna elsewhere only in *Ham.* 3.2.248–9 (2106–7): "this play is the Image of a murther doone in *Vienna, Gonzago* is the Dukes name."

2940 **The names of all the Actors**] ROWE (ed. 1709) adds "*Varrius, a Gentleman, Servant to the Duke*" and "*Guards, Officers, and other Attendants.*" THEOBALD (ed. 1733) adds "*A Justice*" from 2.1. JOHNSON (ed. 1765): "*Varrius* might be omitted, for he is only once spoken to [2320–2; cf. SDs 2319, 2346], and says nothing." LASCELLES (1953, p. 165): "I believe that we should not associate this list with him [Sh.], nor build on it any surmise as to the form in which he found his plot, or left his play." GREG (1955, p. 355): The only other lists in F1 are for *Tmp., TGV, WT, 2H4, Tim.,* and *Oth.* It is "likely that they were specially drawn up by the editor when preparing the copy for the collection." "Unless the scribe omitted this name [Vincentio] from the direction at I. i. 1 he apparently invented it for the list. If he did, he may also have invented the names of Thomas and Francisca in the directions. It would be much more like Shakespeare to call for a Friar and a Nun in the directions and then give them names in the text than vice versa." HONIGMANN (1965, p. 46): "The purpose, I imagine, was to aid the author in his plotting." LEVER (ed. 1965, p. xxv): "'Vincentio' might have been copied for his [Crane's] list from the original heading of I. i before it disappeared in transcription." HOWARD-HILL (1972, p. 78): "It is probably significant that four of the five plays with which Crane has been associated supply lists of actors. (There was insufficient space on the page for a list to be printed for *Wiv.*) Similar lists for *Witch* and quarto *Duchess of Malfi,* which was printed from a Crane transcript, suggest that it was his practice to supply his transcripts with lists of characters, though whether he compiled them himself or copied them cannot be determined." [He is more likely to have copied than to have originated the list printed in *Duchess* in 1623, since it names earlier actors such as William Ostler, who had died in 1614, and Richard Burbage, who had died in 1619. But whoever drew up the list for *MM,* it was probably not Sh.]

2941 *Vincentio*] JOHNSON (ed. 1765, 1:382): "Since the Duke has no name in the play, nor is ever mentioned but by his title, why should he be called *Vincentio* among the *Persons,* but because the name was copied from the story . . . ? It is therefore likely that there was then a story of *Vincentio* Duke of Vienna." SARRAZIN (1895, pp. 165–9): The Duke seems almost like a portrait, somewhat idealized, of course, of Vincenzio Gonzaga, Duke of Mantua from 1587 to 1612. He was often in Vienna or fighting in Hungary [cf. 98, 101], and his divorced wife became a nun. [Gonzaga was quite unlike Sh.'s Duke, for an English traveler in 1592 wrote that he was "given to more delights then all the Dukes of Italye," and another in 1610 that he was "much delighted with Commedies and Mistresses" (LEA, 1934, 2:342–3). He was a patron of Tasso, Monteverdi, Rubens, and a company of players that traveled through Italy, France, and Spain and included Tristano Martinelli, who may have been the first to play Harlequin (Lea, 1:83–8, 276–8; BELLONCI, 1947, tr. 1956, pp. 108–10, 199–203, 214, 235–6, 245). Though he killed the Admirable Crichton for killing his friend, he won no glory in war, and never succeeded in being elected king of Poland, despite sending envoys disguised as merchants to buy votes, or in being declared heir to his cousin the Emperor Rudolf II (Bellonci, pp. 62–6, 176, 246–7).] ERLER (1913, p. 55): It is not necessary to suppose that Sh. had Vincenzio Gonzaga in mind, since he had already used the name in *Shr.* LASCELLES (1953, p. 165): The name does not occur among the known sources and analogues. MUIR (1956, p. 424) thinks that "the case in which Vincentius appears" as a friar in Erasmus's *Colloquia* (ed. 1571, p. 504, "*Barnardino, tandundem Vincentio*") "would seem to have given Shakespeare" the name. See nn. 2954, 353. It is unwise to assume that Sh. found the name in only one place when he could have seen it in many, since Vincentio was a common Italian name.

2942 *Angelo*] MALONE (1780, 1:100): "Here [in line 1757] we see what induced the author to give the outward-sainted deputy [1303] the name of Angelo." EMPSON (1951, p. 272): "My own guess is that he saw the wicked deputy as one of the Cold People of Sonnet 94, the lilies that fester and smell worse than weeds; he christened him Angel." SCHANZER (1963, p. 94): "He is both the 'angel on the outward side', as the Duke puts it (3.2.[286 (1757)]), who is inwardly a devil, and also a false coin, not the angel (a ten-shilling gold coin in Shakespeare's day) that he appears to be." HOY (1964, p. 11): "Angelo is engaged in a desperate struggle with his baser self, his private devil. He is well named; and his name gives us the clue to what he aspires to be, which is nothing less than angelic."

2943 *Escalus*] ERLER (1913, pp. 30, 71, 75, 138): Arthur Brooke in *Romeus and Iuliet* (1562) makes a Latin form out of "Escale" in Boaistuau, from "Scala" in Bandello. Sh. keeps the name for the Prince of Verona in *Rom.* and mentions another Escalus in *AWW* 3.5.80 (1700). He uses this and other Italian names to give *MM* Italian coloring, a strange and romantic setting. [A pun on "scales of justice" would be more likely if "Escalus" were accented on the second syllable, but it is not.]

2944 *Claudio*] Sh. had used this name for a Florentine in *Ado* and for a Dane in *Ham.* 4.7.40 (3051).

2945 *Lucio*] MALONE (in Var. 1821, 9:14): "This name may have been suggested by Turberville's *Tragical Tales* [1587], p. 103, where we find: 'One *Luzio* a roysting roague'." Sh. had used Lucio in *Rom.* 1.2.73 (319). BATTENHOUSE (1946, p. 1036 n.): " 'Light' in both morals and wit." Cf. Lucio's pun in 2658.

fantastique] *OED* (Fantastic *sb.* 2): "One given to fine or showy dress; a fop," quoting Overbury, *Characters* (1614; ed. 1936, p. 60): "A Phantastique. An Improvident Young Gallant." See also Burton, *Anatomy of Melancholy* (1621, 2.2.6.3): "some light *inamorato*, some idle phantasticke." LASCELLES (1953, p. 165): Sh. uses the adj. *fantastique* in a corresponding sense (*TGV* 2.7.47 [1022]), but his form for the noun is *fantastico* (*Rom.* 2.4.30 [1132–3]) [prob. not Sh.'s form, since it is only in Q1; *phantacies* in Q2 and in F]. NOSWORTHY (ed. 1969, on 96): "The word may imply a fop, but in Lucio's case it seems more likely to signify someone with an unbridled fantasy or imagination." See n. 877–8 on *phantastique tricks.* But the term in this list may not be Sh.'s. In Crane's transcript of Middleton's *Witch* (MSR) one of "The Persons" is "Almachildes a fantasticall Gentleman."

2947 *Prouost*] STEEVENS (Var. 1785, 2:33): "A *provost* is generally the executioner of an army." This is JOHNSON's definition in 1755, but his quotation is not for *provost* but for *provost marshal.* DOUCE (in Var. 1793, 4:215): "The *Provost* here, is not a *military officer*, but a kind of sheriff or gaoler, so called in foreign countries." HALLIWELL (ed. 1854, 3:81): In *Captaine Thomas Stukeley* (1605, sig. F2) "the keeper of the prison is called the provost. . . . The Provost Marshal was a different officer." [Many eds. still confuse the two.] *OED* (*sb.* 6): "An officer charged with the apprehension, custody, and punishment of offenders," quoting 203. Sh. uses the word only in *MM.*

2948–9 *Thomas. Peter.*] JOHNSON (ed. 1765, 1:359–60): "This play has two *Friars*, either of whom might singly have served. I should therefore imagine that *Friar Thomas*, in the first act, might be changed, without any harm, to *Friar Peter;* for why should the Duke unnecessarily trust two in an affair which required only one. The name of *Friar Thomas* is never mentioned in the dialogue, and therefore seems arbitrarily placed at the head of the scene [289]." THISELTON (1901, p. 42): " '*Thomas*' may well have been a kind of Superior in charge of a Religious House . . . who told off '*Peter*' to assist the Duke." LASCELLES (1953, p. 56): "I think there is some reason for believing that Shakespeare intended a difference. The Duke addresses 'Thomas' as 'holy Father', 'holy Sir', 'pious Sir', and uses him as a friend: [quotes 297–8]. 'Peter', on the other hand, is nothing more than an agent, to be dispatched on business without the show either of ceremony or of intimacy. If the name to which the dialogue bears no witness, Thomas, is of the scrivener's providing, his care may yet reflect stage practice: the playing of the two as distinct parts." GREG (1955, p. 354): Thomas and Peter are probably the same, as Johnson suggested, "the author having merely forgotten the name." LEVER (ed. 1965, p. xix): "Probably 'Frier Thomas' was tentatively written in the scene heading to I. iii (like 'Francisca a Nun' in I. iv), but the name, not having been used in the dialogue, may well have been forgotten by the time Act IV was written; so that when a friar's name was again called for, 'Peter' took its place." See n. 2958.

2950 *Elbow*] BATTENHOUSE (1946, p. 1036 n.): "An arm-of-the-law with no brain." His name fits him because he leans upon justice (503) and because "he's out at Elbow" (516: see n.). He may also be stooped and bent like an elbow. See n. 1502.

2951 *Froth*] ERLER (1913, pp. 108–9): His brain is empty as foam. [Cf. *Luc.* 212, "a froth of fleeting ioy." His name suggests a haunter of alehouses. Froth is an alehouse-keeper's wife in Massinger's *A New Way to Pay Old Debts.*]

2952 *Clowne*] RITSON (1783, p. 17): "The clown of this play is a different personage [from other clowns in Sh.], the tapster to a bawdy-house." DOUCE (1807, 1:151–2): "The clown in this play officiates as the tapster of a brothel; whence it has been concluded that he is not a domestic fool, nor ought to appear in the dress of that character. A little consideration will serve to shew that the opinion is erroneous, that *this* clown is *altogether* a domestic fool, and that he should be habited accordingly. In Act ii. Sc. i [568, 622] Escalus calls him a *tedious fool,* and *Iniquity,* a name for one of the old stage buffoons. . . . In [*Tim.* 2.2] we have a *strumpet's fool,* and a similar character is mentioned in the first speech in [*Ant.*]." Ancient prints "furnish instances of the common use of the domestic fool in brothels." But Ritson is right: this clown, Pompey Bum (see n. 661–3), makes his living not as a professional fool or jester but as Mrs. Overdone's tapster and *parcell Baud* (518).

2953 *Abborson*] ERLER (1913, p. 117): The name is associated with "whoreson." PARTRIDGE (1947, p. 63): "A composite name, meaning 'son from (L[atin] *ab*) a whore'." KÖKERITZ (1950, p. 240 n.): "Obvious quibble on *abhor* and *ab whoreson.*"

2954 *Barnardine*] HALLIWELL (ed. 1854, 3:175): "One of the friars, in Marlowe's *Jew of Malta,* is termed Barnardine." MUIR (1956, p. 424): Bernardinus, a Franciscan friar in Erasmus's *Colloquia* (ed. 1571, p. 504, ablative *"Barnardino"*) "would seem to have given" Sh. the name. Cf. nn. 2941, 353. But *The Jew of Malta* is the most likely source. Bernardine, often spelled and pronounced Barnardine, was a well-known name. Cf. St. Bernardine of Siena, *The Chirche of the Euill Men and Women,* tr. 1511, *STC* 1966, and "Bernardin," a "captain," in William Thomas's *Historie of Italie* (1549; ed. 1963, p. 61). Sh. had used *Barnardo* in *Ham.* 1.1.

2955 *Isabella*] FARMER (1767, p. 15): Madam Isabella tells the story of Promos and Cassandra in Whetstone, *An Heptameron of Ciuill Discourses* (1582). THISELTON (1901, p. 42): " '*Isabella*' may have been suggested by the Isabella of Ariosto's *Orlando Furioso,* who 'gave her selfe to praier and pure divinity, And vow'd to God her life and her virginity' (Harington XXIV. 73)." HUNTER (1964, pp. 167–9): Isabella, sister to St. Louis of France, founded a convent of Poor Clares, and the order in England observed the "Isabella Rule." See n. 353. The usual form in F1 is *Isabell,* which occurs in speeches twenty-one times, besides *Isabel* in 2576, 2829, 2834, with *Isabella* five times (357, 368, 373, 1374, 2244). *Isabella* appears in eight SDs, *Isabell* in three. Each compositor set both *Isabell* and *Isabella.* Sh. seems to have preferred *Isabell.*

2956 *Mariana*] BULLOUGH (1958, 2:410): "Mariana's name comes from the warning matron's in *AWW* III.5, so well-versed in male seductions."

2957 *Iuliet*] This name, like *Escalus,* Sh. found in Arthur Brooke. She is *Iuliet* here and in 204, 206 SD, 247, 395, 753, 962 SD, 1154; *Iulieta* in 238; and *Iulietta* in 164, 2875 SD. Compositor B set 1154 and C seems to have set all the rest.

2958 *Francisca*] GREG (1955, p. 355): "The nun Francisca (not named in the text) speaks only nine lines in I. iv, but her presence is justified." See Greg in n. 2940. LEVER (ed. 1965, p. xxv): "The names Thomas and Francisca do not appear in the dialogue; it would seem that Shakespeare wrote them at the head of the scenes in case he should later decide to use them, while Crane allowed them to stay." See n. 353.

2959 *Mistris Ouer-don*] COLLINS (i.e., STEEVENS, in Var. 1778, 2:16) compares the meaning of *done* in 177: see n. 177–8. HALLIWELL-PHILLIPPS (1880, p. 7): "There is a Mrs. Overdon in Dryden's *Kind Keeper,* 1680, p. 37 [4.1]." PARTRIDGE (1947, p. 161): "Many whores, when they are *overdone* (worn out), become bawds or procuresses." Master Overdon is an elderly suitor in Middleton's *No Wit, No Help Like a Womans.* See 199 *worne . . . almost out* and n. 650.

MEASVRE,
For Measure.

Actus primus, Scena prima.

---

1 *a Palace.* ROWE1,POPE1-SIS (*subst.*); *Vienna. An open place.* RLTR; *Within Vienna.*
ARD2

0.1–0.2 **MEASVRE, For Measure.**] STEEVENS (Var. 1778 on 2799): So in *3H6*
2.6.55 (1338): "Measure for measure, must be answered." MALONE (ibid.) quotes
A Warning for Faire Women (1599, sig. G3): "Measure for measure, and lost bloud
for bloud." M. S. (1795, p. 645): "I believe, the very name had its origin in that
passage, that 'with whatever measure you mete, it shall be meted to you again' "
(Matt. 7:2; also Mark 4:24, Luke 6:38). NARES (1822): "Equivalent to *like for like,*
denoting the law of retaliation, or equal justice. . . . The title of Shakespeare's comedy
implies that the same law should be enforced against Angelo, which he enforced
against others." COLLIER (1831, 3:66): Sh. may have taken the idea of the title from
Whetstone's play (*1 Promos,* 5.4, p. 335 below): "who others doth deceyue, Deserues
himselfe, lyke measure to receyue." ULRICI (1839, tr. 1846, p. 315): "The title
. . . is not intended . . . to convey the meaning that like ought to be repaid with like.
. . . Such is its purport in an ironical sense alone. Its true sense is that of the beautiful
petition in the prayer which Our Lord has taught us:—'Forgive us our trespasses as
we forgive them that trespass against us'. None of us, in short, ought mentally even
to judge another: for not one of us is without sin." GERVINUS (1849–50, tr. 1875,
p. 504): The Duke "awards punishment not *measure for measure*, but *with* measure."
TILLEY (M800, M801) quotes *Tit.* 5.3.66 (2570): "Ther's meede for meede."
SIEGEL (1953, p. 318): " 'Measure for measure' refers not only to Angelo's method
of dispensing justice, the scales for the measuring out of the penalty in precise
proportion to the crime, in which the time comes for his own misdeeds to be weighed
—only for them to be discarded by the Duke at the crucial moment; it refers not only
to the opposite of Angelo's procedure, the Christian forgiveness of the Sermon on
the Mount, with the Christian meaning superseding the Mosaic one, mercy being
returned for severity; it refers also to the retribution, ironically and sometimes humorously appropriate, which is visited upon each of the misdoers even though mercy is
granted to him." LEVER (ed. 1965): "A commonplace signifying (i) just retribution

Enter Duke, Escalus, Lords.   (F1

Duke.
Escalus.
    Esc. My Lord.   5
    Duk. Of Gouernment, the properties to vnfold,
Would seeme in me t'affect speech & discourse,
Since I am put to know, that your owne Science
Exceedes (in that) the lists of all aduice
My strength can giue you: Then no more remaines   10

---

8 put] not POPE1-CAP; apt COLNE, COL2, COL3, COL4; not yet KTLY

---

and reward, . . . (ii) moderation or temperance as a virtue." See n. 1728–9 on *measure*.
WILSON (1970, p. 520) quotes *A Myrroure for Magistrates* (1559; ed. Campbell, p.
99): "For looke what measure we other awarde, The same for vs agayne is preparde."
    2 WILSON (ed. 1922): "The important business of this scene involves the pres-
ence of the Duke's 'Privy Council'." LASCELLES (1953, p. 47): "The dialogue gives
no warrant for this. . . . Suppose the Duke to enter . . . dressed for travel. . . . Let
him come attended by Escalus, and followed, at a discreet distance, by some humbler
personal attendant—the one who will be needed to fetch Angelo. . . . Surely all this
takes place at the very moment of parting, in privacy, perhaps even in secrecy?" But
the *Lords* in SD do not suggest secrecy.
    3 WILSON (ed. 1922): "The play opens with an abruptness quite unusual with
Shakespeare, and it is still more unusual for him to begin his first scene with a broken
line of verse. [But he does so in *Ham.* and *Tim.*] It is strange also that the Duke
vouchsafes no reason for his sudden departure from Vienna. Yet we learn from Lucio
[402–7] that such reasons had been given, albeit 'of an infinite distance from his
true-meant design' (cf. [304–6]). It seems natural to suppose, therefore, that these
'givings-out' were uttered at the beginning of 1. 1. in its unabridged form and that
the received text only preserves for us the second half of the scene." LEVER (ed. 1965,
p. xiv): "Such an elaborate theory of revision is no longer generally accepted." See
nn. 76–81, 1027–33.
    6 **properties**] LEISI (ed. 1964): " 'Essential qualities' (OED 5)."
        vnfold] See *OED* (*v.* 1 2): "Explain."
    7 **affect**] SCHMIDT (1874): "Love" (*OED, v.* 1 2). RIDLEY (ed. 1935): "Imply an
affectation of." LEISI (ed. 1964): " 'Be (very) fond of' (OED 2, 5), mostly used by
Sh. in a non-derogatory sense." LEVER (ed. 1965): "Often used by Shakespeare in
the modern sense of 'practise artificially'." But more often it means "love," as here
and in 81.
        discourse] Talk (*OED, sb.* 3).
    8 **put to know**] STEEVENS (Var. 1773): "*Obliged to acknowledge.*" OED (Put
v. 1 28b): "To oblige, compel," first quotation in this sense. See p. 278 for conjectures.
        Science] LEISI (ed. 1964): " 'Knowledge (in some special field)' (OED 2)."
    9 **lists**] JOHNSON (ed. 1765): "Bounds, Limits" (*OED, sb.* 3 8).
    10 **strength**] SCHMIDT (1875): "Power of mind" (*OED, sb.* 1c).
    10–12 **Then . . . worke**] THEOBALD (ed. 1733): "The Sense is manifestly lame

But that, to your sufficiency, as your worth is able,   11

---

11 Put that to your Sufficiency, as your Worth is able, ROWE, POPE, THEO, WARB; But that to your sufficiency you joyn A will to serve us as . . . able, HAN1; But that your . . . able, v1773-RANN; But thereto your . . . able, SINGER (1852) *conj.,* SING2; But add to your sufficiency your worth, COLNE, COL2, COL3, COL4; But that to your sufficiency, as Your worth is able, you add diligence, KTLY; But t'add sufficiency, . . . able, HUD2; But add sufficiency, as your worth is, ample, HENL; But that. To . . . able, SIS

---

and defective, and as the Versification is so too, they concur to make me think, a Line has accidentally been left out." WARBURTON (ed. 1747): "By *sufficiency* is meant *authority,* the power delegated by the Duke to *Escalus.* The plain meaning of the word being this; *Put your skill in governing* (says the Duke) *to the power which I give you to exercise it, and let them work together."* JOHNSON (ed. 1765): "I am not convinced that a line is lost. . . . I therefore suspect that the Authour wrote thus,—*Then no more remains, But that to your* sufficiencies *your worth is* abled, *And let them work. Then nothing remains more than to tell you that your Virtue is now invested with power equal to your knowledge and wisdom. Let therefore your knowledge and your virtue now work together."* WARBURTON (MS n. in JOHNSON, ed. 1765): "Obscure only for want of a stage direction. I would read thus . . . < pointing to the Roll in his hand > ." ANON. (1785, p. 37): "There is not an omission here, as has been generally supposed: *and* means *so.* The sense is, 'having both power and integrity, exert both'." MALONE (ed. 1790): "I have not the smallest doubt that the compositor's eye glanced from the middle of the second of these lines to that under it in the Ms. and that by this means two half lines have been omitted. . . . *And let them work,* a figurative expression; *Let them ferment."* DOUCE (1807, 1:120): *"Sufficiency* is, no doubt, *ability,* and not *authority."* HARNESS (ed. 1825): "May it not mean—That the Duke has no further counsel to give, but that Escalus should apply himself *to his sufficiency?* i.e. his skill and knowledge of law and government, as *his worth is able,* to the best of his ability." KNIGHT (ed. 1840): *"Then, no more remains:* (to say on government) *But that,* (your science) *to your sufficiency,* (joined to your authority) *as your worth* (as well as your virtue) *is able;* (equal to the duty) *and let them work* (call them into action)." VERPLANCK (ed. 1847): "I take it, that the 'that' refers to the commission, which the Duke must have in his hand, or before him. . . . 'That' authority is all that is wanted to his full 'sufficiency' to duties which his 'worth' and ability fit him for." CLARKE (ed. 1864): " 'Then no more remains < there is nothing more required > but *that* < meaning the "strength" mentioned in the previous line, the governing power embodied in the "commission" he gives him > to your sufficiency < sufficing authority > , as your worth is able < your excellence rendering you competent > , and let them work' < let them operate in combination > ." HUNTER (ed. 1873): "But that legal document. Here the duke holds out the commission." PERRING (1885, pp. 36–9): "The Duke exhorts Escalus to have recourse to (some such phrase has to be supplied) his sufficiency (intellectual capability) to the utmost ability of his worth (high character)." LEE (ed. 1907): "Nothing more remains for me to tell you except to commit my authority to your own fit knowledge, with which your moral worth is on a level, and to let the principles or properties of government work out their way." WILSON (ed. 1922): *"Sufficiency,* qualifications, competency [*OED,* 4]. Cf. *Oth.* 1.3.224 [572]." *"Worth,* . . . standing, authority [*OED, sb.* 1 3]." *"Able,* suitable, appropriate (v. N.E.D. 'able' 2)." "It was

And let them worke: The nature of our People,
Our *Cities Institutions*, and the Termes
For Common Iustice, y'are as pregnant in
As Art, and practise, hath inriched any　　　　　　　　15
That we remember: There is our Commission,

---

12 And let them] You let it HAL
14 For] Of POPE1-THEO4
15 hath] has BUL, SIS

---

perhaps necessary to 'cut' a reference to previously deleted matter (W. W. Greg, privately)." TERRY (1924, p. 686): *That* refers to *strength, them* to *science* and *strength.* HARDING (ed. 1954): "Nothing remains, then, except that Escalus apply his best abilities to his *sufficiency*—that is, his fitness for government—and let them work together." BREWER (1955, p. 425): "But that *that* (my strength, i.e. my power) should be added to your ability, since your merit is ready and willing." SISSON (1956, 1:74): *"Read . . . But that. To your sufficiency*, . . . an imperative phrase, like the familiar 'To it'. . . . 'Now betake you to your competence, to the full extent of your personal qualities . . . and let your skill and your character go to work together on this task'." See p. 278.

12, 13 **our**] SCHMIDT (1875): "My, in the royal style" (*OED, poss. pron.* 1c). So *we* in 16 and often, *vs* in 18 and often, and cf. n. 49.

13 *Institutions*] SCHMIDT (1874): "Rules and forms of government." PORTER & CLARKE (ed. 1909): "The legal knowledge of the various offices and the prerogatives of different courts." LEVER (ed. 1965): "Political or social customs [*OED*, 6]. A 16th-cent. innovation and only here in Shakespeare."

Termes] JOHNSON (ed. 1765): "I rather think the Duke meant to say, that *Escalus* was *pregnant,* that is, *ready* and knowing in all the forms of law, and, among other things, in the *terms* or *times set apart* for its administration." BLACKSTONE (in MALONE, 1780, 1:94): *"Terms* mean the technical language of the courts. An old book called *Les Termes de la Ley,* (written in Henry the Eighth's time) was in Shakspeare's days, and is now, the accidence of young students in the law" (John Rastell's *Exposicions of the Termes of the Lawes, STC* 20701–18). DELIUS (ed. 1860): It is rather in connection with the following: the condition or the manner of administering justice. ORGER (1890, p. 16): "Limits." ONIONS (1911): "(a) conditions of the ordinary administration of justice, (b) 'technical terms of the courts' " (*OED, sb.* 10, 13). EVANS (ed. 1974): "Modes of procedure."

14 **Common**] SCHMIDT (1874): "Public," as in 305, 1863 (*OED, a.* 6).

y'are] FRANZ (§52): *MM* has *y'are* here [and in 769], *you'r* in 1147 for "you are."

pregnant] NARES (1822): "Stored with information." SCHMIDT (1875): "Expert." HUDSON (ed. 1880): *"Ripe,* well-informed, or *full of learning* and experience." ONIONS (1911): "Resourceful, ready" (*OED, a.*[2] 3a).

15 **Art**] KELLNER (1931, p. 244): Theory. LEISI (ed. 1964): " 'Skill', 'learning', studies' " (*OED, sb.* 1, 3b).

practise] SCHMIDT (1875): "Experience, skill acquired by experience (opposed to theory)" (*OED,* Practice 3).

hath] See ABBOTT §334, *"Third person plural in -th,"* and FRANZ §156.

16 **Commission**] Warrant conferring delegated authority (*OED, sb.*[1] 3).

From which, we would not haue you warpe; call hither,
I say, bid come before vs *Angelo*:
What figure of vs thinke you, he will beare.
For you must know, we haue with speciall soule   20
Elected him our absence to supply;
Lent him our terror, drest him with our loue,
And giuen his Deputation all the Organs

---

18 *Exit an Attendant.* CAP, MAL+
19 he will] will he v1785
20 soule] roll WARB

---

17 **would**] SCHMIDT (1875, p. 1370): Subjunctive "expressing a present wish in a conditional form" (*OED*, Will *v.*[1] 40).

warpe] *OED* (*v.* 19): "Deviate, swerve, go astray," first use in this fig. sense.

18 WINNY (ed. 1959): "The Duke softens his command to suit Angelo's new dignity."

19 **figure**] SCHMIDT (1874): "Image in general, representation" (*OED, sb.* 9). LEVER (ed. 1965): "Suggested perhaps by the ducal stamp on the seal of the commission, and introducing the iterative 'stamp' or 'coin' image for the first time." Cf. 56.

beare] SCHMIDT (1874, p. 87): "Be marked with," "show" (*OED, v.*[1] 23).

20 **soule**] EDWARDS (1758, p. 29): "With great thought, upon mature deliberation." HEATH (1765, p. 77): "The *soul* is put for one of its principal faculties, the judgment; or, at least for one of its principal operations, deliberation." STEEVENS (Var. 1773): "I believe, the poet meant no more than *that he was the immediate choice of his heart.*" Cf. *full soule* in *Tmp.* 3.1.44 (1288). MALONE (in Var. 1778): "This seems to be only a translation of the usual formal words inserted in all royal grants —'De *gratia* nostra *speciali* et ex mero motu—'." CAPELL (1780, 2:3:31-2): "An equivocal expression, and will signify either—special thought, or special design; the latter the speaker's latent intention, though to Escalus it bears the face of the first: we see in it, and likewise in his address [33–5] which is also equivocal, a dawn of that suspicion of Angelo which breaks out at full in the latter lines of scene IV." LEVER (ed. 1965): "All the powers of the mind, intuitive and rational (*O.E.D.* 5)." Cf. 75, 2353.

21 **Elected**] *OED* (Elect *v.* 1): "To pick out, choose (usually, for a particular purpose or function)."

our absence to supply] SCHMIDT (1875, pp. 1156, 1424): To fill the place of us in our absence (*OED*, Supply *v.*[1] 4, "make up for").

22 **Lent him our terror**] WINNY (ed. 1959): "Invested him with power of life and death." LEVER (ed. 1965): "Cf. *Sir Thomas More,* 'for to the king god hath his offyc lent / of dread of Iustyce, power and Comaund' (*M.S.R.*, Addition II, lines 221-2)," and *H8* 5.5.48 (3418). See *OED* (Lend *v.*[2] 2): "Give, grant."

drest . . . loue] WINNY (ed. 1959): "Transferred to him the people's affection for their ruler." LEVER (ed. 1965): " 'Adorned him with the outward signs of our love'. Cf. *1H4,* III. ii. 51 [1870]." See *OED* (Dress *v.* 7e *fig.*) and 875.

23 **Deputation**] SCHMIDT (1874): "The office of a substitute, vicegerency." See *OED* (*sb.* 2): "Appointment to act on behalf of another."

Organs] SCHMIDT (1875): "Any instrument." HART (ed. 1905): "Means of operation, machinery" (*OED, sb.*[1] 7).

Of our owne powre: What thinke you of it?
 Esc. If any in *Vienna* be of worth   25
To vndergoe such ample grace, and honour,
It is Lord *Angelo.*

       Enter Angelo.

 Duk. Looke where he comes.
 Ang. Always obedient to your Graces will,   30
I come to know your pleasure.
 Duke. Angelo:
There is a kinde of Character in thy life,
That to th'obseruer, doth thy history
Fully vnfold: Thy selfe, and thy belongings   35

---

24 What] say, what POPE1-v1773 (−CAP)
28 SCENE II. POPE, HAN1, WARB, JOHN *Enter Angelo.*] *After* 29 DYCE, CAM,
GLO, HUD2-ARD1
 31 your] your Graces F2-ROWE3

---

 25 **worth**] See n. 10–12.
 26 **vndergoe**] SCHMIDT (1875): "To partake of, to enjoy," as in *Ham.* 1.4.34
(Q2). So *OED* (*v.* 6d), quoting only *MM* and *Ham.* ONIONS (1911): "Bear the
weight of " (*OED, v.* 5b). CAMPBELL (ed. 1949): "Sustain."
 grace] "Manifestation of favour" (*OED, sb.* 8).
 33 **Character**] KNIGHT (ed. 1840): "Surely *character* has here the original meaning of something engraved or inscribed—*thy life* is thy habits." HART (ed. 1905):
"Cipher for hidden or secret writing or correspondence. Compare Ben Jonson, *Epigr.*
xciii. . . . *New Eng. Dict.* [*sb.* 7] quotes the passage in the text doubtfully, the next
illustration being *Pepys,* 1659[/60]." PORTER & CLARKE (ed. 1909): "By certain
signs appearing in him, the Duke reads him, as in the common saying 'I read you,
like a book'." CAMPBELL (ed. 1949): "Hand-writing, hence, stamp." LEVER (ed.
1965): " 'Character' was primarily an engraving or inscription, hence fig. for appearance or behaviour. . . . The observer, says the Duke, can infer Angelo's history from
his present behaviour." See n. 247.
 thy] BYRNE (1936, p. 94): "The Duke says *thy* to Angelo in affectionate
intimacy conferring the power of government upon him, and *you* in official language
of business."
 34 **obseruer**] JOHNSON (1755): "One who looks vigilantly on persons and
things; close remarker," quoting this and *JC* 1.2.202 (304). So *OED* (3).
 history] THIRLBY (1723–33): Cf. *2H4* 3.1.80 ff. (1498 ff.). "Does he mean
unfold what he will do, how he will behave himself?" IDEM (1747–53): "Does he
mean future?" JOHNSON (Var. 1773): "*History* may be taken in a more diffuse and
licentious meaning, for *future occurrences,* or the part of life yet to come." WHITE (ed.
1857): " 'The character of your present life shows what your past life must have
been'." HART (ed. 1905): "Record." LEISI (ed. 1964): " 'Story'."
 35 **vnfold**] See n. 6.
 belongings] MALONE (ed. 1790): "Endowments." *OED* (*vbl. sb.* 1): "Circum-

Are not thine owne so proper, as to waste
Thy selfe vpon thy vertues; they on thee:
Heauen doth with vs, as we, with Torches doe,
Not light them for themselues: For if our vertues
Did not goe forth of vs, 'twere all alike   40

---

37 they] them DAWSON *and* THEOBALD *conj.*, HAN1, JOHN, v1773-v1821, SING,
COL, STAU, KTLY, HUD2
40-1 all . . . we] all as if We HAN1

---

stances connected with a person or thing; relations with another person or thing,"
first use as sb. HARDING (ed. 1954): "Qualities." LEISI (ed. 1964): "The substantive
occurs [in Sh.] only here and in *Coriolanus* I 9 62 [818]." Cf. *concernings* in 64,
aduisings in 1419, *thankings* in 2351, and *becommings* in *Ant.* 1.3.96 (417).

36 **thine owne so proper**] STEEVENS (Var. 1778): "So much thy own property."
ONIONS (1911): *Proper*, "belonging distinctly or exclusively (*to*), peculiar" (*OED,
a.* 2). Cf. 1233.

waste] SCHMIDT (1875): "To consume, to spend [*OED, v.* 3,9] . . . (to bestow
all thy powers on perfectioning thyself)."

37 **they on thee**] THEOBALD (1726, p. 40): "It is requisite, to make it true
English, to read, *Them on Thee.*" THIRLBY (1747-53): "That worthy wight Dʳ Dawson was pleased to tell me he read *them.*" KNIGHT (ed. 1840): "But as Angelo might
waste himself upon his virtues, *they* might waste themselves on him." HALLIWELL
(ed. 1854): "Thyself and thy endowments are not so exclusively your own, belonging
to yourself, that either you are to waste your exertions upon your own virtues, or that
they are to be solely exercised for your own advantage. Or, as the pronoun was
frequently used somewhat capriciously,—you are not to employ your own gifts for
selfish purposes. There is a slight ambiguity, which is either to be explained philo-
sophically or grammatically."

38-9 **Heauen . . . themselues**] M. S. (1795, p. 645): Suggested by Matt. 5:
15-16. [See also Mark 4:21, Luke 8:16 and 11:33.] BOND (1902, 2:316, 542): Cf.
Lyly's *Campaspe* (1584), Prologue at Court: "these torches, which giuing light to
others, consume themselues." TILLEY (C39): "A candle (torch) lights others and
consumes itself." Cf. B141, "We are not born for ourselves." LEVER (ed. 1965):
"The parable had become a secular commonplace."

39-41 **For . . . not**] THEOBALD (ed. 1733): Cf. Horace, *Odes,* 4.9: "Paullum
sepultae distat inertiae Celata virtus [In the tomb, hidden worth is little different from
sloth]." So W. THEOBALD (1909, pp. 217-18). BALDWIN (1944, 2:510): "There
is nothing conclusive about [this] parallel. . . . The parallel is of the most general
kind."

39-42 **For . . . issues**] WHITER (1794, p. 254): "Every one perceives that the
Poet here alludes to the narrative in the Gospel, where Jesus is conscious 'that *Virtue*
had *gone out of him*', when the woman was cured of an *issue* of blood by *touching* his
garment. (Mark 5. v. 25, &c.) Would the reader believe that these latter words, *issue*
—*touch*, are used in the [succeeding] lines, though they are applied by the Poet to
the operations of intellect?"

40 **forth of**] SCHMIDT (1874): "Out of " (*OED, adv.* 9).

'twere] It would be. See ABBOTT §301, FRANZ §638, and nn. 2150, 2260.

As if we had them not: Spirits are not finely touch'd,
But to fine issues: nor nature neuer lends
The smallest scruple of her excellence,
But like a thrifty goddesse, she determines
Her selfe the glory of a creditour,   45
Both thanks, and vse; but I do bend my speech

---

42 nor] *Om.* POPE, HAN1

---

41 **Spirits**] SOULS (*OED, sb.* 11).
    finely touch'd] HUNTER (ed. 1873): "Made of fine touch. An allusion to the touchstone, a slaty kind of stone, which was thought to indicate the purity of gold by the marks which the metal made upon it." SCHMIDT (1875): *Touch,* "to paint or to form as an artist," as in *Son.* 17. CLARKE (1879, p. 599): " 'Gifted with acute perception', 'endowed . . . with keen sense'." HUDSON (ed. 1880): "Kindled or quickened." CAMPBELL (ed. 1949): "Accurately tested." HARDING (ed. 1954): "Nobly endowed." WINNY (ed. 1959): "(1) gifted. (2) tried by assay." LEVER (ed. 1965): " 'Touched' and 'issues', with 'fine' (=refined) suggest the 'touch' placed on gold coins of standard fineness before they were passed into circulation (*O.E.D. v.* 8)." See also *OED* (*v.* 23), "To affect mentally or morally, to imbue *with* some quality," and cf. nn. 2007, 2407.
    42 **to fine issues**] JOHNSON (1755): *Issue,* "Event; consequence." IDEM (ed. 1765): "To great consequences. For high purposes." SCHMIDT (1874): *Issue,* "that which proceeds from a man; action, deed." So ONIONS (1911) (*OED, sb.* 8b, sense only in Sh.).
    nor] See *OED* (*conj.*[1] 1): "Continuing the force of a negative."
    nature] M. S. (1795, p. 645): "An allusion to the parable of the talents" (Matt. 25:14-30). ROBERTSON (1897, pp. 62-3): Cf. Seneca, *De Beneficiis,* 5.8-10, 22-5. HANKINS (1953, p. 215) quotes Palingenius, *The Zodiake of Life,* tr. Googe (ed. 1576, p. 105): "For vnto vs these are but lent, the vse doth nature giue." LEVER (ed. 1965): "Nature's action here corresponds with Heaven's, [38]; together they show a blending of Christian ethics and Stoic philosophy. The implied coin image in [41-2] may have suggested Nature as creditor, who 'determines' (ordains) thanks and 'use' (usury). . . . Death as the repayment of nature's loan, and the conceit of nature as a usurer, are Senecan ideas taken up in the Renaissance by Palingenius, Montaigne [bk. 2, ch. 37], Spenser, *Faerie Queene,* II. xi. 45, and Shakespeare, *Sonn.,* IV, VI, and IX, where Nature lends life for man to 'invest' in progeny." *Nature* is personified (*OED, sb.* 11b).
    43 **scruple**] JOHNSON (1755): "Proverbially, any small quantity." So *OED* (*sb.*[1] 6). DURHAM (ed. 1926): "Small measure of weight used by goldsmiths."
    44-6 **determines . . . vse**] CAPELL (1780, 2:3:32): "Adjudges to herself that which is a creditor's glory,—both the thanks of her debtor, and her loan's interest or use." See *OED* (Determine *v.* 7): "To ordain, decree."
    46 **vse**] SCHMIDT (1875): "Interest paid for borrowed money" (*OED, sb.* 5b *fig.*).
    46-7 **I . . . aduertise**] WARBURTON (ed. 1747): "I direct my speech to one who is able to teach me how to govern: *my part in him,* signifying my office, which I have delegated to him." TYRWHITT (in Var. 1778): "I am speaking *to one, that can in him* < in, or by himself > apprehend *my part* < all that I have to say > ." RANN (ed. 1786): "Is well apprised of the part I have in him, of my claim to his services; or,

To one that can my part in him aduertise; (F1^b)
Hold therefore *Angelo*:
In our remoue, be thou at full, our selfe:
Mortallitie and Mercie in *Vienna* 50
Liue in thy tongue, and heart: Old *Escalus*
Though first in question, is thy secondary.

---

47 my part in him] in my part me HAN1
48 Hold therefore.—Angelo; TYRWHITT *conj.*, SING, STAU; Hold, therefore, Angelo, our place and power: WH1; Hold therefore, Angelo, thy deputation; KTLY; Hold therefore, Angelo, our power and place. WH2
50 Mortallitie] Morality POPE

---

of all that I could wish to impart to him." SEYMOUR (1805, 1:83): "To one that can already declare or make known all those precepts which I would impart to him." KNIGHT (ed. 1840): "My part deputed to him, which he can *advertise*—direct his attention to,—without my speech." VERPLANCK (ed. 1847): "One that can of himself declare the duty he owes to me." ROLFE (ed. 1882): "For *advertise* = instruct, cf. *Hen. VIII.* ii. 4. 178 [1544]. . . . The accent in S. is regularly on the penult." ONIONS (1911): "Inform, instruct." HARDING (ed. 1954): "One who can, in his own right, make known his abilities as my deputy." GRIVELET (ed. 1957): Show in himself how my role should be acted. LEVER (ed. 1965): " 'Make my function (*part*) generally known through his own example'. In [49] the Duke plays on 'part' in contrast to 'at full'." See *OED*, Bend (*v.* 18), "direct," and Advertise (*v.* 4), "notify," "inform." Cf. 2767 and n.

48 **Hold therefore *Angelo***] THIRLBY (1723–33): Cf. *Take* 53. JOHNSON (ed. 1765): "That is, continue to be *Angelo, hold* as thou art." TYRWHITT (in Var. 1778): "If a full point be put after *therefore*, the duke may be understood to speak of himself." STEEVENS (ibid.): "I believe that—*Hold therefore Angelo*, are the words which the duke utters on tendering his commission to him." HUNTER (ed. 1873): "Hold office for us." HART (ed. 1905): "Keep firm and true for the purposes I have stated" (*therefore* "concerning this," *hold* as in 1394). WILSON (ed. 1922): "It seems simpler to take it, with Hanmer and Steevens, as the first proffer of the commission. Angelo's hesitancy is underlined by Shakespeare." PARROTT (ed. 1938): "Retain (what follows)." HARRISON (ed. 1948): "Observe, remember." LEISI (ed. 1964): "As an imperative without an object the word is always concrete in Sh.: it means: 'here! Take it' " (*OED, v.* 15b).

49 **remoue**] *OED* (*sb.* 5c): "A period of absence from a place," only example in this sense.
    at full] ONIONS (1911): "Fully" (*OED*, Full B. 1a). CRAIG (ed. 1951): "In every respect."
    our selfe] SCHMIDT (1875): "Myself, in the regal style" (*OED, pron.* 1). See n. 12, 13.

50-1 **Mortallitie . . . heart**] JOHNSON (1755): "Power of destruction" (*OED*, 3). DOUCE (1807, 1:120–1): "I delegate to thy tongue the power of pronouncing sentence of death, and to thy heart the privilege of exercising mercy."

51 **Liue**] SCHMIDT (1874): "Exist" (*OED, v.*¹ 1b *fig.*).

52 **first in question**] JOHNSON (ed. 1765): "First called for; first appointed." SCHMIDT (1875, p. 930): "First in consideration" (*OED*, Question *sb.* 1d). NEILSON

Take thy Commission.

Ang. Now good my Lord
Let there be some more test, made of my mettle,   55
Before so noble, and so great a figure
Be stamp't vpon it.

Duk. No more euasion:
We haue with a leauen'd, and prepared choice

---

55 mettle] Metal ROWE1+ (−CAM3, SIS, PEL1, EVNS)

57-9 *Lines ending* evasion: . . . choice v1793-KTLY, KNT3, DEL4, COL4, WH2+; we . . . choice DYCE2, DYCE3, HUD2

57 vpon it] upon't CAP, DYCE2, DYCE3, HUD2, PEN2

58 No] Come, no POPE1-v1773 (−CAP)

59 a] *Om.* DENT MS *conj. in* HAL, PEN2   leauen'd, and prepared] prepar'd and leaven'd POPE, THEO, HAN1; prepar'd and level'd WARB

& HILL (ed. 1942): "Consideration (because the elder)."

secondary] *OED* (*sb.* 1): "One who acts in subordination to another." HART (ed. 1905): Cf. *Jn.* 5.2.80 (2333). [Also *2 Promos,* 3.3 (p. 354 below), *"Phallax,* Lord *Promos* secondary."]

53 **Commission**] See n. 16. HUNTER (ed. 1873): "We have here one of the rare examples, in Shakspeare, of the dissyllabic orthoepy of such terminations as *-tion, -sion,* &c. in the *middle* of a line." ABBOTT §479 finds only three examples. ROLFE (ed. 1882) adds this and three more. But it seems more likely that *Commission* is spoken with the usual three syllables, like *Commission* in 16 and *Commissions* in 68, followed by a pause (see ABBOTT §506).

54 **good my Lord**] "My good lord." See ABBOTT §13, FRANZ §328, *OED* (Good *a.* 2b). See nn. 902, 2818.

55 **test**] JOHNSON (1755): "Trial; examination: as by the cupel" (*OED, sb.*[1] 2). LEISI (ed. 1964, p. 31): "Not an abstract word in Shakespeare's time but a word which referred to the examination (by melting) of precious metals." See n. 908.

mettle] SCHMIDT (1875): *Metal* or *Mettle,* "substance or material," "the simile taken from minting." See *OED* (Metal *sb.* 1f *fig.*). WILSON (ed. 1922): "Courage, disposition, the stuff of life, vital energy. . . . A quibble upon 'metal' is intended," as in 1052 and 1564. LEISI (ed. 1964): *"Metal* and *mettle* were spelling variants of one and the same word. . . . This, therefore, is a metaphor and not a pun."

56 **noble**] JORGENSEN (1962, p. 80) sees a pun on *noble* as a coin.

figure] See n. 19.

58 **euasion**] LEVER (ed. 1965): "Evasive argument, excuse (*O.E.D.* 3b)."

59 **leauen'd**] UPTON (1746, p. 211): "Before hand prepared and rightly season'd." WARBURTON (ed. 1747) reads *level'd,* but withdraws his emendation in a MS note printed by BENNET (1893, pp. 141-2): "If *leaven'd* be the true reading, the author used it for *digested. Leaven* makes a fermentation, and fermentation produces one kind of digestion." JOHNSON (ed. 1765): *"I have proceeded to you with choice* mature, concocted, fermented, *leavened.* When Bread is *leavened,* it is left to ferment: a *leavened* choice is therefore a choice not hasty, but considerate, not declared as soon as it fell into the imagination, but suffered to work long in the mind." HUDSON (ed. 1880): "Probably an implied image or idea of ale *well fermented,* and so made fit for

Proceeded to you; therefore take your honors: 60
Our haste from hence is of so quicke condition,
That it prefers it selfe, and leaues vnquestion'd
Matters of needfull value: We shall write to you
As time, and our concernings shall importune,
How it goes with vs, and doe looke to know   65
What doth befall you here. So fare you well:
To th'hopefull execution doe I leaue you,
Of your Commissions.
     Ang. Yet giue leaue (my Lord,)
That we may bring you something on the way.   70
     Duk. My haste may not admit it,
Nor neede you (on mine honor) haue to doe
With any scruple: your scope is as mine owne,

---

63 to you] *Om.* HAN1
64 concernings] concerns mF2FL *conj.,* v1785
66 fare you] fare ye JOHN
68 your] our ROWE2-POPE2, HAN1   Commissions] Commission F2-POPE2,
HAN1, HUD2
69 giue] give me THEO, WARB

---

use." SYMONS (in IRVING & MARSHALL, ed. 1889): "The metaphor may no doubt
have [the meaning given by Johnson,] but may it not mean as well, or more primarily,
that the choice was based on a thorough and searching scrutiny, as leaven works up
through and permeates the whole mass of dough?" HART (ed. 1905): "Well fermented, *i.e.* tempered, considered."
     61 **of so quicke condition**] DURHAM (ed. 1926): " 'Of a nature which demands
such extreme haste'." LEVER (ed. 1965): "Probably with play on 'quick' as pregnant.
. . . *condition:* quality" (*OED, sb.* 12, 13).
     62 **prefers it selfe**] ROLFE (ed. 1882): "Places itself before the most important
business." LEE (ed. 1907): "Takes precedence of everything else."
          vnquestion'd] LEE (ed. 1907): "Undiscussed." *OED (ppl. a.* 2): "Unexam-
ined." CRAIG (ed. 1951): "Not yet considered." See n. 52.
     64 **concernings**] SCHMIDT (1874): Affairs, as in *Ham.* 3.4.191 (2567). See n.
35.
          importune] *OED (v.* 2): "Press, urge, impel," first of two quotations in this
sense. See n. 2824.
     65 **looke**] LEISI (ed. 1964): " 'Expect' (OED 3c)."
     67 **hopefull**] SCHMIDT (1874): "Exciting good hopes, likely to obtain or ensure
success" (*OED, a.* 2).
          execution] SCHMIDT (1874): "Carrying into effect" (*OED,* 1c).
     70 **bring**] REED (in Var. 1785): "Accompany" (*OED, v.* 2).
          something] SCHMIDT (1875): "Somewhat" (*OED, adv.* 1b).
     71 **admit**] SCHMIDT (1874): "Permit" (*OED, v.* 2a).
     72 **Nor**] See n. 42.
          haue to doe] Have concern (*OED,* Do *v.* 33c).
     73 **scruple**] *OED (sb.* 2 1): "A doubt, uncertainty or hesitation in regard to right

So to inforce, or qualifie the Lawes
As to your soule seemes good: Giue me your hand,   75
Ile priuily away: I loue the people,
But doe not like to stage me to their eyes:
Though it doe well, I doe not rellish well

---

74 Lawes] Law ROWE3, POPE, HAN1

---

and wrong, duty, propriety, etc."

   scope] THIRLBY (1723-33): "Does he mean power?" JOHNSON (1755): "Aim; intention; drift." IDEM (ed. 1765): "Amplitude of power." See *OED* (*sb.* ² 7): "Liberty to act." LEISI (ed. 1964): "It is used more often in *M/M* than in any other play, and is indeed one of its key-words," citing 218, 327, 1281, 2610.

   74 **inforce**] LEISI (ed. 1964): " 'Strengthen, make more severe'." More likely "compel the observance of " (*OED,* Enforce *v.* 14, quoting 2293). See n. 1328.

   qualifie] SCHMIDT (1875): "To temper, to moderate" (*OED, v.* 8). See n. 1943.

   75 **soule**] See n. 20.

   76-81 TYRWHITT (1766, pp. 36-7): "I cannot help thinking that *Shakespeare* [here and in 1030-33], intended to flatter that unkingly weakness of *James the first,* which made him so impatient of the crowds that flocked to see him, especially upon his first coming, that . . . he restrained them by a Proclamation. Sir *Symonds D'Ewes,* in his Memoirs of his own Life, has a remarkable passage with regard to this humour of *James.* After taking notice, that the King going to Parliament, on the 30*th of January,* 1620-1, 'spake lovingly to the people, and said, *God bless ye, God bless ye';* he adds these words, *'contrary to his former hasty and passionate custom, which often, in his sudden distemper, would bid a pox or a plague on such as flocked to see him'."* NICHOLS (1828, 1:188) quotes a letter by Thomas Wilson, 22 June 1603: "The people, according to the honest English nature, approve all their Princes actions and words, savinge that they desyre some more of that generous affabilitye wch ther good old Queene did afford them." PORTER & CLARKE (ed. 1909): "This reference reminds one of Coriolanus, as Shakespeare shows his dislike of public adulation . . . , rather than of James." WILSON (ed. 1922): "James I's dislike of crowds is a historic fact, and it has been generally agreed that Shakespeare is here flattering the king's weakness, a weakness with which he himself is likely to have had some sympathy (cf. *Son.* 110, 111; *Cor.* 4.6.128-32 [3054-8]). . . . It seems probable that both passages were *additions,* written expressly for the Court performance of 1604. That at [1027-33] is almost certainly so, while it should be noticed that the lines at present under consideration involve a double leave-taking on the part of the Duke, the second one being a broken line of verse." See nn. 3, 1027-33.

   76 **Ile**] I'll go. See *OED* (Will *v.* ¹ 18), ABBOTT §405, FRANZ §621, and cf. 1523 and n.

   priuily] "Secretly, privately" (*OED, adv.* 1).

   77 **stage**] JOHNSON (1755): "Exhibit publickly" (*OED, v.* 3, 1st fig. use). LEVER (ed. 1965): "Shakespeare twice uses this figure (*Ant.* III. [xiii]. 30 [2186]; v. ii. [217 (3460)]), each time in a context of distaste."

   78 **doe well**] RANN (ed. 1786): "Afford the populace a momentary gratification." HULL (in HALLIWELL, ed. 1854): "Tho' it may be politically usefull in a

Their lowd applause, and Aues vehement:
Nor doe I thinke the man of safe discretion   80
That do's affect it. Once more fare you well.
    Ang. The heauens giue safety to your purposes.
    Esc. Lead forth, and bring you backe in happi-|nesse.   83–4
                                                                Exit.
    Duk. I thanke you, fare you well.   85
    Esc. I shall desire you, Sir, to giue me leaue
To haue free speech with you; and it concernes me
To looke into the bottome of my place:
A powre I haue, but of what strength and nature,
I am not yet instructed.   90
    Ang. 'Tis so with me: Let vs with-draw together,
And we may soone our satisfaction haue
Touching that point.
    Esc. Ile wait vpon your honor.   *Exeunt.*

---

81 Once] One v1773   you] ye JOHN
84 *Exit.*] *After* 85 F2+
85 fare you] fare ye JOHN
93–4 *One verse line* v1793+ (−WH2, NLSN)
94 your] you F2

Regent, to shew himself to his subjects occasionally." SCHMIDT (1874, p. 325): "To be convenient, to fit, to succeed, to thrive." So *OED* (*v.* 20). EVANS (ed. 1974): "Show their good will."
    rellish] SCHMIDT (1875): "Like" (*OED, v.*[1] 3b).
    79 **Aues**] CAPELL (1779, 1:glossary, 4): "Salutations, Hailings, from the Latin Word—*aue*, hail!" *OED* (*sb.* 1a): "Shout of welcome." LEVER (ed. 1965): "For Elizabethan writers it often suggested crowd enthusiasms. Cf. Webster, *Appius and Virginia*, V. ii. 6–7."
    80 **safe**] SCHMIDT (1875): "Sound" (*OED, a.* 4).
    81 **do's affect it**] HUNTER (ed. 1873): "Is fond of it." See n. 7. LEVER (ed. 1965, p. xii): The apostrophe is characteristic of Crane. See HOWARD-HILL (1972), pp. 43 ff. and nn. 114, 131, 207. F1 has *do's* seven times, *does* once in 813, and *doe's* once in 1023.
    82 **safety**] "Protection" (*OED,* 3).
    83 **Lead forth**] May they conduct you (*OED,* Lead *v.*[1] 2).
    happinesse] SCHMIDT (1874): "Good fortune" (*OED,* 1).
    84 *Exit.*] The Duke exits after his speech in 85.
    87 **free**] SCHMIDT (1874): "Open, candid, unreserved" (*OED, a.* 25).
    88 **To . . . bottome**] SCHMIDT (1874, p. 132): "To know it throughout." *OED* (*sb.* 12): "*To search, etc., to the bottom:* to examine thoroughly." Cf. *OED,* Look (*v.* 16, *Look into*).
    place] SCHMIDT (1875): "Office" (*OED, sb.* 14).
    90 **instructed**] *OED* (*v.* 2): "To apprise, inform."
    92 **satisfaction**] SCHMIDT (1875): "Full information, release from uncertainty and suspense" (*OED,* 6). Cf. 1988.
    94 **wait vpon**] Accompany, escort (*OED, v.*[1] 14k).

Scena Secunda.   1.2

Enter Lucio, and two other Gentlemen.   96

Luc. If the *Duke*, with the other Dukes, come not to
composition with the King of *Hungary*, why then all the
Dukes fall vpon the King.
1. *Gent.* Heauen grant vs its peace, but not the King   100

---

95 *Scena Secunda*] SCENE III POPE, HAN1, WARB, JOHN   *The Street.* ROWE1-
SIS; *The same. A public place.* ARD2
96 *other*] *Om.* ROWE1-CAM2, ARD1, CAM3

---

95 *Scena Secunda*] CAPELL (1780, 2:3:33): This scene "is a sort of battle at
sharps, or a give-and-take plate between wits of the same cast, their wit turning all
upon their debaucheries: Lucio is the first setter-out . . . and the first Gentleman joins
him, in two speeches, in a run upon their other companion: after which, Lucio (whose
tongue pardons nobody) turns suddenly upon the one who had join'd him, and, by
wire-drawing the last of his speeches, finds means to run his wit upon him."
    97 **the other Dukes**] LEVER (ed. 1965, p. xxxii): " 'The other dukes' might
suggest any continental potentates, and could well have hinted at the presence in
London [in 1604] of envoys from the Austrian Archdukes, Albert and Isabel, who
also held the titles of Dukes of Burgundy, Styria, and other provinces."
    98 **composition**] SCHMIDT (1874): "Compact, agreement, accord" (*OED*, 23b).
See n. 2593–4.
    King of *Hungary*] WHITE (1854, pp. 126–32): Since Whetstone dates his
story in *Heptameron* "At what time *Coruinus* the scourge of the *Turkes*, rayned as
Kinge of *Bohemia*" (see p. 370 below), the period of *MM* is evidently between 1476,
when Mathias Corvinus overran Austria, and 1490, when he died. As he marched
on Vienna in 1485, we are able to determine almost the very year required. [But Sh.
was not writing annals.] LASCELLES (1953, p. 54): "The King of Hungary . . . looks
much like an elusive half-memory of Corvinus King of Hungary, the overlord of Julio
in Whetstone's play."
    99 **fall vpon**] Attack (*OED*, Fall *v.* 64b, 69b).
    100 **Heauen . . . peace**] "Dona nobis pacem," "Grant us thy peace" (*OED*,
Peace *sb.* 5, "Calmness; *peace of mind, soul,* or *conscience*").
    its] *OED* (*poss. pron.*): "*Its* does not appear in any of the works of Shakspere
published during his life-time . . . but there are 9 examples of *it's,* and 1 of *its,* in
the plays first printed in the folio of 1623." This is the only *its.* ABBOTT (§228): Here

20

of *Hungaries.*

2. *Gent.* Amen.

Luc. Thou conclud'st like the Sanctimonious Pirat,
that went to sea with the ten Commandements, but
scrap'd one out of the Table.   105

2. *Gent.* Thou shalt not Steale?

Luc. I, that he raz'd.

1. *Gent.* Why? 'twas a commandement, to command

---

103 conclud'st] could'st F4   Sanctimonious] testimonious POPE2
106 Thou . . . Steale?] *Marked as quotation* DYCE, WH, STAU, CAM, GLO,
DEL4+ (−SIS)
108 1. *Gent.* Why? 'twas] 1. *Gent.* Why? *Lucio.* 'Twas COL1 *conj.,* COL2, SING2,
KTLY   Why?] ~ , POPE+ (−v1821, COL1, SING2, KTLY, COL4, SIS)

---

it is emphatic. See FRANZ §320.

100–1 L. L. K. (1915, pp. 98–9): An allusion to *A Declaration of the Lordes and
States of the Realme of Hungarie* (1605) may have been added after the play was first
acted in 1604. WILSON (ed. 1922, pp. 104–5): "After a war of thirteen years, the
Empire concluded peace with the Turks . . . on Nov. 11, 1606. This peace was signed,
against the Emperor's will, by his brother Archduke Matthias, King of Hungary.
. . . The words, at once so pointed and so irrelevant, must be a topical allusion
. . . proving that the play was lengthened sometime after Nov. 11, 1606." DURHAM
(ed. 1926): "The context, however, renders it unnecessary to assume that Shakespeare had specific continental events in mind." CHAMBERS (1930, 1:454): "It may
as well be the peace made and treacherously broken by Sigismund of Hungary in
2 Tamburlaine, i. 2; ii. 1. 2." LEVER (ed. 1965, pp. xxxi–ii): "It is more likely that
the dialogue here turned upon King James's negotiations for a settlement with Spain.
. . . The anxiety of Lucio's companions at the imminence of an end to the war reflected
a mood prevalent amongst gentlemen of fortune who feared for their occupation as
soldiers or pirates. . . . Hungary . . . also supplied a familiar pun on 'hungry' soldiers,
a 'hungry' peace, etc."

103–5 LEVER (ed. 1965): "The pirate took the Ten Commandments, traditionally
pictured on the 'tables' of stone, as his figurehead. The joke seems to be echoed in
Middleton's *Your Five Gallants* [1608], III. v." But Lucio says nothing about a figurehead. The *Table* means a wooden tablet such as hung on the wall in English churches:
see *OED* (Commandment 2b) and BRINKWORTH (1972, pp. 123, 127).

103 **Sanctimonious**] *OED* (*a.* 2): "Making a show of sanctity, affecting the
appearance of sanctity," first quotation in this sense. Cf. *sanctimony* in *Oth.* 1.3.362
(706).

104 **Commandements**] WALKER (1854, p. 126): "In the Folio . . . *commandment,*
is, when used as a trisyllable, printed *command'ment;* the entire word being a quadrisyl-
lable, *commandement.*" *OED:* "Originally 4 syllables. . . . Shaks., 1st fol., has *commandement* 4 times, *command'ment* 6 times, *commandment* 3 times."

107 **I**] Ay (*OED,* Aye, ay *interj.*), always spelled *I* in this text, as usually in Sh.'s
time.

   raz'd] Erased (*OED, v.* 3). Cf. *razure* 2361.

108 **Why?**] DYCE (1844, p. 17): "Here, as in very many passages of early books,

21

the Captaine and all the rest from their functions: they
put forth to steale: There's not a Souldier of vs all, that   110
in the thanks-giuing before meate, do rallish the petition
well, that praies for peace.

2. *Gent.* I neuer heard any Souldier dislike it.

Luc. I beleeue thee: for I thinke thou neuer was't
where Grace was said.   115

2. *Gent.* No? a dozen times at least.

1. *Gent.* What? In meeter?

---

111 before] after HAN1   do] does WARB, CAP; doth HAN1, JOHN, v1773-
STAU, KTLY-HUD2, ARD1

---

the compositor has put a point of interrogation after 'Why', when the word is merely
used emphatically." HOWARD-HILL (1972, pp. 82, 85): *MM* in F has 347 interrogation marks and no exclamation marks. "Jaggard's compositors at least did not trouble
themselves to distinguish exclamation from interrogation marks when setting from
manuscript copy."

109 **functions**] See *OED* (*sb.* 4): "Profession, calling." LEVER (ed. 1965): Cf.
1H4 1.2.116–17 (212–13). See n. 1734.

110 **put forth**] See *OED* (Put *v.* [1] 42k): "Set out . . . to sea."

111 **thanks-giuing before meate**] EMERSON (1856; ed. 1966, p. 129) heard at
Oxford "the ancient form of grace before meals." See n. 115. STAUNTON (ed. 1859):
"It is found in ancient rituals in the very words of the text, 'Heaven grant us its
peace'." *Preces Privatae,* published by the authority of Elizabeth in 1564 [ed. 1573,
sig. Gg6], directs that "the Acts of Thanksgiving in Eating shall always be concluded
by these short prayers," ending "pacem nobis donet perpetuam. Amen." CLARK &
GLOVER (ed. 1863): "Hanmer's reading [*after meat*] is recommended by the fact that
in the old forms of 'graces' used in many colleges, and, as we are informed, at the
Inns of Court, the prayer for peace comes always after, and never before, meat. But
as the mistake may easily have been made by Shakespeare, or else deliberately put
into the mouth of the 'First Gentleman', we have not altered the text." WORDS-
WORTH (1864, pp. 176–8): Cf. *Cor.* 4.7.3–4 (3093–4), "the Grace 'fore meate";
1H4 1.2.19–23 (131–5); and *Shr.* 4.1.162 (1788). LEVER (ed. 1965) quotes Montaigne (1603, bk. 1, ch. 21): "no Souldier is pleased with the peace of his Citie." In
The Tryall of Cheualry (1605), sig. C1[v], Cavaliero Dick Bowyer says, "A pox a peace."

meate] See *OED* (*sb.* 4b): "A meal."

rallish] "Relish," spelled *rellish* in 78 (see n.) and usually in Sh., but *Rallish*
in *Cor.* 2.1.206 (1099).

113 **dislike**] *OED* (*v.* 3b): "Show or express aversion to."

114 **was't**] The redundant apostrophe characteristic of Crane (see n. 81), printed
again in 2758.

115 **Grace**] See *OED* (*sb.* 20): "A short prayer either asking a blessing before,
or rendering thanks after, a meal." Cf. n. 111.

117 **In meeter**] JOHNSON (ed. 1765): "In the primers, there are metrical graces,
such as, I suppose, were used in *Shakespear*'s time." CAPELL (1780, 2:3:33): "This
can only relate to some lewd graces, pen'd by such debauchees as the speaker for their

Luc. In any proportion: or in any language.

1. *Gent.* I thinke, or in any Religion.

Luc. I, why not? Grace, is Grace, despight of all con- 120
trouersie: as for example; Thou thy selfe art a wicked
villaine, despight of all Grace.

1. *Gent.* Well: there went but a paire of sheeres betweene vs.

118-21 In . . . as] Not in any profession, or in any language, I think, or in any religion. 2 *Gent.* And why not? . . . controversie. *Lucio.* As HAN1
123 1. *Gent.*] 2 *Gent.* HAN1, PEL1

---

disorderly banquets." NARES (1822, p. 210): "In the play of *Timon,* there is an instance of a metrical grace said by Apemantus [1.2.63-72 (404-14)]." HALLIWELL (ed. 1854) quotes two metrical graces from Holyband, *The French Schoole-Maister* (ed. 1612). HART (ed. 1905): "For a metrical grace, . . . perhaps a burlesque, see the old play *How a Man may choose a Good Wife from a Bad* (Hazlitt's *Dods*[*ley,*] ix. 58, 59), 1602."

118-22 CLARK & GLOVER (ed. 1863): "In the remainder of this scene Hanmer and other Editors have made capricious changes in the distribution of the dialogue. . . . It is impossible to discern any difference of character in the three speakers, or to introduce logical sequence into their buffoonery."

118 **proportion**] WARBURTON (ed. 1747): *"Measure."* JOHNSON (ed. 1765): "Form." WORDSWORTH (1864, p. 177): "I rather think it means *prose or verse, chant or hymn,* as 'in any language' means especially, I imagine, *Latin or English.* " SCHMIDT (1875): "Metre, cadence." HART (ed. 1905): "Refers perhaps to the tediously long graces in vogue at this time." ONIONS (1911): "Metrical or musical rhythm" (*OED, sb.* 10).

language] LEVER (ed. 1965): " 'Language' and 'religion' probably hint at Latin graces and hence Roman Catholic practice, as a dig at the religion of 2 Gent." But the point seems rather that he is too indifferent to care about the language or kind of religion.

120 **Grace**] See *OED* (*sb.* 11a): "The free and unmerited favour of God," and (11b) "The divine influence which operates in men."

120-1 **controuersie**] WARBURTON (ed. 1747): "Satirically insinuating that the *controversies* about *grace* were so intricate and endless, that the disputants unsettled every thing but this, that *grace was grace.* " JOHNSON (ed. 1765): "I am in doubt whether *Shakespear*'s thoughts reached so far into ecclesiastical disputes. . . . The nature of things is unalterable; Grace is as immutably Grace, as his [Lucio's] merry antagonist is a *wicked villain.* Difference of religion cannot make a *Grace* not to be *Grace,* a *Prayer* not to be *holy.* " LEVER (ed. 1965): "Lucio evades a major theological dispute between Catholics and Reformers, while playing on grace as (i) thanksgiving, (ii) propriety, (iii) divine mercy manifested towards sinners."

123 **Well**] EVANS (ed. 1974): "Often used to show that note has been taken of an insult; cf. [153]." See TILLEY (W269) and WILSON (p. 879): "Well, well is a word of malice."

123-4 **there . . . vs**] JOHNSON (ed. 1765): "We are both of the same piece." A common proverb: see TILLEY (P36) and WILSON (p. 607).

Luc. I grant: as there may betweene the Lists, and   125
the Veluet. Thou art the List.

1. *Gent.* And thou the Veluet; thou art good veluet;
thou'rt a three pild-peece I warrant thee: I had as liefe
be a Lyst of an English Kersey, as be pil'd, as thou art
pil'd, for a French Veluet. Do I speake feelingly now?   130

Luc. I thinke thou do'st: and indeed with most pain-

---

125 Lists] list COL3, DYCE2, DYCE3, HUD2
129 an] *Om.* CAP
130 pil'd] pilled ARD2

---

125 **Lists**] *OED* (*sb.* ³ 2): "The selvage, border, or edge of a cloth."
128 **three pild-peece**] JOHNSON (1755): *Three-piled*, "Set with a thick pile."
NARES (1822): *"Three-pile.* The finest and most costly kind of velvet. . . . Hence
Shakespeare gives the name of *Three-pile* to a mercer [2087], as dealing in that
commodity. *Three-pil'd, a.* Refined, approaching or pretending to perfection; metaphorically." *OED* (Piled *ppl. a.*³ 2): "Having a pile or long nap, as velvet." LIN-
THICUM (1936, p. 126): "Velvet was made also in two piles upon a ground of satin.
Since this makes three heights, if the satin ground be counted as one, it is probably
the 'three pile velvet' mentioned in *Westward Hoe* [Dekker, 1.1.64], *Winter's Tale*
[4.3.14 (1681–2)], and many other plays, and used as a figure of perfection in *Measure
for Measure.*"
     warrant] SCHMIDT (1875): "Assure" (*OED, v.* 5).
     I had as liefe] SCHMIDT (1874, p. 649): "I should like as much; followed by
an inf. without *to.*" See n. 224.
129 **Kersey**] ONIONS (1911): "Kind of coarse cloth," as in *LLL* 5.2.413 (2345).
LINTHICUM (1936, pp. 79–81): "Kersey was a light-weight, narrow, wool cloth in
many colours, costing from one to three shillings a yard. It was probably manufac-
tured originally at Kersey, Suffolk. . . . Broad-list kersies . . . had very wide selvedge
or 'list' . . . and they were held in contempt. The First Gentleman's statement . . .
may have had these wasteful cloths in mind."
     pil'd] JOHNSON (ed. 1765): "Alludes to the loss of hair in the *French* disease
[syphilis]." STEEVENS (Var. 1773): "The jest lies between the similar sound of the
words *pill'd* and *pil'd.*" DYCE (1867): "A quibble between *piled* = *peeled,* 'stripped
of hair, bald' (from the French disease), and *piled* as applied to velvet." LEVER (ed.
1965): *"Pilled,* deprived of hair [*OED, ppl. a.* 2]: a frequent effect of the mercury
treatment then given for venereal disease." ROSEBURY (1973, p. 103): "We have a
word play on the disease commonly called piles [*OED, sb.* ⁶], on the French disease,
and on not drinking out of the same cup to avoid infection."
130 **for**] HART (ed. 1905): "After the manner of."
     French Veluet] COLMAN (1974, p. 195): "Quibble, (a) costly and soft velvet,
the opposite of a rough 'English kersey'; (b) patch of velvet used in treating syphilis,
to cover lanced chancres." Cf. *AWW* 4.5.100–2 (2577–9).
     feelingly] SCHMIDT (1874): "So as to hit home." ONIONS (1911): "Appro-
priately, to the purpose" (*OED, adv.* 2). COLMAN (1974, p. 193): "Quibble, (a) to
the point, (b) probingly, painfully (because of venereal disease)."
131 **do'st**] HOWARD-HILL (1972, p. 89): The apostrophe is characteristic of
Crane. See n. 81.

full feeling of thy speech: I will, out of thine owne confession, learne to begin thy health; but, whilst I liue forget to drinke after thee.

1. *Gen.* I think I haue done my selfe wrong, haue I not?   135

2. *Gent.* Yes, that thou hast; whether thou art tainted,
or free.   *Enter Bawde.*

Luc. Behold, behold, where Madam *Mitigation* comes.
I haue purchas'd as many diseases vnder her Roofe,
As come to   140

2. *Gent.* To what, I pray?

Luc. Iudge.

135–6 1. *Gen.* . . . 2. *Gent.*] 2 *Gent.* . . . 1 *Gent.* HAN1
136 art] are F4
137 SCENE IV. POPE, HAN1, WARB   *Enter Bawde.*] *After* 150 THEO, WARB,
JOHN, v1773-ARD1
138 *Luc.*] *1 Gent.* MAL, v1821   Behold . . . comes.] *Prose* CAP+
139–40 *Prose* POPE2+
139 I haue] *1 Gent.* I have THEOBALD (1726, p. 156) *conj.,* POPE2-JOHN2,
v1821, COL, SING2, WH1, STAU, KTLY, DYCE2, DEL4, DYCE3, HUD2, BUL, ARD1,
KIT1, SIS+ (−ARD2); He has HAL
140 to_] ~ — F2+
141 I] *Om.* ROWE2-POPE2, HAN1
142 *Luc.*] *1 Gent.* POPE2-JOHN2, v1773-v1821, SING, KTLY, DYCE2, DYCE3,
HUD2, BUL, ALEX, SIS

---

132 **feeling**] See *OED* (*vbl. sb.* 3): "Knowledge of an object through having felt
its effects."

133 **begin**] SCHMIDT (1874): "Drink to . . . cf. Sonn. 114, 14."

134 **drinke after thee**] HART (1908, p. 63): Cf. Montaigne (1603, bk. 1, ch.
40): "hee would not drinke after him, for feare hee should take the pox of him."

135 **done . . . wrong**] HUNTER (ed. 1873): "Put myself in the wrong."
SCHMIDT (1875): *To do wrong,* "not to do justice" (*OED,* Wrong *sb.*² 2c), as in
709–10, 1617. HART (ed. 1905): "Discredited myself, 'given myself away'." Cf.
Tmp. 1.2.443 (595).

136 **tainted**] SCHMIDT (1875): *Taint,* "to infect with a disease" (*OED, ppl. a.*
1b).

138 **Madam**] *OED* (*sb.* 2d): First example of the word "in playful or derisive
uses." NEWCOMER (1929, p. 22): Cf. such titles as "lady *Disdaine*" in *Ado* 1.1.119
(115).

Mitigation] PARTRIDGE (1947, p. 155): "She provides the means of mitigat-
ing sexual desire."

139–40 Prose set as verse.

140 **to_**] THISELTON (1901, p. 37): "The use of dashes is rare in the Folio. The
uncompleted sentence is, therefore, indicated by the absence of a stop [here and in
2335]. . . . Such cases suggest careful attention to the punctuation of the manuscript
on the part of the printer." But often the compositor sets a full stop or colon after
an incomplete speech, as in 1518, 2140. Cf. 1272 and n.

142 **Iudge**] SCHMIDT (1874): "Guess."

2. *Gent.* To three thousand Dollours a yeare.

1. *Gent.* I, and more.

Luc. A French crowne more.   145

1. *Gent.* Thou art alwayes figuring diseases in me; but
thou art full of error, I am sound.

Luc. Nay, not (as one would say) healthy: but so
sound, as things that are hollow; thy bones are hollow;
Impiety has made a feast of thee.   150

1. *Gent.* How now, which of your hips has the most
profound Ciatica?

Bawd. Well, well: there's one yonder arrested, and

---

143 Dollours] Ff.; Dollars ROWE3-STAU (−CAP, WH1), DEL4, COL4; Dolours
ROWE1 *etc.*
146 1. *Gent.*] 2 *Gent.* COL1, COL2, COL3, STAU
150 has] hath POPE1-v1773 (−CAP)
151 SCENE IV. JOHN

---

143 **Dollours**] HANMER (ed. 1743): *"A quibble intended between* dollars *and*
dolours." JOHNSON (ed. 1765): Cf. *Tmp.* 2.1.18–19 (693–4). SCHMIDT (1874):
Also *Lr.* 2.4.54 (1326). KÖKERITZ (1953, p. 234): The pun shows that *dolour* was
pronounced like *dollar:* see *OED*.
145 **French crowne**] THEOBALD (ed. 1733): *"Lucio* means here not the piece
of mony so call'd, but that *Venerial* Scab which among the Surgeons is stil'd *Corona
Veneris."* Cf. *MND* 1.2.99 (358). NARES (1822): *"French crown.* This was a most
tempting word for equivocation, as it might mean three things:—1. The crown of a
Frenchman's head; 2. A piece of French money; 3. The baldness produced by a
disease, supposed to be French [syphilis]."
146-7 ROSENBAUM (1975) assigns this speech to Bawd, citing *diseases* in 139.
146 **figuring**] *OED* (*v.* 3): "Imagine," first quotation in this sense. EVANS (ed.
1974): "(1) reckoning (with reference to the preceding lines); (2) imagining."
149 **sound**] SCHMIDT (1875, pp. 1091, 1421): "Clear, shrill." Quibbling here
and in *Ado* 3.2.13 (1219), "sound as a bell." CAMPBELL (ed. 1949): "(1) in good
health, (2) the sound given by hollow things when struck."
    bones are hollow] UPTON (1748, p. 148): Cf. *Rom.* 2.4.36–7 (1138–9) and
Tro. 2.3.21 (1222) [also 5.1.26 in Q]. STEEVENS (Var. 1793) adds *Tim.* 4.3.152
(1768). ROSEBURY (1973, p. 109) notes that Timon gives "a vivid picture of severe
secondary and late syphilis, with destructive lesions of bones."
150 **Impiety**] SCHMIDT (1874): "Sin, wickedness."
151 **How now**] See *OED* (How *adv.* 4b): " 'How is it now?' "
152 **profound**] *OED* (*a.* 1b): "Deep-seated."
    Ciatica] JOHNSON (1755): *Sciatica,* "The hip gout," quoting this and *Tim.*
4.1.23 (1526). SCHMIDT (1875): "Considered as a symptom of syphilis," as in *Tro.*
(Q) 5.1.25. LEVER (ed. 1965): "While sciatica was associated with bawds in Latin
comedy, the remark here is surely a reply to Lucio's taunt." But *How now* shows that
1 Gent. is speaking to Mrs. Overdone. Cf. Skelton, *Magnyfycence,* line 1956: "Allasse,
I haue the cyatyca full euyll in my hyppe."
153 **Well**] See n. 123.
    yonder] EVANS (ed. 1974): "Back there (not limited to what is in view)." See
n. 176.

carried to prison, was worth fiue thousand of you all.

2. *Gent.* Who's that I pray'thee?   155

Bawd. Marry Sir, that's *Claudio*, Signior *Claudio*.

1. *Gent.* *Claudio* to prison? 'tis not so.   (F1ᵛb)

Bawd. Nay, but I know 'tis so: I saw him arrested:
saw him carried away: and which is more, within these
three daies his head to be chop'd off.   160

Luc. But, after all this fooling, I would not haue it so:
Art thou sure of this?

Bawd. I am too sure of it: and it is for getting Madam
Iulietta with childe.

Luc. Beleeue me this may be: he promis'd to meete   165
me two howres since, and he was euer precise in promise
keeping.

2. *Gent.* Besides you know, it drawes somthing neere
to the speech we had to such a purpose.

1. *Gent.* But most of all agreeing with the proclamatiō.   170

Luc. Away: let's goe learne the truth of it.   *Exit.*

Bawd. Thus, what with the war; what with the sweat,

---

155 2 *Gent.*] 1 *Gent.* ROWE2-KNT2 (−CAP), HAL, SING2, KTLY, KNT3, ALEX
   Who's] And who is v1785
160 head] Head is ROWE1-JOHN2, v1773-RANN, COL3; head's CAP, MAL-v1821,
SING, KNT, WH, KTLY, DYCE2, DYCE3-HUD2
171 *Exit.*] *Exeunt* LUCIO, *and* Gentlemen. CAP, MAL+

---

154 **carried**] See *OED* (*v.* 5b): "To take by force, as a prisoner." See n. 208.
   was] Who was. See ABBOTT §244, FRANZ §348.
155 **pray'thee**] HOWARD-HILL (1972, p. 128) notes that the apostrophe shows
Crane's influence, as in *pre'thee* 269.
156 **Marry**] See *OED* (*int.*): "An exclamation of asseveration, surprise, indignation, etc."
   Signior] SCHMIDT (1875): "A title of respect among the Italians. . . . Applied
to people of other countries:" to Claudio in 156, 203, 1256, and to Lucio in 2638,
2705.
159 **which**] FRANZ (§337): "What." See *OED* (*pron.* 11): "That which."
161 **after**] *OED* (*prep.* 10): "Subsequent to and notwithstanding," quoting
2723–4 as first example.
   would] See n. 17.
163 **Madam**] See *OED* (*sb.* 2a): "As a prefixed title," with a given name.
166 **precise**] See n. 342.
168 **drawes . . . neere**] Approaches (*OED, v.* 83).
   somthing] See n. 70.
169 **to . . . purpose**] SCHMIDT (1875, p. 921): "With respect to this."
171 ***Exit***] For *Exeunt,* as in 346, 1400, 1489, 1833, 1913, 2075, 2762.
172–204 WILSON (ed. 1922): "The style of this section is markedly different

what with the gallowes, and what with pouerty, I am
Custom-shrunke. How now? what's the newes with
you.   *Enter Clowne.*   175
   Clo. Yonder man is carried to prison.
   Baw. Well: what has he done?
   Clo. A Woman.
   Baw. But what's his offence?

---

175 you.] ~ ? F2 + (−v1785)   *Enter*] SCENE V. *Enter* POPE, HAN1, WARB,
JOHN   *Enter Clowne.*] *After* poverty, (173) CAP; *after* custom-shrunk. (174) DYCE,
STAU-GLO, DEL4, HUD2+   *Ad. A Gaoler and Prisoner pass over the stage* PEN2

---

from that which goes before. The dialogue seems suddenly to come alive."
   172 **what**] JOHNSON (1755): "Used adverbially for partly; in part." *OED*
(D.II.2b): "Introducing advb. phrases formed with prepositions," implying "in consequence of, on account of, as a result of." See FRANZ §342.
   war;] BROOK (1976, p. 157): "The semicolon shows that *war* has stronger
emphasis than the other nouns." But the semicolon is prob. not Sh.'s: see HOWARD-
HILL (1972), pp. 82–5.
   the sweat] JOHNSON (ed. 1765): "This may allude to the *Sweating sickness*
. . . but more probably to the method of cure then used for the diseases contracted
in Brothels." CAPELL (1780, 2:3:34): "The plague. . . . We have in these circumstances a picture of the situation of England, and of her sentiments also, in the latter
end of 1603." HART (ed. 1905): "See Dekker's account of the 1603 epidemic in
A Wonderfull Yeere." LEVER (ed. 1965, p. xxxii): "Overdone's complaint links a
number of factors operative in the winter of 1603–4: the continuance of the war with
Spain; the plague in London; the treason trials and executions at Winchester in
connection with the plots of Raleigh and others; the slackness of trade in the deserted
capital."
   174 **Custom-shrunke**] SCHMIDT (1874): "Having fewer customers than formerly" (*OED,* Custom *sb.* 6).
   176 **Yonder man**] WILSON (ed. 1922): " 'Yonder man' is curious, since Claudio
has not yet appeared. Possibly Shakespeare placed this dialogue after the verse which
now follows it." LASCELLES (1953, p. 51): "I do not, however, find it necessary to
suppose that 'yonder man' is Claudio." LEVER (ed. 1965, pp. xix–xx): The audience
"would undoubtedly assume that Claudio was meant." The suspicion that 176–82
"were not meant to be printed is strengthened by the abnormally crowded appearance of sig. F1ᵛ where the passage occurs, with its extremely compressed spaces for
stage directions and scene headings." NOSWORTHY (ed. 1969): *Yonder man* "must
surely, on internal evidence, be some other victim of Angelo's *proclamation.*" But it
may be that Pompey had seen Claudio in custody, as Mrs. Overdone had seen or
heard of him when she said, "there's one yonder arrested, and carried to prison.
. . . Signior *Claudio*" (153–4, 156). See n. 153.
   177–8 THEOBALD (1729, in NICHOLS, 1817, 2:285): "Downright indecency"
(in the original letter, "Downright Bawdry"). Cf. *Tit.,* Q 1611 [and Q1, 4.2.76].
COLLINS (i.e., STEEVENS, in MALONE, 1780, 1:94): Cf. *WT* 1.2.311–12 (408–9)
and Marlowe's tr. of Ovid's *Elegies.* SCHMIDT (1874, p. 324): *Do,* "used for the act
of cohabitation." LEVER (ed. 1965): Cf. 569 ff. See nn. 570, 2959.

Clo. Groping for Trowts, in a peculiar Riuer. 180

Baw. What? is there a maid with child by him?

Clo. No: but there's a woman with maid by him:
you haue not heard of the proclamation, haue you?

Baw. What proclamation, man?

Clow. All howses in the Suburbs of *Vienna* must bee 185
pluck'd downe.

Bawd. And what shall become of those in the Citie?

Clow. They shall stand for seed: they had gon down

---

185 howses] bawdy-houses TYRWHITT *conj. in* v1778, COLNE, COL2, COL3, COL4; houses of resort TYRWHITT *conj. in* v1778, OXF1

---

180 **Groping**] HALLIWELL (1847): "A mode of catching trout by tickling them with the hands under rocks or banks." IDEM (ed. 1854): Cf. *Locrine* (1595, *Sh. Apoc.*, 3.3.18, "to fish her belly"). *OED* (*v.* 2b): "Feeling for them in the water," first quotation, but see Marston, *Antonio and Mellida* (1602), 2.1.115–17. HART (ed. 1905): Cf. *tickling* in *TN* 2.5.25 (1037) and *grope and tickle* in Chapman's *Al Fooles* (1605, 3.1.119). A periphrasis for "copulating."

peculiar Riuer] MALONE (1780, 1:94): "A river belonging to an individual; not publick property." HART (ed. 1905): "In private water—poaching." LEVER (ed. 1965): "*Peculiar:* own (*O.E.D.* 1); 'yonder man's' own river, i.e. his own wife; implicitly contrasting the 'offence' to that of Mistress Overdone's customers. Cf. *Oth.* IV. i. 68–70 [2448–50]." Malone's explanation is more probable.

182 **with maid**] SEYMOUR (1805, 1:84): "I suspect that a quibble is intended; a woman *with-made* by him, *i. e. made* by him according to the sense in which to make or to *do* has already been used." But KÖKERITZ (1953, p. 126) notes that *withmade* is not recorded as a word. HART (ed. 1905): "Can maid mean child here, not girl?" WILSON (ed. 1922): " 'Maids' are the young of skate and other fish (v. N.E.D. 'maid' *sb.*[1] 7) and Pompey has just been speaking of 'groping for trouts'." HARDING (ed. 1954): "The explanation, if correct, adds little point and much coarseness to the quibble." It is not likely to be correct. Pompey jokes that a pregnant woman is not a virgin, but that the child she carries is. Cf. *TN* 5.1.270 (2429), where Sebastian is both "a maid and man" (*OED*, Maid *sb.*[1] 2c).

185 **howses**] SEYMOUR (1805, 1:84): "Mr. Tyrwhitt proposes that we should read bawdy-houses; but in this colloquy between the bawd and her tapster, the distinction seems superfluous; and there is, perhaps, more humour and character in its omission: no other kind of houses was in the clown's thoughts."

Suburbs] HART (ed. 1905): "The usual situation for houses of ill-fame and resort of disreputable people in all walled cities." *OED* (1) quotes Nashe, *Christs Teares* (1593, 2:148): "*London,* what are thy Suburbs but licensed Stewes?"

186 **pluck'd downe**] See *OED* (*v.* 2b): *Pluck down,* "demolish." LEVER (ed. 1965): "Pompey's talk of demolitions may have been suggested by the proclamation of 16 September 1603, intended as a precaution against plague, but directed chiefly against the brothel quarters of the suburbs."

188 **stand for seed**] EVANS (ed. 1974): "Remain standing to assure the continuance of prostitution (like grain left uncut to provide seed for another season), with a bawdy equivoque."

had] Would have. Past subjunctive (*OED,* Have *v.* 22). Cf. 2250.

to, but that a wise Burger put in for them.

Bawd. But shall all our houses of resort in the Sub-   190
urbs be puld downe?

Clow. To the ground, Mistris.

Bawd. Why heere's a change indeed in the Common-
wealth: what shall become of me?

Clow. Come: feare not you: good Counsellors lacke   195
no Clients: though you change your place, you neede
not change your Trade: Ile bee your Tapster still; courage, there will bee pitty taken on you; you that haue
worne your eyes almost out in the seruice, you will bee
considered.   200

Bawd. What's to doe heere, *Thomas* Tapster? let's

---

190 all] *Om.* ROWE2-POPE2, HAN1, KTLY

---

189 **Burger**] See *OED* (Burgher *sb.* 1): "A citizen. Chiefly used of continental
towns."

put in] JOHNSON (1755): "To offer a claim." HART (ed. 1905): "Applied."
OED (*v.*[1] 44d): "To interpose on behalf of some one or something, to plead or
intercede *for,*" only quotation in this sense. LEVER (ed. 1965): "(i) He interceded
for them. . . . (ii) He made a bid to acquire them. Both senses may well be present."

193–4 **Common-wealth**] See *OED* (5 *fig.*): "A number of persons united by
some common interest." COLMAN (1974, p. 188): "With pun on *common.*" Cf. 497
Common-weale, 498 *common houses.*

195–6 **good . . . Clients**] CAMPBELL (1859, p. 36): "This comparison is not very
flattering to the bar, but it seems to show a familiarity with both the professions
alluded to." *OED* (Counsellor 3): "A counselling lawyer."

197 **Tapster**] JOHNSON (1755): "One whose business is to draw beer in an
alehouse." Cf. n. 656.

199 **worne . . . seruice**] LEVER (ed. 1965): "A sly allusion to 'Blind Cupid',
traditionally the sign in front of brothels. . . . Prostitution is 'the service', as if it were
a public service maintained for the good of the state. Cf. III. ii. 116 [1608]."

200 **considered**] SCHMIDT (1874): "To have regard to." *OED* (*v.* 8): "To
requite, recompense, remunerate."

201 **What's to doe**] *OED* (Do *v.* 33): "What is the matter?"

Thomas **Tapster**] THEOBALD (1729, in NICHOLS, 1817, 2:286): "Does not
the Poet here a little forget himself? The Clown afterwards, upon examination
. . . says his name is Pompey Bum." THIRLBY (1747–53): "It will be said perhaps
that the Customers gave him the name of Pompey and perhaps of Bum too." DOUCE
(1807, 1:122): "Perhaps she is only quoting some old saying or ballad." BOSWELL
(Var. 1821): "Names were, and still are, applied to different occupations, such as
Tom Tapster, Tom Toss-pot, &c." DYCE (1853, p. 24): "*Thomas* or *Tom* was the name
commonly applied to a *Tapster;* for the sake of the alliteration, it would seem." See
Greene, *A Quip for an Upstart Courtier* (1592; ed. Grosart, 11:275): "You, Tom
tapster, that tap your smale cannes of beere." SYMONS (in IRVING & MARSHALL, ed.
1889): "But of course it is a mere class-name, no more peculiar to one man than John
Barleycorn or Tommy Atkins."

withdraw?

Clo. Here comes Signior *Claudio*, led by the Prouost
to prison: and there's Madam *Iuliet*.   *Exeunt.*

Scena Tertia.   205

Enter Prouost, Claudio, Iuliet, Officers, Lucio, & 2. Gent.

---

202 withdraw?] ∼ . F2+
205 *Scena Tertia*] SCENE VI POPE, HAN1, WARB, JOHN; *om.* ROWE, THEO, HAL,
DYCE, STAU-GLO, HUD2+
206 *Claudio*] *Claudia* F4-ROWE2   *Iuliet*] GAOLER T. WHITE MS *conj.*, HAL; *om.*
COLNE, COL2, HUD2   *Lucio, & 2. Gent.*] *Om.* ROWE, DYCE, STAU-GLO, DEL4,
HUD2-NLSN, SIS, EVNS

---

203 **led**] Conducted. See nn. 83, 1534.
205 DYCE (1844, p. 18): "As there is no change of *place* here, a new 'Scene'
ought not to have been marked." IDEM (ed. 1857): F marks "the *entrance of all the
persons who are successively to take part in the scene.*" LASCELLES (1953, pp. 52–3): "The
Folio scene-division at Pompey's exit signifies no more than the departure of one set
of characters and appearance on the stage of another." GREG (1955, p. 356): "F
marks a new scene at I. ii. 120 because there is a clear stage. But in the previous line
Pompey announces the approach of the Provost and his prisoners, who now enter,
so that there can be no change of locality and the action is continuous, and modern
editors continue the scene." See n. 1490.
206 *Iuliet*] STEEVENS (Var. 1773): "This speech [237–47] is surely too indelicate to be spoken concerning Juliet, before her face, for she appears to be brought
in with the rest, tho' she has nothing to say. The Clown points her out as they enter;
and yet, from Claudio's telling Lucio, *that he knows the lady,* &c. one would think she
was not meant to have made her personal appearance on the scene." RITSON (1783,
p. 17): "The little seeming impropriety there is will be entirely removed by supposing, that, when Claudio stops to speak to Lucio, the provosts officers depart with
Julietta." MALONE (ed. 1790): "Claudio may be supposed to speak to Lucio apart."
T. WHITE (1793, fol. 15ᵛ): "I have little doubt that by a mistake Juliet was printed
for *Jailor.*" MARSHALL (ed. 1889): "It looks very much here as if the author had
originally intended to make some use of Julietta or Juliet in this scene, but in the
course of working it out had changed that intention." LASCELLES (1953, p. 53): "Did
Shakespeare intend to bring Juliet on, but change his mind and forget to erase the
tell-tale reference? Or, did he bring her on for a brief scene of farewell, afterwards
cut?" GREG (1955, p. 355): "Juliet is certainly present (see [204]) but does not
speak. This in the circumstances may be modesty, but her presence is curiously
ignored by the other characters." MIKKELSEN (1958, p. 267 n.) finds her presence
dramatically effective: "by attracting our sympathy, Juliet's humiliation would help

Cla. Fellow, why do'st thou show me thus to th'world?
Beare me to prison, where I am committed.

Pro. I do it not in euill disposition,
But from Lord *Angelo* by speciall charge.   210

Clau. Thus can the demy-god (Authority)
Make vs pay downe, for our offence, by waight
The words of heauen; on whom it will, it will,

---

210 Lord] *Om.* F2-F4
212 offence] offence' (*plural*) WALKER (1854, pp. 264–5) *conj.,* HUD2
waight‸] ~ ; HAN1; ~ . WARB-STAU, KTLY-IRV, BUL, RLTR, ARD2
213 The words] I'th' words WARBURTON *conj.* (*see* HAN2), HAN1; The sword
ROBERTS *conj. in* v1773, STAU, DYCE2, DYCE3, HUD2; The word HAL; The bonds
SIS

---

to condemn Angelo's arrest of Claudio." LEVER (ed. 1965, pp. 14, xvii): Juliet would
be "onstage, but far enough away to have no part in the dialogue." "Until her
situation has been fully explained by Claudio, it is more effective for her to be seen
than heard."

207 do'st] HOWARD-HILL (1972, p. 89): The apostrophe is characteristic of
Crane. See n. 81.

world] JOHNSON (1755): "Mankind; an hyperbolical expression for many."
IDEM (1773): "The publick." So *OED* (*sb.* 15), first quotation in this sense.

208 Beare] See *OED* (*v.* 1), "carry," and n. 154.

211 demy-god] ONIONS (1911): *Demi-*, "= half (often contemptuous)."
SCHANZER (1963, p. 78): "Authority, pretending to be like God"; cf. 875. LEVER
(ed. 1965): "No sarcasm need be inferred. 'Demi-god' (a person raised to near-
divine rank) follows the Elizabethan commonplace based on Exodus, xxii. 9 (Geneva)
and Psalm lxxxii. 6, that rulers and judges had the attributes of gods."

Authority] Printed with a capital also in 892, 1975, 2297.

212 WARBURTON (ed. 1747): "A fine expression, to signify paying the full
penalty. The metaphor is taken from paying money by *weight*, which is always exact;
not so by *tale*, on account of the practice of diminishing the species [i.e., specie]."
OED (*sb.*[1] 1, *By weight*) overlooks this fig. sense. JOHNSON (ed. 1765): "I suspect
that a line is lost." SCHMIDT (1875): *By weight*, "in just proportion, exactly," as in
Tro. 5.2.168 (3165) and *Ham.* (F) 4.5.156 (2909). HUDSON (ed. 1880): *"Offence'*
for *offences.* The Poet often has words thus elided." LEE (ed. 1907): The punctuation
of F "is clearly right. Authority can make us suffer for our offence precisely the
retribution described in the Bible." Cf. TILLEY (G186) and WILSON (p. 309): "God
gives his wrath by weight and without weight his mercy."

213–14 WILSON (ed. 1922): "The resignation of [these lines] is ill-suited with
Claudio's fierce temper at this point." SCHANZER (1963, p. 78): "The mood of these
lines is not one of resignation but of bitter indignation."

213 The words of heauen] THIRLBY (1733–47): "He will have mercy on whom
he will have mercy and whom he will he hardens." HENLEY (1780, p. 22): "The poet
applies a passage from St. Paul to the Romans, *ch.* ix. *v.* 15, 18 . . . For he saith to
Moses, I will have mercy on whom I will have mercy, &c. And again: Therefore hath
he mercy on whom he will have mercy, &c. [and whom he will he hardeneth]."

On whom it will not (soe) yet still 'tis iust.

   Luc. Why how now *Claudio?* whence comes this restraint.   215

   Cla. From too much liberty, (my *Lucio*) Liberty

As surfet is the father of much fast,

So euery Scope by the immoderate vse

Turnes to restraint: Our Natures doe pursue

Like Rats that rauyn downe their proper Bane,   220   (F2ᵃ)

A thirsty euill, and when we drinke, we die.

---

214 still 'tis iust] 'tis just still WALKER *conj. in* DYCE1 (*and* 1860, 2:249), DYCE2,
DYCE3   *Enter* Lucio. DAV; *Re-enter* LUCIO *and two* Gentlemen. DYCE, STAU-GLO,
DEL4, HUD2-NLSN, SIS, EVNS

   216–17 *Lucio*) Liberty‸ As surfet‸] F1; ~) ~ , ~~ ‸ F2-F4; ~ . ~ , ~~ ,
ARD2; ~ , ~ ; ~~ ‸ ROWE1 *etc.*

NOBLE (1935, pp. 68, 222): This line "agrees with the Genevan of Rom. ix. 15
rather than with the Bishops'." "St. Paul is quoting God, as in Exod. xxxiii. 19;
Claudio referred first to the demi-god Authority and that reminded him of the words
of God himself." See p. 280.

   214 **soe**] LEISI (ed. 1964): "Perhaps accompanied by a gesture denoting casting
away, beheading etc." EVANS (ed. 1974): "Similarly, i.e. it will not."

     still] SCHMIDT (1875): "Always" (*OED, adv.* 3).

   215 **restraint**] SCHMIDT (1875): "Confinement, detention" (*OED, sb.* 2c). Cf.
n. 1279.

   216 **liberty**] BROWN (1864, p. 49): Cf. *Err.* 2.1.15 (289), "headstrong liberty
is lasht with woe." *OED* (*sb.* 5): "Unrestrained action, conduct, or expression; freedom of behaviour or speech, beyond what is granted or recognized as proper; licence.
(*Occas.* personified)," quoting 319. TILLEY (L225) and WILSON (p. 831): "Too much
liberty spoils all." See n. 414.

   217 **surfet**] SCHMIDT (1875): "Excess in eating and drinking, gluttony; and
sickness and satiety caused by it" (*OED, sb.* 4, 5). TILLEY (S1011): "Every surfeit
foreruns a fast." Cf. 2469 *surfetting.*

   218 **Scope**] SCHMIDT (1875): "Liberty, license," as in 327. *OED* (*sb.* ² 7b): "An
instance of liberty or licence," only quotation in this sense. See n. 73.

   219 **Natures**] SCHMIDT (1875): "The physical and moral constitution of man."

   220–1 THIRLBY (1723–33): "Ratsbane makes thirsty and I think I have heard that
rats drink till they burst if they can get water." STEEVENS (Var. 1778): "So in *Revenge
for Honour*" [by Henry Glapthorne, 1654, 2.1.111–12]. TILLEY (F585) and SMITH
(1963, p. 39): "What is forbidden (baneful) is desired." DENT (1966, p. 349) quotes
Joseph Hall, *Meditations and Vowes Diuine and Morall* (1605), no. 95: Ambition makes
men "like poysoned Rats, which when they haue tasted of their bane, cannot rest till
they drinke, and then can much lesse rest, till their death."

   220 **rauyn**] JOHNSON (1755): "Devour with great eagerness and rapacity"
(*OED,* Raven *v.* 2b).

     proper] JOHNSON (ed. 1765): *"Own,"* quoting 2687 and 2796.

     Bane] See *OED* (*sb.* ¹ 2): "That which causes death," (2b) *"esp.* Poison."
TRAVERSI (1942, pp. 40–1) and CAMPBELL (1948, pp. 91–3) discuss this image.

   221 **thirsty**] *OED* (*a.* 3): "That causes thirst."

     euill] WALKER (1860, 2:197): One syllable. KÖKERITZ (1953, p. 204):

Luc. If I could speake so wisely vnder an arrest, I
would send for certaine of my Creditors: and yet, to say
the truth, I had as lief haue the foppery of freedome, as
the mortality of imprisonment: what's thy offence,   225
Claudio?
    Cla. What (but to speake of) would offend againe.
    Luc. What, is't murder?
    Cla. No.
    Luc. Lecherie?   230
    Cla. Call it so.
    Pro. Away, Sir, you must goe.
    Cla. One word, good friend:

---

225 mortality] Ff., ARD1, RLTR, SIS, PEN2, EVNS; Morality DAV, ROWE1 *etc.*
228-31 *One verse line* ARD2
228 What, is't‸] ~ ‸ ~ ‸ F2-F4; ~ ‸ ~ , ROWE1-v1821, SING, COL, WH1,
KTLY, CAM3
233-4 *One line* POPE1+ (−CAP)

"Monosyllabic . . . and may have been pronounced in the same way as the famous
eale" in *Ham.* (Q2) 1.4.36. LEVER (ed. 1965): "Not lechery but liberty, which
encourages desire."
    224 **lief**] JOHNSON (1755): "Willingly." See n. 128.
    foppery] SCHMIDT (1874): "Folly" (*OED,* 1).
    225 **mortality**] HART (ed. 1905): "Shakespeare has the word 'mortality' very
often, 'morality' [see textual notes] nowhere. In *Henry V.* IV. iii. 107 [2354], 'mortality' has the meaning of 'deadliness', which is the sense here, and forms a better
antithesis to the lively folly implied in the word 'foppery' than 'morality' does, which
at this time signified 'philosophy', or some such sense." PORTER & CLARKE (ed.
1909): "It was the dead earnest of imprisonment that struck serious wisdom out of
Claudio." RIDLEY (ed. 1935): "Almost universally emended to *morality,* but as
neither seems to make any particular sense, one may as well retain F. *Morality* if it
means anything must mean the faculty of moralising in imprisonment." PARROTT
(ed. 1938): "Death." HARDING (ed. 1954): "The word is ultimately derived from
Latin *mortalitas* which Cooper (*Thesaurus,* 1578) defines: 'Mortality, frailety, estate
subject to decay'." SISSON (1956, 1:76): " 'Freedom may be an illusion', says Lucio,
'but I would rather be free and enjoy the illusion than suffer under the undoubted
and deadly pangs of imprisonment'." STEVENSON (1956, *SQ* 7:451): Lucio prolongs
"the tone of paradox with a comment that he prefers the foolishness of being alive
to the captivity of death." WINNY (ed. 1959): *Morality,* "moral justice." LEVER (ed.
1965): "Morality = moral instruction (*O.E.D.* 3). Lucio prefers the foolish or flippant
talk of freedom to the moralizing of people under arrest. F 'mortality' has never been
convincingly defended." NOSWORTHY (ed. 1969): "The F reading, signifying 'deadliness' or 'mortification', is quite acceptable."
    227 LEVER (ed. 1965): Cf. *Per.* 4.6.75.
    233-5 HART (ed. 1905): Cf. the anon. *Timon* (ed. 1875, p. 405): "My ffreind,
a word or two. *Pseud.* Yes, yf thou wilt, three hundred."

Lucio, a word with you.

   Luc. A hundred: 235

If they'll doe you any good: Is *Lechery* so look'd after?

   Cla. Thus stands it with me: vpon a true contract

I got possession of *Iulietas* bed,

You know the Lady, she is fast my wife,

235–6 *Prose* POPE, THEO1, THEO2, WARB, COL, ALEX; *verse lines ending* good:
. . . after? HAN1, THEO4-KNT2, HAL-WH1, STAU-DYCE3, HUD2-KIT1, SIS+

---

236 **look'd after**] SCHMIDT (1874): "To keep in the eye." *OED* (*v.* 12g): "To keep watch upon," first quotation.

237 **a true contract**] DAVIS (1884, p. 70) believes that the distinction between a contract of marriage *per verba de presenti* (by words in the present tense) and one *per verba de futuro* (by words in the future tense) "was plainly drawn in Shakespeare's mind" and that Claudio's was the latter, a precontract (see n. 1850). UNDERHILL (1916, 1:407) and GREENWOOD (1920, pp. 411–14) consider the contract between Claudio and Juliet a valid marriage by words *de presenti*. LUCAS (1927, 2:40): Cf. Webster, *The Dutchesse of Malfy,* 1.1.547–8: "I have heard Lawyers say, a contract in a Chamber, (*Per verba <de> presenti*) is absolute marriage." LAWRENCE (1931, pp. 97–8): "An understanding of the binding force of the Elizabethan betrothal is important. Spousals, or betrothals, and the final celebration of marriage were separate and distinct ceremonies. . . . Such a union [as Claudio's with Juliet] was recognized by both ecclesiastical and state authorities as valid. . . . The custom explains completely the apparent irregularity in the relations of Shakespeare and Anne Hathaway." HOTSON (1937, pp. 138–40, 203 ff.): Sh.'s friend Thomas Russell and Mrs. Anne Digges were contracted about 1600 and lived as man and wife, but did not marry until 1603 because marriage ended an annuity left her by her first husband. EMPSON (1951, p. 286) and SCOUTEN (1975, pp. 70–1) follow Hotson in comparing this betrothal with Claudio's. HARDING (1950, pp. 154, 156): "Claudio and Julietta have been betrothed *per verba de praesenti.* . . . Claudio had violated the moral code by consummating his betrothal before the nuptials. In the eyes of the church, he was a sinner." SCHANZER (1960, p. 83): "Claudio and Juliet are guilty in the eyes of the Church of two transgressions—of having contracted a secret marriage and of having consummated it. Being technically guilty of fornication, Claudio is therefore punishable under the law which Angelo has revived." NAGARAJAN (1963, pp. 116–17) argues that Claudio was betrothed *de futuro,* and "a *de futuro* betrothal did not confer the right of sexual union on the partners." LEVER (ed. 1965, p. lv): "While Angelo had broken his matrimonial vows and abandoned his intended wife when her dowry was lost, Claudio had kept his pledge and married Juliet in law, postponing the consecration only until the dowry became available." BIRJE-PATIL (1969, p. 111): "It is the clandestine nature of Claudio's contract that makes his punishment dramatically valid in view of the fact that he is reprehensible according to the Church's edict." The whole question calls for further study, though HAWKINS (1974, p. 177) considers it a question "that Shakespeare himself chose to raise, not to answer."

239 **fast**] SCHMIDT (1874): "Firmly." *OED* (*adv.* 2): "Securely." WILSON (ed. 1922): "I.e. by 'handfasting' or betrothal, which was considered valid without religious ceremony (cf. *pre-contract*)" (1850).

Saue that we doe the denunciation lacke   240
Of outward Order. This we came not to,
Onely for propogation of a Dowre
Remaining in the Coffer of her friends,
From whom we thought it meet to hide our Loue
Till Time had made them for vs. But it chances   245
The stealth of our most mutuall entertainment
With Character too grosse, is writ on *Iuliet.*

---

240 the] *Om.* MEREDITH (1883, p. 8) *conj.,* PEN2   denunciation] pronunciation COLNE, COL2

242 propogation] preservation mTBY1 *conj.,* WH1; prorogation MAL *conj.,* SIS;
procuration mF2FL *and* JACKSON (1819) *conj.,* COLNE, COL2, COL3

246 most] *Om.* HAN1

247 on] in F2-POPE2, HAN1

---

240 **denunciation**] RANN (ed. 1786): "Due solemnization." TODD (1818):
"Publication, sanction." *OED* (1): "Official, formal, or public announcement; declaration, proclamation."

241 **Order**] See *OED* (*sb.* 17): "Administration of a rite or ceremony."

242 **propogation**] RANN (ed. 1786): "A report propagated." LUCIUS (1786, p.
356): *"Propagation* being here used to signify *payment,* must have its root in the Italian
word *pagare."* STEEVENS (Var. 1793): "I suppose the speaker means—for the sake
of *getting* such a dower as her friends might hereafter bestow on her, when time had
reconciled them to her clandestine marriage." HUDSON (ed. 1851): "Either fixing,
securing, or continuing (to keep up the chance of a dower)." HALLIWELL (ed. 1854):
"Literally, increase. We delayed to celebrate our marriage, merely because we
desired to add to our means from a portion in the hands of friends, whose favour we
were first anxious to secure. Perhaps a better meaning is found in the other ordinary
sense of *propagate,* to promote." SCHMIDT (1875): "Augmentation, increase." *OED*
(3): "Increase in amount or extent," first fig. use. DEROCQUIGNY (1926–7, pp.
338–40): Delay, prorogation. LEVER (ed. 1965): "Breeding; used for a figurative
gestation, i.e. actualizing of what was potential, and suggested here by the idea of the
dowry having to be 'born' out of the coffer (not, as *O.E.D.* 3, 'increase')." But the
usual meaning of *to propagate* in Sh. is "to increase," as in "To propagate their states,"
Tim. 1.1.67 (86). See p. 280.

243 **friends**] ONIONS (1911): "Relatives, kinsfolk" (*OED, sb.* 3).

245 **made them for vs**] SCHMIDT (1875, p. 683): "Disposed them in our favour."

246 **stealth**] *OED* (4): "Furtive or underhand action," quoting this and *Lr.*
1.2.11 (345).

mutuall] SCHMIDT (1875): "Intimate, cordial." So *OED* (*a.* 3). More likely
"reciprocal" (*a.* 1); cf. *mutually,* "on both sides," 982, 983.

entertainment] BOWDLER prints this word in 1818 and 1820 but changes it
in 1823 and later eds. to *intercourse.* SCHMIDT (1874) prefers the euphemisms "hos-
pitable reception, kind treatment." LEVER (ed. 1965): "Cf. *Per.*, IV. ii. 60." See n.
1288.

247 **Character**] SCHMIDT (1874): "Writing." LEVER (ed. 1965): "Signs of preg-

Luc. With childe, perhaps?
Cla. Vnhappely, euen so.
And the new Deputie, now for the Duke,   250
Whether it be the fault and glimpse of newnes,
Or whether that the body publique, be
A horse whereon the Gouernor doth ride,
Who newly in the Seate, that it may know
He can command; lets it strait feele the spur: 255
Whether the Tirranny be in his place,
Or in his Eminence that fills it vp
I stagger in: But this new Gouernor
Awakes me all the inrolled penalties

248-9 *One verse line* KNT1, KNT2, HAL, DYCE1+ (−COL3, KNT3, COL4)

---

nancy." See n. 33.
    grosse] ONIONS (1911): "Plain, evident" (*OED, a.* 3). Cf. 1090.
    248-9 Note the wordplay on *perhaps* and *Vnhappely.*
    251 **fault and glimpse**] THEOBALD (1729, in NICHOLS, 1817, 2:286): "The
little insight he has in his duty, from being so *fresh in the office.*" JOHNSON (ed. 1765):
"*Fault* and *glimpse* have so little relation to each other, that both can scarcely be right;
we may read *flash* for *fault.*" IDEM (Var. 1773): "Or, perhaps we may read, *Whether
it be the fault* or *glimpse*—That is, whether it be the seeming enormity of the action,
or the glare of new authority. Yet the same sense follows in the next lines." MALONE
(1780, 1:95): "The *fault and glimpse* is the same as *the faulty glimpse.* And the meaning
seems to be—*whether it be* the fault of newness, *a fault arising from the mind being dazled
by a novel authority, of which the new governour has yet had only* a glimpse; *has yet only taken
a hasty survey.*" HART (ed. 1905): "The imperfection awaiting upon the sudden and
unaccustomed brightness or flash of novelty." LEE (ed. 1907): "Inherent defect and
hasty vision of one in a new position." PARROTT (ed. 1938): "Faulty glance, imperfect vision." NEILSON & HILL (ed. 1942): "Harmful glamour." LEVER (ed. 1965):
"Probably a hendiadys, i.e. faulty glimpse ('flash or momentary shining', *O.E.D. sb.*
1)." See p. 280.
    255 **strait**] ONIONS (1911): "*Straight* adv.: immediately, straightway" (*OED,
adv.* 2). So *strait* 442, *straight* 733.
    256-8 WINNY (ed. 1959): "Whether his tyrannous behaviour springs from his
office or from the homage he receives, I cannot decide. The construction of the
passage is curiously like that of Aufidius' speech in *Coriolanus* IV.vii.37 ff. [3128 ff.]."
    257 **Eminence**] SCHMIDT (1874): "Excellence." *OED* (4a): "Distinguished su-
periority, elevated rank," first use in this sense. PARROTT (ed. 1938): "Moral lofti-
ness." LEVER (ed. 1965): "Self-importance." But this sense is not in Sh. Cf. 2293
eminent, "of high rank."
    258 **stagger in**] *OED* (*v.* 2b): "Begin to doubt or waver in an argument, opinion,
or purpose." PARROTT (ed. 1938): "Hesitate to say."
    259 **Awakes**] See *OED* (*v.* 6 *fig.*): "Make active."
    me] SCHMIDT (1874, p. 565): "Like the Latin dativus ethicus, superfluous as
to the general sense, but imparting a lively colour to the expression." So in 570, 1861.

Which haue (like vn-scowr'd Armor) hung by th'wall   260
So long, that ninteene Zodiacks haue gone round,
And none of them beene worne; and for a name
Now puts the drowsie and neglected Act
Freshly on me: 'tis surely for a name.
    Luc.   I warrant it is: And thy head stands so tickle on   265

---

261 ninteene] fourteen THEO1 *conj.*, RANN
264 on] in WARB
265-7 *Verse lines ending* stands . . . milk-maid, . . . off. . . . him. HAN1
265 it is] so it is HAN1   And] an PEN2

See ABBOTT §220, FRANZ §294. GILLETT (1974, pp. 299 f.): Here *me* may imply "a tone of amazement or incredulity."
    inrolled] See ONIONS (1911): *"Enrolled:* written, as a deed, on a roll or parchment."
    260 **like vn-scowr'd Armor**] STEEVENS (Var. 1778): Cf. *Tro.* 3.3.152-3 (2005-6). See *OED* (Scoured *ppl. a.* 1): "Polished by rubbing."
    261 **ninteene Zodiacks**] THEOBALD (1729, in NICHOLS, 1817, 2:286): Both this line and 311 "must be restor'd either to 19, or 14." IDEM (ed. 1733): "The Author could not so disagree with himself, in so narrow a Compass. The Numbers must have been wrote in Figures, and so mistaken: for which reason, 'tis necessary to make the two Accounts correspond." RITSON (1783, p. 18): "But there is no reason to charge the author with inconsistency, neither is it necessary that the two speakers should agree in their calculation. If it were, the dukes account should most certainly be preferred, as he was doubtless much better acquainted with the exact time of the disuse of those laws than Claudio can be reasonably supposed to have been." HUNTER (ed. 1873): Years. "The ecliptic, or the sun's apparent path through the zodiac, was formerly supposed to be his actual orbit round the earth." *OED* (Zodiac *sb.* 3a): "A year." LEVER (ed. 1965): "The discrepancy may be due to a confusing of the figures 4 and 9; or Shakespeare may simply have forgotten what he wrote." [Or "xiv" and "xix" may have been confused.] NATHAN (1969, p. 84): "Nineteen years or zodiacs is a cycle, a revolution, a re-beginning. Claudio is saying that the particular law has not been enforced for as long a time as it would take the sun and the moon to run their full cycle into realignment. This seems similar to saying that the law is enforced once in a blue moon."
    262 **for a name**] THIRLBY (1723-33): "Does he mean to get fame?" HALLIWELL (ed. 1854): "To establish his reputation as a strict judge." *OED* (*sb.* 6c): "A distinguished name; a reputation."
    263 **drowsie**] PARROTT (ed. 1938): "I.e. from long disuse." LEVER (ed. 1965): "Cf. the figure of the sleeping lion [415-16]." See nn. 416, 845.
    Act] SCHMIDT (1874): "Decree, law, edict" (*OED, sb.* 5).
    265-7 COLLIER (ed. 1842): "This speech seems to have been originally meant for verse." But all Lucio's speeches so far have been in prose except for 215 and possibly 235-6 through *good.*
    265 **I warrant**] I'm sure. See n. 128.
    tickle] JOHNSON (1755): "Tottering; unfixed; unstable; easily overthrown" (*OED, a.* 6).

thy shoulders, that a milke-maid, if she be in loue, may
sigh it off: Send after the Duke, and appeale to him.
   Cla. I haue done so, but hee's not to be found.
I pre'thee (*Lucio*) doe me this kinde seruice:
This day, my sister should the Cloyster enter,   270
And there receiue her approbation.
Acquaint her with the danger of my state,
Implore her, in my voice, that she make friends
To the strict deputie: bid her selfe assay him,
I haue great hope in that: for in her youth   275
There is a prone and speechlesse dialect,

---

266 be] be but HAN1
268 hee's] he is MAL
276 prone] grace SIS

266–7 **that . . . off**] LEVER (ed. 1965): " 'If the milkmaid's "head" [maidenhead]
were as tickle (i.e. unstable) as yours she would sigh it off'." See n. 1859. EVANS (ed.
1974): "The merest breath of wind (a lovesick milkmaid's sigh) will blow it off (?)."
   269 **pre'thee**] See *OED* (Prithee *int. phr.*): "Archaic colloquialism for '(I) pray
thee'." See nn. 155, 337.
   270 **should**] SCHMIDT (1875, Shall 2 and 4): "To be going to, to be to." Cf.
OED (Shall *v.* 13): "Was to." So 1434, 2861, 2887.
   271 **approbation**] MALONE (1780, 1:95): "Enter on her *probation*, or *noviciate*."
OED (4): "Probation, trial," first quotation in this sense. Cf. *probation* 2432.
   273 **in my voice**] *OED* (*sb.* 7c): "*In my voice*, in my name. *Obs. rare,*" quoting
only this and *AYL* 2.4.87 (872). EVANS (ed. 1974): "As persuasively as I would."
   273–4 **make friends To**] *OED* (Friend *sb.* 6b): "Get on good terms with."
   274 **assay**] *OED* (*v.* 15): "To assail: *a.* with words, or arguments; to accost,
address." DURHAM (ed. 1926): "Make trial of." LEISI (ed. 1964): "It combines the
meanings of 'try' and 'assail'. Note also the contemporary technical meaning 'test
precious metals'," as in 1384: see n.
   276 **prone**] THIRLBY (1733–47): "Apt (Nam facile et pronum est [For it is easy
and natural, Juvenal 9:43 and 13:75])." IDEM (1747–53): "Apt, easy, natural."
JOHNSON (ed. 1765): This may mean "a dialect which men are *prone* to regard, or
a dialect natural and unforced, as those actions seem to which we are *prone*. Either
of these interpretations is sufficiently strained; but such distortion of words is not
uncommon in our authour." STEEVENS (Var. 1773): "*Prone*, perhaps, may stand for
humble, as *a prone posture* is *a posture of supplication*." MALONE (ed. 1790): "*Prone*, I
believe, is used here for *prompt, significant, expressive.*" SEYMOUR (1805, 1:85): "Spontaneous, apt, intuitive, congenial, natural." DOUCE (1807, 1:122): "*Easily moving.*
. . . See Cotgrave's *Dictionary* [1611]." HALLIWELL (ed. 1854): " '*Prone*, prone,
readie, nimble, quicke, wheeme, easily moving', Cotgrave. . . . 'Prone or apt',
Howell's *Lex[icon] Tet[raglotton]*." STAUNTON (ed. 1859): "The poet has obviously
intended it to imply a power of bending or inclining another by the exertion of a
strong yet silent personal influence." CLARKE (ed. 1864): "Deferential, gently submissive and supplicatory." SCHMIDT (1875): Hendiadys, "speaking fervently and
eagerly without words." HART (ed. 1905): "Inciting. This adjective had a use with

Such as moue men: beside, she hath prosperous Art
When she will play with reason, and discourse,
And well she can perswade.

   Luc. I pray shee may; aswell for the encouragement   280
of the like, which else would stand vnder greeuous imposition: as for the enioying of thy life, who I would be

---

277 moue] moves DAV, ROWE1-HUD2 (−CAM1, GLO)   beside] besides CAP,
SING, KTLY, HUD2

279–85 *Verse lines ending* persuade. . . . may; . . . like, . . . imposition; . . . be
. . . tick-tack. . . . her strait. . . . *Lucio.* HAN1; *one verse line ending* may; (*then prose as*
F1, *then one verse line*) I'll . . . Lucio. CAM3

281 vnder] upon F2-POPE2; on HAN1

282 the enioying of] *Om.* HAN1   who I would] which I'd HAN1; which I
would mTBY1 *conj.,* SING2, WH1, HUD2

---

reference to the passions, or desires, which probably influences the sense here."
HARDING (ed. 1954): "Shakespeare deliberately makes it ambiguous: *prone,* suggesting the posture of supplication, a familiar meaning of Latin *pronus,* but with overtones
of an indelicate sexual connotation." LEISI (ed. 1964, p. 22): "The meaning 'eager'
[*OED, a.* 7] makes very good sense in our passage; an indelicate overtone appears
improbable and an emendation becomes unnecessary." LEVER (ed. 1965): "Often
'eager' or 'apt'; but Claudio means here the abject posture of submission or helpless-
ness (*O.E.D.* 4)." "There is an undercurrent of irony in the equivocal words 'prone',
'move', and 'play', all capable of suggesting sexual provocation. The overt drift,
however, is an application of psychology to the art of rhetoric." COOPER (1565)
defines Latin *pronus* as "prone: inclined: stouping downe: readie: easie. . . ." FLORIO
(1598) defines Italian *prono* as "inclined, readie, easie, quicke, light, prompt. . . ."
See p. 281.

     speechlesse] RANN (ed. 1786): Cf. *WT* 2.2.41-2 (867–8): "The silence often
of pure innocence Perswades, when speaking failes."

     dialect] JOHNSON (1755): "Language; speech." *OED* (1): "Manner of speak-
ing, language, speech," first fig. use. NOSWORTHY (ed. 1969): "Language (but here
conveying also the sense of 'dialectic', logical persuasion)."

     277 **moue**] ABBOTT (§367): *"Subjunctive used indefinitely after the Relative."* LEVER
(ed. 1965): "Perhaps 'moves', but the plural may be due to the influence of the two
precedent adjectives." See nn. 833, 909, 1347.

     she hath] KÖKERITZ (1953, p. 277): Pronounced *sh'ath.* Cf. 426, 2387.

     prosperous] See *OED* (*a.* 1): "Consistently successful."

     Art] See n. 15.

     278 **discourse**] SCHMIDT (1874): "Thought, reflection" (*OED, sb.* 2). LEISI (ed.
1964): " 'Arguing' or 'conversation' cf. [7]."

     280 **aswell**] See *OED:* "Obs. way of writing *as well.*"

     281 **the like**] PARROTT (ed. 1938): "I.e. lechery." LEISI (ed. 1964): " 'Similar
offenders'."

     else] See *OED* (*adv.* 4): "Otherwise."

     281-2 **imposition**] JOHNSON (ed. 1765): "Penalties imposed." SCHMIDT
(1874): "Charge, accusation, imputation" (*OED,* 3), as in *WT* 1.2.74 (137).
ONIONS (1911): This sense only in Sh.

     282 **who**] Which. See ABBOTT §264, *OED* (*pron.* 11c).

sorry should bee thus foolishly lost, at a game of ticke-
tacke: Ile to her.

 Cla. I thanke you good friend *Lucio.*　　　　　　　　285

 Luc. Within two houres.　　　　　　　　　　　　　(F2ᵇ)

 Cla. Come Officer, away.　　　　　　　*Exeunt.*

Scena Quarta.   1.3

Enter Duke and Frier Thomas.

 Duk. No: holy Father, throw away that thought,　　　290
Beleeue not that the dribling dart of Loue
Can pierce a compleat bosome: why, I desire thee

---

284 her.] her strait. HAN1; her—WH1

286–7 *One verse line* COL1, DYCE1+ (−KTLY, KNT3, ARD2)

286 houres.] ～ ,— THEO, WARB-v1821, SING, COL, HAL, DYCE2, DEL4-HUD2,
BUL

288 *Scena Quarta*] SCENE III ROWE, HAL, DYCE, STAU, CAM1, GLO, HUD2,
IRV+; SCENE VII POPE, HAN1, WARB, JOHN; *SCENE* VI MAL (*corrected in errata*)
 A Monastery. ROWE1-SIS (−CAP, CAM3); *A Cell.* CAP, CAM3, ARD2

292 bosome] breast POPE, HAN1

283–4 **ticke-tacke**] MALONE (1780, 1:95): "*Tick-tack* is a game at tables. Jouer
au *tric-trac* is used in French, in a wanton sense." STEEVENS (Var. 1785): "The same
phrase in Lucio's wanton sense occurs in *Lusty Juventus*" (c. 1550–60, MSR, 827).
HALLIWELL (ed. 1854): "Another instance may be seen in a catch" in Lyly's *Mother
Bombie,* ed. 1632 (5.3.66). See *OED* (2): "An old variety of backgammon, played on
a board with holes along the edge, in which pegs were placed for scoring. Also *fig.*"
See also John Day, *Law-Trickes* (1608), MSR, 1588–9.

 284 **Ile to**] I'll go to. See *OED* To (*prep.* 1c [*a*]), and n. 76.

 288 *Scena Quarta*] WILSON (ed. 1922): "Capell reads 'A Cell'. Cf. 'Patrick's
cell', *Two Gent.* 4. 3. 43 [1813], 'Friar Laurence's cell', *Rom.* 2. 4. 193 [1276]."

 291 **dribling**] JOHNSON (1755): *Dribble,* "To fall weakly and slowly." IDEM
(ed. 1765): "*Fluttering without force.*" STEEVENS (in Var. 1803): Cf. Sidney, "dribbed
shot." COLLIER (ed. 1842): "Dribling" in *Astrophil and Stella,* ed. 1591, Sonnet 2.
OED (Dribble v. 5 = Drib v. 4): "To shoot (an arrow) so that it falls short or wide
of the mark." RINGLER (1962, p. 459): "Ineffectual or at random."

 292 **compleat bosome**] JOHNSON (ed. 1765): "A breast *compleatly armed.*"
SCHMIDT (1874–5, pp. 227, 1413): "Perfect." "The form *cómplete* always precedes
a noun accented on the first syllable." LEISI (ed. 1964): "For the connotation 'invulnerable' cf. *complete armour* (*Rich. III,* IV 4 189 [2969]) and *in complete steel* (*Hamlet*

To giue me secret harbour, hath a purpose
More graue, and wrinkled, then the aimes, and ends
Of burning youth.   295
   Fri. May your Grace speake of it?
   Duk. My holy Sir, none better knowes then you
How I haue euer lou'd the life remoued
And held in idle price, to haunt assemblies
Where youth, and cost, witlesse brauery keepes.   300
I haue deliuerd to Lord *Angelo*
(A man of stricture and firme abstinence)

---

295 youth] youths POPE2
300 witlesse] and witlesse F2-NLSN, KIT1; a witless NICHOLSON (1885) *conj.*,
CAM3, ALEX, PEN2   keepes] keep HAN1, HAL, DYCE2, DYCE3, HUD2
302 stricture] strictness DAV; strict ure WARB

I 4 52 [637]."
   why] The reason why (*OED, adv.* 5d). The clause *why . . . harbour* is the subject
of *hath.*
   293 **harbour**] See *OED* (*sb.* 1): "Shelter, lodging."
   294 **graue, and wrinkled**] *OED* (Wrinkled *a.* 3): first use in transferred sense.
LEISI (ed. 1964): "Probably connoting '(politically) serious', 'wise', 'mature', cf.
[2341] and *the graue wrinkled senate, T. of Athens* IV 1 5 [1508]."
   then] Than, always so spelled in this text. See ABBOTT §70.
   295 **burning youth**] Cf. *Ham.* 3.4.84 (2459).
   298 **remoued**] THIRLBY (1733–47): "Retir'd. Cotgrave *remouuer*, to remove,
retire, withdraw." STEEVENS (Var. 1778): "A life of retirement."
   299 **in idle price**] PARROTT (ed. 1938): "As little worth" (*OED,* Price *sb.* 6).
   haunt] See *OED* (*v.* 3): "To resort to frequently or habitually."
   assemblies] See *OED* (7): "A gathering of persons for purposes of social
entertainment," sense first found in Sh.
   300 **cost**] WILSON (ed. 1922): "Extravagance, display." LEISI (ed. 1964): "Connoting 'expense' " (*OED, sb.*² 1b).
   witlesse] JOHNSON (1755): "Wanting understanding." IDEM (1773): "Inconsiderate; wanting thought." See *OED* (*a.* 1): "Foolish, heedless." LEVER (ed.
1965): "The momentary pause may allow for a brief gesture of contempt, followed
by strong stress on 'witless'."
   brauery] MALONE (ed. 1790): *"Splendour of dress."* STAUNTON (ed. 1859):
"Ostentation" (*OED,* 3).
   keepes] Cf. JOHNSON (1755): "To dwell; to live constantly," quoting 1213.
REED (in Var. 1793): "In this sense it is still used at Cambridge." VERPLANCK (ed.
1847): "This Shakespearian and collegiate term is common in many parts of the
United States." See *OED* (*v.* 37). LEVER (ed. 1965): "The quasi-singular form was
a common Elizabethan usage (Abbott §333)." See FRANZ §673. EVANS (ed. 1974):
"Maintains."
   302 **stricture**] THEOBALD (ed. 1733): *"Strictness."* THIRLBY (1747–53): Cf.
prompture (1192: see n.). *OED* (*sb.*²): "Strictness," only example. LEVER (ed. 1965):
"But the common and more likely meaning was 'restriction' (*O.E.D. sb.*¹ 2). The

My absolute power, and place here in *Vienna*,
And he supposes me trauaild to *Poland*,
(For so I haue strewd it in the common eare) 305
And so it is receiu'd: Now (pious Sir)
You will demand of me, why I do this.
Fri. Gladly, my Lord.
Duk. We haue strict Statutes, and most biting Laws,
(The needfull bits and curbes to headstrong weedes,) 310

---

303 here] *Om.* F4-ROWE2
305 For] Far F2
307 this.] ~ ? DAV, POPE1-ARD1 (−CAP, HAL, CAM2), CAM3, SIS, PEL1
310 to] for F2-SING1 (−MAL), CAM3   weedes] Steeds THEO1-STAU
(−COL1), DYCE2-WH2, NLSN, KIT1, ALEX; wills mTBY1 *and* WALKER *conj. in*
DYCE1 (*and* 1860, 2:66), BUL, CAM3, PEL1; jades ORGER *conj.,* ARD2

---

word here alludes to Angelo's self-repression rather than to his strictness towards others." SCHÄFER (1973, p. 159) notes other nouns in *-ure* among Sh.'s once-used words in *Ham., Tro., Cor.* See also *razure* 2361.
305 **strewd**] SCHMIDT (1875): "Spread by scattering." *OED* (*v.* 1c *fig.*): "To scatter, spread loosely."
common] See n. 14.
306 **receiu'd**] SCHMIDT (1875, p. 948): *Receive,* "to believe" (*OED, v.* 15b). The parenthesis should have been closed here.
309 **strict**] LEVER (ed. 1965): " 'Strict' retains the Latin sense of 'drawn tight'; hence the figure of bits and curbs [310]. Cf. *2H6,* IV. vii. 18–19 [2649]."
biting] SCHMIDT (1874): "Sharp, severe."
310 **weedes**] THEOBALD (ed. 1733): "I do not think, the Author would have talk'd of *Bits* and *Curbs* for *Weeds.* On the other hand, nothing can be more proper, than to compare Persons of *unbridled Licentiousness* to headstrong *Steeds.*" COLLIER (ed. 1842): "*Weed* is a term still commonly applied to an ill-conditioned horse." STONE (in IRVING & MARSHALL, ed. 1889): "Shakespeare was careless in linking metaphors. I think it possible that he combined the idea of a well-bitted horse (literally equivalent to enforcement of law), and the picture of a rank, noisome growth of weeds, suffered to spring up in a fair garden (literally equivalent to relaxation of law)." HART (ed. 1905): " 'Steeds' is a most desirable alteration. . . . 'Weed' . . . applied to an ill-conditioned horse . . . refers to a spiritless beast, and is probably quite modern [*OED, sb.* 5 records no instance before 1845]. To apply bits and curbs to garden weeds is an intolerable confusion of metaphors to our ears. But the whole speech is a jumble of them. The text is countenanced by the fact that Whetstone has the same metaphor in the same situation. Promos says [*1 Promos*] (ii.3): 'So that the way, is by severity Such wicked weedes even by the rootes to teare' " [see p. 314 below]. WILSON (ed. 1922): *Weedes* is impossible. *Wills* [see textual notes] "makes better sense and at least begins with a *w.*" EMPSON (1930; 1953, pp. 84–5): "It is in keeping with the tone of this period of his development that he should start with 'steeds' and then change, with a twinge of disgust, to *weeds. Biting* . . . besides making a sort of pun with *bits,* expresses both the effect of a *curb* on a 'steed' and the effect of a scythe on a *weed.*" RIDLEY (ed. 1935): "This, the F

Which for this foureteene yeares, we haue let slip,   311
Euen like an ore-growne Lyon in a Caue

---

311 this] these THEO, WARB-v1821, SING, HAL, STAU, KTLY, CAM3   foure-
teene] nineteen DAV, GIL, THEO1-v1778 (−CAP), GLO, WH2, NLSN   slip] sleep
DAV, GIL, THEO1-WH2 (−KNT, CAM1, GLO), CAM3, KIT1

---

reading, has been characterised as 'impossible'. But if we are going to regard as
impossible any word which involves Shakespeare in a violence of mixed metaphor we
shall certainly need bits and curbs for headstrong emendation." SISSON (1956, 1:78):
"I cannot see difficulty in *weeds,* which here is itself a metaphor for evil wills, or
venture to correct and improve Shakespeare's later compressed imagery." MAHOOD
(1957, p. 18): "Shakespeare may have intended to write *steed,* but *weed* is, I think,
his word rather than the copyist's or compositor's, because in its double meaning of
'tare' and 'dress' it fits excellently into the thematic pattern of the play. The idea of
society as an unweeded garden had haunted Shakespeare since he wrote *Richard II.*"
HUNTER (1964, p. 167): "In fact, a stronger case can be made out for the Folio
reading, for the mixture of the two ideas recurs commonly enough in Shakespeare:"
weeds and *curb* in *Ham.* 3.4.151–5 (2534–8) and *2H4* 4.4.54–62 (2432–40), *weed*
and *unbitted* in *Oth.* 1.3.326–35 (675–84). See n. 1755.
   311 **foureteene**] MALONE (1780, 1:95–6): "The two readings which Mr. Theobald has introduced into the text, he might have found in an alteration of this play,
published in 1700, by Charles Gildon . . . 'Which I have suffer'd *nineteen* years to
sleep'." DAVENANT in 1673 makes both changes. WHALLEY (in Var. 1785): "Theobald's correction is misplaced. If any correction is really necessary, it should have been
made where Claudio, in [261], says *nineteen* years. I am disposed to take the Duke's
words." See n. 261.
   slip] THEOBALD (ed. 1733) emends to *sleep,* citing other references to the law
sleeping or waking (259, 263, 845, 848). MALONE in Var. 1778 defends *slip,* but
in ed. 1790 prefers *sleep.* SCHMIDT (1875): "Pass unnoticed." HARDING (ed. 1954):
"Both meanings are in this passage metaphorically appropriate—perhaps reflecting
Shakespeare's intention." LEISI (ed. 1964): "*Slip* in the sense of 'pass out of one's
hand' (OED 10, *Coriolanus* I 6 39 [650], *J. C.* III 1 273 [1501]) goes very well with
the *bits and curbs;* in the sense of 'pass unnoticed', 'steal away' (OED 2, [*AYL*] IV
3 113 [2263]), it fits in with the *ore-growne Lyon* who lets his prey escape, an image
which is repeated in [415–16]. *Slip,* then, with its two meanings, provides a hinge
between the two metaphors." LEVER (ed. 1965): " 'Withdraw the head from the
collar' (*O.E.D. v.* [1] 17). Cf. *R3,* IV. iv. 112–13 [2883–4]." But *slip* refers to *Statutes*
and *Laws* (309) and may mean "To fail to hold or stick; to slide" (*OED, v.* [1] 9).
   312–13 **Euen . . . prey**] KNIGHT (ed. 1840, p. 282): Cf. Job 4:11, "The Lion
perisheth for lacke of pray." SCHMIDT (1875): *O'ergrown,* "having become too old."
ORGER (1890, p. 20): " 'O'ergrown' is, I suppose, only a superlative, meaning
'huge'." *OED (ppl. a.* 2): "Too big, abnormally large." HART (ed. 1905): "Compare
Whitney's *Choice of Emblems,* 1586, (ed. Green, p. 210)," which cites Horace and
pictures "The Lion oulde that could not get his praye." POTTS (1958, p. 170): Cf.
Spenser, *F.Q.* 3.3.30.1–5. LEVER (ed. 1965): "Originally Horace, *Epist.*, I. i. 73–5,
through Camerarius, *Fabellae Aesopicae,* a favourite schoolbook (Baldwin [1944], I,
622 f.)." See n. 416.

That goes not out to prey: Now, as fond Fathers,
Hauing bound vp the threatning twigs of birch,
Onely to sticke it in their childrens sight,   315
For terror, not to vse: in time the rod
More mock'd, then fear'd: so our Decrees,
Dead to infliction, to themselues are dead,
And libertie, plucks Iustice by the nose;
The Baby beates the Nurse, and quite athwart   320
Goes all decorum.

---

316 terror] errour F2-ROWE2   in time the rod] Till it in time DAV; in time the
rod's mTBY1 *and* ANON. MS *in* HAL *conj.,* COLNE, COL2, COL3, KTLY, IRV; do find
in time The rod HUD2
317 More mock'd] become more markt DAV; Becomes more mock'd POPE1-GLO
(—COL3), DYCE2-COL4, WH2, CAM2+ (—CAM3); More mocked at KTLY
     Decrees] most just decrees COLNE, COL2, COL3

---

313 **fond**] SCHMIDT (1874): "Foolish" and "doting," "(significations blent)"
(*OED, a.* 5a). See n. 1031.
317 PORTER & CLARKE (ed. 1909): "After *fear'd:* there is in speaking the line
an impressive vacant foot, one of the *moræ vacuæ* [empty pauses] effective in Greek
dramatic verse, and often used in Shakespeare, especially in the mouths of such
thoughtful speakers as the Duke in this play, or such headlong and impulsive speakers
of rapid ideas as Leontes in *The Winter's Tale.*" Davenant adds *become* and Pope
Becomes, which most eds. follow.
318 **Dead to infliction**] JOHNSON (1755): *Infliction,* "The act of using punishments." *OED:* "The fact of being inflicted," only quotation in this sense. HARRISON
(ed. 1954): "Which have become a dead letter." BALD (ed. 1956): "Completely
unenforced."
319 **libertie**] See nn. 216, 414.
     plucks . . . nose] HART (ed. 1905): "So 'tweaks me by the nose', *Hamlet,* II.
ii. 601 [1614]." Cf. 2720–1.
320 **The Baby . . . Nurse**] STEEVENS (Var. 1793): "This allusion was borrowed
from an ancient print, entitled *The World turn'd upside down,* where an infant is thus
employed." HART (1908, p. 63): Cf. Nashe, 1589 (ed. McKerrow, 3:315): "it is no
maruaile if euery Alehouse vaunt the table of the world turned vpside downe, since
the child beateth his father, and the Asse whippeth his Master." [See also Guilpin,
Skialetheia (1598), Satire 6, 29–30: "The ale-house *Ethicks,* the worlds vpside downe
Is verefied: the prince now serues the clowne."] ROSSITER (1961, p. 157): "This
inversion-figure does symbolize the essential clash or disharmony in [*MM*]. . . . The
inverted world is the subject of . . . *(Sonnet 66).* It is the subject too of the 'cryptic'
sentences of the Duke at [1708–15]."
     athwart] SCHMIDT (1874): "Crossly, wrongly." *OED (adv.* 4): "Crosswise,
perversely, awry," fig. sense first in *1H4* 1.1.36 (40).
321 **decorum**] SCHMIDT (1874): "Propriety, decency" (*OED,* 1c). CAMPBELL
(ed. 1949): "Social order." Italicized as a Latin word in the other two instances in
F, *Ant.* 1.2.77 (150–1) and 5.2.17 (3220), as it is in Ascham and others quoted in
OED and in Whetstone's dedication of *Promos.*

45

Fri. It rested in your Grace
To vnloose this tyde-vp Iustice, when you pleas'd:
And it in you more dreadfull would haue seem'd
Then in Lord *Angelo.*   325
   Duk. I doe feare: too dreadfull:
Sith 'twas my fault, to giue the people scope,
'T would be my tirrany to strike and gall them,
For what I bid them doe: For, we bid this be done
When euill deedes haue their permissiue passe,   330
And not the punishment: therefore indeede (my father)
I haue on *Angelo* impos'd the office,
Who may in th'ambush of my name, strike home,

---

326 doe] *Om.* POPE, HAN1
329 I bid] I bade mTBY2 *conj.,* COL3   be done] *Om.* POPE, HAN1
331 the] their mTBY3 *and* DYCE1 *conj.,* KTLY, DYCE2, DYCE3, HUD2
    indeede] *Om.* POPE, HAN1

---

   322 **rested**] SCHMIDT (1875): "To be in the power of." *OED* (*v.*¹ 6d): "To lie *in* or remain *with* one, as something to be accomplished or determined," sense first used by Sh.
   323 **tyde-vp**] *OED* (Tied *ppl. a.* 3), first fig. use of *tied up.* HOWARD-HILL (1972, p. 128): The hyphen shows Crane's influence.
   324 **dreadfull**] See n. 22.
   327 **Sith**] Since (*OED, conj.* 2).
      scope] JOHNSON (1755): "Liberty beyond just limits; licence." See nn. 73, 218.
   328 **gall**] SCHMIDT (1874): "To injure, to harass" (*OED, v.*¹ 4). EVANS (ed. 1974): "Chafe, cause physical irritation" (*OED, v.*¹ 1). See n. 858.
   329 **we . . . done**] CHEDWORTH (1805, p. 33): "Qui non prohibet cum prohibere potest, jubet [He who does not forbid when he can forbid, commands]." SMITH (1963, p. 77): "Too much lenity encourages wrongdoing." LEVER (ed. 1965): "Cf. Seneca, *Troades,* 291: *'Qui non vetat peccare cum possit, iubet* [He who does not forbid sin when he could, commands it]'."
   330 **permissiue**] *OED* (*a.* 1): "Not forbidding," first quotation in this sense. Sh. uses the word only here.
      passe] JOHNSON (1755): "A permission to go or come any where." SCHMIDT (1875): "Permission or right of going, license" (*OED, sb.*² 8). LEISI (ed. 1964): "'Free passage' (as in *give pass, H. V,* II Prol. 39 [501], *Hamlet* II 2 77 [1102])."
   331 **punishment**] ABBOTT (§467): "I in the middle of a trisyllable, if unaccented, is frequently dropped, or . . . nearly dropped," as here and in *Officer* 1520, *minister* 2313. See n. 2360.
   332 **office**] See *OED* (*sb.* 2b): "Duty."
   333 **in th'ambush**] THIRLBY (1747–53): "Under cover." See *OED* (*sb.* 4 *fig.*).
      strike home] See *OED,* Strike (*v.* 80), "Make an effective stroke," *fig.,* and Home (*adv.* 4, 5). See n. 2234.

And yet, my nature neuer in the fight
To do in slander: And to behold his sway 335
I will, as 'twere a brother of your Order,
Visit both Prince, and People: Therefore I pre'thee
Supply me with the habit, and instruct me
How I may formally in person beare
Like a true *Frier*: Moe reasons for this action 340

334–5 fight To do in] sight To do in POPE, WARB, COL4; fight So do in THEO;
sight To do it HAN1, JOHN1-v1785, v1793-SING1, DYCE2, DYCE3, NLSN, CAM3,
PEL1, PEN2; fight To do it DAWSON *conj.*, RANN, MAL, DYCE1, DEL4, IRV, BUL,
KIT1, SIS; fight, To do me HAL, RLF1; sight To draw on COLNE, COL2, COL3; fight
have To do in KTLY
335 And] *Om.* POPE, HAN1
337 I] *Om.* POPE1-v1773 (−CAP)
339 in] my POPE, HAN1   beare] bear me CAP, v1778-SIS (−KNT, COL1,
WH1, STAU, IRV, KIT1), PEN2
340 Moe] More ROWE1-IRV, ARD1

---

334 **nature**] SCHMIDT (1875): "Personal character" (*OED, sb.* 2).
    fight] MALONE (in Var. 1778): "The words in the preceding line—*ambush*
and *strike*, shew that *fight* is the true reading." COLLIER (ed. 1842): " 'And yet my
nature never in the fight, or contest, with crime, to do what is necessary under an
imputation, or slander, of too great severity'." STONE (1884, p. 114*): *"Open war-
fare,* as opposed to *ambush."* WILSON (ed. 1922): "Malone noted that 'fight' is
supported by the words 'ambush' and 'strike'; but they may, on the other hand, have
themselves been the cause of the error." See p. 281.
    335 **To do in slander**] KNIGHT (ed. 1840): "To be prominent in action, and
thus exposed to slander." WHITE (ed. 1857): " 'To perform this office in the face of
slander'." HUNTER (ed. 1873): "To have anything to do with what is slandered."
SCHMIDT (1875, p. 1070): "Perhaps = to act in danger of being misjudged." HART
(ed. 1905): "Perhaps 'do in' has the sense of bring in, work in." LEVER (ed. 1965):
"To put in a discreditable position? 'Do': put or place (*O.E.D.* I. 1b), 'slander': ill
repute (*O.E.D. sb.* 3)." See p. 281.
    sway] SCHMIDT (1875): "Rule." CAMPBELL (ed. 1949): "Methods of gov-
erning." Cf. *OED* (*sb.* 6, 6c).
    336 **as**] As if (*OED, conj.* 9, ABBOTT §107). See n. 737.
    337 **Prince**] LEVER (ed. 1965): "The person with sovereign authority, irrespec-
tive of his title" (*OED, sb.* 2).
    pre'thee] See n. 269.
    339 **formally**] See *OED* (1c): "In outward appearance, seemingly."
    person] See *OED* (*sb.* 1): "Character sustained or assumed," quoting *AYL*
4.1.92 (2004).
    beare] JOHNSON (1755): "Act in character." SCHMIDT (1874): "Behave."
Cf. *OED* (*v.*[1] 4 *refl.*) and ONIONS (1911), refl. and intr. WILSON (ed. 1922): "W.
W. Greg (privately) suggests that the lost 'me' has got wrongly tacked on to [338],
where it is not needed." It is not needed here either.
    340 **Moe**] See *OED* (Mo *a.* 3): "Further, other." See n. 1243.

At our more leysure, shall I render you;
Onely, this one: Lord *Angelo* is precise,
Stands at a guard with Enuie: scarce confesses
That his blood flowes: or that his appetite
Is more to bread then stone: hence shall we see 345
If power change purpose: what our Seemers be. *Exit.*

(F2va

Scena Quinta. 1.4

Enter Isabell and Francisca a Nun.

341 our] your F2-POPE2, HAN1
342 one] one now KTLY
346 *Exit.*] *Om.* CAP-MAL (*Exeunt. ad. in* MAL 10:562)
347 *Scena Quinta*] SCENE IV ROWE, HAL, DYCE, STAU, CAM, GLO, HUD2, IRV+; SCENE VIII POPE, HAN1, WARB, JOHN   *A Nunnery.* ROWE1-SIS, ARD2
348 *Isabell*] *Isabella* ROWE1+ (−CAP, EVNS)   *a Nun*] *Om.* ROWE1-CAM2 (−CAP, COL4), ARD1, ALEX, SIS

342 **precise**] SCHMIDT (1875): "Exact, nice, punctilious" (*OED, a.* 2), as in 166. WILSON (ed. 1922): "I.e. Puritanical" (*OED, a.* 2b). See n. 509.
343 **at a guard**] THIRLBY (1747–53): "At bay, at defiance." JOHNSON (ed. 1765): "On terms of defiance." MASON (1785, p. 33): "This rather means to stand cautiously on his defence." ROLFE (ed. 1882): "On his guard against." PORTER & CLARKE (ed. 1909): "In a position to parry the criticism of envy, i.e., not open to attack." ONIONS (1911): "On his defence" (*OED, sb.* 3, 5a).
    Enuie] SCHMIDT (1874): "Malice. . . . Especially malice shown by calumny and depreciation" (*OED, sb.* 1), as in 1628. LEVER (ed. 1965): "Here personified."
345 **more . . . stone**] CARTER (1905, p. 403): "Figure drawn from the words in Matt. vii.9." LEVER (ed. 1965): " 'Possessed of natural desires' seems to be the meaning." SAUNDERS (ed. 1971): Cf. Matt. 4:3.
    hence] SCHMIDT (1874): "Out of this, from this source or cause" (*OED,* 5), as in 1974. LEISI (ed. 1964): " 'Henceforth' " (*OED,* 4).
346 CAMPBELL (ed. 1949): "If power changes its aim, whether he is what he seems to be." LEISI (ed. 1964): Cf. *Jn.* 2.1.567 (888), "that same purpose-changer, that slye diuel" (Commodity). NOSWORTHY (ed. 1969): "Shakespeare often uses 'seem' in the sense of 'pretend' or 'dissemble', and the present usage strongly suggests that Vincentio already suspects Angelo of hypocrisy."
    Seemers] *OED:* "One who seems, or makes a pretence or show," first quotation. See nn. 1017, 1163, 1443.

Isa. And haue you *Nuns* no farther priuiledges?

Nun. Are not these large enough?   350

Isa. Yes truely; I speake not as desiring more,
But rather wishing a more strict restraint
Vpon the Sisterstood, the Votarists of Saint *Clare.*

Lucio within.

Luc. Hoa? peace be in this place.   355

Isa. Who's that which cals?

Nun. It is a mans voice: gentle *Isabella*
Turne you the key, and know his businesse of him;
You may; I may not: you are yet vnsworne:

---

349 farther] further DAV, THEO2, WARB-JOHN2, v1773, v1793-DYCE1 (−COL1), KTLY-DYCE3, HUD2, IRV, BUL, ARD1, SIS
353 Sisterstood, the] F1; sister POPE, HAN1; sisterhood, CAP, DYCE2, DYCE3, COL4; sisters stood, the ARD2; Sisterhood, the F2 *etc.*   Votarists] votaries WH2, NLSN

---

353 **Sisterstood**]JOHNSON (1755): *Sisterhood,* "A number of women of the same order" (*OED,* 2). PORTER & CLARKE (ed. 1909): "She would desire that a more strict restraint stood upon the sisters." So LEVER (ed. 1965), but a misprint or misreading of *h* as *st* is more likely: cf. 761 *Sister-hood,* 2432 *Sisterhood, Rom.* 5.3.157 (3020), *AYL* 3.4.17 (1726).

Votarists]JOHNSON (1755): "One devoted to any person or thing; one given up by a vow to any service or worship." *OED,* first quotation; also in *Oth.* 4.2.190 (2905), *Tim.* 4.3.27 (1629). Here two syllables, like *Votresse* in *MND* 2.1.123, 163 (499, 540).

Saint *Clare*] MUIR (1956, p. 424): "The idea of making Isabella a votaress of St. Clare, and the name of the nun, Francisca, may be suggested by" Erasmus's *Colloquia* (ed. 1571, p. 503, "*S. Fransisco,*" "*S. Clarae*"). [Not necessarily: see nn. 2941, 2954.] HUNTER (1964, pp. 167–8): "I have discovered no other references to the Order among Shakespeare's English contemporaries. . . . He seems aware that the Poor Clares were an enclosed order." But see Webster, *The Deuils Law-case* (1623), 5.5.38: "This is a white Nun, of the Order of Saint *Clare.*" Cf. nn. 2955, 2958.

354 HOWARD-HILL (1972, p. 123): "Crane's practice with 'within' directions was to write 'within' after the speech-prefix when the dialogue was to be spoken off-stage." See p. 295 and 2101.

355 **Hoa**] See *OED* (Ho *int.* 1 2): "An exclamation to attract attention."

355, 365 **peace**] See *OED* (*sb.* 3b).

356 **that which**] SCHMIDT (1875, p. 1360): "He who." See ABBOTT §265, FRANZ §335.

357 **gentle**] SCHMIDT (1874): "Good, dear, sweet." Cf. *OED* (*a.* 3b): "A complimentary epithet." Again in 374 and often.

358 **of**] From (*OED, prep.* 10b).

When you haue vowd, you must not speake with men,   360
But in the presence of the *Prioresse*;
Then if you speake, you must not show your face;
Or if you show your face, you must not speake.
He cals againe: I pray you answere him.
    Isa. Peace and prosperitie: who is't that cals?   365
    Luc. Haile Virgin, (if you be) as those cheeke-Roses
Proclaime you are no lesse: can you so steed me,
As bring me to the sight of *Isabella*,
A Nouice of this place, and the faire Sister
To her vnhappie brother *Claudio*?   370
    Isa. Why her vnhappy Brother? Let me aske,
The rather for I now must make you know
I am that *Isabella*, and his Sister.
    Luc. Gentle & faire: your Brother kindly greets you;
Not to be weary with you; he's in prison.   375
    Isa. Woe me; for what?
    Luc. For that, which if my selfe might be his Iudge,
He should receiue his punishment, in thankes:

---

   364 *Exit marked by* ROWE1+ (−CAP, ARD2); *veils.* CAP; *Retires.* ARD2
   365 is't that] is it COL4
   366 *Enter* Lucio. ROWE1+   (if you be)] ‸ ~ ~ ~ ‸ POPE; ‸ ~ ~ ~ ! KTLY
   371 her vnhappy Brother] *Marked as quotation* CAM, GLO, DYCE2, DYCE3, HUD2,
IRV+ (−NLSN, SIS)   vnhappy] *Italic* STAU
   376 Woe] Woe's mTBY3 *conj.,* COL4
   377 For that, which] That, for which MALONE (1780, 1:96) *conj.,* RANN   his]
the CAP

---

   364 LEVER (ed. 1965, p. xxvi): "Francisca the nun surely does not leave the
novice Isabella alone with Lucio: she will retire to the door until the interview is over,
and the two women will then make a joint exit."
   366 (**if you be**)] LEISI (ed. 1964): "An aside."
      cheeke-Roses] SCHMIDT (1874): "Blooming cheeks." Cf. *TGV* 4.4.159
(1973), *MND* 1.1.129 (139). LEISI (ed. 1964): "Blushes."
   367 **steed**] JOHNSON (1755): *Stead,* "To help" (*OED, v.* 1c). The verb is spelled
steed seven times in F, *stead* twice, and *sted* once. See n. 1471.
   368 **As**] As to (*OED, adv.* 20).
   370 **vnhappie**] SCHMIDT (1875): "Unfortunate" (*OED, a.* 2). Cf. 249.
   372 **The rather for**] SCHMIDT (1875): "The more so because" (*OED,* Rather
adv. 4).
   374 **Gentle**] See n. 357.
   375 **weary**] *OED* (*a.* 6b): "Tedious, wearisome."
   376 **Woe me**] ABBOTT (§230): " 'Woe is (to) me'."

He hath got his friend with childe.

    Isa. Sir, make me not your storie.   380

    Luc. 'Tis true; I would not, though 'tis my familiar sin,

With Maids to seeme the Lapwing, and to iest

Tongue, far from heart: play with all Virgins so:

I hold you as a thing en-skied, and sainted,

By your renouncement, an imortall spirit   385

And to be talk'd with in sincerity,

As with a Saint.

    Isa. You doe blaspheme the good, in mocking me.

    Luc. Doe not beleeue it: fewnes, and truth; tis thus,

Your brother, and his louer haue embrac'd;   390

380–1 *Lines ending* true: . . . sin CAP, v1793-v1813, CAM, GLO, DYCE2, DEL4, DYCE3, HUD2+

380 make . . . storie] make me not your scorn DAV, COLNE, COL2, DYCE, COL3, COL4, HUD2; make me not your sport mTBY3 *conj.,* SING2; mock me not:—your story MALONE (1783) *conj.,* MAL, v1821, SING1

381 'Tis true;] *Om.* POPE, HAN1; Nay, 'tis true: CAP; It is true. v1793-v1813, CAM, GLO, DEL4, WH2, ARD1-ALEX, PEN2

385 By] Be ROWE

390 haue] having ROWE1-v1773 (−CAP)

---

379 **friend**] DYCE (1867): "Lover—a term applied to both sexes." So *OED* (*sb.* 4).

380 **make . . . storie**] JOHNSON (ed. 1765): "Do not, by deceiving me, make me a subject for a tale." STEEVENS (Var. 1773): *"Do not divert yourself with me, as you would with a story."* RITSON (1783, p. 18): "Do not make a *jest of me.*" STEEVENS (Var. 1793): Cf. 570, "Come *me* to what was done to her." " 'Make *me* not your story', may therefore signify—*invent not your story on purpose to deceive me."* OED (Story *sb.*[1] 5e): "A theme for mirth, a dupe," first use in this sense.

381 **familiar**] SCHMIDT (1874): "Accustomed, habitual" (*OED, a.* 6b).

382 **Lapwing**] THIRLBY (1733–47) cites Ray, *Proverbs* (1678, p. 256; cf. TILLEY, L68, and WILSON, p. 442). HANMER (ed. 1743): *"The Lapwings fly with seeming fright and anxiety far from their nests to deceive those who seek their young."* GREY (1754, 1:113–14) quotes *Err.* 4.2.27 (1133); Lyly, *Campaspe,* 2.2.9.

383 **Tongue . . . heart**] RUSHTON (1872, p. 183): Cf. Lyly, *Euphues* (1:279, 2:4).

384 **en-skied**] CAPELL (1779, 1:glossary, 22): "Seated in Sky." *OED* (Ensky *v.*): "To place in the sky or in heaven; *pass.* only," first quotation.

    sainted] JOHNSON (1755): "Holy; sacred" (*OED, ppl. a.* 2). Cf. 1303.

388 **the good**] LEVER (ed. 1965): "In contrast, not in apposition, to 'me'."

389 **fewnes**] JOHNSON (1755): "Paucity of words; brevity; conciseness." *OED* (1b): "In few words," only quotation. LEVER (ed. 1965): " 'Truth is told in few words'." Cf. 1540, "sad, and few words."

390 **louer**] JOHNSON (1755): "Friend." ROLFE (ed. 1882): "For the feminine use, cf. *A.Y.L.* iii.4.46 [1749], *A. and C.* iv.14.101 [2943], and *Cymb.* v.5.172

As those that feed, grow full: as blossoming Time
That from the seednes, the bare fallow brings
To teeming foyson: euen so her plenteous wombe
Expresseth his full Tilth, and husbandry.
    Isa. Some one with childe by him? my cosen *Iuliet?*   395
    Luc. Is she your cosen?
    Isa. Adoptedly, as schoole-maids change their names

---

391 blossoming Time] Ff.; blossoming-time DYCE2, DYCE3, HUD2, BUL, SIS;
blossoming time ROWE *etc.*
    392 That . . . brings] Doth . . . bring HAN1   seednes] seeding COL3
    393 euen] *Om.* POPE1-RANN (—CAP)
    394 his] its HAN1

[3452]. The poet's *Lover's Complaint* is the lament of a deserted maiden."
    391 **as blossoming Time**] JOHNSON (ed. 1765): "As the sentence now stands
it is apparently ungrammatical, I read, At *blossoming time.*" MASON (1785, p. 34):
"This passage seems to me to require no amendment; and the meaning of it is this:
'As blossoming time proves the good tillage of the farmer, so the fertility of her womb
expresses Claudio's full tilth and husbandry'. By *blossoming time* is meant, the time
when the ears of corn are formed." MALONE (ed. 1790): "I suspect two half lines
have been lost. Perhaps however an imperfect sentence was intended, of which there
are many instances in these plays:—or, *as* might have been used in the sense of
like." HART (ed. 1905): " 'As the bare fallow brings on the blossoming time from
the seed time to the teeming rich harvest, even so', etc. I think it is difficult to find
a difficulty."
    392 **seednes**] WARBURTON (ed. 1747): "An old word for seed-time." HAL-
LIWELL (ed. 1854): "A word of unusual occurrence. It is, however, still in use in some
parts of Yorkshire." SCHMIDT (1875): "Sowing with seeds," revised by SARRAZIN
in 1902 to "The state of being sown." HART (ed. 1905): "In frequent provincial use;
see *English Dialect Dictionary*" and Holland's Pliny (1601), 18.14, 17. *OED* (1): "The
action of sowing, the state of being sown." LEVER (ed. 1965): "The imagery of
increase is typically Shakespearean."
    fallow] SCHMIDT (1874): "Arable land untilled." ONIONS (1911): "Ground
ploughed and harrowed but left uncropped for a time" (*OED, sb.* 2).
    393 **foyson**] GILDON (1710, glossary, p. lxix): "Plenty, Abundance." So JOHN-
SON (1755). POPE (ed. 1723): "Harvest." COLLIER (ed. 1858): *"Plenty, abundance,*
and figuratively *autumn.*" ONIONS (1911): "Plentiful crop or harvest" (*OED,* 1b),
as in *Tmp.* 4.1.110 (1771).
    394 **Expresseth**] SCHMIDT (1874): "To indicate by signs, to exhibit" (*OED, v.*
7).
    Tilth] JOHNSON (1755): "Husbandry." CAPELL (1779, 1:glossary, 69):
"Tillage, Act of tilling" (*OED, sb.* 2).
    husbandry] JOHNSON (1755): "Tillage; manner of cultivating land" (*OED,
sb.* 2). MALONE (ed. 1790, 10:562): Cf. *Son.* 3. LEISI (ed. 1964): "With a pun on
husband."
    397 **Adoptedly**] JOHNSON (1755): "After the manner of something adopted."
OED: "By adoption," only quotation. HART (ed. 1905): Cf. *AWW* 1.1.188 (178):

By vaine, though apt affection.
   Luc. She it is.
   Isa. Oh, let him marry her. 400
   Luc. This is the point.
The Duke is very strangely gone from hence;
Bore many gentlemen (my selfe being one)
In hand, and hope of action: but we doe learne,
By those that know the very Nerues of State, 405
His giuing-out, were of an infinite distance
From his true meant designe: vpon his place,
(And with full line of his authority)   (F2vb)
Gouernes Lord *Angelo*; A man, whose blood
Is very snow-broth: one, who neuer feeles 410
The wanton stings, and motions of the sence;

---

400 Oh, let him] Let him F2-ROWE3; Let him then POPE, HAN1; Then let him
RANN
402 is] who's COL3; who is KTLY; has KNT3
404 and] in KTLY, NLSN   doe] *Om.* POPE1-JOHN2
406 giuing-out] givings out ROWE1+ (−COL1, COL4, IRV, ARD2)   were] was
COL1, COL4

"pretty fond adoptious christendomes."
    change] HUDSON (ed. 1880): *"Exchange* or *interchange"* (*OED, v.* 3), as in
Ham. 1.2.163 (351). See also 1013, 2717, *AYL* 1.3.93 (553), *Tmp.* 1.2.441 (593).
    398 **apt**] SCHMIDT (1874): "Easily accounted for, natural." LEISI (ed. 1964):
" 'Willing', 'ready', cf. [2897]." More likely *OED* (*a.* 3), "Suitable, becoming,
appropriate."
    403-4 **Bore . . . hope**] JOHNSON (ed. 1765): *"To bear in hand* is a common
phrase for *to keep in expectation and dependance."* See *OED* (Bear *v.* [1] 3e): "To delude,
abuse with false pretences." Cf. TILLEY (H94) and WILSON (p. 34). LEISI (ed. 1964):
"Probably a construction mixing *bore in hand . . .* and *bore* (= 'kept') *in hope."*
    404 **action**] SCHMIDT (1874): "Warlike occupation" (*OED,* 10, first used in this
sense by Sh.).
    405 **Nerues**] *OED* (*sb.* 2): "Those things, parts, or elements, which constitute the
main strength or vigour *of* something," first fig. use in plural. LEVER (ed. 1965):
"Sinews, so fig. for the chief motivations of policy."
    406 **giuing-out**] SCHMIDT (1874): "Anything uttered, assertion." Cf. *Ham.*
1.5.178 (874), *Oth.* 4.1.131 (2514), and 1632 *bringings forth.* HOWARD-HILL (1972,
p. 128): The hyphen shows Crane's influence.
    407 **vpon**] On the strength of (ONIONS, 1911; cf. *OED, prep.* 11c).
    408 **line**] JOHNSON (ed. 1765): "Extent." Cf. *2H4* (F) 4.4.39 (2413) and *OED*
(*sb.* [2] 2b).
    410 **very**] See *OED* (*a.* 3): "In the fullest sense of the term."
    snow-broth] JOHNSON (1755): "Very cold liquor." *OED:* "Melted snow."
    411 **stings**] SCHMIDT (1875): "Impulse, incitement," esp. "sexual desire," as in
AYL 2.7.66 (1040), *Oth.* 1.3.335 (684). *OED* (*sb.* [2] 5): "Something which goads to

But doth rebate, and blunt his naturall edge
With profits of the minde: Studie, and fast
He (to giue feare to vse, and libertie,
Which haue, for long, run-by the hideous law,   415
As Myce, by Lyons) hath pickt out an act,
Vnder whose heauy sence, your brothers life
Fals into forfeit: he arrests him on it,
And followes close the rigor of the Statute
To make him an example: all hope is gone,   420
Vnlesse you haue the grace, by your faire praier

---

412 his] it's CAP
413 fast‸] ∼ . F2+
415 for long] long time POPE1-JOHN2   run-by] run up ROWE2

---

action or appetite."
    motions] SCHMIDT (1875): "Impulse." ONIONS (1911): "Inward prompting or impulse, (hence) desire, inclination, emotion" (*OED, sb.* 9).
    sence] DYCE (1867): "Sensual passion." ONIONS (1911): "Sensual nature, sexual desire." See *OED* (*sb.* 4b *collective sing.*) and nn. 900–1, 932.
    412 **rebate**] JOHNSON (1755): "To blunt; to beat to obtuseness; to deprive of keenness" (*OED, v.* 1 4a).
    naturall] SCHMIDT (1875): "Subject to, or caused by, the laws of nature." Cf. *OED* (*a.* 8): "Inherent in the very constitution of a person or thing, innate." See n. 897.
    edge] SCHMIDT (1874): "Keenness, desire" (*OED, sb.* 2b), as in *Luc.* 9, *batelesse edge.*
    413 **profits**] *OED* (*sb.* 1b): "That which is to the advantage or benefit of some one or something," first use in transferred sense, only in Sh.
    414 **to vse, and libertie**] JOHNSON (ed. 1765): *Use,* "practices long countenanced by *custom*" (*OED, sb.* 9). SCHMIDT (1875, p. 1304): "To the practice of liberty, or to licentious practice." ONIONS (1911): *Liberty,* "improper freedom, licence." See n. 216.
    415 **run-by**] HOWARD-HILL (1972, p. 128): The hyphen shows Crane's influence.
    hideous] SCHMIDT (1874): "Frightful" (*OED, a.* 1).
    416 **As Myce, by Lyons**] HART (ed. 1905) quotes Caxton's Aesop, 1484 (ed. Jacobs, 2:26), bk. 1.18, "Of a lyon whiche slepte in a forest and the rats desported and playd aboute hym." See nn. 263, 845. BALDWIN (1944, 1:618–19): Sh. prob. read Aesop in an ed. by Camerarius. See n. 312–13.
    pickt] JOHNSON (1755): "To cull; to chuse; to select" (*OED, v.* 1 19b, *pick out*).
    act] See n. 263.
    417 **heauy sence**] SCHMIDT (1874–5): *Heavy,* "severe." *Sense,* "meaning, import" (*OED, sb.* 20).
    418 **forfeit**] SCHMIDT (1874): "Forfeiture" (*OED, sb.* 4).
    421 **grace**] JOHNSON (ed. 1765): "Power of gaining favour." SCHMIDT (1874): "Good fortune" (*OED, sb.* 10).

To soften *Angelo*: And that's my pith of businesse
'Twixt you, and your poore brother.
   Isa. Doth he so,
Seeke his life?   425
   Luc. Has censur'd him already,
And as I heare, the Prouost hath a warrant
For's execution.
   Isa. Alas: what poore
Abilitie's in me, to doe him good.   430

422–33 *Lines ending* pith . . . brother. . . . life? . . . him . . . hath . . . execution.
. . . me . . . good? . . . have. . . . doubt. . . . traitors, HAN1, CAP, v1778-MAL; pith
. . . brother. . . . so . . . life? . . . already; . . . warrant . . . execution. (*then as* HAN1)
v1773; pith . . . brother. . . . him . . . hath . . . execution. . . . me . . . have. . . . traitors,
v1793-v1821, SING, COL, DYCE, WH1, KTLY, HUD2, BUL, NLSN, SIS, EVNS; business
. . . so . . . already, . . . warrant . . . poor . . . good? . . . My power? . . . traitors,
KNT1, (*last lines ending* doubt— . . . traitors, KNT2, KNT3, have. . . . traitors, HAL);
business . . . brother. . . . already: . . . warrant . . . execution. (*then as* v1793) STAU;
business . . . brother. (*then as* v1793) CAM, GLO, DEL4, WH2, IRV, ARD1, KIT1, ALEX,
PEL1, PEN2; business . . . so, . . . already: . . . warrant . . . execution. (*then as* v1793)
ARD2
   422 pith of] *Om.* POPE
   423 'Twixt] betwixt HAN1, CAP, v1773
   424 so,] ~ ∧ ROWE1+ (−ARD2)
   425 Seeke] Seek for THEO, WARB, JOHN, v1773
   426 Has] H'as THEO1-JOHN2, RANN, EVNS; He has mTBY1 *and* MALONE (1780,
1:96) *conj.*, KTLY; Hath KNT; 'Has DYCE2, DYCE3, HUD2; He's OXF1
   427 as] *Om.* HAN1
   428 For's] for his HAN1, CAP+ (−HAL, ARD2, EVNS)
   430 good.] F1, PEN2; ~ ! DYCE, HUD2, BUL, ARD2, EVNS; ~ ? F2 *etc.*

---

422 **pith**] THIRLBY (1733–47): "Marrow, substance." JOHNSON (ed. 1765):
"The inmost part, the main of my message." *OED* (*sb.* 4 *fig.*): "The essential or vital
part."
   424–5 LEVER (ed. 1965): "Usually arranged as one line. The F division into
half-lines is not only better for the metre: it also suggests Isabella's hesitation at
putting her fear into words." J. J. HOGAN (1968, p. 229): "It is likely that the F
compositor simply wanted to fill an extra line for casting-off reasons."
   426 **Has**] MALONE (1780, 1:96): "I would wish to read: He has censur'd him
already. Which according to the old fashion was written: *H' as* censur'd." IDEM (in
Var. 1821): "Yet after all as Shakspeare and the writers of his time frequently omit
the personal pronoun, this emendation may be unnecessary." ABBOTT (§400): " 'He
has' is frequently pronounced and sometimes written 'has'." See n. 1111.
      censur'd] STEEVENS (*Var.* 1773): "Sentenced" (*OED, v.* 4). So in 466, 480.
   428 **For's**] FRANZ (§53): Cf. *in's* (2604).
   430 **good.**] NOSWORTHY (ed. 1969): "Most editors print an interrogation mark
after *good,* but the F pointing, which conveys Isabella's conviction of her own helpless-
ness, seems convincing."

Luc. Assay the powre you haue.

Isa. My power? alas, I doubt.

Luc. Our doubts are traitors
And makes vs loose the good we oft might win,
By fearing to attempt: Goe to Lord *Angelo*   435
And let him learne to know, when Maidens sue
Men giue like gods: but when they weepe and kneele,
All their petitions, are as freely theirs
As they themselues would owe them.

Isa. Ile see what I can doe.   440

Luc. But speedily.

Isa. I will about it strait;
No longer staying, but to giue the Mother
Notice of my affaire: I humbly thanke you:
Commend me to my brother: soone at night   445
Ile send him certaine word of my successe.

Luc. I take my leaue of you.

Isa. Good sir, adieu.   *Exeunt.*

---

432 doubt.] ~ ,— mTBY1 *conj.,* CAP+ (−COL, ALEX, ARD2, PEN2)

434 makes] F1-ROWE2, NLSN, ARD2, EVNS; made THEO4, JOHN, v1773; make ROWE3 *etc.*

438 freely] truely F2-RANN

448 *Exeunt.*] *Om.* v1778-RANN

---

431 **Assay**] SCHMIDT (1874): "Try" (*OED, v.* 1). See n. 274.

432 This line may be unfinished: see textual notes.

434 **makes**] LEVER (ed. 1965): "Quasi-singular verb to plural subject (Abbott §333)." See n. 879.

435 **attempt**] *OED* (*v.* 1c): Only instance of absolute use.

439 PARROTT (ed. 1938): "As if they themselves possessed them." Rather "as they themselves would wish to have them." See n. 17.

442 **strait**] See n. 255.

443 **but**] Than. See ABBOTT §127, *OED* (*conj.* 5).

Mother] JOHNSON (ed. 1765): "The abbess, or prioress." *OED* (*sb.* 3b): "The head or superior of a female religious community," first quotation.

445 **soone at night**] DYCE (1867): About night. SCHMIDT (1875): "This very night." HART (ed. 1905): "Early to-night." See *OED* (*adv.* 3).

446 **successe**] SCHMIDT (1875): "Issue, result, fortune." ONIONS (1911): "Fortune (good or bad)" (*OED, sb.* 2).

Actus Secundus. Scœna Prima.   2.1

Enter Angelo, Escalus, and seruants, Iustice.   450

Ang. We must not make a scar-crow of the Law,
Setting it vp to feare the Birds of prey,
And let it keepe one shape, till custome make it
Their pearch, and not their terror.
    Esc. I, but yet   455
Let vs be keene, and rather cut a little
Then fall, and bruise to death: alas, this gentleman

---

449 *the Palace.* ROWE1-JOHN2; *A Hall in* Angelo's *House.* CAP-NLSN, KIT1-SIS (*subst.*); *A Court of Justice* CAM3, ARD2

450 *Enter . . .*] *Enter* ANGELO, ESCALUS, *and a Justice*; Provost, *Officers, and others, attending.* CAP-SIS (−v1773, COL, WH1, NLSN, KIT1) (*subst.*)

---

449 LEVER (ed. 1965): "The scene is usually located in Angelo's house, but the dialogue suggests a session in court."

450 *Iustice*] GREG (1955, p. 355): "Seems to be a later addition," as suggested by WILSON (ed. 1922).

452 **feare**] JOHNSON (1755): "To fright; to terrify." *OED* (*v.* 2a): "To drive away by fear, frighten away."

455 **I, but**] See *OED* (Aye, ay *interj.* 2b): Aye, *but*, "Indicating provisional assent to a statement for the sake of rebutting it." Cf. 1337.

457 **fall**] WARBURTON (ed. 1747): "I should rather read *fell, i.e.* strike down." STEEVENS (Var. 1773): "Let fall," as in *Err.* 2.2.127 (520) and *AYL* 3.5.5 (1775). KNIGHT (ed. 1840): "The verb is here used actively. We still say *to fall a tree;* and probably Shakspere had this image in his mind." HUNTER (ed. 1873): "Escalus desires that Angelo and he should act as keen instruments and cut a little rather than fall as heavy weights on an offender and crush him to death." WILSON (ed. 1922): "Let fall (the sword of justice)." HARDING (ed. 1954): "Let fall, as an executioner's ax." LEVER (ed. 1965): " 'Let fall', as of felling a tree" (*OED, v.* 51c). SAUNDERS (ed. 1971): "Let us use the law as a surgeon's knife (which will promote cure) and not as a bludgeon which only deals out death."

Whom I would saue, had a most noble father,
Let but your honour know
(Whom I beleeue to be most strait in vertue)   460
That in the working of your owne affections,
Had time coheard with Place, or place with wishing,
Or that the resolute acting of our blood
Could haue attaind th'effect of your owne purpose,
Whether you had not sometime in your life   465
Er'd in this point, which now you censure him,
And puld the Law vpon you.

459–61 *Lines ending* believe . . . whether in . . . affections, HAN1; believe . . . virtue) and consider . . . affections, CAP; believe . . . virtue) . . . affections, v1773-RANN

460 strait] straight KNT, HAL, STAU

460–1 vertue) That in] virtue, whether in HAN1; virtue) and consider This, In CAP

463 our] Ff., KNT1, KNT2, IRV, ALEX; your DAV, ROWE *etc.*

465 not] *Om.* F4

466 which . . . him] For which you censure him DAV, RANN; you censure now in him HAN1; which now you censure him for CAP, KTLY; where now you censure him WH1, HUD2

---

459 **know**]JOHNSON (ed. 1765): "To *know* is here to *examine,* to take *cognisance.*" CLARKE (ed. 1864): "Used here for reflect, consider." See *OED* (*v.* 11): "To be cognizant, conscious, or aware of . . . to understand."

460 **strait**] *OED* (*a.* 7b): "Rigorous in principles; strict or scrupulous in morality or religious observance." See n. 1741.

461 **affections**] SCHMIDT (1874): "Feelings, passions" (*OED, sb.* 3). LEVER (ed. 1965): "Physical desires."

462 **coheard**] JOHNSON (1755): *Cohere,* "To suit; to fit; to be fitted to." *OED* (*v.* 4b): "Agree."

463 **our blood**] ROLFE (ed. 1882): "Animal passion" (*OED, sb.* 6), as in 1017, 1192, 2869. STONE (in IRVING & MARSHALL, ed. 1889): "By exchanging *your* for *our,* when using a word which might have a general application to human frailty, Escalus avoided a too personal reference in a supposititious case." LEVER (ed. 1965): *Your blood,* " 'your sensual desires'. Alexander keeps F 'our', which however jars with the rhetorically iterated 'your' throughout this speech."

464 **effect**] SCHMIDT (1874): "Performance, realization." ONIONS (1911): "Accomplishment, fulfilment" (*OED,* 7).

465 **had**] See n. 188.

465–6 M.S. (1795, p. 646): Cf. John 8:7. See n. 894–9.

466 **which . . . him**] MALONE (ed. 1790, 10:562): "The sense undoubtedly requires,'—which now you censure him *for',* but the text certainly appears as the poet left it. I have elsewhere shewn that he frequently uses these elliptical expressions." See ABBOTT §394, FRANZ §542, and nn. 2149, 2222.

    censure] *OED* (*v.* 4): "To pronounce judicial sentence on," first quotation in this sense. See n. 426.

Ang. 'Tis one thing to be tempted (*Escalus*)
Another thing to fall: I not deny   (F3a)
The Iury passing on the Prisoners life   470
May in the sworne-twelue haue a thiefe, or two
Guiltier then him they try; what's open made to Iustice,
That Iustice ceizes; What knowes the Lawes
That theeues do passe on theeues? 'Tis very pregnant,
The Iewell that we finde, we stoope, and take't,   475
Because we see it; but what we doe not see,
We tread vpon, and neuer thinke of it.
You may not so extenuate his offence,
For I haue had such faults; but rather tell me
When I, that censure him, do so offend,   480
Let mine owne Iudgement patterne out my death,

472–4 *Lines ending* made . . . know . . . pregnant, HAN1; made . . . laws, . . .
pregnant, MAL, HAL, DYCE, WH1, COL3, KTLY, HUD2
473 Iustice ceizes] justice seizes on POPE1-THEO2, WARB-v1773; it seizes on
HAN1   What] who CAM3   knowes] know ROWE3-ARD1 (—WH1, KTLY,
DYCE2, DYCE3, HUD2, IRV)   Lawes] Law DAV, WH1, DYCE2, DYCE3, HUD2, IRV,
KIT1
474 very] *Om.* HAN1
475 take't] take it CAP-v1821, SING, KNT, COL, HAL, KTLY, DEL4, ARD1

---

469 **not**] On *not* before a verb see ABBOTT §305, FRANZ §405, *OED* (*adv.* 1b).
470 **passing**] STEEVENS (Var. 1793): "So, in *King Lear* [3.7.24 (2084)] . . . '*pass
upon* his life'." DYCE (1867): "*Pass,* to pass sentence." See *OED* (*v.* 21): "Give a
verdict *for* or *against.*"
472 SEYMOUR (1805, 1:87): "This line is, at once, exuberant and ungrammatical." For *then him,* "than he whom," see ABBOTT §208, FRANZ §284.
472–3 **what's . . . ceizes**] LEVER (ed. 1965, pp. xxix, 28): These words look like
an afterthought. "A more probable arrangement would be 'What's open made / To
justice, justice seizes'." STEEVENS suggested this change in 1793.
473–4 **What . . . on theeues**] MALONE (ed. 1790): "How can the administra-
tor[s] of the laws take cognizance of what I have just mentioned? How can they know,
whether the jurymen who *decide* on the life or death of thieves be themselves as
criminal as those whom they try?" HART (ed. 1905): "The laws are ignorant that
thieves have passed judgment upon thieves." WILSON (ed. 1922): " 'What' may very
easily have been caught by the compositor's eye from 'what's open' immediately
above." DURHAM (ed. 1926): "*Knows* (= know) is the Northern English verbal
plural, common in Shakespeare." LEVER (ed. 1965): "Plural subject with quasi-
singular verb (Abbott, §333)." See FRANZ §672.
474 **pregnant**] JOHNSON (ed. 1765): "*Plain.*" ONIONS (1911): "Clear, obvious" (*OED, a.*[1]), from Old Fr., not the same word as *pregnant,* "resourceful," from
Latin in 14 (*OED, a.*[2]).
479 **For**] JOHNSON (ed. 1765): "*Because*" (ABBOTT §151, *OED, conj.* 1).
481 **patterne**] JOHNSON (1755): "Serve as an example to be followed." *OED*
(*v.* 1b): "Give an example or precedent for." See n. 1748–9.

And nothing come in partiall. Sir, he must dye.

Enter Prouost.

Esc. Be it as your wisedome will.
Ang. Where is the *Prouost?*   485
Pro. Here if it like your honour.
Ang. See that *Claudio*
Be executed by nine to morrow morning,
Bring him his Confessor, let him be prepar'd,
For that's the vtmost of his pilgrimage.   490
  Esc. Well: heauen forgiue him; and forgiue vs all:
Some rise by sinne, and some by vertue fall:

---

482 Sir,] *Om.* POPE, HAN1
483 *Enter* . . .] *Om.* CAP, v1778-KNT2, HAL-DYCE1, STAU-DYCE3, HUD2-ARD1,
CAM3, ALEX, SIS; *after* 485 COL, WH1; *after* 484 KIT1
486 [*coming from behind*] DYCE2, DYCE3, HUD2, IRV, CAM3 (*subst.*)
488 nine] *Om.* PEN2
489 Bring him] Bring PEN2
490 *Exit* Provost. ROWE1+
491-4 [*Aside*] WALKER (1860, 3:16) *conj.*, CAM, GLO, DYCE2, DYCE3, WH2-BUL,
NLSN, ALEX, SIS

---

482 **And . . . partiall**] ROLFE (ed. 1882): "And no partiality be urged or
allowed."
486 **like**] SCHMIDT (1874): "Please" (*OED, v.*[1] 1), as in 612, 2435.
488 **by nine**] LEVER (ed. 1965): "The Provost tells Claudio: 'by eight . . .'
[1919]. An hour would elapse before the prisoner was judicially considered dead."
489 **Confessor**] ABBOTT (§492): "The accent on the first syllable was the proper
noun accent; the accent on the second (which . . . ultimately prevailed) was derived
from the verb."
490 **pilgrimage**] HART (ed. 1905): "Human life [*OED, sb.* 1c *fig.*]. See Genesis
xlvii. 9." TILLEY (L249), WHITING (P201), and WILSON (p. 461): "Life is a pilgrimage."
491-4 HUDSON (ed. 1880): "This is, to me, one of the most perplexing passages
in Shakespeare. . . . I strongly suspect the two couplets to be an interpolation, or at
least the work of some other hand than Shakespeare's." WILSON (ed. 1922): "We
ascribe these couplets to the reviser. . . . They do not assist the action."
492 JOHNSON (ed. 1765): "This line is in the first folio printed in Italicks as a
quotation." HUDSON (ed. 1880): "In Italic type, as if to mark it either as a quotation
or as a proverbial saying." THISELTON (1901, p. 14): "The italics show that this is
a 'maxime'." HUNTER (1951, p. 179): Crane uses italic script twice to set off sayings
in Malone MS 25. See n. 1199. Escalus is not quoting a proverb but inventing a
sententia, sharpened by antithesis.
  some by vertue fall] HORNE (ed. 1840, 1:209): "Virtue being frequently
overwhelmed by the vices of the world, falls into error or ruin. Some fall by the very

Some run from brakes of Ice, and answere none,   493
And some condemned for a fault alone.

---

493 from brakes of Ice] Ff., KNT, CAM, GLO, OXF1, ARD2, EVNS; through Brakes
of Vice ROWE1-JOHN2, v1773, WH2; from brakes of justice CAP, RANN; from breaks
of ice STEEVENS (v1773) *conj.,* COL, IRV, ALEX-PEL1; from wreaks o' vice KTLY; from
brakes of office PEN2; from brakes of vice v1778 *etc.*   and] *Om.* CAP, RANN
    494 condemned] are condemn'd KTLY   a] one HAN1, SIS

---

strength of their best feelings and virtue."
    493 **brakes of Ice**] STEEVENS (Var. 1773): *"Some run away from danger, and stay
to answer none of their faults. . . .* If this be the true reading, it should be printed
. . . breaks <i.e. fractures> *of ice. . . .* A *brake* anciently meant not only a *sharp bit,*
a *snaffle,* but also . . . a smith's *brake.*" IDEM (Var. 1778): Brakes were also *"engines
of punishment."* MALONE (ed. 1790): Cf. "the rough Brake" [i.e., thicket] in *H8*
1.2.75–6 (410–11). NARES (1822): "The plainest interpretation seems to be, 'from
thorns and perplexities of vice'." TIECK (ed. 1831, 5:381): "From ice that breaks."
COLLIER (ed. 1842): "Some escape without responsibility, even though the danger
seem as imminent as when the ice breaks under them." FIELD (1845, p. 48): *Brakes*
means *"tortures, traps, or thorny hedges."* INGLEBY (1875, p. 147): *Brakes,* fixed forms.
"Some, whose *characters* are set in brakes of ice, *i.e.,* with no shew of passion whatever, do run from them, under the heat of lust." STONE (1884, p. 114*): "Dangerous
places in the ice." LEE (ed. 1907): " 'Brakes of ice' may mean 'frozen ground
rendered dangerous by traps of ice', and hence 'danger' generally." PORTER &
CLARKE (ed. 1909): "The implication is that Angelo curbs his heat with snaffles of
ice." Some *"run from brakes* of Ice, and answer nobody just as an unruly steed, kept
in by the stiffest brake, will break from its control and run and not answer to the rein
and bit of any driver." WILSON (ed. 1922): " 'Brakes of ice' belong to the same hell
as the 'thrilling region of thick-ribbéd ice' [1342]. A 'brake' was a sort of cage, and,
as N.E.D. [*sb.* 6] quotes two references to 'the Devil's brake', such a cage was perhaps
a familiar piece of furniture in the miracle-plays." [Not so: "the Devil's brake" in
these passages, both 16th-c., means only "the Devil's snare."] NUTT (1942, pp.
253–4): Cf. *The Three Voyages of William Barents to the Arctic Regions (1594, 1595, and
1596),* Hakluyt Soc. 54 (1876), 208: "the ice whereon we lay . . . brake and ran one
peece vpon another," "the ice brake vnder our owne feet," "the ice brake vnder vs."
SISSON (1956, 1:78–9): "Read *breaks of ice."* Cf. *Tro.* 3.3.215 (2070). STEVENSON
(1956, *SQ* 7:452): "Angelo is one who in the chill of his inhumanity seems quite
literally to take his origins in (to 'run from') brakes or thickets of ice." Cf. 342–4,
409–10. LEVER (ed. 1965): "The F reading may possibly be understood as a reference to punishment in hell or purgatory, with 'brakes' as constrictions. . . . The
meaning would then be 'hell pains'." See p. 282.
    answere none] HENLEY (in Var. 1793): *"Make no confession of guilt."* IDEM
(in Var. 1821): *"Are not called to account for their conduct."* HART (ed. 1905): "Pay no
penalty." See *OED* (Answer *v.* 6b): "Atone for." See nn. 848, 1080.
    494 **a fault alone**] STEEVENS (Var. 1773): *"A single frailty."* LEVER (ed. 1965):
"With the stress on 'fault' as distinguished from 'offence'." J. J. HOGAN (1968, p.
229): "I think rather that *a,* in the frequent sense of 'one', is stressed."

Enter Elbow, Froth, Clowne, Officers.   495

Elb. Come, bring them away: if these be good people in a Common-weale, that doe nothing but vse their
abuses in common houses, I know no law: bring them
away.

Ang. How now Sir, what's your name? And what's   500
the matter?

Elb. If it please your honour, I am the poore Dukes
Constable, and my name is *Elbow*; I doe leane vpon Iustice Sir, and doe bring in here before your good honor,
two notorious Benefactors.   505

Ang. Benefactors? Well: What Benefactors are they?
Are they not Malefactors?

Elb. If it please your honour, I know not well what
they are: But precise villaines they are, that I am sure of,
and void of all prophanation in the world, that good   510
Christians ought to haue.

Esc. This comes off well: here's a wise Officer.

---

495 SCENE II. POPE, HAN1, WARB, JOHN

---

496 **away**] See *OED* (*adv.* 1): "Onward, on."

498 **abuses**] SCHMIDT (1874): "Corrupt practice" (*OED, sb.* 3).

  common houses] *OED* (Common house 4b): "A brothel, stews." Elbow
contrasts them with *Common-weale.* See n. 193–4.

501 **the matter**] See *OED* (*sb.* 1 25b): "The circumstance or state of things." So
in 741. Cf. n. 778.

502–3 **the poore Dukes Constable**] DELIUS (ed. 1860): He means *the duke's
poor constable:* cf. *Ado* 3.5.22 (1615) and Dogberry's misunderstanding of *malefactors*
in 4.2.3–4 (2001–2). HART (ed. 1905): "Hardly a transposition, though parallels are
common. 'Duke's constable' may be regarded as one term or title." LEVER (ed.
1965): "But a transposition . . . is characteristic of Elbow." Cf. 627–8.

503 **leane**] SCHMIDT (1874): "Depend. . . . Quibbling" (*OED, v.* 3, "To trust
to for support"). EVANS (ed. 1974): "Probably a blunder for *uphold* or some such
word that means the opposite of what he says."

506 **What**] What kind of (ABBOTT §86, *OED, a.* 1 15). See n. 1167.

509 **precise**] FARMER (in Var. 1773, 10:Oo5ᵛ): "A stroke at the *puritans.*" See
n. 342. SCHMIDT (1875): "In the language of Elbow, = decided, doubtless." KELL-
NER (1931, p. 250): He means *precious.* [Cf. *pretious villaine* in *Oth.* 5.2.235 (3531).]
HARDING (ed. 1954): "Precious, arrant." LEVER (ed. 1965): "Elbow's 'misplacings'
form an ironic commentary on Angelo's principles."

510 **prophanation**] DELIUS (ed. 1860): Elbow uses *profanation* for the opposite,
fear of God. CLARKE (ed. 1864): "For 'profession' . . . (as is proved by Angelo's
asking, 'What *quality* are they of ?')." PARROTT (ed. 1938): " 'Irreverence', for
'reverence'."

512 **This comes off well**] JOHNSON (ed. 1765): "This is nimbly spoken; this is

Ang. Goe to: What quality are they of? *Elbow* is
your name?

Why do'st thou not speake *Elbow*? 515

Clo. He cannot Sir: he's out at Elbow.

Ang. What are you Sir?

Elb. He Sir: a Tapster Sir: parcell Baud: one that
serues a bad woman: whose house Sir was (as they say)
pluckt downe in the Suburbs: and now shee professes a 520
hot-house; which, I thinke is a very ill house too.

Esc. How know you that?

Elb. My wife Sir? whom I detest before heauen, and

513–15 *Prose* POPE1+
513 they] you ROWE, POPE, HAN1
518 He◠ Sir:] F1; ∼ ◠ ∼ , F2-F4, PEL1; ∼ , ∼ ! DYCE, STAU-GLO, HUD2-NLSN,
EVNS; ∼ , ∼ ? ROWE1 *etc.*
523 Sir?] ∼ , F2+

---

volubly uttered." STEEVENS (Var. 1778): "This is well delivered, this story is well
told." ONIONS (1911): *Come off,* "to come to the issue, turn out" (*OED, v.* 61i), as
in *Tim.* 1.1.29 (42).

513 **Goe to**] SCHMIDT (1874, p. 482): "Come! (a phrase of exhortation or
reproof)." See *OED* (Go *v.* 91b).

quality] RANN (ed. 1786): "Calling" (*OED, sb.* 5). LEVER (ed. 1965): "Occupation, business, or rank."

514–15 LEVER (ed. 1965): "The separate lineation in F suggests a pause for
Elbow to answer." Cf. 2241–2.

516 **out at Elbow**] THIRLBY (1747–53): "A carawichet upon his faltering or
silence after being called by his name n.b. his cue." FARMER (in Var. 1773, 10:
Oo5ᵛ): "I know not whether this quibble be generally observed: he is *out* at the word
elbow, and *out* at the *elbow* of his coat." HART (ed. 1905): " 'Elbow' is singular for
the sake of the pun. The expression (in rags) is always plural. The passage in the text
is the earliest in *New Eng. Dict.,* but it occurs in Nashe, *Foure Letters Confuted,* " 1593
[ed. McKerrow, 1:332, and see index]. TILLEY (E102) and WILSON (p. 601) cite
earlier uses. LEVER (ed. 1965): "Without the wit to reply."

518 **parcell Baud**] NARES (1822): "A person, one part of whose profession was
being a bawd." *OED* (Parcel *adv.* 1c): "In part, partly."

520 **professes**] HUDSON (ed. 1851): "Pretends, *to keep.*" SCHMIDT (1875): "To
make it one's business or trade" (*OED, v.* 5). Cf. 1722 and n. LEVER (ed. 1965):
"Jocularly suggesting the 'professed houses' of monks and nuns, 'to profess' being to
take the vows of an order." See n. 2079.

521 **hot-house**] JOHNSON (1755): "A bagnio; a place to sweat and cup in,"
quoting this and, as a second meaning, "brothel" in Jonson (*Epigram* 7). *OED* (2):
"Brothel." LEVER (ed. 1965): "Elbow's remark is a mere gag: what Mistress Overdone actually 'professed' was a tavern." Not so: no one in the play says anything about
a tavern, which sold wine. Johnson is right: she claimed to be keeping a bathhouse,
as does the bawd in Dekker's *West-ward Hoe,* 1.1.8.

523 **detest**] THIRLBY (1733–47): "Blunder for protest," as in *Wiv.* 1.4.160

your honour.

    Esc. How? thy wife?   525

    Elb. I Sir: whom I thanke heauen is an honest wo-
man.

    Esc. Do'st thou detest her therefore?

    Elb. I say sir, I will detest my selfe also, as well as she,
that this house, if it be not a Bauds house, it is pitty of her   530
life, for it is a naughty house.

    Esc. How do'st thou know that, Constable?

    Elb. Marry sir, by my wife, who, if she had bin a wo-
man Cardinally giuen, might haue bin accus'd in forni-
cation, adultery, and all vncleanlinesse there.   535   (F3

    Esc. By the womans meanes?

    Elb. I sir, by Mistris *Ouer-dons* meanes: but as she spit

---

524 honour.] ~ ,— THEO, WARB+
526-7 woman.] ~ ;— THEO, WARB+ (−KIT1, SIS, EVNS)
535 vncleanlinesse] uncleannesse F2-MAL
536 the] that HAN1

---

(535). MALONE (ed. 1790): "He means—*protest.*" MASON (1798, app. p. 10): "I think that Elbow uses it for *Attest,* that is call to witness." DYCE (1867): "A blunder for *protest.*"

525 **How**] SCHMIDT (1874): "Used . . . to express surprise." *OED* (*adv.* 4): "*Ellipt.* for 'How is it?' or 'How say you?' " So in 905, 2670.

526 **whom**] See *OED* (*pron.* 3): "Used ungrammatically for the nominative *Who.*" See FRANZ §334.

528 **therefore**] For that reason (*OED, adv.* 1b).

529 **she**] Her (FRANZ §287d). Cf. 1434, 2504, 2924.

530-1 **pitty of her life**] A great pity. Elbow misuses an idiom used by comic characters like Bottom and Snug in *MND* 3.1.44, 5.1.229 (853, 2029) and Aguecheek in *TN* 2.5.14 (1027). See n. 1000.

531 **naughty**] SCHMIDT (1875): "Bad, wicked." So *OED* (*a.* 3).

534 **Cardinally**] *OED* (*adv.*): "Humorous perversion of *carnally* (cf. *cardinal sins*)." KÖKERITZ (1953, p. 63): "Henslowe's persistent spelling of *cardinal* without the medial syllable *-di-* . . . and the *MM* malapropism prove beyond any doubt that this *d* was no longer used in colloquial pronunciation, that consequently *cardinal* and *carnal* were homonyms." [See also *the verie diuell incardinate* in *TN* 5.1.185 (2344).]

    giuen] See *OED* (*ppl. a.* 2): "Inclined, disposed."

    accus'd] THIRLBY (1747-53): "Abused." Cf. *abuses* (498). SCHMIDT (1874): "To charge with a fault or crime." KELLNER (1931, p. 250): For *seduced.* [Cf. *2 Promos,* 4.2 (p. 360 below): "*Casgandra* scusde (meaning 'accused'), *Promos* of honestie."]

534-5 **fornication . . . vncleanlinesse**] ANDERS (1904, p. 221): Cf. Gal. 5:19, "adultery, fornication, vncleannesse."

537-8 JOHNSON (ed. 1765): "Here seems to have been some mention made of

in his face, so she defide him.

Clo. Sir, if it please your honor, this is not so.

Elb. Proue it before these varlets here, thou honora-   540
ble man, proue it.

Esc. Doe you heare how he misplaces?

Clo. Sir, she came in great with childe: and longing
(sauing your honors reuerence) for stewd prewyns; sir,
we had but two in the house, which at that very distant   545
time stood, as it were in a fruit dish (a dish of some three
pence; your honours haue seene such dishes) they are not

---

544 sir,] *Om.* F4-POPE2, HAN1
545 distant] instant F2-POPE2, HAN1
547 haue] having F4-ROWE2

Froth, who was to be accused, and some words therefore may have been lost, unless
the irregularity of the narrative may be better imputed to the ignorance of the
constable." Elbow forgets to name Froth, as in 594 he merely points to "this man."

537 **meanes**] LEVER (ed. 1965): "Go-between or pimp. (*O.E.D.* 'mean' *sb.* [2]
9b)." I think that makes too much sense for Elbow. Perhaps he misunderstands it as
"man, servant" (Pompey).

540-1 VICKERS (1968, p. 316): Elbow "has that variation on malapropism, *hypal-
lage,* the right words in the wrong place."

540 **varlets**] SCHMIDT (1875): Rascals (*OED,* 2), misused for "honorable men."

542 **misplaces**] *OED* (*v.* 1c): "Misplace one's words," only quotation in absolute
sense.

543-85 TIECK (c. 1794; 1920, p. 233): The citation of these small insignificant
details produces extraordinarily rich comic effects, like the speech of Mrs. Quickly
in *2H4* (2.1.92-112 [688-704]). LEVER (ed. 1965): "The humour in Pompey's
rambling story depends mainly on its run of equivocal words and phrases—'stewed
prunes', 'but two', 'stood', 'dish', 'pin', 'point', 'cracking the stones', and perhaps
others."

544 **sauing . . . reuerence**] See *OED* (Reverence *sb.* 5b): "An apologetic phrase
introducing . . . some remark that might offend the hearer."

stewd prewyns] STEEVENS (Var. 1778): "*Stewed prunes* were to be found in
every brothel. See a note on [*1H4* 3.3.128 (2120), quoting Lodge, Clowes, and
others]. In the old copy *prunes* are spelt, according to vulgar pronunciation, *prewyns.*"
OED (*ppl. a.* [1] c): "With pun on *Stewed ppl. a.* [2]," "Belonging to the stews." HARDING
(ed. 1954): "There seems to have been a theory that this fruit was effective both in
the prevention and cure of venereal disease, hence its popularity in brothels." Cf.
SHUGG (1977), pp. 303, 311.

545 **distant**] THIRLBY (1747-53): "Blunder for instant?" MALONE (ed. 1790):
"He means *instant.*" CLARKE (ed. 1864): "Probably the Clown intends to say 'distinct', or, perhaps, 'instant'." *OED* (*a.* 4) cites this passage as the earliest use of *distant*
meaning "Far apart or remote in time," but since it finds no other example before
1732, this seems unlikely. LEVER (ed. 1965): "A contracted MS. spelling of 'instant'
as 'ĩstant' might well have prompted 'correction' to 'distant'." But Pompey simply
misplaces, as in 606, 615, 620.

China-dishes, but very good dishes.

Esc. Go too: go too: no matter for the dish sir.

Clo. No indeede sir not of a pin; you are therein in   550
the right: but, to the point: As I say, this Mistris *Elbow*,
being (as I say) with childe, and being great bellied, and
longing (as I said) for prewyns: and hauing but two in
the dish (as I said) Master *Froth* here, this very man, hauing eaten the rest (as I said) & (as I say) paying for them   555
very honestly: for, as you know Master *Froth*, I could not
giue you three pence againe.

Fro. No indeede.

Clo. Very well: you being then (if you be remembred) cracking the stones of the foresaid prewyns.   560

Fro. I, so I did indeede.

Clo. Why, very well: I telling you then (if you be
remembred) that such a one, and such a one, were past
cure of the thing you wot of, vnlesse they kept very good
diet, as I told you.   565

Fro. All this is true.

Clo. Why very well then.

Esc. Come: you are a tedious foole: to the purpose:

---

548 dishes.] ~ ,— DYCE, STAU-GLO, HUD2-BUL, NLSN, PEL1, ARD2
553 but two] no more F2-POPE2, HAN1
557 againe.] ~ : CAP, MAL, DYCE, STAU, COL4, HUD2, BUL, KIT1-ARD2
560 foresaid] aforesaid SING, KTLY   prewyns.] ~ ; CAP, MAL, DYCE, STAU+
(−KNT3, COL4)
562 telling] tell v1821
564 very] *Om.* ROWE3, POPE, HAN1
565 you.] ~ ; CAP, MAL, v1793, DYCE, STAU+ (−KTLY, KNT3, COL4)
567 then.] ~ : CAP, STAU+ (−KNT3, COL4, KIT1, SIS)

---

548 **China-dishes**] HALLIWELL (ed. 1854) quotes references to China or porce-
lain from Marco Polo to *The Country Wife* (1675, 4.3).

549 **Go too**] See n. 513.

550 **not of a pin**] TILLEY (P334) and WILSON (p. 626): "Not worth a pin."
WHITING (P211) quotes a closer parallel from More's *Workes* (1557, p. 1158): "not
please hym of a pynne." Cf. 792, 1323, and *OED* (*sb.*[1] 3b).

557 **giue...againe**] See *OED* (*v.* 53a): "Give back." THISELTON (1901, p. 15):
"Pompey, clearly, had pretended that he had no change."

559–60 **be remembred**] See *OED* (*v.* 6c): "Remember."

564 **wot**] SCHMIDT (1875): "Know." Cf. Launce's "the thing you wot of" in
TGV 4.4.30 (1845).

565 **diet**] DYCE (1867): "The regimen prescribed for those suffering from the
lues venerea." *OED* (*sb.*[1] 3): "Prescribed course of food . . . regimen."

568 **the purpose**] *OED* (*sb.* 5): "The matter in hand."

what was done to *Elbowes* wife, that hee hath cause to
complaine of ? Come me to what was done to her.   570
   Clo. Sir, your honor cannot come to that yet.
   Esc. No sir, nor I meane it not.
   Clo. Sir, but you shall come to it, by your honours
leaue: And I beseech you, looke into Master *Froth* here
sir, a man of foure-score pound a yeare; whose father   575
died at *Hallowmas*: Was't not at *Hallowmas* Master
Froth?
   Fro. Allhallond-Eue.
   Clo. Why very well: I hope here be truthes: he Sir,
sitting (as I say) in a lower chaire, Sir, 'twas in the bunch   580

---

570 me] *Om.* POPE1-v1773 (−CAP); we WH, KNT3
572 nor] *Om.* POPE, HAN1
575 pound] pounds v1785
580 chaire] chamber mTBY1 *and* CAPN *conj.,* RANN

---

570 **me**] See n. 259.
   done] HART (ed. 1905): " 'Done' in this line quibbles upon an obscene sense
which frequently occurs, as above in [177: see n. 177–8], and in the name of the
Bawd."
   571 Pompey pretends to be shocked that Escalus can't wait to have intercourse.
   572 **nor**] See n. 42.
   574 **looke into**] LEVER (ed. 1965): "Consider." Or perhaps "look at"; cf. *looke
in* 598, *looke vpon* 599.
   575 **foure-score pound a yeare**] WINNY (ed. 1959): "A decent sum, giving
Froth social respectability." LEVER (ed. 1965): "A modest income, allowing little
scope for vice or extravagance." But James I in 1603 required all Englishmen who
owned land worth forty pounds a year to accept knighthood or be fined, which shows
that they were considered well-to-do, and Froth had twice that income. On *pound* see
FRANZ §190.
   578 **Allhallond-Eue**] *OED* (All-hallow 4): "*All hallow eve:* the eve of All Saints.
(See also *Hallow e'en.*)" Cf. *Alhallowne* (Q1), *Alhollown* (F), *1H4* 1.2.178 (261),
other forms derived from ME *al halwen.*
   579 **hope**] See *OED* (*v.* 2): "Trust."
   580 **lower chaire**] MALONE (ed. 1790): "A *lower* chair is a chair lower than
ordinary." STEEVENS (Var. 1793): "Every house had formerly, among its other
furniture, what was called—a *low chair,* designed for the ease of sick people, and,
occasionally, occupied by lazy ones. Of these conveniencies I have seen many."
HALLIWELL (ed. 1854): "Low chairs are occasionally mentioned in old inventories."
He gives a print of one and cites Barnabe Barnes, *The Diuils Charter,* 1607 (ed.
McKerrow, 2460). "*Lower,* in the text, is used merely, by an ordinary license, instead
of *low.*" [But it may be a misprint.] ROLFE (ed. 1905): Cf. *Chaires of ease* in *Tim.*
5.4.11 (2521), *drooping Chaire* in *1H6* 4.5.5. (2118).
   580–1 **bunch of Grapes**] ROLFE (ed. 1882): "It was the custom in the time of
S., and long after, to give names to particular rooms in taverns. See *1 Hen. IV.* [2.4.30
(990)]."

of Grapes, where indeede you haue a delight to sit, haue
you not?

   Fro. I haue so, because it is an open roome, and good
for winter.

   Clo. Why very well then: I hope here be truthes.   585

   Ang. This will last out a night in *Russia*
When nights are longest there: Ile take my leaue,
And leaue you to the hearing of the cause;
Hoping youle finde good cause to whip them all.   *Exit.*

   Esc. I thinke no lesse: good morrow to your Lord-   590

---

584 winter] windows COLNE, COL2
585 truthes.] ~ — CAM3
589 *Exit.*] *Exit* Angelo. (*after* Lordship. [591]) THEO, WARB+
590 SCENE III. POPE, HAN1, WARB, JOHN
590-1 I . . . Lordship.] *Verse* THEO, WARB+

---

   583 an open roome] KNIGHT (ed. 1840): "A *common* room, which is also a warm room." HALLIWELL (ed. 1854): "An open room was, possibly, a room leading into an outer gallery, and unprotected by windows or lattices. Such a room would of course be 'good for summer', and hence the absurdity of poor Froth's observation. . . . At the same time, the ordinary meaning of *open*, airy, would make perfect sense." HUNTER (ed. 1873): "Here Master Froth is intentionally made to blunder." ROLFE (ed. 1882): "The confusion of ideas is sufficiently characteristic of the speaker, but some of the critics have tried to make the passage logical." HART (ed. 1905): "Public room," as in "open court" (*OED, a.* 14, 21). LEVER (ed. 1965): "In winter a fire would burn there all day, whereas in the private rooms, which Froth could not afford, fires would only be lit to order. Cf. *The London Prodigal,* I. ii. 110 ff. *(Sh. Apoc.)* ['fye, sit in the open roome?']."

   586-9 CLARKE (ed. 1864): "We may here observe how perfectly characteristic of Angelo is this casually introduced little speech and incident of withdrawal; indicating his selfishly leaving his colleague to fulfil a wearisome task, and his own hard intolerance of spirit, on which intolerance he moreover plumes himself, as if it were a virtue." COGHILL (1955, p. 19): "Instead of doing his duty he exhibits the insolence of office, refuses the tedium of sifting evidence and departs with a pun and a flick of cruelty." LEVER (ed. 1965): "Angelo does not show neglect of duty or marked severity. Scene ii, with no lapse of time indicated, has him 'hearing of a cause' when the Provost arrives; and whipping was a normal punishment for bawds." Cf. "an vnpittied whipping" in 1867.

   586 last] *OED* (*v.* 1 3c): "Continue in vigour as long as or longer than (something else)," first quotation with *out* (see Out *adv.* 7).

   Russia] ROLFE (ed. 1882): "Metrically a trisyllable." LEVER (ed. 1965): "Cf. *Err.,* III. ii. [100 (890)], on 'a Poland winter'; Webster, *Duchess of Malfi,* IV. i. 115 ff., on 'a Russian winter'."

   588 cause] Case: see *OED* (*sb.* 8), "action, process, suit." Cf. 2214, 2231. In 589 Angelo plays on *cause,* "reason," as in 587-8 he plays on *leaue.*

   590 I . . . lesse] I am of the same opinion: see *OED* (Think *v.* 2 9c), "hold the opinion."

ship. Now Sir, come on: What was done to *Elbowes*
wife, once more?

Clo. Once Sir? there was nothing done to her once.

Elb. I beseech you Sir, aske him what this man did to
my wife.   595

Clo. I beseech your honor, aske me.

Esc. Well sir, what did this Gentleman to her?

Clo. I beseech you sir, looke in this Gentlemans face:
good Master *Froth* looke vpon his honor; 'tis for a good
purpose: doth your honor marke his face?   600

Esc. I sir, very well.   (F3va)

Clo. Nay, I beseech you marke it well.

Esc. Well, I doe so.

Clo. Doth your honor see any harme in his face?

Esc. Why no.   605

Clo. Ile be supposd vpon a booke, his face is the worst
thing about him: good then: if his face be the worst
thing about him, how could Master *Froth* doe the Constables wife any harme? I would know that of your
honour.   610

Esc. He's in the right (Constable) what say you to it?

Elb. First, and it like you, the house is a respected
house; next, this is a respected fellow; and his Mistris is
a respected woman.

Clo. By this hand Sir, his wife is a more respected per-   615
son then any of vs all.

---

611 right (Constable)] F1-ROWE2, SIS; ⁓ , ⁓ : CAP, WH1, KIT1, ALEX, ARD2,
EVNS; ⁓ ; ⁓ , ROWE3 *etc.*

---

598 **this Gentlemans face**] NOSWORTHY (ed. 1969): "It is conceivable that, like
Bardolph in the historical plays, he was given a very red face."

600 **marke**] See *OED* (*v.* 14): "Give heed or attention to."

606 **supposd**] THIRLBY (1723-33): "Blunder for depos'd." MALONE (ed.
1790): "He means *deposed.*" HUDSON (ed. 1880): " '*Deposed',* that is, *sworn;* according to the old practice of requiring witnesses to make oath upon the Bible."

606-7 **his face . . . him**] LEVER (ed. 1965): "This sounds proverbial. Cf. [664-
5]."

612 **and**] LEVER (ed. 1965): " 'If. The usual spelling of the time, now too often
rendered as 'an'." See *OED* (*conj.* C.1).

like] See n. 486.

respected] HART (ed. 1905): "Suspected. So Ben Jonson's 'high constable of
Kentish Town' in *Tale of a Tub* [3.1.17]: . . . 'And held of all as a respected person'."
LEVER (ed. 1965): "Dogberry uses a converse 'misplacing' in *Ado,* IV. ii. [76-7
(2064-5)]."

Elb. Varlet, thou lyest; thou lyest wicked varlet: the
time is yet to come that shee was euer respected with
man, woman, or childe.

Clo. Sir, she was respected with him, before he mar-   620
ried with her.

Esc. Which is the wiser here; *Iustice* or *Iniquitie?* Is
this true?

Elb. O thou caytiffe: O thou varlet: O thou wick-
ed *Hanniball*; I respected with her, before I was married   625
to her? If euer I was respected with her, or she with me,
let not your worship thinke mee the poore *Dukes* Officer: proue this, thou wicked *Hanniball*, or ile haue
mine action of battry on thee.

Esc. If he tooke you a box 'oth'eare, you might haue   630
your action of slander too.

Elb. Marry I thanke your good worship for it: what
is't your Worships pleasure I shall doe with this wicked Caitiffe?

---

629 mine] my PEL1
630 'oth'eare] of the ear MAL; o' ear v1803
633 shall] should v1785, v1803-SING1, KNT

---

617 **Varlet**] See n. 540.
618 **that**] When. See ABBOTT §284.

622 *Iustice* or *Iniquitie*] JOHNSON (ed. 1765): "These were, I suppose, two
personages well known to the audience by their frequent appearance in the old
moralities." RITSON (1783, p. 19): "The *constable* or the *fool* . . . *Iniquity* in allusion
to the old *Vice.*" IDEM (in Var. 1793): Cf. Iniquitie in *Kyng Daryus* (1565) and *1H4*
2.4.500 (1411–12). SCHMIDT (1874): Cf. the "Vice, *Iniquitie*" in *R3* 3.1.82 (1661),
and *Per.* 4.6.28. HART (ed. 1905): "In *Nice Wanton,* 1560, there is a contest between
'Judge' and 'Iniquity' (Hazlitt's *Dods[ley,]* ii. 178)."

624 **thou . . . thou . . . thou**] Cf. *TN* 3.2.48 (1423–4), "if thou thou'st him some
thrice."

624, 634 **caytiffe**] JOHNSON (1755): "A mean villain; a despicable knave,"
quoting 2409. So *OED* (*sb.* 3). Used as adj. in 2454.

625 *Hanniball*] THIRLBY (1723–33): "Meaning Canibal." HANMER (ed.
1743): "*He means to say* Animal." JOHNSON (ed. 1765): "Mistaken by the constable
for *Cannibal.*" ADAMS (1895, p. 203): "Malapropism for Ananias." HART (ed.
1905): "Cannibal." Cf. *2H4* 2.4.180 (1188) and Jonson, *Euery Man in his Humor*
(3.4.53). WINNY (ed. 1959): "In confusion for Pompey, another famous general."

629 **action of battry**] SCHMIDT (1874): Law suit for unlawful beating (*OED,*
Battery 1), as in *TN* 4.1.36–7 (1950–1), "Ile haue an action of Battery against him
. . . though I stroke him first."

630 **tooke**] *OED* (Take *v.* 5b): "Strike, hit."

'oth'] See *OED* (O, o' *prep.* ¹ c): On, "esp. in *o' th'* for 'on the'," sense first
in Sh. *O' th'* is printed *'oth'* in *Tmp.* 1.2.389 (532) and *'oth* in *Tmp.* 2.2.151 (1193).

Esc. Truly Officer, because he hath some offences in   635
him, that thou wouldst discouer, if thou couldst, let him
continue in his courses, till thou knowst what they are.

Elb. Marry I thanke your worship for it: Thou seest
thou wicked varlet now, what's come vpon thee. Thou
art to continue now thou Varlet, thou art to continue.   640

Esc. Where were you borne, friend?

Froth. Here in *Vienna*, Sir.

Esc. Are you of fourescore pounds a yeere?

Froth. Yes, and't please you sir.

Esc. So: what trade are you of, sir?   645

Clo. A Tapster, a poore widdowes Tapster.

Esc. Your Mistris name?

Clo. Mistris *Ouer-don.*

Esc. Hath she had any more then one husband?

Clo. Nine, sir: *Ouer-don* by the last.   650

Esc. Nine? come hether to me, Master *Froth*; Master
Froth, I would not haue you acquainted with Tapsters;
they will draw you Master *Froth*, and you wil hang them:

---

635 hath] has SING1
640 now . . . continue] *Om.* F4-ROWE2
645 you] ye F4
653 them] then PEN2

---

636 **discouer**] SCHMIDT (1874): "Detect." LEISI (ed. 1964): " 'Expose' " (*OED,*
v. 3, 4). See n. 1414.

637 **courses**] See *OED* (*sb.* 21b): "*Pl.* Ways of action, proceedings; personal
conduct or behaviour, *esp.* of a reprehensible kind; 'goings on'."

640 **continue**] THIRLBY (1747–53): "[Be] continued upon your recogni-
zances." STEEVENS (Var. 1793): "Perhaps Elbow . . . supposes the Clown is to
continue in confinement; at least, he conceives some severe punishment or other to be
implied by the word." WILSON (ed. 1922): "Elbow seems to interpret this as 'contain', i.e. be continent." EVANS (ed. 1974): "But perhaps he simply confuses the
word with its opposite, as elsewhere."

644 **and't**] See n. 612.

650 ***Ouer-don* by the last**] DELIUS (ed. 1860): With two meanings: "She is
named Overdone from her last husband," and "She has been exhausted, worn out
by the last." See n. 2959.

652 **would**] See n. 17.

653 **draw**] THIRLBY (1723–33): "I suppose playing upon Froth's name." JOHN-
SON (ed. 1765): "*Draw* has here a cluster of senses. As it refers to the tapster, it
signifies *to drain, to empty;* as it is related to *hang,* it means *to embowel* or *exenterate.*
In *Froth's* answer it is the same as *to bring along by some motive or power.*" IDEM (Var.
1773): "As it is related to *hang,* it means *to be conveyed to execution on a hurdle.*" CLARKE
(ed. 1864): " 'Draw' is here quibblingly used in allusion to the tapsters when *drawing*

get you gon, and let me heare no more of you.

Fro. I thanke your worship: for mine owne part, I   655
neuer come into any roome in a Tap-house, but I am
drawne in.

Esc. Well: no more of it Master *Froth*: farewell:
Come you hether to me, M^r. Tapster: what's your name
M^r. Tapster?   660

    Clo. Pompey.

    Esc. What else?

    Clo. Bum, Sir.

    Esc. Troth, and your bum is the greatest thing about
you, so that in the beastliest sence, you are *Pompey* the   665

---

658 *Exit* Froth. ROWE1-JOHN2, v1793+
659 SCENE IV. POPE, HAN1, WARB, JOHN

---

beer, and when *drawing* (or as we should now say 'taking') in their customers;
likewise in allusion to the *drawing* felons on a hurdle to be hanged" (*OED, v.* 4). Or
it may be, as Johnson first suggested, to being "hanged and drawn" or disembow-
eled (*OED, v.* 50). Cf. the puns in *Jn.* 2.1.504–5 (821–2) and *Ado* 3.2.22–5 (1229–
31).

       hang them] HUDSON (ed. 1880): *"Hang* is here used as a causative verb; the
sense being, you shall *cause* them *to be hanged.* This would be done by accusing them,
or bearing witness against them, for having swindled him out of money." *OED*
overlooks this sense, but SCHMIDT (1874) cites *MND* 1.2.79, 80 (339, 340), *Lr.*
4.6.167 (2606).

    656 **Tap-house**] *OED:* "A house where beer drawn from the tap is sold in small
quantities; an ale-house." HART's (ed. 1905) gloss "tavern" is wrong, since a tavern
sold wine and Sh. never confuses it with an alehouse.

    657 **drawne in**] DELIUS (ed. 1860): Pulled in by force, and enticed, cheated.
SCHMIDT (1874): "Swindled out of my money" (*OED, v.* 82d *fig.*).

    659, 660 **M^r.**] Escalus stresses "Master Tapster" with ironic politeness, because
the Clown has been making much of Froth's social standing by referring again and
again to "Master Froth." Escalus has some good-humored fun with the Clown by
repeating "Master Froth" four times and "Pompey" ten times, then returns to his
ironic courtesy with "Master Elbow," "Master Constable" (701, 702). Angelo uses
plain "Elbow" (515).

    661–3 His name begins with "pomp" and ends with the anticlimactic "bum"
(bottom). Cf. the clown Costard, who plays Pompey "the big" in *LLL* 5.2.553
(2497), and Pompey Doodle, the clown in *Wit at Several Weapons* (printed in the
Beaumont & Fletcher Folio but prob. written by Middleton & Rowley). See n. 2952.

    664 **Troth**] *OED (sb.* 4c as *int.):* In truth, quoting 1545.

    bum] DYCE (1867): "An allusion to Pompey's large trunk-hose, round swell-
ing breeches." TILLEY (P73): Cf. Heywood, *Prouerbes* (1546), 1:10. HARDING (ed.
1954): "The buttocks, but also the fantastically stuffed trunk hose which emphasized
the buttocks and which were very much in vogue at the time."

    665 **beastliest**] *OED* (Beastly *a.* 5): "Abominable; disgusting." See n. 1513.

great; *Pompey*, you are partly a bawd, *Pompey*; howso-   (F3vb)
euer you colour it in being a Tapster, are you not? come,
tell me true, it shall be the better for you.

Clo. Truly sir, I am a poore fellow that would liue.

Esc. How would you liue *Pompey*? by being a bawd?   670
what doe you thinke of the trade *Pompey*? is it a lawfull
trade?

Clo. If the Law would allow it, sir.

Esc. But the Law will not allow it *Pompey*; nor it
shall not be allowed in *Vienna*.   675

Clo. Do's your Worship meane to geld and splay all
the youth of the City?

Esc. No, *Pompey*.

Clo. Truely Sir, in my poore opinion they will too't
then: if your worship will take order for the drabs and   680
the knaues, you need not to feare the bawds.

Esc. There is pretty orders beginning I can tell you:
It is but heading, and hanging.

Clo. If you head, and hang all that offend that way

---

667 in] *Om.* F2-ROWE2   a] *Om.* v1778-RANN
673 would] will ROWE2-MAL (−CAP)   sir.] ~ ? SING
674 nor] and POPE, HAN1
676 splay] spay v1773-KNT1, COL, HAL, SING2, WH, KTLY, KNT3
677 of] in F2-SING1 (−MAL), CAM3
681 the knaues] Knaves F2-POPE2, HAN1   to] *Om.* v1785
682 is] F1, DYCE1, BUL, NLSN+; are F2 *etc.*

666-7 **howsoeuer**] See *OED* (However *adv.* 1c): "However much; notwithstanding that; although."

667 **colour**] ONIONS (1911): "Gloss, disguise" (*OED, v.* 3). BALD (ed. 1956):
"Camouflage."

669 **would liue**] Wants to make a living (*OED*, Will *v.*[1] 40, Live *v.*[1] 3).

674 **nor**] See n. 42.

676 **splay**] KNIGHT (ed. 1842): "Used in Chapman's Homer and Holland's
Pliny." Both are quoted in RICHARDSON (1837) and Holland in *OED* (*v.*[2]). HART
(ed. 1905): Cf. COTGRAVE (1611), "Chastrer. *To geld, lib, cut, spey, splay,*" and
FLORIO (1611) on *castrare.*

679 **will**] Will go. See n. 284.

    too't] SCHMIDT (1875, p. 1234): "To work . . . in an obscene sense." See n.
2247-8.

680 **take order**] HALLIWELL (ed. 1854): "Take measures" (*OED, sb.* 1d).

    drabs] JOHNSON (1755): "A whore; a strumpet" (*OED, sb.*[1] 2).

682 **is**] See nn. 434, 473-4.

683 **but**] See *OED* (*conj.* 6b): "Neither more nor less than."

684 **head**] JOHNSON (1755): "Behead." Also quoted in *OED* (*v.* 1). LEVER (ed.

but for ten yeare together; you'll be glad to giue out a   685
Commission for more heads: if this law hold in *Vienna*
ten yeare, ile rent the fairest house in it after three pence
a Bay: if you liue to see this come to passe, say *Pompey*
told you so.

    Esc. Thanke you good *Pompey*; and in requitall of   690
your prophesie, harke you: I aduise you let me not finde
you before me againe vpon any complaint whatsoeuer;
no, not for dwelling where you doe: if I doe *Pompey*, I
shall beat you to your Tent, and proue a shrewd *Cæsar*
to you: in plaine dealing *Pompey*, I shall haue you whipt;   695
so for this time, *Pompey*, fare you well.

    Clo. I thanke your Worship for your good counsell;

---

685 yeare] Years ROWE1-v1773 (−CAP)
687 yeare] yeares F2-RANN
688 Bay] Day ROWE3, POPE, WH, NLSN
695 *Pompey*] *Om.* F4-ROWE2   shall] will ROWE2

1965): "Hanging was the death penalty for common felons, beheading for gentlemen." See Marlowe, *Edward II,* 2.5.30.
    685, 687 **yeare**] Years: see FRANZ §190. So *yeere* in 704 but *yeares* or *ye(e)res*
elsewhere in *MM.*
    685 **together**] See *OED* (*adv.* 5): "Without intermission, continuously." So in
706–7.
    686 **Commission**] Warrant: see n. 16.
      hold] See *OED* (*v.* 23c): "Remain valid," "be in force."
    687 **after**] SCHMIDT (1874): "At the rate of " (*OED,* 16).
    688 **Bay**] THEOBALD (ed. 1733): "Semi-circular juttings out in Front." WAR-
BURTON (1734, in NICHOLS, 1817, 2:645–6): "It means a *division of a house. . . .* And
even to this day with us in Nottinghamshire (though houses are now built otherwise),
when a new house is spoke of as built or to be let, the common question is, how many
bays has it, or how many *bays* of building." IDEM (ed. 1747): "The squared frame
of a timber house; each of which divisions or squares is called a *Bay."* JOHNSON
(1755): "In architecture, a term used to signify the magnitude of a building. . . . These
bays are from fourteen to twenty feet long," quoting *Builder's Dictionary* and this
passage. IDEM (ed. 1765): "A *Bay* of building is in many parts of *England* a common
term, of which the best conception that I could ever attain, is, that it is the space
between the main beams of the roof; so that a barn crossed twice with beams is a barn
of three *bays." OED* (*sb.*[3] 2): "Applied to a house, it appears to be the space lying
under one gable, or included between two party-walls."
    690 **requitall of**] Return for (*OED,* 1b).
    694 **shrewd**] See *OED* (*a.* 7): "Severe, harsh, stern."
    Cæsar] HUDSON (ed. 1880): "Escalus is laughing *inwardly.* He has humour;
not so Angelo." HART (ed. 1905): Cf. 1533–4. DURHAM (ed. 1926): "Alluding to
Cæsar's defeat of Pompey the Great at Pharsalia."

but I shall follow it as the flesh and fortune shall better
determine. Whip me? no, no, let Carman whip his Iade,
The valiant heart's not whipt out of his trade.   *Exit.*   700

    Esc. Come hether to me, Master *Elbow*: come hither
Master Constable: how long haue you bin in this place
of Constable?

    Elb. Seuen yeere, and a halfe sir.

    Esc. I thought by the readinesse in the office, you had   705
continued in it some time: you say seauen yeares together.

    Elb. And a halfe sir.

    Esc. Alas, it hath beene great paines to you: they do
you wrong to put you so oft vpon't. Are there not men   710
in your Ward sufficient to serue it?

    Elb. 'Faith sir, few of any wit in such matters: as they
are chosen, they are glad to choose me for them; I do it

698–700 [*aside.*] JOHN, v1773, STAU+ (−KNT3, COL4, PEN2)
699–700 Whip . . . trade.] *Verse* ROWE3+
700 heart's] heart is CAM1, GLO, WH2
701 SCENE˚V. POPE, HAN1, WARB, JOHN
704 yeere] years WARB, JOHN, v1773
705 by the] F1-ROWE3, CAP, COL1, DEL4, NLSN, ALEX-ARD2, EVNS; by your
POPE1 *etc.*
706–7 together.] — ? ROWE3+

698–700 LEVER (ed. 1965): "The 'aside' is spoken while Pompey is retiring from
the courtroom. At a safe distance, he turns and declaims his couplet to the audience."
    698 **the flesh**] See *OED* (*sb.* 10): "The animal or physical nature of man."
    699–700 WHITE (ed. 1883): "This couplet is probably an interpolation." But cf.
"tis no sinne for a man to labor in his vocation," *1H4* 1.2.116–17 (212–13).
    699 **Carman**] SCHMIDT (1874): "A man whose employment it is to drive a cart"
(*OED*, Carman[1]). PARROTT (ed. 1938): "Teamster."
    Iade] SCHMIDT (1874): "A term of contempt or pity for a worthless, or
wicked, or maltreated horse" (*OED*, *sb.*[1] 1).
    705 **the readinesse**] MALONE (ed. 1790): "In the Mss. of our author's age,
y^e. and y^r. (for so they were frequently written) were easily confounded." COLLIER
(ed. 1842): "Escalus means 'by the readiness you showed in the office'." SCHMIDT
(1875): "Facility, ease" (*OED*, 2b).
    office] See *OED* (*sb.* 2c): "Performance of a duty or function."
    711 **sufficient**] CLARKE (ed. 1864): " 'Of sufficient capacity', 'sufficingly compe-
tent'." SCHMIDT (1875): "Fit, able" (*OED*, *a.* 3b). Cf. 11, 716.
    712 **'Faith**] In truth (*OED*, *sb.* 12b used as *interj.*). Also in 1551, 2903. HOW-
ARD-HILL (1972, p. 128): The apostrophe shows Crane's influence.
    wit] *OED* (*sb.* 5): "Mental quickness or sharpness, acumen."

for some peece of money, and goe through with all.

 Esc. Looke you bring mee in the names of some sixe   715
or seuen, the most sufficient of your parish.

 Elb. To your Worships house sir?

 Esc. To my house: fare you well: what's a clocke,
thinke you?

 Iust. Eleuen, Sir.   720

 Esc. I pray you home to dinner with me.

 Iust. I humbly thanke you.

 Esc. It grieues me for the death of *Claudio*
But there's no remedie.

 Iust. Lord *Angelo* is seuere.   725

 Esc. It is but needfull.
Mercy is not it selfe, that oft lookes so,

---

714 with all] withal CLN2
715 Looke⌃ you⌃] ~ ⌃ ~ , ROWE1-v1821, SING, COL3, KTLY, ALEX; ~ ,
~ ⌃ KNT1, KNT3
716 of] in v1785
719 *Exit* Elbow. ROWE1-THEO4; (*after* Fare you well. [718]) JOHN, v1773,
v1793+
721 home] goe home F2-POPE2, HAN1, CAP

---

714 **goe through**] See *OED* (Go *v.* 89b), *Go through,* "complete what is entered
upon," and (90a) *Go through with,* "perform thoroughly."
 with all] LEISI (ed. 1964): " 'With'; cf. [2813]." HOUGHTON (ed. 1970):
"*Withal:* with it. I have substituted this for the 'with all' hitherto printed." MAXWELL
(1972, p. 461): " 'With all' meaning 'withal' is common in the Folio." ECCLES (1972,
p. 461): "The sense 'with everything', however, seems to me to have more force.
. . . The actor may choose whether to put the stress on *through* or on *all.*" See n. 2813.
 715 **Looke**] SCHMIDT (1874): Take care, see that (*OED, v.* 3b), as in 2675,
2896, 2924.
 720 **Eleuen**] NARES (1822): *"Dinner-time.* The proper hour for dinner is laid
down by Thomas Cogan, a physician," in *The Hauen of Health* (1584, ch. 211): "The
most conuenient time for dinner is about eleuen of the clocke before noone." So in
The Knight of the Burning Pestle (1613, 1.1.352) [and in *Mucedorus* (1598, *Sh. Apoc.,*
3.2.11)]. HALLIWELL (ed. 1854): "Eleven o'clock was the usual dinner hour in
Shakespeare's time, and the manners of his own country and day are introduced into
this play, although the scene is laid at Vienna. Harrison, in his *Description of England,*
written about the year 1580, says, 'the nobilitie, gentrie, and students, do ordinarilie
go to dinner at eleven before noone'."
 721 **pray you**] *OED* (*v.* 2): "To beg or entreat (a person) to come to a feast, or
the like; to invite," latest quotation in this sense.
 home] Come home. See n. 76.
 727–8 DELIUS (ed. 1860): Cf. *Rom.* 3.1.202 (1642). TILLEY (P50) and WILSON
(p. 609): "Pardon makes offenders." Cf. *Luc.* 1687, *Tim.* 3.5.3 (1260). LEVER (ed.
1965): " 'Seeming mercy is often not merciful in the long run'." Cf. Angelo in

Pardon is still the nurse of second woe:
But yet, poore *Claudio*; there is no remedie.
Come Sir.   *Exeunt.*   730

Scena Secunda.   2.2

Enter *Prouost, Seruant.*

Ser. Hee's hearing of a Cause; he will come straight,
I'le tell him of you.
    Pro. 'Pray you doe; Ile know   735
His pleasure, may be he will relent; alas
He hath but as offended in a dreame,
All Sects, all Ages smack of this vice, and he
To die for't?

---

729 there is] there's POPE1-v1821, SING, KTLY, DYCE2, DYCE3, HUD2
731 *Scena Secunda*] SCENE VI POPE, HAN1, WARB, JOHN   Angelo's *House.*
JOHN, v1773-RANN; *A Room in the same.* CAP, MAL-NLSN, KIT1-SIS (*subst.*); (*no change
from A Court of Justice*) CAM3; *An ante-room to the same.* ARD2
734-5 *One line* COL, DYCE, WH, CAM1+ (−KNT3)
735 *Exit* Serv. CAP, v1778+
736 may be] 't may be, THEO2, WARB-JOHN2
737 but as offended] offended but as mTBY3 *conj.*, WH, KNT3
738 of this] o'th' HAN1
739 for't?] F1; ~ ! F2-ROWE3, CAM1, GLO, WH2-BUL, NLSN-ARD2, EVNS; ~ —
KNT, HAL; for it! POPE1 *etc.*

856-60 and *R2* 5.3.57-8, 83-4 (2556-7, 2583-4).
    728 **still**] SCHMIDT (1875): "Always" (*OED, adv.* 3).
    729 **there is**] Pronounced *there's,* as in 724.
    733 **straight**] See n. 255.
    734 **of**] About (*OED, prep.* 26, 27). See nn. 1143, 2229.
    735 **'Pray**] On the apostrophe see n. 768.
    736 **he will**] Pronounced *he'll,* not as in 733.
    737 **but as offended**] Offended only as if: see n. 336.
    738 **Sects**] ONIONS (1911): "Class (of people), rank" (*OED, sb.* 1 1).
        Ages] LEVER (ed. 1965): "Either periods of history [*OED, sb.* 11], or of a
person's life [5]."
        smack] JOHNSON (1755): "Have a tincture or quality infused." *OED* (*v.* 1 2b):
"Partake or savour *of.*"

Enter Angelo.   740

Ang. Now, what's the matter *Prouost?*

Pro. Is it your will *Claudio* shall die to morrow?

Ang. Did not I tell thee yea? hadst thou not order?

Why do'st thou aske againe?

Pro. Lest I might be too rash: 745

Vnder your good correction, I haue seene

When after execution, Iudgement hath

Repented ore his doome.

Ang. Goe to; let that be mine,

Doe you your office, or giue vp your Place,   750

And you shall well be spar'd.

Pro. I craue your Honours pardon:

What shall be done Sir, with the groaning *Iuliet?*

Shee's very neere her howre.

Ang. Dispose of her   755

To some more fitter place; and that with speed.

Ser. Here is the sister of the man condemn'd,

---

742 Is it . . . shall] It is . . . should POPE2

743 not I] I not v1778-KNT1, COL, SING2, WH1, KTLY, KNT3, DEL4, ARD, CAM3

744 do'st thou] *Om.* HAN1

749 Goe to;] *Om.* HAN1

752 Honours] *Om.* POPE1-JOHN2

756 fitter] fitting POPE1-RANN (−CAP)

757 *Re-enter* Servant. CAP, v1778+

---

741 **the matter**] See n. 501.

743–4 WINNY (ed. 1959): "His three abrupt questions suggest how quickly Angelo has become imperious and autocratic."

746 **Vnder . . . correction**] SCHMIDT (1874, p. 248): "If you do not take it ill." CRAIG (ed. 1951): "Allow me to say." See *OED* (Corre·tion 1b): "Subject to correction; a formula expressing deference to superior information, or critical authority."

748 **doome**] SCHMIDT (1874): "Sentence" (*OED, sb.* 2).

749 **Goe to**] See n. 513.

   mine] ABBOTT (§418): "Perhaps . . . an imitation of 'meum est', 'It is my business'." FRANZ (§327a): An absolute use of *mine.*

750 **office**] See n. 332.

751 **well**] SCHMIDT (1875): "Easily."

   spar'd] See *OED* (*v.* 1 8): "To do without."

753 **groaning**] SCHMIDT (1874): "Used of a woman in labour." Cf. *Ham.* 3.2.259 (2117).

754 **howre**] *OED* (4): "Appointed time" (of delivery).

756 **more fitter**] Sh. often doubles the comparative, as again in 2613. See ABBOTT §11, FRANZ §217a.

Desires accesse to you.

    Ang. Hath he a Sister?

    Pro. I my good Lord, a very vertuous maid,   760
And to be shortlie of a Sister-hood,
If not alreadie.

    Ang. Well: let her be admitted,
See you the Fornicatresse be remou'd,
Let her haue needfull, but not lauish meanes,   765
There shall be order for't.

           Enter Lucio and Isabella.

    Pro. 'Saue your Honour.

    Ang. Stay a little while: y'are welcome: what's your will?

---

763 Well:] *Om.* POPE, HAN1   admitted,] — . ROWE1+   *Exit Servant.* DAV, THEO1+

766–9 *Lines ending* honour! . . . will? DYCE, CAM1, GLO, DEL4, WH2+; for't. . . . while. . . . will? HUD2

766 for't] for it POPE1-v1821, SING, KNT, COL, DYCE, STAU, KTLY, ARD1

767 SCENE VII. POPE, HAN1, WARB, JOHN   *Enter . . .*] *After* while (769) RANN

768 'Saue] God save mTBY3 *and* WALKER *conj.,* CAM1, GLO, DEL4, HUD2, WH2, CAM2, NLSN, KIT1, PEN2   *offering to retire.* MAL-IRV (—CAM1, GLO, DEL4, WH2), CAM3-ALEX, ARD2 (*subst.*)

769 a little] yet a POPE1-v1778 (—CAP)   while: y'are] while.—[*To* Isab. Y'are JOHN, v1773+

---

758 **Desires**] Who desires. ABBOTT (§244): "The relative is frequently omitted." See FRANZ §348.

    accesse] SCHMIDT (1874) marks the accent on the second syllable, as usually in Sh.

764 **Fornicatresse**] JOHNSON (1755): "A woman who without marriage cohabits with a man." *OED* quotes this and two more instances.

765 **meanes**] *OED* (*sb.*[2] 12 *pl.*): "Resources," first quotation in this sense. LEVER (ed. 1965): "Conditions of living in imprisonment."

766 **order**] SCHMIDT (1875): "Command . . . (or = arrangement?)." *OED* (*sb.* 14): "Suitable action." Prob. "command," as in 743, 2861.

768 **'Saue**] WALKER (1860, 1:214, 263): Read *God save,* "the name of God having been omitted by the editor of the folio in deference to the well-known act of parliament against profaneness; or having been, perhaps, struck out by the licensers of the press." Cf. 924, 996, 2782. HOWARD-HILL (1972, pp. 89, 128): The five comedies Crane transcribed have six instances of *'saue* "with the apostrophe denoting the omission of 'God' whereas none of the four instances in the later comedies has the apostrophe." Cf. *'pray* 735, *'Please* 771, *'blesse* 1500.

769 **Stay**] JOHNSON (ed. 1765): "It is not clear why the *Provost* is bidden to stay, nor when he goes out." RITSON (1783, p. 19): "The entrance of Lucio and Isabella

Isab. I am a wofull Sutor to your Honour,   770
'Please but your Honor heare me.
Ang. Well: what's your suite.
Isab. There is a vice that most I doe abhorre,
And most desire should meet the blow of Iustice;
For which I would not plead, but that I must,   775
For which I must not plead, but that I am
At warre, twixt will, and will not.
Ang. Well: the matter?
Isab. I haue a brother is condemn'd to die,
I doe beseech you let it be his fault,   780

---

772 Well:] *Om.* POPE, HAN1   suite.] ~ ? F2+
774 most] more ROWE, POPE
776 must not plead, but that] must plead, albeit HAN1
779 to die] to-day HAN1
780 you$_\wedge$] ~ , THEO1+ (−SIS, EVNS)

---

should not, perhaps, be made till after Angelos speech to the provost, who had only announced *a lady,* and seems to be detained as a witness to the purity of the deputys conversation with her. His *exit* may be fixed with that of Lucio and Isabella [924]." MALONE (ed. 1790): *"Stay a little while* is said by Angelo, in answer to the words, *'Save your honour';* which denoted the Provost's intention to *depart."*
  y'are] See n. 14.
771 **'Please but**] If only it may please. ABBOTT (§361): *Please* "represents our modern 'may it please?' and expresses a modest doubt." See nn. 768, 1071.
775 **would not**] Do not wish to: see n. 17.
776 JOHNSON (ed. 1765): "This is obscure, perhaps it may be mended by reading, *For which I must* now *plead, but* yet *I am.... Yet* and *yt* are almost undistinguishable in a manuscript." IDEM (Var. 1773): "Yet no alteration is necessary, since the speech is not unintelligible as it now stands." MALONE (ed. 1790): "For which I must not plead, but that there is a conflict in my breast betwixt my affection for my brother, which induces me to plead for him, and my regard to virtue, which forbids me to intercede for one guilty of such a crime; and I find the former more powerful than the latter." M. S. (1795, p. 646): Suggested by Rom. 7. NOBLE (1935, pp. 222–3): "This passage gave Johnson some difficulty which a reference to Rom. vii. might have resolved. St. Paul laments that owing to his carnal nature he does that of which he does not approve, and that which is against his will (verse 15), so that in verse 23 he is 'rebelling against the lawe of my mind'.... Isabella means she is disinclined to plead but that she is compelled by natural ties; yet her pleading is forbidden by principle, but that the law of her affections conflicts with the law of her mind and inclination."
777 Cf. 2305.
778 **matter**] SCHMIDT (1875): "Point in question" (*OED, sb.*[1] 25a). Cf. n. 501.
779 **is**] Who is. See n. 758.
780–1 **let . . . brother**] MALONE (ed. 1790): "Let his fault be condemned, or extirpated but let not my brother himself suffer." CLARKE (ed. 1864): "Isabella means, 'Let my brother's fault be condemned to extinction, not his life'; but Angelo

And not my brother.

   Pro. Heauen giue thee mouing graces.

   Ang. Condemne the fault, and not the actor of it,

Why euery fault's condemnd ere it be done:

Mine were the verie Cipher of a Function   785

To fine the faults, whose fine stands in record,

And let goe by the Actor.

   Isab. Oh iust, but seuere Law:

I had a brother then; heauen keepe your honour.

   Luc. Giue't not ore so: to him againe, entreat him,   790

---

783 it,] F1-F3; ～ : F4-ROWE2; ～ ! CAP-v1821, SING, KTLY, ALEX; ～ ? ROWE3 *etc.*

785 verie] *Om.* ROWE1, ROWE2

786 To fine] To find THEO, WARB-v1813 (−MAL)   faults] fault mTBY1 *conj.,* DYCE, STAU, HUD2

789 *retiring.* MAL-IRV (−CAM1, GLO, DEL4, WH2), CAM3, KIT1, ARD2 (*subst.*)

790 Giue't] Give THEO, WARB, JOHN

---

answers as if she had only implied 'condemned', or censured." TILLEY (P238) and WILSON (p. 358): "Hate not the person but the vice."

782 **mouing graces**] SCHMIDT (1874, p. 488): "The gift of persuasion." Cf. *moue men* 277 and *grace* 421.

783, 787 **actor**] *OED* (3): "Doer," quoting 787.

785 **were**] See n. 40.

   verie] SCHMIDT (1875): "Mere" (*OED, a.* 9b).

   Cipher] *OED* (*sb.* 2b): Zero, a "mere nothing." TILLEY (C391) and WILSON (p. 124): "He is a cipher among numbers."

   Function] See n. 109.

786 **fine**] MALONE (ed. 1790): "To *fine* means, I think, to pronounce the *fine* or sentence of the law, appointed for certain crimes. . . . The repetition is much in our author's manner." KNIGHT (ed. 1840): "To *fine* is to sentence—to bring to an end." *OED* (*v.*² 8): "To punish," quoting 1333. PORTER & CLARKE (ed. 1909): "Used in a double sense, first, 'to punish', then to 'conclude', and also as 'the finis'." WILSON (ed. 1922): "To put a stop to the crime, for which the penalty has already been adjudged." LEVER (ed. 1965): "The faults have their punishment ('fine'), by being recorded as faults; his task as a judge is not to punish ('fine') them again, but to deal with the wrong-doer."

   stands in record] SCHMIDT (1875): *Stand,* "to be written"; *in record,* "set down, registered." ROLFE (ed. 1882): "Is set down in the statute. S. accents the noun *record* on either syllable, as suits the measure."

787 **let goe by**] SCHMIDT (1874, p. 481): "Leave him unpunished." Cf. *run-by* 415.

788 **seuere**] ROLFE (ed. 1882): "Accented on the first syllable because coming before the noun." See SCHMIDT (1875), pp. 1413–15.

789 **I had a brother**] THIRLBY (1723–33): "Fuimus Troes, fuit Ilium" (*Aeneid* 2:324). TILLEY (T529, 540): "We were Trojans," "Troy was" (but is no longer).

790 **Giue't not ore**] See *OED* (Give *v.* 63a): *Give over,* "give up, abandon."

790, 794 **to him**] See n. 284 and FRANZ §530.

Kneele downe before him, hang vpon his gowne,
You are too cold: if you should need a pin,
You could not with more tame a tongue desire it: 〈F4ᵇ
To him, I say.

Isab. Must he needs die?   795

Ang. Maiden, no remedie.

Isab. Yes: I doe thinke that you might pardon him,
And neither heauen, nor man grieue at the mercy.

Ang. I will not doe't.

Isab. But can you if you would?   800

Ang. Looke what I will not, that I cannot doe.

Isab. But might you doe't & do the world no wrong
If so your heart were touch'd with that remorse,
As mine is to him?

Ang. Hee's sentenc'd, tis too late.   805

Luc. You are too cold.

Isab. Too late? why no: I that doe speak a word
May call it againe: well, beleeue this

---

793 more tame a] a more tame ROWE, POPE, HAN1
797 might] may ROWE1, ROWE2
801 Look‸] ～ , F4-ARD2 (−SIS)
802 might you] you might WALKER *conj. in* DYCE1 (*and* 1860, 2:250), KTLY,
DYCE2, DYCE3-HUD2
804–6 *Lines ending* late. . . . cold. v1793-DYCE1, COL3-SIS, ARD2, EVNS; him?
. . . cold. WH1, PEL1, PEN2
804 him?] ～ . CAM1, KTLY, DYCE2, DYCE3-HUD2, BUL, ARD1, CAM3
806 You are] Yo art F2
807 no:] so: F3; so? F4-ROWE2
808 againe] F1, SIS, ARD2, EVNS; in again CAM3; backe againe F2 *etc.*   well,
beleeue] ～ ‸ ～ THEO, WARB, JOHN, v1778-v1821, KNT, COL, STAU

---

791 **hang vpon**] THIRLBY (1723–33): As in *Tmp.* 1.2.474 (635). SCHMIDT
(1874): "Cling to" (*OED, v.* 14a).
792 **pin**] See n. 550.
800 **would**] Were willing to (*OED,* Will *v.* ¹ 34).
801 **Looke what**] DEROCQUIGNY (1907, p. 72): An indefinite relative meaning
"whatever" (*OED,* Look *v.* 4b). Sh.'s use of this idiom is discussed by ECCLES (1943,
pp. 386–400). See also *LLL* 5.2.24 (1911). All editors before Sisson (1954) mispunc-
tuate as *Look, what* or *Look; what.*
803 **remorse**] STEEVENS (Var. 1778): "*Pity* [*OED, sb.* 3]. So in [2467]."
808 **againe**] F2 reads *backe againe.* WILSON (ed. 1922) "We read 'in' as being
more likely to have been overlooked (coming as it does after 'it') than a word like
'back'." SISSON (1956, 1:79): "There is in fact a marked and dramatic pause in the
middle of the line, and no irregularity is felt in the speaking of the passage."
     well, beleeue this] GILDON omits the comma when he quotes this speech

No ceremony that to great ones longs,
Not the Kings Crowne; nor the deputed sword,   810
The Marshalls Truncheon, nor the Iudges Robe
Become them with one halfe so good a grace
As mercie does: If he had bin as you, and you as he,
You would haue slipt like him, but he like you
Would not haue beene so sterne.   815
  Ang. Pray you be gone.

---

809 longs] belongs DAV, ROWE3, POPE, HAN1
812 Become] Becomes GIL, HAL
813–16 *Lines ending* as you, . . . him; . . . stern. . . . gone. DAV, POPE1-JOHN2,
v1773, MAL-v1813, SING, KNT1, DYCE1, KTLY, KNT3; does: . . . as he, . . . you,
. . . stern. . . . gone. CAP, v1778-RANN; as he, . . . you, . . . begone. v1821, COL1,
STAU, COL4; does: . . . as he, . . . you, . . . gone. KNT2, WH1, COL3, CAM1, GLO,
DYCE2, DEL4, DYCE3, HUD2+; as you, . . . him; . . . begone. HAL

(1710, "Remarks," p. 294). THEOBALD (1729, in NICHOLS, 1817, 2:287): "This,
well, &c. is not the style in which inferiors address the great: it is too familiar. The
fault is only in the pointing, and Isabella will speak with much more solemnity and
propriety.—'Well believe this', &c. *i. e.* be most assured, &c." HALLIWELL (ed.
1854): "*Well* seems to be here merely a strong expletive." LEVER (ed. 1965):
"Perhaps in answer to some gesture of refusal which occupies the missing 'foot': or
there may be a transposition from 'Believe this well'."
  809–13 TILLEY (M898): "It is in their mercy that kings come closest to gods,"
quoting *Tit.* 1.1.117–19 (139–41) and *MV* 4.1.196–7 (2107–8). SONNENSCHEIN
(1905, p. 27) compares Seneca, *De Clementia.*
  809 **ceremony**] *OED* (4): "An external accessory or symbolical 'attribute' of
worship, state, or pomp." Cf. *H5* 4.1.256 ff. (2089 ff.).
    longs] ROLFE (ed. 1882): "Belongs; but not a contraction of that word." Most
eds. wrongly print *'longs*, but see *OED* (Long *v.* ² 1): "To be appropriate *to* . . . to
pertain *to.* "
  810 **the deputed sword**] WILSON (ed. 1922): "The pause before 'nor the
deputed sword' (Angelo's) is dramatic." LEVER (ed. 1965): "The sword of justice
committed to mayors or governors in token of their office. In *1 Prom.*, I. i [p. 309
below], the Mayor invests Promos with it."
  811 **Marshalls**] SCHMIDT (1875): "The chief officer of arms, who regulates
combats in the lists and establishes rank and order at royal feasts and processions"
(*OED, sb.* 5). Cf. *R2* 1.3. The marshal in *2 Promos,* 5.2, is commanded by the King
to behead Promos (see p. 364 below).
    Truncheon] JOHNSON (1755): "A staff of command." *OED* (*sb.* 3): "A staff
carried as a symbol of office, command, or authority; a marshal's baton."
  812 **Become**] Plural because several nouns follow the subject, *ceremony.* See
FRANZ §675.
    grace] LEVER (ed. 1965): "Isabella plays on 'grace', as seemliness [*OED, sb.*
1b] and as a divine attribute, much as Lucio does in [120] ff." See n. 120.
  813 **as you . . . as he**] In your situation and you in his.
  814 **slipt**] *OED* (*v.* ¹ 8c): "To err, to sin," quoting 2869.

Isab. I would to heauen I had your potencie,
And you were *Isabell*: should it then be thus?
No: I would tell what 'twere to be a Iudge,
And what a prisoner.   820
  Luc. I, touch him: there's the vaine.
  Ang. Your Brother is a forfeit of the Law,
And you but waste your words.
  Isab. Alas, alas:
Why all the soules that were, were forfeit once,   825
And he that might the vantage best haue tooke,
Found out the remedie: how would you be,

820–1 *One line* ARD1-CAM3, ARD2+
821 I,] ~ ‸ F2, F3
825 that were] that are WARB, KTLY

---

817 **would**] See n. 17.
818 *Isabell*] WALKER (1860, 1:232): "*Isabel* . . . appears to be sometimes pronounced as Isbel." SCHMIDT (1874): Disyllabic here and elsewhere, like *Isbel* in *AWW* 1.3.20, 25 (347, 352), 3.2.13–15 (1413–15).
  should] Would. See ABBOTT §322 and *OED* (Shall *v.* 19a).
819 **tell**] LEVER (ed. 1965): "Know." Rather "make known" (*OED, v.* 3).
  'twere] See n. 40.
821 **touch**] SCHMIDT (1875): "To hit, to come near" (*OED, v.* 19b), as in *AYL* 2.7.94 (1070).
  there's the vaine] SCHMIDT (1875): "Strain, style, manner of speech or action" (*OED,* Vein *sb.* 12, 13). LEVER (ed. 1965): " 'That is the right approach'. Perhaps fig. from the action of the physician seeking the vein for blood-letting. 'Vein' also signifies a style in writing or speech." See n. 887.
822 **forfeit**] JOHNSON (1755): "A person obnoxious to punishment; one whose life is forfeited by his offence" (*OED, sb.* 2b). See n. 2024.
825 **all . . . that were**] WARBURTON (ed. 1747): "This is false divinity. We should read *are.*" GRIFFITH (1775, pp. 39–40): "But are we not taught that the *redemption* had released the *forfeit?*" PRICE (1839, p. 122): Cf. Rom. 3:10–26, John 3:16. HALLIWELL (ed. 1854): "All the souls that ever existed."
  forfeit] JOHNSON (1755): "Liable to penal seizure; alienated by a crime." ONIONS (1911): "Lost by reason of breach of an obligation" (*OED, a.*). See n. 1680–1.
826 **vantage**] SCHMIDT (1875): "Good opportunity." HARDING (ed. 1954): "Advantage (to punish mankind)." LEISI (ed. 1964): "The image represents Christ as a magnanimous creditor who renounces his profits although the souls are forfeited." See *OED* (*sb.* 1): "Advantage, benefit, profit, gain," and Matt. 25:27, "with vantage." Cf. 2801.
  tooke] Taken. See ABBOTT §343 and *OED* (Take *v.* A.5δ).
827–31 **how . . . made**] T. WHITE (1793, fol. 16ᵛ): "Shakspeare very probably had his eye upon a passage in Sir Thomas Elyots *Boke named the Governour*" (1531, bk. 2, ch. 7): "But nowe to speke of the inestimable price and value of mercy. . . ." PRICE (1839, p. 122): Cf. Ps. 130:3. TILLEY (M895): "He shall find mercy that merciful is," quoting Matt. 5:7 and *MV* 4.1.200–2 (2111–13).

If he, which is the top of Iudgement, should
But iudge you, as you are? Oh, thinke on that,
And mercie then will breathe within your lips   830
Like man new made.
    Ang. Be you content, (faire Maid)
It is the Law, not I, condemne your brother,
Were he my kinsman, brother, or my sonne,
It should be thus with him: he must die to morrow.   835
    Isab. To morrow? oh, that's sodaine,
Spare him, spare him:
Hee's not prepar'd for death; euen for our kitchins
We kill the fowle of season: shall we serue heauen

---

828 top] God COLNE, COL2
833 condemne] condemns ROWE1-HUD2 (−CAM1, GLO, DEL4), ARD1, CAM3,
PEL1, PEN2
835 must die] dies POPE1-JOHN2
836–7 *One line* POPE1+ (−CAM3, ARD2)
839 shall we serue] serve we POPE, HAN1

---

828 which] Who (*OED, pron.* 9a).
    the top of Iudgement] JOHNSON (1755): *Top,* "The highest person." DYCE
(1853, p. 25): "That very expression . . . occurs in another mighty poet," Dante,
Purgatorio 6:37. *OED* (Top *sb.* [1] 15b): "The most perfect example or type."
    830–1 THIRLBY (1733–47): Cf. Gen. 2:7. WARBURTON (ed. 1747): "This is a
fine thought, and finely expressed. The meaning is, that *mercy will add such grace to your
person, that you will appear as amiable as man come fresh out of the hands of his creator.*"
HEATH (1765, p. 82): "As if a new man were formed within you." JOHNSON (Var.
1773): "I rather think the meaning is, *You would then change the severity of your present
character.* In familiar speech, *You would be quite another man.*" CAPELL (1780, 2:3:39):
"As it would have done within the lips of the first man, ere his fall had subjected him
to the infirmities of passion." T. H. WHITE (in Var. 1793): *"And you, Angelo, will
breathe new life into Claudio, as the Creator animated Adam, by* 'breathing into his nostrils
the breath of life' [Gen. 2:7]." T. WHITE (1793, fol. 16ᵛ): " 'As a *new baptized*
soule'." M. S. (1795, p. 646) and PRICE (1839, p. 122): Cf. Eph. 4:24, "put on the
newe man." WORDSWORTH (1864, p. 132): *"Like man redeemed, like the redemption of
man."* LEE (ed. 1907): Cf. John 3:3–8. NOBLE (1935, p. 223): "Made new by
Baptism." Cf. the Book of Common Prayer (1559) service for baptism: "that the
newe man may be raysed vp in them." TILLEY (M170): "He is now become a new
man," quoting 2 Cor. 5:17. See also Col. 3:10.
    833 **condemne**] LEVER (ed. 1965): "The form of the verb may be 1st person by
attraction of the pronoun 'I', or plural by influence of the precedent noun and
pronoun (cf. [277])." See FRANZ §677 and nn. 277, 1347.
    835 **should**] See n. 818.
    836–7 Compositor C set this as two lines because it was too long for one line. Cf.
1127–8.
    839 **of season**] STEEVENS (Var. 1793): "When it is in season." *OED* (*sb.* 5): *"Of
(the) season* = in season (see 15b) . . . in the best state for eating."

With lesse respect then we doe minister   840
To our grosse-selues? good, good my Lord, bethink you;
Who is it that hath di'd for this offence?
There's many haue committed it.
    Luc. I, well said.
    Ang. The Law hath not bin dead, thogh it hath slept: 845
Those many had not dar'd to doe that euill
If the first, that did th'Edict infringe
Had answer'd for his deed. Now 'tis awake,
Takes note of what is done, and like a Prophet
Lookes in a glasse that shewes what future euils   850
Either now, or by remissenesse, new conceiu'd,

---

847 the first,] the first man POPE1-JOHN2, v1773-v1821, SING; that the first mTBY1 *and* DENT MS *in* HAL *and* WALKER (1860, 2:264) *conj.*, DYCE2, DYCE3, HUD2, BUL, CAM3, KIT1, PEL1, PEN2; he, the first TYRWHITT *conj. in* v1773, CAP; the first one COL2, COL3; but the first WH, NLSN   the first, that] he who first DAV; he that first COL4   did th'Edict] the edict did KTLY, COL4
    850 that shewes what] which shews that HAN1
    851 Either now] Or new POPE1-v1773; Either new COL2, DYCE, COL3, STAU, GLO, DEL4-ARD2 (−CAM2, ARD1, CAM3, ALEX); Either now born KTLY

---

840 **respect**] SCHMIDT (1875): "Care" (*OED, sb.* 13c).
    841 **good, good my Lord**] Emphatic repetition. See n. 54.
    bethink] *OED* (*v. refl.* 8): "Reflect, consider," quoting 903.
    843 **haue**] Who have: see n. 758.
    844 DELIUS (ed. 1860): Lucio thinks of himself, since he finds Isabella's last words especially pertinent.
    845 MALONE (ed. 1790, 10:562): Cf. *The Spanish Tragedie* (1592, ed. Boas, 3.15.22). T. H. WHITE (in Var. 1793): "*Dormiunt aliquando leges, moriuntur nunquam* [Laws sometimes sleep, never die], is a maxim in our law." HART (ed. 1905): "This maxim is attributed to Sir Edward Coke." PHILLIPS (1972, p. 43) cites "Coke's Second Institute . . . 161." See nn. 263, 416.
    846-8 **Those . . . deed**] Cf. *Tim.* 3.5.3 (1260) and WILSON (p. 116), "He that chastises one amends many."
    847 **If the first**] KNIGHT (ed. 1840): "The necessary retardation of the original [F] adds to the force of the line." COLLIER (ed. 1842): "The sense is here complete without *man.*" See textual notes.
    Edict] DELIUS (ed. 1860): Sh. usually accents *edict* on the last syllable, though the other accentuation is not unknown to him.
    848 **answer'd for**] JOHNSON (1773): "To be accountable for." SCHMIDT (1874): "To atone for." CAMPBELL (ed. 1949): "Paid the penalty for" (*OED, v.* 6b). Cf. 493 (see n.), 859.
    849-50 **like . . . glasse**] THIRLBY (1733-47): "Dr. Dee." WARBURTON (ed. 1747): "This alludes to the fopperies of the *Berril,* much used at that time by cheats and fortune-tellers to predict by." HART (ed. 1905): "An allusion to the method of divination by looking into a crystal, such as Dr. Dee's famous beryl."
    851-2 RANN (ed. 1786): "Either in actual existence at present, or in embryo

And so in progresse to be hatch'd, and borne,
Are now to haue no successiue degrees,
But here they liue to end.

   Isab. Yet shew some pittie.   855

   Ang. I shew it most of all, when I show Iustice;
For then I pittie those I doe not know,
Which a dismis'd offence, would after gaule
And doe him right, that answering one foule wrong   (F4va)

---

854 here] F1-POPE2, THEO, COL1, ALEX, EVNS; where TYRWHITT *conj. in* v1773,
MAL-KNT2, HAL, ARD1; ere mTBY1 *conj.*, HAN1 *etc.*
855 *Kneeling.* IRV, RLTR

---

only." RIDLEY (ed. 1935): "A sense can be extracted; 'either now hatch'd and born,
or new-conceived and so in progress . . .'; the trouble with this is that if the simile
is to work out fully the evils are to be ended before they get as far as being hatched.
The New Cambridge editors, with perhaps more heroism than discretion, would read
Eggs for *Either.*" LEISI (ed. 1964): " 'Future sins that have either been conceived
already or might, through negligence, be conceived later on, and consequently
hatched and born . . .'." " 'Hatching' or 'breeding' of sin is a frequent metaphor in
MfM and indeed in Sh.; cf. [901, 1009]. This may be an echo of James 1 15." LEVER
(ed. 1965): "A recurrent image-cluster where prophecy and hatching are associated."
" 'New' and 'new conceiv'd' are well balanced, whereas F 'now' leads to an awkward
repetition in [853]. . . . 'Either' may be a sophistication for 'Or'."

   851 **Either**] KÖKERITZ (1953, p. 322): Monosyllabic, with loss of medial consonant. See nn. 1082, 1208, 1240.

   853 **no successiue degrees**] THIRLBY (1747–53): "*Gradus* [steps]." CAPELL
(1780, 2:3:39): "No progress from bad to worse." ABBOTT (§492): *Successive* is
accented on the first syllable. TERRELL (1871, p. 16): "The phrase refers to inheri-
tances passing to the son from the father. Angelo means that existing evils should not
be propagated." PARROTT (ed. 1938): "Descendants." HARRISON (ed. 1948):
"Successors." BALD (ed. 1956): *Degrees,* "Stages."

   854 MALONE (1780, 1:96): "They should *end where* they *began;* i.e. with the
criminal. . . . It is more likely that a letter should have been omitted at the press, than
that one should have been added." IDEM (ed. 1790, 10:562): Cf. *Cor.* 5.6.65–6
(3728–9) and *JC* 5.3.24 (2504). COLLIER (ed. 1842): "There is no need of alteration. Angelo is referring to the place of his own rule, and contrasts what the state of
the law there had been with what it then was: . . . here crimes live only that they may
be brought to an end." LEISI (ed. 1964): " 'Live only to die out'."

   856–7 JOHNSON (ed. 1765): "This was one of [Sir Matthew] *Hale*'s memorials.
*When I find myself swayed to mercy, let me remember, that there is a mercy likewise due to the
Country.*" TILLEY (E200), SMITH (1963, p. 69), and WILSON (p. 368): "He that
helps the evil hurts the good" (Publilius Syrus).

   858 **Which**] ABBOTT (§266): "*Which,* like *that,* is less definite than *who. Who*
indicates an individual, *which* a 'kind of person'." Here "unknown persons."

      dismis'd] OED (*v.* 8b): "Forgive," first use in this sense.

      gaule] JOHNSON (1755): *Gall,* "vex." SCHMIDT (1874): "To injure, to
harass." See n. 328.

   859 **doe him right**] SCHMIDT (1875, p. 979): "To give him his due, to do him
justice."

Liues not to act another. Be satisfied; 860
Your Brother dies to morrow; be content.
   Isab. So you must be yᵉ first that giues this sentence,
And hee, that suffers: Oh, it is excellent
To haue a Giants strength: but it is tyrannous
To vse it like a Giant. 865
   Luc. That's well said.
   Isab. Could great men thunder
As *Ioue* himselfe do's, *Ioue* would neuer be quiet,
For euery pelting petty Officer

---

860 Be] Then be POPE, HAN1   satisfied;] — ∧ PEN2
861 *He raises her.* IRV
863 it is] 'tis POPE1-JOHN2, HUD2, WH2, PEN2
864 it is] *Om.* HAN1, HUD2
865-7 *Lines ending* said. . . . thunder v1793-NLSN, KIT1-SIS, EVNS; giant. . . .
thunder CAM3, ARD2

---

862 yᵉ] The compositor uses the common abbreviation for *the* because the line
is full. Cf. yᵘ 2473.
   863-5 **Oh . . . Giant**] TILLEY (H170): "To be able to do harm and not to do
it is noble," quoting *Son.* 94, *LLL* 2.1.58 (550).
   863, 864 **it is**] LEVER (ed. 1965): " 'It is' in [863] seems to be a sophistication
of "tis', and in [864] unnecessary."
   865 **like a Giant**] THIRLBY (1733-47): "Giants in romances generally cruel and
likewise in the Bible and old poets." STEEVENS (Var. 1793): "Isabella alludes to the
savage conduct of *giants* in ancient romances." DELIUS (ed. 1860): But perhaps Sh.
thought of the heaven-storming Titans; cf. *Wiv.* 2.1.81 (622). LEVER (ed. 1965):
"The revolt of the giants against Jove was a familiar myth, especially as told in Ovid,
Metamorphoses, I."
   867-80 LLOYD (1877, p. 143): Cf. Marcellus Palingenius, *Zodiacus Vitae* (1531),
"Jupiter Omnipotens . . . ," and Googe's tr. (1561, 1576, sig. D7ᵛ), esp. these lines:
"And as the Ape that counterfets, to vs doth laughter moue: So we likewise doe cause
and moue the Saintes to laugh aboue, As oft as stately steps we treade with looke of
proude disdaine." HANKINS (1953, p. 143) cites also another passage in *The Zodiake
of Life* (ed. 1576, p. 87): "An Ape (quoth shee) and iesting stock is man to God in
skye . . . ."
   867-70 DOUCE (1807, 1:127): "This fine sentiment . . . appears to have been
suggested by the following lines in Ovid's *Tristia,* lib. ii. [33-4] that Shakspeare
might have read in Churchyard's translation [1572]: 'Si quoties peccant homines sua
fulmina mittat Jupiter, exiguo tempore inermis erit'." HART (ed. 1905): Ovid is
quoted and translated in Robert Laneham's *Letter* (1575, rpt. 1968, p. 58): "If Ioue
shoold shoot hiz thunderbollts az oft az men offend, Assure yoo hiz artillary wold soon
be at an end."
   868 **neuer**] Pronounced *ne'er,* as in 946, 2597.
   869 **pelting**] JOHNSON (1755): "This word in *Shakespeare* signifies, I know not
why, mean; paltry; pitiful." *OED (a.)*: "Paltry, petty, contemptible."

Would vse his heauen for thunder;   870
Nothing but thunder: Mercifull heauen,
Thou rather with thy sharpe and sulpherous bolt
Splits the vn-wedgable and gnarled Oke,
Then the soft Mertill: But man, proud man,
Drest in a little briefe authoritie,   875
Most ignorant of what he's most assur'd,
(His glassie Essence) like an angry Ape

870–1 *Lines ending* but thunder:— . . . heaven, mTBY1 *conj.,* CAP-SING1, KNT,
HAL, DYCE, KTLY, DEL4, BUL, ARD, KIT1, SIS
870 Would] Incessantly would HAN1
871 heauen] sweet heav'n HAN1
874 Mertill] yielding myrtle KTLY   But] O But F2-v1813 (−MAL)
876 assur'd] assur'd of mTBY3 *conj.,* KTLY

871–4 **Mercifull . . . Mertill**] DOUCE (1807, 1:127): Cf. Persius, *Satire* 2, but
this author was not then translated. HART (ed. 1905): Greene contrasts the "Myrtle
tree" with "the hard Oake" (*Mamillia,* 1583, ed. Grosart, 2:61). CAMPBELL (ed.
1949): "*Soft,* delicate, because it cannot stand the cold."
   872 **sulpherous**] SCHMIDT (1875): "Made of brimstone, or impregnated with
it; considered as a quality of thunder and lightning." So *OED* (*a.* 2b).
   873 **Splits**] WALKER (1860, 2:126): "*S* is not unfrequently substituted for *st* in
the second person singular of a verb." See ABBOTT §340, FRANZ §152, KÖKERITZ
(1953, p. 303), DOBSON §398, and nn. 998, 1223.
   vn-wedgable] JOHNSON (1755): "Not to be cloven." Sh. is first to use the
word; cf. *wedged,* "cleft as with a wedge," *Tro.* 1.1.35 (70).
   gnarled] JOHNSON (1755): "Knotty," recalling from his boyhood that *"gnar,
nar,* or *nurr,* is in Staffordshire a hard knot of wood which boys drive with sticks"
(OED, Knur 3, first quotations 1852 "Nurr" and 1855 *"Knor* or *Gnar").* OED *(ppl.
a.):* "Var. of *Knurled* . . . the sole authority is the folio of 1623." LEVER (ed. 1965):
"A unique variant if not a misprint." It is not a misprint but a dialect form: see *Eng.
Dial. Dict., gnarl, gnarly,* KÖKERITZ (1953, p. 304), DOBSON §§417–18.
   874–9 **But . . . weepe**] TILLEY (A402) and WILSON (p. 382): "Authority shows
what a man is" (Bias). HUXLEY (1949, p. 25) quotes these lines, which provide the
title for *Ape and Essence.*
   875 **Drest**] See n. 22.
   876–7 DELIUS (ed. 1860): Man thinks of least, what he should know best, how
fragile, like glass, is his existence. *Of* belongs both to *ignorant* and to *assured.* HUDSON
(ed. 1880): "Most ignorant of that which *is most certain,* namely, his natural infirmity."
LASCELLES (1951, p. 140): "Of that in which he most confides, his very nature."
LEVER (ed. 1965): " 'Most ignorant of his own spiritual entity, though religion
should make him most certain of it'."
   876 **assur'd**] PARROTT (ed. 1938): "Sure of, dogmatic about" (*OED, ppl. a.* 6,
7). See ABBOTT §394, FRANZ §542.
   877 **His glassie Essence**] THIRLBY (1723–33): "Brittle." HEATH (1765, p. 82):
Either "his brittle essence" or "his essence like a looking-glass." HORNE (ed. 1840,

Plaies such phantastique tricks before high heauen,   878
As makes the Angels weepe: who with our spleenes,

---

879 makes] make mTBY3 *conj.,* JOHN1-SIS (−CAP, KTLY, IRV, NLSN, ALEX)

1:209): "The soul, or essence, of a substance easily shattered to atoms; yet, which man ignorantly thinks he sees through, and is thus made conversant with all the depths of heaven beyond. The full meaning, in its peculiar subtilty, does not admit of literal explanation, and vanishes before the rude materiality of analysis." CLARKE (ed. 1864): "That essential nature of man which is like glass from its faculty to reflect the image of others in its own, and from its fragility, its liability to injury or destruction." *OED* (Essence *sb.* 3): "Specific being, manner of existing, 'what a thing is'; nature, character." PLATT (1906, pp. 465–6): "His own essence which he can only see in a glass darkly" (1 Cor. 13:12). LASCELLES (1951, p. 141): This image "should make visible the antithesis between the epithet (with its twofold implication, deceptive, brittle) and the noun (signifying inescapable, indestructible reality: the very self)." CUNNINGHAM (1952, p. 266): "This is the scholastic notion in a scholastic context: man's essence is his intellectual soul, which is an image of God, and hence is *glassy* for it mirrors God. *Glassy* is used in this sense in [*Ham.* 4.7.168 (3159) and *1H6* 5.3.62 (2499)]. The full context of the notion here involved is given in . . . Ralegh's *History of the World:* 'But man . . . that is ignorant of the essence of his own soul . . . .'. *Works* (Oxford, 1829, II, xlvi)." HANKINS (1953, p. 143): "The 'glassy essence' of which man is so ignorant is his physical nature, as in [*The Zodiake of Life* (1576, p. 86)]. . . . His earthly being is as an image in a mirror." HALL (1964, pp. 161–2): This line is "the most compressed and cryptic statement Shakespeare made on the illusion of identity. Proud man's glassy essence is the image of his identity reflected both in and by his pride, and his pride in turn, as the associations of the speech make quite clear, is the reflection of himself in the image and likeness of authoritarian deity." HUNTER (1964, p. 169): " 'What the < looking > glass assures him is his essence'." Cf. 1136–7.

877–8 **like . . . tricks**] HART (ed. 1905): Sh. recalled Dekker, *Old Fortunatus,* 1600 (2.2.25): "like a young Ape, full of fantasticke trickes." ONIONS (1911): *Fantastic,* "extravagant, grotesque" (*OED, a.* 6). *OED* (Trick *sb.* 2b): "A capricious, foolish, or stupid act; a thing done without full thought or consideration." Cf. *fantasticall tricke,* 1581, and nn. 1332, 2249–50, 2903–4.

879 **As . . . weepe**] THEOBALD (ed. 1733): "This Notion of the Angels weeping for the Sins of Men is purely *Rabbinical.—Ob peccatum flentes Angelos inducunt* Hebræorum *Magistri* [Jewish rabbis represent angels as weeping on account of sin]" (Grotius on Luke 15:7–10). STEEVENS (Var. 1785, 10:662): Cf. "deeds to make Heauen weepe," *Oth.* 3.3.371 (2015). LEVER (ed. 1965): Grotius was "perhaps alluding to the Talmudic story that God rebuked his angels for rejoicing at the drowning of the Egyptians, telling them that they should rather weep at the destruction of his creatures."

makes] See n. 434. ABBOTT (§337): "Often, however, a verb preceded by a plural noun (the apparent nominative) has for its real nominative, not the noun, but the noun clause."

879–80 **who . . . mortall**] THEOBALD (ed. 1733): "Who, if they were endued with our Spleens and perishable Organs, would laugh themselves out of Immortality; or, as we say in common Life, laugh themselves dead." WARBURTON (ed. 1747): "By

Would all themselues laugh mortall.   880
   Luc. Oh, to him, to him wench: he will relent,
Hee's comming: I perceiue't.
   Pro. Pray heauen she win him.
   Isab. We cannot weigh our brother with our selfe,
Great men may iest with Saints: tis wit in them,   885
But in the lesse fowle prophanation.
   Luc. Thou'rt i'th right (Girle) more o'that.
   Isab. That in the Captaine's but a chollericke word,

---

883 [*To* Lucio.] JOHN, v1773; [*Aside.*] COL1+ (−HAL, KNT3)
884 our selfe] your self WARBURTON *conj. in* THEO1, THEO1-CAP, COL4, HUD2
887 i'th] i' F3-ROWE3; *om.* POPE1-JOHN2; in the v1773-SING2, COL3, KTLY, KNT3, DEL4, COL4

---

spleens, he [Sh.] meant that peculiar turn of the human mind, that always violently inclines it to a spiteful, unseasonable mirth. Had the angels *that,* says *Shakespear,* they would laugh themselves out of their immortality, by indulging a passion which does not deserve that prerogative. The ancients thought, that immoderate laughter was caused by the bigness of the spleen." KNIGHT (ed. 1840): "If they had our spleens, they would *laugh,* as mortals." LASCELLES (1951, p. 140): "Were they endowed only as man himself is, they would be moved to nothing but the satirist's harsh laughter." HALL (1964, p. 162): "Would laugh themselves not to death . . . but out of heaven into our ignobly deluded state."
   879 **spleenes**] See *OED* (*sb.* 1c): "Regarded as the seat of laughter or mirth. *Obs.* (Freq. *c* 1600.)"
   881 **wench**] LEISI (ed. 1964): "The word was not necessarily disparaging, but certainly not respectful, cf. *Girle* in [887]."
   882 **comming**] SCHMIDT (1874, p. 216): "About to yield." *OED* (*v.* 16): "To yield, be favourably moved."
   884 THIRLBY (1723–33): Cf. 2479. WARBURTON (in THEOBALD, ed. 1733): "Why not?" JOHNSON (Var. 1773): *"We* mortals proud and foolish cannot prevail on our passions to *weigh* or compare *our brother,* a being of like nature and like frailty, *with ourself.* We have different names and different judgments for the same faults committed by persons of different condition." HART (ed. 1905): "Judge of others by ourselves." LEE (ed. 1907): "One cannot treat one's neighbour as on precisely the same level with one's self; we are not all of the same scale." WILSON (ed. 1922): "We do not (as we ought) put ourselves in our brother's place." LEVER (ed. 1965): " 'We cannot judge our fellow-man by the standards we use for ourselves'. . . . Isabella is speaking of human behaviour in general."
   885–6 This may be a reminiscence of *1 Promos,* 3.5, p. 324 below: *"Non bonus est, ludere cum sanctis* [It is not good to play with saints (or sacred things)]. The quietest, and the thryftiest course they say, Is, not to checke, but prayse great mens amys." THIRLBY (1723–33): *Saints,* "holy things." LEVER (ed. 1965): *Jest,* "trifle" (*OED, v.* 3).
   887 Cf. Middleton, *The Familie of Loue* (1608, 3.2.38–9): "Thou'rt in the right, sweet wench; more of that vein." Cf. *vaine* 821. BYRNE (1936, p. 95): "Lucio says *you* to Isabella, then a *thou* of approval" [or of familiarity: see n. 2245].

Which in the Souldier is flat blasphemie.

   Luc. Art auis'd o'that? more on't.   890

   Ang. Why doe you put these sayings vpon me?

   Isab. Because Authoritie, though it erre like others,

Hath yet a kinde of medicine in it selfe

That skins the vice o'th top; goe to your bosome,

Knock there, and aske your heart what it doth know   895

That's like my brothers fault: if it confesse

A naturall guiltinesse, such as is his,

Let it not sound a thought vpon your tongue

Against my brothers life.

   Ang. Shee speakes, and 'tis such sence   900

---

890 auis'd] thou advis'd HAN1   on't] on't, yet more HAN1
898 your] you F2
899–901 *Lines ending* life. . . . 'tis . . . well. HAN1, CAP-MAL; 'tis . . . well.
v1793-COL1, SING2-COL3, CAM1-NLSN, KIT1, ALEX, PEL1, PEN2, EVNS; 'tis . . . it.
. . . well. HAL; sense, . . . well. STAU, CAM3, SIS, ARD2
900–1 Shee . . . it;] *Marked as aside* JOHN1-RANN, COL1+ (−KNT3)

---

890 **Art auis'd o'that?**] ROLFE (ed. 1882): "Advised, or aware" (*OED,* Advised
ppl. a. 1, quoting *Wiv.* 1.4.106 [490]). HART (ed. 1905): "Have you learnt that
truth?"

890 **on't**] Of it (*OED,* On *prep.* 27).

891 **put . . . vpon me**] LEVER (ed. 1965): " 'Make these sayings applicable to
me'." See *OED* (Put *v.* 1 23): "Impose."

    vpon] BROOK (1976, p. 165): "Many disyllabic words could be pronounced
with the chief stress on either syllable" (here on the first).

894 **skins**] JOHNSON (1755): "To cover with the skin," quoting this and *Ham.*
3.4.147 (2530). HORNE (ed. 1840, 1:209): "Brings a new skin or covering over the
sore place." CLARKE (ed. 1864): "A metaphor borrowed from surgery; in a case
where superficial application produces a false skin over an unhealed wound." *OED*
(*v.* 1c): "Cover *(over)* in some slight or superficial manner," first use in this sense.

    o'th] On the. See n. 630.

894–9 **goe . . . life**] BIRCH (1848, pp. 361–2): Cf. John 8:3–11. See n. 465–6.
BROWN (1864, pp. 15–17) adds Gal. 6:1 and *2H6* 3.3.31 (2165): "Forbeare to
iudge, for we are sinners all." WORDSWORTH (1864, p. 237): "This is in keeping
with what S. Paul has taught us, viz. that in judging others the consequence is we
condemn ourselves, Rom. ii.1; an idea which our poet has again caught and admirably
intensified, when he makes Timon ask,—Wilt thou whip thine own faults in other
men? [5.1.40–1 (2245)]." TILLEY (I27): "He that speaks ill of another let him first
think of himself " (Italian proverb).

897 **naturall**] Cf. *OED* (*a.* 8), "innate." Perhaps a reference to man's fallen
nature. See n. 412.

898 **sound**] See *OED* (*v.* 1 8): "Utter."

900–1 JOHNSON (ed. 1765): "New thoughts are stirring in my mind, new conceptions are *hatched* in my imagination." STEEVENS (Var. 1778): *"Davenant's* altera-

That my Sence breeds with it; fare you well.

Isab. Gentle my Lord, turne backe.

Ang. I will bethinke me: come againe to morrow.

Isa. Hark, how Ile bribe you: good my Lord turn back.

Ang. How? bribe me? 905

Is. I, with such gifts that heauen shall share with you.

Luc. You had mar'd all else.

Isab. Not with fond Sickles of the tested-gold,

---

901 breeds] bleeds POPE, HAN1, WARB   with it] with't HAN1, DYCE2, DYCE3, HUD2, BUL, SIS

908 Sickles] F1-ROWE3, ARD2; circles COLNE, COL2; sicles CAM2, CAM3-ALEX, PEL1, PEN2, EVNS; shekles POPE1 *etc.*

---

tion favours the sense of the old reading:—*She speaks such sense As with my reason breeds such images As she has excellently form'd.*" CAPELL (1780, 2:3:40): "Sensation or appetite, sensual appetite . . . excited by the '*sense*' and good qualities of the person haranguing him." RITSON (1783, p. 20): "Does not the deputy plainly mean, that *her wisdom* raised *his desires?*" HALLIWELL (ed. 1854): "Her eloquence is so great, her address so noble, my sense (passion) increases in proportion as I admire it." *OED* (Breed *v.* 3c): Fig. "to have offspring," quoting this and *Ado* 1.3.4 (347). HART (ed. 1905): *Speaks*, "speaks to the purpose," as in *Cor.* 1.1.124 (123). EMPSON (1951, p. 274): "Angelo's first use of the word [*sense*] is 'wise or reasonable meaning' [*OED, sb.* 28], and then the meaning 'sensuality', which Lucio has made dominant for this stage of the play [see n. 411], pokes itself forward and is gratified by the second use of the word as a pun." Cf. HARRISON (1954, p. 5). LEVER (ed. 1965): "But the main meaning of 'such sense' here is surely 'such import'. Isabella has directed Angelo's attention to his own 'natural guiltiness' and increased his desire by making him conscious of it."

902 **Gentle my Lord**] My gracious lord. See nn. 54, 357, 2818.

903 be**t**hinke] Consider. See n. 841.

906 **such gifts that**] FRANZ (§340): "*Such gifts as.*" Cf. *OED* (Such *dem. adj.* 12).

907 **else**] See n. 281.

908 **fond**] JOHNSON (1755): "Trifling; valued by folly." *OED* (*a.* 4): "Valued only by fools, trifling," first quotation in this sense, but ONIONS (1911) finds the same meaning in *Ham.* 1.5.99 (784), *triuiall fond Records.*

Sickles] FIELD (1845, pp. 47–8): "The Latin word is *siclus,* and in Coverdale's Bible we find the word *sicle* and *sycle,* and not *shekel.* So in Peele's *David and Bethsabe, sickles* is printed for *shekels* [1599, ed. Blistein, lines 1492, 1493]." WRIGHT (ed. 1891, 1:435): "So he [Sh.] would hear it read in Church from the Bishops' Bible, where it is spelt 'sicles' [cf. *OED*]. . . . The Hebraic form 'shekels' was introduced in the Geneva Bible of 1560 and adopted by King James's Translators."

tested-gold] WARBURTON (ed. 1747): "Attested, or marked with the standard stamp." JOHNSON (ed. 1765): "Rather copelled, brought to the *test,* refined." HAWKINS (in Var. 1778): "Tried by the cuppell, which is called by the refiners a *test.*" *OED* (Test *v.*[2] 1): "To subject (gold or silver) to a process of separation and refining in a test or cupel; to assay," first quotation for any form of the verb. See n. 55.

Or Stones, whose rate are either rich, or poore
As fancie values them: but with true prayers,   910
That shall be vp at heauen, and enter there
Ere Sunne rise: prayers from preserued soules,
From fasting Maides, whose mindes are dedicate
To nothing temporall.
    Ang. Well: come to me to morrow.   915
    Luc. Goe to: 'tis well; away.
    Isab. Heauen keepe your honour safe.

---

909 rate are] rate is HAN1; rates are JOHN1-PEL1 (−ALEX)

914–25 *Lines ending* me . . . away. . . . I . . . temptation, . . . to-morrow . . . noon.
. . . virtue! v1793-v1813; me . . . Tomorrow. . . . away. . . . Amen: (*then as* v1793)
v1821, SING1, KNT3; to-morrow. . . . away. . . . Amen: (*then as* v1793) KNT1-GLO,
DEL4, COL4, WH2-CAM2, ARD1-CAM3, SIS+ (*last lines ending* I . . . noon. . . . virtue!
KTLY); to-morrow. . . . away. . . . I (*then as* v1793) DYCE2, DYCE3, HUD2, BUL, ALEX;
to-morrow. . . . away! . . . I . . . temptation . . . to-morrow . . . lordship? . . . honour!
. . . virtue! KIT1

915 to me to morrow] to-morrow POPE1-JOHN2

916 *Om.* HAN1   'tis well; away] it is well; away v1793-v1821, KNT1, KTLY,
KNT3; it is well away SING1

909–10 KELLNER (1931, p. 251): The same idea of value in *Tim.* 1.1.168–72
(210–14). TILLEY (W923) and WILSON (p. 922): "The worth of a thing is as it is
esteemed (valued)," quoting *Tro.* 2.2.52 (1037).

909 **rate are**] LEVER (ed. 1965): "All editors except Alexander emend to 'rates'
or 'is' to improve the grammar, but the F form is quite Shakespearean." See nn. 277,
812.

910 **fancie**] See *OED* (*sb.* 8): "Capricious or arbitrary preference; individual
taste."

912 **preserued**] WARBURTON (ed. 1747): "Preserved from the corruption of
the world. The metaphor is taken from fruits preserved in sugar." EDWARDS (1748,
p. 53) remarks ironically, "In order to continue the metaphor, we should alter *fasting*
maids to *pickled* maids." BOSWELL (Var. 1821): "Surely our author had 'no such stuff
in his thoughts'." SCHMIDT (1875): "Kept pure." LEVER (ed. 1965): " 'Kept safe
from harm' (*O.E.D.* 1)."

913 **dedicate**] JOHNSON (1755): "Consecrate; devote; dedicated" (*OED, pa.
pple.*).

916 **Goe to**] See n. 513.

917 MAHOOD (1957, p. 179): "At first this seems a piece of direct, negative
irony; Angelo's honour is merely his title as judge, and does not correspond to any
real quality in his character. But if honour is a mere scutcheon to Angelo in the depths
of his self-discovery, it is for Isabella the concept which preserves them both. Her
conventional phrase is also a prayer which is answered when the Duke, in his Providential aspect, preserves Angelo from the seduction of Isabella and from the murder
of her brother."

Ang. Amen.

For I am that way going to temptation,

Where prayers crosse.   920

    Isab. At what hower to morrow,

Shall I attend your Lordship?

    Ang. At any time 'fore-noone.

    Isab. 'Saue your Honour.

    Ang. From thee: euen from thy vertue.   925   (F4vb)

What's this? what's this? is this her fault, or mine?

The Tempter, or the Tempted, who sins most? ha?

918–20 *Marked as aside* HAN1, CAP, COL, DYCE1+ (−KTLY, CAM3)
918 Amen.] Amen! I say: HAN1
919–20 [*Aside.*] JOHN, v1773-v1821, SING, KNT, HAL, KTLY
920 prayers crosse] prayer's cross'd KELLNER (1931) *conj.*, ARD2
921 morrow] marrow F2
922 your Lordship] you lordship F2; you HAN1
923 'fore-noone] 'fore Noon ROWE1+ (−CAM3, PEL1, PEN2)
924 'Saue] God save mTBY3 *and* WALKER (1860, 1:214) *conj.*, HUD2, KIT1,
PEN2; Heaven save KTLY   *Exeunt.* F2-F4; *Exeunt* Lucio *and* Isabella ROWE1-
JOHN2, v1773-RANN; *Exeunt* Provost, LUCIO, *and* ISABELLA. CAP, MAL+ (*subst.*)
925 SCENE VIII. POPE, HAN1, WARB, JOHN
927 ha?] *Om.* POPE1-JOHN2; Ha! (*separate line*) CAM1, GLO, DEL4, WH2-CAM2,
ARD1, NLSN, ALEX, PEL1, PEN2; Ha! (*beginning* 928) CAM3

---

920 CAPELL (1780, 2:3:40): "Meaning—that they had a *cross* or contrary effect
to that which should be produc'd by them; esteem their natural one, but their real
one—lust." MALONE (ed. 1790): "Where prayers *only* can *thwart* the temptation,
and prevent it from overcoming me. . . . Or, perhaps, the speaker means,—I am going
into the road of temptation, into which we daily pray that we may not be led. Our
Lord's prayer may have been here in Shakspeare's thoughts." COLLIER (ed. 1842):
"Angelo answers, 'Amen; for, tempted as I am, I pray for one thing, you for another;
you pray heaven to keep my honour safe, I the contrary, and thus our prayers cross'."
PORTER & CLARKE (ed. 1909): "Yet this is not all; her genuine prayer that his
honour be kept safe is crossed by his spurious prayer that the interview to-morrow
be successful, and yet that he keep the honour of his name safe."

    923 '**fore-noone**] Before noon: *OED* (Fore *prep.* 2), latest quotation in this sense.
HOWARD-HILL (1972, p. 128): The apostrophe and hyphen show Crane's influence.

    924 '**Saue**] See n. 768. All but Angelo go out after this speech.

    927 **ha?**] STEEVENS (Var. 1793): "This tragedy—*Ha!* (which clogs the metre)
was certainly thrown in by the player editors." HART (ed. 1905): "I should like to
throw it out." See *OED* (*int.* 2): "Used as an interjectional interrogative, esp. after
a question; = *Eh* 2. (Chiefly in Shakspere.)." SISSON (1956, 1:80): "Read . . . *who
sins most, ha?* It is a most natural and effective Elizabethan turn of phrase, giving the
question dramatic emphasis, and spoken without pause." LEVER (ed. 1965): "This
little word has been persecuted by editors. . . . As an Elizabethan half-query, half-
grunt, 'ha?' is unobtrusive and metrically harmless." Sh. uses it again in 1046, 1162,
1537, 1539, 1544, 1568.

Not she: nor doth she tempt: but it is I,
That, lying by the Violet in the Sunne,
Doe as the Carrion do's, not as the flowre,   930
Corrupt with vertuous season: Can it be,
That Modesty may more betray our Sence
Then womans lightnesse? hauing waste ground enough,
Shall we desire to raze the Sanctuary
And pitch our euils there? oh fie, fie, fie: 935

---

929 by] with CAP
930 Doe] Does ROWE3
935 euils] offals COLNE, COL2

928-31 WARBURTON (ed. 1747, 8:166): "The same *thought*" as in *Ham.*
2.2.181-2 (1218-19). JOHNSON (ed. 1765): "I am not corrupted by her, but by my
own heart, which excites foul desires under the same benign influences that exalt her
purity; as the carrion grows putrid by those beams which encrease the fragrance of
the violet."
    929 **by the Violet**] CAPELL (1780, 2:3:40): "Isabel . . . is the *'sun'*, and by the
'violet' is meant—'the uncorrupted, the man of firmness and virtue'." LEVER (ed.
1965): "The sun typifies chaste influences ('sun-like chastity'); the violet, true virtues."
    931 **vertuous season**] WHITER (1794, pp. 142, 147): "Shakspeare is frequent
in the metaphorical application of the word [*season* . . . that which *preserves*]. . . . The
following beautiful image in [*MM*] must be thus explained," quoting 926-31.
SCHMIDT (1875): *Season*, "the benign influence of summer-weather and sunshine."
WILSON (ed. 1922): "The effect of the sun which brings the flower to . . . maturity."
EMPSON (1951, pp. 275-6): "This idea is certainly present. . . . But if the violet is
giving the *season*, the idea seems to be the smell of it, like *'seasoning'* in food." LEISI
(ed. 1964): "*Vertuous* combines the meanings of 'morally good' and 'powerful'."
[The same double sense is possible in 948.] LEVER (ed. 1965): "(i) the season when
the sun's rays give the plants their strength to grow . . . (ii) the preservative for meats,
etc. The meanings reinforce one another."
    932 **betray**] SCHMIDT (1874): "To ensnare: . . . almost = to seduce" (*OED, v.*
4).
        Sence] MALONE (ed. 1790): "*Sense* has in this passage the same signification
as in that above" (901: see n.). DYCE (1867): "Sensual passion," as in 411: see n.
    933 **lightnesse**] JOHNSON (1755): "Unchastity" (*OED*, Lightness¹ 7b). See nn.
2596, 2658-9.
        waste ground] THIRLBY (1747-53): "Common in the Lord's wast." See *OED*
(*a.* 1c) and (*sb.* 2): "Land not in any man's occupation, but lying common." GREY
(1754, 2:77): "Having common women enough." See n. 498.
    935 **euils**] GREY (1754, 2:76-7): "*Houses of office* [i.e., privies], which *Shakespeare,*
in his metaphorical way, might call *evils,* because they are *nusances.*" So in *H8* 2.1.67
(908). MALONE (ed. 1790): *Evil* has this meaning in Sir John Birkenhead, *Two
Centuries of Pauls Churchyard* (ed. 1653, p. 61). HENLEY (ibid., 10:563): "The
desecration of edifices devoted to religion, by converting them to the most abject
purposes of nature, was an eastern method of expressing contempt. See 2 Kings, x.

What dost thou? or what art thou *Angelo*?
Dost thou desire her fowly, for those things
That make her good? oh, let her brother liue:
Theeues for their robbery haue authority,
When Iudges steale themselues: what, doe I loue her,   940
That I desire to heare her speake againe?
And feast vpon her eyes? what is't I dreame on?
Oh cunning enemy, that to catch a Saint,
With Saints dost bait thy hooke: most dangerous
Is that temptation, that doth goad vs on   945

---

942 is't] is it F4-ROWE2
944 thy] thou F4, ROWE1
945 doth] dost JOHN

27." HALLIWELL (ed. 1854): "Having regard to the use of *evils* as *vices* just previously, it is natural to conclude that at least the double meaning of the term was referred to, the whole passage being emblematical:—Having spare ground enough (alluding to light women), why desire to invade the sanctuary of purity with our evil actions?" WILLIAMS (1862, p. 442): "The Perkins folio alters 'evils' to *'offals';* but Mr. Collier prints 'evils', remarking that the meaning of the two words is the same. It would not be difficult to show that by 'evil' or 'evils' our forefathers designated *physical* as well as moral corruption and impurity. I am told that the word retains this sense among the Americans; and I find that a newspaper correspondent, writing from the camp of General M'Clellan after his late defeat before Richmond, and detailing the distress of the Federal army, speaks of 'the *offal* of hecatombs of oxen, impossible to cart away', and afterwards varies his phraseology by describing the 'grinning heads of oxen, hides mosaic'd into *evil* by rains'." OED (*sb.* [2]): "Meaning uncertain." THISELTON (1905, 2:22–3): Cf. Charles Fitz-Geffrey, *Sir Francis Drake* (1596, ed. Grosart, p. 49): "overturne Their big-bon'd carcasses to *Orcus* evils." WILSON (ed. 1922): "The 'privy' interpretation may be right and is certainly most forcible." NOBLE (1935, p. 32): "The word 'evils', as used by Angelo, appears to have no other meaning than wickedness. He used it as an antithesis to 'sanctuary', and therefore as the abode of vice. Why was vice not content with its own indulgence without destroying that which was holy?" LEVER (ed. 1965): "Privies, a lost word."
    fie, fie, fie:] SANDMANN (1882, p. 272): Cf. *1 Promos,* 2.3 (p. 315 below): "What didst thou say? fie *Promos* fie: of hir auoide the thought."
    939–40 **Theeues . . . themselues**] TILLEY (T119) and WILSON (p. 335): "The great thieves hang the little ones" (Diogenes). Cf. 470–2, *Lr.* 4.6.155–8 (2595–8), and *1 Promos,* 3.2, p. 321 below.
    939 **authority**] See *OED* (2): "Authorization."
    942–4 LEVER (ed. 1965): "Angelo imagines himself as an anchorite tempted in a dream by Satan disguised as a virgin saint."
    943 **enemy**] See *OED* (*sb.* 1b): "The Devil."
    Saint] See *OED* (*sb.* 4): "A person of extraordinary holiness of life," and (3) "one of the elect," "a Christian," quoting Hooker as well as Puritan writers. Cf. 1303.

To sinne, in louing vertue: neuer could the Strumpet
With all her double vigor, Art, and Nature
Once stir my temper: but this vertuous Maid
Subdues me quite: Euer till now
When men were fond, I smild, and wondred how.   *Exit.*   950

Scena Tertia.   2.3

Enter Duke and Prouost.

Duke. Haile to you, *Prouost*, so I thinke you are.
Pro. I am the Prouost: whats your will, good Frier?
Duke. Bound by my charity, and my blest order,   955

---

949 Euer till now] Even till now F2-ROWE3, ARD2; Ev'n 'till this very Now POPE,
HAN1; Ever 'till this very Now THEO, WARB, JOHN
   950 *Exit.*] *Om.* CAP, MAL
   951 *Scena Tertia*] SCENE IX POPE, HAN1, WARB, JOHN   *A Prison.* ROWE1-
SIS, ARD2
   952 *Enter . . . Prouost*] *Enter* Duke *in disguise of a Fryar, and* Provost DAV, ROWE1
+ (*subst.*)
   953 are.] ∼ ? HENL
   954 your] you ROWE2, ROWE3

---

946 **To . . . vertue**] WINNY (ed. 1959): "Beyond love of virtue to desire of the
virtuous person."
   neuer] See n. 868.
   947 WINNY (ed. 1959): "With her double power of alluring men; skill and
physical charm."
   948 **temper**] SCHMIDT (1875): "Disposition, constitution, temperament." *OED*
(*sb.* 3): "Mental balance or composure . . . moderation in or command over the
emotions," first use in this sense. Cf. *Lr.* 1.5.51 (919).
   949-50 DYCE (ed. 1857): "Frequently, when our early dramatists introduce a
couplet, they make *the first line shorter* (sometimes *much shorter*) than the second."
   950 **fond**] See n. 313.
   Exit] JOHNSON (ed. 1765): "As a day must now intervene between this
conference of *Isabella* with *Angelo*, and the next, the act might more properly end
here, and here, in my opinion, it was ended by the poet." See n. 2305. RHODES
(1923, p. 122): "The division of plays was posthumous and has no authority."
HEUSER (1956) and JEWKES (1958, pp. 97–8) show that Sh. did not normally divide
a play into acts.
   953 **so . . . are**] LEVER (ed. 1965): "Added to support his disguise. The Duke-as-
Duke would recognize his own Provost."

I come to visite the afflicted spirits
Here in the prison: doe me the common right
To let me see them: and to make me know
The nature of their crimes, that I may minister
To them accordingly.   960
  Pro. I would do more then that, if more were needfull.

      Enter Iuliet.

Looke here comes one: a Gentlewoman of mine,
Who falling in the flawes of her owne youth,
Hath blisterd her report: She is with childe,   965
And he that got it, sentenc'd: a yong man,
More fit to doe another such offence,
Then dye for this.

---

959 crimes] Crime ROWE1, ROWE2
962 *Enter Iuliet.*] *After* 968 DYCE, STAU, DEL4, HUD2, IRV, BUL
964 flawes] flames DAV, WARB, CAP, RANN-WH2 (−KNT, CAM1, GLO), NLSN
968–70 *Lines ending* he die? . . . to-morrow. v1793-v1821, SING, KNT; this.
. . . to-morrow. COL, HAL, DYCE1-DYCE2, DEL4+

---

956 **spirits**] THIRLBY (1723–33): "N.T. Preach'd to the spirits in prison." So
WHALLEY (in Var. 1785), citing 1 Pet. 3:19. See *OED* (*sb.* 9a): "One who has a spirit
of a specified nature."
 957 **common right**] *OED* (*a.* 5c): "*Common right:* the right of every citizen."
 963–70 LEISI (ed. 1964): "These words are spoken out of Juliet's hearing."
 964 **flawes**] THEOBALD (ed. 1733): "As, *blister'd,* follows in the *second* Line, Mr.
Warburton ingeniously advises to read *Flames* in the *first.* And it is the Metaphor our
Author elsewhere chooses to use." WARBURTON (ed. 1747): "Who doth not see that
the integrity of the metaphor requires we should read *flames of her own youth.*"
JOHNSON (ed. 1765): "Who does not see that upon such principles there is no end
of correction." FARMER (in Var. 1773, 10:Oo5ᵛ): "*Davenant* reads *flames.*" STEEV-
ENS (Var. 1778): "Shakespeare has *flaming youth* in *Hamlet* [3.4.84 (2459)] and
Greene, in his *Never Too Late* [1590, p. 35] . . . 'the *flames of youth'.*" KNIGHT (ed.
1840): "Shakspere, in the superabundance of his thought, makes one metaphor run
into another; and thus Juliet may yield to the *flaws*—storms—of her own youth, and
so *blister* her reputation." SCHMIDT (1874): "Storm of passion," as in *Mac.* 3.4.63
(1332). WILSON (ed. 1922): " 'Flaws' could mean 'flakes' or 'sparks of fire' (v.
N.E.D. 'flaw' sb.¹ 1)." LEISI (ed. 1964): "*Flaw* in Sh. can mean 'crack' . . . or
'fragment' . . . but the dominant sense is 'blast', 'squall', 'storm' " (*OED, sb.*² 1).
 965 **blisterd**] JOHNSON (1755): "To raise blisters by some hurt, as a burn, or
rubbing." *OED* (*v.* 1): "To raise blisters on," first fig. use. LEISI (ed. 1964): "*Blister*
(vb.) never refers [in Sh.] to the effects of heat; it means 'blast', 'blight' in *Tempest*
I 2 324 [462]. . . . *Blister* (sb. and vb.) can also refer to the effects of poison or
infection," as in *Mac.* 4.3.12 (1827).
 report] *OED* (*sb.* 1c): "Repute, fame, reputation,"

Duk. When must he dye?

Pro. As I do thinke to morrow.   970

I haue prouided for you, stay a while

And you shall be conducted.

    Duk. Repent you (faire one) of the sin you carry?

    Iul. I doe; and beare the shame most patiently.

    Du. Ile teach you how you shal araign your consciēce   975

And try your penitence, if it be sound,

Or hollowly put on.

    Iul. Ile gladly learne.

    Duk. Loue you the man that wrong'd you?

    Iul. Yes, as I loue the woman that wrong'd him.   980

    Duk. So then it seemes your most offencefull act

Was mutually committed.

    Iul. Mutually.

    Duk. Then was your sin of heauier kinde then his.

    Iul. I doe confesse it, and repent it (Father.)   985

    Duk. 'Tis meet so (daughter) but least you do repent   (F5a)

As that the sin hath brought you to this shame,

---

973 carry?] ⁓ . F4-ROWE2
982 committed.] ⁓ ? v1773+ (−KIT1, ALEX)
984 his.] ⁓ ? F4, ROWE
986 least you do repent] repent you not POPE1-JOHN2; unless you do repent
RLTR
987 shame,] ⁓ ? POPE1-THEO4

---

971 **prouided**] RANN (ed. 1786): "A place to lie in at."

973 **carry**] See n. 997-9. J. J. HOGAN (1968, p. 230): *"Carry* here means 'have on one's conscience'; *carry OED* 26c 'to be pregnant with' first appears in 1776."

975 **araign**] LEISI (ed. 1964): " 'Accuse' " (*OED, v.*[1] 2). LEVER (ed. 1965): "Interrogate, examine" [but *OED, v.*[1] 1, cites no instance of this meaning after 1447].

977 **hollowly**] JOHNSON (1755): "Insincerely." So *OED*, first fig. use.

981 **offencefull**] *OED* (*a.*): "Full of offence, sinful," only quotation. ROLFE (ed. 1905): Cf. *offencelesse* in *Oth.* 2.3.275 (1398-9) [first quotation in *OED*].

982 **mutually**] See n. 246.

984 **heauier**] THIRLBY (1733-47): "Why so? Greater shame in the eye of the foolish world, but sure not greater sin." ONIONS (1911): *Heavy,* "grievous, heinous, wicked." WINNY (ed. 1959): "Woman's nature did not permit her being over-whelmed by passion like a man; hence Juliet must deliberately have consented to her seduction."

986 **least you do repent**] STEEVENS (Var. 1785): "Is only a kind of negative imperative—*Ne te pœniteat,*—and means, repent not on this account." SCHMIDT (1874): *Lest,* "for fear that, in order that not" (*OED*, Lest *conj.* 1).

987 **As that**] SCHMIDT (1874): "In as much as" (*OED*, As *adv.* 18). ROLFE (ed. 1882): "For the reason that, because that."

Which sorrow is alwaies toward our selues, not heauen,
Showing we would not spare heauen, as we loue it,
But as we stand in feare. 990
    Iul. I doe repent me, as it is an euill,
And take the shame with ioy.
    Duke. There rest:
Your partner (as I heare) must die to morrow,
And I am going with instruction to him: 995
Grace goe with you, *Benedicite.*   *Exit.*
    Iul. Must die to morrow? oh iniurious Loue

---

988 toward] towards ROWE1-RANN (−CAP), SING1, CAM1, GLO, WH2, NLSN
989 we would not spare] we'd not spare ROWE3, v1793-v1821, SING; we'd not seek POPE1-v1773 (−CAP); we would not serve COLNE, COL2, COL3, COL4
990 feare.] ⁓ ,— CAP+ (−COL1, COL3, DEL4, RLTR)
993 There] 'Tis well, there HAN1
996 Grace . . . *Benedicite.*] *Jul.* Grace go with you! *Duke. Benedicite!* RITSON (1783) *conj.,* DYCE; *Juliet.* May grace go with you! *Duke. Benedicite!* STEEVENS (v1793) *conj.,* KTLY; *Jul.* God's grace go with you! Duke. *Benedicite!* WALKER (1860, 1:214) *conj.,* HUD2   Grace] So grace POPE1-CAP
997 Loue] law mTBY1 *conj.,* HAN1, SING2-WH1, KTLY-KNT3, COL4-WH2, BUL, NLSN-SIS

---

989 **spare heauen**] CAPELL (1780, 2:3:40): *"Spare* to offend it." HUDSON (ed. 1880): " *'Forbear to offend* Heaven', or spare Heaven the offence of our sin."
990 **feare.**] FRYE (1963, p. 237): Cf. *R2* 5.3.56 (2555). See textual notes for changes in punctuation.
993 **There rest**] JOHNSON (ed. 1765): "Keep yourself in this temper." Cf. 1394.
995 **instruction**] SCHMIDT (1874): "Spiritual advice," as in 1521.
996 **Grace**] SCHMIDT (1874): "Divine favour" (*OED, sb.* 6b).
    Benedicite] OED (*interj.* 1): "Bless you."
997–9 **oh . . . horror**] JOHNSON (ed. 1765): "Her execution was respited on account of her pregnancy, the effects of her love: therefore she calls it *injurious;* not that it brought her to shame, but that it hindered her freeing herself from it. Is not this all very natural?" TOLLET (in Var. 1778): "Oh, love, that is injurious in expediting Claudio's death, and that respites me a life, which is a burthen to me worse than death!" MASON (1785, p. 34) prefers Hanmer's change of *Loue* to *law,* "which removes every difficulty, and can scarcely be considered as an alteration, the trace of the letters in the words *law* and *love* being so much alike.—The law affected the life of the man only, not that of the woman; and this is the injury that Juliet complains of, as she wished to die with him." RANN (ed. 1786): "Cruel kindness of *Angelo,* not to include me in Claudio's doom." HARNESS (ed. 1825): "The old folio has *Love,* printed with a capital, which I have restored.—Love is here spoken of by Juliet as the deity who had injuriously appointed her destiny." ARROWSMITH (1865, p. 12): " 'Injurious love', which respites a sentenced criminal for a few hours from execution, to spend the interim, as Spenser has it, 'half dead with dying fear'." DURHAM (ed. 1926): "Malicious love, which deprives Claudio of life, forces Juliet to prolong her existence for a time." LEVER (ed. 1965): "Juliet is not alluding to abstract love, but

That respits me a life, whose very comfort
Is still a dying horror.
Pro. 'Tis pitty of him.   *Exeunt.*   1000

Scena Quarta.   2.4

Enter Angelo.

An. When I would pray, & think, I thinke, and pray
To seuerall subiects: heauen hath my empty words,
Whilst my Inuention, hearing not my Tongue,   1005
Anchors on *Isabell*: heauen in my mouth,

1001 *Scena Quarta*] SCENE X POPE, HAN1, WARB, JOHN   *The Palace.*
ROWE1-JOHN2; *A Room in* Angelo's *House.* CAP-SIS (*subst.*); *The Ante-room.* ARD2
     ANGELO *discovered, seated.* IRV; *ANGELO, on his knees* CAM3
     1005 Inuention] intention POPE, HAN1, WARB, JOHN, v1773-RANN, DYCE2,
DYCE3-HUD2
     1006 heauen] Heav'n's ROWE1-JOHN2; God mTBY3 *and* WHITE (1854) *conj.*,
PEN2; heaven is CAP-RANN

---

to its physical effects: cf. 'the sin you carry' [973]." But see n. 973. Cf. *1 Promos,* 5.3
(p. 335 below): "Great shame redounds to thee, O *Loue,* in leauing vs in thrall."
     998 **respits**] LEISI (ed. 1964): "For *respitst,* for the sake of euphony, cf. *splits*
[873: see n.]."
     1000 **pitty**] *OED* (*sb.* 3b): "A ground or cause for pity. . . . Idiomatically with
of (= in relation to, in respect of, about)," quoting this and *Oth.* 4.1.206–7 (2581).
'Tis pitty of him occurs again in *Ant.* 1.4.71 (508) and *Oth.* 2.3.130 (1237). See n.
530–1.
     1003–19 **When . . . Crest:**] THEOBALD (MS n. in F2): Cf. *Ham.* 3.3.36–72
(2312–48). GENTLEMAN (ed. 1773): "This soliloquy has some similitude to that of
the King in *Hamlet;* to which it is certainly inferior, yet wants not considerable merit."
     1003 **thinke, and pray**] SCHMIDT (1875, p. 1419): "Syllepsis of the preposition:
. . . I think of and pray to."
     1004 **seuerall**] SCHMIDT (1875): "Separate, different, distinct" (*OED, a.* 1).
     1005 **Inuention**] STEEVENS (Var. 1778): *"Imagination."* SCHMIDT (1874): "Ac-
tivity of the mind generally, faculty of thinking." HART (ed. 1905): "Inventive
power, conception." LEVER (ed. 1965): "Fancy, rather than will or understanding."
See *OED* (4): "The faculty of inventing or devising; power of mental creation or
construction; inventiveness."
     1006 **Anchors on**] JOHNSON (1755): "To stop at; to rest on." MALONE (1783,
p. 4): "We have the same singular expression" in *Ant.* 1.5.33 (560). STEEVENS (Var.

As if I did but onely chew his name,
And in my heart the strong and swelling euill
Of my conception: the state whereon I studied
Is like a good thing, being often read   1010
Growne feard, and tedious: yea, my Grauitie

1007 his] its POPE1-RANN
1011 feard] sear'd HAN1, WARB, COL1-COL4 (−CAM1, GLO, KNT3), WH2, BUL, NLSN, PEN2; sere HEATH *conj.,* HUD2, CAM3-ALEX, PEL1, ARD2, EVNS; frayed (*spelled* fraid) KELLNER (1925, p. 56) *conj.,* SIS

1793): Cf. *Cym.* 5.5.393 (3714). *OED* (*v.* 4 *fig.*): "To fix oneself, one's attention, thought."

heauen] WHITE (1854, p. 153): "We should evidently read *God.* . . . The change was made by the publishers of the first folio, in conformity with the statute of James I [Act to Restrain the Abuses of Players, 1606] . . .; but they neglected to make a corresponding change in the pronoun." REES (1876, p. 64): Cf. Matt. 15:8. NOBLE (1935, p. 225): "It is very evident that 'Heaven' has been substituted for 'God' and that Shakespeare originally wrote 'God in my mouth'. See Isa. xxix. 14 [13] . . . , Matt. xv. 8." LEVER (ed. 1965): "Cf. *Basilicon Doron* [ed. Craigie], p. 51: 'Keepe God more sparingly in your mouth, but aboundantly in your harte'." See n. 1316–17.

1007 chew] JOHNSON (1755): "Taste without swallowing." *OED* (*v.* 3e): "Keep saying or mumbling over," first use in this sense. HUNTER (1964, pp. 170–1): *Chew* can be interpreted as "chew over, keep in the mouth and not digest"; but *"God in my mouth* sounds like a reference to the Eucharist," and "reception of the sacrament was mere *chewing* if the heart lacked faith; in such a case the *evil* in the heart was unaffected by Grace." But the texts quoted in n. 1006 support the meaning given in *OED.*

1009 conception] SCHMIDT (1874): "Idea, thought" (*OED,* 7). SARRAZIN in his 1902 revision limits the sense to "An evil thought," but *evil* has already been specified.

state] BALD (ed. 1956): "Statecraft." See *OED* (*sb.* 32): "All that concerns the government or ruling power of a country," quoting *TN* 2.5.163–4 (1155–6), "arguments of state"; cf. 2.5.175–6 (1165), "I will reade politicke Authours."

1011 feard] GILDON (1710, "Remarks," p. 295) prints *sear'd* in quoting this line. WARBURTON (ed. 1747): "We should read *sear'd: i.e.* old. So *Shakespear* uses, *in the sear,* to signify old age." JOHNSON (ed. 1765): "I think *fear'd* may stand, what we go to with reluctance may be said to be *fear'd."* HEATH (1765, pp. 83–4): *"Sear'd* . . . signifies *scorched,* not *old.* . . . He [Warburton] should have carried his correction a little farther, and given us, *sear,* or, *sere,* which indeed signifies, *dry,* and by a metaphor, *old."* COLLIER (1841, p. 4): "Warburton suggested *seared* for 'feared' or 'fear'd', as it stands in most copies of F1: that belonging to Lord Francis Egerton has it *sear'd,* as if the letter *s* had been substituted for *f,* as the sheet was going through the press." INGLEBY (1861, p. 24) shows that this change was made, not during printing, but by erasing the cross of the *f.* HUDSON (ed. 1880): *"Sere is dry, withered.* So in *Macbeth* [5.3.23 (2240)]." SISSON (1956, 1:81): "The accepted emendation . . . is Hudson's *sere,* from Warburton's *seared.* . . . I suggest *frayed,* assuming the spelling *fraid* in the underlying copy, and this would seem to be more consonant with the image of a book often read, worn and dog-eared from use, and tedious from

Wherein (let no man heare me) I take pride,
Could I, with boote, change for an idle plume
Which the ayre beats for vaine: oh place, oh forme,
How often dost thou with thy case, thy habit   1015
Wrench awe from fooles, and tye the wiser soules
To thy false seeming? Blood, thou art blood,

1014 vaine] vane MALONE (1783) *and* MASON (1785) *conj.,* RANN
1017 thou art blood] thou art but blood POPE-v1785 (−CAP); thou still art blood
MAL-SING1, DYCE2, DYCE3, HUD2; thou art blood still KTLY

---

over-familiarity." But *OED* (Fray *v.*[2] 2) records no example of this sense before 1710.
LEVER (ed. 1965): "Rowe's 'sear'd' for F 'feard' appears only in his first edition of
1709 and may have been a misprint." [It is not in any Folger copy of Rowe, ed. 1709.
Lever may refer to Gildon's quotation in 1710.] See p. 283.
    Grauitie] SCHMIDT (1874): "Dignity, solemnity of deportment or character"
(*OED,* 3). HART (ed. 1905): "An assumed decorum here." Promos refers to "my
Grauity" in *1 Promos,* 2.5 (p. 317 below).
    1013 **Could**] Could readily. See *OED* (Can *v.*[1] 7): "Expressing an inclination in
a conditional form."
    boote] JOHNSON (1755): "Profit; gain; advantage." IDEM (1773): "Some-
thing given to mend the exchange" (*OED, sb.*[1] 2).
    change] Exchange: see n. 397.
    plume] HARDING (ed. 1954): "A feather or panache, emblematic of frivol-
ity."
    1014 **for vaine**] STEEVENS (Var. 1793): "As *fair* is known to have been repeat-
edly used by Shakspeare, Marston, &c. for *fairness, vain* might have been employed
on the present occasion, instead of *vanity.* . . . The air is represented by Angelo as
chastising the plume for being vain." HALLIWELL (ed. 1854): "In vain, to no purpose." ORGER (1890, p. 22): "Angelo will match his gravity 'for vain', or in point
of vanity, with a feather which the air beats; nay, will on comparison of either choose
the feather, and give something over. This sense, which requires no verbal alteration,
is obscured by the omission of a comma, which should be marked after 'beats'."
WILSON (ed. 1922): "A quibble upon 'vane'. Cf. *L.L.L.* 4.1 [97-8 (1074-5)]."
    forme] SCHMIDT (1874): "External appearance, empty show," as in 2412. See
OED (*sb.* 15): "Observance of etiquette, ceremony, or decorum."
    1015 **case**] JOHNSON (ed. 1765): "Outside; garb, external shew." ONIONS
(1911): "Clothes" (*OED, sb.*[2] 4b).
    habit] SCHMIDT (1874): "Dress" (*OED, sb.* 1).
    1016-17 **Wrench . . . seeming**] JOHNSON (ed. 1765): "Here *Shakespear* judi-
ciously distinguishes the different operations of high place upon different minds.
Fools are frighted, and wise men are allured. Those who cannot judge but by the eye,
are easily awed by splendour, those who consider men as well as conditions, are easily
persuaded to love the appearance of virtue dignified with power." *OED* (Wrench
v. 6): "To twist or wrest out; to force," fig. use, as in *Lr.* 1.4.290 (781).
    1017 **seeming**] *OED* (*vbl. sb.* 3): "External appearance considered as deceptive,"
quoting 1528. See nn. 346, 1163.
    Blood . . . blood] JOHNSON (ed. 1765): "*Blood,* says he, *thou art but blood,*

Let's write good Angell on the Deuills horne
'Tis not the Deuills Crest: how now? who's there?

Enter Seruant.   1020

1019–22 *Lines ending* crest. . . . there? . . . you. . . . heav'ns! THEO, WARB-MAL
(−CAP); crest. . . . sister, . . . way. . . . heavens! v1793-v1813, SING, COL, WH1,
DYCE2, DEL4, DYCE3, HUD2, BUL; crest. . . . sister, . . . heavens! v1821, HAL, DYCE1;
crest. . . . sister, . . . you. . . . heavens! KNT, STAU
     1019 'Tis . . . Crest:] Is't . . . crest? HAN1   Crest:] ⁓ :— CAP, HENL, PEN2
     1020 *Enter* . . .] *After* crest. (1019) THEO, WARB, JOHN, v1773-SIS, EVNS; *after*
horn, (1018) CAP

---

however concealed with appearances and decorations. Title and character do not alter
nature, which is still corrupt, however dignified." CAPELL (1780, 2:3:41): "As well
in me as in others; place, and outward appearance, have no allaying effect on thy
inflammable quality." MALONE (ed. 1790): *"Blood* is used here, as in other places,
for *temperament of body."* COLLIER (ed. 1842): "The pause after the mark of admiration [*seeming!*] amply fills up the time." MAHOOD (1957, p. 53): "That is, neither
high birth nor his seemingly phlegmatic temper of mind exempts Angelo from
common human appetite." WINNY (ed. 1959): "Angelo now recognises that blood,
the bodily fluid, is the medium of impulses and emotions from which he is not exempt
—that, after all, his blood is not snow-broth." See n. 463.
     1018–19 **Let's . . . Crest**] WARBURTON (ed. 1747): "Let the most wicked thing
have but a virtuous pretence, and it shall pass for innocent." JOHNSON (Var. 1773):
"O place, how dost thou impose upon the world by false appearances! so much, that
if we *write good angel on the devil's horn, 'tis not* taken any longer to be *the devil's crest."*
CAPELL (1780, 2:3:41): "His blood is his leader; and the horn his own crest, and
not the devil's, and to be born by him in signal of what he is—his own tempter."
MASON (1785, p. 35): " 'Though we should write good angel on the devil's horn,
it will not change his nature, so as to give him the right to wear that crest'." BROWN
(1864, pp. 176–7): Cf. 2 Cor. 11:14. ROLFE (ed. 1882): "Mr. [Joseph] Crosby
suggests that Angelo here plays upon his own name." HART (ed. 1905): "Good angel
or fair seeming is really the devil's motto, and the strongest weapon in his armoury.
' 'Tis' refers to horn. That (the horn) is not his crest, but the words good angel."
WILSON (ed. 1922): "By Angelo's fall 'good Angel' has become 'the devil's crest'.
The simplest emendation is to read 'now' for 'not'." NEILSON & HILL (ed. 1942):
"Angelo, talking about 'false seeming', appears to say cynically, 'Let hypocrisy thrive'.
I.e., we may (safely) write 'good angel' on the devil's horn, because it ('good angel')
is not the true crest (insignia) of the devil (and thus will deceive)." HARRISON (ed.
1948): " 'Since desire *(blood)* is natural, let us call the Devil a good angel, and then
his horn is the badge of an angel and not a devil'." HARDING (ed. 1954): "Angelo
here seems to be drawing a parallel between himself and the devil, the master-
hypocrite." CRAIK (1958, pp. 50–1): "Shakespeare is perhaps referring to such a
practice" as that in *Like Will to Like* (ed. 1587, sig. A3): "This name Lucifer, must
be written on his back and on his brest." SCHANZER (1963, p. 94 n.): "That Shakespeare wrote 'yet' for F's 'not', as was first suggested by Johnson, seems to me a
near-certainty." LEVER (ed. 1965): "Angelo will reveal the diabolical side of his
nature, 'the devil's horn', while designating it with his own name 'angel', though this
is not his real title." See p. 284.

Ser. One *Isabell*, a Sister, desires accesse to you.

Ang. Teach her the way: oh, heauens
Why doe's my bloud thus muster to my heart,
Making both it vnable for it selfe,
And dispossessing all my other parts   1025
Of necessary fitnesse?
So play the foolish throngs with one that swounds,

1021 desires] asks POPE, HAN1
1022-6 *Lines ending* blood . . . both that . . . dispossessing . . . fitness? mTBY1
conj., HAN1, KTLY (*reading* both it)
1022 way:] way. [*Solus.*] JOHN, v1773-RANN; way. [*Exit* Serv.] CAP, MAL+
(—CAM1, KTLY, CAM2)
1024 Making both it] Making both that POPE1-JOHN2; Both making it HENL
1025 all my] My HAN1; all the v1803-v1821, SING

1021 *Isabell*] See n. 818.
    Sister] CLARKE (ed. 1864): "The servant, imagining the novice's habit worn
by Isabella to be that of a nun, announces her as if she had already taken the vows."
POEL (1931, p. 564) argues that she is not yet a novice but that "in this scene she
wears the dress of a novice for self-protection." SPEAIGHT (1954, p. 92): "No one,
however, seems to have considered that Isabella might have been a *postulant;* for no
woman is admitted to the novitiate of the Poor Clares, the order to which Isabella
is said to aspire, without a period of probation. When she speaks of herself as a
probationer [2432], this is surely what she means. But even as a postulant she would
still have worn a simplified habit, or dark costume. . . . It is quite possible that she
would have worn a postulant's dress within the enclosure, and a secular attire when
she was visiting the prison or the deputy's house." But most critics, like BRADBROOK
(1941, p. 391), believe that she is a novice.
    1022 Teach] SCHMIDT (1875): "Show" (*OED, v.* 3).
    1023 muster] JOHNSON (1755): "Assemble in order to form an army" (*OED,*
v.[1] 2c). CRAIG (ed. 1951): "According to Elizabethan psychology and physiology,
this is what happens to a victim of passion. . . . The blood rushes *(musters)* to the heart,
and the parts of the soul . . . 'change and become hurtfull'." LEISI (ed. 1964): "This
military metaphor is also found in *Lucrece* 442." Also in *Luc.* 720, *2H4* 4.3.120
(2347).
    1024 vnable] See *OED* (*a.* 2b): "Ineffectual."
    1027-33 WARBURTON (MS n. in JOHNSON, ed. 1765): "It is possible this pas-
sage may allude to the *obsequious* fondness of the people crouding to the presence of
K. James, on his entrance into England, and whose *untaught love* was rebuked by
Proclamations." See n. 76–81. MALONE (in Var. 1778, 1: < 320 >): Imitated by
William Barksted, *Mirrha the Mother of Adonis* (1607, sig. B7): "And like as when
some suddaine extasie, seisth the nature of a sicklie man, When hee's discernd to
swoune, straite by and by folke by [*read* to] his helpe confusedly haue ran, And
seeking with their art to fetch him backe: so many throng, that he the ayre doth
lacke." CAPELL (1780, 2:3:42): "This set simile, differing from Shakespeare's manner and that of the best dramatists, has the look of a thing engrafted; an after-birth
of the poet's upon some occasion or other during his play's run, and he pay'd his court

Come all to help him, and so stop the ayre
By which hee should reuiue: and euen so
The generall subiect to a wel-wisht King   1030
Quit their owne part, and in obsequious fondnesse
Crowd to his presence, where their vn-taught loue
Must needs appear offence: how now faire Maid.

Enter Isabella.

Isab. I am come to know your pleasure.   1035

1030 generall subiect] general subjects F4-THEO4; general, subject v1778-PEN2
(−CAM2, NLSN, ALEX, ARD2)
1031 part] path COL2, COL3, COL4
1033–5 *Verse lines ending* offence. . . . pleasure. v1793-COL3, DYCE2-HUD2, BUL,
ARD1
1034 SCENE XI. POPE, HAN1, WARB, JOHN   *Enter . . .*] *After* offence.
(1033) JOHN1+

---

by it well." WILSON (ed. 1922): "These lines, which have been generally taken as
a complimentary reference to King James's hatred of crowds, read like a later addition." LEVER (ed. 1965): "The continuity of thought and imagery rebuts Wilson's
view *(N.C.S.)* that [these lines] were additions tacked on for a special performance."
See n. 3.
1027 play] See *OED* (*v.* 1): "Be busily engaged; to act."
  swounds] See *OED* (*v.*): "To swoon, faint."
1029 should] Would. See n. 818.
1030 **The generall subiect**] JOHNSON (ed. 1765): "The *general subject* seems a
harsh expression, but *general subjects* has no sense at all; and *general* was in our
Authour's time a word for *people,* so that the *general* is the *people* or *multitude subject*
to a King. So in *Hamlet* [2.2.457 (1482)]." SCHMIDT (1875): *Subject,* "the people
under the dominion of a sovereign," as in 1624, 2362. Cf. *OED* (*sb.* 1b): "Collect-
[*ive*] *sing.* The subjects of a realm. . . . (Only Shaks.)," quoting *Ham.* 1.2.33 (212),
MM 1624, and *Per.* 2.1.52. FRANZ §358 explains *subiect* in 1624 as an adj. LEVER
(ed. 1965): "The common people."
  wel-wisht] *OED* (Well-wished *ppl. a.*): "Attended by good wishes," only
quotation.
1031 **Quit . . . part**] SCHMIDT (1875): *Quit,* "leave." *Part,* "particular business."
LEVER (ed. 1965): "Abandon their own functions; 'part' also as member of the body
(cf. [1025]), and, by analogy, the body politic." ["Part" could also mean "role," as
in 2327; cf. *play* 1027.]
  obsequious] SCHMIDT (1875): "Zealous, officious, devoted." ONIONS
(1911): "Dutiful, obedient" (*OED, a.* 1). LEISI (ed. 1964): "Eager to serve."
  fondnesse] SCHMIDT (1874): "Love." *OED* (3): "Affectionateness, tenderness," first use in this sense. CAMPBELL (ed. 1949): "Folly." LEVER (ed. 1965):
"Obsequious fondness: loyalty of an affectionate but foolish kind." See n. 313.
1032 **vn-taught**] SCHMIDT (1875): "Unmannerly." LEISI (ed. 1964): "This
always connotes 'ignorant', 'rude' " (*OED, ppl. a.* 1).

An. That you might know it, wold much better please me,
Then to demand what 'tis: your Brother cannot liue.
   Isab. Euen so: heauen keepe your Honor.
   Ang. Yet may he liue a while: and it may be
As long as you, or I: yet he must die.   1040
   Isab. Vnder your Sentence?
   Ang. Yea.
   Isab. When, I beseech you: that in his Reprieue
(Longer, or shorter) he may be so fitted
That his soule sicken not.   1045
   Ang. Ha? fie, these filthy vices: It were as good
To pardon him, that hath from nature stolne   (F5
A man already made, as to remit
Their sawcie sweetnes, that do coyne heauens Image

1037 demand] declare HAN1   your Brother] He HAN1
1038 so:] ~ ? ROWE3-v1821, SING, HAL, KTLY   your Honor.] you! HAN1
  Going. ROWE1-KIT1 (−CAP, CAM1, GLO, WH2, CAM2, ARD1, NLSN)
1039–40 *Lines ending* while; . . . I; . . . die. HAN1
1042 Yea] Yes v1785
1046 It were] 'twere POPE1-JOHN2, DYCE2, DYCE3, HUD2
1049 sweetnes] lewdness HAN1   heauens] God's PEN2

1036 **know it**] HART (ed. 1905): "Angelo gives the meaning of sensual gratification to Isabella's word pleasure, in his own thoughts." HARRISON (ed. 1948): "Angelo cynically sees a double meaning in *pleasure* and *know*—i.e., have carnal knowledge."
   1037 **Then to demand**] Than for you to ask.
   1040 **he must die**] TILLEY (M505) and WILSON (p. 10): "All men must die."
Cf. *2 Promos,* 5.4 (p. 365 below): "Death, is but death, and all in fyne shall dye";
Heywood, *2 Edward IV* (1600; ed. 1874, 1:176), "I am mortal and must die, When
my time comes; but that I thinks not yet"; *Ham.* 1.2.72 (252), "all that liues must
dye."
   1043 **Reprieue**] *OED* (*sb.* 1c): "The time during which one is reprieved," only
quotation in this sense.
   1044 **fitted**] SCHMIDT (1874): "To prepare," as in 1201, 2122.
   1045 **sicken**] Decline in spiritual health. Cf. *OED* (*v.* 1b *fig.*).
   1046 **Ha**] SCHMIDT (1874): Expressive of indignation (*OED, int.* 1), as in 1162.
See n. 927.
   It were] See n. 40.
   1048 **remit**] SCHMIDT (1875): "Pardon" (*OED, v.* 1).
   1049 **sawcie**] *OED* (*a.* 1 2b): "Wanton, lascivious," first use in this sense.
   sweetnes] MALONE (ed. 1790): Cf. 1058. STEEVENS (Var. 1793): *"Lickerish-
ness." OED* (8): "Addiction to sweet things; self-indulgence. *Obs. rare."*
   1049–50 **coyne . . . forbid**] MALONE (1783, p. 5): "We meet with nearly the
same words in *King Edward III"* (*Sh. Apoc.,* 2.1.257–8): "Comit high treason against
the King of heauen, To stamp his Image in forbidden mettel." "These lines are

In stamps that are forbid: 'tis all as easie,   1050
Falsely to take away a life true made,
As to put mettle in restrained meanes
To make a false one.

Isab. 'Tis set downe so in heauen, but not in earth.

Ang. Say you so: then I shall poze you quickly.   1055
Which had you rather, that the most iust Law

1050 easie] just HAN1
1052 mettle] Metal THEO, WARB-RANN (−CAP), COL1, WH1-KTLY, DEL4,
COL4-SIS (−IRV, CAM3), PEN2, EVNS   restrained] restained ROWE1   meanes]
mints STEEVENS (v1773) *conj.,* CAM3
1055 Say] And say POPE1-v1773 (−CAP); Ha! Say KTLY; Ay, say HUD2   so:]
∼ ? DAV, F4+

---

spoken by the countess of Salisbury, whose chastity (like Isabel's) was assailed by her
sovereign." WINNY (ed. 1959): "A complex passage, dominated by images of coun-
terfeiting. Its immediate sense is 'who beget illegitimate children', but much else is
implied. 'Heaven's image' is man, made in God's likeness" (Gen. 1:27). COLMAN
(1974, p. 188): Cf. *Cym.* 2.5.5–6 (1342–3).

1050 **stamps**] *OED* (*sb.*[3] 12b): "The design or combination of marks stamped by
authority on a piece of metal in the process of minting or coining into money."

easie] WARBURTON (ed. 1747): *"Easie* is here put for light or trifling" (*OED,*
a. 15). More likely *a.* 11, "Not difficult."

1051 **Falsely**] JOHNSON (ed. 1765): *"Falsely* is the same with *dishonestly, illegally,*
so *false* in the next lines is *illegal, illegitimate"* (*OED, a.* 13, "counterfeit").

1052 **mettle**] See n. 55.

in restrained meanes] THIRLBY (1747–53): "Forbidden" (*OED, v.* 5a).
JOHNSON (ed. 1765): "In forbidden moulds. I suspect *means* not to be the right
word, but I cannot find another." STEEVENS (Var. 1773): "I should suspect that the
author wrote,—*in restrained* mints, as the allusion is to *coining."* MALONE (in Var.
1778): "The sense is clear, and *means* may stand without alteration. . . . The thought
is simply, that murder is as easy as fornication, and it is as improper to pardon the
latter as the former." IDEM (1780, 1:97): *"Means,* I suppose, is here used for *medium*
or *object."* LEE (ed. 1907): "After forbidden methods." WILSON (ed. 1922): "The
whole context demands 'mints' and the word is palaeographically quite possible."
HARDING (ed. 1954): "For 'meanes' as a variant spelling of 'mints', see Kökeritz
[1953], . . . p. 215." LEVER (ed. 1965): "Instruments (*O.E.D.* 'mean' *sb.*[2] [10]).
. . . 'Means' implies both minting and procreation through the instrumentality of a
woman, thus answering to the two senses of 'mettle-metal'."

1054 JOHNSON (Var. 1773): "I would have it considered, whether the train of
the discourse does not rather require Isabel to say, *'Tis so set down in* earth, *but not
in* heaven." MALONE (ed. 1790): "What you have stated is undoubtedly the divine
law: murder and fornication are both forbid by the *canon of scripture;*—but on *earth*
the latter offence is considered as less heinous than the former."

1055 **poze**] JOHNSON (1755): "Puzzle. See *Pose* and *Appose."* LEVER (ed. 1965):
"Non-plus with a question (*O.E.D. v.*[2] 2)."

Now tooke your brothers life, and to redeeme him
Giue vp your body to such sweet vncleannesse
As she that he hath staind?
 Isab. Sir, beleeue this.   1060
I had rather giue my body, then my soule.
 Ang. I talke not of your soule: our compel'd sins
Stand more for number, then for accompt.
 Isab. How say you?
 Ang. Nay Ile not warrant that: for I can speake 1065
Against the thing I say: Answere to this,
I (now the voyce of the recorded Law)
Pronounce a sentence on your Brothers life,
Might there not be a charitie in sinne,
To saue this Brothers life?   1070
 Isab. Please you to doo't,
Ile take it as a perill to my soule,
It is no sinne at all, but charitie.
 Ang. Pleas'd you to doo't, at perill of your soule

1057 and] or DAV, ROWE1+
1063 for accompt] accompt ROWE3-THEO4, CAP, v1773, v1793-v1821, SING,
KTLY, DYCE2, DYCE3-HUD2, BUL, CAM3, PEN2; for compt JOHN
 1074 at] at the v1785

 1057 **and**] Error for *or*, corrected by DAVENANT (1673).
 1061 MALONE (ed. 1790): "She means, I think, *I had rather* die, *than forfeit my eternal happiness by the prostitution of my person.*" STEEVENS (Var. 1793): "She may mean—I had rather *give up my body to imprisonment, than my soul to perdition.*"
 1062-3 **our . . . accompt**] MALONE (ed. 1790): "Actions to which we are compelled, however *numerous*, are not *imputed* to us by heaven as crimes." HAL-LIWELL (ed. 1854): Cf. *1 Promos*, 3.4 (p. 323 below): "*Iustice* wyll say, thou dost no cryme commit: For in forst faultes is no intent of yll." TILLEY (S475): "Compelled sins are no sins." WHITAKER (1953, p. 207) cites Richard Hooker, *Of the Lawes of Ecclesiasticall Politie* (1594, 1.9.1): "What we do against our wills, or constrainedly, we are not properly said to do it." See n. 1117.
 1062 **compel'd**] WALKER (1854, p. 293): Accented on the first syllable.
 1063 **Stand . . . for**] See *OED* (*v.* 71f): "To be counted or considered as."
  accompt] See *OED* (Account *sb.* 1): "Counting, reckoning" (at the day of judgment).
 1067 **recorded**] *OED* (*ppl. a.*): "Put on record, preserved in writing." Cf. 786.
 1071 **Please you**] If it please you. See n. 771.
 1074-5 JOHNSON (ed. 1765): "*Angelo* replies, that if *Isabella* would *save him at the hazard of her soul, it would be not indeed no sin, but a sin to which the charity would be equivalent.*"

Were equall poize of sinne, and charitie.   1075
   Isab. That I do beg his life, if it be sinne
Heauen let me beare it: you granting of my suit,
If that be sin, Ile make it my Morne-praier,
To haue it added to the faults of mine,
And nothing of your answere.   1080
   Ang. Nay, but heare me,
Your sence pursues not mine: either you are ignorant,
Or seeme so crafty; and that's not good.
   Isab. Let be ignorant, and in nothing good,

1075 Were . . . charitie.] Were't . . . charity? HAN1; 'Twere . . . charity. SEYMOUR
conj., KTLY
  1077 Heauen‸] ~ , THEO, WARB-KNT1, COL, SING2, WH1, STAU, KTLY, KNT3
    of] *Om.* POPE1-JOHN2
  1078 make it] make't HAN1   Morne-praier] morning-pray'r HAN1, KTLY
  1083 crafty] Ff., COL, HAL, WH1, STAU, KTLY, ARD2; craftily DAV, ROWE1 *etc.*
    that's] that is COL, WH1, STAU, KTLY
  1084 Let] Let me F2+

  1075 **equall poize**] JOHNSON (1755): *Poize,* "Balance; equipoize; equilibrium"
(*OED, sb.* 5). HART (ed. 1905): Cf. *1 Promos,* 2.3 (p. 315 below): "herein, renowned
Lorde, Iustice with pitie payse: . . . in equal ballance waide."
  1077 **you granting of**] Supposing you grant. See ABBOTT §377, FRANZ §663.
  1080 STEEVENS (Var. 1773): *"And make no part of those which you shall be called
to answer for."* HALLIWELL (ed. 1854): "A harsh elliptical construction, meaning
apparently,—and nothing of those sins for which you have to answer." SCHMIDT
(1874): *Answer,* "account." See n. 493.
  1082 **Your . . . mine**] SCHMIDT (1875, p. 1027): "You do not understand my
meaning." EMPSON (1951, p. 276): "Her meaning does not follow his, and also her
desires do not start running when his do. . . . The immediate context very definitely
imposes 'interpretation' ('the sense you put on my words') as the chief meaning;
indeed to suppose it means 'sensuality' is a satire on Angelo; but by this time it is so
strong a dominant meaning that it arises easily." SCHANZER (1963, p. 91): "Angelo
is now thoroughly exasperated. He feels like the chess-player who finds his most
skilful and carefully calculated moves come to nothing, simply because his opponent
fails to understand their purpose and therefore does not reply in the expected manner.
Or is it possible that this girl is not really so slow-witted but is merely outmanœuvring
him by pretending not to understand his meaning?"
     either] ABBOTT (§503): " 'Either' may be a monosyllable" (see §466). See
also nn. 851, 1208. Or *you are* may be pronounced *you're,* as in 1147.
  1083 **crafty**] HALLIWELL (ed. 1854): "Davenant alters *crafty* to *craftily,* but this
seems merely a modernization, the adjective frequently being used for the adverb by
Elizabethan writers." THISELTON (1901, p. 21): Cf. *crafty sicke, 2H4* Ind. 37 (40).
LEISI (ed. 1964): "Probably adverb; most edd. emend to *craftily,* which is more in
keeping with the metre."
  1084–5 TILLEY (N276) and WILSON (p. 434): "I know nothing except that I

But graciously to know I am no better.   1085
  Ang. Thus wisdome wishes to appeare most bright,
When it doth taxe it selfe: As these blacke Masques
Proclaime an en-shield beauty ten times louder

1088 an] *Om.* KIT1   en-shield] enshell'd mTBY1 *and* TYRWHITT *conj. in*
v1773, KTLY, RID; in-shell'd TYRWHITT *conj. in* v1773, COLNE, COL2, COL3, COL4;
enshielded KIT1, ALEX; enciel'd ARD2

---

know not" (Socrates).
    1084 Let be] F2 corrects to *Let me be,* as it also corrects *let me* to *let me be* in *AYL*
4.1.1 (1917).
    1085 graciously] HUNTER (ed. 1873): "Through divine grace." So *OED (adv.*
3).
    1086-7 Thus . . . selfe] NEWCOMER (1929, p. 115): Cf. *Ado* 2.3.48-9 (880-1).
    1087 taxe] SCHMIDT (1875): "Reproach" (*OED, v.* 6).
    these blacke Masques] TYRWHITT (in Var. 1773, 10:Ll4ᵛ): "These *Masks*
must mean, I think the *Masks of the audience;* however improperly a compliment to
them is put into the mouth of Angelo. As Shakespeare would hardly have been guilty
of such an *indecorum* to flatter a common audience, I think this passage affords ground
for supposing that the play was written to be acted at court. Some strokes of particular
flattery to the king have been pointed out in the *Observations and Conjectures printed
at Oxford,* 1766 [see n. 76-81]; and there are several other general reflections, in the
Character of the duke especially, which seem calculated for the royal ear." STEEVENS
(Var. 1778): "*Davenant* reads—*as a black mask;* but I am afraid Mr. Tyrwhitt is too
well supported in his first supposition, by a passage [in *Rom.* 1.1.236-7 (238-9)]."
RITSON (1783, p. 20): "The idea in Angelos speech might be easyly communicated
by the mask which Isabella held in her hand. And *these black masks* will, in that case,
onely be *such masks as these,* or *this kind of masks.*" TYRWHITT (in Var. 1785): "I do
not think so well of the conjecture in the latter part of this note as I did some years
ago; and therefore I should wish to withdraw it. . . . My notion at present is, that the
phrase *these black masks* signifies nothing more than *black masks;* according to an old
idiom of our language, by which the demonstrative pronoun is put for the prepositive
article." See *OED* (These *dem. a.* 1c). JACKSON (1819, p. 42): "Isabella is in her
probation, and habited in the *sables* of the sisterhood . . . covered with a black veil."
So PORTER & CLARKE (ed. 1909). WILSON (ed. 1922, pp. 101-2): "On Twelfth
Night (i.e. Jan. 5), 1605, Ben Jonson's *Masque of Blackness* was given at Court by
Queen Anne and eleven of her maids of honour, all wearing black masks. . . . The
masquers were placed in a great concave shell. . . . This vision of 'an enshelled beauty'
. . . Jonson ascribes to 'Master Inigo Jones's design and act'." CHAMBERS (1924, p.
110): "As it happens, they did not wear masks." LAWRENCE (1928, p. 140): "All
this is pure fallacy. The most remarkable thing about this masque was that the ladies
in it wore no masks." CRAIG (ed. 1951): "A metaphor to signify pretense of ignorance or modesty; *these* is probably generic." LEVER (ed. 1965): " 'These' might
merely indicate something in vogue. . . . 'Masks' here are probably veils: cf. *Gent.*
IV. iv. 160 [1972]" [and *OED,* Mask *sb.*³ 1b].
    1088 en-shield] HANMER (ed. 1743, 6, glossary): "Shielded, protected." So
JOHNSON (1755). STEEVENS (Var. 1773): *"A beauty covered as with a shield."* TYR-
WHITT (ibid. 10:Ll4ᵛ): "This should be written *en-shell'd* or *in-shell'd* as it is in [*Cor.*

Then beauty could displaied: But marke me,
To be receiued plaine, Ile speake more grosse: 1090
Your Brother is to dye.
    Isab. So.
    Ang. And his offence is so, as it appeares,
Accountant to the Law, vpon that paine.
    Isab. True.   1095
    Ang. Admit no other way to saue his life
(As I subscribe not that, nor any other,
But in the losse of question) that you, his Sister,

1089 me] me well HAN1; you me mTBY3 *conj.,* HUD2

1093 appeares,] ~ ‸ DAV, POPE1-v1813, SING, KNT, COL, HAL, WH1, KTLY, DEL4, ARD1, KIT1

1098 losse] toss JOHN1 *conj.,* BUL; force COLNE, COL2, COL3, COL4; loose ANON. *conj. in* SINGER (1853), KIT1

4.6.45 (2948)]." CAPELL (1779, 1:glossary, 22): "For *enshielded,* immask'd, guarded, cover'd as with a Shield." *OED (a.):* "?Shielded, concealed," only quotation.

1090 **receiued**] SCHMIDT (1875): "To conceive, to understand," as in *TN* 3.1.131 (1333). So *OED (v. 7).*

   grosse] CLARKE (1879, p. 557): " 'Openly', 'plainly' " (adj. as adv., cf. *OED, a.* 3). See n. 247.

1094 **Accountant**] THIRLBY (1723–33): "Debtor." JOHNSON (1755): "Accountable to." SCHMIDT (1874): "Liable to penalty." *OED (a.):* "Accountable, responsible."

   paine] JOHNSON (ed. 1765): *"Penalty, punishment" (OED, sb.*[1] *1).*

1096 **Admit**] SCHMIDT (1874): "Grant," "suppose" (*OED, v.* 2d). Cf. *1 Promos,* 3.6 (p. 326 below): "Well, I admit it so, onelie to argue in your case."

1097 **subscribe**] STEEVENS (Var. 1778): *"Agree to."* SCHMIDT (1875): "To admit of, to grant, to acknowledge." *OED (v.* 4): "Give one's assent or adhesion to."

1098 **in the losse of question**] THIRLBY (1723–33): "For want of discourse." STEEVENS (Var. 1773): *"In idle supposition,* or *conversation that tends to nothing."* HARNESS (ed. 1825): "For the sake of argument." HORNE (ed. 1840, 1:210): "Loss of the argument, point, or object at issue." BRAE (1852, p. 217): "The *casus quaestionis* of the logicians. . . . the refutation of the arguments urged by Isabella." SINGER (1853, *Text,* p. 11): "In my corrected copy of the second folio I find *losse* altered to *loose,* and the meaning would then be 'in the *looseness of conversation'.*" WHITE (ed. 1857): " 'The very waste of words', 'supposing an unsupposable case'." HUNTER (ed. 1873): "Without disowning the right of calling him to answer for his crime." SCHMIDT (1874, p. 671): "As no better arguments present themselves to my mind, to make the point clear." *OED* (Loss *sb.*[1] 7): "Lack, default, want [first use in this sense]. *In the loss of question:* provided there is no dispute." WILSON (ed. 1922): "Singer's conjecture seems to remove all difficulties." *"Question,* discussion, debate." BALD (ed. 1956): "Except that discussion would flag." LEISI (ed. 1964): " 'For want of topic or argument'." LEVER (ed. 1965): " 'Provided nothing more can be said for the defence'." See p. 284.

Finding your selfe desir'd of such a person,
Whose creadit with the Iudge, or owne great place,   1100
Could fetch your Brother from the Manacles
Of the all-building-Law: and that there were
No earthly meane to saue him, but that either
You must lay downe the treasures of your body,
To this supposed, or else to let him suffer: 1105
What would you doe?
    Isab. As much for my poore Brother, as my selfe;
That is: were I vnder the tearmes of death,

1102 all-building-Law] all-holding Law ROWE1-THEO4, WH1; all-binding law
mTBY1 *and* mTHEO *conj.*, JOHN1-v1821, SING, KNT, COL3, STAU, DYCE2, DYCE3-
HUD2, CAM3+; all-bridling law BUL
    1105 to] *Om.* HAN1, JOHN1-v1813 (−MAL), HUD2

    1099 of] SCHMIDT (1875, p. 795): "By" (*OED, prep.* 15).
    1102 **all-building-Law**] JOHNSON (ed. 1765): "Mr. *Theobald* has *binding* in one
of his copies." Theobald never printed *all-binding,* but it is written in the Theobald-
Johnson copy of F2 at the Folger Library. Thirlby wrote it in his copies of the eds.
of Pope, Theobald, and Warburton, the last of which was also used by Johnson.
Thirlby was prob. the first to propose it, since Theobald does not mention it in his
ed. (1733). COLLIER (ed. 1842): "Shakespeare seems to use 'all-building' in reference to the constructive and constantly repairing power of the law." KEIGHTLEY
(1853, p. 362): "The law that builds, maintains, and repairs the whole social edifice."
HALLIWELL (ed. 1854): "*Building* is used in any signification implying increase or
active growth. The all-building law is, therefore, the ever active, the ever growing
law, a law which is never completed or built, but which is always throwing out new
efforts, which is ever building." SCHMIDT (1874): "Being the ground and foundation
of all." WILSON (ed. 1922): " 'All-building' can hardly be right after 'manacles'."
PRAZ (1937, p. 111): "I do not see that anybody has suggested 'all-bridling'."
[Bullen printed it in his text in 1904, and JONES (1907, p. 505) compared *bits and
curbes* in 3.10.] SISSON (1956, 1:82): "Read *all-binding,* as proposed by Theobald and
now generally accepted by modern editors. The pattern of writing makes the misprint
credible, and emendation is necessary. *ld* and *d* are confusable in current writing, and
ui and *in* are each three minims." [Since *bridling* could equally well be misread as
building, either emendation is possible.] LEVER (ed. 1965): "The same reading of
'build' where 'bind' is evidently meant occurs in Webster's *Duchess of Malfi,* I. i. 562:
'How can the Church build faster?' " See BROWN (1964), p. 37 n.
    1103 **meane**] See *OED* (*sb.* 2 10a): "Method, or course of action."
    1105 **supposed**] SCHMIDT (1875): "To lay down or state as a proposition
. . . for the sake of argument." *OED* (*ppl. a.* 1): Only absolute use. LEVER (ed. 1965):
"Hypothetical person."
    1108–12 MUIR (1954, *London Mag.,* p. 106): "At the beginning of this quotation
Death is a beadle whipping a harlot; Isabella thinks of stripping herself for punishment, but the image takes on a sexual meaning." WINNY (ed. 1959): "The imagery
suggests the woman coming to life beneath the nun's habit."
    1108 **tearmes**] ONIONS (1911): "State, condition, position, circumstances"
(*OED, sb.* 10). LEVER (ed. 1965): "*Under the terms*] under sentence."

Th'impression of keene whips, I'ld weare as Rubies,
And strip my selfe to death, as to a bed, 1110
That longing haue bin sicke for, ere I'ld yeeld
My body vp to shame.
Ang. Then must your brother die. (F5va)
Isa. And 'twer the cheaper way:
Better it were a brother dide at once, 1115
Then that a sister, by redeeming him
Should die for euer.
Ang. Were not you then as cruell as the Sentence,
That you haue slander'd so?
Isa. Ignomie in ransome, and free pardon 1120

1111 longing haue] longing I've ROWE1-JOHN2, SING2, WH1, COL3, KNT3, DYCE3, COL4; longing I have CAP-SING1, COL1; longing had KNT1, KNT2; long I have HUD1, SIS, PEN2; long I had LETTSOM *conj. in* DYCE2, DYCE2, HUD2; longings have THOMPSON *conj. in* CAM3, CAM3, KIT1   sicke] seek JOHN
1112–14 *Lines ending* die. . . . way: v1793-KNT2, HAL-DYCE1, STAU-KTLY, KNT3, DEL4, WH2-CAM2, ARD1-CAM3, ALEX, PEL1+; must . . . die. . . . way. COL, WH1; must . . . way: DYCE2, DYCE3, HUD2, BUL, KIT1, SIS
1120 Ignomie in] Ignominy in F2-ROWE3, JOHN, v1773, v1778, RANN, RLTR, ALEX; An ignominious POPE, THEO, HAN1, CAP; As ignominious WARB; No; ignomy in KTLY

1111 **longing haue**] KNIGHT (ed. 1840): *"Longing* is clearly a *substantive,—*desire." DYCE (ed. 1857): "In this line, by an ellipsis not unfrequent with our old writers, *'have'* is equivalent to *'I have'."* CLARK & GLOVER (ed. 1863, 1:393): "The second person singular of the governing pronoun is frequently omitted by Shakespeare in familiar questions, but, as to the first and third persons, his usage rarely differs from the modern. If the text be genuine, we have an instance in this play of the omission of the third person singular [426: see n.], 'Has censured him'." LEVER (ed. 1965): "Cf. [277] and other instances of sing. subject with pl. verb."
1113 WILSON (ed. 1922): "F. begins a new page with this line. The catch-word of the previous page is *'Ang. That'.*" Compositor D prob. set this catchword, the only wrong one in this text. Compositor B set the correct *Then* in 1113. See p. 297.
1114 **'twer**] See n. 40.
cheaper way] *OED* (*a.* 3): "Costing little labour, trouble, effort." LEVER (ed. 1965): "This is not Isabella's meaning," which is " 'better bargain' " (*OED, a.* 2).
1115 **at once**] T. WHITE (1793, fol. 17): " 'Without any more ado, or . . . with a stroke'." MAXWELL (1954, p. 464): See *OED* (*adv. phr.* 1), "At one stroke, . . . once for all." HULME (1962, p. 268): " 'At one time', suffering death once only."
1117 **die for euer**] MAXWELL (1966, pp. 254–5): "Within the ethic of the play, Isabella would have committed mortal sin in yielding to Angelo. . . . Any competent Elizabethan casuist would have made short work of the notion that Isabella's fornication would have been 'compelled' in any defensible sense." IDEM (1974, p. 214): "The contrast with *Promos and Cassandra* is worth emphasizing here." See n. 1062–3.
1120 **Ignomie**] REED (in Var. 1793): "So the word *ignominy* was formerly written," as in *Tro.* 5.10.33 (3570), *ignomy.* See *OED.*

Are of two houses: lawfull mercie,
Is nothing kin to fowle redemption.
    Ang. You seem'd of late to make the Law a tirant,
And rather prou'd the sliding of your brother
A merriment, then a vice.   1125
    Isa. Oh pardon me my Lord, it oft fals out
To haue, what we would haue,
We speake not what vve meane;
I something do excuse the thing I hate,
For his aduantage that I dearely loue.   1130
    Ang. We are all fraile.
    Isa. Else let my brother die,
If not a fedarie but onely he

1121–2 *Lines ending* is . . . redemption. COT (p. 193), v1793–v1821, SING, COL,
DYCE, WH1, STAU, KTLY, HUD2, PEN2
    1121 mercie] mercy sure POPE1–v1773
    1122 kin] akin mTBY3 *conj.,* v1793–v1821, SING, COL, DYCE, WH1, STAU, KTLY,
HUD2
    1125–8 *Lines ending* me, . . . to have . . . mean: HAN1
    1126 oft] very oft HAN1
    1127–8. *One line* ROWE3, POPE, THEO, WARB+
    1127 To haue] T' have DYCE2, DYCE3   we would] we'd v1793–SING1,
DYCE2, DYCE3
    1133 fedarie] feodary F2–COL1, SING2–COL4 (−DYCE, DEL4), WH2, CAM2, SIS,
ARD2; foedary MASON (1785) *conj.,* HAL, EV1

1121 **of two houses**] THIRLBY (1723–33): "Not kin." SCHMIDT (1874): *House,*
"family" (*OED, sb.* [1] 6). HUNTER (1964, p. 172): "Isabella is using a social distinction
to mirror the moral distinction: 'you may, if you wish give things the same name, but
that is not to give them a real relationship'. We may also compare *Edward III* [*Sh.
Apoc.*], II. i. [262–3]."
    1122 **nothing**] SCHMIDT (1875): "Not at all" (*OED, adv.* 2).
    1124 **prou'd**] SCHMIDT (1875): "To show to be" (*OED, v.* 5b), as in 1372,
1891. LEISI (ed. 1964): " 'Argued' hence 'represented as', cf. [1518]."
    sliding] HART (ed. 1905): "Backsliding. See 'slipp'd' [814]." ONIONS
(1911): "Lapse, moral slip" (cf. *OED, v.* 9).
    1125 **merriment**] SCHMIDT (1875): "Diversion, amusement" (*OED,* 1). BALD
(ed. 1956): "Light matter."
    1127–8 LEVER (ed. 1965): "The exceptionally long line (divided into two in F)
may be due to a sophistication of the idiomatic contractions 'T' have', 'we'd'."
    1127 **would**] Wish to. See n. 17.
    1129 **something**] See n. 70.
    1131 NOBLE (1935, p. 225): Cf. Ecclus. 8:5, "but remember that wee are fraile
euery one" (Bishops' Bible, 1585). TILLEY (F363) and WILSON (p. 268): "Flesh is
frail." Cf. Matt. 26:41; *H8* 5.3.10–12 (3058–60); *1H4* 3.3.188–9 (2173–4); *2H6*
3.3.31 (2165); *1 Promos,* 2.5 (p. 317 below), "*Cassandras* flesh is as her brothers,
frayle." See n. 1406.
    1133–4 MALONE (ed. 1790, 10:564): "If he has not one associate in his crime,

Owe, and succeed thy weaknesse.
Ang. Nay, women are fraile too.   1135
Isa. I, as the glasses where they view themselues,

1134–5 *One line* v1793-STAU, KTLY-HUD2, IRV, BUL, SIS, ARD2
1134 thy] by ROWE1-JOHN2, v1773-SING1; to, CAP; this MALONE *conj.,* HARN,
COL, SING2, KTLY, DYCE2, DYCE3, HUD2, BUL, NLSN

---

if no other person own and follow the same criminal courses which you are now
pursuing, let my brother suffer death. I think it, however, extremely probable that
something is omitted. . . . It may be conjectured that the compositor's eye glanced
from the word *succeed* to *weakness* in a subsequent hemistich." KNIGHT (ed. 1840):
"When Angelo says, 'We are all frail', he makes a confession of his own frailty, and
of that particular frailty of which, from the tenor of what has preceded, Isabella begins
to suspect him. She answers, otherwise [*OED,* Else *adv.* 4] let my brother die, if we
be not all frail—if . . . only *he* be found to own and succeed *thy* weakness, which thou
hast confessed by implication." HART (ed. 1905): "Malone implies in the words 'you
are now pursuing'—they can mean nothing else—that Isabella is fully awake to
Angelo's baseness. She is not to be assumed to be so till [1162]. She would not call
him 'gentle my lord' at [1151] were it so. 'Thy weakness' refers to the frailty that
Angelo accuses all men of having. Isabella refers to it then as man's characteristic, and
Angelo, perceiving that, says, 'but women are just as bad'. 'Thy weakness' means the
weakness of thy sex." DURHAM (ed. 1926): "If only he possesses and inherits the
weakness of mankind." EVANS (ed. 1974): "This frailty you speak of (but with an
unintended second meaning)."
    1133 **fedarie**] WARBURTON (in THEOBALD, ed. 1733): "A *Feodary* was One,
that, in the Times of Vassalage, held Lands of the chief Lord, under the Tenure of
paying Rent and Service. . . . And the comparing Mankind, (who, according to some
Divines, lye under the Weight of Original Sin,) to a *Feodary,* who owes *Suit* and *Service*
to his Lord, is, I think, one of the most beautiful Allusions imaginable." KENRICK
(1765, p. 25): "An *accomplice,* a *confederate,* a *companion equally guilty,"* as in *Cym.*
3.2.21 (1489). HALLIWELL (ed. 1854): In *Cym.* it is spelt *Fœdarie* in F1. "It is, in
all probability, a Latinism (from *fœdus*), and is synonymous with *federary* in the
Winter's Tale, an accomplice, a confederate. The old law term *feodary* . . . is a different
word, and is altogether unsuited to the context of the present passage." *OED* (Fedarie): "A confederate, accomplice," first quotation. LEVER (ed. 1965): "Combines
two meanings: (i) confederate, accomplice . . . ; (ii) feudatory, i.e. hereditary tenant."
This is wrong, as Kenrick, Halliwell, and *OED* make clear.
    1134 **Owe**] THIRLBY (1723-33): "Own." JOHNSON (ed. 1765): "To *own,* to
hold, to have possession" (*OED, v.* 1).
    succeed] SCHMIDT (1875): "Inherit." So *OED* (*v.* 3).
    thy] MALONE (ed. 1790): "The emendation [*by*] was made by Mr. Rowe. I
am by no means satisfied with it. *Thy* is much more likely to have been printed by
mistake for *this,* than the word which has been substituted." Malone may well be
right, since Isabel always uses the respectful *you* and *your* to Angelo until 1164: see
n.
    1136-7 TILLEY (W646) and WILSON (pp. 907-8): "A woman and a glass are
ever in danger." WINNY (ed. 1959): "Which are shattered as easily as they reflect
images."

Which are as easie broke as they make formes:
Women? Helpe heauen; men their creation marre
In profiting by them: Nay, call vs ten times fraile,
For we are soft, as our complexions are,   1140
And credulous to false prints.
    Ang. I thinke it well:
And from this testimonie of your owne sex
(Since I suppose we are made to be no stronger
Then faults may shake our frames) let me be bold;   1145
I do arrest your words. Be that you are,

1140 soft, as] as soft as v1773-RANN

1137 **formes**] SCHMIDT (1874): "Image" (*OED, sb.* 2). See n. 877.
1138 **Women**] KÖNIG (1888, p. 78): The trochee sharpens the exclamation.
    Helpe heauen] Heaven help them: see *OED* (Help *v.* 1c).
1138-9 **men . . . them**] THIRLBY (1733–47): "Genesis." JOHNSON (ed. 1765):
"In imitating them, in taking them for examples." KENRICK (1765, p. 26): "Taking
advantage of female weakness." CAPELL (1780, 2:3:43): "Learning from them things
that are hurtful." LUCIUS (1786, p. 359): "Men debase their nature by taking advantage of such pitiful weak creatures." HARNESS (ed. 1825): "The nature of men suffers
deterioration from its being generated by the means of woman." SCHMIDT (1874):
Creation, "the thing created . . . (viz women)." HARDING (ed. 1954): "When men
take advantage of woman's frailty, they are marring the sex which brought them into
being." LEVER (ed. 1965): "Men mar their creation in God's likeness by taking
advantage of women" (*OED*, Profit *v.* 4b).
1139 **ten times**] SCHMIDT (1875, p. 1230): "Simply used by way of multiplication" ("many times over," as often in Sh.). Cf. *OED* (Ten *a.* 1c).
1140 **complexions**] SCHMIDT (1874): "External appearance, particularly when
expressive of some natural disposition," as in 1227, 1404. LEISI (ed. 1964): " 'Combination of qualities or "humours" in the human body' (orig. a technical term of
mediaeval medicine)" (*OED, sb.* 1). See n. 1227.
1141 WARBURTON (ed. 1747): "Take any impression." MALONE (ed. 1790): So
in *TN* 2.2.30-3 (685-8). DELIUS (ed. 1860): Two ideas are here blended: we
believe too readily false assurances, and we are susceptible, yielding to false impressions. LEVER (ed. 1965): " 'Prints' for any impress, especially the stamp on a coin,
is fig. for conception, as in [1049-50], and is thus a variant on the recurrent coin
image."
1143 **of**] About. See n. 734.
1144 **we**] All men and women, as in 1131.
1145 **Then**] ABBOTT (§ 390): "*Than* (that)." LEISI (ed. 1964): Cf. 2399.
    frames] ONIONS (1911): "The human body" (*OED, sb.* 9), as in *Son.* 59.
1146 **arrest your words**] SCHMIDT (1874): "Take you at your word." *OED*
(*v.* 12): "Take as security." HART (ed. 1905): Cf. *LLL* 2.1.160 (656) and Sidney's
Arcadia (1590, 1.15; ed. Feuillerat, 1:99). DURHAM (ed. 1926): "Seize upon."
    that] SCHMIDT (1875, p. 1196): "What, that which" (*OED, dem. pron.* 7,
ABBOTT §244, FRANZ §348). Cf. *TN* 5.1.152 (2309) and n. 2229.

That is a woman; if you be more, you'r none.
If you be one (as you are well exprest
By all externall warrants) shew it now,
By putting on the destin'd Liuerie.   1150
   Isa. I haue no tongue but one; gentle my Lord,
Let me entreate you speake the former language.
   Ang. Plainlie conceiue I loue you.
   Isa. My brother did loue *Iuliet*,
And you tell me that he shall die for't.   1155
   Ang. He shall not *Isabell* if you giue me loue.
   Isa. I know your vertue hath a licence in't,
Which seemes a little fouler then it is,
To plucke on others.

1147 you be] you're POPE1-JOHN2
1152 former] formal WARB
1154-5 *Lines ending* me, . . . for it. v1793-COL3, KTLY-HUD2, IRV, BUL, ARD1, KIT1, SIS
1155 for't] for it DAV, ROWE3-v1821, SING, KNT, STAU-KTLY, WH2, CAM2, NLSN

1147 **if . . . none**] THIRLBY (1723-33) Cf. 2414. THEOBALD (MS n. in F2): Cf. *Mac.* 1.7.47 (525). WINNY (ed. 1959): "If you haven't the nature you have ascribed to woman, you are no woman at all."

1148 **exprest**] BALD (ed. 1956): "Shown to be." LEVER (ed. 1965): "Revealed, manifested" (*OED, v.* 7).

1149 **warrants**] LEVER (ed. 1965): "Tokens" (*OED, sb.* [1] 7b).

1150 **destin'd Liuerie**] SCHMIDT (1874): *Livery,* "any particular dress or garb" (*OED, sb.* 2). PARROTT (ed. 1938): "I.e., frailty." CAMPBELL (ed. 1949): "Of submission to man." BALD (ed. 1956): "Behavior which properly belongs to you." JENKINS (in LEVER, ed. 1965): "The uniform of her kind, the frailty which is the natural destiny of women." See n. 1310.

1151 **I . . . one**] WINNY (ed. 1959): Cf. 1187-8.

1156 *Isabell*] See n. 818.

1157-9 HALLIWELL (ed. 1854): Cf. *1 Promos,* 3.2 (p. 321 below): "Renowned Lorde, you vse this speach (I hope) your thrall to trye."

1157 **licence**] WARBURTON (ed. 1747): "Alluding to the licences given by Ministers to their Spies, to go into all suspected companies and join in the language of Malecontents." LUCIUS (1786, p. 359): "I suspect this interpretation is more ingenious than just. The obvious meaning is, 'I know your virtue assumes an air of licentiousness which is not natural to you, on purpose to try me'." DELIUS (ed. 1860): Your worth has the privilege that it can make itself somewhat more ugly or sullied than it is. SCHMIDT (1874): "Authorization, privilege." ONIONS (1911): "Leave, permission" (*OED, sb.* 1). WILSON (ed. 1922): "Liberty of action."

1159 DELIUS (ed. 1860): To draw others to confession. LEE (ed. 1907): "In order to test other people, to draw them into damaging admissions." DURHAM (ed. 1926): "Lead on, mislead." PARROTT (ed. 1938): "Stir up, incite." BALD (ed. 1956): "Lure." LEISI (ed. 1964): "'Drag on' (OED 2), hence 'seduce'."

Ang. Beleeue me on mine Honor,   1160
My words expresse my purpose.
    Isa. Ha? Little honor, to be much beleeu'd,
And most pernitious purpose: Seeming, seeming.
I will proclaime thee *Angelo*, looke for't.
Signe me a present pardon for my brother,   1165
Or with an out-stretcht throate Ile tell the world aloud
What man thou art.
    Ang. Who will beleeue thee *Isabell*?
My vnsoild name, th'austeerenesse of my life,
My vouch against you, and my place i'th State,   1170
Will so your accusation ouer-weigh,
That you shall stifle in your owne report,

1166–8 *Lines ending* World . . . art. . . . *Isabel?* ROWE3-MAL; world . . . Isabel?
v1793-KNT1, COL, SING2, DYCE1, KTLY-DYCE3, BUL, PEN2; aloud, . . . Isabel?
KNT2, HAL, WH, STAU-GLO, IRV, CAM2, ARD1-ARD2, EVNS
  1166 aloud] *Om.* DYCE2 *conj.,* HUD2, PEN2
  1168 *Isabell*] *Om.* COL4
  1170 My] May mTBY3 *conj.,* COL3

  1162 **Ha**] See nn. 927, 1046.
  1163 **Seeming**] JOHNSON (ed. 1765): "Hypocrisy; counterfeit virtue." LEVER
(ed. 1965): "False appearance personified, as in *Ado* IV. i. [57 (1713)], and in the
allegorical figure *Faux-semblant.*" Cf. 346, 1017, 1158, 1443, 1528.
  1164 **proclaime**] *OED* (*v.* 2b): "Denounce."
    thee] BYRNE (1936, pp. 95–6): "Isabella moves to *thee* in anger and scorn
towards Angelo."
    looke for't] Expect it (*OED, v.* 15).
  1165 **present**] SCHMIDT (1875): "Instant, immediate" (*OED, a.* 9).
  1166 **out-stretcht**] SCHMIDT (1875): "To strain to the utmost" (*OED, v.* 3).
OED (*ppl. a.* 2): "Stretched in area or compass," only use in this sense. LEVER (ed.
1965): "Opened wide (*O.E.D.* 'stretch', *v.* 21b)."
    aloud] LEVER (ed. 1965): "The word is hypermetrical; consequently the line
has been much doctored. Isabella is suiting her voice to her words, and needs an extra
long line for the purpose."
  1167 **What**] ABBOTT (§86): " 'What kind of '." See n. 506.
  1168 *Isabell*] COLLIER (ed. 1875): "Quite needless, and interpolated by the old
actor, or printer, as the measure establishes." KÖKERITZ (1953, p. 286): "Disyllabic." See n. 818.
  1170–3 **My . . . calumnie**] THIRLBY (1733–47): Cf. 2297–9.
  1170 **vouch**] WARBURTON (ed. 1747): "The testimony one man bears for another . . . his *denial.*" ROBERTS (in Var. 1821): "*Assertion.*" *OED* (*sb.* 2): "An
assertion, allegation, or declaration; a formal statement or attestation," first quotation.
See n. 2519.
  1172–3 **That . . . calumnie**] WARBURTON (ed. 1747): "Metaphor taken from
a lamp or candle going out." HORNE (ed. 1840, 1:210): "Shakspere has most

And smell of calumnie. I haue begun,
And now I giue my sensuall race, the reine,
Fit thy consent to my sharpe appetite,   1175
Lay by all nicetie, and prolixious blushes
That banish what they sue for: Redeeme thy brother,
By yeelding vp thy bodie to my will,
Or else he must not onelie die the death,   (F5vb)

1177 Redeeme] save POPE, HAN1

---

egregiously suffered from the love of the literal in his commentators. . . . The word *smell* is, however, used here in a sense common with Shakspere, as though he had said *smacks* of *calumny*" (*OED*, Smell *v.* 9b). WINNY (ed. 1959): "You will choke yourself with seeming falsehood." LEVER (ed. 1965): "A play on 'report' as (i) narration, (ii) reputation, as in [965]."

1174 HEATH (1765, p. 85): "And since now I give my senses the rein in the race they are now actually running." HALLIWELL (ed. 1854): *"Race,* disposition," as in *Tmp.* 1.2.358 (499). HART (ed. 1905): "But the word 'rein' rather implies the meaning 'running, course'." *OED* (*sb.*[2] 7) and ONIONS (1911): "Natural or inherited disposition," sense only in Sh. LEISI (ed. 1964): " 'Run', 'course' . . . , but 'kind', 'nature' . . . is also possible."

1176 **Lay by**] SCHMIDT (1874): "Put off" (*OED, v.*[1] 48a, 50a).

nicetie] THIRLBY (1723–33): "Coyness." *OED* (3): "Reserve, shyness, coyness."

prolixious] THIRLBY (1747–53): "Dilatory." JOHNSON (1755): "Dilatory; tedious. A word of *Shakespeare's* coining." STEEVENS (Var. 1778): Cf. *Nashes Lenten Stuffe* (1599, 3:203), *Haue with You to Saffron-walden* (1596, 3:5), and Drayton, *Moyses his Miracles* (1604, 475). MALONE (ed. 1790): "That maiden modesty, which is *slow* in yielding to the wishes of a lover." STEEVENS (Var. 1793): *"Prolixious blushes* mean what Milton has elegantly called '—sweet reluctant [amorous] *delay' "* (*P.L.* 4:311). DELIUS (ed. 1860): Lengthy, superfluous. SYMONS (in IRVING & MARSHALL, ed. 1889): "The word is here evidently used, by a certain license of language, for 'tiresomely prudish'." *OED* (*a.* 2): "Long in extent or duration." LEVER (ed. 1965): "Time-wasting."

1177 **banish . . . for**] SCHANZER (1963, pp. 87–8): "Angelo can either mean that Isabel's blushes at his infamous proposal, while suing for a change of heart in him, are banishing all chance of this (since they make her seem all the more desirable); or he can mean that Isabel's 'nicety and prolixious blushes' are a mere pose, that she is actually suing for what she pretends to banish, his embraces." LEVER (ed. 1965): " 'Drive away the compunction for which they plead'."

1178 **will**] *OED* (*sb.*[1] 2): "Carnal desire or appetite."

1179 **die the death**] JOHNSON (ed. 1765): "This seems to be a solemn phrase for death inflicted by law." STEEVENS (Var. 1773): "It is a phrase taken from scripture." TYRWHITT (in Var. 1778): "The phrase is *a good phrase,* as Shallow says, but I do not conceive it to be either of *legal* or *scriptural* origin. Chaucer uses it frequently." [Chaucer uses *the death,* but never *die the death.*] HART (ed. 1905): It is in Bale, *God's Promises,* 1538 (Hazlitt's Dodsley, 1:290), and *Ferrex and Porrex* [*Gorboduc*], 1565, 4.2. See WORDSWORTH (1864, pp. 10–11) and *OED* (*v.*[1] 2c),

But thy vnkindnesse shall his death draw out   1180
To lingring sufferance: Answer me to morrow,
Or by the affection that now guides me most,
Ile proue a Tirant to him. As for you,
Say what you can; my false, ore-weighs your true.   *Exit*
    Isa. To whom should I complaine? Did I tell this,   1185
Who would beleeue me? O perilous mouthes
That beare in them, one and the selfesame tongue,
Either of condemnation, or approofe,
Bidding the Law make curtsie to their will,
Hooking both right and wrong to th'appetite,   1190
To follow as it drawes. Ile to my brother,
Though he hath falne by prompture of the blood,
Yet hath he in him such a minde of Honor,

1185 should] shall DAV, v1803-SING1
1186 perilous] most perilous THEO, WARB, JOHN, v1773; these perilous SEY-
MOUR *conj.*, KTLY

"Suffer death, be put to death," first cited from Coverdale, 1535. The Geneva Bible
has it in Exod. 21:12–17, Lev. 20 passim, Num. 35:16–21, but A.V. keeps it, in this
absolute sense, only in Matt. 15:4, Mark 7:10, and Ecclus. 14:17.
    1180 **vnkindnesse**] LEVER (ed. 1965): " 'Unnatural behaviour': whether to-
wards Claudio or Angelo himself" (*OED,* 1). See n. 1461.
    1181 **sufferance**] SCHMIDT (1875): "Pain, torment." *OED* (4): "Suffering."
    Answer] SCHMIDT (1875, p. 1451): "Satisfy." See *OED* (*v.* 19): "Reply
favourably to."
    to morrow] LEVER (ed. 1965, pp. xvi, 64): "Angelo's unnecessary 'to-mor-
row' is easily explained as the slip of a writer too closely following his sources."
Contrast 1317, "This night's the time."
    1182 **affection**] See n. 461.
    1187–8 WINNY (ed. 1959): "Containing a single tongue, yet able to speak both
for and against a cause." SIMS (1966, p. 41): Cf. Jas. 3:10. See TILLEY (M1258) and
WILSON (p. 70): "Out of one mouth to blow hot and cold" (Aesop).
    1188 **approofe**] HANMER (ed. 1743): "Approbation." JOHNSON (1755): "Ap-
probation; commendation." *OED* (2): "Sanction, approval, approbation."
    1189 **make curtsie**] Bow in reverence (*OED,* Curtsy *sb.* 2).
    1190 **Hooking**] THIRLBY (1723–33): "Joining, fastening." SCHMIDT (1874):
"To draw as with a hook," but SARRAZIN (1902) defines it better: "To attach with
a hook" (*OED, v.* 8b). WILSON (ed. 1922) notes that "hookers" were rogues who
used a staff with an iron hook to steal from windows open at night, but that has
nothing to do with this line. Cf. *hooke* in 944 and *WT* 2.3.7 (906).
    1192 **prompture**] JOHNSON (1755): "Suggestion; motion given by another;
instigation." HART (ed. 1905): "Probably a coinage of Shakespeare's. Compare
'stricture' " (302: see n. and n. 2361). *OED:* "Prompting, suggestion, instigation,"
first use.

That had he twentie heads to tender downe
On twentie bloodie blockes, hee'ld yeeld them vp,   1195
Before his sister should her bodie stoope
To such abhord pollution.
Then *Isabell* liue chaste, and brother die;
"More then our Brother, is our Chastitie.
Ile tell him yet of *Angelo*'s request,   1200
And fit his minde to death, for his soules rest.   *Exit.*

1197 pollution] pollution as this KTLY
1199 "More] More ROWE3+ (−CAM3)

1194 **tender downe**] *OED* (*v.*[1] 1b): "Lay down (money) in payment," first fig. use.
1196 **stoope**] SCHMIDT (1875): "To bow down . . . to humiliate, to subdue" (*OED, v.*[1] 7).
1198–9 LASCELLES (1953, p. 166): "The couplet is surely delivered to the audience; it may be designed principally to enlighten them as to the new course the story is to take." SCHANZER (1963, p. 99): "The thought of sacrifice also evokes in Isabel something of the gaiety of the Christian martyrs, as is suggested, to me at least, by the couplet which has repelled so many readers."
1199 SIMPSON (1911, pp. 101–2): "A favourite device to call attention to them [proverbs and moral maxims] was the use of inverted commas at the beginning, but not at the end, of the line." See n. 492. HUNTER (1951, p. 177): "The books in which the *sententiae* are systematically marked are usually books in which there is some evidence of editorial care, so that we may attribute responsibility for the marking to the 'editor'." LEVER (ed. 1965): "Isabella's affirmation derives from Cinthio," quoting *Hecatommithi* [1565, 2:421] where Epitia says, "My brother's life is very dear to me, but even dearer to me is my honor."
1201 **fit**] See n. 1044.

Actus Tertius. Scena Prima.   3.1

Enter Duke, Claudio, and Prouost.

Du. So then you hope of pardon from Lord *Angelo?*
Cla. The miserable haue no other medicine   1205
But onely hope: I'haue hope to liue, and am prepar'd to
die.
Duke. Be absolute for death: either death or life

1202 *The Prison.* ROWE1-SIS, ARD2
1204 you] you've JOHN   of] for HAN1
1205–11 *Lines ending* medicine . . . am . . . die. . . . life . . . thus . . . lose . . .
breath HAN1; medicine, . . . hope: . . . dye. (*then as* F1) CAP-KNT2, HAL-WH1,
STAU-GLO, DYCE2-DYCE3, HUD2+; have . . . hope. . . . die. (*then as* F1) COL;
medicine, . . . am . . . death; . . . sweeter. . . . Life: . . . thing . . . art, mTBY1 *conj.*,
KTLY
1206 I'haue] I've ROWE1-JOHN2, WH, CAM1, GLO, DYCE2, DYCE3, HUD2,
CAM2, ARD1, NLSN   hope to] hop'd to BLAIR
1208 either] or COT (p. 173), POPE1-JOHN2

1204 **hope of**] Hope for (*OED, v.* 1), as in *Ant.* 1.1.61–2 (75–6).
1205–7 THEOBALD (1909, p. 283): Cf. Palingenius, *Zodiacus Vitae* (ed. 1832,
7:353–4): "Ignorance and hope are the two medicines which have been bestowed
on us." [So in *The Zodiake of Life* (1576, pp. 114–15): "Man of all creatures most
miserable. . . . *Hope* and *Follie* medicines be."] Cf. TILLEY (H602).
1206 **I'haue**] WILSON (ed. 1922): "N.E.D. quotes no examples of mod. contracted form 'I've' before eighteenth century." But FRANZ §52 cites *I'ue* in *Ham.* (F)
5.2.237 (3678) and KÖKERITZ (1953, p. 277) adds *Ham.* (F) 4.7.84 (3080). HOW-
ARD-HILL (1972, pp. 44, 48–50, 89) notes that Crane wrote *I'haue* in two transcripts
of Middleton's *Game at Chesse* and that the only two Jonsonian apostrophes in ten
Folio comedies are this and *I'am* in *Tmp.* 1.1.58 (64).
1208–44 ROBERTSON (1897, p. 52): "The whole speech may be said to be a
synthesis of favourite propositions of Montaigne." HOOKER (1902, p. 326): It
"seems to collect many of Montaigne's remarks" (citing parallels on pp. 326–47,
358–62). HARRISON (1934, pp. 2–3) compares Lucretius, *De Rerum Natura,* 3:

Shall thereby be the sweeter. Reason thus with life:
If I do loose thee, I do loose a thing   1210
That none but fooles would keepe: a breath thou art,
Seruile to all the skyie-influences,

1211 keepe] reck THEO, WARB   thou art,] *Om.* HAN1
1212 *In parentheses* PORSON *conj. in* MALONE (1780, 1:98), RANN-v1821, SING, KNT1, KNT2, HAL, HENL

830–1094. HARMON (1942, pp. 1000–1): "The Duke's speech is, as Robertson says, made up of Stoic comments on life and death. Most of these were universally familiar as commonplaces of consolation against the fear of death." Sh. could have read some of them in Cicero, Seneca, Lucretius, Pliny, or Marcus Aurelius, and many were gathered in Erasmus's *Adagia* and in English books. "No one passage which I cite can be pointed out definitely as Shakespeare's source—indeed in this speech he has adapted, fused, and compressed his material more perhaps than in any of the passages from his plays quoted above. . . . Seneca's commonplaces are probably a main source." MARTIN (1945, pp. 177–9): "The arguments may be chiefly of Stoical origin, but . . . some of the notions recommended by the Duke to Claudio are at least as near to Lucretius the heretic, as they are to Seneca." BALDWIN (1944, 2:84–6): Sh.'s *argumentatio* or reasoning "is in clear-cut conformity with the type" described in *Ad Herennium: propositio* (1208–9), *ratio* (1210–11), *rationis confirmatio* (1211–44), *conclusio* (1245–7). "The Duke has emphasized his confirmations." DUNCAN-JONES (1977, p. 442): Sh. "might also have cast his eye over" *A Discourse of Life and Death,* written in French by Philippe du Plessis-Mornay and tr. by Mary Sidney, Countess of Pembroke (1592), "which could have served him as a quarry for the Duke's arguments." HARMON (1942, p. 1006) notes that Mornay's *Discourse* "itself depends to a great extent upon Seneca."
    1208 Be . . . death] JOHNSON (ed. 1765): "Be determined to die, without any hope of life." *OED* (Absolute *a.* 11): "Positive, perfectly certain, decided," first quotation in this sense.
        either] Monosyllabic. See nn. 851, 1082.
    1211 keepe] WARBURTON (in THEOBALD, ed. 1733): "But this Reading is not only contrary to all Sense and Reason; but to the Drift of this moral Discourse. . . . The Sense of the Lines, in this Reading, is a direct Perswasive to *Suicide!* I make no Doubt, but the Poet wrote, *That none but Fools would* reck. i.e. care for, be anxious about, regret the Loss of." JOHNSON (ed. 1765): "The meaning seems plainly this, that *none but fools would* wish *to keep life;* or, *none but fools would keepe* it, if choice were allowed. A sense, which, whether true or not, is certainly innocent." STEEVENS (Var. 1778): *"Keep . . . may not signify preserve,* but *care for."* MALONE (1780, 1:97): Cf. Webster, *Dutchesse of Malfy,* 4.2.188: "Of what is't fools make such vain keeping?", "apparently used for *account, estimation."* HALLIWELL (ed. 1854): "The word is here used in its ordinary sense, in contrast with *lose."* Cf. Daniel, *Cleopatra* (1601, 5.2.1): "What doe I lose, that haue but life to lose?" HANKINS (1953, pp. 136–7): Cf. *The Zodiake of Life* (1576, p. 107): "who fears to dye Is but a foole."
    1212 Seruile] SCHMIDT (1875): "Meanly subject." *OED* (*a.* 5): "Subject *to* the control of something else; not free."
        skyie] JOHNSON (1755): *"Adj.* <from *sky.* Not very elegantly formed.> Ethereal." SCHMIDT (1875): "Pertaining to the sky (as the cause of the weather)."

That dost this habitation where thou keepst
Hourely afflict: Meerely, thou art deaths foole,
For him thou labourst by thy flight to shun,   1215
And yet runst toward him still. Thou art not noble,
For all th'accommodations that thou bearst,
Are nurst by basenesse: Thou'rt by no meanes valiant,

1213 dost] do HAN1, WARB, JOHN1-v1785, DYCE, STAU, DEL4-HUD2, BUL,
ARD1, KIT1, SIS; doth KTLY
1218 by no meanes] no way F4-ROWE2

OED (*a.* 1): "Of or pertaining to the sky; emanating from the sky," first quotation,
but DYCE (1853, p. 26) finds "skyey carte" in Anthony Copley, *A Fig for Fortune*
(1596, p. 20).

    influences] See *OED* (*sb.* 2): "The supposed flowing or streaming from the
stars or heavens of an etherial fluid acting upon the character and destiny of men."
HANKINS (1953, pp. 257–66) has a chapter on "The Skyey Influences" in Sh.

    1213 dost] PORSON (in MALONE, 1780, 1:98): "The construction is not, 'the
skiey influences, that do', but, 'a breath thou art, that dost &c.'. If [1212] be inclosed
in a parenthesis, all the difficulty will vanish." DYCE (ed. 1857): "Can any thing be
plainer than the poet's meaning here, viz. that 'the skyey influences hourly afflict' the
body ('this habitation')?" LEISI (ed. 1964): *"Dost* was often confused with *doth*
. . . and Sh. frequently uses the singular of the verb after a plural subject. It is probable,
therefore, that *dost* refers to *influences* and not to *life."*

    habitation] EVANS (ed. 1974): "(1) the earth; (2) the body."

    keepst] See n. 300.

    1214 Meerely] DYCE (1867): "Absolutely, entirely." SCHMIDT (1875):
"Only." WILSON (ed. 1922): "As a matter of fact." LEISI (ed. 1964): " 'Altogether'
(the earlier sense [historically] . . .) or 'only' (the later sense)." See nn. 1233, 2846.

    deaths foole] WARBURTON (in HANMER, ed. 1743; marked "Warburton"
ed. 1745): *"In the simplicity of the ancient shews upon our stage it was common to bring in
two figures, one representing a* Fool, *the other* Death *or* Fate: *The turn and contrivance of
the piece was to make the* Fool *lay many stratagems to avoid* Death *which yet brought him
more immediately into the jaws of it."* STEEVENS (Var. 1778, 5:419): Cf. *1H4* 5.4.81
(3046), "Life, Times foole." RITSON (in Var. 1793): "There are no such characters
as *Death* and *the Fool,* in any old *Morality* now extant. They seem to have existed only
in the *dumb Shows."* STEEVENS (ibid., 13:498–9): Cf. *Per.* 3.2.42, "To please the
Foole and Death." GREEN (1870, pp. 471–3): Sh. may have seen the picture of
Death and the Fool in Holbein's *Imagines* (1566). HART (ed. 1905): "One that death
makes a fool of. The early commentators endeavoured to fix a meaning here from
Moralities, Dumb Shows, or The Dance of Death. I am doubtful of any such reference, any more than there is in 'Love's not Time's fool . . . ,' *Sonnet* cxvi."

    1216 still] See n. 728.

    1217 accommodations] SCHMIDT (1874): "Supply of conveniences, comfort"
(*OED*, 6). HART (ed. 1905): "The earliest example of the word (in any sense) in
New Eng. Dict. is that in *Othello,* I. iii. 239 [586]."

    1218 Are . . . basenesse] WARBURTON (ed. 1747): *"Thy most virtuous actions have
a selfish motive, and even those of them which appear most generous, are but the more artful*

For thou dost feare the soft and tender forke
Of a poore worme: thy best of rest is sleepe, 1220

---

disguises of self-love." EDWARDS (1748, pp. 43–4): "Shakespear is not here considering man as a moral agent, but is speaking of animal life, the *accommodations* < conveniencies > of which, he says, are *nurs'd* < supplied and supported > by *baseness* . . . such as wool, silk, the excrements of beasts and insects, &c. or by the labour and service of the meanest people." IDEM (1750, p. 99): Cf. *Lr.* 3.4.107–13 (1882–8). See also MAXWELL (1952, p. 126). JOHNSON (ed. 1765): "*Shakespear* meant only to observe, that a minute analysis of life at once destroys that splendour which dazzles the imagination. Whatever grandeur can display, or luxury enjoy, is procured by *baseness,* by offices of which the mind shrinks from the contemplation. All the delicacies of the table may be traced back to the shambles and the dunghill, all magnificence of building was hewn from the quarry, and all the pomp of ornaments, dug from among the damps and darkness of the mine." STEEVENS (Var. 1778): "This is a thought which Shakespeare delights to express." Cf. *Ant.* 1.1.35–6 and 5.2.7 (46–7, 3207). *OED* (Nurse *v.* 3): "To foster, tend." HARDING (ed. 1954): " 'Provided by the base offices and occupations of others'." WINNY (ed. 1959): "Derived from ignoble sources (as shoe-leather from cattle, silk from worms)."

1219–20 **the . . . worme**] JOHNSON (ed. 1765): "*Worm* is put for any creeping thing or *serpent. Shakespear* supposes falsely, but according to the vulgar notion, that a serpent wounds with his tongue, and that his tongue is *forked.* He confounds reality and fiction, a serpent's tongue is *soft* but not *forked* nor hurtful." KNIGHT (ed. 1840): "It appears to us that the fear here described is that of the *worm of the grave.*" HALLIWELL (ed. 1854): "The fork is merely the single sharpened end, the soft and tender insertion of the common earth-worm." *OED* (Fork *sb.* 1c): "The forked tongue (popularly supposed to be the sting) of a snake," first quotation in this sense. HARDING (ed. 1954): "Shakespeare may mean the grave or coffin worm to which, by analogy with 'snake', he ascribes a forked tongue." LEISI (ed. 1964): "The question whether 'grave-worm' or 'poisonous snake' is meant here, is not relevant since grave worms were often thought of, and represented in pictorial art, as snakes."

1220–2 **thy . . . more**] WARBURTON (1734, in NICHOLS, 1817, 2:639; cf. ed. 1747): "Evidently translated from this of Tully: 'Habes somnum, imaginem mortis, eamque quotidie induis, & dubitas quin sensus in morte nullus sit, cùm in ejus simulacro videas esse nullum sensum [You look on sleep as an image of death, and you take that on you daily; and have you, then, any doubt that there is no sensation in death, when you see there is none in sleep, which is its near resemblance?, *Tusculan Disputations,* 1.38, tr. C. D. Yonge]'. Again, 'Thou hast nor youth, nor age, &c.' So Tully: 'Quae vero aetas longa est? aut quid omnino homini longum? nonne modo pueros, modo adolescentes, in cursu a tergo insequens, nec opinantes assecuta est senectus [but what age is long? or what is there at all long to a man? Does not Old age, though unregarded, still attend On childhood's pastimes, as the cares of men?, ibid., 1.39]'." JOHNSON (ed. 1765): "I cannot without indignation find *Shakespear* saying, that *death is only sleep,* lengthening out his exhortation by a sentence which in the *Friar* is impious, in the reasoner is foolish, and in the poet trite and vulgar." KENRICK (1765, p. 27): "The duke . . . speaks of the mere *sense of death,* the parting of the soul from the body." So HALLIWELL (ed. 1854). STEEVENS (Var. 1778): "This was an oversight in Shakespeare; for in [2008–9] the Provost speaks of the desperate Barnardine, as one who regards death only as a *drunken sleep.*" MALONE (ed. 1790, 10:564): "I apprehend Shakspeare means to say no more, than that the passage from this life to another is as easy as sleep; a position in which there is surely

And that thou oft prouoakst, yet grosselie fearst
Thy death, which is no more. Thou art not thy selfe,
For thou exists on manie a thousand graines
That issue out of dust. Happie thou art not,
For what thou hast not, still thou striu'st to get,   1225
And what thou hast forgetst. Thou art not certaine,
For thy complexion shifts to strange effects,

1227 effects] affects JOHN1 *conj.*, RANN, SING, KTLY, DYCE2, DYCE3, HUD2, BUL

---

neither folly nor impiety." BECKET (1815, 1:229): "In death every thing in respect
of *this world* is forgotten or lost as it is in sleep." WORDSWORTH (1864, pp. 266–7):
Cf. Lucretius, 3:1058 ff. and 990, and *Ham.* 3.1.60–1 (1714–15). NOBLE (1935, p.
226): Cf. Job 14:12: "So man sleepeth and riseth not: for he shall not wake againe,
nor be raysed from his sleepe till the heauen be no more." BALDWIN (1944, 2:602):
"The reader will notice how skilfully Shakspere has 'cut over' and Christianized this
passage in Cicero [quoted by Warburton]. . . . Unquestionably, I think, Shakspere's
sententia is an 'imitation' of this passage." See also TILLEY (S526, 527) and WILSON
(p. 741): "Sleep is the brother of death" (Homer), "Sleep is the image of death."
   1221 **prouoakst**] MALONE (ed. 1790): "Solicitest, procurest." HORNE (ed.
1840, 1:210): "By courting it, or inducing it by narcotics." CLARKE (ed. 1864): "For
invok'st, or encouragest." SCHMIDT (1875): "Call forth" (*OED, v.* 1). HART (ed.
1905): "Challengest, defiest to combat. A technical sense from the duello." LEVER
(ed. 1965): " 'Dost invoke', 'summon'."
   grosselie] SCHMIDT (1874): "Stupidly" (*OED, adv.* 6a). WINNY (ed. 1959):
"Excessively." Cf. 2869.
   1222 **Thou art not thy selfe**] JOHNSON (ed. 1765): "Thou art perpetually
repaired and renovated by external assistance, thou subsistest upon foreign matter,
and hast no power of producing or continuing thy own being." KÖNIG (1888, p. 56):
Thou art is one syllable here and in 1239. COTGRAVE (1655, p. 173) prints *Th'art.*
   1223 **exists**] WILSON (ed. 1922): "Shakespearian 2nd pers. sing. Cf. [873: see
n.]. Shakespeare did not write for the eye. All mod. edd. print the monster 'exist'st';
they could not pronounce it if they tried." See nn. 873, 1311.
   graines] JOHNSON (1755): *Grain,* "Any minute particle." CLARKE (ed.
1864): "The corn of which daily bread is made." WINNY (ed. 1959): "Grains of dust,
the substance of the body." LEVER (ed. 1965): "Seeds (*O.E.D. sb.* [1] 1)."
   1224 **out of dust**] HANKINS (1953, p. 40): Cf. Gen. 3:19. LEVER (ed. 1965):
"Recalling Gen. ii. 7."
   1226 **certaine**] DURHAM (ed. 1926): "Steadfast." HARDING (ed. 1954): "Constant."
   1227 **complexion**] WHITE (ed. 1883): "Constitution, the making up, here, of
the body." HART (ed. 1905): "Disposition, temperament." WILSON (ed. 1922):
"According to the old medical theory the 'complexion' or composition of man's body
was made up of four humours or fluids (blood, phlegm, choler, and melancholy) and
if the proportion of these was disturbed, disease of mind or body followed. The
moon, which influenced the tides, was likewise supposed to influence the human
fluids." See n. 1140.
   strange] SCHMIDT (1875): "New." See nn. 2060, 2523.
   effects] HALLIWELL (ed. 1854) quotes Bartholomaeus, *De Proprietatibus Rerum*

After the Moone: If thou art rich, thou'rt poore,
For like an Asse, whose backe with Ingots bowes;
Thou bearst thy heauie riches but a iournie,   1230
And death vnloads thee; Friend hast thou none.
For thine owne bowels which do call thee, fire
The meere effusion of thy proper loines
Do curse the Gowt, Sapego, and the Rheume

1228 If] Though HAN1
1231 vnloads] unloadeth ROWE3-v1773 (−CAP), HUD2; in fine unloads KTLY
hast thou] thou hast THEO, WARB
1232 thine] thy THEO, WARB, JOHN1-RANN (−CAP)   thee, fire] thee sire?
F4; thee sire, COT (p. 174), ROWE1+

(1535, 8.29, fol. cxxx): "Vnder the moone is conteyned sykenesse, losse, fere and
drede, and dommage. Therfore aboute the chaungynge of mans bodye, the vertue
of the moone werketh principallye. . . . And therfore a phisicyon knowethe not
perfyghtlye the chaungyng of syckenes, but if he knowe the effectes and werkynge
of the moone in mannes bodye." STAUNTON (ed. 1859): *"Results, consequences, conclu-
sions."* CLARKE (ed. 1864): " 'Strange effects of colour (indicating alteration of
mind), according as the moon changes'." SCHMIDT (1874): "Outward manifestation" (*OED, sb.* 3). Cf. 2570. HART (ed. 1905): "Tendencies, aims, things to be
effected."

1228 **After**] See *OED* (*prep.* 12): "In obedience to."

If . . . poore] NOBLE (1935, p. 227): Cf. Rev. 3:17.

1229 MALONE (in Var. 1821): Cf. Whitney's *Emblems* (1586; ed. Green, p. 18):
"the foolishe asse Whose backe is fraighte with cates, and daintie cheare." [Tr. from
Alciati's *Emblemata,* "In Avaros," ed. 1531, sig. C6-6ᵛ, ed. Green, 1870.] HAL-
LIWELL (ed. 1854): Cf. Dekker, *Old Fortunatus,* 1600 (1.2.96-8, 152-6). WAHL
(1888, pp. 81-2): Cf. *JC* 4.1.21-7 (1876-82). HART (ed. 1905): Cf. La Primau-
daye's *French Academie,* tr. T. B., 1586, chap. 42, p. 446: "They [covetous men] are
like Mules that carie great burthens of golde and siluer on their backes, and yet eate
but hay." See TILLEY (A360) and WILSON (p. 22): "The ass though laden with gold
still eats thistles."

1231 **death vnloads thee**] WORDSWORTH (1880, p. 373): Cf. 1 Tim. 6:7.

1231-5 **Friend . . . sooner**] HANKINS (1953, pp. 213-14): Cf. *The Zodiake of
Life* (1576, p. 73): "Who shall thy wearied age relieue? who shall thy hurts lament?
Thy brother or thy kinsman nere, or will doe this thy frende? No sure, for to be heyre
to thee they rather wish thine ende."

1232 **bowels**] *OED* (*sb.* 1 5): "Offspring, children," a biblical idiom first used in
English by Tyndale in translating Philem. 12, "myne awne bowels."

fire] F4 corrects to *sire.*

1233 **meere**] BALD (ed. 1956): "Very." LEVER (ed. 1965): "Absolute, unmodified." See nn. 1214, 2846.

effusion] *OED* (1): "Pouring out." WINNY (ed. 1959): "Issue."

proper] Own. See n. 36.

1234 **Sapego**] JOHNSON (1755): *Serpigo,* "A kind of tetter." CAPELL (1779, 1:
glossary, 61): "Properly,—an eruptive Disorder, call'd vulgarly—Tetter or Ringworm: but the Word is us'd here for . . . the *Mal François* [syphilis] ; and *Rheum*

For ending thee no sooner. Thou hast nor youth, nor age   1235
But as it were an after-dinners sleepe
Dreaming on both, for all thy blessed youth

1235, 1240 Thou hast] Thou'st DYCE2, DYCE3, HUD2
1235 nor youth] not youth F4-ROWE2
1237 all thy blessed] pall'd, thy blazed WARB; all thy boasted COLNE, COL2

. . . is taken in the same Sense." *OED:* "A general term (cf. *Herpes*) for creeping or spreading skin diseases; *spec.* ringworm." KÖKERITZ (1953, pp. 20, 201): Sh.'s pronunciation is indicated by the phonetic spelling here and by *Suppeago* in *Tro.* 2.3.81 (1277, F only).

    Rheume] ONIONS (1911): "Morbid defluxion of humours (such as was supposed to cause rheumatism), also, catarrh" (*OED, sb.* [1] 1, 2).

    1235-7 **Thou . . . both**] JOHNSON (ed. 1765): "This is exquisitely imagined. When we are young we busy ourselves in forming schemes for succeeding time, and miss the gratifications that are before us; when we are old we amuse the languour of age with the recollection of youthful pleasures or performances; so that our life, of which no part is filled with the business of the present time, resembles our dreams after dinner, when the events of the morning are mingled with the designs of the evening." ELIOT quotes these lines as the epigraph to "Gerontion" (1920).

    1235 **nor . . . nor**] SCHMIDT (1875): "For *neither . . . nor,*" as in 2213. See FRANZ §587 and *OED* (Nor *conj.* [1] 2b), "Chiefly *poet.*" See n. 2744.

    1236 **after-dinners**] JOHNSON (1755): "The hour passing just after dinner, which is generally allowed to indulgence and amusement." *OED:* "Afternoon." Cf. *Tro.* 2.3.121 (1316), "An after Dinners breath."

    1237 **Dreaming**] Cf. *Tmp.* 4.1.156-7 (1827-8).

    1237-9 **for . . . Eld**] THIRLBY (1747-53): "Youth lives upon the (generally scanty) allowance of parents and according to the proverb have no bread (of their own) to eat till they have no teeth to eat it with." EDWARDS (1758, pp. 31-2): "In your Youth you are in as bad a condition as an old man; for tho' you have Appetites to enjoy the pleasures of life, yet you are unable to enjoy them for want of the Means to purchase them, *viz.* Riches; not being come to your estate, being dependent on your Elders for subsistence." JOHNSON (ed. 1765): "In *youth,* which is the *happiest* time, or which might be the happiest, he [man] commonly wants means to obtain what he could enjoy; he is dependant on *palsied eld; must beg alms* from the coffers of hoary avarice; and being very niggardly supplied *becomes as aged,* looks, like an old man, on happiness, which is beyond his reach." CAPELL (1780, 2:3:44): "Is as much a *beggar,* as *'eld'* is, lives, as do the *'palsy'd'* and old, on *'alms'* gotten from others, meaning—it's exhibition from parents before it's fortunes descend to it: . . . or *as* if it was *aged,* is in the condition that some are who are *aged."* MALONE (1783, p. 5): Cf. *Lr.* 1.2.48-51 (382-4). CLARKE (ed. 1864): " 'Thy youth becomes as if it were aged, carkingly coveting those things that belong to old people'." HUNTER (ed. 1873): "Thy youth devotes all its freshness, vigour, &c., to make provision for old age; as if old age were present in youth and then craving sustenance." HART (ed. 1905): "The meaning appears to be that in our youth we are compelled to seek help from old age—acting like palsied old age in begging alms." WILSON (ed. 1922): "Perhaps the corruption lies in 'becomes as' since 'aged' appears to be required by the context. The general meaning seems to be 'youth's desire is to grow up and gain the prerogatives of age'. Possibly a line is lost." See p. 285.

Becomes as aged, and doth begge the almes
Of palsied-Eld: and when thou art old, and rich
Thou hast neither heate, affection, limbe, nor beautie   1240   (F6a)
To make thy riches pleasant: what's yet in this
That beares the name of life? Yet in this life
Lie hid moe thousand deaths; yet death we feare
That makes these oddes, all euen.

1238 as aged] an indigent mTBY2 *conj.*, HAN1; assuaged WARB; engaged STAU *conj.*, KTLY
1240 beautie] bounty WARB
1241 yet] *Om.* POPE, HAN1, CAP, DYCE2, DYCE3-HUD2
1242 Yet] Yea, KTLY
1243 moe] more COT (p. 174), ROWE1-THEO2, WARB-CAM1, DYCE2-HUD2, ARD1, PEN2; a mTBY1 *conj.*, HAN1; some KTLY

1239–41 HARMON (1942, p. 1007 n.): "The description of old age . . . is clearly Senecan for the most part." Cf. *Epistles*, 120.15–18.
1239 **Eld**] GILDON (1710, glossary, p. lxix): "Age." POPE (ed. 1723): *"Old age."* JOHNSON (1755): "Old people; persons worn out with years" (*OED, sb.* 2 3b). STEEVENS (Var. 1778): Cf. *Wiv.* 4.4.36 (2158).
1240 **neither**] WILSON (ed. 1922): "Read 'not' or 'nor' and the line runs smoothly. 'Neither' is possibly a scribal substitution." But *neither* could be pronounced as one syllable: see ABBOTT §466 and n. 851.
heate] CAMPBELL (ed. 1949): "Ardor." BALD (ed. 1956): "Warmth of blood." LEVER (ed. 1965): "Desire."
affection] See n. 461.
limbe] LEVER (ed. 1965): "Any organ of the body" (*OED, sb.* 1).
1241–3 **what's . . . deaths**] HARMON (1942, pp. 1006–7): "Shakespeare's sources for this passage are probably Senecan." Cf. *Epistles*, 101.10–14.
1241 **yet**] DYCE (ed. 1864) agrees with Pope in omitting *yet*, "an error undoubtedly caused by the occurrence of *'yet'* in the next line and in the line after that." LLOYD (1884, p. 728): "The three *yets* towards the ends of three consecutive lines confuse each other, and the immediate repetition of 'yet in this' betrays a manifest compositor's blunder."
1242–4 **Yet . . . euen**] TILLEY (C774): "A coward dies many deaths, a brave man but one." Cf. *JC* 2.2.32–3 (1020–1). Cf. 1291, 2783–4.
1243 **moe thousand**] RANN (ed. 1786): "More by a thousand than are here recited." ROLFE (ed. 1882): "A thousand more." See n. 340.
1244 TILLEY (D143, E117) and WILSON (pp. 174, 220): "Death is the grand leveler"; "The end makes all equal." Cf. *F.Q.* 2.1.59, "Death is an equall doome." WHITING (D99): "Death makes all things alike."
oddes, all euen] HANKINS (1953, p. 137): "Shakespeare's implied reference to odd and even numbers is probably derived directly or indirectly" from Seneca, *Epistulae Morales*, 91.16, "Inpares nascimur, pares morimur [We are born unequal, we die equal]"; *De Ira*, 3.43.1, "Venit ecce mors quae vos pares faciat [Behold, death comes, which makes you equal]." "In life we may be 'odds', i.e., of unequal fortunes; but at death we become 'evens', i.e., equal in fortune." Cf. *Ant.* 4.15.66 (3078), "The oddes is gone."

Cla. I humblie thanke you.   1245
To sue to liue, I finde I seeke to die,
And seeking death, finde life: Let it come on.

Enter Isabella.

Isab. What hoa? Peace heere; Grace, and good companie.   1250
Pro. Who's there? Come in, the wish deserues a
welcome.

1248 *Enter Isabella.*] *After* 1252 CAP, COL, HAL, SING2, WH1, KTLY, CAM3; *after*
1254 DYCE, STAU-GLO, DEL4, HUD2, WH2, CAM2-NLSN, ARD2, EVNS; *after* very
welcome. (1256) IRV
   1249 [*within*] CAP, COL1-CAM3 (−KNT3), ALEX, ARD2, EVNS (*subst.*)

1246–7 MASON (1785, p. 38): "Had the Friar, in reconciling Claudio to death,
urged to him the certainty of happiness hereafter, this speech would have been
introduced with more propriety; but the Friar says nothing of that subject, and argues
more like a philosopher than a Christian divine." STEEVENS (Var. 1793): "Mr. M.
Mason seems to forget that no actual Friar was the speaker, but the Duke, who might
reasonably be supposed to have more of the philosopher than the divine in his
composition." BOSWELL (Var. 1821): "Surely the Duke may be supposed to have
as much of the divine in his composition as Claudio; but I cannot think Mr. Mason's
censure well founded: Claudio's answer is the inference which the Duke intended
should be drawn from his arguments." BROWN (1864, p. 57): Cf. Luke 17:33, John
12:25. WORDSWORTH (1864, p. 343): See Matt. 16:25. NOBLE (1935, p. 227): Also
Matt. 10:39. MUIR (1953, p. 47): Cf. *Edward III* (*Sh. Apoc.,* 4.4.158-9): "Since for
to liue is but to seeke to die, And dying but beginning of new lyfe." COGHILL (1955,
p. 20): "The Duke has been criticized by some for preaching a stoical rather than a
Christian sermon; yet John Donne was a Christian preacher, and one has only to finger
through his sermons to find passages of no less stoical admonition on the contempt
of life." WINNY (ed. 1959): "Because life is one long act of dying, from which death
delivers us, by death we avoid dying and so live." MAXWELL (1974, p. 211): "A
friar-like concern with the state of Claudio's soul would have been dramatically
inappropriate. The dialogue must centre on death, as such."
   1246 **To sue**] ABBOTT (§357): *"As regards suing."* HUDSON (ed. 1880): *"To sue*
is another instance of the infinitive used gerundively, or like the Latin *gerund,* and
so is equivalent to *in* or *by suing.* So again, [1272]." FRANZ (§655): " *<In >* suing."
DURHAM (ed. 1926): "If I sue."
   1248 Isabel speaks "within" (offstage) but does not enter till after 1252 or 1254.
See HOWARD-HILL (1972, p. 123).
   1249–52, 1256–7 LEVER (ed. 1965, p. xxviii) calls these lines verse set as prose,
but I think they are verse lines run on, as in 1206–7, 1260–1, 2200–1, all set by
Compositor B, who in *MM* never indents the second line.
   1249 **Peace**] See n. 355.
      Grace] See n. 996.
   1249–50 **good companie**] May the companionship of angels be with you (*OED,*

Duke. Deere sir, ere long Ile visit you againe.

Cla. Most holie Sir, I thanke you.

Isa. My businesse is a word or two with *Claudio.*   1255

Pro. And verie welcom: looke Signior, here's your
sister.

Duke. Prouost, a word with you.

Pro. As manie as you please.

Duke. Bring them to heare me speak, where I may be   1260
conceal'd.

Cla. Now sister, what's the comfort?

Isa. Why,

1253 sir] son MASON *conj. in* v1803, KTLY, DYCE2, DYCE3-HUD2, KIT1   Ile]
I RANN

1256 looke] *Om.* POPE, HAN1

1258-9 *One verse line* v1793-ARD1 (−COL, CAM1, GLO, WH2, CAM2)

1260-1 Bring . . . conceal'd] Bring them to speake, where I may be conceal'd,
yet heare them F2-ROWE3; Bring me where I conceal'd May hear them speak DAV;
Bring them to speak where I may be conceal'd, Yet hear them POPE1-JOHN2,
v1773-RANN, v1793-v1813; Bring me to stand where I may be conceal'd Yet hear
them speak CAP; Bring me to hear them speak, where I may be Conceal'd MAL, DYCE,
HUD2, BUL; Bring me to hear them speak, where I may be conceal'd, Yet hear them
mTBY3 *conj.,* v1821, SING1; Bring me to hear them speak, where I may be conceal'd
STEEVENS (v1778) *conj.,* KNT1-SING2, WH1-KTLY, KNT3, DEL4, COL4, WH2-CAM2,
ARD1+

1261 *Exeunt.* F2-F4; *Ex. Duke, Provost.* DAV, ROWE1-NLSN, KIT1-SIS, EVNS; *the
Duke and Provost withdraw* CAM3, PEL1-PEN2

1262 SCENE II. POPE, HAN1, WARB, JOHN

1262-4 *Lines ending* comfort? . . . indeed: POPE1-KNT2 (−MAL), HAL, WH1,
STAU, KTLY, KNT3, DEL4, HUD2; all . . . indeed. COL; Why, . . . indeed. DYCE, GLO,
WH2, IRV

1262 sister] good sister HAN1

Company *sb.* 1).

1260 **Bring . . . speak**] STEEVENS (Var. 1778): "I believe we should read: Bring
me to hear *them* speak." SISSON (1956, 1:83): "There can be no reasonable doubt
that this error is a mere slip of the compositor carrying his line in his head, and
transposing *them* and *me.* It is perhaps typical of F2 that it emends by adding the words
'Yet hear them', a shallow piece of officious editing." BECKERMAN (1962, p. 195)
suggests "that the Duke, like the King and Polonius [*Ham.* 3.1], withdraws behind
the arras." LEVER (ed. 1965, p. xxvi): "In this scene the two older men must merely
retire while Claudio and Isabella confer (if the Duke left the stage, he would not be
able to 'hear them speak')."

1263-4 LEE (ed. 1907): "The line scans ill. But Isabella's perturbation justifies
the irregularity." ABBOTT §512 gives many instances of "interjectional lines" of one
or two syllables, as in 1263.

As all comforts are: most good, most good indeede,
Lord *Angelo* hauing affaires to heauen   1265
Intends you for his swift Ambassador,
Where you shall be an euerlasting Leiger;
Therefore your best appointment make with speed,
To Morrow you set on.
    Clau. Is there no remedie?   1270
    Isa. None, but such remedie, as to saue a head
To cleaue a heart in twaine.
    Clau. But is there anie?
    Isa. Yes brother, you may liue;
There is a diuellish mercie in the Iudge,   1275
If you'l implore it, that will free your life,
But fetter you till death.

1264 most good, most good indeede] most good indeed POPE, CAP, v1821, SING1; most good in Deed THEO, WARB, JOHN, v1773-v1785, v1793-v1813; most good in speed HAN1; most good. Indeed BLACKSTONE *conj. in* MALONE (1780, 1:98), RANN; most good, most good, in deed MAL
    1269 on] out POPE, HAN1
    1272–4 *Lines ending* any? . . . live; v1793-NLSN, KIT1+; twain. . . . live; CAM3
    1272 To] Must HAN1

1264 **most good indeede**] TILLEY (H347): "He is well since he is in heaven." Cf. WILSON (p. 878).
    1266 **Ambassador**] Cf. "an Embassage From my Redeemer," *R3* 2.1.3–4 (1126–7).
    1267 **Leiger**] KNIGHT (ed. 1840): "A resident ambassador—not one sent on a brief and special mission." *OED* (Ledger *sb.* 7a): "A (permanent) representative," first use in fig. sense.
    1268 **appointment**] THEOBALD (1726, sig. I3ᵛ): *"Reconciliation."* Cf. *disappointed* in *Ham.* 1.5.77 (762). JOHNSON (ed. 1765): "Preparation" (cf. *OED*, Appoint *v.* 14d). STEEVENS (Var. 1773): "The word . . . on this occasion comprehends confession, communion, and absolution." HALLIWELL (ed. 1854) quotes COOPER (1565): *"Instructus ad mortem contemnendam. Cic.* Perfitely apointed to contemne death." CLARKE (ed. 1864): "Here used in the sense of outfit, or equipment for a voyage, and in that of spiritual supplyment." LEVER (ed. 1965): "Arrangement."
    1269 **set on**] THIRLBY (1723-33): "Set forward" (*OED, v.* 148g). SCHMIDT (1875, p. 1035): "Begin a march or journey."
    1272 WINNY (ed. 1959): "By splitting a heart in two; *sc.,* to avoid death in one form by choosing it in another; or, to save yourself at the cost of another person's life."
    To cleaue] *OED* (*v.*¹ 1b): "To hew asunder; to split." LEVER (ed. 1965): "Perhaps a misreading of 'To-cleaves', the intensive prefix." But see n. 1246.
    twaine.] SIMPSON (1911, pp. 71–2) interprets the colon in F1 (see p. 277) as *"marking an interrupted speech."* That does not seem to be true here, though it may be in 2140. See n. 140.

Cla. Perpetuall durance?

Isa. I iust, perpetuall durance, a restraint
Through all the worlds vastiditie you had   1280
To a determin'd scope.

Clau. But in what nature?

Isa. In such a one, as you consenting too't,
Would barke your honor from that trunke you beare,
And leaue you naked.   1285

Clau. Let me know the point.

Isa. Oh, I do feare thee *Claudio*, and I quake,
Least thou a feauorous life shouldst entertaine,
And six or seuen winters more respect
Then a perpetuall Honor. Dar'st thou die?   1290

1280 Through] Tho' ROWE3+ (−SIS)

1278 **durance**] SCHMIDT (1874): "Imprisonment" (*OED, sb.* 5).

1279 **I iust**] HART (ed. 1905): " 'Yes, that's exactly it' " (*OED,* Just *adv.* 3). See n. 2574.

restraint] JOHNSON (ed. 1765): "A confinement of your mind to one painful idea; to ignominy, of which the remembrance can be neither suppressed nor escaped." See n. 215.

1280-1 SISSON (1956, 1:83): "Rowe read *though* for *through,* and this is generally accepted. I see no need for the emendation, and read *Through,* the sense being clearly 'reducing the vastidity you once had to a fixed limit'." LEVER (ed. 1965): " 'Though all the immensity of the world were yours to wander in, your mind would be tied to one fixed thought'."

1280 **vastiditie**] JOHNSON (1755): "Wideness, immensity. A barbarous word." *OED:* "Vastness," first quotation.

1281 **a determin'd scope**] HUDSON (ed. 1880): *"Determined* in its old sense of *limited, confined,* or *narrow;* literally, fenced-in with *terms,* that is, *bounds."* OED (*ppl. a.* [2]): "Limited, restricted," first use in this sense. See n. 73 on *scope.*

1283 **you consenting**] See n. 1077.

1284 **barke**] *OED* (*v.* [2] 3b): "Strip off the bark from," only use in fig. sense. HART (ed. 1905): Cf. *barkt* in *Ant.* 4.12.23 (2779).

trunke] LEVER (ed. 1965): "A play on 'trunk' as body and as tree-trunk."

1288 **feauorous**] *OED* (*a.* 2): first use in fig. sense; = *Feverish* (2), "Excited, fitful, restless, now hot now cold."

entertaine] CLARKE (ed. 1864): "Used for 'hold too dear', 'estimate too highly', 'overprize'." SCHMIDT (1874): "To maintain, to keep." HART (ed. 1905): "Endure, put up with, live through." MORRIS (ed. 1912): "Think upon." NEILSON & HILL (ed. 1942): "Favor." CRAIG (ed. 1951): "Possibly, desire." LEVER (ed. 1965): "Keep up, maintain (*O.E.D.* 3); or, admit to consideration (*O.E.D.* 14b)." See also *OED, v.* 14c, "To keep, hold, or maintain in the mind with favour; to harbour; to cherish." See n. 246.

1289 **respect**] JOHNSON (1755): "To regard; to have regard to" (*OED, v.* 2). SCHMIDT (1875): "Care for." See n. 1827.

The sence of death is most in apprehension,
And the poore Beetle that we treade vpon
In corporall sufferance, finds a pang as great,
As when a Giant dies.
   Cla. Why giue you me this shame?   1295
Thinke you I can a resolution fetch
From flowrie tendernesse? If I must die,

1296 can a resolution fetch] want a resolution fetch'd HAN1; cannot resolution
fetch KTLY

1291 **sence**] See *OED* (*sb.* 14): "Consciousness or impression *of* . . . as present
or impending."
    apprehension] SCHMIDT (1874): "Conception, imagination." *OED* (11):
"Anticipation; *chiefly* of things adverse," first use in this sense. See n. 2008. SMITH
(1963, p. 37) and WILSON (p. 250): "The fear of death is worse than death itself."
Cf. 1242–4, 2783–4, and Montaigne, bk. 1, ch. 40.
    1292–4 JOHNSON (ed. 1765): "The Reasoning is, *that death is no more than every
being must suffer, though the dread of it is peculiar to man,* or perhaps, *that* we are
inconsistent with ourselves when we so much dread that which we carelessly inflict
on other creatures, that feel the pain as acutely as we." GENTLEMAN (ed. 1773):
"*Shakespeare's* darling principle of humanity, is delightfully expressed here; in four
lines we are instructed, as we fear death ourselves, not to be forward in administring
it even to insects." DOUCE (in Var. 1793): "The meaning is—fear is the principal
sensation in death, which has no pain; and the giant when he dies feels no greater
pain than the beetle." PATTERSON (1842, pp. 77–81) quotes Charles S. Bird, "On
the Want of Analogy between the Sensations of Insects and Our Own," *Entomological
Magazine,* no. 2, p. 113: "It is somewhat amusing that [Sh.'s] words should, in this
case, be entirely wrested from their original purpose. His purpose was to show how
little a man feels in dying; that the sense of death is most in apprehension, not in the
act; and that even a beetle, which feels so little, feels as much as a giant does." "The
less, therefore, the beetle is supposed to feel, the more force we give to the sentiment
of Shakespeare." WHITE (1854, p. 159): "The almost universal perversion of these
lines to a plea for long life to beetles, justifies a repetition of the explanation of the
passage previously made by others. *Isabella* is not reading *Claudio* a lecture upon
cruelty to animals." HALLIWELL (ed. 1854): "The contrast is evidently between the
mental and physical pain, and, without the former, that the death of an insect would
be as horrible as that of the highest order of man. This is probably an exaggeration,
but Isabel is endeavouring to impress upon her brother the slight pain there is in a
violent death." TAYLOR (1945, p. 499) repeats the point made by Douce.
    1293 **sufferance**] See n. 1181.
    1297 **flowrie tendernesse**] HALLIWELL (ed. 1854): "Eloquent pathos." DELIUS
(ed. 1860): Softness or delicacy such as is proper to flowers; cf. *Ant.* 2.2.215 (923).
ARROWSMITH (1865, p. 11): "An abstract for woman." SYMONS (in IRVING &
MARSHALL, ed. 1889): The phrase "appears to be used by Claudio in mockery or
resentment of his sister's stoic counsels, coming, as they do, from her, a mere woman,
a creature tender as a flower, to him, a man, supposing himself valiant." *OED* (*a.* 6):
"Abounding in flowers of speech; full of fine words and showy expressions, florid,"
first use in fig. sense.

I will encounter darknesse as a bride,
And hugge it in mine armes.

   Isa. There spake my brother: there my fathers graue   1300
Did vtter forth a voice. Yes, thou must die:
Thou art too noble, to conserue a life
In base appliances. This outward sainted Deputie,
Whose setled visage, and deliberate word
Nips youth i'th head, and follies doth emmew   1305

1300 graue] gave F4
1303 appliances] appliance HAN1
1305 emmew] enmew v1793-SING1, COL, OXF1; enew KTLY, HUD2, ARD, CAM3+

1298–9 MALONE (ed. 1790): Cf. *Ant.* 4.14.99–101 (2941–3). SPENCER (1936, p. 76): On death as a bride or bridegroom see the Greek Anthology, 7:182–8, and *Lr.* 4.6.202 (2640–1).

   1298 **encounter**] JOHNSON (1755): "Meet face to face." *OED* (*v.* 6): "Go to meet," citing only this and *Cym.* 1.3.32 (301). WINNY (ed. 1959): "Embrace." LEISI (ed. 1964): "Often used in a very definite erotic sense." See n. 1472.

   darknesse] *OED* (4b): "Absence of the 'light' of life; death," as in Job 10:21. ONIONS (1911): "Cf. the biblical phrase 'darkness and the shadow of death' " [Job 3:5, 10:21, 22, 28:3, Ps. 107:10, 14].

   1303 **appliances**] DAVENANT (1673) modernizes *In base appliances* to *By wretched remedies.* THIRLBY (1747–53): Perhaps for "remedies." *OED* (1): "Compliance, willing service; subservience." LEISI (ed. 1964): " 'Medicine', 'medical application', as always in Sh." See SCHMIDT (1874).

   outward sainted] Outwardly holy. See nn. 384, 943, 1756–7.

   1304 **setled**] SCHMIDT (1875): "Composed, calm, sober, grave." *OED* (*ppl. a.* 1c): "Indicating a settled purpose, mind, character." WINNY (ed. 1959): "Unmoved."

   1305 **Nips . . . head**] HART (ed. 1905): "A recognised expression for killing a bird." *OED* (*v.*[1] 3b): *"To nip by, in,* or *on* the *neck, head* or *pate* . . . To give a decisive or final check to." WILSON (1970, p. 567) quotes Osorius, *A Pearle for a Prynce* (1565), tr. R. Shacklock: "Princes doe vnwisely which doo not nyp wickednes in the hed, So sone as it doth begin." HENN (1972, p. 31): "Strike at youth, as the falcon strikes at the neck with those deadly sickle-shaped talons."

   emmew] HANMER (ed. 1743, 6, glossary): "To *Emmew,* to mew up, to coop up." So JOHNSON (1755). JOHNSON (ed. 1765): "Forces follies to lie in cover without daring to show themselves." STEEVENS (Var. 1778): "To *enmew* is a term in falconry used by B[eaumont] and Fletcher," in *The Knight of Malta* (ed. Glover & Waller, 2.2): 'And at his pitch inmew the Town below him'." STAUNTON (ed. 1859): "To *emmew* or *enmew* is a hawking technical, and as here used signifies, we believe, to paralyse and disable, as the falcon does the frightened bird over and around which it wheels preparatory to making the deadly swoop by which the prey is transfixed." But *OED* finds no evidence for this guess. KEIGHTLEY (1863, p. 263): "It is the falcon, and not the fowl, that *emmewed.* The right word, then is *enew.*" BAYNES (1872, pp. 354–5): "The hawk *enewed* the fowl; that is, forced it back to the

As Falcon doth the Fowle, is yet a diuell: (F6
His filth within being cast, he would appeare
A pond, as deepe as hell.
  Cla. The prenzie, *Angelo*?   1309

1309, 1312 prenzie] Princely F2-THEO2, THEO4-SING1, COL1, HAL, DEL4, SIS;
priestly WARBURTON (*see* HAN2) *conj.,* HAN1, WARB, COLNE, COL2, DYCE, WH,
COL3, COL4, HUD2, BUL; precise TIECK *conj.,* KNT, VERP, KTLY, ALEX, ARD2, PEN2
(1309 *only*); primzie CEBES *conj.,* SING2, HENL; rev'rend STAU

---

water again, from which it had to be driven afresh by the falconer and landed [i.e.,
forced to solid ground] before the hawk could stoop and seize, or strike and truss her
quarry. The fowl was often enewed once or twice before it was landed effectively
enough for the final swoop." Turberville, "In Commendation of Hawking" (1575),
spells the verb *eneaw,* and Drayton explains *ineawe* as "Lay the Fowles againe into the
water" (*Poly-Olbion,* 1613, 20:234). Cf. *eneauer,* "turne into water," in COTGRAVE
(1611). "From this primary sense it seems to have acquired the secondary signification of 'to check', 'to drive back', and 'relentlessly pursue'. . . . The imagery is that
of the penal law, or rather perhaps of despotic power . . . pursuing its victims with
reiterated strokes, and allowing them little chance of ultimate escape." *OED* (Enew
v.): "Of a hawk: To drive (a fowl) into the water. . . . (In Shaks. spelt *emmew,* either
by confusion with *emmew* Enmew, or merely by a misprint.)" MADDEN (1897, p. 202
n.): " 'Enmew' in the sense of 'to cause to lie close and keep concealed, as hawk in
mew' " (cf. *OED,* Inmew). HART (ed. 1905): "I think the passage requires the more
violent and destructive sense implied by 'enew'." LASCELLES (1916, 2:363 n.): "To
'enew' was to drive the quarry into covert or water, where it was kept down, till again
roused by the falconer with his spaniels. The term occurs once in Shakespeare . . .
but in the Folios is disguised under the erroneous form 'emmew'." HENN (1972, p.
31 and n.): " 'Drive into hiding'." Cf. *The Boke of Saint Albans* (1486, sig. d2, facs.
1881): "And if it dooth oftimes the fowle for fere of yowre hawke woll
spryng and fall ayen in to the Ryuer. or [i.e., before] the hawke sees hir. and so [the
fowle] lie styll and dare not arise. ye shall say then yowre hawke hath ennewed the
fowle in to the Ryuer."
    1307-8 JOHNSON (ed. 1765): "To *cast* a pond, is to empty it of mud." MASON
(1785, p. 38): "Isabella continues to borrow her images from falconry; when a hawk
disgorges, she is said to *cast.* " LUCIUS (1786, p. 359): *"Sounded,* or having its depth
fathomed." BAYNES (1872, p. 356): "The hawk when first taken out of the mew
. . . was subjected to a course of scouring diet. The technical name for such diet was
casting, and as the result the hawk was said to have *cast* her filth." CARTER (1905,
p. 410): Cf. Matt. 23:27: "whited tombes, which appeare beautifull outward, but are
within full of dead mens bones, and of all filthines." HART (ed. 1905): "Computed,
estimated. Perhaps a reference to the medical use 'casting water' is understood." LEE
(ed. 1907): "Diagnosed." RIDLEY (ed. 1935): "Cast up (*i.e.* thrown out)." WINNY
(ed. 1959): "If his foulness were measured, Angelo would seem a bottomless cess-
pool. Compare *Macbeth* IV.iii.60-1 [1883-4]." LEVER (ed. 1965): *"Cast*] a word of
many meanings. . . . *O.E.D. v* 28, 29, 'dig up with a spade (as of a ditch etc.)' is the
most fitting." WILSON (1970, pp. 175-6): Cf. "as deepe as hell," *Wiv.* 3.5.14
(1691). EVANS (ed. 1974): Cf. *MV* 1.1.88-9 (97-8).
    1309 **prenzie**] F2 *Princely* is the reading in 1309 and 1312 of all subsequent eds.

Isa. Oh 'tis the cunning Liuerie of hell,   1310

---

before Knight except Hanmer and Warburton, who print *priestly* (marked "Warb. emend." in the 1745 ed. of Hanmer). TIECK (ed. 1831, 5:381) proposes *precise,* meaning "puritanical." KNIGHT (ed. 1840): "Tieck has suggested, as we think very happily, the word *precise.* It will be seen at once that this word has a much closer resemblance to *prenzie* than either of the others:—prenzie. precise. princelie. priestlie. Angelo has already been called *precise;* and the term, so familiar to Shakspere's contemporaries, of *precisian,* would make Claudio's epithet perfectly appropriate and intelligible." COLLIER (ed. 1842): "But for this repetition [at 1312] it might have been thought that Shakespeare meant to introduce the Italian word *prence,* as applied to Angelo, to designate his rank. . . . Tieck suggests *precise* . . . and the emendation deserves attention." BRAE (1851, p. 455): " 'Precise' has the immeasurable advantage of repetition by Shakspeare himself, in the same play [342], applied to the same person, and coupled with the same word 'guard'." SINGER (1851, p. 456): " 'Precise' is peculiarly applicable to the assumed sanctity of Angelo." It may have been accented on the first syllable. CEBES (1851, p. 522): Burns uses *primsie* to mean "demure, precise." [See *OED* and *Scottish National Dict.*] H. C. K. (1853, p. 195): "It will be observed that there is a comma after *prenzie* in the original, indicating that the word is a substantive, not an adjective. Now what is the Italian for a prince? Not only *principe,* but also *prenze.* . . . I have no doubt that what Shakspeare *did* write was— 'The prenzie, Angelo?' while a little lower down he converted the word into an adjective." So NICHOLSON (1883, p. 464), SULLIVAN (1926, p. 537), HOTSON (1947, p. 603). KEIGHTLEY (1853, p. 362): "As to the Italian *prenze,* I cannot receive it. I very much doubt Shakspeare's knowledge of Italian, and am sure that he would not, if he understood the word, use it as an adjective." SCHMIDT (1875): "Probably = too nice, precise, demure, prim." McGINN (1948, p. 132): *Precise,* "if correct, would indicate . . . by the repetition of the adjective that Shakespeare wishes to impress upon his audience the puritanical character of the deputy." SISSON (1956, 1:83–4): *"Prenzie* is meaningless and demands emendation. . . . Angelo is *princely,* though not Prince, for he has all the functions of the Prince." LEVER (ed. 1965): " 'Precise' could have been misread as 'prenzie', was sometimes accented on the first syllable (with 'i' normally pronounced as in French), and makes good sense in the second instance." McINTOSH (1969, p. 355): "I would suggest that the available evidence would support a hypothesis, that Shakespeare's *prenzie* is likely to be genuine, that it was a highly colloquial word, sardonic in tone, current in Elizabethan English and meaning 'strait-laced' or 'prim and proper'." But his evidence (pp. 352–6) does not support this. *Precise* gives precisely the right sense, "strict, scrupulous" (*OED, a.* 2). An adj. of two syllables is regularly accented by Sh. on the first when it precedes a noun accented on the first syllable (SCHMIDT, pp. 1413–15): cf. 725, *Lord Angelo is seuére,* but 788, *Oh iust, but séuere Law.* In Elizabethan handwriting *ci* can easily be mistaken for *n* and *se* for *zie,* or the MS spelling may have been *precize,* quoted in *OED* from Daniel in 1594 and Quarles in 1640, and also printed in *Greenes Vision* (1592, sig. H1ᵛ) and *West-ward Hoe* by Dekker and Webster (1607, 4.2.49). EDWARDS & JENKINS (1976, pp. 333–4) cite *prenselles,* n., and *pryncy,* a., but these are not *prenzie.* See p. 286.

1310 WAHL (1887, pp. 121–3): Cf. *Ham.* 2.2.628–9, 3.1.47–9 (1639–40, 1698–1700); *Oth.* 2.3.357–8 (1477–8); *LLL* 4.3.254, 257 (1603, 1606).

Liuerie] MAHOOD (1957, pp. 46–7): "Here the whole of Isabella's dilemma is conveyed in a single word of multiple and contradictory meanings. *Livery* sends our minds back to Angelo's words in [1150] . . . 'the destin'd *Liuerie'.* This meaning of

The damnest bodie to inuest, and couer
In prenzie gardes; dost thou thinke *Claudio*,
If I would yeeld him my virginitie
Thou might'st be freed?
   Cla. Oh heauens, it cannot be.   1315
   Isa. Yes, he would giu't thee; from this rank offence

1311 damnest] damnedst F2, ROWE1+; damned F3, F4   bodie] bodies KTLY
1312 prenzie] prenzie's IRV; precious PEN2   gardes] garb COLNE, COL2, COL3, COL4; garbs KTLY
1316 giu't] grant mTBY2 *conj.*, HAN1; give WARB, CAP; give it v1773-v1821, SING, KTLY, DEL4, ARD1   thee;] ~ ‸ JOHN, v1773, COL1, WH1, COL3   from] for HAN1-RANN

'token of servitude' thus mingles with the sense of 'disguise' in Isabella's words to Claudio to suggest that Angelo is enslaved to the passion from which he pretends to be exempt; and the lines which follow show that here *livery* is also used to mean 'delivery'; that is, in the legal sense of 'delivery of property into a person's possession' (*N.E.D.* 5a). Isabella can deliver Claudio from death by delivering herself into Angelo's possession, but this would in fact be 'the cunning livery of hell', since it would purchase damnation for both of them." LEVER (ed. 1965): "A verbal noun, 'the dispensing of clothing to retainers or servants' (*O.E.D.* 1a)." See n. 1150. The lines may mean: "It is the subtle disguise of the devil to dress and conceal his most wicked servant in strait-laced trimmings."
   1311 **damnest**] LEVER (ed. 1965): "F. 'damnest' may be an elocutionary simplification, like 'exists' [1223: see n.]."
   inuest] SCHMIDT (1874): "To array, to dress' (*OED, v.* 1).
   1312 **prenzie gardes**] HANMER (ed. 1743, 6, glossary): "*Guarde,* the hem or welt of a garment: also, any lace or galloon upon the seams or borders of it." WARBURTON (ed. 1747): "*Guards* here signifies *lace,* as referring to *livery*. . . . *Priestly guards* means *sanctity.*" STEEVENS (Var. 1773): "*Princely guards* mean no more than the ornaments of royalty." MALONE (ed. 1790): "*A guard,* in old language, meant a welt or border of a garment; 'because (says Minsheu [*The Guide into Tongues,* 1617]) it *gards* and keeps the garment from tearing'." NARES (1822): "Trimmings, facings, or other ornaments applied upon a dress [*OED, sb.* 11b]. . . . *Guards* stand for ornaments in general, or by synecdoche, for dress, in [this] passage." SIEGEL (1950, p. 443) quotes Marston's *Scourge of Villanie* (1598), Satire 7, on "yon garded man" who looks like "some grave sober Cato Vtican" but is "naught but budge, old gards, brown fox-fur face." See n. 1498.
   dost thou thinke] HART (ed. 1905): "Do you understand." HARRISON (ed. 1948): "Would you believe it." See *OED* (*v.*[2] 12): "To believe possible or likely," quoting *Oth.* 3.3.339 (1982).
   1316-17 **Yes . . . still**] HEATH (1765, p. 89): "Yes, he would put it in your power, from the advantage this rank offence of his would give you over him, to go on in the commission of the same sin." STEEVENS (Var. 1778): "*From the time* of my committing this offence, you might persist in sinning with safety." HART (ed. 1905): "He would give you freedom as a result of this rank transgression (he proposes to me), and give you power to go on sinning in the self-same way." If *heauens* in 1315 was originally *God* (see n. 1006), *offend him* may have referred to God rather than

So to offend him still. This night's the time
That I should do what I abhorre to name,
Or else thou diest to morrow.
  Clau. Thou shalt not do't.   1320
  Isa. O, were it but my life,
I'de throw it downe for your deliuerance
As frankely as a pin.
  Clau. Thankes deere *Isabell.*
  Isa. Be readie *Claudio*, for your death to morrow.   1325
  Clau. Yes. Has he affections in him,
That thus can make him bite the Law by th'nose,
When he would force it? Sure it is no sinne,

1322 I'de] I'le F3, F4
1324 deere] dearest POPE1-v1773 (−CAP)
1326 Yes] I will KTLY he] he then HAN1
1327–8 th'nose, . . . it?] ∼ ? . . . ∼ , v1773-v1785

---

to Angelo.
 1316 **giu't**] SCHMIDT (1874): *Give,* "To grant, to allow" (*OED, v.* 39).
 1317 **still**] SCHMIDT (1875): "In future (no less than formerly); for ever."
DURHAM (ed. 1926): "Continually" (*OED, adv.* 3).
 1318 **abhorre to name**] LEVER (ed. 1965): "Cf. [227] and *Per.,* IV. vi. 75–6."
See also *Oth.* (F) 4.2.162 (2876), "It do's abhorre me now I speake the word."
 1321–3 HALLIWELL (ed. 1854) quotes *1 Promos,* 3.4 (p. 323 below): "O would
my life, would satisfie his yre, *Cassandra* then, would cancell soone thy band."
 1323 **frankely**] JOHNSON (1755): "Liberally; freely; kindly; readily." *OED* (*adv.*
2): "Unreservedly."
  as a pin] STEEVENS (Var. 1778): So in *Ham.* 1.4.65 (654). See n. 550.
 1326 This line has only four stresses. Claudio pauses after *Yes* to think it over.
  affections] See n. 461.
 1327 **bite . . . nose**] WARBURTON (ed. 1747): "This is but a kind of bear-garden
phrase, taken from the custom of driving cattle, and setting a dog upon them to catch
them by the nose, and stop them when they go astray." MALONE (1780, 1:98): *"Is
he actuated by passions that impel him to transgress the law, at the very moment that he is
enforcing it against others?"* ROLFE (ed. 1882): *"To bite the law by the nose* is rather
to treat it with contempt." So *OED* (Nose *sb.* 9e). THISELTON (1901, p. 26): "To
'bite the Law by th' nose' is much more than to 'plucke Justice by the nose' (I. iii.
29 [319]). It is rather to arrest violently the course of the Law." HART (ed. 1905):
"Cause it to weep, grieve it." PARROTT (ed. 1938): "Mock the law." LEVER (ed.
1965): "A proverbial expression (Tilley N 241)." But "to bite off one's nose" (to
reply sharply) is not the same thing.
 1328 **force**] WARBURTON (ed. 1747): "Inforce." *OED* (*v.*¹ 9b): "To lay stress
upon, press home, urge. *Obs.* Also, To enforce (a law. etc.)." WINNY (ed. 1959):
"Violate." See n. 74.
  it is no sinne] LEVER (ed. 1965): "In Lodge's *Wits Miserie* (1596) . . .
Fornication says, 'Tut . . . lechery is no sinne . . .' (sig. G3ᵛ)."

Or of the deadly seuen it is the least.
   Isa. Which is the least?   1330
   Cla. If it were damnable, he being so wise,
Why would he for the momentarie tricke
Be perdurablie fin'de? Oh *Isabell.*
   Isa. What saies my brother?
   Cla. Death is a fearefull thing.   1335
   Isa. And shamed life, a hatefull.
   Cla. I, but to die, and go we know not where,

1332 Why‸] ∼ , HAN1, CAP, MAL-1821, SING, HAL   momentarie] momentany F3, F4
   1335 Death is] Death's POPE1-JOHN2, DYCE2, DYCE3-HUD2

1329 **the deadly seuen**] See Morton W. Bloomfield, *The Seven Deadly Sins* (1952).

1331-3 JOHNSON (ed. 1765): "*Shakespear* shows his knowledge of human nature in the conduct of *Claudio*. When *Isabella* first tells him of *Angelo*'s proposal he answers with honest indignation. . . . But the love of life being permitted to operate, soon furnishes him with sophistical arguments." PARTRIDGE (1947, p. 155): "Cf. the elaboration on this theme in *Lucrece*, vv. 211–218."

1332 **tricke**] SCHMIDT (1875): "Any thing done not deliberately, but out of passion or caprice." See n. 877–8. DURHAM (ed. 1926): "Trifle." PARTRIDGE (1947, p. 208): "A bout of love-making."

1333 **perdurablie**] JOHNSON (1755): "Lastingly." *OED* (*adv.*): "Permanently, lastingly; everlastingly, eternally."
   fin'de] Punished. THIRLBY (1723–33): Cf. 786 (see n.).

1337-51 THEOBALD (1726, pp. 46–7): Here and in *Ham.* 1.5 Sh. "had those fine Verses of *Virgil* in his Eye" (*Aeneid* 6:736 ff.). THIRLBY (1733–47): "Purgatory." UPTON (1746, p. 216): "These passages of Shakespeare and Milton [*P.L.* 2:596 ff., 178 ff.] will bear comparison with what Virgil has written of the punishment of the damned, from Plato's *Phaedo.*" So WHALLEY (1748, pp. 55–6). HURD (1757, p. 20): "We see in this passage a mixture of Christian and Pagan ideas; all of them very susceptible of poetical ornament, and conducive to the argument of the Scene; but such as Shakespear had never dreamt of but for Virgil's Platonic hell." FARMER (1767, p. 24): "I am not sure, that they came from the *Platonick* hell of *Virgil.* The Monks also had their hot and their cold Hell." CAPELL (1780, 2:3:46): Cf. the famous speech of Achilles in the *Odyssey*, bk. 11. W. R. (1780, p. 518): Cf. Euripides, *Iphigenia in Aulis*, 1252 [Better to live miserably than to die nobly]. DOUCE (1807, 1:132): "It is difficult to decide whether Shakspeare is here alluding to the pains of hell or purgatory. May not the whole be a mere poetical rhapsody originating in the recollection of what he had read in books of Catholic divinity?" TODD (1809, 2:384): Cf. Milton, *P.L.* 2:146–51. BALDWIN (1944, 2:492): "Virgil and Shakspere follow the triple purgation of the philosophers. . . . As Claudio's sin has been corporal he must first be purged with fire, and thence progress to betterment through water and air." HANKINS (1956, pp. 490–1): "Shakespeare's use of 'howling' to designate souls in hell may proceed from the groans *(gemitus)* and great cries *(tantus plangor* [or *clangor*]) of Virgil's souls in Tartarus (*Aen.* VI. 557, 561) and from the later visions

To lie in cold obstruction, and to rot,
This sensible warme motion, to become
A kneaded clod; And the delighted spirit   1340

1339 sensible warme] sensible-warm WALKER (1860, 1:35) *conj.*, HUD2
1340 delighted] dilated HAN1

---

which follow the same convention. . . . If Claudio's howling ones refer to souls in
hell, then his fire, wind, and ice afford a clear parallel to Virgil's purgatorial punishments of fire, wind, and water." NOSWORTHY (ed. 1969): "Claudio's meditations are
upon Purgatory rather than Hell since he is, by inference, a Catholic, like his sister."
See FLUCHÈRE (1948), p. 454 below.
    1337 STEEVENS (in Var. 1803): Cf. Dryden, *Aurengzebe,* 4.1.3–4: "Death, in
itself, is nothing; but we fear To be we know not what, we know not where." MARTIN
(1945, p. 180): Claudio reflects "the mental state of the man who, according to
Lucretius [3:870–8], has failed to banish care because he cannot use himself to the
thought of complete extinction." FRYE (1957, p. 271) finds four kinds of rhythm in
this line.
    I, but] See n. 455.
    1338 THIRLBY (1747–53): "Does he mean pent up in a close coffin or grave?"
JOHNSON (1755): *Obstruction,* "something heaped together." HALLIWELL (ed.
1854): "To lie in the cold earth which obstructs every movement or vital action of
the body; or, possibly, to lie a lifeless mass, when the circulation of the body is entirely
stopped." HART (ed. 1905): "Stagnation (of the blood)," as in *TN* 3.4.22 (1542).
OED (Obstruction 1): *Cold obstruction,* "stoppage or cessation of the vital functions;
the condition of the body in death." LEISI (ed. 1964): " 'Stoppage', either of the
blood . . . or of light, hence '(utter) darkness' (as *Tw. Night* IV 2 43 [2024–5]). As
this passage contains traditional ideas similar to those of *Inferno* V 28–42 (cf. [1344]),
the meaning 'darkness' is more appropriate, since Dante speaks of a place deprived
of light." Cf. Shelley, *The Cenci,* 5.4.49–51: "so young to go Under the obscure, cold,
rotting, wormy ground! To be nailed down into a narrow place." See p. 286 and
RYLANDS (1928), p. 453 below.
    1339 **sensible**] SCHMIDT (1875): "Capable of perception, endowed with feel-
ing." ONIONS (1911): "Endowed with sensibility, sensitive" (*OED, a.* 8).
    motion] MALONE (ed. 1790): *"Organized body."* SCHMIDT (1875): "Sense,
perceptivity, mental sight." GRAY (1888, p. 342): "The human body is a motion, or
automaton," as in 1599. *OED* (*sb.* 2c): "Power of movement," first use in this sense.
WILSON (ed. 1922): "The body, conceived as a puppet moved by 'the delighted
spirit'." CAMPBELL (ed. 1949): "Movement of the mind; hence, mind." BALD (ed.
1956): "Organism."
    1340 **kneaded**] ABBOTT (§375): "Seems used for 'knead*able'.'' OED* (Knead v.),
first quotation for Kneaded *(ppl. a.).* LEVER (ed. 1965): "Compressed into a lump
of earth."
    delighted] WARBURTON (ed. 1747): "The spirit accustomed here to ease and
delights." EDWARDS (1748, p. 17): "Shakespear used *delighted,* either for *delightful,*
or *which is delighted in."* UPTON (1748, p. 217 n.): "Its being capable of delight; or
its formerly being delighted; not the actual possession of delight." ANON. (1780, p.
260): "The spirit now delighted or pleased with its situation and enjoyments in the
body." A gentleman offers a modest query: "May not *delighted* bear the same meaning
as the word *alighted* . . . a spirit *discharged* from the body." ANON. (1786, p. 165 n.):

To bath in fierie floods, or to recide   1341
In thrilling Region of thicke-ribbed Ice,
To be imprison'd in the viewlesse windes

1341 bath] bathe F2+ (−CAP, ARD2)
1342 Region] Regions ROWE1-v1773 (−CAP), MAL-KNT2, SING2, KTLY-DYCE3, HUD2   thicke-ribbed] thick-ribb'd THEO, WARB, JOHN

"We think *'delighted'* is used for *'delighted in':* the preposition *in* being omitted *euphoniæ gratia."* So in *Cym.* 5.4.102 (3138); *Oth.* 1.3.290 (642). "The spirit in which we delight—in which we so much pride ourselves as our noblest part." NARES (1822): "Used . . . for *delightful,* or causing delight; delighted in." KNIGHT (ed. 1840): A correspondent suggests: "Does not the word *delighted (de-lighted)* mean removed from the regions of light . . . ?" So in *N&Q* 4 May 1861 (p. 358), 3 Aug. 1878 (p. 83). HICKSON (1850, p. 113): *"Lightened,* made light, relieved from the weight of matter." KENNEDY (1850, p. 139): "The word *delighted* in Shakspeare represents the Latin participle *delectus* (from *deligere*), 'select, choice, exquisite, refined'." WALKER (1860, 2:11−12): *"The spirit engaged in earthly delights, enjoying the pleasures of this world."* ABBOTT (§375): " 'That once took its delight in this world'." SCHMIDT (1874): "Having the power of giving delight, rich in delight." *OED (ppl. a.* 2): "Endowed or attended with delight; affording delight, delightful. . . . cf. *Delightful* 2 . . . Full of or experiencing delight; delighting *in,* delighted *with."* SMITHERS (1970, p. 31): "Evidently a Shakespearian coinage in [*OED*] sense 2, which is to be regarded as an adjective formed on the noun," not as ppl. a. See p. 286.

    1341 **bath**] A variant spelling of *bathe (OED, v.).*

    fierie floods] HANKINS (1953, p. 136): "It seems likely that the word 'floods' " is recalled from *The Zodiake of Life* (1576, p. 27), "Where flames the flouds of *Phlegeton,"* though other sources have doubtless contributed.

    recide] Cf. *recides* 1485.

    1342 FARMER (1767, p. 24) quotes "an old Homily" on a part of hell "passynge colde, that yf a greate hyll of fyre were cast therin, it sholde torne to yce." STEEVENS (Var. 1778) quotes *The Kalender of Shepherdes* (1506; ed. Sommer, 3:68–9): "I sawe in hell . . . a flode of frosone yce . . . & than sodenly came acolde wynde ryght great." T. H. WHITE (1785, p. 277): Sh. read Hakluyt's *Voyages* (ed. 1598, 1:562) on Iceland, where [according to Sebastian Münster's *Cosmographia*] "The inhabitants are of opinion that in mount Hecla and in the ise, there are places wherein the soules of their countreymen are tormented." DOUCE (1807, 1:134): "In the old legend of *Saint Patrick's purgatory* mention is made of a lake of ice and snow, into which persons were plunged up to their necks." BLAKEWAY (in Var. 1821): Cf. Jonson, *Catiline* (1.1.213–14): "W'are spirit-bound, In ribs of ice." "Milton seems to have had Shakspeare before him" when he wrote *P.L.* 2:595–603. HART (ed. 1905): "The thrilling region may well be identified with Iceland." NUTT (1942, p. 256): Sh. could have found many references to thick ice in the Dutch voyages to the Arctic Ocean (see n. 493). But HANKINS (1956, pp. 482–95) traces the ice of hell or purgatory from Gregory and Bede down to Palingenius.

    thrilling] *OED (ppl. a.* 1b): "Piercing or penetrating, as cold; causing shivering or shuddering." ROLFE (ed. 1905): Cf. *Rom.* 4.3.15 (2496).

    1343 **viewlesse**] JOHNSON (1755): "Unseen." MALONE (ed. 1790, 3:164 n.): Cf. *AYL* 2.7.178 (1158) and *LLL* 4.3.105–6 (1442–3). STEEVENS (in Var. 1803):

And blowne with restlesse violence round about
The pendant world: or to be worse then worst   1345
Of those, that lawlesse and incertaine thought,
Imagine howling, 'tis too horrible.

1345 be worse then worst] be, worse than worst, WH, NLSN
1346 Of those—that lawless and incertain thought— HAN1; Of those that, lawless
and incertain, thought COL2   incertaine] uncertain ROWE1, ROWE2   thought]
thoughts THEO, WARB-HUD2 (—CAP, HAL, CAM1, GLO), CAM3
1347 Imagine] Imagines DAV, HAL, COL2, KIT1

Cf. Milton, *Comus,* 92. [Milton also uses the word in "The Passion," 50, and *P.L.*
3:518.] *OED* (*a.* 1): "Invisible," first quotation.
    1344–5 **blowne . . . world**] T. WHITE (1793, app.) and DOUCE (1807, 1:134)
quote Chaucer (*Parlement of Foules,* ed. Robinson, 78 ff.), from Cicero's *Dream of
Scipio:* "Shul whirle aboute th'erthe alwey in peyne." STONE (1879, pp. 286–7)
quotes Cicero (in Macrobius) and Dante, *Inferno* 5:31–2. ROLFE (ed. 1882): "Cf.
Oth. v. 2. 279 [3579]." THALER (1929, p. 195): Cf. *P.L.* 3:487–9. HANKINS (1956,
p. 494): "Claudio's phrase 'viewless winds' could very well proceed from Virgil's
'inanes ventos'. But Claudio envisions an image unlike Virgil's, for his sinners are not
attached to any fixed point and can be blown all the way around the world. There
is nothing quite like this in Virgil or in any of the medieval visions, though Plato has
a somewhat similar description in the *Phaedo* (109–114). Much the closest resemblance that I have observed anywhere is Cicero's account of the punishment of the
wicked at the very end of his *Somnium Scipionis* . . . (IX.3)." VELZ (1968, p. 159):
"Stone does not observe how appropriate this Ciceronian punishment for the lustful
is to Claudio and to the entire theme of the play."
    1345 **pendant**] TODD (1801, 2:174): Cf. Milton, *P.L.* 2:1052. *OED* (*a.* 3):
"Hanging or floating unsupported in the air or in space."
    worst] *OED* (*a.* 4): "Most unfortunate or badly off," this sense only here and
in *Lr.* 4.1.2 (2180).
    1346 **lawlesse . . . thought**] JOHNSON (ed. 1765): "Conjecture sent out to
wander without any certain direction, and ranging through all possibilities of pain."
CAPELL (1780, 2:3:46): "An undefinable and uncircumscribable thought." SCHMIDT
(1874): *Lawless,* "unruly, licentious." *Incertain,* "not knowing what to think or to
do." INGLEBY (1875, p. 99): "Who body forth—or render objective—their own
lawless and distracted mind." PERRING (1885, pp. 45–6): "A periphrasis expressive
of the mental idiosyncracy of lunatics. It is they who fancy they hear the damned ones
howl." HANKINS (1956, p. 490): "Unrestrained thought which, uncertain of the
exact punishments of hell, imagines the worst of horrors and takes the outcries to be
the screams of tortured sufferers." LEVER (ed. 1965): "Lawless, because unwarranted
by Christian teaching."
    1347 **Imagine**] LEISI (ed. 1964): "The lack of concord is probably Shake-
speare's, not the printer's (cf. *Englische Studien* 30, 1902, p. 13), especially as *lawlesse
thought* and *incertaine thought* can be taken as two separate subjects." LEVER (ed.
1965): "Plural form after two adjectives, cf. [277] and note." See also n. 833.
    howling] THIRLBY (1733–47): Cf. *Ham.* 5.1.265 (3433) and *2H4* 2.4.374
(1371). LASCELLES (1953, p. 166): "Claudio is (I believe) speaking of sounds,
supposedly supernatural, in which he fears, but is forbidden [by the denial of purga-

The weariest, and most loathed worldly life
That Age, Ache, periury, and imprisonment
Can lay on nature, is a Paradise   1350
To what we feare of death.
   Isa. Alas, alas.
   Cla. Sweet Sister, let me liue.
What sinne you do, to saue a brothers life,
Nature dispenses with the deede so farre,   1355
That it becomes a vertue.
   Isa. Oh you beast,

1349 periury] penury F2+   and] *Om.* POPE1-JOHN2
1351-3 *Lines ending* death. . . . live: v1793-NLSN, KIT1-PEL1, PEN2, EVNS; alas!
. . . live. CAM3, ARD2

---

tory in reformed doctrine], to hear the voices of the unhappy dead." HANKINS
(1956, p. 488): "Who these howling ones are is indicated by Romeo's words" in
Rom. 3.3.47–8 (1849–50): "the damned vse that word in hell: Howling attends it."
   1349 **periury**] A scribal or compositorial error for *penury,* corrected in F2.
   1350 **nature**] See n. 219.
   1351 **To**] Compared to. See SCHMIDT (1875, p. 1236), ABBOTT §187, FRANZ
§529.
   1354 **What**] Whatever, any . . . that (*OED, a.*[1] C.9).
   1355 **Nature**] SCHMIDT (1875): "Innate and involuntary affection" (*OED, sb.*
9e). HART (ed. 1905): "Nature is here 'Natura naturans', the creative power of the
schoolmen." This seems unlikely. TILLEY (N41) and WILSON (p. 273): "He that
follows nature is never out of his way" (Cicero). Cf. *2 Promos,* 4.4 (p. 362 below):
"Nature wyld mee, my Brother loue."
   dispenses with] JOHNSON (1755): "To excuse; to grant dispensation for; to
allow." *OED* (*v.* 15): "To deal with (a breach of law) so as to condone it . . . to excuse,
pardon."
   1357–68 JOHNSON (ed. 1765): "In *Isabella*'s declamation there is something
harsh, and something forced and far-fetched. But her indignation cannot be thought
violent when we consider her not only as a virgin but as a nun." CLARKE (ed. 1864):
"Shakespeare uses the word 'beast', in numerous instances, to express 'inconsistent
with human nature', 'wanting in manhood'. Here, Claudio pleading nature's leniency
to sin, suggests to his sister the retort that he is *unnatural* and *unmanly* in his plea.
The very vehemence of Isabella's indignation in this speech might surely redeem her
from the charge of 'coldness'; and can we need stronger proof of her warm affection
for her brother than those glowing words of passionate earnestness? [Quotes 1321–
3.]" WITTING (1941; 1976, p. 65): "The real character of Isabella is as great a
mystery to the student as Hamlet's [the narrator in a novel writes]. My own opinion,
for what it is worth, is that in neither case was Shakespeare able to make up his mind
—and the effect is bi-focal. Is Isabella, one is forced to ask, a saint or a waspish prude?
Take her denunciation of the unhappy Claudio [quotes 1357–62]. . . . Elizabeth's
interpretation did not suggest outraged modesty or spiteful prudery; but rather a
frantic consciousness that she must not weaken; that she must crush her love for
Claudio, even by a savage and over-coloured outburst, directed as much against

Oh faithlesse Coward, oh dishonest wretch,
Wilt thou be made a man, out of my vice?
Is't not a kinde of Incest, to take life   1360
From thine owne sisters shame? What should I thinke,
Heauen shield my Mother plaid my Father faire:
For such a warped slip of wildernesse
Nere issu'd from his blood. Take my defiance,
Die, perish: Might but my bending downe   1365
Repreeue thee from thy fate, it should proceede.
Ile pray a thousand praiers for thy death,
No word to saue thee.
   Cla. Nay heare me *Isabell.*
   Isa. Oh fie, fie, fie: 1370

1362 shield] grant POPE1-v1773 (−CAP)
1365 but my] my only POPE1-JOHN2
1367 pray] pay F4-POPE2, HAN1
1368–70 *Lines ending* thee. . . . fie! v1793-GLO, DYCE2-NLSN, KIT1-PEL1, PEN2, EVNS; Isabel. . . . fye! KTLY, CAM3, ARD2
1369 Nay] *Om.* POPE, HAN1

---

herself as her brother. . . . Elizabeth caught the desperate mood of Isabella." See HUDSON (1872), CHAMBERS (1937), and CAMPBELL (ed. 1949), pp. 441, 444, and 445 below.

   1358 **faithlesse**] *OED* (*a.* 3): "That cannot be trusted or relied on," first quotation in this sense.

      dishonest] SCHMIDT (1874): "Dishonourable" (*OED, a.* 1).

   1359 **made a man**] LEVER (ed. 1965): "Given life again. Cf. [831, 1048]."

   1362 THIRLBY (1747–53): "God shield 'tis false." SCHMIDT (1875): *Shield,* "To forefend, to forbid, to avert . . . (i.e. God grant that thou wert not my father's son)" (*OED, v.* 5). HART (ed. 1905): "I prefer to explain it as a sudden doubt, shield meaning guard, protect. God protect my mother from such a suspicion, but it would seem almost necessary. Isabella uses the expression later, [2487]." LEVER (ed. 1965): " 'Heaven forbid that my mother should have been faithful to my father when you were conceived'."

   1363 **warped slip**] SCHMIDT (1875): *Warped,* "perverse, unnatural." *Slip,* "scion." HARRISON (ed. 1948): "The metaphor is of a cultivated fruit tree which reverts to the original wild stock." See n. 17. Cf. *2H6* 3.2.211–15 (1916–20).

      wildernesse] STEEVENS (Var. 1773): "Here used for *wildness,* the state of being disorderly." IDEM (Var. 1778): "Again, in old *Old Fortunatus,* 1600: 'But I in *wilderness* totter'd out my youth' " (Bowers in his ed. of Dekker, 1:172, emends Q to read *wildnesse*). ONIONS (1911): "*Of wilderness* (=barren, worthless)." *OED* (5b): "Wildness of character, licentiousness. *Obs. nonce-use.*"

   1364 **defiance**] STEEVENS (Var. 1778): "*Refusal.*" SCHMIDT (1874): "Rejection." *OED* (5): "Declaration of aversion or contempt; rejection," only quotation in this sense. HART (ed. 1905): "Renunciation, disownment."

   1370 **fie**] Cf. 935, 1046, 1508, 1881.

Thy sinn's not accidentall, but a Trade;

Mercy to thee would proue it selfe a Bawd,   (F6ᵛ

'Tis best that thou diest quickly.

    Cla. Oh heare me *Isabella.*

    Duk. Vouchsafe a word, yong sister, but one word.   1375

    Isa. What is your Will.

    Duk. Might you dispense with your leysure, I would by and by haue some speech with you: the satisfaction I would require, is likewise your owne benefit.

    Isa. I haue no superfluous leysure, my stay must be   1380
stolen out of other affaires: but I will attend you a while.

    Duke. Son, I haue ouer-heard what hath past between you & your sister. *Angelo* had neuer the purpose to corrupt her; onely he hath made an assay of her vertue, to

---

1373 quickly] quietly ROWE1, ROWE2   *going.* CAP, MAL-ARD1 (−CAM1, GLO, WH2, CAM2), PEL1-PEN2

1374 *Isabella*] *Isabel* JOHN

1375 SCENE III. POPE, HAN1, WARB, JOHN   *Duke steps in.* F2-F4; *om.* F1; *Enter* Duke *and* Provost. ROWE1-JOHN2, v1773, STAU (*subst.*); *The DUKE comes forward* CAM3, PEL1-PEN2; *Re-enter* Duke. CAP *etc.* (*subst.*)

1381 *walks apart.* CAP, CAM1, GLO, WH2-CAM2, ARD1-ALEX (−CAM3), ARD2, EVNS (*subst.*)

1384 assay] Essay ROWE, POPE, HAN1, v1803-SING1, COL1, COL4

1371 **accidentall**]JOHNSON (1755): "Casual, fortuitous, happening by chance." *OED* (*a.* 2): "Casual, occasional."

    Trade] JOHNSON (ed. 1765): "A custom; a practice; an established habit." *OED* (*sb.* 3c): "A regular or habitual course of action." LEVER (ed. 1965): " 'Trade' also links Claudio's situation with Pompey's and Overdone's."

1372 **proue**] See n. 1124.

1375-1489 VICKERS (1968, p. 319): "The function of prose here is important as a contrast in mood, in that it has a definite dampening effect after such great emotional stress—and the detail of the language reinforces our impression of its coolness and steadiness."

1377 **dispense with**] SCHMIDT (1874): "To do without, to spare." *OED* (*v.* 14) quotes this sense first from *Tim.* 3.2.93 (1069).

1378 **by and by**] SCHMIDT (1874, p. 162): "Presently," as in 1926. HARRISON (ed. 1948): "At once." LEVER (ed. 1965): "Soon."

    satisfaction] SCHMIDT (1875): "Gratification" (*OED* 5b). CAMPBELL (ed. 1949): "Payment." See n. 1484.

1381 **attend**] See *OED* (*v.* 1a): "Listen to."

    a while] THIRLBY (1733-47): "Does she go out?" LEVER (ed. 1965): "She has only to remain at the back of the stage (where the Provost is still waiting) to be conventionally out of earshot."

1384 **assay**] SCHMIDT (1874): "Examination, probation, trial." So *OED* (*sb.* 1). LEISI (ed. 1964): "The original meaning 'test of metal' may still have been felt." See n. 274.

practise his iudgement with the disposition of natures.   1385
She (hauing the truth of honour in her) hath made him
that gracious deniall, which he is most glad to receiue: I
am Confessor to *Angelo*, and I know this to be true, therfore prepare your selfe to death: do not satisfie your resolution with hopes that are fallible, to morrow you   1390
must die, goe to your knees, and make ready.

    Cla. Let me ask my sister pardon, I am so out of loue
with life, that I will sue to be rid of it.

    Duke. Hold you there: farewell: *Prouost*, a word
with you.   1395

    Pro. What's your will (father?)

    Duk. That now you are come, you wil be gone: leaue

    1389 satisfie] falsifie mTBY1 *and* WARBURTON (*see* HAN2) *conj.*, HAN1, WARB, CAP; qualify mTBY1 *and* BAILEY (1866) *conj.*, HUD2

    1391 goe‸] ~ ; COL1, DEL4, COL4

    1393 *Exit.* F2-RANN; *after* Farewell. (1394) *Exit* CLAUDIO. MAL-PEL1, PEN2, EVNS; *after* farewell. (1394) *Claudio retires.* ARD2

    1394 *Re-enter* Provost. *after* Farewel. CAP, MAL-SING2, WH1, COL3, KTLY, KNT3, DEL4, COL4, ARD1, CAM3, SIS, PEL1, PEN2; *after* 1393 v1778, v1785, RANN; *after* 1395 DYCE, CAM1, GLO, HUD2-BUL, NLSN, KIT1, ALEX, EVNS

    1385 **disposition**] SCHMIDT (1874): "Quality in general, manner of thinking and acting." CAMPBELL (ed. 1949): "Constitution." HARDING (ed. 1954): "Evaluation." LEVER (ed. 1965): "Control, ordering."

    1387 **gracious**] SCHMIDT (1874): "In a state of heavenly grace, pious, virtuous, holy" (*OED, a.* 6). Cf. *grace* 1403, *gracious* 1423, 1705, *graciously* 1085 and n.

    1389 **satisfie**] STEEVENS (Var. 1773): "Rest with satisfaction." MALONE (ed. 1790): "Content yourself." CLARKE (ed. 1864): " 'Feed your resolution (or sustain your courage)'." SCHMIDT (1875): "Set yourself at ease," "gratify yourself." *OED* (*v.* 4b): "Content."

    1390 **fallible**] JOHNSON (1755): "Liable to errour; such as may be deceived." So *OED* (*a.* 2).

    1393 **sue**] Cf. 1246.

    1394 **Hold you there**] JOHNSON (ed. 1765): "Continue in that resolution." SCHMIDT (1874, p. 546): "Cf. *there rest* [993]."

    1394–1400 ***Prouost . . . Exit.***] LYONS (1962, pp. 267-8): "Why should the Provost enter only to be told to leave again? . . . Is it not possible that one function of this brief dialogue may be to draw the Duke aside and leave the stage focally to Claudio and Isabella? Most editors add a direction, as here cited, to indicate that Claudio exits immediately after the Duke's 'Farewell'. But Claudio's 'Let me ask my sister pardon' in the preceding line evokes audience anticipation which no dialogue fulfills. A brief tableau, however, can effectively cap the Isabella-Claudio prison scene. Claudio approaches Isabella and in mime asks pardon of his sister; she lovingly responds, giving her blessing to a brother penitently kneeling and now prepared for death." LEVER (ed. 1965): "This summons leaves Claudio alone with Isabella for a mimed reconciliation."

me a while with the Maid, my minde promises with my
habit, no losse shall touch her by my company.

Pro. In good time.   *Exit.*   1400

Duk. The hand that hath made you faire, hath made
you good: the goodnes that is cheape in beauty, makes
beauty briefe in goodnes; but grace being the soule of
your complexion, shall keepe the body of it euer faire:
the assault that *Angelo* hath made to you, Fortune hath   1405
conuaid to my vnderstanding; and but that frailty hath

1402 cheape] chief DAWSON *conj.,* COLNE, COL2, COL4
1403 in] in such HAN1
1404 shall] should v1778-v1813, SING1, KNT
1405 to] on HAN1, WARB, JOHN

1398 **promises**] See *OED* (*v.* 6 *fig.*): "To afford ground of expectation of."
1398-9 **with my habit**] BALD (ed. 1956): "As well as my priestly robes." Cf. 338 *the habit* (*OED, sb.* 2), 2055 *my coate.*
1399 **losse**] *OED* (*sb.*[1] 5): "Detriment or disadvantage."
     touch] SCHMIDT (1875): "To hurt, to injure" (*OED, v.* 25a), as in 2298.
1400 **In good time**] STEEVENS (Var. 1778): "*A la bonne heure,* so be it, very well" (*OED,* Time *sb.* 42c[*d*]).
1401-4 VICKERS (1968, pp. 320-1): "A remarkably careful pattern, using the familiar rhetorical devices (*parison* throughout, *antimetabole* for a crucial hinge-effect in the second clause, disjunction in the third) to define and clarify a distinction essential to the action and to the character of Isabella."
1402-3 **the goodnes . . . in goodnes**] CAPELL (1780, 2:3:47): "If beauty holds goodness (or virtue) cheap, such beauty will be brief in it's own goodness, maintain it good a short time." CLARKE (ed. 1864): " 'The virtue of a beautiful woman that is parted with on easy terms, makes her beauty of short duration'." HUDSON (ed. 1880): "I do not well understand this. Does it mean, 'she who, in her pride or confidence of beauty, holds virtue in light esteem, will easily part with her virtue'?" Cf. *Ham.* 3.1.111-14 (1766-8). MIRIAM JOSEPH (1947, p. 81): "Shakespeare's interest in this figure [antimetabole] is revealed by the variations which he introduces in the repetition." Cf. n. 1721-2. LEVER (ed. 1965): " 'The pleasing qualities that cost little effort when you are beautiful make beauty soon cease to be good'." Cf. TILLEY (B163) and WILSON (p. 37): "Beauty and chastity seldom meet."
1403 **grace**] SCHMIDT (1874, p. 489): "Virtue" (*OED, sb.* 13b), as in 1749, 2304.
1404 **complexion**] WHITE (ed. 1883): "As in [1227], but here having reference to the constitution of both soul and body." LEISI (ed. 1964): " 'Temperament', . . . hence: 'character'." LEVER (ed. 1965): " 'Your disposition' [*OED, sb.* 3]; with play on 'complexion' in the modern sense." See nn. 1140, 1227.
     faire] See *OED* (*a.* 9): "Free from moral stain, spotless, unblemished."
1405 **assault**] SCHMIDT (1874): "Attempt on the chastity of a woman." See n. 1476.
1406 **frailty**] See *OED* (2): "Liability to err or yield to temptation." See n. 1131.

examples for his falling, I should wonder at *Angelo*: how
will you doe to content this Substitute, and to saue your
Brother?

Isab. I am now going to resolue him: I had rather   1410
my brother die by the Law, then my sonne should be vn-
lawfullie borne. But (oh) how much is the good Duke
deceiu'd in *Angelo*: if euer he returne, and I can speake
to him, I will open my lips in vaine, or discouer his gouernment.   1415

Duke. That shall not be much amisse: yet, as the matter now stands, he will auoid your accusation: he made
triall of you onelie. Therefore fasten your eare on my
aduisings, to the loue I haue in doing good; a remedie
presents it selfe. I doe make my selfe beleeue that you   1420
may most vprighteously do a poor wronged Lady a me-

1408 will] would v1778-SING1, OXF1, CAM3
1410 him:] ~ , HAL, DYCE, IRV, BUL
1413 returne] returns v1773-RANN
1419 aduisings, . . . good;] ~ : . . . ~ , POPE1-v1821, SING, COL, DYCE, WH,
STAU-KTLY, DEL4+ (−ARD2)
1421 vprighteously] uprightly POPE1-JOHN2

1407 **examples**] SCHMIDT (1874): "Precedent." See *OED* (*sb.* 4): "A parallel
case in the past." See n. 1959. LEVER (ed. 1965): "Referring either to the fall of the
angels, with play on Angelo's name, or to the fall of Adam tempted by Eve, or both."
 his] LEISI (ed. 1964): *"His* is probably the neuter possessive (Modern Engl.
'its'), as often in Sh., and consequently refers to *frailty.*" It is more likely to refer to
Angelo.
 1410 **resolue**] DYCE (1867): "To satisfy, to inform, to remove perplexity or
uncertainty, to convince." *OED* (*v.* 15): "To free (one) from doubt or perplexity,"
quoting 2074–5. WILSON (ed. 1922): "Set the mind at rest."
 1414 **discouer**] SCHMIDT (1874): "Reveal" (*OED, v.* 4). ROLFE (ed. 1882):
"Uncover, expose." See n. 636.
 1414–15 **gouernment**] SCHMIDT (1874): "Administration of public affairs."
PARROTT (ed. 1938): "Conduct." HARRISON (ed. 1948): "Misgovernment." LEVER
(ed. 1965): "(i) moral conduct (*O.E.D.* 2b . . .); (ii) his way of governing."
 1417 **auoid**] CROSBY (1872 letter): "Defeat, or evade," a legal term used in
pleading. *OED* (*v.* 2): "To make void or of no effect; to refute, disprove. In *Law,*
to defeat (a pleading)."
 1417–18 **he . . . onelie**] MASON (1785, p. 39): "That is, he will say he made
trial of you only." LEISI (ed. 1964): "An early instance of 'reported speech'."
 1419 **aduisings**] *OED* (*vbl. sb.*): "Counselling." See n. 35.
 1420–4 **I . . . Duke**] VICKERS (1968, p. 321): "His remedy is formally stated,
almost like a *propositio* in a formal oration, and gains more clarity by its parallel
structure."
 1421 **vprighteously**] *OED:* "In an upright manner," only quotation; cf. *Upright-
eousness.*

rited benefit; redeem your brother from the angry Law;
doe no staine to your owne gracious person, and much
please the absent Duke, if peraduenture he shall euer re-
turne to haue hearing of this businesse.   1425

   Isab. Let me heare you speake farther; I haue spirit to
do any thing that appeares not fowle in the truth of my
spirit.

   Duke. Vertue is bold, and goodnes neuer fearefull:
Haue you not heard speake of *Mariana* the sister of *Fre-*   1430
dericke the great Souldier, who miscarried at Sea?

   Isa. I haue heard of the Lady, and good words went
with her name.

   Duke. Shee should this *Angelo* haue married: was affianced to her oath, and the nuptiall appointed: between   1435
which time of the contract, and limit of the solemnitie,

1425 hearing] a hearing KNT2
1426 speake farther] speak, father F4-POPE2, HAN1; speak further JOHN1-ARD1
(—CAP, COL, WH, CAM1, GLO, CAM2), SIS
   1434 Shee] Her POPE1-SING1, COL3, HUD2   was] he was HAN1, COL
   1435 to her oath] F1, IRV, RLTR, ARD2; by her oath KELLNER (1931) *conj.*, PEL1;
to her by oath F2 *etc.*   and] *Om.* F4, ROWE1

   1426–8 **spirit . . . spirit**] CLARKE (ed. 1864): "Here 'spirit' is used, the first time,
in the sense of courage or courageous enterprise; the second in the sense of conscience, spiritual perception of right and wrong." *OED* (*sb.* 13) defines *spirit* in 1426
as "Mettle; vigour of mind; ardour; courage," first used in this sense by Sh. For *spirit*
meaning "soul" in 1428 see n. 41.
   1427 **truth**] SCHMIDT (1875): "Honesty, righteousness" (*OED, sb.* 4). Cf. 1386.
   1429 **Vertue is bold**] BROWN (1864, pp. 22–3): Cf. Prov. 28:1. TILLEY (I82):
"Innocence is bold." Cf. *2H6* 4.4.59–60 (2596–7), *Luc.* 87–8.
   1430–1 **Fredericke**] Sh. gave this name to the usurping duke in *AYL*. The name
was rare in England, but in 1594 King James named his first son Henry Frederick
for the child's grandfathers Henry Stuart and Frederick II of Denmark. Cf. *The
Weakest Goeth to the Wall* (1600), MSR, 66: "Miscarried not young *Fredericke* my
sonne?"
   1431 **miscarried**] JOHNSON (1755): "To fail"; "to be lost in an enterprise"
(*OED, v.* 1).
   1434 **Shee**] DYCE (ed. 1857): "Here '*She*' is used for '*Her*'." Cf. FRANZ §287g
and 529, 2504, 2924.
      should . . . haue married] Was to have married. Cf. *WT* 4.4.793–4 (2648–9),
"that should haue marryed a Shepheards Daughter." See n. 270.
   1434–5 **was . . . oath**] LEVER (ed. 1965): "Mariana had pledged herself in
betrothal (Angelo's reciprocal oath being assumed)." But F1 makes no sense, since
betrothal is not to an oath but by oath. F2 reads *by oath.* Cf. Barry, *Ram-Alley* (1611),
1076: "Shee is my wife by oth." Cf. 1447, 2581, 2602–3.
   1436 **limit**] *OED* (*sb.* 2f): "Used by Shaks. for: Prescribed time." See n. 2030–1.

her brother *Fredericke* was wrackt at Sea, hauing in that
perished vessell, the dowry of his sister: but marke how   (F6vb)
heauily this befell to the poore Gentlewoman, there she
lost a noble and renowned brother, in his loue toward   1440
her, euer most kinde and naturall: with him the portion
and sinew of her fortune, her marriage dowry: with
both, her combynate-husband, this well-seeming
Angelo.

Isab. Can this be so? did *Angelo* so leaue her?   1445

Duke. Left her in her teares, & dried not one of them
with his comfort: swallowed his vowes whole, pretending in her, discoueries of dishonor: in few, bestow'd
her on her owne lamentation, which she yet weares for
his sake: and he, a marble to her teares, is washed with   1450
them, but relents not.

Isab. What a merit were it in death to take this poore
maid from the world? what corruption in this life, that

1441–2 the portion and] her portion, the JOHN
1446 her teares] tears THEO2, WARB-JOHN2
1448 few] few words F3-POPE2, HAN1
1449 she yet] yet she v1773-MAL
1450 teares] eares F2-F4

1437 **wrackt**] SCHMIDT (1875): "Shipwrecked" (*OED*, Wrack *v.* 2 2).

1441 **naturall**] *OED* (*a.* 16): "Having natural feeling." See n. 1355.

portion] SCHMIDT (1875): "Inheritance settled on a person" (*OED, sb.* 2, 3).

1442 **sinew**] SCHMIDT (1875): "Considered as the seat of strength, and hence
= strength." ONIONS (1911): "Main strength or support, mainstay" (*OED, sb.* 4).

1443 **combynate**] THIRLBY (1733–47): Cf. *combined* in 2235 (see n.). JOHNSON
(1755): "Betrothed; promised; settled by compact. A word of *Shakespeare.*" So *OED*
(*a.* b).

well-seeming] *OED (ppl. a.):* "Presenting a good or specious appearance." Cf.
welsee[m]ing in *Rom.* 1.1.185 (184). See nn. 346, 1163.

1447 **swallowed**] THIRLBY (1747–53): Cf. "eat your words." SCHMIDT (1875):
"To devour . . . (retracted, disavowed)." So *OED* (*v.* 8), first used in this sense by
Sh.

1447–8 **pretending**] SCHMIDT (1875): "To alledge falsely, to use as a pretext"
(*OED, v.* 6).

1448 **in few**] SCHMIDT (1874): "In short" (*OED, a.* 1g).

1448–9 **bestow'd her on**] MALONE (ed. 1790): "Left her to." STEEVENS (Var.
1793): " '*Gave* her up' to" (*OED, v.* 6). HART (ed. 1905): "Handed her over to."
CRAIG (ed. 1951): "With quibble on *bestowed* meaning 'gave in marriage'."

1449 **weares**] See *OED* (*v.* 1 8): "To carry about with one in one's heart, mind,
or memory."

1450 **marble**] SCHMIDT (1875): "Emblem of hardness" (*OED, sb.* 1d), as in
marble-breasted, marble-hearted.

it will let this man liue? But how out of this can shee a-
uaile?   1455
   Duke. It is a rupture that you may easily heale: and the
cure of it not onely saues your brother, but keepes you
from dishonor in doing it.
   Isab. Shew me how (good Father.)
   Duk. This fore-named Maid hath yet in her the con-   1460
tinuance of her first affection: his vniust vnkindenesse
(that in all reason should haue quenched her loue) hath
(like an impediment in the Current) made it more violent and vnruly: Goe you to *Angelo*, answere his requiring with a plausible obedience, agree with his demands   1465
to the point: onely referre your selfe to this aduantage;
first, that your stay with him may not be long: that the
time may haue all shadow, and silence in it: and the place

1459 good] *Om.* ROWE2
1461 vnkindenesse] kindness POPE, HAN1
1464 answere] answering ROWE
1466 aduantage;] — ˄ KTLY
1468 time . . . place] place . . . time RID *conj.*, ARD2

   1454–5 **auaile**] *OED* (*v.* 5a): "Benefit oneself or profit by," elliptically, first use
in this sense.
   1456 **rupture**] SCHMIDT (1875): "A breach, a gap, an injury." LEVER (ed.
1965): "Breach of agreement." More likely "a breach of harmony or friendly relations between two persons" (*OED, sb.* 1b), like "An vnkind breach" in *Oth.* 4.1.238
(2614).
   1461 **vnkindenesse**] JOHNSON (1755): "Malignity; ill-will; want of affection."
See *OED* (3) and n. 1180.
   1462–4 **hath . . . vnruly**] WALKER (1860, 1:155): Cf. Ovid, *Metam.* 3:568.
THISELTON (1901, p. 27): So *AWW* 5.3.214–15 (2941–2), "As all impediments in
fancies course Are motives of more fancie." TILLEY (S929) and WILSON (p. 780):
"The stream (current, tide) stopped swells the higher."
   1465 **plausible**] SCHMIDT (1875): "Pleased, contented, willing, ready." ON-
IONS (1911): "Laudable, acceptable." DEROCQUIGNY (1926–7, p. 439): "Affable,
agreeable, ingratiating, winning." *OED* notes that this last sense (*a.* 2) was "Common
in late 16th and 17th c.," whereas (*a.* 3) "fair-seeming, specious," was used "chiefly
of arguments or statements" before the 19th c.
   1466 **to the point**] THIRLBY (1747–53): "Exactly" (*OED, sb.* 1 D. 6b, quoting
Tmp. 1.2.194 [306], "to point").
   referre . . . to] JOHNSON (ed. 1765): "This is scarcely to be reconciled with
any established mode of speech." STEEVENS (Var. 1793): *"Have recourse to, betake
yourself to."* LEVER (ed. 1965): " 'Entrust yourself to this favourable condition'. Cf.
Wint., III. ii. 116 [1294]" (*OED, v.* 5 *refl.*).
   1467–8 **stay . . . silence**] PORTER & CLARKE (ed. 1909): "These are the conditions of the similar situation" in *AWW* 3.7.36–9, 4.2.54–8 (1896–9, 2082–6).
   1468 **time . . . place**] RIDLEY (ed. 1935): "The sense would be much improved

answere to conuenience: this being granted in course,
and now followes all: wee shall aduise this wronged   1470
maid to steed vp your appointment, goe in your place:
if the encounter acknowledge it selfe heereafter, it may
compell him to her recompence; and heere, by this is
your brother saued, your honor vntainted, the poore
Mariana aduantaged, and the corrupt Deputy scaled.   1475
The Maid will I frame, and make fit for his attempt: if

1469 conuenience] all Convenience ROWE2
1469–70 granted in course, and now] granted, in Course now ROWE3-JOHN2,
HUD2; granted in course, now CAP-KNT2, SING2, DYCE2, KNT3, DYCE3; granted,
in course and now STAU
1471 goe] and go KTLY
1473 heere] hear ARD2
1475 scaled] foiled WH, DYCE2, HUD2
1476 his] this mTBY3 *and* WALKER (1860, 2:222) *conj.,* HUD2

---

by transposing these two words." LEVER (ed. 1965) so emends.
   shadow] SCHMIDT (1875): "Darkness." *OED* (*sb.* 1): "Comparative darkness."
   1469 **answere**] SCHMIDT (1874): "To agree with, to correspond" (*OED, v.* 28),
as in 1741.
   conuenience] ONIONS (1911): "Fitness" (*OED, sb.* 5). See n. 2187.
   in course] ONIONS (1911): "In due course, as a matter of course" (*OED, sb.*
34b).
   1471 **steed vp**] JOHNSON (1755): *Stead,* "To fill the place of another." *OED*
(*v.* 3): "*To stead up:* to fulfil in the stead of another," only quotation. HARDING (ed.
1954): "Assume." LEVER (ed. 1965): " 'Serve to keep up'; cf. 'stead me' [367]." See
n. 367.
   goe in your place] WARBURTON (MS n. in JOHNSON, ed. 1765): "An explanation, I would guess, crept in from the margin."
   1472 **encounter**] SCHMIDT (1874): "An amorous meeting, a rendezvous"
(*OED, sb.* 2b, sense first in Sh.). See n. 1298.
   acknowledge it selfe] LEISI (ed. 1964): "The word often connotes 'confess'
. . . , hence: 'makes itself known'."
   1473–5 **by . . . aduantaged**] HORNE (1962, pp. 112–13): Cf. Giraldi, *Epitia*
(1583), 5.7: "Vico is saved, Iuriste is saved, Epitia's honour is saved."
   1475 **aduantaged**] *OED* (*ppl. a.*): "Benefited, profited," first quotation.
   scaled] GILDON (1710, glossary, p. lxxii): "To *Scale* a thing. To weigh it in
Scales." JOHNSON (ed. 1765): "*To scale the Deputy* may be, *to reach him notwithstanding
the elevation of his place; or it may be, to strip him and discover his nakedness, though armed
and concealed by the investments of authority.*" STEEVENS (Var. 1773): "*Put into confusion.*" NARES (1822): "To weigh as in scales, to estimate aright," as in *Cor.* 2.3.257
(1652). KNIGHT (ed. 1841 on *Cor.* 1.1.95 [93], p. 152 n.): "We have precisely the
same meaning in the Scriptures" [Dan. 5:27, "Thou art wayed in the balance, and
art found too light"]. HALLIWELL (ed. 1854): "Scaled as a fish, his scales of sanctity
being stripped off." *OED* (*v.* 1 2a): "To weigh as in scales," first quotation in this
sense. LEVER (ed. 1965): "This suits the recurrent imagery of testing." See p. 287.
   1476 **frame**] SCHMIDT (1874): "To mould, to fashion." Cf. *OED* (*v.* 5c): "To

155

you thinke well to carry this as you may, the doublenes
of the benefit defends the deceit from reproofe. What
thinke you of it?

   Isab. The image of it giues me content already, and I   1480
trust it will grow to a most prosperous perfection.

   Duk. It lies much in your holding vp: haste you speedily to *Angelo*, if for this night he intreat you to his bed,
giue him promise of satisfaction: I will presently to S.
Lukes, there at the moated-Grange recides this deie-   1485

  1477 this₍₎] ~ , F4, ROWE, COL, HAL, WH1, STAU, DEL4, OXF1, ARD1, PEL1,
PEN2
  1478 from] and ROWE, POPE, HAN1

---

shape . . . ; to dispose." HARRISON (ed. 1948): "Prepare." Cf. 1730 and n.
   fit] *OED* (*a.* 5): "Ready."
   attempt] *OED* (*sb.* 3b): "Assault made upon . . . a woman's honour," first
quoted from *Luc.* 491. See n. 1405.
   1477 **carry**] SCHMIDT (1874): "To manage, to execute" (*OED, v.* 22, sense first
in Sh.).
   1477–8 **the doublenes . . . reproofe**] TILLEY (E112): "The end justifies the
means." Cf. *Luc.* 528–9, *MV* 4.1.216 (2127), and see 1851–3.
   1480 **image**] SCHMIDT (1874): "Idea, conception, imagination" (*OED, sb.* 5).
   1481 **perfection**] SCHMIDT (1875): "Performance." More likely "completion,"
"full growth" (*OED, sb.* 2, 2b).
   1482 **lies . . . in**] See *OED* (*v.* ¹ 12h): "*To lie in:* to consist in, to have its ground
or basis in."
    holding vp] HART (ed. 1905): "Supporting, carrying it through." CAMPBELL
(ed. 1949): "Sustaining your part." LEVER (ed. 1965): "Power of sustaining (the
scheme)" (*OED,* Hold *v.* 44b). See n. 1820.
   1484 **satisfaction**] SCHMIDT (1875): "Gratification." So *OED* (5). See n. 1378.
    presently] SCHMIDT (1875): "Immediately" (*OED, adv.* 3).
   1484–5 **S. *Lukes***] Cf. "Saint *Lukes*" in *Shr.* 4.4.88 (2287).
   1485 **Grange**] JOHNSON (1755): "A farm: generally a farm with a house at a
distance from neighbours." STEEVENS (Var. 1778): "A solitary farm-house. So in
Othello" (1.1.105 [118]). MALONE (ed. 1790): "A *grange,* in its original signification,
meant the farm-house of a monastery. . . . Being placed at a distance from the
monastery, and not connected with any other buildings, Shakspeare, with his wonted
licence, uses it, both here and in *Othello,* in the sense of a *solitary* farm-house."
KNIGHT (ed. 1840) quotes Tennyson's "Mariana" (1830), where "the idea of
loneliness and desolation, suggested by these simple words of Shakspere, is worked
out with the most striking effect." HORNE (ed. 1840, 1:211) also quotes from the
poem. HALLIWELL (ed. 1854) cites Stephen Skinner, *Etymologicon Linguæ Anglicanæ*
(1671): "Grange . . . in Lincolnshire, signifies a house or barn by itself, situated far
from any other houses." [See also Henry Cockeram's *English Dictionarie* (1623):
"*Graunge.* A lone house in the Countrey."] LEVER (ed. 1965): "Usually, country
house; but in conjunction with 'Saint Luke's', probably 'an outlying farm-house

cted *Mariana*; at that place call vpon me, and dispatch
with *Angelo*, that it may be quickly.

Isab. I thank you for this comfort: fare you well good
father.   *Exit.*

Enter Elbow, Clowne, Officers.   **3.2**

Elb. Nay, if there be no remedy for it, but that you   1491
will needes buy and sell men and women like beasts, we
shall haue all the world drinke browne & white bastard.

1489 *Exit.*] F1-POPE2, CAM3, SIS+; *Exeunt severally.* (*or Exeunt.*) THEO1 *etc.*
1490 SCENE IV. POPE, HAN1, WARB, JOHN; *SCENE* II. CAP+   Enter . . .]
The Street. Enter Duke, Elbow, Clown, *and officers.* POPE1-ALEX (—CAM3) (*subst.*)

---

belonging to a religious establishment' (*O.E.D.* 2b).''
      recides] See n. 1341.
      1485–6 **deiected**] SCHMIDT (1874): ''Cast down, low-spirited.'' HART (ed.
1905): ''Depreciated, fallen from her estate.'' LEVER (ed. 1965): ''Lowered (i) in
spirits, (ii) in estate'' (*OED, ppl. a.* 2, 3).
      1486 **dispatch**] *OED* (*v.* 10): ''Conclude or settle a business,'' first use in absolute
sense. LEVER (ed. 1965): ''Settle matters with, combining the sense of 'make haste'.''
Cf. 2160, 2175, and the noun in 2282 (see n.).
      1490 DYCE (ed. 1857): ''As soon as Isabella had quitted the stage, the audience
were to suppose that the scene was changed from the interior to the outside of the
prison.'' KOPPEL (1874, p. 287): Pope and later eds. change the scene, but it should
continue, as in F and Rowe. FLEAY (1891, 2:199): ''III.1 was acted as in the prison;
the traverse was then drawn, and the Duke was supposed to be in the street outside.''
WILSON (ed. 1922): ''F. makes no scene-division here, and there seems no good
reason for Capell's [in fact Pope's] introducing one; the Duke remains 'on'.''
HUNTER (1926, p. 298): ''This is a particularly bad example of arbitrary editorial
methods, for the dialogue and the Folio stage-direction alike make it perfectly clear
that the Duke does not at this point leave the stage, and that consequently there is
no change of scene. The editors, however, in their anxiety to convey exact impressions of locality, not warranted by the text, have decided that before line [1490] the
place represented is A Room in a Prison, and after that point A Street before the
Prison, and, to give effect to this decision, deliberately altered stage-directions which
are in full conformity with the dialogue, and which even a modern producer might
find sufficient. [Note:] Rowe, rightly treating the whole as one scene, was content
with the simple description 'The Prison'.'' GREG (1955, p. 356): ''Modern editors,
familiar with the picture-stage, have felt constrained to mark a fresh scene, giving the
Duke an exit and immediate re-entry contrary to Elizabethan custom. On Shakespeare's stage with the drawing of the traverse the prison gates closed, leaving the
Duke outside, another instance of dramatic *enjambement*.'' See n. 205.
      1493 **drinke . . . bastard**] WARBURTON (ed. 1747): ''A kind of sweet wine then
much in vogue'' (*OED, sb.* 4). STEEVENS (Var. 1773, 5:274–5) cites *1H4* 2.4.30
(989), Dekker's *1 Honest Whore* (1604, 2.1.232–4) and *Match Mee in London* (1631,

Duk. Oh heauens, what stuffe is heere.

Clow. Twas neuer merry world since of two vsuries   1495
the merriest was put downe, and the worser allow'd by
order of Law; a fur'd gowne to keepe him warme; and
furd with Foxe and Lamb-skins too, to signifie, that craft

1495 vsuries] usurers HAN1; usances COLNE, COL2

1497 Law;] Fl-ROWE2, RID, ARD2, EVNS; ~ , ROWE3, HAN1, JOHN, v1773, SING1, COL3; ~ . POPE, THEO; ~ . *** (*lacuna*) WARB; ~ ₐ mTBY1 *conj.,* CAP *etc.*
fur'd] fur'd lamb-skin CAP

1498 Foxe and Lamb-skins] Fox and Lambs-skins ROWE, POPE, HAN1; ox and lamb-skins JOHN; fox-skins CAP; fox on lamb-skins mTBY3 *and* MASON (1785) *conj.,* RANN, HUD2, HENL, CAM3-ALEX, ARD2

2.2.3), and other plays. HALLIWELL (ed. 1854): "The double meaning here intended will be apparent from a passage in Middleton's *Faire Quarrell,* 1617, . . . 'thy daughter has drunk bastard' " (5.1.166–7; cf. 123–4). LEVER (ed. 1965): "Procreate bastards of all races." More likely it means "of dark and light complexions," as in Heywood's *1 Fair Maid of the West* (1631, ed. Turner, 3.3.93–5): "bastard, white or browne, according to the complexion of your bedfellow."

1494 **stuffe**] Rubbish (*OED, sb.*[1] 7c). Cf. *Tmp.* 2.1.254 (949), "What stuffe is this?", and Middleton, *Michaelmas Terme* (1607, 3.1.205), "How now? what piece of stuff comes here?"

1495 **Twas . . . world**] HART (ed. 1905): Cf. *TN* 3.1.109 (1309), *2H6* 4.2.9 (2327), and Dekker's *Old Fortunatus* (1600, 1.2.75–6).

vsuries] JOHNSON (ed. 1765): "*Usury* may be used by an easy licence for the *Professors of Usury.*" HALLIWELL (ed. 1854): "The two 'usuries' meant are, of course, law and lechery, both of which are usurers, in the sense of their habit of extracting money." HART (ed. 1905): "The merriest usury . . . is that sin that was interdicted by the proclamation [183]. . . . But Pompey (a Londoner born) alludes probably to events much nearer home—to the putting down of the public Stews, or Bordello, on the Bankside" in 1546. *The worser,* moneylending. HUNTER (1964, p. 172): "The 'worser' usury here is the ordinary 'copulation of metals'; the 'merriest' would seem to be that of the fleshmonger, who not only keeps the principal of the flesh, but draws a regular profit from it." Cf. *Tim.* 2.2.103–8 (765–9) and *2 Promos,* 2.5 (p. 349 below): "a double knaue he is: A couetous churle, and a lecher too."

1496 **the merriest**] The one causing most pleasure (*OED,* Merry *a.* 1a).

worser] See *OED (a.):* "A double comparative," " 'worse'."

put downe] *OED* (*v.*[1] 41b): "To put an end to by force or authority, to suppress, repress, crush," quoting 1591.

1496–7 **by order of Law**] HART (ed. 1905): "A statute of 13th Elizabeth confirmed that passed in 3rd Henry V., which reduced all legal interest to ten per cent."

1497 **fur'd**] THIRLBY (1723–33): Cf. *Lr.* 4.6.169 (2608).

1498 **Foxe and Lamb-skins**] MASON (1785, p. 39): "We ought to read, furred with fox *on* lamb-skins . . . for otherwise, craft will not stand for the facing." MALONE (ed. 1790, 10:565): "Fox-skins and lamb-skins were both used as facings to cloth in Shakspeare's time. . . . Hence *fox-furr'd* slave is used as an opprobrious epithet in *Wily Beguiled,* [Prologue,] 1606, and in other old comedies." CLARKE (ed. 1864): "The passage seems to us to imply, 'Furred (that is, lined with lamb-skin fur inside,

being richer than Innocency, stands for the facing.

Elb. Come your way sir: 'blesse you good Father   1500
Frier.

Duk. And you good Brother Father; what offence
hath this man made you, Sir?

Elb. Marry Sir, he hath offended the Law; and Sir,   (G1ᵃ)
we take him to be a Theefe too Sir: for wee haue found   1505
vpon him Sir, a strange Pick-lock, which we haue sent
to the Deputie.

Duke. Fie, sirrah, a Bawd, a wicked bawd,

1502 Brother Father] father brother HARN
1502–3 *Verse lines ending* offence . . . sir? CAM3, KIT1
1508 Fie, sirrah,] Fie, sirrah, fie! DYCE2 *conj.,* COL4, HUD2, HENL

---

and trimmed with fox-skin fur outside) with both kinds of fur, to show that craft
(fox-skin), being richer than innocency (lamb-skin), is used for the decoration'."
HART (ed. 1905): "Fox-fur (brown, not black or white) and budge (or lamb-skin)
facings was the recognised garb of usurers," quoting Nashe, *Pierce Penilesse,* 1592
(1:162). SISSON (1956, 1:84): "I see no need to change *and* to *on.*" LEVER (ed.
1965): "Mason's 'on' for F's 'and' is necessary to make the point about 'facing', i.e.
outer covering." See also Dekker, *1 Honest Whore,* 1604 (2.1.104): "fac'st all with
conny before, and within nothing but Foxe." Cf. 2677 and n. 1312.

1499 **stands for**] Represents (*OED, v.* 71h).

facing] See *OED* (*vbl. sb.* 4): "Something with which a garment is faced"
(covered or trimmed).

1500 **Come your way**] Come on (*OED,* Way *sb.* ¹ 23b).

'blesse] SCHMIDT (1874): Usually "God bless" in Sh. See n. 768.

1502 **Father**] JOHNSON (ed. 1765): "This word should be expunged." TYR-
WHITT (in Var. 1778): "In return to Elbow's blundering address of *good father friar,*
i.e. *good father brother,* the duke humorously calls him, in his own style, *good brother
father.*" The Duke calls a friar *Father* in 290, 331. SCHMIDT (1874): "Appellation
given to any old man." HART (ed. 1905): "Probably Elbow is represented as a very
old man."

1506 **Pick-lock**] RITSON (in Var. 1793): "As we hear no more of this charge,
it is necessary to prevent honest Pompey from being taken for a house-breaker. The
locks which he had occasion to *pick,* were by no means common, in this country at
least. They were . . . so well known in Edinburgh, that in one of Sir David Lindsay's
plays, represented to thousands in the open air, such a *lock* is actually opened on the
stage." [This was not acted at Edinburgh but is in the 1552 Cupar Banns for *Ane Satyre
of the Thrie Estaitis:* see *The Works of Sir David Lindsay,* ed. Hamer, 2:22, 4:164–5.]
STEEVENS (in Var. 1803) quotes Jonson's *Volpone* (1607, 2.5.57). LEVER (ed. 1965):
"A sly reference to 'chastity belts'. . . . The 'lock' is referred to figuratively in *Cym.,*
II. ii. 41 f. [948–9]." See also Middleton, *A Chast Mayd in Cheap-side* (1630,
4.3.31–3), and Robert Tofte, *Ariosto's Satyres* (1608, p. 67): "The slie Venetian lockt
his Ladies ware" with "a most wonderfull, strange and artificiall locke & key" which
Tofte says can still be seen in St. Mark's Palace, but she "got a false key for the lock."
OED (Picklock *sb.* ¹ 2) quotes *MM* and Percyvall's Spanish dictionary (1591), "a false
keye, a picke-locke."

The euill that thou causest to be done,
That is thy meanes to liue. Do thou but thinke   1510
What 'tis to cram a maw, or cloath a backe
From such a filthie vice: say to thy selfe,
From their abhominable and beastly touches
I drinke, I eate away my selfe, and liue:
Canst thou beleeue thy liuing is a life,   1515
So stinkingly depending? Go mend, go mend.
    Clo. Indeed, it do's stinke in some sort, Sir:
But yet Sir I would proue.
    Duke. Nay, if the diuell haue giuen thee proofs for sin
Thou wilt proue his. Take him to prison Officer: 1520

1510 Do] Dost THEO, WARB, JOHN
1513–14 From . . . liue:] *Marked as quotation* CAM3-ALEX
1514 eate away] eat, array BISHOP *conj.,* THEO1+
1516 Go mend, go mend] go mend, mend POPE1-CAP; Mend, go mend v1773
1517–18 *Prose* POPE1+
1517 do's] doth POPE1-v1773 (−CAP)
1518 proue.] ~ — F2+
1519 haue] hath THEO4-RANN (−CAP); had ARD1   thee] the ARD1

1513 **abhominable**] *OED* (Abominable *a.*): "Regularly spelt *abhominable. . . .*
No other spelling occurs in the first folio of Shaks." LEVER (ed. 1965): "F 'abhominable' brings out the old, popular derivation from *ab homine,* 'inhuman', which
'beastly' reinforces." See n. 665 and 1492, 1522.

    touches] HALLIWELL (ed. 1854): "The last word is somewhat technical. So
Ovid." SCHMIDT (1875): "Euphemistically, = sexual commerce," as in 2511 (see
n.), *Oth.* 4.2.84 (2781), *Son.* 141.

    1514 **eate away**] THEOBALD (ed. 1733): "The ingenious Mr. [Hawley] *Bishop,*
when we read this Play together, gave me that most certain Emendation [*eat, array*],
which I have substituted in the Room of the former foolish Reading." See textual
notes. Cf. *Oth.* 4.1.95–6 (2478–9) and Jonson's epigram on Lieut. Shift (*Epigram* 12):
"By that one spell he liues, eates, drinkes, arrayes Himself." Theobald first printed
his emendation *array* in the *Daily Journal,* 17 Apr. 1729, in a letter reprinted by
NICHOLS (1817), 2:214–22. Only PORTER & CLARKE (ed. 1909) defend F's reading: "That is 'eat myselfe away', waste my life away through eating by such diseased
means. The expression is a strong one referring to the oft-referred-to disease of vice
that eats the bones and tissues of the flesh." All other mod. eds. print *array.*

    1516 **depending**] SCHMIDT (1874): *Depend,* "to serve." PARROTT (ed. 1938):
"Supported" (*OED, v.*[1] 4, "To be sustained by; to be dependent *on*").

    mend] See *OED* (*v.* 1c *intr.* for *refl.*): "Reform."

    1517–18 Prose set as verse by Compositor B.

    1518 **proue**] SCHMIDT (1875): "Demonstrate" (*OED, v.* 5). The Duke seems
to interrupt before Pompey finishes. See n. 140.

    1520 **proue**] See *OED* (*v.* 8): "Be shown or found by experience or trial to be."
    Officer] See n. 331.

Correction, and Instruction must both worke
Ere this rude beast will profit.

Elb. He must before the Deputy Sir, he ha's giuen
him warning: the Deputy cannot abide a Whore-ma-
ster: if he be a Whore-monger, and comes before him,　　　　1525
he were as good go a mile on his errand.

Duke. That we were all, as some would seeme to bee
From our faults, as faults from seeming free.

1528 From our] Free from our F2, F3, CAP, v1793-v1813, SING, HAL, WH, COL3, STAU, KTLY, DYCE2, DYCE3-HUD2, NLSN-KIT1, SIS, PEL1, PEN2; Free from all F4-JOHN2, v1773-RANN　　as faults from] as from faults THEOBALD (1729) *conj. in* NICHOLS (2:289), HAN1, CAP, RANN, WH, DYCE2, DYCE3, HUD2, KIT1; or faults from JOHN1 *conj.*, BUL, SIS; as his faults from ALEX

1521 **Correction, and Instruction**] ANON. (1872, *Congregationalist*, p. 411): Cf. 2 Tim. 3:16. See *OED* (Correction 4), "corporal punishment," and n. 995.

1522 **rude**] See *OED* (*a.* 3b): "Uncivilized, barbarous."

1523 **must**] Must go: see n. 76.

ha's] The only instance in *MM* of *ha's* for *has.* See n. 2744.

1526 BUTLER (1891, p. 83): "He will fare badly, or have a hard time." INGLEBY (1891, p. 283): " 'He is half sentenced already'." JEAKES (1891, p. 283): " 'He has made a sad mistake'." NICHOLSON (1891, p. 464): He "is sent a mile or more on an errand not to be performed. . . . has been made an April fool of." LLOYD (1891, p. 204): "What Elbow really has in his mind and intends to say is that Pompey had better have gone a mile in another direction." KELLNER (1931, p. 257): He had better stay away as long as possible. NEILSON & HILL (ed. 1942): "He has no chance." HARRISON (ed. 1948): "Make a fruitless journey." TILLEY (M927): Cf. Ray, *Proverbs* (1670, p. 177): "I'll go twenty miles on your errand first." HARDING (ed. 1954): "Give himself up for lost." BALD (ed. 1956): "He has a hard road ahead." LEVER (ed. 1965): " 'Do anything rather than that'." [Cf. Benedick's wish to "go on the slightest arrand now to the Antypodes," *Ado* 2.1.272-3 (666-7).]

1527 TILLEY (S214) and WILSON (p. 33): "Be what thou would seem to be" (Erasmus).

That] Would that (*OED, conj.* 3c).

1528 JOHNSON (ed. 1765) suggests *"Free from all faults, or faults from seeming free; that men were really good, or that their faults were known,* that men were free from faults, *or* faults from *hypocrisy."* MALONE (ed. 1790): *"Free . . .* was added unnecessarily by the editor of the second folio, who did not perceive that *our,* like many words of the same kind, was used by Shakspeare as a dissyllable. . . . Dr. Johnson's conjectural reading, *or,* appears to me very probable. The compositor might have caught the word *as* from the preceding line." IDEM (ed. 1790, 10:565): "This line is rendered harsh and obscure by the word *free* being dragged from its proper place for the sake of the rhyme." COLLIER (ed. 1842): "The Duke wishes that we were all as free from faults, as faults are from seeming to be so." HALLIWELL (ed. 1854): "Oh that all of us were, as some appear to be, as free from our faults, as we seem to be in appearance free from them." HUNTER (ed. 1873): "O that we had no more faults than those we seem to have." STONE (1884, p. 115*): "Would that we were as free from faults,

Enter Lucio.

Elb. His necke will come to your wast, a Cord sir.   1530

Clo. I spy comfort, I cry baile: Here's a Gentleman,
and a friend of mine.

Luc. How now noble *Pompey*? What, at the wheels
of *Cæsar*? Art thou led in triumph? What is there none
of *Pigmalions* Images newly made woman to bee had   1535
now, for putting the hand in the pocket, and extracting

1529 SCENE V. POPE1, HAN1, WARB, JOHN; SCENE IV. POPE2   *Enter*
. . .] *After* 1532 DYCE, STAU-GLO, DEL4-ARD1; *after* 1530 ALEX, SIS, ARD2
1533 wheels] heels v1773-SING1
1536 extracting] extracting it ROWE3+ (−IRV, RLTR, ARD2)

---

as our faults are from seeming (hypocrisy)." WILSON (ed. 1922): "F2 reading restores sense, rhythm and balance to the line, and we believe it to be correct. The Duke
means: 'Would that all men were as free from sin as Angelo seems, or as Pompey is
free from hypocrisy'." See n. 1163 and p. 287.

   seeming] See n. 1017.

   1529 Lucio prob. enters after 1530. See HOWARD-HILL (1972, p. 123).

   1530 JOHNSON (ed. 1765): "His neck will be tied like your waist with a rope.
The Friers of the *Franciscan* order, perhaps of others, wear a hempen cord for a
girdle." HART (ed. 1905): Cf. *The Troublesome Raigne of King Iohn*, 1591 (Part 1, sig.
E4ᵛ): "Ner trust me for a groate, If this waste girdle hang thee not, that girdleth in
thy coate."

   1531 **cry**] See *OED* (*v.* 1a): "Entreat."

   1533 **noble**] CLARKE (1879, p. 420): "Mockingly applied," as in *Ant.* 3.2.6
(1545).

   1533–4 **at the wheels of *Cæsar***] HART (ed. 1905): Cf. 694 and *Ant.* 4.14.75–6
(2911–12). LEVER (ed. 1965): "The historical Pompey was not led in triumph by
Caesar, but his sons were, after their defeat at Munda. Cf. *Cæs.,* I. i. [56 (58)]." See
n. 694.

   1534 **led**] *OED* (Lead *v.* ¹ 2): "To conduct." See nn. 83, 203.

   1535 *Pigmalions . . . woman*] WARBURTON (ed. 1747): "Come out cured from
a salivation [treatment of venereal disease by mercury]." HEATH (1765, p. 89): "Are
there no fresh women, no maidenheads, to be had now?" KENRICK (1765, p. 34):
"Young girls newly debauched." STEEVENS (Var. 1778): "Have you no women now
to recommend to your customers, as fresh and untouched as *Pygmalion's* statue was,
at the moment when it became flesh and blood?'." Perhaps an allusion to Marston,
The Metamorphosis of Pigmalions Image (1598), or Lyly, *The Woman in the Moone*
(1597). MALONE (1780, 1:99): "Is there no courtezan, who being *newly made woman,*
< i.e. *lately debauched,* > still retains the appearance of chastity, and looks as cold as
a statue, to be had." DOUCE (in Var. 1793): *"Pygmalion's images,* &c. may mean
new-coined money with the Queen's image upon it." HARDING (ed. 1954): "Lucio
mocks the tendency of bawds to exaggerate the beauty and chastity of the prostitutes
they represent." LEVER (ed. 1965): "Because the Elizabethan statue was often
painted, Pygmalion's beloved suggested the idea of a prostitute." Cf. 1568.

   1536 **extracting**] ROWE (ed. 1714) adds *it,* followed by most eds.

clutch'd? What reply? Ha? What saist thou to this
Tune, Matter, and Method? Is't not drown'd i'th last
raine? Ha? What saist thou Trot? Is the world as it was
Man? Which is the vvay? Is it sad, and few words?   1540
Or how? The tricke of it?

1538 Matter, and] the matter, and the HAN1
1538–9 Is't . . . raine?] It's not down i'th' last reign. WARB
  1539 saist] says KTLY   Trot] to't GREY *conj.*, RANN, SING2, DYCE, KTLY,
COL4, HUD2; troth JACKSON (1819) *conj.*, COLNE, COL2, COL3

  1537 **clutch'd**] HART (ed. 1905): "Clenched (and holding money)." Cf. *Jn.*
2.1.589 (910). "It was a new use, and it is one of the terms that Jonson reprehends
Marston for in his *Poetaster* [1602, 5.3.292]" (*OED, v.*¹ 2, 5).
  1537, 1539, 1544, 1568 Ha] See n. 927.
  1537–8 **to . . . Method**] THIRLBY (1733–47): "Chinking money." RANN (ed.
1786): "To a ready money customer (chinking his purse in *Pompey's* ear)." SCHMIDT
(1875): *Tune,* "humour." *Matter,* "argument." *Method,* "manner of acting."
  1538–9 **drown'd . . . raine**] EDWARDS (1750, p. 22): "Is it <*his reply or answer*> not drown'd in the last rain? A proverbial phrase to express a thing which is
lost." JOHNSON (ed. 1765): "It is a common phrase used in low raillery of a man
crest-fallen and dejected, that *he looks like a drown'd puppy. Lucio,* therefore, asks him
whether he was *drowned in the last rain,* and therefore cannot speak." STEEVENS (Var.
1778): "He rather asks him whether his *answer* was not drown'd in the last rain, for
Pompey returns *no answer* to any of his questions: or, perhaps, he means to compare
Pompey's miserable appearance to a *drown'd mouse.*" HALLIWELL (ed. 1854): "There
can be little doubt but that this is a proverbial expression for being lost, but *it* may
refer to 'this tune', ready money, as Lucio may here be supposed to flourish his purse
in the face of the Clown, or it may merely allude to Pompey's reply." HART (ed.
1905): "This probably alludes to destructive floods which took place in London some
time in the winter of 1602–03 [actually 1603–4]," according to Dekker in *The
Magnificent Entertainment* (ed. Bowers, 2:258). "It is not unlikely that a quibble in 'the
last rain' (reign) is intended, alluding to these changes due to the new king." LEE
(ed. 1907): "A colloquial expression for 'are our prospects damped?' " WILSON (ed.
1922): "All such pretended allusions to a variable climate like that of England seem
to us very dubious." LEVER (ed. 1965): "Probably 'now out of fashion'."
  1539 **Trot**] GREY (1754, 1:118): "Seldom (if ever) us'd to a man." JOHNSON
(ed. 1765, 8:Hh8ᵛ): "*Trot,* or as it is now often pronounced *honest trout,* is a familiar
address to a man among the provincial vulgar." HALLIWELL (ed. 1854): "The term
trot was generally applied in contempt to an old woman [*OED,* Trot *sb.*², which quotes
Shr. 1.2.80 (645)], and sometimes to a bawd. If the text is correct, it is here used
to Pompey with the implication of the utmost derision, as engaged in the occupation
of a bawd." WHITE (ed. 1857): "There surely could be no name given to a Bawd's
assistant more appropriate than Trot." HART (ed. 1905): "I know no other example
of its use to a man. . . . Old age seems to be the essential sense. . . . We are told
presently that Pompey is a bawd of antiquity." [But that means "of long standing,"
not "old": see n. 1557.]
  1540 **Which . . . vvay**] JOHNSON (ed. 1765): "*What is the* mode *now?*"
      sad, and few words] Cf. *MV* 1.1.88–99 (97–108) and TILLEY (W798–9).
  1541 **tricke**] JOHNSON (1755): "A practice; a manner; a habit" (*OED, sb.* 7).

Duke. Still thus, and thus: still vvorse?

Luc. How doth my deere Morsell, thy Mistris? Pro-
cures she still? Ha?

Clo. Troth sir, shee hath eaten vp all her beefe, and   1545
she is her selfe in the tub.

Luc. Why 'tis good: It is the right of it: it must be
so. Euer your fresh Whore, and your pouder'd Baud, an
vnshun'd consequence, it must be so. Art going to prison *Pompey?*   1550

Clo. Yes faith sir.

1543 Morsell,] — ? F3-ROWE2
1545 her] the ROWE3, POPE, HAN1

HART (ed. 1905): "The fashion, or custom, of it. Equivalent to 'this tune', above."
See n. 2903–4.

1542 Still . . . thus] Always like this, and like this, perhaps gesturing towards
Lucio and Pompey. Cf. *thus and thus* in *Sir Thomas More (Sh. Apoc.,* 3.2.1), *thus, or
thus* in *Oth.* 1.3.323 (673), *thus, and thus* in *Lr.* 1.2.114 (435).

1543 Morsell] HALLIWELL (ed. 1854) notes "a morsel of flesh" in Middleton
(*Familie of Loue,* 1608, 1.1.45). SCHMIDT (1875): "Piece in general, remnant," as in
Tmp. 2.1.286 (985). LEVER (ed. 1965): "Used in a lecherous sense for a woman; cf.
. . . *Ant.,* III. [xiii.] 116 f. [2293; also 1.5.31 (558) and *Per.* 4.2.142]. Modern
analogies might be 'bit' or 'piece'." [Sh. uses *peece* in this sense in *Tro.* 4.1.62 (2238)
and *Per.* 4.2.48 and 151.]

1543–4 Procures] *OED* (*v.* 5b): "To obtain (women) for the gratification of
lust," first quotation in this sense.

1545 Troth] See n. 664.

beefe] PARTRIDGE (1947, pp. 72–3): "Women that, being prostitutes, serve
as the flesh-food . . . for the *satisfaction* of the *appetite* of *brothel*-frequenters. . . . *Beef.*
not *flesh*, because they have been prepared for consumption." See n. 1667.

1546 in the tub] JOHNSON (ed. 1765): "The method of cure for venereal
complaints is grosly called the *powdering-tub.*" NARES (1822): "The discipline of
sweating in a heated tub, for a considerable time, accompanied with strict abstinence,
was formerly thought necessary for the cure of the venereal taint. . . . As beef was
also usually salted down, or powdered in a tub, the one process was, by comic or
satiric writers, jocularly compared to the other." ROSEBURY (1973, p. 106): " 'Pow-
dering tub' refers to treatment with mercury by fumigation."

1548 Euer . . . Baud] LEVER (ed. 1965): " 'The young prostitute always grows
into the old brothel-keeper, "powdered" like beef in the tub'."

your] GILLETT (1974, p. 306): " 'Your', in what Schmidt calls its indefinite
use, appears most often in sentencious statements like Lucio's" and in many lines in
4.2 (1890–1904). Cf. *your beggar,* 1613.

pouder'd] *OED* (*ppl. a.* 2b): "Salted, pickled," only quotation in this sense.
PARTRIDGE (1947, p. 170): "Face-powdered to hide the ravages of age and her
former profession (prostitution) and subjected to the treatment of the *powdering-tub.*"

1549 vnshun'd] THIRLBY (1723–33): "Unavoidable." HALLIWELL (ed. 1854):
"Inevitable." Cf. *vnshunnable* in *Oth.* 3.3.275 (1906).

1551 faith] See n. 712.

Luc. Why 'tis not amisse *Pompey*: farewell: goe say
I sent thee thether: for debt *Pompey*? Or how?

Elb. For being a baud, for being a baud.

Luc. Well, then imprison him: If imprisonment be   1555
the due of a baud, why 'tis his right. Baud is he doubt-
lesse, and of antiquity too: Baud borne. Farwell good
Pompey: Commend me to the prison *Pompey*, you will
turne good husband now *Pompey*, you vvill keepe the
house.   1560

Clo. I hope Sir, your good Worship wil be my baile?

Luc. No indeed vvil I not *Pompey*, it is not the wear:
I will pray (*Pompey*) to encrease your bondage if you
take it not patiently: Why, your mettle is the more:
Adieu trustie *Pompey*.   1565
Blesse you Friar.

Duke. And you.

Luc. Do's *Bridget* paint still, *Pompey*? Ha?

Elb. Come your waies sir, come.

1552 goe‸] ~ , ROWE3+ (−POPE2, CAM2, SIS, EVNS)
1561 baile?] F1-F3, CAM3, KIT1, SIS, ARD2; ~ . F4 *etc.*
1563–4 bondage‸ . . . patiently:] ~ ; . . . ~ , THEO1+
1565–6 *Continuous* POPE1+

1552–3 **say . . . thether**] MASON (1785, p. 40): "He speaks as one who had some
interest there, and was well known to the keepers." HART (ed. 1905): "This may be
merely a piece of chaff, like the modern 'mention my name'. But at [1685–6]
Overdone tells us that Lucio was the cause of her arrest, in his anxiety to do away
with evidence against himself for acts of incontinence. Pompey was Overdone's
servant . . . and Pompey was included probably in the informations. At [161] Lucio
seems anxious for his own safety. Now, being a braggart, he cannot refrain from his
triumph."

1557 **Baud borne**] SCHMIDT (1874): *"Bawd-born,* born as a bawd, a bawd from
birth." WHITE (1885, p. 322): " 'Born of a bawd'." But *of antiquity* (see n. 1539)
supports the first sense; cf. 1996 "A Bohemian borne," *Tmp.* 4.1.188 (1862), "A
Deuill, a borne-Deuill," and *Tro.* 5.7.17 (3488–9), "bastard begot."

1559 **husband**] MALONE (1780, 1:99): "Alluding to the etymology of the
word" (as JOHNSON [1755] says, "from *house*").

1559–60 **keepe the house**] HALLIWELL (ed. 1854): "A play upon words, to
keep the house meaning, to keep within doors, as well as to take care of it, like a good
economist." Cf. *Tim.* 3.3.42 (1116).

1562 **the wear**] THIRLBY (1747–53): "The fashion." *OED* (*sb.* 3b): "What one
wears or should wear," in fig. sense. Cf. *AWW* 1.1.219 (211–12), *AYL* 2.7.34
(1007).

1563–4 **if . . . more**] HART (ed. 1905): "If you give trouble in jail your shackles
(metal) will be the heavier." See n. 55.

1566 **Blesse**] See n. 1500. The new line indicates that Lucio turns to the Duke.

Clo. You will not baile me then Sir?   1570   (G1ᵛ

Luc. Then *Pompey*, nor now: what newes abroad *Frier*? What newes?

Elb. Come your waies sir, come.

Luc. Goe to kennell (*Pompey*) goe:
What newes *Frier* of the Duke?   1575

Duke. I know none: can you tell me of any?

Luc. Some say he is with the Emperor of *Russia*: other
some, he is in *Rome*: but where is he thinke you?

Duke. I know not where: but wheresoeuer, I wish
him well.   1580

Luc. It was a mad fantasticall tricke of him to steale
from the State, and vsurpe the beggerie hee was neuer
borne to: Lord *Angelo* Dukes it well in his absence: he
puts transgression too't.

1571 Then] Neither then KTLY   *Pompey,*] ~ ? CAP-v1821 (−RANN, MAL),
SING, STAU, HUD2   nor now] no, nor now WALKER (1860, 2:257) *conj.*, HUD2
1574-5 *Continuous* CAP
1574 Goe . . . (*Pompey*)] ~ — . . . , ~ — JOHN, v1773-RANN; ~ , — . . . ,
~ , MAL-STAU, HUD2, WH2, BUL   *Exeunt.* F2-F4; *Exeunt* Elbow, Clown *and
Officers.* ROWE1+ (*after* 1573 CAP)
1575 SCENE VI. POPE, HAN1, WARB, JOHN   *Duke turns his face away.* IRV
1576 none] of none KTLY   of] *Om.* ROWE1, ROWE2
1581 mad fantasticall] mad-fantastical WALKER (1860, 1:32, 51) *conj.*, HUD2
1582 the State] his state DYCE2, DYCE3

1574 **kennell**] JOHNSON (Var. 1773): "It should be remembered, that *Pompey*
is the common name of a dog." HART (ed. 1905): "No doubt it is now a common
name, but, although I have noted down every dog name I ever met in Elizabethan
literature, Pompey is not one. . . . I think kennell refers merely to his jail."
1577-8 **other some**] Some others. Cf. *othersome* in *MND* 1.1.226 (240).
1581 **mad . . . tricke**] HART (ed. 1905): "Absurd whim." See n. 877-8.
of him] On his part (*OED, prep.* 16).
1582 **beggerie**] LASCELLES (1953, p. 48 n.): "For a duke to have taken leave in
this manner is mere beggary—that is, a condition below that of a private gentleman
—in Lucio's estimation." COGHILL (1955, p. 24): "How did Lucio know the Duke
had become a mendicant? . . . If he did not know, but was pretending to, it was an
amazing guess." LEVER (ed. 1965): "It is more likely to be what Coghill rejects, 'a
stage situation contrived to raise a laugh', with a latent irony for the audience."
1583 **Dukes it**] ABBOTT (§226): "*It* is often added to nouns or words that are
not generally used as verbs, in order to give them the force of verbs." Cf. "Prince
it" in *Cym.* 3.3.85 (1646), "Queene it" in *WT* 4.4.460 (2294) and *H8* 2.3.37
(1246). SCHMIDT (1874): "To play the duke." So *OED (v.).*
1584 **puts . . . too't**] JOHNSON (1755): *Put to it,* "To distress; to perplex; to press
hard." *OED* (*v.* 28c < *b* >): "To reduce to straits; to drive to extremities," first
quotation in this sense.

Duke. He do's well in't.   1585

Luc. A little more lenitie to Lecherie would doe no
harme in him: Something too crabbed that way, *Frier.*

Duk. It is too general a vice, and seueritie must cure it.

Luc. Yes in good sooth, the vice is of a great kindred;
it is vvell allied, but it is impossible to extirpe it quite,   1590
Frier, till eating and drinking be put downe. They say
this *Angelo* vvas not made by Man and Woman, after
this downe-right vvay of Creation: is it true, thinke
you?

Duke. How should he be made then?   1595

Luc. Some report, a Sea-maid spawn'd him. Some,
that he vvas begot betweene two Stock-fishes. But it

1588 general] gentle WARB
1589 a] *Om.* ROWE, POPE, HAN1
1590 but] and HAN1
1593 this] the POPE1-v1821, SING, DYCE, COL3, KTLY, HUD2, BUL, CAM3, KIT1, SIS
1597 begot] got THEO2, WARB-JOHN2

1587 **Something**] See n. 70.

crabbed] LEISI (ed. 1964): " 'Cross-tempered', 'harsh' (OED 1b), as *Tempest* III 1 8 [1243]."

1588 **general**] See *OED* (*a.* 4): "Prevalent, widespread."

1589 **in good sooth**] Indeed (*OED,* Sooth *sb.* 4b).

is . . . kindred] EDWARDS (1750, p. 25): "The greatest men have it as well as we little folks." CRAIG (ed. 1951): "Belongs to a numerous race."

1590 **allied**] *OED* (*ppl. a.* 2 *fig.*): "Related."

extirpe] DYCE (1867): "To extirpate, to root out." So *OED* (*v.* 3). HART (ed. 1905): Cf. *1H6* 3.3.24 (1609).

1591 **put downe**] See n. 1496.

1592 **after**] See *OED* (*prep.* 13): "In accordance with."

1593 **this**] See *OED* (*dem. adj.* 1d): "Referring to something as known."

downe-right] *OED* (*a.* 2): "Direct, straightforward." Cf. *H5* 5.2.150–1 (3134); *Oth.* 1.3.250 (599).

1595 **should**] See *OED* (Shall *v.* 15): "Forming with the inf. a substitute for the pa. t. indic. . . . in the oblique report of another's statement in order to imply that the speaker does not commit himself to the truth of the alleged fact."

1596 **Sea-maid**] *OED:* "Mermaid," first found in *MND* 2.1.154 (530).

spawn'd] JOHNSON (1755): "To produce as fishes do eggs." *OED* (*v.* 5): "In contemptuous use, to give birth to (a person)," first use in this sense.

1597 **Stock-fishes**] HART (ed. 1905): "A kind of small cod imported from Newfoundland, Iceland, and Scandinavia. Hence, besides insensibility, it conveyed the idea of coldness." CASE (in rev. Arden ed. 1925, p. 151) doubts Hart's definition and quotes Richard Eden, *Decades* (ed. Arber, p. 303): "Haddockes or hakes indurate and dryed with coulde, and beaten with clubbes or stockes, by reason whereof the

is certaine, that when he makes water, his Vrine is congeal'd ice, that I know to bee true: and he is a motion
generatiue, that's infallible.   1600

Duke. You are pleasant sir, and speake apace.

Luc. Why, what a ruthlesse thing is this in him, for
the rebellion of a Cod-peece, to take away the life of a
man? Would the Duke that is absent haue done this?
Ere he vvould haue hang'd a man for the getting a hun-   1605
dred Bastards, he vvould haue paide for the Nursing a
thousand. He had some feeling of the sport, hee knew
the seruice, and that instructed him to mercie.

Duke. I neuer heard the absent Duke much detected

1599 is a] has no mTBY1 *conj.,* HAN1; is not a CAP
1600 generatiue] ungenerative THEO, WARB-v1821 (−CAP), SING, WH, STAU,
KTLY, DYCE2, DYCE3, HUD2, BUL, ARD2; ingenerative COLNE, COL2, COL3, COL4
1606 a] of a SING1, HUD1
1609 detected] detracted CAP

Germayns caule them stockefysshe." See *OED.* NOSWORTHY (ed. 1969): "Monstrous births of the kind glanced at by Lucio were a favourite theme in ballads and
pamphlets of the period." Cf. *WT* 4.4.265–86 (2084–2103) on ballads of a usurer's
wife and of a woman turned into a cold fish.

1599–1600 **a motion generatiue**] THEOBALD (1729, in NICHOLS, 1817, 2:
289): "Lucio, perhaps, means, that though Angelo have the organs of generation, yet
that he makes no more use of them than if he were an inanimate puppet. But I rather
think this was our Author's reading: and he is a motion *ungenerative.*" Cf. *vngenitur'd*
(1660). STEEVENS (Var. 1778): "A *motion generative* certainly means a *puppet of the
masculine gender.*" HALLIWELL (ed. 1854): "A generative puppet, a person as generative as a puppet." SCHMIDT (1874, p. 470): "A puppet born of a female being."
HART (ed. 1905): "A puppet appearing to be generative or possessed of breeding
powers. An imitation, or a fraud." PARROTT (ed. 1938): "A puppet, capable of
procreation." LEVER (ed. 1965): *"A motion ungenerative*] 'a puppet without power of
generation'." See p. 287.

1601 **pleasant**] SCHMIDT (1875): "Merry, facetious" (*OED, a.* 3).

apace] SCHMIDT (1874): "Quickly [*OED, adv.*]," "at random," as in *LLL*
5.2.369 (2296). HARRISON (ed. 1948): "Excessively." CAMPBELL (ed. 1949):
"Speak apace, talk nonsense." LEISI (ed. 1964): " 'Fast' (as always), connoting 'idly',
'to no purpose'."

1603 **rebellion**] DELIUS (ed. 1860): Cf. *rebels* in *MV* 3.1.38 (1250). [Also
AWW 4.3.23, 5.3.6 (2125, 2703), *Oth.* 3.4.43 (2186). "Insurrection," with a pun
on "rising."]

Cod-peece] *OED* (1c): "A bagged appendage to the front of the close-fitting
hose or breeches worn by men," first quotation in fig. sense.

1607 **feeling**] See *OED* (*vbl. sb.* 6): "Emotional appreciation or sense."

1608 **the seruice**] See n. 199.

1609 **detected**] THIRLBY (1747–53): "Reflected on, suspected, affected, detracted." MALONE (in Var. 1778): *"Suspected.*" IDEM (ed. 1790, 10:565): *"Detected,
however, may mean, notoriously charged,* or guilty." RICHARDSON (1836): *Detect,*

for Women, he was not enclin'd that vvay.   1610

Luc. Oh Sir, you are deceiu'd.

Duke. 'Tis not possible.

Luc. Who, not the Duke? Yes, your beggar of fifty:
and his vse was, to put a ducket in her Clack-dish; the
Duke had Crochets in him. Hee would be drunke too,   1615
that let me informe you.

Duke. You do him wrong, surely.

Luc. Sir, I vvas an inward of his: a shie fellow vvas
the Duke, and I' beleeue I know the cause of his vvith-
drawing.   1620

Duke. What (I prethee) might be the cause?

Luc. No, pardon: 'Tis a secret must bee lockt within the teeth and the lippes: but this I can let you vnderstand, the greater file of the subiect held the Duke to be
vvise.   1625

1613 your] with your KTLY
1618 shie] sly mTBY1 *conj.,* HAN1, CAP, DYCE2, DYCE3, HUD2, WH2, BUL
1621 I] *Om.* ROWE1-JOHN2, v1773

---

accuse. HALLIWELL (ed. 1854) and *OED* (*v.* 2) quote many instances of this sense.

1613–16 HART (ed. 1905): Cf. Jonson, *Volpone* (1607, 1.5.43–5). On *your* see
n. 1548.

1613 **fifty**] See *OED* (*sb.* 2a): "The age of fifty years."

1614 **vse**] See *OED* (*sb.* 7c): "Custom."

ducket] LEVER (ed. 1965): "The ducat (Italian *ducato,* ducal coin) would serve
almost as the Duke's visiting card. The Duke's secret charities are made by Lucio into
occasions for slander."

Clack-dish] STEEVENS (Var. 1773): "The beggars, two or three centuries ago,
used to proclaim their want by a wooden dish with a moveable cover, which they
clacked to shew that their vessel was empty." Cf. Middleton, *The Familie of Loue,* 1608
(4.2.29, 30). COLMAN (1974, p. 188): "Possibly a quibble, (a) beggar's wooden
bowl with noisy lid, (b) female pudendum."

1615 **Crochets**] *OED* (Crotchet *sb.*[1] 9): "A whimsical fancy." See TILLEY
(C843), "He has crotchets in his head," and *Wiv.* 2.1.159 (691).

1618 **inward**] THIRLBY (1747–53): "An intimate." JOHNSON (1755): "Intimate; near acquaintance." *OED* (*sb.* 3): "An intimate or familiar acquaintance," first
quotation in this sense.

shie] JOHNSON (1755): "Keeping at a distance." *OED* (*a.* 4): "Cautiously
reserved; wary in speech or action," first used in this sense here and in 2410.

1622–3 **'Tis...lippes**] TILLEY (T424): "Good that the teeth guard the tongue."
Cf. *R2* 1.3.167 (460).

1624 **the greater file**] JOHNSON (ed. 1765): "The larger list, the greater number." HUNTER (ed. 1873): "The higher class of the people." HART (ed. 1905): *File,*
" 'a row of persons' " (*OED, sb.*[2] 8, first use in this sense). "The greater file, the
majority."

subiect] See n. 1030.

Duke. Wise? Why no question but he was.

Luc. A very superficiall, ignorant, vnweighing fellow.

Duke. Either this is Enuie in you, Folly, or mista-
king: The very streame of his life, and the businesse he
hath helmed, must vppon a warranted neede, giue him   1630
a better proclamation. Let him be but testimonied in
his owne bringings forth, and hee shall appeare to the
enuious, a Scholler, a Statesman, and a Soldier: therefore you speake vnskilfully: or, if your knowledge bee
more, it is much darkned in your malice.   1635

Luc. Sir, I know him, and I loue him.   (G1v

Duke. Loue talkes with better knowledge, & knowledge with deare loue.

1638 deare] dearer mTHEO *conj.*, HAN1+

1627 **vnweighing**] JOHNSON (1755): "Inconsiderate; thoughtless." So *OED*,
only quotation. LEVER (ed. 1965): "Injudicious. Another figure of 'measuring'; cf.
'scaled' [1475], 'weighing' [1751], etc." Cf. *vnwaied* in *Wiv.* 2.1.23 (570).

1628 **Enuie**] See n. 343.

1629 **streame**] THIRLBY (1733–47): "Course, current." JOHNSON (1755):
"Any thing forcible and continued," but the revision of 1773 defines as "Course,
current." *OED* overlooks this meaning.

1630 **helmed**] HANMER (ed. 1743, 6, glossary): "Guided, conducted." STEEV-
ENS (Var. 1773): *"Steer'd through."* *OED* (*v.* 2): "To steer," first quotation.

vppon a warranted need] SCHMIDT (1875, pp. 1335, 1418): "If a warrant
is needed." *OED* (Warranted *ppl. a.*): "Approved, justified." LEVER (ed. 1965): " 'In
a proven (or truly sufficient) case of necessity'." Cf. *well-warranted* 2632.

1631 **proclamation**] SCHMIDT (1875): "Open declaration" (*OED*, 4). LEVER
(ed. 1965): "Reputation."

testimonied] JOHNSON (1755): "To witness." *OED* (*v.* 2): "To test or prove
by evidence," only quotation.

1632 **bringings forth**] SCHMIDT (1874): "Achievement." STEVENSON (1959,
p. 200): "James's pride in his own 'bringings-forth' was sufficiently obvious." LEISI
(ed. 1964): " 'His fruits' (as in Matth. 7 16)." Cf. n. 406.

appeare] SCHMIDT (1874): "Become evident" (*OED, v.* 9).

1633 **Scholler . . . Soldier**] HARRIS (1909, p. 43): Cf. *Ham.* 1.5.141, 3.1.159
(834, 1807). HARBAGE (1948, pp. 70–1): Cf. *MV* 1.2.124 (303). Sh. means by
scholar one "intelligent and well-informed, educated, schooled, whether formally or
by natural aptitude and experience of the world." ZEEVELD (1974, p. 83): Sh. uses
the new word *statesman* only here and in *Oth.* 1.2.99 (322) and *WT* 1.2.168 (248).

1634 **vnskilfully**] JOHNSON (1755): "Without knowledge; without art." *OED*
(*adv.* 2): "Without discernment; foolishly; ignorantly."

1635 **darkned**] SCHMIDT (1874): *Darken,* "to deprive of intellectual vision"
(*OED, v.* 7). More likely "To cloud with something evil" (*OED, v.* 9).

1637–8 CARTER (1905, p. 411): Cf. Phil. 1:9. VICKERS (1968, p. 328): "The
Duke returns a biting *antimetabole."* See n. 1721–2.

1638 **deare**] I.e., dearer. VAN DAM (1900, pp. 110–11) suggests apocope of

Luc. Come Sir, I know what I know.

Duke. I can hardly beleeue that, since you know not   1640
what you speake. But if euer the Duke returne (as our
praiers are he may) let mee desire you to make your answer before him: if it bee honest you haue spoke, you
haue courage to maintaine it; I am bound to call vppon
you, and I pray you your name?   1645

Luc. Sir my name is *Lucio*, wel known to the Duke.

Duke. He shall know you better Sir, if I may liue to
report you.

Luc. I feare you not.

Duke. O, you hope the Duke will returne no more: 1650
or you imagine me to vnhurtfull an opposite: but indeed
I can doe you little harme: You'll for-sweare this a-
gaine?

Luc. Ile be hang'd first: Thou art deceiu'd in mee
Friar. But no more of this: Canst thou tell if *Claudio*   1655
die to morrow, or no?

Duke. Why should he die Sir?

Luc. Why? For filling a bottle with a Tunne-dish:
I would the Duke we talke of were return'd againe: this

1639 what] I what ROWE1
1652 little] a little HAN1, CAP
1652-3 againe?] ~ . JOHN1+ (−CAP, ARD2)

-er from *dearer;* cf. *Farre* for *farther* in *WT* 4.4.442 (2275), *neere* for *nearer* in *R2*
3.2.64 (1420).

1639 TILLEY (K173): "I know (wot) what I know."

1643 **you haue spoke**] See n. 758.

1648 **report**] See *OED* (*v.* 1c): "To give an account of (a person), to describe."

1651 **vnhurtfull**] SCHMIDT (1875): "Wanting the power of doing harm" *(OED,
a.).*

   opposite] STEEVENS (Var. 1793): "Opponent, adversary" (*OED, sb.* 3).

1652 **for-sweare**] See *OED* (*v.* 2): "Deny or repudiate."

1652-3 **againe**] See *OED* (*adv.* 4): "Another time."

1654 **Thou**] BYRNE (1936, p. 96): "Lucio and the Duke (as Friar) exchange
conversational *you,* then in bragging defiance and easy familiarity Lucio moves to
thou."

1658 **Tunne-dish**] STAUNTON (ed. 1859): "An old Warwickshire name for a
funnel." *OED:* "A kind of funnel used in brewing," from *tun* "cask" and *dish.*
HALLIWELL (ed. 1854) gives an illustration. JOYCE (1916, pp. 219–20) mentions the
word *tundish* as current in Ireland. TANNENBAUM (1933, p. 107) says that
"'Tunner-dish' . . . occurs in some copies of the Folio," but HINMAN (1963,
1:257) finds no such variant. PARTRIDGE (1947, p. 112): "Penis."

1659 **would**] Wish. See n. 17.

   againe] See *OED* (*adv.* 1d): "Back," with a verb of motion.

vngenitur'd Agent will vn-people the Prouince with   1660
Continencie. Sparrowes must not build in his house-
eeues, because they are lecherous: The Duke yet would
haue darke deeds darkelie answered, hee would neuer
bring them to light: would hee were return'd. Marrie
this *Claudio* is condemned for vntrussing. Farwell good   1665
Friar, I prethee pray for me: The Duke (I say to thee
againe) would eate Mutton on Fridaies. He's now past
it, yet (and I say to thee) hee would mouth with a beggar, though she smelt browne-bread and Garlicke: say

---

1667–8 now past it, yet] not past it yet; HAN1, WARB, JOHN, SING2, COL3,
CAM1-DYCE2, DYCE3, HUD2, WH2, CAM2, ARD1, CAM3-ALEX, PEL1, PEN2; now
past it: yea, CAP; not past it; COL4
    1668 say] say't v1773, NLSN
    1669 smelt] smelt of ROWE1-v1773 (−CAP)

    1660 **vngenitur'd**] CAPELL (1779, 1:glossary, 73): "Unfurnish'd with the Or-
gans of Geniture or Generation." RICHARDSON (1837): *"Ungenerated. Ungenitured.*
Not begotten, or borne into existence; not procreated." HUDSON (ed. 1851): *"Unfa-*
thered, not begotten after the ordinary course of nature." SCHMIDT (1875): "Impotent." BALD (ed. 1956): "Sexless." LEVER (ed. 1965): "Sterile, seedless; or without
genitals." Cf. *vnseminar'd, Ant.* 1.5.11 (537), and *vnpaued Eunuch, Cym.* 2.3.34 (992).
    1661–2 **Sparrowes . . . lecherous**] TILLEY (S715) and WILSON (p. 497): "As
lustful as sparrows." Cf. Chaucer, *C.T. Prol.* 626, "lecherous as a sparwe."
    1663 **darke deeds**] Cf. *Per.* 4.6.32, *Lr.* 3.4.90 (1867). See n. 2250.
    darkelie] SCHMIDT (1874): "Secretly" (*OED, adv.* 1), as in *AWW* 4.3.13
(2117). ONIONS (1911): "S. is earliest for 'secretly'." Again in 2657.
    1664 **would**] See *OED* (Will *v.*[1] 36): "With ellipsis of 1st pers. pron. as an
expression of longing = 'I wish'." Cf. 2303.
    1665 **vntrussing**] HALLIWELL (ed. 1854): "To untruss was to untie the tags
which united the doublet and hose" (*OED, v.* 3 and *vbl. sb.*).
    1667 **eate . . . Fridaies**] THEOBALD (ed. 1733) compares *lac'd-Mutton* in *TGV*
1.1.102 (101), and a note on that passage quotes *1 Promos,* 1.3 (p. 312 below), "he
lou'd lase mutton well." STEEVENS (Var. 1778) quotes Marlowe's *Dr. Faustus* (1604,
708–10). NARES (1822): *Mutton,* "A loose woman" (*OED,* 4). TILLEY (M1338) and
WILSON (p. 552): "He loves laced mutton." Lucio means that "The Duke would not
give up women, fast-day or no fast-day, law or no law." See n. 1545.
    now] JOHNSON (Var. 1773): Hanmer's emendation *not* "was received in the
former edition, but seems not necessary. It were to be wished, that we all explained
more, and amended less." HART (ed. 1905): "I agree with M. Mason [1785, p. 40]
that 'Hanmer's amendment appears absolutely necessary'. Otherwise there is no force
in the previous sentence, or rather there would be contradiction." RIDLEY (ed.
1935): "There is an additional insult in the picture of the now *impotent* old lecher."
LEISI (ed. 1964): "Most edd. emend to *not,* putting a semicolon after *yet.* Cf. the
present tense in *he's a better woodman,* [2255]."
    past] See *OED* (*prep.* 1): "Beyond the age for."
    1668 **mouth**] *OED* (*v.* 6): "Join lips," first quotation in this sense.
    1669 **smelt**] HALLIWELL (ed. 1854): "We should now write, *smelt of,* but a

that I said so: Farewell.   *Exit.*   1670
   Duke. No might, nor greatnesse in mortality
Can censure scape: Back-wounding calumnie
The whitest vertue strikes. What King so strong,
Can tie the gall vp in the slanderous tong?
But who comes heere?   1675

Enter Escalus, Prouost, and Bawd.

   Esc. Go, away with her to prison.
   Bawd. Good my Lord be good to mee, your Honor
is accounted a mercifull man: good my Lord.
   Esc. Double, and trebble admonition, and still for-   1680

1670 said] say POPE, HAN1   *Exit.*] *Om.* F4
1676 SCENE VII. POPE, HAN1, WARB, JOHN   *Enter . . .*] *Enter* Escalus,
Provost, Bawd, *and Officers.* THEO2+ *(subst.)*

---

similar phraseology occurs in [*Wiv.* 3.2.69 (1329)], 'he smells April and May' [*OED,
v.* 10]. Cf. Powell's *Art of Thriving,* 1635, p. 93,—'if the clowne be predominant, he
will smell all browne bread and garlicke'. Lucio's reason perhaps for so pertinaciously
accusing the Duke of lechery, is the desire to render Claudio's crime more venial."
    browne-bread] LEVER (ed. 1965): "Coarse rye, or rye and wheat bread, the
food of the poor, which rapidly turned musty and affected the breath" (*OED,* Brown
bread).
    1669–70 **say that I said so**] Cf. 688–9.
    1671–4 KÖNIG (1888, p. 124): *Sententiae* are often in rhyme. Cf. 491–4. LAS-
CELLES (1953, p. 107) writes of *"sentence* clinched with a couplet," but there are two
couplets, since *mortality* rhymes with *calumnie.* See n. 1834–9.
    1671 **mortality**] SCHMIDT (1875): "Human life." LEVER (ed. 1965): "Mortal
beings" (*OED,* 1b).
    1672 **censure**] *OED (sb.* 4): "An adverse judgment, unfavourable opinion, hos-
tile criticism," first quotation in this sense.
    Back-wounding] THIRLBY (1723–33): "Backbiting." ONIONS (1911): "In-
juring treacherously from behind."
    1672–3 **Back-wounding . . . strikes**] TILLEY (E175): "Envy (Calumny) shoots
at the fairest mark (flowers, virtue)." Cf. *Son.* 70, *Ham.* 1.3.38 and 3.1.141 (501,
1791–2), *WT* 2.1.73–4 (675–6).
    1673 **so**] ONIONS (1911): "Be he or it never so . . . , however. . . ." Cf. *OED
(adv.* 24): "To such an extent, that," and (25) "With omission of *that.*"
    1674 **Can**] That he can. On ellipses see ABBOTT §382. Cf. n. 2067.
    gall] SCHMIDT (1874): "Bitterness of mind, rancor" (*OED, sb.*[1] 3).
    1679 **a mercifull man**] NEWCOMER (1929, p. 161): Like Dogberry in *Ado*
3.3.64–5 (1389).
    1680 **Double . . . admonition**] GREY (1754, 1:119): *"Escalus* exceeds the apos-
tle's direction to *Titus* iii.10. 'After a first and second admonition reject'."
    1680–1 **forfeite**] STEEVENS (Var. 1793): "Transgress, offend." SCHMIDT
(1874) explains it as adj., "liable to penal seizure," as in 825 (see n.). EVANS (ed.
1974): "Found guilty."

feite in the same kinde? This would make mercy sweare
and play the Tirant.

Pro. A Bawd of eleuen yeares continuance, may it
please your Honor.

Bawd. My Lord, this is one *Lucio*'s information a-   1685
gainst me, Mistris *Kate Keepe-downe* was with childe by
him in the Dukes time, he promis'd her marriage: his
Childe is a yeere and a quarter olde come *Philip* and *Iacob*: I haue kept it my selfe; and see how hee goes about
to abuse me.   1690

Esc. That fellow is a fellow of much License: Let
him be call'd before vs. Away with her to prison: Goe

1681 sweare] swerve mTHEO *conj.*, HAN1, WARB
1688 and a] and v1773-RANN
1691 That] This THEO2, WARB-JOHN2

1681 **kinde**] SCHMIDT (1874): "Way" (*OED, sb.* 8).

sweare] STEEVENS (Var. 1773): "We say at present, Such a thing *is enough to
make a parson swear,* i.e. deviate from a proper respect to decency, and the sanctity
of his character." IDEM (Var. 1778): "The idea of swearing agrees very well with
that of a *tyrant* in our ancient mysteries." RITSON (1783, pp. 21–2): "We still say
to swear like an emperor; and, from some old book, of which the writer unfortunately
neglected to copy the title, he has noted, *to swear like a tyrant.*" Cf. *AYL* 4.3.13–14
(2161–2). DOUCE (1807, 1:136–7): "The old belief certainly was that tyrants in
general swore lustily; but here seems to be a particular allusion to the character of
Herod, in the mystery of *The slaughter of the innocents,*" quoting the Coventry play.
Cf. *Ham.* 3.2.15–16 (1862) and see TILLEY (S28) and WILSON (p. 696): "Enough
to make a saint swear."

1685 **information**] SCHMIDT (1874): "Accusation" (*OED,* 5).

1686 *Kate Keepe-downe*] PARTRIDGE (1947, p. 136): *Kate,* "a common name for
whores; *Keep-Down* may well imply that she kept men down (on the bed)." [Or it
could mean "stay down" (*OED, v.* 39, 48e). Cf. *1H4* 3.1.229–30 (1769).] HOWARD-
HILL (1972, p. 128): The hyphen shows Crane's influence.

1688–9 **come *Philip* and *Iacob*]** HALLIWELL (ed. 1854): "That is, on the arrival
of the feast of Philip and James, Apostles, May 1st. This day is called that of Philip
and Jacob in the old calendars." HART (ed. 1905): "*Come*] next, when the time
arrives." So "come *Lammas* Eue," *Rom.* 1.3.17 (371–2) and "come Pescod-time,"
2H4 2.4.413 (1412). See FRANZ §660. LEVER (ed. 1965): "The style of reckoning
age indicates that Lucio's child owed its origin to a more pagan way of celebrating
May Day."

1689 **kept it my selfe**] SHUGG (1977, p. 296): "The motherly solicitude shown
by Mistress Overdone in caring for Kate Keepdown's bastard . . . may not have been
entirely altruistic. The child, if female, could easily be prostituted at a very young
age," quoting *Per.* 4.2.15–18.

goes about] See *OED* (About *adv.* 10): To go about, "to busy oneself, to
endeavour."

1692–3 **Goe too**] See n. 513.

too, no more words. Prouost, my Brother *Angelo* will
not be alter'd, *Claudio* must die to morrow: Let him be
furnish'd with Diuines, and haue all charitable prepara-   1695
tion. If my brother wrought by my pitie, it should not
be so with him.
    Pro. So please you, this Friar hath beene with him,
and aduis'd him for th'entertainment of death.
    Esc. Good'euen, good Father.   1700
    Duke. Blisse, and goodnesse on you.
    Esc. Of whence are you?   (G1vb)
    Duke. Not of this Countrie, though my chance is now
To vse it for my time: I am a brother
Of gracious Order, late come from the Sea,   1705
In speciall businesse from his Holinesse.
    Esc. What newes abroad i'th World?
    Duke. None, but that there is so great a Feauor on

1693 words.] Words. *Exeunt with the* Bawd. ROWE1+ (*subst.*)
1698 So please you] So, please you F4, IRV, RLTR; My lord, so please you KTLY
    hath] has THEO2, WARB-RANN (−CAP)
1705 Sea] F1-POPE2, RLTR; See of Rome KTLY; See THEO1 *etc.*

    1693 **Brother**] SCHMIDT (1874): "Associate, colleague" (*OED, sb.* 4), as in
1737.
    1696 **wrought . . . pitie**] HARRISON (ed. 1948): "Acted as mercifully as I
would" (*OED*, Work *v.* 21).
    by] ABBOTT (§145): "According to" (*OED, prep.* 23).
    1699 **entertainment**] SCHMIDT (1874): "Conception, expectation." WHITE
(ed. 1883): "Reception." EVANS (ed. 1974): "Acceptance" (*OED,* 12a).
    1700 **Good'euen**] HOWARD-HILL (1972, p. 127): " 'Good'euen' at 1700 and
2241 shows Crane's variation of hyphen and apostrophe: the hyphenated form is
more common in his dramatic transcripts. Such expressions may change colloquial-
isms in his copy which editors should be prepared to restore in appropriate circumstances."
    1701 Cf. "Blisse be vpon you," *Rom.* 5.3.124 (2982).
    1704 **vse**] *OED* (*v.* 16): "Resort to," "dwell in."
    time] PARROTT (ed. 1938): "Present time." LEVER (ed. 1965): "Occasion"
(*OED, sb.* 16).
    1705 **gracious**] See n. 1387.
    Sea] THIRLBY (1723-33): "Without doubt see is the true reading." THEO-
BALD (1729, in NICHOLS, 1817, 2:289): "His being lately come from *sea* is, I think,
a very idle circumstance here. The third line seems to determine, that the Poet wrote,
—late come from the *See, i. e.* the see of Rome." RITSON (1783, p. 22) defends *sea*
in its usual sense. WILSON (ed. 1922): "So spelt in the three other places where [the
noun] 'see' occurs in the canon" (*Jn.* 3.1.144, 5.2.72 [1071, 2325], *2H4* 4.1.42
[1910]).
    1708-9 **there is . . . cure it**] HORNE (ed. 1840, 1:211): "Virtue has become so

goodnesse, that the dissolution of it must cure it. Noueltie is onely in request, and as it is as dangerous to be   1710
aged in any kinde of course, as it is vertuous to be constant in any vndertaking. There is scarse truth enough
aliue to make Societies secure, but Securitie enough to

1710 and as it is as] and it is as F3-DYCE3 (—COL, HAL), WH2-KIT1, PEL1-PEN2;
and, as it is HUD2; and, as it is, as ALEX, SIS, EVNS
    1711–12 constant] inconstant STAUNTON (1872, p. 867) *conj.*, HUD2, BUL,
CAM3, SIS

---

extreme and outrageous, that it must have a speedy end." VERPLANCK (ed. 1847):
"The reference is to the overstrained sanctity and zeal of Angelo." MORRIS (ed.
1912): "Goodness has so high a fever that only death will cure it." See n. 320.
    1709–10 **Noueltie**] ALBRECHT (1914, p. 160): James I wrote of the common
people of Scotland "euer wearying of the present estate, and desirous of nouelties"
[*Basilicon Doron,* ed. Craigie, 1:93, and in 1604 of "An inconsiderate and childish
affectation of Noueltie," quoted in *OED* (3). See also *Tro.* 3.3.175–80 (2027–32),
AWW 1.2.61–3 (308–10)]. Cf. GROSS (1965, pp. 104–5).
    1710 **onely**] SCHMIDT (1875): "Alone" ("only novelty"). HART (ed. 1905):
"Pre-eminently, specially."
        in request] In demand (*OED, sb.*[1] 6a), as in 2085.
    1710–11 **as it . . . vertuous**] HALLIWELL (ed. 1854): The first *as* is one of the
redundant particles in Sh. "The meaning implied is that it is dangerous not to vary
with the times." WHITE (ed. 1857): "The *Duke* himself calls what he says a 'riddle',
i.e., a paradox." CROSBY (MS n. in DYCE, ed. 1866, on "It is as dangerous"): "(I.e.
to the reputation) as it is virtuous < indeed >." See p. 288.
    1710 **dangerous**] CAPELL (1780, 2:3:49): "Danger to a reputation for spirit, if
we want changeableness and the virtue of volatility."
    1711–12 **it is . . . vndertaking**] DELIUS (ed. 1860): It is now a proof of virtue
if one only perseveres in any enterprise. RIDLEY (ed. 1935): "Either, I think, we must
suppose an ironic twist to *virtuous* (*i.e.* the Duke means that the novelty-mad age
sneers at the 'virtue' of constancy), or else with Staunton read *inconstant.*" BALD (ed.
1956): "To be constant is as dangerous as it is virtuous."
    1713 **Societies**] See *OED* (8): *Society,* "an association."
        Securitie] THIRLBY (1747–53): "Suretyship." JOHNSON (1773): "Any thing
given as a pledge or caution." MALONE (ed. 1790, 10:566): "Those legal securities
into which 'fellowship' leads men to enter for each other." T. H. WHITE (in Var.
1793): "In excuse of this quibble, Shakspeare may plead high authority.—'He that
hateth *suretiship* is sure'. Prov. xi. 15." KNIGHT (1930, p. 81): "Ignorant self-confidence (i.e. in matters of justice) enough to make human intercourse within a society
a miserable thing." BALD (ed. 1956): "Endorsing bonds has become the curse of
friendship." LEISI (ed. 1964): " 'There is hardly enough loyalty to make friendships
secure, but there are enough (financial) securities to make partnership a burden'."
LEVER (ed. 1965): "The 'riddle' [1714] lies in the quibble on (i) security, as the
pledges demanded in return for advances of capital, and (ii) fellowships, as the
corporations formed for trading ventures. Such corporations are 'accurst' by the high
security they must offer to have their ventures financed."

make Fellowships accurst: Much vpon this riddle runs
the wisedome of the world: This newes is old enough,   1715
yet it is euerie daies newes. I pray you Sir, of what disposition was the Duke?

Esc. One, that aboue all other strifes,
Contended especially to know himselfe.

Duke. What pleasure was he giuen to?   1720

Esc. Rather reioycing to see another merry, then
merrie at anie thing which profest to make him reioice.
A Gentleman of all temperance. But leaue wee him to
his euents, with a praier they may proue prosperous, &
let me desire to know, how you finde *Claudio* prepar'd?   1725
I am made to vnderstand, that you haue lent him visita-
tion.

Duke. He professes to haue receiued no sinister measure from his Iudge, but most willingly humbles him-
selfe to the determination of Iustice: yet had he framed   1730

1718–19 *Prose* CAP+
1719 especially] specially POPE1-JOHN2
1723 wee] *Om.* F3-POPE2, HAN1

1714 **Fellowships**] SCHMIDT (1874): *Fellowship,* "association, alliance, partnership" (*OED, sb.* 1a). PARROTT (ed. 1938): "Friendships."

Much] SCHMIDT (1875): "Pretty nearly" (*OED, adv.* 3).

vpon] See *OED* (*prep.* 11b): "According to."

1718–19 Prose set as verse by Compositor B.

1718 **strifes**] SCHMIDT (1875): *Strife,* "endeavour." *OED* (4): "The act of striv-
ing; strong effort," sense first in Sh.

1719 **Contended**] ONIONS (1911): "To strive earnestly" (*OED,* 1).

know himselfe] See TILLEY (K175), SMITH (1963, p. 76), and WILSON (p.
435): "Know thyself" (Thales).

1721–2 RUSHTON (1868, 2:50–1): "Shakespeare sometimes uses this figure Antimetabole or the Counterchange [as Puttenham calls it] . . . he takes a couple of words
to play with in a verse, and making them to change and shift one into another's place,
exchange and shift the sense." Cf. nn. 1402–3, 1637–8.

1722 **profest**] SCHMIDT (1875): "To make it one's business," as in 520 (see n.).
WINNY (ed. 1959): "Attempted."

1724 **his euents**] ONIONS (1911): "The issue of his affairs" (*OED, sb.* 3).

1726 **lent**] See n. 22.

1728 **sinister**] JOHNSON (1755): "Unfair" (*OED, a.* 3).

1728–9 **measure**] *OED* (*sb.* 15): "Treatment (of a certain kind) 'meted out' to
a person." See n. 0.1–0.2.

1730 **determination**] SCHMIDT (1874): "Decision" (*OED,* 2).

framed] SCHMIDT (1874): "To devise" (*OED, v.* 8). HARDING (ed. 1954):
"Fabricated." See n. 1476.

to himselfe (by the instruction of his frailty) manie de-
ceyuing promises of life, which I (by my good leisure)
haue discredited to him, and now is he resolu'd to die.

Esc. You haue paid the heauens your Function, and
the prisoner the verie debt of your Calling. I haue la-   1735
bour'd for the poore Gentleman, to the extremest shore
of my modestie, but my brother-Iustice haue I found so
seuere, that he hath forc'd me to tell him, hee is indeede
Iustice.

Duke. If his owne life,   1740
Answere the straitnesse of his proceeding,
It shall become him well: wherein if he chance to faile
he hath sentenc'd himselfe.

Esc. I am going to visit the prisoner, Fare you well.

1734 your] the due of your COLNE, COL2, COL3
1740–1 *Prose* POPE1+
1741 straitnesse] straightness COL4
1744 *Exit.* F2-JOHN2, v1773-RANN; *Exeunt* ESCALUS, *and* Provost. (*after* 1745)
CAP, MAL+

1731 **instruction**] SCHMIDT (1874): "Prompting." See rather *OED* (1): "Teaching," as in 1871.

   frailty] See n. 1406.

1732 **by my good leisure**] SCHMIDT (1874): "I. e. taking an opportunity of
doing so." LEVER (ed. 1965): " 'In my own time'." See *OED* (5c): *By good leisure,*
"at one's leisure."

1733 **discredited**] JOHNSON (1755): "To deprive of credibility; to make not
trusted" (*OED, v.* 2).

   resolu'd] REED (Var. 1785): "Satisfied." DOUCE (1807, 1:137): *"Resolute,
firm, determined."* ONIONS (1911): "Prepared in mind (esp. for some evil)."

1734 **Function**] JOHNSON (1755): "Employment; office." HUDSON (ed. 1880):
"Duty." See n. 109 and *OED* (*sb.* 4): "The kind of action proper to a person as
belonging to a particular class."

1736–7 **extremest . . . modestie**] SCHMIDT (1875): *Modesty,* "freedom from
arrogance or obtrusive impudence" (*OED,* 2). CAMPBELL (ed. 1949): "Just as far as
I could without being offensively insistent." BALD (ed. 1956): "Furthest limits of
propriety."

1737 **brother-Iustice**] See n. 1693.

1738–9 **indeede Iustice**] TERRELL (1871, p. 22): "We may suppose a legal pun:
he is indeed *just-ice.*" ROLFE (ed. 1882): "The very embodiment of justice pure and
simple, with no mingling of mercy." MIRIAM JOSEPH (1947, p. 153): An example
of "Emphasis . . . a figure which gives prominence to a quality or trait by conceiving
it as constituting the very substance in which it inheres."

1740–1 Prose set as verse by Compositor B.

1741 **Answere**] See n. 1469.

   straitnesse] JOHNSON (1755): "Strictness; rigour." So *OED* (1c). Cf. *strait*
460 and n.

Duke. Peace be with you.   1745
He who the sword of Heauen will beare,
Should be as holy, as seueare:

1745 SCENE VIII. POPE, HAN1, WARB, JOHN

1745 **Peace**] See n. 355.

1746–67 CAPELL (1780, 2:3:49–50): "Speeches, and parts of speeches, in rime, (some in measures properly lyrical, like the sententious one here) are found in all parts of Shakespeare; and should be look'd upon as the time's vices, sacrifices of judgment to profit, but not always unwilling ones; for such speeches are not of ill effect in all places, of which the present is instance. . . . In these lyrical speeches, as we may call them, there is almost always in Shakespeare an interchange of those iso-dunamous measures—the Iambic and the Trochaic: in this, the intermixture is equal; eleven lines of each measure being the speech's whole complement, which is mention'd as a memento to the reciter." WHITE (ed. 1857): "I more than doubt that this and the following lines are Shakespeare's. . . . They are entirely superfluous, having no dramatic purpose. . . . The lines may have been added with Shakespeare's consent." THISELTON (1901, p. 29): "These much-abused lines do not constitute a soliloquy. . . . They are rather of the nature of a chorus summarising the drama's import for the benefit of the audience. . . . The reason for their position is that we are now passing from the domain of tragedy to that of comedy, but before the transition is complete the poet wishes to emphasise the moral which might be lost sight of in the approaching reign of comic method." HART (ed. 1905): "This un-Shakespearian chorus of the Duke's is not justified (like those in *Pericles*) by its assistance to the business in hand. It is a needless interpolation." PORTER & CLARKE (ed. 1909): "This four-stressed verse, terse and gnomic, suits the bitter wisdom and the righteous indignation of the Duke upon witnessing the foul ways of spurious yet pretentious justice in his city." KELLNER (1931, p. 259): These lines are out of place here. They belong to [1834: see n.]. EMPSON (1951, p. 281): "The unreal style lets the Duke act as a sort of chorus." LASCELLES (1953, p. 104): "The staple is a line of seven syllables, which proceeds with a rocking motion from a strong beat in the opening to a strong beat in the close [quotes 1748]. It is capable of easy expansion, in any of three ways: by a light syllable at the end, giving a disyllabic rhyme [quotes 1750]; by a light syllable at the beginning, giving a regular octosyllabic line [quotes 1755]; by a heavy syllable at the beginning, leading to a ripple of light syllables before the rhythm re-establishes itself [quotes 1762]. . . . The only place where verse of this sort would be proper is prologue or epilogue—or, . . . here, a formal pause midway. . . . One conjecture remains permissible; at some performance, Shakespeare's play was given in two parts, a pause intervening, and on this occasion it was judged prudent to remind the audience, on renewal of the performance, of the theme and situation." LEVER (ed. 1965): "The Duke's rhyming speech provides a sententious *finale* to an act full of surprises, and affords a much-needed point of rest. It falls into four parts. . . . Each part except (iii) [1758–61] consists of three couplets; (iii) has almost certainly lost two lines [after 1759]." NOSWORTHY (ed. 1969): "These rhyming couplets have often been stigmatized as a non-Shakespearian insertion but their authenticity is nowadays generally accepted."

1746–7 WATSON (1843, pp. 84–5): Cf. 2 Sam. 23:3. WORDSWORTH (1864, p. 284): "We are reminded of S. Paul, Rom. xiii.4." LEVER (ed. 1965): "Cf. 'the

Patterne in himselfe to know,
Grace to stand, and Vertue go:
More, nor lesse to others paying,
Then by selfe-offences weighing.

1750

1749 Grace . . . go] In grace to stand, in virtue go JOHN1 *conj.*, KTLY; Grace to stand, virtue to go COLERIDGE (1836, 2:124) *conj.*, COLNE, COL2, HENL, RID and] an ARD1, CAM3

---

deputed sword' [810]." See TILLEY (L118) and WILSON (p. 446): "They that make laws must not break them."
    1748–9 JOHNSON (ed. 1765): "These lines I cannot understand, but believe that they should be read thus: Patterning *himself to know*, In *Grace to stand*, in *Virtue go*. . . . *One that after good examples labours to know himself, to live with innocence, and to act with virtue.*" STEEVENS (Var. 1773): "*Should be able to discover in himself a pattern of such grace as can avoid temptation, together with such virtue as dares venture abroad into the world without danger of seduction.*" MALONE (1783, p. 6): "To experience in his own bosom an *original* principle of action, which, instead of being borrowed or copied from others, might serve as a *pattern* to them." Cf. *WT* 4.4.393 (2211). CLARKE (ed. 1864): " 'Should be himself a pattern whereby to know how grace ought to bear itself, and how virtue ought to proceed'." PORTER & CLARKE (ed. 1909): "In himself to recognize Heaven's *patterne*, in himself bear *Grace* to hold himself upright, and *Vertue* upon which to go forward." LEVER (ed. 1965): " 'To know that the precedent for his judgments lies in his own conduct'. 'Pattern' as a precedent (*O.E.D. sb.* 7) rather than a model for imitation, is a Shakespearean usage; cf. . . . (as a verb) [481: see n.]." See p. 288.
    1749 COLERIDGE (1836, 2:124): "Worse metre, indeed, but better English would be,—Grace to stand, virtue to go." FIELD (1845, p. 50): " 'Should have grace to stand and virtue to go'." STAUNTON (ed. 1859): "To show grace how to stand and virtue how to go." ABBOTT (§504): " 'He ought to have grace for the purpose of standing upright, and virtue <for the purpose of> walking in the straight path'. 'Go' is often used for 'walk'. 'To' is omitted before 'go'." STONE (1884, p. 115*): "Grace to *withstand* temptation, and virtue to *go* (walk) uprightly." HART (ed. 1905): " 'An', the conjunction meaning 'if', is almost invariably written 'and' in the early editions. It appears to me to give excellent sense here where none obtained before. He should know in himself a pattern for others, and virtuous disposition to stand upright if it fails elsewhere. This may be a quotation from an educational text-book of the time. Nashe has nearly identical words . . . 'In grace and vertue, to proceed' " (ed. McKerrow, 2:209, 3:247, and see n. on the hornbook in 4:205). RIDLEY (ed. 1935): Hart's emendation "seems singularly infelicitous, missing as it does the contrast, much more pointed to the Elizabethans than to us, between *stand* and *go* (*i.e.* 'walk'), with which *Grace* and *virtue* are exactly appropriate. *Virtue to go* is probably the easiest reading."
    Grace] See n. 1403.
    1750 FIELD (1845, p. 50): " 'Punishing others neither more nor less'."
    1751 CAPELL (1780, 2:3:50): "Than conscience shall teach him, after weighing his own offences."
    selfe-offences] *OED* (2): "One's own offence." Used in a different sense (*OED*, 1) by Milton, *Samson Agonistes*, 515.

Shame to him, whose cruell striking,
Kils for faults of his owne liking:
Twice trebble shame on *Angelo*,
To vveede my vice, and let his grow.   1755
Oh, what may Man within him hide,
Though Angel on the outward side?
How may likenesse made in crimes,

1758 may] many HARN, OXF1   likenesse made in] that likeness, made in
WARBURTON *conj. in* THEO1, THEO, WARB-v1785 (—CAP); that likeness shading
HAN1; that likeness wade in MALONE (1780, 1:100) *conj. (withdrawn* 1790 ed.),
RANN; likeness wade in HAL, SING2, WH1, DYCE2, DYCE3, BUL, SIS; likeness work,
in HUD2

1752-3 SMITH (1963, pp. 50–1): "What you find fault with in others you should
not be guilty of." Cf. TILLEY (F107).
  1753 **liking**] SCHMIDT (1874): "Inclination" (*OED, vbl. sb.* 3).
  1755 STEEVENS (Var. 1778): "To weed faults out of my dukedom, and yet
indulge himself in his own private vices." MALONE (1780, 1:99–100): *"My,* does
not, I apprehend, relate to the duke in particular, who had not been guilty of any vice,
but to any indefinite person. . . . The speaker, for the sake of argument, puts himself
in the case of an offending person." HENLEY (in Var. 1793): "The Duke is plainly
speaking in his own person. What he here terms '*my* vice', may be explained from
his conversation in Act I. sc.iv. with Friar Thomas, and especially the following line:
'—'twas *my* fault to give the people scope'." JACKSON (1819, p. 45): "The Duke
charges himself with the vices of his people." FIELD (1845, p. 50): " 'To weed *my*
vice' means 'the vice of my dominions'." HART (ed. 1905): "To weed vice in every
one else, and cherish his own." HANKINS (1953, p. 191): "The use of 'weeds' for
vices occurs several other times in Shakespeare," as in *Ham.* 1.2.135 and 3.4.151
(319, 2534). See n. 310. JENKINS (in LEVER, ed. 1965) : "The Duke is . . . speaking
chorically as an 'everyman'. 'My vice' here signifies that of other persons in contrast
to Angelo's own."
  1756-7 M. S. (1795, p. 646): Cf. Matt. 23:28. NOBLE (1935, pp. 227–8): "A
common thought, but see the comparison of the Scribes and Pharisees with painted
sepulchres" (Matt. 23:27, quoted in n. 1307–8) and "This outward sainted Deputie"
(1303). See n. 2942.
  1758 **likenesse . . . crimes**] THIRLBY (1733–47): "Seeming." IDEM (1747–53):
"Image." MALONE (1780, 1:100): *"Likeness* is here used for *specious* or *seeming*
virtue." CAPELL (1780, 2:3:50): "Virtue's likeness . . . drawn upon wickedness, for
there is in both those expressions an allusion to painting." MASON (1785, p. 41):
"Made in crimes . . . means, trained in iniquity, and perfect in it: thus we say, a made
horse; a made pointer; meaning one well trained." STEEVENS (Var. 1785): *"Likeness*
may mean *seemliness,* fair appearance, as we say, a likely man." COLLIER (ed. 1842):
This phrase "may refer to the resemblance in vicious inclination between Angelo and
Claudio. . . . The sense seems to be, 'how may persons of similar criminality, by
making practice on the times, draw to themselves, as it were with spiders' webs, the
ponderous and substantial benefits of the world'." STAUNTON (ed. 1859): *"Likeness*
means *false seeming."* PORTER & CLARKE (ed. 1909): "How may man make use of
that outward likeness to an angel, inwardly made up of crimes. . . . The compact and

Making practise on the Times,
To draw with ydle Spiders strings   1760
Most ponderous and substantiall things?
Craft against vice, I must applie.
With *Angelo* to night shall lye
His old betroathed (but despised:)
So disguise shall by th'disguised   1765

1759 Making] Mocking, MAL, v1821, SING1, KIT1; Masking COLNE, COL2, COL4; Make a ALEX   Times,] times (*two lines missing*) NICHOLSON (1866) *conj.*, ARD2

1760 To draw] Draw WARBURTON *conj. in* THEO1, THEO1-v1813 (−MAL), HARN, KTLY; To-draw PERRING (1885) *and* SPENCE *and* GOW *conj. in* CAM2, CAM3, PEN2   strings] stings F1(u)

1765 by] to HUD2

---

trochaic make-up of the lines carries the weight of the speaker's indignation most fitly." PARROTT (ed. 1938): "False seeming, composed of guilt within." CAMPBELL (ed. 1949): "False appearance (deceit), assumed to hide crime." See p. 288.

1759 WARBURTON (in THEOBALD, ed. 1733): "Imposing on the World." SMITH (in GREY, 1754, 1:119): "Making it a practice of letting great rogues break through the laws with impunity, and hanging up little ones for the same crimes." PARROTT (ed. 1938): "Using stratagems" (*OED*, Practice 6c). See n. 2475.

1760–1 WARBURTON (in THEOBALD, ed. 1733): "Draw with its false and empty Pretences . . . the most ponderous and substantial Things of the World, as Riches, Honour, Power, Reputation, &c." SMITH (in GREY, 1754, 1:119): "Draw away in time with idle spiders strings (For no better do the cords of the law become, according to the old saying, *Leges similes aranearum telis* [Laws like spiders' webs], to which the allusion is) justice and equity the most ponderous, and substantial bases, and pillars of government." HALLIWELL (ed. 1854): "To obtain the gratification of the grossest and most absolute desires under the slender web of deceptive appearances." PERRING (1885, p. 47) and SPENCE (1888, p. 444) suggest, as Spence writes, that " 'To', before 'draw', is not the sign of the infinitive, but an archaic prefix, as in 'to-pinch' " in *Wiv.* 4.4.57 (2180). GOLLANCZ (ed. 1894): Perhaps "to-draw," "pull to pieces." WILSON (ed. 1922): " 'To-draw' is a clumsy way . . . of saying 'draw to itself '." HARDING (ed. 1954): "The Duke asks himself how, by adopting spider-like methods of deceit, roughly similar to those of Angelo . . . he can take advantage of the current situation to encompass (*To draw* meaning 'draw together') the *substantial* ends he had earlier outlined to Isabella." SISSON (1956, 1:85): "*To draw* = Drawing, or By drawing.*" LEVER (ed. 1965): "Alludes to the Renaissance commonplace, supposedly a saying of Anacharsis [or Solon], that the laws were like spiders' webs which caught the small flies but let the big insects break through" (TILLEY L116, WILSON, pp. 446–7).

1760 strings] HINMAN (1968, p. xxi): A press correction in F1 from *stings.* "No Folger copy shows the uncorrected reading but the Elizabethan Club copy at Yale does."

1765–6 JOHNSON (ed. 1765): "So *disguise* shall by means of a person *disguised,* return an *injurious demand* with a *counterfeit person.*" HALLIWELL (ed. 1854): "In this

Pay with falsehood, false exacting,   1766
And performe an olde contracting.   *Exit*

---

way disguise (I, a disguised friar) shall, by the agency of a lady disguised, meet an injurious demand by a stratagem." LEE (ed. 1907): "The meaning seems to be that the disguise which Mariana is assuming will, by the agency of the vicious Angelo, who wears the *false guise* of sanctity, satisfy deceptively his base demand." LEVER (ed. 1965): "Mariana's physical disguise (as Isabella) will pay with 'falsehood' (illusion) the false exaction by Angelo, in his moral disguise of 'seeming'."

1766 **Pay**] See n. 2798.

    exacting] *OED (vbl. sb.),* first quotation.

Actus Quartus. Scæna Prima.   4.1

Enter Mariana, and Boy singing.

Song. *Take, oh take those lips away,*   1770

1768 *a Grange.* THEO1-JOHN2, v1773-RANN, CAM1, GLO, WH2-NLSN, KIT1-SIS, ARD2 (*subst.*); *A Room in* Mariana's *House.* CAP, MAL-SING2, WH1-STAU, KTLY, KNT3, DEL4, COL4 (*subst.*); *Before MARIANA'S house.* DYCE, HUD2; *The garden of a moated grange.* CAM3

1769 *Enter . . .*] MARIANA *discovered sitting; a Boy singing.* v1793-STAU, KTLY-HUD2, CAM3 (*subst.*)

1770 **Song**] THEOBALD (ed. 1733): "This Song . . . is inserted in *Beaumont* and *Fletcher's* [*Rollo, Duke of Normandy; or The*] *Bloody Brother*" (1639, 5.2) with an additional stanza, omitted in *MM* because it is addressed from a lover to his mistress. [This is the second stanza in *Rollo*, ed. Jump, 1948, p. 67: "*Hide ô hide those hills of Snow, That thy frozen bosome beares, On whose tops the pincks that grow, Are yet of those that Aprill wears, But first set my poore heart free, Bound in those Icy chaines by thee.*"] WARBURTON (ed. 1747): "This is part of a little sonnet of *Shakespear's* own writing, consisting of two Stanzas, and so extremely sweet, that the reader won't be displeased to have the other." MALONE (ed. 1790): "I believe that both these stanzas were written by our author." BOSWELL (Var. 1821, 20:420): "I have grave doubts whether this delicate little poem may not, from its popularity at the time, have been introduced by the printer, to fill up the gap, and gratify his readers, from some now forgotten author." COLLIER (ed. 1842): "It may be doubted whether either stanza was the authorship of Shakespeare, as it certainly was the frequent custom of dramatists of that day to insert songs in their plays which were not of their own writing; but, on the other hand, we have no proof that such was the usual practice of Shakespeare." WHITE (1854, p. 164): "Shakespeare evidently wrote the first stanza, and some one else,—probably Fletcher, the second." REES (1876, pp. 101–2): Cf. a Latin poem by Gallus, published at Venice in 1558. HUDSON (ed. 1880): "To this stanza, which I am sure none but Shakespeare could have written, is commonly appended another, which I am equally sure Shakespeare did not write." MONTAGUE (1911, p. 242): "The song sung to Mariana is a possible candidate for the place of finest lyric in the English language." DE LA MARE (1929, p. xxvii): The song "evokes in the imagination a face—pale, grey-eyed, dark, phantasmal—seen in dream; and despite its 'lips'

> *that so sweetly were forsworne,*   1771
> *And those eyes: the breake of day*
> *lights that doe mislead the Morne;*

---

and its 'sweetly' and its 'kisses', it is spiritual in effect." CHAMBERS (1930, 1:455): "A musical interpolation in a Jacobean revival is always possible." HOUSMAN (1933, pp. 39–40): "Even Shakespeare, who had so much to say, would sometimes pour out his loveliest poetry in saying nothing. [Quotes this song.] That is nonsense; but it is ravishing poetry." JUMP (1948, p. 105): "Shakespeare must be recognised as the author of the stanza." AUDEN (1957, p. 38): "Mariana, unlike Katharine [in *H8* 3.1], is not trying to forget her unhappiness; she is indulging it. Being the deserted lady has become a rôle. The words of the song, *Take, O take, those lips away,* mirror her situation exactly, and her apology to the Duke when he surprises her, gives her away." LONG (1961, p. 20): "The dramatic function of the song seems to be aimed at an immediate characterization of Mariana upon her entry. The probability that she is an addition to Shakespeare's gallery of melancholics appears when we compare her remark about the music, it 'pleas'd my woe', to [*AYL* 2.5.12–14 (901–2) and *TN* 1.1.2–3 (6–7)]. Thus, from the effect of the song and knowledge previously given us of Mariana's plight, our sympathies are instantly drawn to her before she speaks a line." STERNFELD (1963, p. 91): "The economy, poignancy and integration of the music into the dramatic structure is in accord with Shakespeare's observance in the tragedies." IDEM (in LEVER, ed. 1965, p. 201): "The ancestor of Shakespeare's verse was probably [as Rees noted] the popular Latin poem, 'Ad Lydiam', much admired in the sixteenth century. . . . Such lines as *porrige labra* [reach out your lips] and *da columbatim mitia basia* [give gentle kisses like a dove] were likely points of departure for Shakespeare's muse." SENG (1967, p. 183) suggests that Sh. "might have borrowed" from a hypothetical English poem imitating "Ad Lydiam," and NAEF (1976, pp. 222–3) agrees. NOSWORTHY (ed. 1969): "It appears to have been Shakespeare's normal practice to write his own songs, and this one is certainly worthy of his genius." See also p. 478 on the music.

    1770–5   CAPELL (1780, 2:3:51): This song has "such a sweetness of language and imag'ry, as might even work the effect ascrib'd to it here [in line 1783], without other assistance: What the moderns could mean by their suppression of the final couplet's repeatings, cannot be conceiv'd; for it may be easily seen that such repeatings may be made, with some art, to have the best effect possible." NOBLE (1923, pp. 90–1): The repetition of *bring againe* and *seal'd in vaine* lends "some colour to the idea that, when Shakespeare wrote his lyrics, he did so with some melody in view." EMPSON (1930; 1953, pp. 180–1): "The main logical structure of this exquisite song is a contrast; *take, but bring;* which involves a contradiction; and there is another in the idea of 'returning' a kiss. . . . He must not bring her new kisses, but only her old ones back, so as to restore her to her original unkissed condition." [Cf. *Rom.* 1.5.112 (689).] SITWELL (1948, pp. 129–30): "Part of the poignance of this marvellous song . . . is due to the repetition, to the echoes which sound throughout the verse, and part to the way in which the imploring stretching outward of the long vowels in 'Take' and its internal assonance 'againe' (and other words with long high vowels) are succeeded, in nearly every case, in the next stressed foot, by a word which seems drooping hopelessly, as with 'lips' and 'forsworne'. . . . A singular beauty, too, is given by the variation in the length and depth of the pauses."

    1773 *lights*] HART (ed. 1905): "A favourite poetical term for the eyes," as in Sidney's *Astrophil and Stella,* Sonnet 9.

    mislead the Morne] J. G. B. (1886, p. 319): The image was suggested by

> *But my kisses bring againe, bring againe,*
> *Seales of loue, but seal'd in vaine, seal'd in vaine.*   1775

> *Enter Duke.*

Mar. Breake off thy song, and haste thee quick away,
Here comes a man of comfort, whose aduice
Hath often still'd my brawling discontent.
I cry you mercie, Sir, and well could wish   1780
You had not found me here so musicall.
Let me excuse me, and beleeue me so,
My mirth it much displeas'd, but pleas'd my woe.

1774 *bring againe, bring againe,*] *bring again,* ROWE1-JOHN2
1775 *seal'd in vaine, seal'd in vaine.*] *seal'd in vain.* F4-JOHN2
1776 *Enter Duke.*] *After* 1779 CAP, v1778-ARD1
1778 [*Exit* Boy.] *after* comfort, CAP; *after* 1779 MAL-CAM3, ALEX+; *after* 1777 KIT1
1783 it] is THEO2, WARB, THEO4

Marlowe's *Hero and Leander* (1598, 2:321–2): "this false morne Brought foorth the day before the day was borne." EMPSON (1930; 1953, pp. 181–2): *"They mislead the morn* is in main idea a simple hyperbole; 'when your eyes arrive at a place nature thinks it is the sun rising'. But *mislead* is a word already well suited to the situation; she was herself in a state of *morning* before he came to her, because of her youth, freshness, and lack of experience; just as she was *day* in the previous line, either when she was happy in his love for her, so that the promise of her *morning* had been achieved, or before she met him." [More Empson than Sh.]
     1774 *againe*] Back (*OED, adv.* 3).
     1775 *Seales of loue*] STEEVENS (Var. 1778): Cf. *Son.* 142. MALONE (1780, 1:100): Cf. *Ven.* 511, "Pure lips, sweet seales in my soft lips imprinted." REED (in Var. 1785): Cf. "the old Black Letter Translation of *Amadis of Gaule,* 4to. p. 171 [tr. Anthony Munday, c. 1590; 1619, bk. 1, p. 215] . . . *'kisses* (which are counted the *seales of Love*)'." SCHMIDT (1875): Seal, "confirmation, sanction, pledge." *OED (sb.* [2] li): "An impressed mark serving as visible evidence of something." See n. 2622 and "seales of loue" (1601) in *Campion's Works,* ed. Vivian (1909), pp. 350, 377.
     1777 **Breake . . . song**] KNIGHT (ed. 1840): These words "would lead one to infer that . . . it is not complete." WHITE (1854, p. 166): "Her command to the boy to break off his song, is no evidence that Shakespeare had written more than one stanza. It is but a dramatic contrivance to produce the effect of an intrusion upon her solitude." LEVER (ed. 1965): "Suggesting that a second stanza was expected."
     1779 **brawling**] JOHNSON (1755): "To quarrel noisily." ONIONS (1911): "Clamorous" (*OED, ppl. a.* b).
     1780 **cry you mercie**] SCHMIDT (1874, p. 265): "Beg your pardon" (*OED, v.* 1b).
     1782 **so**] THIRLBY (1747–53): "So far." SCHMIDT (1875): "This." See *OED (adv.* 2c): "In this way; thus; as follows."
     1783 JOHNSON (ed. 1765): "Though the musick soothed my sorrows, it had no tendency to produce light merriment." CAPELL (1780, 2:3:50): "The musick I was

Duk. 'Tis good; though Musick oft hath such a charme
To make bad, good; and good prouoake to harme.   1785
I pray you tell me, hath any body enquir'd for mee here
to day; much vpon this time haue I promis'd here to
meete.

Mar. You haue not bin enquir'd after: I haue sat
here all day.   1790

Enter Isabell.

Duk. I doe constantly beleeue you: the time is come
euen now. I shall craue your forbearance alittle, may be
I will call vpon you anone for some aduantage to your
selfe.   1795
    Mar. I am always bound to you.   *Exit.*
    Duk. Very well met, and well come:
What is the newes from this good Deputie?
    Isab. He hath a Garden circummur'd with Bricke,

1788 meete.] meet one. HAN1; meet— WALKER (1860, 3:20) *conj.*, KTLY
1790 all] all the CAP
1791 *Enter Isabell.*] *After* you: (1792) JOHN, v1773; *after* 1796 SING2, DYCE,
STAU, KTLY, DEL4, HUD2, IRV, BUL, ARD1; *after* now. (1793) SIS
    1797 SCENE II. POPE, HAN1, WARB, JOHN   well come] wellcome THEO2;
welcome WARB-BUL (−CAM, GLO, WH2), SIS, PEL1, PEN2

---

attending to, was of a kind to damp mirth; but sooth'd, and fed pleasingly, the
melancholy passion that now governs me." CRAIG (ed. 1951): "These lines reflect
the Renaissance conception of the psychological effects of music; cf. Burton's description: '. . . Many men are melancholy by hearing Musick, but it is a pleasing melancholy
that it causeth; and therefore to such as are discontent, in woe, fear, sorrow, or
dejected, it is a most present remedy; it expels cares, alters their grieved minds, and
easeth in an instant'. (*Anatomy of Melancholy,* II, 2, vi, 3.).”
    1784 **charme**] SCHMIDT (1874): "Magic power." See ONIONS (1911): "The
orig. sense 'incantation, enchantment, magic spell' . . . runs through the fig. applica-
tions" (*OED, sb.*¹ 2).
    1785 LEVER (ed. 1965): " 'To give sin a pleasing aspect and lead virtue into
harm'."
    1787 **much**] See n. 1714.
    vpon] ONIONS (1911): "At or just about." See n. 1805.
    1788 **meete**] *OED* (*v.* 8c): "Keep an appointment."
    1792 **constantly**] JOHNSON (ed. 1765): "Certainly; without fluctuation of
mind." *OED* (*adv.* 1b): "Confidently, firmly, assuredly."
    1793 **forbearance**] SCHMIDT (1874): "Withdrawing, keeping aloof," as in *Lr.*
1.2.182 (488). *OED* overlooks this sense.
    1799 **circummur'd**] JOHNSON (1755): "Walled round." *OED* (*v.*), first quota-
tion.

Whose westerne side is with a Vineyard back't;   1800
And to that Vineyard is a planched gate,
That makes his opening with this bigger Key:
This other doth command a little doore,
Which from the Vineyard to the Garden leades,
There haue I made my promise, vpon the   1805
Heauy midle of the night, to call vpon him.
    Duk. But shall you on your knowledge find this way?
    Isab. I haue t'ane a due, and wary note vpon't,
With whispering, and most guiltie diligence,
In action all of precept, he did show me   1810

1805-6 There . . . him.] There on the heavy middle of the night, Have I my
promise made to call upon him. POPE1-JOHN2; There have I made my promise to
call on him, Upon the heavy middle of the night. CAP-SING1 (upon him mTBY1 *conj.,*
KTLY); There have I made my promise upon the heavy Middle of the night to call
upon him. COL1, KNT3, EVNS (in the heavy SING2, on the heavy DYCE1, COL3); *prose*
WH, STAU, DEL4; *three lines ending* promise . . . night . . . him. WALKER (1860, 3:20–1)
conj., CAM, GLO, DYCE2, DYCE3-HUD2, IRV-PEN2
    1810 all of] of all ROWE1, ROWE2

    1801 **planched gate**] HANMER (ed. 1743, 6, glossary): "A Gate of boards."
STEEVENS (Var. 1778): Cf. "planched floore" in Sir Arthur Gorges's tr. of Lucan,
1614 (1:18). MOOR (1823, p. 282): "A paled gate, we called a *planched-gate:* as does
Shakespeare." HALLIWELL (ed. 1854) quotes COTGRAVE (1611): "*Planché,* planked,
boorded, floored with plankes." *OED (v.),* first quotation as ppl. a.
    1802 **his**] Its. See ABBOTT §228, *OED (poss. pron.* 3), FRANZ §320. Cf. 1974.
    1805-6 WHITE (ed. 1857): "These lines are prose, although printed as verse."
DYCE (ed. 1864): "This arrangement [lines ending *promise . . . night . . . him.*] was
recommended to me in 1844 by a true poet (the present Laureate [Tennyson]): and
see Walker's *Crit[ical] Exam[ination]* &c. vol. iii. p. 21." RIDLEY (1933, p. 116):
Keats echoes this line, which he underlines in his 1814 ed. [SPURGEON, 1928, p.
115], in "The Eve of St. Agnes," 49, "Upon the honied middle of the night."
    1805 **vpon**] *OED (prep.* 6b): "In, at, or during." See n. 1787.
    1806 **Heauy**] CLARKE (ed. 1864): "Shakespeare applies the epithet 'heavy' to
'night' here, and in [*Oth.* 5.1.42 (3132)] to express darkness that seems ponderous."
DYCE (1867): "Thick, cloudy, dark." SCHMIDT (1874): "(The different significations often scarce distinguishable, as they afford much scope to quibbling) . . . weary,
drowsy, sleepy" (*OED, a.*[1] 28).
    1807 **shall**] Will. See ABBOTT §315, *OED* (8c), FRANZ §611. Cf. 1956, 2210.
    1808 **t'ane**] Taken. HOWARD-HILL (1972, p. 89): " 'Tane' with the apostrophe
in different positions in the word occurs five times in the five comedies" transcribed
by Crane. Cf. *ta'ne* in 2301.
    wary] See *OED (a.* 2): "Careful."
    1810 **In . . . precept**] WARBURTON (ed. 1747): "Shewing the several turnings
of the way with his hand; which action contained so many precepts, being given for
my direction." JOHNSON (ed. 1765): "I rather think we should read, *in precept all*

The way twice ore.

   Duk. Are there no other tokens
Betweene you 'greed, concerning her obseruance?
   Isab. No: none but onely a repaire ith' darke,
And that I haue possest him, my most stay   1815
Can be but briefe: for I haue made him know,
I haue a Seruant comes with me along
That staies vpon me; whose perswasion is,
I come about my Brother.
   Duk. 'Tis well borne vp.   1820
I haue not yet made knowne to *Mariana*

              Enter Mariana.

A word of this: what hoa, within; come forth,
I pray you be acquainted with this Maid,
She comes to doe you good.   1825
   Isab. I doe desire the like.

1822 *Enter Mariana.*] *After* 1823 ROWE1+
1824 SCENE III. POPE, HAN1, WARB, JOHN

---

of action; that is, *in direction given not by words but by mute signs.*" CLARKE (ed. 1864): "Conveying all his directions in action, rather than in speech." SCHMIDT (1874–5): *Action,* "gesticulation." *Precept,* "instruction, lesson." DURHAM (ed. 1926): "With instructive gestures." BALD (ed. 1956): "Teaching by demonstration." LEVER (ed. 1965): "Angelo showed the way not by leading Isabella to it ('action') but by detailed directions ('precept', *O.E.D.* 2b)."

   1813 **'greed**] ONIONS (1911): "Agreed or determined upon" (*OED,* Gree *v.*).

   concerning her obseruance] HUNTER (ed. 1873): "Which it concerns her to observe." Cf. *OED* (Concern *v.* 4): "To be of importance to," as in 87.

   obseruance] SCHMIDT (1875): "The act of keeping or adhering to" (*OED,* 1), as in *Ham.* 1.4.16 (621). LEE (ed. 1907): "Keeping the appointment." BALD (ed. 1956): "Prescribed conduct."

   1814 **repaire**] ONIONS (1911): "Going or coming to a place" (*OED, sb.*[1] 4).

   1815 **possest him**] JOHNSON (ed. 1765): "Made him clearly and strongly comprehend." DYCE (1867): "To inform precisely." ONIONS (1911): "To inform, acquaint" (*OED, v.* 10). See also *OED* (9b): "To persuade, convince."

   most] See *OED* (*a.* 1b): "Greatest."

   1818 **staies vpon me**] HALLIWELL (ed. 1854): "Waits for my leisure." So *OED* (*v.*[1] 16).

   perswasion] SCHMIDT (1875): "Belief" (*OED,* 2a). Cf. *perswade* 1827.

   1820 **borne vp**] THIRLBY (1723–33): Cf. *holding vp* 1482. SCHMIDT (1874, p. 87): "*To bear up* = to arrange, to devise." HART (ed. 1905): "Sustained" (*OED, v.*[1] 13).

   1822 Mariana enters after 1823.

Duk. Do you perswade your selfe that I respect you?

Mar. Good Frier, I know you do, and haue found it.   (G2^v

Duke. Take then this your companion by the hand

Who hath a storie readie for your eare: 1830

I shall attend your leisure, but make haste

The vaporous night approaches.

   Mar. Wilt please you walke aside.   *Exit.*

   Duke. Oh Place, and greatnes: millions of false eies

Are stucke vpon thee: volumes of report   1835

1828 haue] I have POPE1-v1773, KTLY, KIT1; oft have DYCE2, DYCE3, HUD2, OXF1; so have ARD2, PEN2

1832-3 *One line* v1793-STAU, KTLY-COL4, IRV, BUL, ARD1, CAM3, SIS

1833 Wilt] Will't HAN1, v1773+   walke] to walk JOHN, v1773   *Exit.*] *Ex.* Mar. *and* Isab. ROWE3+

1827 **perswade**] See *OED* (*v.* 1b): "To bring oneself to believe."

   respect you] HARRISON (ed. 1948): "Esteem" you (*OED, v.* 4). LEVER (ed. 1965): " 'Have regard for your interests'." See n. 1289.

1833 **walke**] SCHMIDT (1875): "To go away, . . . to withdraw" (*OED, v.*¹ 8a). LEVER (ed. 1965): "An invitation to retire from the centre of the stage, not, as F stage directions imply, to make a full exit." See nn. 1381, 2321.

1834-9 WARBURTON (ed. 1747): "It plainly appears that *this* fine speech belongs to *that* which concludes the preceding Scene, between the *Duke* and *Lucio*. For they are absolutely foreign to the subject of this, and are the natural reflections arising from that. Besides, the very words [quoting 1836] evidently refer to *Lucio*'s scandals just preceding. . . . But that some time might be given to the two women to confer together, the players, I suppose, took part of the speech, beginning at [1671], and put it here." JOHNSON (ed. 1765): "I cannot agree that these lines are placed here by the players. The sentiments are common, and such as a Prince, given to reflection, must have often present. There was a necessity to fill up the time in which the Ladies converse apart, and they must have quick tongues and ready apprehensions, if they understood each other while this speech was uttered." WILSON (ed. 1922, p. 98): "Five and a half lines do not 'fill up the time' required for Isabella to tell her tangled tale." LEVER (1938, p. 232): "The time has obviously been foreshortened, but this was permitted by the theatrical convention that time could be presumed to elapse during a soliloquy." LASCELLES (1953, p. 107): These six lines should precede the other four lines on calumny (1671-4). "All ten lines suit the instant of Lucio's departure much better than the midst of Mariana's business." WINNY (ed. 1959): A. P. Rossiter suggests: "The Duke's couplets closing III.i could equally well go in here —providing a necessary explanation and at a point where the Duke must be alone." See Kellner in n. 1746-67.

1834 **false**] JOHNSON (ed. 1765): "Insidious and trayterous." CLARKE (ed. 1864): "Falsely-judging." SCHMIDT (1874): "Deceitful."

1835 **stucke**] THIRLBY (1747-53): "Fixed" (*OED*, Stick *v.*¹ 20b). HART (ed. 1905): Cf. *Tim.* 4.3.263-6 (1888-91) and Jonson's description of Fame from Virgil's *Aeneid*, bk. 4, in *Poetaster* (1602, 5.2.85 ff.). LEVER (ed. 1965): "The imagery suggests a figure from pageantry or emblem literature."

1835-7 **volumes . . . doings**] WINNY (ed. 1959): "A mass of rumours pursue

Run with these false, and most contrarious Quest
Vpon thy doings: thousand escapes of wit
Make thee the father of their idle dreame,
And racke thee in their fancies. Welcome, how agreed?

> *Enter Mariana and Isabella.*   1840

Isab. Shee'll take the enterprize vpon her father,
If you aduise it.
Duke. It is not my consent,

1836 these] their HAN1, HUD2; base COLNE, COL2, COL3, COL4   Quest]
Quests F2+ (−ALEX, ARD2, EVNS)
1837 escapes] 'scapes POPE1-v1821, SING, KTLY, DYCE2, DYCE3-HUD2
1838 their] an ROWE1, ROWE2   dreame] Dreams ROWE3-v1773 (−CAP),
DYCE, COL3, CAM1, GLO, HUD2, WH2, CAM2, KIT1
1839 Welcome, how agreed?] Well! agreed? HAN1; Welcome! How! agreed?
HAL; Welcome! How greed? WALKER (1860, 3:21) *conj.*, DYCE2, DYCE3
1840 SCENE IV. POPE, HAN1, WARB (*after* fancies! [1839] JOHN)   *Enter
. . .*] *After* fancies! (1839) JOHN, v1773, COL1+ (−HAL, KNT3)
1841 her⌄] ~ , F2+
1843 It is] 'Tis POPE1-v1773 (−CAP), DYCE2, DYCE3, HUD2

---

all your activities, distorting and misrepresenting them."
    1836 THISELTON (1901, p. 31): " 'False' qualifies the verb 'Run', just as 'most
contrarious' qualifies 'Quest'." ONIONS (1953, p. 263): " 'Follow a false scent and
hunt counter'."
    contrarious Quest] F2 reads *Quests,* and most eds. follow. JOHNSON (1755):
"Enquiry; examination." IDEM (ed. 1765): "Different reports *run counter* to each
other." RITSON (1783, p. 22): *"Lying and contradictory messengers."* MALONE (ed.
1790, 10:567): *"Inquisitions."* ROLFE (ed. 1882): "Spyings." THISELTON (1901, pp.
31–2): " 'Quest' is of course the verb . . . which signifies the giving tongue of the
dog on the scent of game." ONIONS (1911): *Contrarious,* adv. "in the contrary
direction." WILSON (1922): "A hunting metaphor; a quest being the cry of the
hound upon the scent (v. N.E.D. 'quest' sb.^{1} 6 *b*)." LEVER (ed. 1965): "To quest
=(i) to search for game, (ii) to bark at the sight of it (*O.E.D.* v.^{1} 1, 2)."
    1837 **escapes**] JOHNSON (1755): "Sally; flight; irregularity." OED (*sb.* ^{1} 5):
"Sally of wit," first quotation in this sense. WILSON (ed. 1922): "Shakespeare seems
rather to mean the little falsehoods that a witty person allows himself in conversation."
    1838 LEVER (ed. 1965): " 'Make you the subject or source of their own fanta-
sies'."
    1839 **racke**] CLARKE (ed. 1864): "Here it seems to mean something equivalent
to 'stretching into enormity', or 'torturing into semblance of evil'. Perhaps the sentence implies, 'mangle thy reputation by their false representations'." ROLFE (ed.
1882): "Probably = strain, distort, misrepresent." ONIONS (1911): "Distort."
    1843 **It is**] Perhaps for *'Tis.* Cf. 1784, 1820.
    1843–4 **not . . . But**] THIRLBY (1723–33): Cf. 2054. SCHMIDT (1875): *Not*
before *but,* "not only." See ABBOTT §54.

But my entreaty too.

    Isa. Little haue you to say   1845
When you depart from him, but soft and low,
Remember now my brother.

    Mar. Feare me not.

    Duk. Nor gentle daughter, feare you not at all:
He is your husband on a pre-contract: 1850
To bring you thus together 'tis no sinne,
Sith that the Iustice of your title to him
Doth flourish the deceit. Come, let vs goe,

1846 low,] ⏜ . ROWE1, ROWE2, POPE
1847 *Marked as quotation* THEO1+ (−SIS)

1850 **pre-contract**] JOHNSON (1755): "A contract previous to another." *OED (sb.):* "A pre-existing contract . . . of marriage." WILSON (ed. 1922): "Formal betrothal." LEVER (ed. 1965): "A future contract of marriage. This signified *sponsalia de futuro,* or betrothal." LAWRENCE (1931, p. 95): "Mariana was fully justified in yielding to the embraces of Angelo, on account of her earlier betrothal to him." HARDING (1950, p. 158): "When the Duke tells Mariana that it is 'no sin', in view of her marital status, to have a sexual relationship with Angelo, he is stretching a point." Cf. 2808–11. SCHANZER (1960, p. 85): "Their bond was not that of a simple or conditional *de futuro* [see n. 237] contract, which could be broken off against the wishes of one of the parties to it. Theirs were *sponsalia iurata,* sworn spousals, as we are told repeatedly [quotes 1434–5, 2581–2, 2602–3]." NAGARAJAN (1963, p. 118): "The Duke insists in the last act on Mariana's marriage with Angelo because, as one who has been well-instructed in the calling of a friar, he knows that nothing ever justifies a sexual union except a proper church wedding." LEVER (ed. 1965, p. lv): "In the view of churchmen, any kind of sexual relationship before a fully conse- crated marriage was, of course, sinful. But the Duke, as the audience knew, was not a friar but a monarch. By secular standards, Mariana's plight fully condoned her deceiving of Angelo." BIRJE-PATIL (1969, p. 110): "One doubts whether the Duke would stake his reputation . . . unless he were quite certain that the alliance between Mariana and Angelo was adequately firm." See nn. 237, 239.

    1851–3 **To . . . deceit**] THIRLBY (1723–33): Cf. 1477–8.

    1852 **Sith**] See n. 327.

    1853 **flourish**] WARBURTON (ed. 1747): "A metaphor taken from embroidery, where a coarse ground is filled up and covered with figures of rich materials and elegant workmanship." JOHNSON (1755): "To adorn; to embellish; to grace." STEEVENS (Var. 1778): *"Flourish is ornament in general."* Cf. *TN* 3.4.404 (1890). DOUCE (1807, 1:139): *"Decorate an action that would otherwise seem ugly. . . . Flourish* may perhaps allude to the ornaments that embellish the *ancient* as well as modern books of penmanship." SCHMIDT (1874): "To colour, to varnish." *OED (v.* 6): "Adorn, decorate, embellish, ornament." DURHAM (ed. 1926): "Justify, grace." PARROTT (ed. 1938): "Gloss over." WINNY (ed. 1959): "Gives formal propriety to . . . flourishes being the decorative embellishment which give[s] elegant finish to a document."

Our Corne's to reape, for yet our Tithes to sow.   *Exeunt.*

Scena Secunda.   4.2

Enter Prouost and Clowne.   1856

Pro. Come hither sirha; can you cut off a mans head?
Clo. If the man be a Bachelor Sir, I can:
But if he be a married man, he's his wiues head,
And I can neuer cut off a womans head.   1860
Pro. Come sir, leaue me your snatches, and yeeld mee

1854 Tithes] F1-ROWE3; Tilth's THEO1-THEO4, CAP, SING, DYCE, WH1-STAU, KTLY, COL4-IRV, BUL, NLSN, CAM3, PEL1, PEN2; tilth VERP; field's COL2; tythe's POPE1 *etc.*
1855 *Scena Secunda*] SCENE V POPE, HAN1, WARB, JOHN   *The Prison.* ROWE1-SIS, ARD2 (*subst.*)
1858-60 *Prose* POPE1+

1854 **Tithes**] THEOBALD (ed. 1733): "It must be *Tilth;* that is, our Tillage is yet to be made; our Grain is yet to be put in the Ground." JOHNSON (ed. 1765): "I believe *tithe* is right, and that the expression is proverbial, in which *tithe* is taken, by an easy metonymy, for *harvest.*" FARMER (in Var. 1773, 10:Oo6): "*Tilth* is provincially used for *land till'd,* prepared for sowing." HENLEY (in HALLIWELL, ed. 1854): "The Duke is speaking in the person of an ecclesiastick; *tythe,* therefore, is a word more in character than *tilth.*" KNIGHT (ed. 1840): "*Tithe* may be also taken in another sense, namely, the proportion that the seed which is sown bears to the harvest. . . . Our *tithe*—our seed which is to produce tenfold." HALLIWELL (ed. 1854): "Our corn (harvest) is certainly yet to be gathered, for even our tithe (a portion of it) is not yet sown." LEE (ed. 1907): " 'Tithe' in the sense of 'grain' makes the line intelligible." LEVER (ed. 1965): "The preliminary work must be done before the reward is forthcoming. . . . 'Tithe', . . . the corn sown for tithe dues, makes good sense."
1858-60 Prose set as verse.
1859 **his wiues head**] T. WHITE (1793, fol. 18): "I fear this is an allusion to Scripture—'the husband is head of the wife'." HALLIWELL (ed. 1854): "See Ephesians, v. 23; 1 Corinthians, xi. 3." MIRIAM JOSEPH (1947, p. 191): "Equivocation, the use of the middle term in two different senses." LEVER (ed. 1965): "With equivocation on 'head' as in [265 ff.: see n. 266-7], and on 'woman' in contrast to 'maid' " [cf. 181-2].
1861 **me**] See n. 259.
    snatches] JOHNSON (1755): "A quip; a shuffling answer." RANN (ed. 1786): "Quibbles." SCHMIDT (1875): "Scraps of wit." ONIONS (1911): "Smart repartee."

a direct answere. To morrow morning are to die *Clau-*
dio and *Barnardine*: heere is in our prison a common executioner, who in his office lacks a helper, if you will take
it on you to assist him, it shall redeeme you from your   1865
Gyues: if not, you shall haue your full time of imprisonment, and your deliuerance with an vnpittied whipping;
for you haue beene a notorious bawd.

   Clo. Sir, I haue beene an vnlawfull bawd, time out of
minde, but yet I will bee content to be a lawfull hang-   1870
man: I would bee glad to receiue some instruction from
my fellow partner.

   Pro. What hoa, *Abhorson*: where's *Abhorson* there?

               Enter Abhorson.

   Abh. Doe you call sir?   1875

   Pro. Sirha, here's a fellow will helpe you to morrow
in your execution: if you thinke it meet, compound with
him by the yeere, and let him abide here with you, if not,
vse him for the present, and dismisse him, hee cannot
plead his estimation with you: he hath beene a Bawd.   1880

   Abh. A Bawd Sir? fie vpon him, he will discredit our
mysterie.

   Pro. Goe too Sir, you waigh equallie: a feather will
turne the Scale.   *Exit.*

   Clo. Pray sir, by your good fauor: for surely sir, a   1885

1864 you] thou ROWE3

OED (*sb.* 9): "A quibble, a captious argument," first quotation in this sense. HARRI-
SON (ed. 1948): "Wisecracks."

   1863 **common**] Public. See n. 14.

   1867 **vnpittied**] STEEVENS (Var. 1793): "An unmerciful one." DOUCE (1807,
1:139): "Rather *a whipping that none shall pity.*" ONIONS (1911): "Unmerciful."

   1876 **will**] Who will: see n. 758.

   1877 **compound**] JOHNSON (1755): "Bargain in the lump." *OED* (*v.* 10):
"Agree, make terms, bargain, contract."

   1880 **estimation**] SCHMIDT (1874): "Reputation" (*OED*, 2b).

   1882 **mysterie**] WARBURTON (ed. 1747): "Trade or manual profession" (*OED,*
Mystery² 2). LEE (ed. 1907): " 'Mystery', in the sense of calling or trade (from the
Latin *ministerium*), has no etymological connection with 'mystery' in the sense of a
secret rite (from the Greek μυστήριον [mystērion]. The two words are here quibblingly confused."

   1885–1900 VICKERS (1968, p. 318): "The sight of a bawd and an executioner

good fauor you haue, but that you haue a hanging look:
Doe you call sir, your occupation a Mysterie?

Abb. I Sir, a Misterie.   (G2va)

Clo. Painting Sir, I haue heard say, is a Misterie; and
your Whores sir, being members of my occupation, v-   1890
sing painting, do proue my Occupation, a Misterie: but
what Misterie there should be in hanging, if I should
be hang'd, I cannot imagine.

Abb. Sir, it is a Misterie.

Clo. Proofe.   1895

1893 imagine.] ~ . **** (*lacuna*) WARB, JOHN
1894 *Abb.* Sir,] *Abhor.* *** *Clown.* *** Sir, HAN1; *Clown.* Sir, WARB
1895 *Clo.*] *Abhor.* HAN1, WARB

---

arguing with the tools of Aristotelian logic is one of the choicest of Shakespearian
inversions."

1886 **fauor**] STEEVENS (Var. 1778): "Countenance." NEILSON & HILL (ed.
1942): "(1) grace, (2) face." LEISI (ed. 1964): "A pun on *favour* 'leave', 'permission'
(OED 3a) and *favour* 'face', 'look' (OED 9, 9b, as in [2039])." The same pun is in
TN 2.4.26 (911).

    a hanging look] JOHNSON (1755): "Foreboding death by the halter." *OED*
(*ppl. a.* 4): "Having a downward cast of countenance; gloomy-looking. (Often with
play on *Hang v.* 3)," first quotation in this sense. HART (ed. 1905): "The quibble
here on a downcast expression and one born to be hanged is probably an old one."
Cf. *Tmp.* 1.1.32 (37–8). LEVER (ed. 1965): "A downcast expression; but quibbling
on Abhorson's occupation."

1890 **your**] See n. 1548.

    occupation] PARTRIDGE (1947, p. 160): Vaguely allusive to *occupy,* "copulate
with," as in *Rom.* 2.4.105 (1199) and *2H4* (Q1) 2.4.161.

1894–1900 WARBURTON (in HANMER, ed. 1743): *"The Text here is plainly
maimed and deficient, the words by which* Abhorson *should prove the Hangman's trade a
mystery are lost. But from what follows the argument may be conjectured to have been this, that
every man's apparel fitted the Hangman: to which we may suppose the* Clown *replied, that for
the same reason the same thing might be said of the Thief's trade.* —Yes, Sir, It is a mystery.
&c. *and this connects the rest that follows."* HEATH (1765, p. 94): A "groundless
supposition. . . . The reading of the old editions is . . . right, except that the last speech
[1897–1900], which makes part of the hangman's argument, is by mistake, . . . given
to the clown or bawd." COLLIER (ed. 1842): "The Clown asks Abhorson for 'proof'
that his occupation is a mystery, and receives for reply, merely, 'Every true man's
(*i. e.* honest man's) apparel fits your thief'. The Clown, who is a quick fellow, instantly
catches at the mode of reasoning passing in Abhorson's mind, and explains in what
way 'every true man's apparel fits your thief'. Abhorson is not a man of many words,
and contents himself with the assertion upon which the Clown enlarges." CLARKE
(ed. 1864): "The speech is much more in character with the clown's snip-snap style
of chop-logic, than with Abhorson's manner, which is remarkably curt and bluff."

Abh. Euerie true mans apparrell fits your Theefe.

Clo. If it be too little for your theefe, your true man thinkes it bigge enough. If it bee too bigge for your Theefe, your Theefe thinkes it little enough: So euerie true mans apparrell fits your Theefe.   1900

Enter Prouost.

Pro. Are you agreed?

Clo. Sir, I will serue him: For I do finde your Hangman is a more penitent Trade then your Bawd: he doth oftner aske forgiuenesse.   1905

Pro. You sirrah, prouide your blocke and your Axe to morrow, foure a clocke.

Abh. Come on (Bawd) I will instruct thee in my

1896–7 *Abh.* Euerie . . . *Clo.* If] *Abhor.* Every . . . thief, Clown: If THEO; *Abho.* Every . . . thief: If HEATH *conj.*, CAP, RANN-v1821, SING, DYCE, CAM1-KTLY, HUD2+ (−IRV)
  1896 *Abh.*] *Clown.* HAN1, WARB
  1897 theefe, your true man] true man, your Thief THEO
  1899 Theefe, your Theefe] true man, your thief THEO
  1903 finde] find that OXF1, PEL1
  1904 your] you F2
  1905 oftner] often OXF1

1896 **fits**] SCHMIDT (1874): "To be of the right measure for, to suit." So *OED* (*v.*[1] 5). WAHL (1888, p. 33) quotes similar German proverbs such as "Dem Diebe passt Alles [Everything fits the thief]." HART (ed. 1905): "A fitter of apparel's occupation is a mystery (a tailor's craft); a thief fits himself from every true man, therefore his business is a mystery." LEVER (ed. 1965): "The true man's apparel 'fits' (satisfies) the thief."

1897–9 THIRLBY (1747–53): "Big enough to lose, for the thief to get. Little enough to get." LEVER (ed. 1965): "Little and big in terms of (i) size, (ii) value."

1900 LASCELLES (1953, p. 108): "A brief passage is surely missing; not necessarily lost, for the whole has the appearance of a first draft, in which what is required may be inserted presently."

1905 **aske forgiuenesse**] GREY (1754, 1:183): "Alluding to the executioner's begging pardon of the criminal, before he does his office," quoting *AYL* 3.5.3–6 (1773–6).

1907 **foure**] LASCELLES (1953, p. 167): "I take it that 'eight' should stand [here], to correspond with [1919], and that Angelo [in 1987] is putting forward the time of the execution, that he may be beforehand with Isabel. A small and natural piece of officiousness on a transcriber's part would lead to the 'correction' (eight to four) in that one passage where a discrepancy with Angelo's order had happened to catch his eye." LEVER (ed. 1965, p. xvi): "The inference is surely that the Provost has arranged for Barnardine to be executed at four, and for Claudio to die at eight."

196

Trade: follow.

Clo. I do desire to learne sir: and I hope, if you haue   1910
occasion to vse me for your owne turne, you shall finde
me y'are. For truly sir, for your kindnesse, I owe you a
good turne.   *Exit*

Pro. Call hether *Barnardine* and *Claudio*:
Th'one has my pitie; not a iot the other,   1915
Being a Murtherer, though he were my brother.

Enter Claudio.

Looke, here's the Warrant *Claudio*, for thy death,
'Tis now dead midnight, and by eight to morrow
Thou must be made immortall. Where's *Barnardine*?   1920
Cla. As fast lock'd vp in sleepe, as guiltlesse labour,

1912 y'are] yours ROWE, POPE; yare mTBY1 *and* THEOBALD (1729) *conj.,*
THEO1+
1913 *Exit*] *Exeunt* Clown, *and* ABHORSON. (*after* 1914) CAP, MAL+ (−NLSN)
1914 *Exit Abhorson.* NLSN
1915 Th'one] One POPE1-KNT1 (−MAL), SING2, KTLY, KNT3
1917 SCENE VI. POPE, HAN1, WARB, JOHN
1920 Where's] Where is CAPN (*errata*)

1912 **y'are**] THIRLBY (1723–33): Read *yare,* as in *Ant.* 3.13.131 (2309). THEO-
BALD (1729, in NICHOLS, 1817, 2:290): "We ought to restore it *yare, i. e.* dexterous
in the office of hanging you." HANMER (ed. 1743, 6, glossary): "Ready, nimble,
quick" (*OED, a.* 1). Cf. *1 Promos,* 2.6 (p. 318 below), where the Hangman says, "I
must be dapper in this my facultie."
1913 **good turne**] THIRLBY (1723–33): "Turning off the ladder." So FARMER
(in Var. 1785). See *OED* (*sb.* 23): *Good turn,* "benefit," quoting Heywood, *Prouerbes*
(1562, ed. Milligan, 1.11.321), "One good tourne askth an other." See TILLEY
(T616) and WILSON (p. 325). LEVER (ed. 1965) quotes the same pun from Dekker,
The Wonderfull Yeare, 1603 (*Plague Pamphlets,* ed. F. P. Wilson, p. 61).
1915-16 WALKER (1860, 2:91–2): "Can these two lines possibly be genuine?
They seem to me to be flatness itself." LEVER (ed. 1965): "The formal couplet
bridges a pause for Claudio's entry while calling to mind Isabella's attitude to her
brother, [1365] ff."
1919 **dead midnight**] HART (ed. 1905): "Midnight that is still as death," citing
Ham. 1.2.198 (389) and *Son.* 43.
1920 **made immortal**] HART (ed. 1905): Cf. Nashe, *The Vnfortunate Traueller*
(1594, 2:258): "deuised the meanes to make me immortall." See also Isabel's words
in 1265–7.
1921-2 CARTER (1905, p. 413) and NOBLE (1935, pp. 69, 228) compare Eccl.
5:11 (5:12 A.V.), "The sleepe of him that trauelleth, is sweete" (in Geneva 1595
and 1598 roman-letter Q eds.; Geneva 1560 and 1583 read "trauaileth" and Bishops'
Bible in 1585 "A labouring man sleepeth sweetely"). BALDWIN (1944, 2:413, 640):

197

When it lies starkely in the Trauellers bones,
He will not wake.
Pro. Who can do good on him?
Well, go, prepare your selfe. But harke, what noise?   1925
Heauen giue your spirits comfort: by, and by,
I hope it is some pardon, or repreeue
For the most gentle *Claudio.* Welcome Father.

                         Enter Duke.

Duke. The best, and wholsomst spirits of the night,   1930
Inuellop you, good Prouost: who call'd heere of late?
Pro. None since the Curphew rung.

1923 He will not wake] He will not awake F3, F4, ROWE3; He'll not awake
POPE1-JOHN2
1925 *Ex.* Claud. (*after* your self.) THEO1-JOHN2, v1773-RANN; (*after* comfort!
[1926]) CAP, MAL-v1821, SING, KNT, HAL, DYCE1, STAU-DYCE3, HUD2+; (*after* By
and by:— [1926]) COL, WH1   *Knock within.* ROWE1+ (*subst.*)
1926 *More knocking* (*after* comfort.) CAM3-SIS, ARD2
1929 *Enter Duke.*] *After* Claudio. DYCE, STAU-GLO, DEL4, HUD2+ (*subst.*)
1932–8 *Lines ending* Isabel?... long.... hope.... deputy. v1793-STAU, KTLY,
KNT3, COL4; rung.... long.... Claudio?... Deputy. CAM1, GLO, DYCE2, DEL4,
DYCE3, HUD2, WH2, BUL-PEL1 (−ALEX), PEN2, EVNS; rung.... long.... hope.
... deputy. IRV, ARD2; rung.... long. (*then as* F1) CAM2; rung.... No.... long.
(*then as* CAM1) ARD1
1932 None] Now F2-F4   rung] run ROWE2

Cf. *2H4* 3.1.9–31 (1430–52).
1921 **labour**] Personified, so that *it lies starkely.*
1922 **starkely**] JOHNSON (ed. 1765): "Stifly. These two lines afford a very
pleasing image." HART (ed. 1905): "Profoundly, perfectly.... I am inclined to refer
starkly here to sleep." Cf. Jonson, *Catiline* (1611, 4.73), "a sleepe, as starke, as
death." *OED* (*adv.* 2): "Stiffly." LEVER (ed. 1965): "Transferred epithet from the
condition of the 'traveller'."
       Trauellers] SCHMIDT (1875): "A labourer" (*OED*, Travailer), as in *LLL*
4.3.308 (1658). LEVER (ed. 1965): "'Travail' and 'travel' were interchangeable
spellings, and 'traveller' here means 'labouring man'." Cf. *H5* 4.1.285 ff. (2118 ff.).
1924 **do good on**] SCHMIDT (1874, p. 485): "To produce effect, to prevail on,"
as in *1H4* 3.1.199–200 (1736), *Rom.* 4.2.13 (2436). LEVER (ed. 1965): "Benefit"
(*OED*, *sb.* 5a [*d*]).
1926 **by, and by**] See n. 1378.
1928 **gentle**] See n. 357.
1930 HART (ed. 1905): Cf. *Oth.* (Q1) 1.2.35 (242): "The goodnesse of the night
vpon your friends."
1931 **Inuellop**] JOHNSON (1755): *Envelop,* "To cover; to hide; to surround."
OED (*v.* 2): "Wrap, cover closely on all sides."
1932 **Curphew**] HALLIWELL (ed. 1854): "The evening curfew, in the [15th and

Duke. Not *Isabell?*
Pro. No.
Duke. They will then er't be long.   1935
Pro. What comfort is for *Claudio?*
Duke. There's some in hope.
Pro. It is a bitter Deputie.
Duke. Not so, not so: his life is paralel'd
Euen with the stroke and line of his great Iustice: 1940
He doth with holie abstinence subdue
That in himselfe, which he spurres on his powre
To qualifie in others: were he meal'd with that

1935 They] She HAWKINS *conj. in* v1778, RANN
1937 There's] There is THEO, WARB
1943–4 *Lines ending* meal'd . . . tyrannous; POPE-v1821, SING, KNT, KTLY

16th] centuries, was usually rung at 8 p.m. for the space of a quarter of an hour."
ROLFE (ed. 1882): "S. transfers the English (and earlier Norman French) curfew bell
to Vienna, as he does to Italy in *R. and J.* iv. 4. 4 [2546]." Elizabeth's proclamation
in July, 1595 (*STC* 8243) sets the curfew in London at nine.

1935 RITSON (in Var. 1793): "The Duke expects *Isabella* and *Mariana.*" Cf.
1945. ROLFE (ed. 1882): "The Duke is expecting both Isabella and the messenger
with a reprieve."

1937 **hope**] Cf. 1204–7.

1938 **It**] See *OED* (*pron.* 2d): "*It* also occurs where *he, she,* or *that* would now
be preferred." Cf. 2197.

1939 **paralel'd**] JOHNSON (1755): "To keep in the same direction; to level."
OED (*v.* 2): "To make parallel, bring into conformity, equalize."

1940 **stroke and line**] THIRLBY (1747–53): "Carpenter's striking his line."
JOHNSON (ed. 1765): "The *stroke* of a pen or a line." STAUNTON (ed. 1859): *"Rule."*
HUNTER (ed. 1873): "Ruled limit." HART (ed. 1905): "Sway, power, or influence."
WILSON (ed. 1922): "Shakespeare is quibbling as usual, since 'stroke' = the blow
of the executioner's axe and 'line' the hangman's cord. . . . Possibly 'paralleled'
. . . 'stroke and line' refers primarily to musical score, where Shakespeare's eyes would
most commonly encounter parallel lines and strokes; if so the idea of 'harmony' would
be present to his mind." WINNY (ed. 1959): "Precise execution." LEISI (ed. 1964):
" 'Straight line', hence 'straight course'."

1943 **qualifie**] JOHNSON (ed. 1765): "To temper, to moderate, as we say wine
is *qualified* with water." ROLFE (ed. 1882): "Abate, control." PARROTT (ed. 1938):
"Check." See n. 74.

meal'd] WARBURTON (ed. 1747): "Mingled." EDWARDS (1750, p. 153): "It
seems to mean *'dawb'd* with the same spots that he finds fault with in others'."
THIRLBY (1747–53): "Tainted, infected." JOHNSON (1755): "To sprinkle; to min-
gle," from Fr. *mêler.* HORNE (ed. 1840, 1:212): "Were he fed, or filled, with that
which he now denounces; or, had he made his meal on this vice, which he now
corrects." WHITE (ed. 1883): "Dusted, smirched as a miller is with the meal in which
he works." HART (ed. 1905): "I imagine the word . . . is used metaphorically to mean
composed, compounded with, as bread is of meal." *OED* (*v.* 3): "To spot, stain," only

Which he corrects, then were he tirrannous,
But this being so, he's iust. Now are they come.   1945
This is a gentle Prouost, sildome when
The steeled Gaoler is the friend of men:
How now? what noise? That spirit's possest with hast,
That wounds th'vnsisting Posterne with these strokes.

   Pro. There he must stay vntil the Officer   1950
Arise to let him in: he is call'd vp.

1945 are they] they are THEO2, WARB-v1773 (−CAP)   *Knock again.* ROWE1-
v1821, SING, KNT, HAL, KTLY, CAM3; (*after* tyrannous; [1944]) COL, WH1; (*after*
just.) DYCE, STAU-GLO, DEL4, HUD2-NLSN, KIT1+   Provost *goes out.* THEO1-
JOHN2, v1773-PEL1, PEN2, EVNS; Provost *goes to the Door.* (*after* come.) CAP, (*after*
just.) ARD2
   1946 sildome when] Seldom-when SING1 *conj.,* SING2, DYCE2, DYCE3, HUD2;
'Tis seldom when KTLY
   1947 *Knocking.* COL, DYCE, WH1-GLO, DEL4+
   1949 th'vnsisting] th' insisting F4; th' unresisting ROWE, POPE, THEO, WARB,
JOHN, v1773-v1785, KTLY, BUL; th' unresting HAN1; the unshifting CAP; th' unlist-
ing MASON (1785) *conj.,* WH1; the resisting COLNE, COL2, COL3, SIS; the unwisting
SING2   Provost *returns.* THEO1-JOHN2, v1773+ (*subst.*)
   1950 he must] must he CAP, v1778-RANN, ARD2
   1951 *Speaking to one at the Door* CAP, v1778-STAU, KTLY-HUD2 (−DEL4), IRV
(*subst.*)

---

quotation; see *mail* in *Eng. Dial. Dict.* So ONIONS (1911). Though doubted by
WILSON (ed. 1922) and LEVER (ed. 1965), this explanation is accepted by most eds.
from Kittredge to Evans.
   1945 **this being so**] RANN (ed. 1786): "As he is thus consistent."
   1946 **gentle**] SCHMIDT (1874): "Kind" (*OED, a.* 8).
   sildome when] SINGER (ed. 1826): "This is absurdly printed Seldom, when,
&c. in all the late editions. '*Seldom-when* (i.e. *rarely, not often*)'." IDEM (1853, *N&Q,*
p. 335): Cf. *2H4* 4.4.79 (2457). HALLIWELL (ed. 1854) quotes Palsgrave (1530),
"Seldom whan, *peu souvent.*" OED (Seldom *adv.* C): *Seldom-when,* "rarely." ONIONS
(1911): *Seldom when,* "seldom that."
   1947 **steeled**] THIRLBY (1747–53): "Harden'd." CAPELL (1779, 1:glossary,
65): "Harden'd, heart-harden'd." So *OED (ppl. a.* 5), sense first in Sh.
   1949 **vnsisting**] JOHNSON (ed. 1765): "What can be made of *unsisting* I know
not; the best that occurs to me is *unfeeling.*" BLACKSTONE (in MALONE, 1780,
1:101): "*Unsisting* may signify 'never at rest', always opening." KNIGHT (ed. 1840):
"Never at rest, from *sisto,* to stand still." ABBOTT (§460): "*Unsisting* for 'unresisting'." SCHMIDT (1875): "Perhaps = unresting, but probably a misprint." HART (ed.
1905): "We should read 'un'sisting' for 'unassisting', *i.e.* unhelping, helpless." POR-
TER & CLARKE (ed. 1909): "Rowe's change of this to 'unresisting' is the best
explanation that has been given of the meaning." ONIONS (1911): "(?) misprint
. . . for *insisting* (F4) = persistent." KITTREDGE (ed. 1936): "Shaken, made to
vibrate." See p. 289.
   1951 **call'd**] See *OED* (Call *v.* 4c): "To rouse from sleep, summon to get up."
So *calles* 2069.

Duke. Haue you no countermand for *Claudio* yet?
But he must die to morrow?   (G2ᵛb)
    Pro. None Sir, none.
    Duke. As neere the dawning Prouost, as it is,   1955
You shall heare more ere Morning.
    Pro. Happely
You something know: yet I beleeue there comes
No countermand: no such example haue we:
Besides, vpon the verie siege of Iustice,   1960
Lord *Angelo* hath to the publike eare
Profest the contrarie.

                    Enter a Messenger.

Duke. This is his Lords man.

1957 Happely] F1, F2, WH, OXF1, CAM3; Haply KNT3, RLTR; Happily F3 *etc.*
1963 SCENE VII. POPE, HAN1, WARB, JOHN
1964–5 *Duke.* This . . . man. *Pro.* And] This . . . man. *Duke.* And mTBY3 *and*
TYRWHITT *conj.,* RANN, KNT, SING2+ (−COL3, COL4, IRV, PEL1, PEN2)
1964 Lords] F1-ROWE2, HAL; *om.* CAP; Lordship's ROWE3 *etc.*

1953 **But**] SCHMIDT (1874, p. 156): "Otherwise than" (*OED, conj.* 7).
1956 **shall**] Will: see n. 1807.
1957 **Happely**] COLLIER (ed. 1842): "For *haply,* three syllables being required
to complete the preceding line." HOWARD-HILL (1972, p. 100) finds this spelling
characteristic of Crane in his transcripts. [Cf. *Vnhappely* 249.]
1959 **example**] SCHMIDT (1874): "Instance." CAMPBELL (ed. 1949): "Precedent." See n. 1407.
1960 **siege**] GREY (1754, 2:311): *"Seat"* (*OED, sb.* 1).
1964–5 *Duke. . . . Pro.*] TYRWHITT (1766, p. 38): "The *Provost* has just declared
a fixed opinion that the execution will not be countermanded, and yet, upon the first
appearance of the Messenger, he immediately guesses that his errand is to bring
Claudio's pardon. It is evident, I think, that the names of the Speakers are misplaced."
JOHNSON (Var. 1773): "When, immediately after the Duke had hinted his expectation of a pardon, the Provost sees the Messenger, he supposes the Duke to have *known
something,* and changes his mind. Either reading may serve equally well." ANON. (in
HALLIWELL, ed. 1854): "Surely the Duke would be likely to know the messenger,
who may be supposed to belong to his court, and the Provost, after what he had heard,
might naturally think the missive was a pardon." LEE (ed. 1907): "The change in the
text, though generally adopted, is not essential." LEVER (ed. 1965): "The presence
of the S.D. for the Messenger's entry between the first and second halves of line 98
[1962–4] probably explains the error."
1964 **This is**] Possibly pronounced as one syllable: see n. 2501. Stresses would
then fall on *-fest, con-, This, Lord-, man.*
    Lords] MALONE (ed. 1790): "In the Ms. plays of our author's time they often
wrote *Lo.* for Lord, and *Lord.* for Lordship; and these contractions were sometimes

Pro. And heere comes *Claudio*'s pardon.   1965
Mess. My Lord hath sent you this note,
And by mee this further charge;
That you swerue not from the smallest Article of it,
Neither in time, matter, or other circumstance.
Good morrow: for as I take it, it is almost day.   1970
    Pro. I shall obey him.
    Duke. This is his Pardon purchas'd by such sin,
For which the Pardoner himselfe is in:
Hence hath offence his quicke celeritie,
When it is borne in high Authority.   1975
When Vice makes Mercie; Mercie's so extended,
That for the faults loue, is th'offender friended.
Now Sir, what newes?
    Pro. I told you:
Lord *Angelo* (be-like) thinking me remisse   1980
In mine Office, awakens mee
With this vnwonted putting on, methinks strangely:
For he hath not vs'd it before.
    Duk. Pray you let's heare.

1966–70 *Prose* POPE1+
1971 *Exit* Messen. ROWE1+
1972–7 [*Aside.* JOHN, v1773+
1979–83 *Prose* POPE1+
1981 mine] my v1778-RANN
1984 you] *Om.* F4, ROWE1

---

improperly followed in the printed copies." Every ed. except Capell and Halliwell
emends to *Lordship's.*

1966–70, 1979–83 Prose set as verse by Compositor B.

1973 **is in**] HEATH (1765, p. 95): " 'Is plunged in guilt'." CAPELL (1780,
2:3:53): "*Is* with*in* the law's danger." ONIONS (1911): "Engaged, involved . . .
(=liable for punishment)."

1974 **his**] Its: see n. 1802.

quicke celeritie] THIRLBY (1723–33): Cf. *swift celeritie* 2780. RANN (ed.
1786): "Speedy propagation, when the magistrate himself is infected with it." PAR-
ROTT (ed. 1938): "Swift speed." Cf. 61, 1482, 1777.

1977 **friended**] JOHNSON (1755): "To favour; to befriend; to countenance."
See *OED* (*ppl. a.* b): "Befriended *(rare),*" quoting a proverb from Camden, 1605,
"As a man is friended, so the law is ended."

1980 **be-like**] JOHNSON (1755): "Probably; likely; perhaps" *(OED, adv.).*
SCHMIDT (1874): "As it seems, it should seem, I suppose." Again in 2495, 2501.

1981 **Office**] See n. 332.

awakens] *OED* (*v.* 5): "To rouse into activity; to stir up."

1982 **putting on**] STEEVENS (Var. 1793): "Spur, incitement." *OED* (*vbl. sb.* [1] 9);
cf. Put *v.* [1] 46h, *Put on,* "To urge onward, encourage; to incite, impel."

                    The Letter.   1985

Whatsoeuer you may heare to the contrary, let Claudio be ex-
ecuted by foure of the clocke, and in the afternoone Bernar-
dine: For my better satisfaction, let mee haue Claudios
head sent me by fiue. Let this be duely performed with a
thought that more depends on it, then we must yet deliuer.   1990
Thus faile not to doe your Office, as you will answere it at
your perill.

What say you to this Sir?
Duke. What is that *Barnardine*, who is to be execu-
ted in th'afternoone?   1995
Pro. A Bohemian borne: But here nurst vp & bred,
One that is a prisoner nine yeeres old.
Duke. How came it, that the absent Duke had not
either deliuer'd him to his libertie, or executed him? I
haue heard it was euer his manner to do so.   2000

1985 *The Letter*] Provost *reads the Letter* ROWE1+ (*subst.*)
1989 duely] truly CAP (duly *in* CAPN)
1991 Thus] This POPE2
1996–7 *Prose* POPE1+ (−CAM3)

1985 *The Letter*] WILSON (ed. 1922): "It looks as if the 'stage-letter' was used
as copy . . . a hypothesis supported by the fact that we have the sp. 'Bernardine' at
[1987–8] and nowhere else in the text." LEVER (ed. 1965, p. xxvii): "The speech-
prefix is omitted for the Provost as the reader of Angelo's letter. . . . [n.] In the Trinity
autograph MS. of Middleton's *A Game at Chess*, the reader of the letter in III.i is not
indicated. 'The Letter' . . . is a customary heading in texts based on 'rough drafts'."
[Middleton wrote this heading, with no reader's name, at 2.1.15 as well as at 3.1.33.
See Bald's ed., pp. 39–40, 64, 80.]
    1988 *satisfaction*] See n. 92.
    1990 *deliuer*] SCHMIDT (1874): "Communicate" (*OED, v.*[1] 11).
    1991 *Thus*] SCHMIDT (1875): "Accordingly" (*OED, adv.* 2).
        Office] See n. 332.
        answere] See n. 493.
    1996–7, 2001 Prose set as verse by Compositor B.
    1996 **Bohemian**] *OED* (*sb.* 1): "A native of Bohemia." HART (ed. 1905): "Com-
pare 'Bohemian-Tartar' in [*Wiv.* 4.5.21 (2238)]. The term was used irrespectively
of country, implying wildness, savagery; in a sense akin to that of gipsy, its late
equivalent." LEISI (ed. 1964): "The meaning 'gipsy' is not found before 1696
(OED)." LEVER (ed. 1965): "Suggested by *2 Prom.*, II.ii[i] [p. 348 below], where
Corvinus is styled 'King of *Hungarie* and *Boemia*'. . . . Shakespeare transfers the
connection to his fictional duchy of Vienna."
    1997 MALONE (1780, 1:101): "That has been confined these nine years." Cf.
Ham. 4.6.14–15 (2988).

Pro. His friends still wrought Repreeues for him:
And indeed his fact till now in the gouerment of Lord
Angelo, came not to an vndoubtfull proofe.

Duke. It is now apparant?

Pro. Most manifest, and not denied by himselfe.   2005

Duke. Hath he borne himselfe penitently in prison?
How seemes he to be touch'd?

Pro. A man that apprehends death no more dread-
fully, but as a drunken sleepe, carelesse, wreaklesse, and
fearelesse of what's past, present, or to come: insensible   2010
of mortality, and desperately mortall.

2001 *Prose* POPE1+
2004 It is] Is it POPE1-v1821 (−CAP), SING, KNT, KTLY
2006 penitently] penitent THEO2, WARB-v1773 (−CAP)
2009 wreaklesse] rechless POPE, HAN1; reckless THEO, WARB-PEN2; reakless
EVNS
2011 desperately mortall] mortally desperate HAN1

2001 **wrought**] See *OED* (Work *v.* 10): "To effect, bring about."

2002 **fact**] SCHMIDT (1874): "Crime" (*OED, sb.* 1c), as in 2825.

   gouernment] *OED* (4b): "Period of rule, tenure of office," first use in this sense.

2007 **touch'd**] LEVER (ed. 1965): "Affected." See nn. 41, 2407, and cf. 803.

2008 **apprehends**] SCHMIDT (1874): "Conceive." *OED* (*v.* 10): "Anticipate," first use in this sense. LEVER (ed. 1965): "Understands." See n. 1291.

2009 **but**] See n. 443.

   wreaklesse] JOHNSON (1755): *Reckless,* "Careless; heedless; mindless." LEVER (ed. 1965): "The F spelling . . . arises from the confusing of 'reck' and 'wreak'. Cf. *AYL.,* II. iv. 81–2 [865–6], which in F reads: 'My master . . . little wreakes . . .'."

2011 **desperately mortall**] JOHNSON (ed. 1765): "This expression is obscure. . . . I am inclined to believe that *desperately mortal* means *desperately mischievous."* KENRICK (1765, pp. 38–9): Either "totally incurable of diseases" or "he looks upon himself as dead to the world." JOHNSON (Var. 1773): It may mean "a man likely to die in a *desperate* state, without reflection or repentance." CAPELL (1780, 2:3:53): *"Desperately* attach'd to the pursuits *of mortality."* So WHITER (1794; ed. 1967, pp. 50–1). ANON. (1786, pp. 85–6): "He has no sense of his approaching fate, and yet that fate is so certain as to be beyond all hope of pardon; he has no chance or expectation of a reprieve." STEEVENS (Var. 1793): "For 'mortally desperate': i. e. desperate in the extreme." HARNESS (ed. 1825): "Subject to divine condemnation without hope of forgiveness—*mortal* is here applied to Barnardine in the same sense, as when we speak of a *mortal* sin." DELIUS (ed. 1860): In desperate condition, so that one must despair of his salvation, he being near death, condemned to death. CLARKE (ed. 1864): "Desperate in his incurring of death." HART (ed. 1905): "Hopelessly [*OED,* Desperately *adv.* 3] devoid of any sense of immortality."

Duke. He wants aduice.

Pro. He wil heare none: he hath euermore had the liberty of the prison: giue him leaue to escape hence, hee
would not. Drunke many times a day, if not many daies   2015
entirely drunke. We haue verie oft awak'd him, as if to
carrie him to execution, and shew'd him a seeming warrant for it, it hath not moued him at all.

Duke. More of him anon: There is written in your   (G3ᵃ)
brow Prouost, honesty and constancie; if I reade it not   2020
truly, my ancient skill beguiles me: but in the boldnes
of my cunning, I will lay my selfe in hazard: *Claudio*,
whom heere you haue warrant to execute, is no greater
forfeit to the Law, then *Angelo* who hath sentenc'd him.
To make you vnderstand this in a manifested effect, I   2025
craue but foure daies respit: for the which, you are to
do me both a present, and a dangerous courtesie.

Pro. Pray Sir, in what?

Duke. In the delaying death.

2016 oft] often JOHN, v1773–SING1 (−MAL)
2023 warrant] a warrant JOHN1-v1821 (−CAP, MAL), SING
2028–9 *One verse line* CAM3

2012 **wants**] Needs (*OED, v.* 4).
    aduice] SCHMIDT (1874): "Spiritual counsel." Cf. 1778, 2073, 2884.
    2013–14 **liberty of**] *OED* (*sb.* 4b): "Unrestricted use of, or access to, permission
to go anywhere within the limits of," first quotation in this sense.
    2019–20 **There . . . constancie**] TILLEY (F5): "A fair face must have good
conditions"; cf. Tilley (F1), "The face is the index of the heart." SCHMIDT (1874):
Constancy, "faithfulness" (*OED,* 2).
    2021–2 **boldnes of my cunning**] STEEVENS (Var. 1793): *"Confidence* of my
sagacity."
    2022 **lay . . . hazard**] HART (ed. 1905): "Stake all I am worth." HARDING (ed.
1954): "Jeopardize myself (a dicing metaphor). Cf. *R3* 5.4.10 (3837) and *OED*
(Hazard *sb.* 5b).
    2024 **forfeit**] See n. 822 and *OED* (*sb.* 2b).
    2025 **in . . . effect**] SCHMIDT (1874, p. 351; cf. pp. 689, 1418): "So that its being
manifest may be the effect or result of my exposition." *OED* (Manifested *ppl. a.*):
"Made manifest," first use as ppl. a. Cf. *manifested* 2173 and n. 1227 on *effects.*
HARDING (ed. 1954): "By presenting concrete evidence." WINNY (ed. 1959): "By
open demonstration."
    2027 **present**] See n. 1165.
    2029 **the delaying**] ABBOTT (§93): *"The* frequently precedes a verbal that is
followed by an object."

Pro. Alacke, how may I do it? Hauing the houre li-   2030
mited, and an expresse command, vnder penaltie, to de-
liuer his head in the view of *Angelo*? I may make my
case as *Claudio*'s, to crosse this in the smallest.
Duke. By the vow of mine Order, I warrant you,
If my instructions may be your guide,   2035
Let this *Barnardine* be this morning executed,
And his head borne to *Angelo*.
Pro. *Angelo* hath seene them both,
And will discouer the fauour.
Duke. Oh, death's a great disguiser, and you may   2040
adde to it; Shaue the head, and tie the beard, and say it

2030-2 it? . . . *Angelo*?] ⌐ ? . . . ⌐ , F4-ROWE2; ⌐ , . . . ⌐ ? ROWE3-v1773
(−CAP), COL1+ (−HAL, KTLY, ARD2)
2034-7 *Prose* POPE1+ (−CAM3)
2034 you,] ⌐ . CAM3
2038-9 *Prose* POPE1+
2041 to it] to F4   tie] dye mTBY3 *and* SYMPSON *conj.,* WH; *om.* mTBY3 *conj.,*
COL4; trim JERVIS (1860) *conj.,* DYCE2, DYCE3, HUD2, KIT1

2030-1 **limited**] SCHMIDT (1874): "To fix, to appoint" (*OED, ppl. a.* 1). See n.
1436.
2033 **crosse**] JOHNSON (1755): "To contravene; to hinder by authority; to countermand." Cf. *OED* (*v.* 14): "To thwart, oppose, go counter to."
    in the smallest] *OED* (Small *a.* 6d): "*In the smallest,* in the least. *rare,*" first
use.
2034-9 Prose set as verse by Compositor B.
2034 **warrant**] SCHMIDT (1875): "To secure (against danger or loss)." HARD-
ING (ed. 1954): "Guarantee your security" (*OED, v.* 8).
2039 **discouer**] SCHMIDT (1874): "Recognise." ONIONS (1911): "Distinguish,
discern" (*OED, v.* 11).
    fauour] SCHMIDT (1874): "Features." See n. 1886.
2041 **tie**] THEOBALD (1729, in NICHOLS, 1817, 2·290): "But would *tieing* the
beard have such an effect to disguise the features of a man? I am persuaded it should
be, Shave the head, and *tire* the beard." JOHNSON (Var. 1773): "A beard tied would
give a very new air to that face, which had never been seen but with the beard loose,
long, and squalid." CLARKE (ed. 1864): "It is probable that the beard was sometimes
tied up out of the way of the axe, previous to beheading, at the request of the sufferer:
as the anecdote of Sir Thomas More may be remembered; who, when laying his neck
on the block, said to the executioner, 'Let me put my beard aside; that hath not
committed treason'." COLLIER (ed. 1875): "It has been objected that to tie the beard
would not be a sufficient disguise: omit 'tie', on the supposition that the scribe or
compositor confounded *the* and *tie,* and no more is required: to shave head and beard
would completely disguise." CRAIG (in HART, ed. 1905): Cf. Dekker's *2 Honest
Whore* (1.2.200-1): "Say I should shaue off this Honor of an old man, or tye it vp
shorter." HARRISON (ed. 1948): "Trim short."

was the desire of the penitent to be so bar'de before his
death: you know the course is common. If any thing
fall to you vpon this, more then thankes and good fortune, by the Saint whom I professe, I will plead against   2045
it with my life.

Pro. Pardon me, good Father, it is against my oath.

Duke. Were you sworne to the Duke, or to the Deputie?

Pro. To him, and to his Substitutes.   2050

Duke. You will thinke you haue made no offence, if
the Duke auouch the iustice of your dealing?

Pro. But what likelihood is in that?

Duke. Not a resemblance, but a certainty; yet since
I see you fearfull, that neither my coate, integrity, nor   2055
perswasion, can with ease attempt you, I wil go further
then I meant, to plucke all feares out of you. Looke
you Sir, heere is the hand and Seale of the Duke: you
know the Charracter I doubt not, and the Signet is not
strange to you?   2060

Pro. I know them both.

Duke. The Contents of this, is the returne of the
Duke; you shall anon ouer-reade it at your pleasure:

2042 so bar'de] so barb'd F4-ROWE2, THEO, WARB-RANN; barb'd ROWE3, POPE,
HAN1

2052 dealing?] ∼ . COL, WH1, STAU, DEL4

2056 perswasion] my Persuasion ROWE1-v1821 (−CAP, MAL), SING, COL, WH1,
KTLY, DEL4   further] farther ROWE2, COL, WH1

2060 you?] ∼ . F3+ (−CAP, KIT1, ARD2)

2042 **bar'de**] I.e., bared. MASON (1797, app. pp. 12–13): "This alludes to a
practice frequent amongst Roman Catholicks, of desiring to receive the tonsure of the
Monks before they die."

2045 **professe**] SCHMIDT (1875): "To avow, to acknowledge." So *OED* (*v.* 4).

2052 **auouch**] JOHNSON (1755): "To vindicate; to justify." SCHMIDT (1874):
"To acknowledge, to answer for" (*OED*, *v.* 9a).

2054 **Not . . . but**] See n. 1843–4.

   resemblance] *OED* (*sb.* 1 4b): "Likelihood or probability." LEVER (ed. 1965):
"Seeming."

2055 **coate**] WINNY (ed. 1959): "Religious habit" (*OED*, *sb.* 6). See n. 1398–9.

2056 **attempt**] SCHMIDT (1874): "Tempt" (*OED*, *v.* 5).

2057–8 **Looke you**] See *OED* (*v.* 4a): "Used to bespeak attention: = 'see'."

2059 **Charracter**] *OED* (*sb.* 4c): "The style of writing peculiar to any individual;
handwriting," first quotation in this sense.

2060 **strange**] *OED* (*a.* 7): "Unknown." See nn. 1227, 2523.

where you shall finde within these two daies, he wil be
heere. This is a thing that *Angelo* knowes not, for hee   2065
this very day receiues letters of strange tenor, perchance
of the Dukes death, perchance entering into some Mo-
nasterie, but by chance nothing of what is writ. Looke,
th'vnfolding Starre calles vp the Shepheard; put not
your selfe into amazement, how these things should be;   2070
all difficulties are but easie vvhen they are knowne. Call
your executioner, and off with *Barnardines* head: I will
giue him a present shrift, and aduise him for a better
place. Yet you are amaz'd, but this shall absolutely re-
solue you: Come away, it is almost cleere dawne.   *Exit.*   2075

2065 that] which F4-v1773 (−CAP)
2067 entering] of his entering POPE1-v1773 (−CAP), HUD2; his entering KTLY,
OXF1
2068 writ] here writ HAN1, WARB, WH, KTLY, DYCE2, HUD2, NLSN

2067 **entering**] Of his entering. See n. 1674.
2068 **nothing . . . writ**] T. WHITE (1793, fol. 19): "Nothing of what is *truth,*
is *gospel.*" So in *Per.* 2, Chorus, 12: "Thinks all is writ he spoken can." ARROWSMITH
(1865, p. 43): "Everything is written conjecturally . . . except as a matter of chance
nothing of what is writ . . . is set down otherwise than uncertainly." LEISI (ed. 1964):
"Probably 'written here'."
2069 **th'vnfolding Starre**] STEEVENS (Var. 1773) quotes Milton's *Comus,* 93,
"The Star that bids the Shepherd fold." *OED* (*ppl. a.* [2] 1): "Indicating the time for
unfolding sheep," only quotation in this sense. KNIGHT (ed. 1840, 2:323): "By a
touch almost magical Shakspere takes us in an instant out of that dark prison, where
we have been surrounded with crime and suffering, to make us see the morning star
bright over the hills, and hear the tinkle of the sheep-bell in the folds."
          calles] See n. 1951.
2070 **amazement**] SCHMIDT (1874): "Perplexity, bewilderment" (*OED,* 2). Cf.
amaz'd 2074.
2071 **all . . . knowne**] TILLEY (D418) and SMITH (1963, p. 42): "Everything
is easy after it has been done" (Erasmus).
2073 **present**] See n. 1165.
          shrift] JOHNSON (1755): "Confession made to a priest." *OED* (*sb.* 2): "Abso-
lution."
2074 **Yet**] RIDLEY (ed. 1935): "Still" (*OED, adv.* 2). Not "now," as explained
by LEISI (ed. 1964).
2074–5 **resolue**] See n. 1410.
2075 **cleere**] *OED* (*a.* 2a): "Fully light, bright."

Scena Tertia.   4.3

Enter Clowne.

Clo. I am as well acquainted heere, as I was in our
house of profession: one would thinke it vvere Mistris
Ouer-dons owne house, for heere be manie of her olde   2080   (G3b)
Customers. First, here's yong Mr *Rash*, hee's in for a
commoditie of browne paper, and olde Ginger, nine

2076 *Scena Tertia.*] *Om.* ROWE, THEO; SCENE VIII. POPE, HAN1, WARB, JOHN;
SCENE IV. v1778, v1785, MAL   *Another Room in the same.* CAP, MAL-WH2, CAM2-
NLSN, KIT1, SIS; *A corridor in the prison* . . . IRV; *The prison* ALEX, ARD2
    2082 paper] Pepper ROWE1-JOHN2

2079 **house of profession**] THIRLBY (1723–33): "Nunnery, profess'd nuns."
Cf. 520. CAPELL (1780, 2:3:53–4): "The wit couch'd in the term *'profession'* may not
strike upon every one: as religious houses, and nunneries chiefly, were call'd—houses
of profession, the title is given here by this speaker to the house that held his mistress's
nuns." MALONE (ed. 1790): "In my late mistress's house, which was a *professed,* a
notorious bawdy-house." HALLIWELL (ed. 1854): "A house of bad character was
frequently termed a nunnery, and hence, as in the present passage, a house of
profession." See n. 520.
    2081–95 JOHNSON (ed. 1765): "This enumeration of the inhabitants of the
prison affords a very striking view of the practices predominant in *Shakespear*'s age.
Besides those whose follies are common to all times, we have four fighting men and
a traveller. It is not unlikely that the originals of these pictures were then known."
LEVER (ed. 1965): "Pompey will probably mime the characters he mentions."
    2081 *Rash*] MALONE (1780, 1:101): "All the names here mentioned are charac-
teristical. *Rash* was a stuff formerly used." CHEDWORTH (1805, p. 41): "I do not
think there is any allusion in this name to the stuff called *rash,* but to the common
significance of the word, *hasty, violent, precipitate.*"
    2082 **commoditie**] *OED* (7b): "A parcel of goods sold on credit by a usurer to
a needy person, who immediately raised some cash by re-selling them at a lower price,
generally to the usurer himself." NARES (1822) and HALLIWELL (ed. 1854) give
many instances.
    browne paper] See *OED* (Brown paper 1), citing COTGRAVE (1611), "Papier
marchand. *Browne paper (wherein Tradesmen fould vp their Wares).*" STEEVENS (Var.

score and seuenteene pounds, of which hee made fiue
Markes readie money: marrie then, Ginger was not
much in request, for the olde Women vvere all dead.   2085
Then is there heere one Mr *Caper*, at the suite of Master
Three-Pile the Mercer, for some foure suites of Peach-
colour'd Satten, which now peaches him a beggar.
Then haue vve heere, yong *Dizie*, and yong Mr *Deepe-*

2085 for] or mTBY3 *conj.,* PEN2
2089 *Dizie*] F1, KIT1, ARD2; *Dizzy* COT (p. 236), POPE1-JOHN2, COL, DYCE,
WH, STAU, DEL4, HUD2, BUL, NLSN, SIS, PEL1, PEN2, EVNS; Dicey STEEVENS *conj.*
in v1803, RLTR; *Dizy* F2 *etc.*

1773): Cf. Middleton, *Michaelmas Terme,* 1607 (2.3.218–20). FARMER (ibid.,
10:Oo6): Also Fennor, *The Compters Common-wealth* (1617, p. 24). STEEVENS (Var.
1778): Also Gascoigne, *The Steele Glas* (1576; *Works,* ed. Cunliffe, 2:163), and other
writers.

    Ginger] THEOBALD (1729, in NICHOLS, 1817, 2:307): Cf. *MV* 3.1.9–10
(1226–7). DOUCE (1807, 1:141–2): The virtues of ginger are described by Sir
Thomas Elyot, *The Castel of Helth* (1541, fol. 30^v), by Henry Buttes, *Dyets Dry Dinner*
(1599, sig. [O]2^v), and by Tobias Venner, *Via Recta ad Vitam Longam* (1620, pp.
108–10). HART (ed. 1905): "Powdered ginger boiled in milk is a favourite warming
drink amongst old women in some country districts."

    2083–4 **fiue Markes**] HART (ed. 1905): A mark was 13*s.* 4*d.* Five would be
£3 6*s.* 8*d.* WILSON (ed. 1922, p. 167): "Pompey is, of course, exaggerating a
little."

    2085 **olde . . . dead**] LEVER (ed. 1965): "Probably a reference to the plague in
1603."

    2086 ***Caper***] HART (ed. 1905): "To caper with grace was a necessary accomplish-
ment of a gallant; either in the lavolta or as a display of activity upon any occasion."
So in *TN* 1.3.129, 150 (229, 247–8).

    2087 ***Three-Pile***] See n. 128.

    2087–8 **Peach-colour'd**] JOHNSON (1755): "Of a colour like a peach." *OED*
(Peach *sb.* ^1 6) gives two senses: *"(a)* the colour of a ripe peach, a soft pale red; *(b)*
the colour of *Peach-blossom,* a delicate rose or pink." HALLIWELL (ed. 1854): Cf.
Riche, *Greenes Newes* (1593, p. 22). LINTHICUM (1936, p. 40): "Peach or peach-
flower colour was a deep, fresh pink. . . . It is descriptive of stockings in [*2H4* 2.2.19
(807), *Euery Man out of his Humour,* 4.6.114,] and *Queen of Corinth* [Beaumont &
Fletcher, ed. Glover & Waller, 2.2.24]; of suits in [*MM*], *London Prodigall* [*Sh. Apoc.,*
1.2.123], and *What You Will* [Marston, 3.3.112]." See also Middleton, *Your Fiue
Gallants,* 3.5.160.

    2088 **peaches him a beggar**] RANN (ed. 1786): "Prefers a charge of beggary
against him." DYCE (1867): "To impeach, to accuse, to inform against" (*OED, v.* 1b).
ONIONS (1911): "To denounce (one) as being (something)." Pompey puns on *peach*
as he does on *suite* in 2086, 2087.

    2089 ***Dizie***] STEEVENS (in Var. 1803): "It might have been corrupted from
Dicey, i. e. one addicted to *dice;* or from *Dizzy,* i. e. giddy, thoughtless." LEVER (ed.
1965) agrees, but LEISI (ed. 1964) calls *Dicey* "improbable on phonetic grounds."

    2089–90 ***Deepe-vow***] ERLER (1913, p. 115): One who takes a solemn oath; here

vow, and Mr *Copperspurre*, and Mr *Starue-Lackey* the Ra-   2090
pier and dagger man, and yong *Drop-heire* that kild lu-
stie *Pudding*, and Mr *Forthlight* the Tilter, and braue M^r

---

2091–2 lustie] the lusty ARD1
2092 *Forthlight*] F1-HAN1, THEO4, JOHN, v1773, v1785, CAM1, GLO, IRV,
CAM2, NLSN, ALEX, EVNS; *Forth-right* WARB *etc.*

---

ironically, a swearer. WILSON (ed. 1922): "A lover." LEVER (ed. 1965): "A heavy
swearer." [Perhaps one who swears earnestly that he will pay back a loan, as in
Chapman's *Al Fooles* (1605, 2.1.58–9), where a prodigal in prison for debt "deeply
swears, As he's a gentleman," to repay 40 crowns next week.]
    2090 *Copperspurre*] HART (ed. 1905): "Simulating gold, like Falstaff's grandfa-
ther's seal-ring." WILSON (ed. 1922): "I.e. Master Pretentious; 'copper' often used
at this period 'with the notion of spurious, pretentious, worthless' (N.E.D.), doubtless
because of its likeness to gold."
        Starue-Lackey] ONIONS (1911): "Descriptive of needy gallants who starved
their pages."
    2090–1 **Rapier and dagger man**] HART (ed. 1905): See *Ham.* 5.2.152 (3614);
Porter, *The Two Angrie Women of Abington* (1599, MSR, 1341–2); and Middleton,
The Phoenix (1607, 2.3.187). MORRIS (ed. 1912): "Man over-anxious to use rapier
and daggers, which he carried; a swashbuckler." HOTSON (1931, pp. 26–31) discovered that Henry Porter, who in *The Two Angrie Women* criticized "this poking fight
of rapier and dagger," was killed with a rapier in 1599 by his fellow playwright John
Day.
    2091 *Drop-heire*] HART (ed. 1905): "Drop-heir, or Droop-heir, here is the
usurer who killed lusty Pudding, or hospitality and good living. Drop has the sense
of cause to droop or pine, bring into a consumption, destroy." WILSON (ed. 1922):
"Master Spendthrift," "an heir who is pining away gradually." LEISI (ed. 1964): "As
heir and *hair* were often pronounced alike (see Kökeritz, *Sh.s Pronunciation* p. 111),
this may also be a pun on *drop-hair* 'bald', in the vein of [128] ff." LEVER (ed. 1965):
" 'Drop-heir' suggests a figure like Middleton's 'Bawd-gallant'; cf. *Father Hubburds
Tales* (VIII.78): '. . . that fed upon young landlords, riotous sons and heirs . . .'. This
is supported by the equivocations 'heir-hair' (cf. [129–30]) and 'Pudding' (= sau-
sage)."
    2092 *Forthlight*] JOHNSON (Var. 1773): "Should not *Forthlight* be *Forthright*
[Warburton's emendation], alluding to the line in which the thrust is made?" STEEV-
ENS (Var. 1778): Sh. uses *forth right* as a noun in *Tro.* 3.3.158 (2011) and *Tmp.* 3.3.3
(1518). RITSON (1783, p. 24): "*Forthlight* may, nevertheless, be the true reading.
. . . It, probably enough, contains an allusion to the fencers threat of making the *light*
shine through his antagonist." This unlikely conjecture misled many editors. NARES
(1822): " 'Master *Forthright*, . . .' Master Straightforward." HART (ed. 1905) quotes
Sidney's description of a tilter "ever going so just with the horse, either foorth right,
or turning" (*Arcadia* 2.5; ed. Feuillerat, 1:179).
        Tilter] SCHMIDT (1875): "One who runs with a lance in a tournament.
. . . [Here] probably = fighter, fencer." *OED* gives no use of the word for "fencer"
and defines *tilter* as "a combatant in a tilt," first quotation 1611, but Sh. uses it in
AYL 3.4.46 (1750).
    braue] SCHMIDT (1874): "Gallant." EVANS (ed. 1974): "Showily dressed"
(*OED, a.* 2).

Shootie the great Traueller, and wilde *Halfe-Canne* that
stabb'd Pots, and I thinke fortie more, all great doers in
our Trade, and are now for the Lords sake.   2095

Enter Abhorson.

Abh. Sirrah, bring *Barnardine* hether.

2093 *Shootie*] F1, ARD1, ALEX; *Shooty* F2-HAN1, THEO4, JOHN, CAM1, GLO, IRV,
CAM2, NLSN; *Shooter* WARB; Suity WH2; *Shoo-tye* CAP *etc.*
2094 Pots] pots HAL, ARD2
2095 now] now in POPE1-v1785 (−CAP), COL2, COL3, COL4   for the Lords
sake] *Marked as quotation* RANN, DYCE, STAU-GLO, HUD2+ (−SIS)

2093 *Shootie*] STEEVENS (Var. 1773): "As most of these are compound names,
I suspect that this was originally written, master *Shoe-tye.*" MALONE (in Var. 1778)
cites Crashaw's "glistring shoo-ty" ["Wishes. To his (Supposed) Mistresse"]. NARES
(1822): "Crashaw writes it *shoo-ty,* and rhymes it to *duty,* as Butler did after him."
HART (ed. 1905): "The shoe-tie usually refers to the roses (rosettes) worn by gallants." LINTHICUM (1936, p. 243): "A yard to a yard and a quarter of ribbon was
allowed for each shoe-tie. . . . These ties gradually developed into roses; or rather,
the dress-shoes were fastened by small ties, and the fastening concealed by rosettes."
    2093–4 *Halfe-Canne . . . Pots*] ERLER (1913, p. 112): *Halfcan,* a small tankard;
Pots, a great lover of drinking. WILSON (ed. 1922): "The context suggests that a
half-can was a larger vessel than a 'pot' which it had put out of fashion among topers."
    2094 Pots] HALLIWELL (ed. 1854): "The last word is generally printed as if it
were a proper name, but the meaning, I think, refers to a person who was so
accustomed to excessive potations, that he hacked at the pots out of which he had been
drinking. The word is not printed, in the first folio, in italics, which is generally the
case with proper names." LEVER (ed. 1965) repeats the point, but his suggestion that
Half-can was a tapster is unlikely.
    fortie more] CLARKE (ed. 1864): "Many more. 'Forty' was often used to
express an indefinite number" (*OED,* A.b).
    doers] MALONE (1783, p. 6): "The word is used here in a wanton sense. See
Mr. Collins's note" (on 2959 *Ouer-don*). SCHMIDT (1874): "One who is wont and
ready to act," as in *R3* 1.3.352 (828).
    2095 for the Lords sake] THIRLBY (1723–33): "The cry of prisoners in a jail."
WARBURTON (ed. 1747): "*I. e.* to beg for the rest of their lives." MALONE (1780,
1:101): Cf. Nashe's *Strange Newes* (1592, 1:300). SINGER (ed. 1826) quotes Baret's
Alvearie (1573), under the word *Interest,* on a prisoner in Ludgate "crauing and crying
at the grate, your woorships charitie for the Lordes sake." SYMONS (in IRVING &
MARSHALL, ed. 1889): Cf. Heywood, *A Woman Kilde with Kindnesse* (1607, sig. D2),
"cry from the grate, Meat for the Lord sake." HALLIWELL (ed. 1854) and HART (ed.
1905) quote other instances.
    2096 *Abhorson*] STYAN (1975, p. 20) imagines "the terrible figure of Abhorson
. . . carrying his gruesome axe," but the axe and block are not onstage, since Abhorson
asks about them (2115).

Clo. Mr *Barnardine*, you must rise and be hang'd,
Mr *Barnardine*.
   Abb. What hoa *Barnardine*.   2100

Barnardine within.

   Bar. A pox o'your throats: who makes that noyse
there? What are you?
   Clo. Your friends Sir, the Hangman:
You must be so good Sir to rise, and be put to death.   2105
   Bar. Away you Rogue, away, I am sleepie.
   Abb. Tell him he must awake,
And that quickly too.
   Clo. Pray Master *Barnardine*, awake till you are ex-
ecuted, and sleepe afterwards.   2110
   Ab. Go in to him, and fetch him out.
   Clo. He is comming Sir, he is comming: I heare his
Straw russle.

Enter Barnardine.

2098–9, 2104–5, 2107–8, 2121–2 *Prose* POPE1+
2104 friends] friend F3–v1773 (−CAP), RANN, HAL, DYCE, STAU, COL4, HUD2
   Hangman] hangmen mTBY2 *conj.,* HUD1
2112 his] the ROWE3–v1773 (−CAP)
2114 *Enter Barnardine.*] *After* 2116 CAP, DYCE, STAU-GLO, DEL4-ARD1

   2098–9, 2104–5, 2107–8, 2117–18, 2121–2, 2130–1 Prose set as verse by Compositor B.
   2098 **rise**] LEVER (ed. 1965): "The point is the play on 'rise', (i) to get up from
bed, (ii) to mount the scaffold."
   be hang'd] Equivocating on the literal meaning and on the imprecation used
in 2735 (*OED,* Hang *v.* 3c).
   2101 *within*] Offstage. See n. 354.
   2102 **A pox . . . throats**] Cf. Lucio in 2734 and Sebastian in *Tmp.* 1.1.43 (49).
   o'] On: see n. 630.
   2104 RITSON (1783, p. 24): "This should be, either—*your* friend, *sir; the hangman;* or—*your friends, sir; the* hangmen." DELIUS (ed. 1860): *Your friends.* So F
rightly, since the Clown answers for himself and for Abhorson, as Barnardine also
had said *throats* in the plural.
   2112–13 **I . . . russle**] CLARKE (ed. 1864): "The effect of these few words, and
of those immediately previous to them, is marvellously strong, though so condensed.
They give the impression of the caged wild-beast-man, with the unwillingness of his
keepers to enter his den and bring him forth."

Abh. Is the Axe vpon the blocke, sirrah?   2115

Clo. Verie readie Sir.

Bar. How now *Abhorson?*

What's the newes vvith you?

Abh. Truly Sir, I would desire you to clap into your

prayers: for looke you, the Warrants come.   2120

Bar. You Rogue, I haue bin drinking all night,

I am not fitted for't.

Clo. Oh, the better Sir: for he that drinkes all night,

and is hanged betimes in the morning, may sleepe the

sounder all the next day.   2125

Enter Duke.

Abh. Looke you Sir, heere comes your ghostly Fa-

ther: do we iest now thinke you?

Duke. Sir, induced by my charitie, and hearing how

hastily you are to depart, I am come to aduise you,   2130

Comfort you, and pray with you.

Bar. Friar, not I: I haue bin drinking hard all night,

and I will haue more time to prepare mee, or they shall

beat out my braines with billets: I will not consent to

2117-18 *One line* POPE1+

2126 *Enter Duke*] *After* 2128 DYCE, STAU-GLO, DEL4, HUD2-ARD1

2129-31 *Verse lines ending* hearing . . . come . . . with you. CAP, KTLY

2131 *Prose* F3+ (−CAP, KTLY)

2133 I] *Om.* DAV, F4-POPE2, HAN1

2115 HALLIWELL (ed. 1854): "There is some little confusion in what the Clown says respecting the mode in which Barnardine is to be executed. The axe and block are spoken of, but the former keeps insisting upon it that he is to be hanged. It is possible this is intentional, to heighten the Clown's humour."

2119 **clap into**] THIRLBY (1723-33): Cf. *AYL* 5.3.11 (2541) and *Ado* 3.4.44 (1543). *OED* (*v.* [1] 15b), citing only Sh., quotes the definition by JOHNSON (1755): "To enter with alacrity and briskness upon any thing."

2120, 2127 **looke you**] See n. 2057-8.

2122 **fitted**] See n. 1044.

2124 **betimes**] JOHNSON (1755): "Early in the day" (*OED, adv.* 2).

2124-5 LEVER (ed. 1965): "Pompey has adapted to Barnardine's situation the proverbial 'He rises over soon who is hanged ere noon' (Tilley N208), which is implicit in 'rise and be hanged', [2098]." Tilley's examples are all from Scotland.

2127-8 **ghostly Father**] Spiritual father. See *OED* (*a.* 1c), "Father confessor," and "Ghostly Fathers" in Whetstone's *Heptameron* (p. 377 below).

2134 **billets**] SCHMIDT (1874): "A small log of wood." WILSON (ed. 1922): "Logs of wood for fuel." *OED* (*sb.* 2) explains as "A (thick) stick used as a weapon,"

die this day, that's certaine. 2135
    Duke. Oh sir, you must: and therefore I beseech you
Looke forward on the iournie you shall go.
    Bar. I sweare I will not die to day for anie mans per-
swasion.
    Duke. But heare you: 2140
    Bar. Not a word: if you haue anie thing to say to me,
come to my Ward: for thence will not I to day.

                                      Exit

                Enter Prouost.

    Duke. Vnfit to liue, or die: oh grauell heart. 2145
After him (Fellowes) bring him to the blocke.   (G3ᵛᵃ)
    Pro. Now Sir, how do you finde the prisoner?
    Duke. A creature vnpre-par'd, vnmeet for death,

2136-7 *Prose* F3-RANN (−CAP), HAL, OXF1, PEL1, PEN2
2140 heare] heaue F2
2144 SCENE IX. POPE, HAN1, WARB, JOHN   *Enter* Prouost.] *After* 2146
CAP, DYCE, STAU-GLO, HUD2-BUL, ALEX, SIS
  2145 grauell heart.] grovelling beast! COLNE, COL2, WH1; gravel-heart! KTLY
2146-7 After . . . *Pro.* Now] *Prov.* After . . . Now HAN1, v1773, RANN, ARD2
2146 *Exeunt* Abhorson *and* Clown. JOHN1+

---

but the usual sense is appropriate here.
  2137 **shall**] Are to. See *OED* (4): "Indicating what is appointed or settled to take
place."
  2140 Barnardine interrupts the Duke. See n. 140.
  2142 **Ward**] SCHMIDT (1875): "Prison-cell." WILSON (ed. 1922): "Generally
explained as 'cell'; but Barnardine had 'the liberty of the prison' [2013–14] and was
not likely, therefore, to be kept in solitary confinement." Cf. *Ham.* 2.2.252 (1292).
DURHAM (ed. 1926): "Section of the prison" (*OED, sb.* ² 17b, like a hospital ward).
  2145 **grauell heart**] NICHOLSON (1866, p. 56): "I believe the 'Oh! gravel heart'
of the thoughtful and religious Duke . . . to be a most beautiful reference to the
parable of the sower, some of whose seed fell by the wayside, and most apposite to
the character, birth, and education of the gipsy Barnardine. But others think differently." SCHMIDT (1874): "Flint heart."
  2146 JOHNSON (ed. 1765): "Here is a line given to the Duke which belongs to
the *Provost.*" HALLIWELL (ed. 1854): "In strict propriety, the line would be more
correctly spoken by the Provost; but it should be recollected that the Duke is speaking
in disgust at Barnardine's language, and may well be imagined to have momentarily
forgotten his resignment of authority." COGHILL (1965, p. 394): "All that has
happened is that the speech-heading [*Pro.*] has slipped a line." LEVER (ed. 1965):
"Spoken by the Provost, lines [2146–7] are an ironic 'I told you so'. . . . The 'Provost'
speech-prefix may have been indicated in MS. by a marginal *'Enter Provost'.* "

And to transport him in the minde he is,
Were damnable.   2150
    Pro. Heere in the prison, Father,
There died this morning of a cruell Feauor,
One *Ragozine*, a most notorious Pirate,
A man of *Claudio*'s yeares: his beard, and head
Iust of his colour. What if we do omit   2155
This Reprobate, til he were wel enclin'd,
And satisfie the Deputie with the visage
Of *Ragozine*, more like to *Claudio*?
    Duke. Oh, 'tis an accident that heauen prouides:
Dispatch it presently, the houre drawes on   2160
Prefixt by *Angelo*: See this be done,
And sent according to command, whiles I
Perswade this rude wretch willingly to die.
    Pro. This shall be done (good Father) presently:
But *Barnardine* must die this afternoone,   2165
And how shall we continue *Claudio*,
To saue me from the danger that might come,

2153 *Ragozine*] *Rogavine* F4; *Rogozine* ROWE1, ROWE2
2155 his] *Om.* F2-F4   do] *Om.* POPE1-JOHN2, HUD2
2158 *Ragozine*] *Rogozine* F4-ROWE2
2162 whiles] while POPE1-v1773 (−CAP)

2149 **transport**] JOHNSON (ed. 1765): "Remove him from one world to another." So *OED* (*v.* 1e), "a euphemism for 'put to death, kill'."
    he is] FRANZ (§544a): "He is in." See n. 466.
2150 **Were**] Would be. See n. 40.
    damnable] JOHNSON (1755): "Deserving damnation."
2153 *Ragozine*] HEATH (1765, p. 111) derives the name, with good reason, from Ragusa on the Adriatic, famous for its *argosies* (*MV* 1.1.9 [12]), or "Ragusyes."
2155 **omit**] *OED* (*v.* 2c): "Leave disregarded, take no notice of," used in this sense only by Sh.
2156 **Reprobate**] JOHNSON (1755): "A man lost to virtue; a wretch abandoned to wickedness." So *OED* (*sb.* 2).
    were] Shall be. ABBOTT (§301): Subjunctive because "a wish is implied."
    enclin'd] SEYMOUR (1805, 1:100): "They must omit him, (or the hanging him) a great while before the prisoner would be well inclined to submit:—but 'inclined' here means 'disposed' or 'prepared' for death, by religious exercises" (*OED*, Inclined *ppl. a.* 3).
2160, 2164 **presently**] See n. 1484.
2161 **Prefixt**] SCHMIDT (1875): "Appointed beforehand" (*OED*, *ppl. a.* 1).
2163 **rude**] See n. 1522.
2166 **continue**] SCHMIDT (1874): "Leave as before," "let live." *OED* (*v.* 3b): "Keep on, maintain, retain," only use in elliptical sense.

If he were knowne aliue?

   Duke. Let this be done,

Put them in secret holds, both *Barnardine* and *Claudio*,   2170

Ere twice the Sun hath made his iournall greeting

To yond generation, you shal finde

Your safetie manifested.

   Pro. I am your free dependant.   *Exit.*

2168–72 *Lines ending* alive? . . . them . . . *Claudio:* . . . greeting . . . find CAP-MAL; alive? . . . holds, . . . twice . . . to . . . find v1793-SING1 (*last lines* greeting . . . find SING2); done: . . . Claudio: . . . greeting . . . find KNT, HAL, DYCE1, STAU-KTLY, DEL4, IRV, CAM2, KIT1-PEL1, EVNS; alive? . . . holds, . . . Claudio: . . . greeting . . . find COL, WH, DYCE2, DYCE3, HUD2, BUL, ARD2; done. . . . Barnardine . . . Claudio. . . . greeting . . . find CAM1 *conj.*, NLSN, CAM3; done: . . . Barnardine . . . made . . . generation, ARD1, PEN2

2170 both . . . *Claudio*] *Claudio* and *Barnardine* HAN1

2172 yond] F1-ROWE2, MAL, COL1, ARD1, PEN2, EVNS; yonder ROWE3, POPE, THEO, KNT, HAL, SING2, COL3, STAU, DEL4, SIS, ARD2; th' under HAN1 *etc.*

2173–5 *Lines ending* manifested. . . . despatch, . . . Angelo. v1793-SING1, KNT, HAL, DYCE, DEL4, HUD2, BUL, ARD1, KIT1, SIS; manifested. . . . Angelo. SING2; dependant. . . . Angelo. KTLY, IRV, ARD2

2173 manifested] manifest HAN1, COL2

2174 *Exit.*] *Exit* Prov. *after* 2175 POPE1+

2170 **holds**] ONIONS (1911): "Prison." BALD (ed. 1956): "Cells" (*OED, sb.* 1 13).

2171 **iournall**] JOHNSON (1755): "Daily; quotidian," quoting this line and *Cym.* 4.2.10 (2257).

2172 **To yond generation**] JOHNSON (ed. 1765): *"To th' under generation.*] So Sir *Tho. Hanmer* with true judgment. It was in all the former editions *to yonder: y*ᵉ *under* and *yonder* were confounded." MALONE (ed. 1790) defends *yond:* "the Duke here speaks of its [the sun's] greeting only those *without* the doors of the jail." STEEVENS (Var. 1793): "By the *under generation* our poet means the *antipodes.* So, in [*R2* 3.2.37–8 (1393–4)]: . . . the *lower world."* KNIGHT (ed. 1840): "The printer no doubt followed the contraction of the writer." DYCE (ed. 1857): " *'The under genera- tion'* is equivalent to 'the generation who live on the earth beneath,—mankind in general'." Cf. *Lr.* 2.2.170 (1240) and *Tmp.* 3.3.54 (1587). HART (ed. 1905): "The rest of the world outside this prison, which admitted no sunlight." GREG (in WILSON, ed. 1922) suggests "that Shakespeare wrote 'yᵉ onder' and that the transcriber or compositor failed to notice the *e."* But *onder* is ME or Scots rather than Shn. HOW-ARD-HILL (1972, p. 127): "Crane, who was apt to omit terminal letters, is as likely as [Compositor] B to have truncated 'yonder'."

2174 **your free dependant**] SCHMIDT (1874, p. 452): "At your free disposal." HARDING (ed. 1954): "Willing servant." COGHILL (1965, p. 395): " 'Released' (*OED* 6) (from his obligations to the Deputy Angelo) because he now knows himself to be *dependant* on the higher authority of the Duke." The Duke must have revealed himself by a gesture after 2173, or "the Provost would have no better reason than he had before, for obeying the Duke." LEVER (ed. 1965): *"Free*] i.e. from guilt or

Duke. Quicke, dispatch, and send the head to *Angelo.*   2175
Now wil I write Letters to *Angelo*,
(The Prouost he shal beare them) whose contents
Shal witnesse to him I am neere at home:
And that by great Iniunctions I am bound
To enter publikely: him Ile desire   2180
To meet me at the consecrated Fount,
A League below the Citie: and from thence,
By cold gradation, and weale-ballanc'd forme.

2175 Quicke, dispatch,] Quick, quick, HAN1; Quick then, dispatch, CAP; Quick, quick, despatch; KTLY; Quick dispatch, ARD1
2176 *Angelo*] Varrius CAM3 *conj.,* PEN2
2183 weale-ballanc'd] Ff., THEO, WARB-COL1, KNT3, ARD1, EVNS; well-ballanc'd ROWE1 *etc.*   forme.] ∼ , F3+

---

blame (*O.E.D.* 7)."
     Exit.] This should follow 2175, but that line had no room even for a final period or colon.
     2176 **Letters**] SCHMIDT (1874): Plural for sing. (*OED, sb.* [1] 4b).
     to *Angelo*] WILSON (ed. 1922): "This can hardly be correct. . . . We are left then with the mysterious Varrius, who meets the Duke, by appointment apparently, in 4. 5." LEVER (ed. 1965, pp. xxiii–iv): "The same phrase appears in the previous line and could have been wrongly repeated by either the scribe or the compositor. . . . A reference to Varrius here would make good dramatic sense in that it would prepare the audience for this character's appearance in IV. v."
     2179 **Iniunctions**] SCHMIDT (1874) explains as "obligation," "urgent motives," but *OED* finds no such meaning. ORGER (1890, pp. 24–5) conjectures "And that by great injunction, as I am bound," and takes the word to refer, not to the Duke, but to Angelo: "The 'injunctions' naturally must be laid on Angelo to meet him." CRAIG (ed. 1951): "Powerful precedent." The sense is prob. the usual one (*OED*, 1), "An authoritative or emphatic admonition or order." The Duke seems to imply that he is bound either by custom or by an imaginary command from the Emperor.
     2181 **the consecrated Fount**] SJÖGREN (1961, pp. 32–3) compares the plan to meet at St. Gregory's well in *TGV* 4.2.84 (1703–4).
     2183 **cold gradation**] *Cold,* "cool, deliberate": see *OED* (*a.* 7b) and James I, *Basilicon Doron* (1599; ed. Craigie, 1:100, 202), "Be cold and forseeing in deuising," "colde in deliberation." JOHNSON (1755): *Gradation,* "Regular advance step by step" (*OED,* 1, as in *Oth.* 1.1.37 [40]). RIDLEY (ed. 1935): "Impersonal procedure." PARROTT (ed. 1938): "Unhurried steps." BALDWIN (1944, 2:165): Sh. connects the word "gradation" in a rhetorical sense with what appears to be an allusion to the rhetorical figure of *compar* or "equal" ("well-balanced"). HARDING (ed. 1954): "Deliberate degrees."
     weale-ballanc'd] CAPELL (1779, 1:glossary, 77): "Balanc'd as in good Weals it should be." MASON (1797, app. p. 13): "Weal-balanced is a pompous Expression, without any meaning; I, therefore, agree with Heath in reading well-balanced." STEEVENS (in Var. 1803): "In Milton's Ode on *The Nativity* [122], we also meet with the same compound epithet:" "And the well-ballanc't world on hinges hung." NARES

We shal proceed with *Angelo.*

Enter Prouost. 2185

Pro. Heere is the head, Ile carrie it my selfe.
Duke. Conuenient is it: Make a swift returne,
For I would commune with you of such things,
That want no eare but yours.
Pro. Ile make all speede.   *Exit* 2190

Isabell within.

Isa. Peace hoa, be heere.
Duke. The tongue of *Isabell.* She's come to know,
If yet her brothers pardon be come hither:
But I will keepe her ignorant of her good, 2195
To make her heauenly comforts of dispaire,
When it is least expected.

2189 eare] ears POPE2, THEO, WARB, JOHN, v1773
2191 SCENE X. POPE, HAN1
2193 She's come] She comes ROWE3-JOHN2
2196 comforts] comfort HAN1, DYCE2, DYCE3, HUD2
2197–9 *One line* DYCE, STAU-KTLY, HUD2+
2197 it is least] least it is v1773

(1822): "*Weal-balanced.* Weighed for the public good. . . . It is possible that this, which is the original, may be also the right reading; but it comes so near *well balanced,* as to create a doubt." SCHMIDT (1875): "With due observance of all forms, which it would be against the public interest not to observe." THISELTON (1901, p. 35): " 'Orderly arrangement that equipoises (or steadies) the weal'." ONIONS (1911): "Adjusted with due regard to the public welfare." *OED* (Well-balanced *ppl. a.*): *Well-balanced* is "prob. the true reading (as suggested by Rowe)."

2187 **Conuenient**] HUNTER (ed. 1873): "Proper or suitable" (*OED, a.* 4b). See n. 1469.

2188 **commune**] JOHNSON (1755): "To converse; to talk together" (*OED, v.* 6c), accented on first syllable.

2189 **want**] See n. 2012.

2191 *within*] See n. 354.

2192 **Peace**] See n. 355 and cf. 1249.

2196–7 JOHNSON (ed. 1765): "A better reason might have been given. It was necessary to keep *Isabella* in ignorance, that she might with more keenness accuse the Deputy."

2196 **of**] From. See *OED* (*prep.* 20, 20b): "After verbs signifying to make," "Expressing transformation from a former condition."

2197 **it**] That. See n. 1938.

Enter Isabella.

Isa. Hoa, by your leaue.

Duke. Good morning to you, faire, and gracious   2200
daughter.

Isa. The better giuen me by so holy a man,
Hath yet the Deputie sent my brothers pardon?

Duke. He hath releasd him, *Isabell*, from the world,
His head is off, and sent to *Angelo*.   2205

Isa. Nay, but it is not so.

Duke. It is no other,
Shew your wisedome daughter in your close patience.

Isa. Oh, I wil to him, and plucke out his eies.

Duk. You shal not be admitted to his sight.   2210

Isa. Vnhappie *Claudio*, wretched *Isabell*,
Iniurious world, most damned *Angelo*.   (G3vb

Duke. This nor hurts him, nor profits you a iot,

2198 SCENE X. WARB, JOHN
2199 Hoa,] *Om.* POPE, HAN1
2202 by] be F2   man,] ∼ : F4+
2206–8 *Lines ending* other: . . . patience. v1793-STAU, KTLY, KNT3, COL4, ARD1,
ALEX, EVNS; so . . . daughter, . . . patience. SPEDDING *conj. in* CAM1, CAM1, GLO,
DYCE2, DEL4, DYCE3, HUD2-BUL; NLSN-KIT1, SIS-PEN2
2208 Shew your wisedome . . . patience.] Shew wisdom . . . patience. POPE,
HAN1; In your close patience, daughter, shew your wisdom. CAP   close] closest
POPE1-v1773 (−CAP)
2212 Iniurious] Perjurious COLNE, COL2
2213 nor hurts] not hurts F4; hurts not ROWE, POPE, HAN1

2199 **by your leaue**] WALKER (1854, p. 191): *"By'r leave,* (pronounce *beer
leave,*)." See KÖKERITZ (1953), p. 272.

2200 **gracious**] See n. 1387.

2202 **holy a**] KÖNIG (1888, p. 46) and KÖKERITZ (1953, p. 291) note that *y*
and *a* are fused in one syllable.

2205 HART (ed. 1905): "The duke deems this lie necessary to spur on Isabella's
vengeance."

2208 LEVER (ed. 1965): "The two 'yours' are non-metrical and suggest 'sophistication'."

   close] SCHMIDT (1874): "Secret." ONIONS (1911): "Practising secrecy, un-
communicative" (*OED, a.* 7).

2209 **I wil to**] See n. 284.

2210 **shal**] Will. See n. 1807.

2213 **nor hurts**] See n. 1235. THIRLBY (1723–33) comments on the change to
hurts not in Rowe and Pope: "Nihil necesse est [It is not at all necessary] odi nimium
diligentes [I hate the too diligent]."

Forbeare it therefore, giue your cause to heauen,
Marke what I say, which you shal finde   2215
By euery sillable a faithful veritie.
The Duke comes home to morrow: nay drie your eyes,
One of our Couent, and his Confessor
Giues me this instance: Already he hath carried
Notice to *Escalus* and *Angelo*,   2220
Who do prepare to meete him at the gates,
There to giue vp their powre: If you can pace your wisdome,
In that good path that I would wish it go,
And you shal haue your bosome on this wretch,
Grace of the Duke, reuenges to your heart,   2225

2215 say] say to you COLNE, COL2, DYCE2, DYCE3-HUD2   finde] surely find
POPE1-CAP; find to be KTLY
2217 nay] *Om.* POPE1-JOHN2
2219 Giues] Gave JOHN, v1773   instance] news GIL, POPE, HAN1; Instant
ROWE2
2221 the] *Om.* ROWE2
2222 If you can pace] Ff., SING, HUD2, RID, ARD2, EVNS; Pace POPE, HAN1;
Pace, if you can, KTLY; If you can, pace ROWE1 *etc.*
2223 wish it go,] wish it, go, CAM1 *conj.,* RLF1, RID; wish it go in, KTLY
2224 And] Then KEIGHTLEY (1867) *conj.,* HUD2

2214, 2231 **cause**] See *OED* (*sb.* 7): "The case of one party in a suit." Cf. nn.
588, 2538-9.
2216 **By**] See *OED* (*prep.* 27): "With respect to."
2218 **Couent**] CLARK & GLOVER (ed. 1863): "We have retained 'covent', which
had grown to be a distinct word from 'convent', and differently pronounced. Shakespeare's ear would hardly have tolerated the harsh-sounding line 'One of our cónvent
and his cónfessor'."
     Confessor] See n. 489.
2219 **instance**] SCHMIDT (1874): "Argument, proof." HUDSON (ed. 1880):
"*Assurance,* or *circumstance in proof.*" Cf. *OED* (*sb.* 7): "A proof, evidence."
2222 **If you can pace**] JOHNSON (1755): "To direct to go." *OED* (*v.* 4): "To
train (a horse) to pace," first use in this sense. PORTER & CLARKE (ed. 1909): "The
image called up is that of a stately and measured advance, like the procession the Duke
has planned. . . . The punctuation of the Folio here, as usually, follows a consistency
of its own, different from that of modern usage, which will bear pondering. Its clew
is to be sought not in grammatical but in oratorical punctuation." LEVER (ed. 1965):
"Editors place a comma after 'can': it is unnecessary, since the construction is merely
an ellipsis of the regular conditional: 'if you can pace, etc. (do so) And . . .'." See
n. 466.
2223 **go**] ABBOTT (§349): *"Infinitive. 'To' omitted."*
2224 **your bosome**] JOHNSON (1755): "Inclination; desire." IDEM (ed. 1765):
"Your wish; your heart's desire." *OED* (*sb.* 6b): "Desire."
2225 **Grace**] See n. 26.
     to] See *OED* (*prep.* 20): "In accordance with."

And general Honor.
 Isa. I am directed by you.
 Duk. This Letter then to Friar *Peter* giue,
'Tis that he sent me of the Dukes returne:
Say, by this token, I desire his companie   2230
At *Mariana*'s house to night. Her cause, and yours
Ile perfect him withall, and he shal bring you
Before the Duke; and to the head of *Angelo*
Accuse him home and home. For my poore selfe,
I am combined by a sacred Vow,   2235
And shall be absent. Wend you with this Letter:

2229 that he] he that v1793, CAM3
2231 to night] *Om.* POPE, HAN1
2235 combined] confined mTHEO *conj.,* COLNE, COL2

2228 **Friar *Peter***] DELIUS (ed. 1860): The same who is previously called "One of our Couent, and his Confessor." LEVER (ed. 1965): "As the Duke's confessor he must be identical with the 'Friar' of I. iii."
 2229 **that**] That which: see n. 1146.
  of] About: see n. 734.
 2231 ABBOTT (§498): This line "must be an Alexandrine, unless in the middle of the line 'Mariana' can be shortened like 'Marian'." Cf. 2791.
 2232 **perfect**] JOHNSON (1755): "Instruct fully." SCHMIDT (1875) marks the verb as always accented by Sh. on first syllable. *OED* (*v.* 4): "Instruct or inform completely," first use in this sense.
  withall] See ABBOTT §196: "The emphatic form of 'with'," quoting 2725.
 2233 **to the head**] SCHMIDT (1874, p. 521): "Without reserve, without any fear of his person and power," as in *Ado* 5.1.62 (2146) and *MND* 1.1.106 (115). *OED* (*sb.* 38): "*To* (one's) *head.* To one's face; directly to the person himself." HART (ed. 1905): Cf. Golding's Ovid, *Metamorphoses* (1567; ed. Rouse, 13:245). See n. 2532 and *Ham.* 3.3.63 (2339).
 2234 **home and home**] HUDSON (ed. 1880): "*Home* is much used by the Poet for *thoroughly, to the uttermost,* or *to the quick.* The repetition here gives a very strong sense." See n. 333. HART (ed. 1905): "With increasing intenseness. Jonson has 'throughly and throughly' [*Volpone*, 1.5.55] in the same sense. The reduplication of the adverb, to enforce it, seems to be commoner in Shakespeare than his contemporaries." Cf. 2396.
 2235 **combined**] JOHNSON (ed. 1765): "I once thought this should be *confined,* but *Shakespear* uses *combine* for to *bind by a pact or agreement,* so he calls *Angelo* the *combinate* husband of *Mariana.*" See n. 1443. *OED* (*v.* 6): "Perh. = To bind [only use in this sense]: cf. *Combind,*" "(A form arising from confusion of *combine* and *bind*)," and *AYL* 5.4.156 (2725). WILSON (ed. 1922): Cf. *Rom.* 2.3.60 (1067). See p. 290.
 2236 **shall**] Must (ABBOTT §315).
  Wend you] GILDON (1710, p. lxxii): "*Wend,* go." *OED* (*v.* 10): "To go off, away, or out; to depart." LEVER (ed. 1965): "Betake yourself (reflexive)."

Command these fretting waters from your eies
With a light heart; trust not my holie Order
If I peruert your course: whose heere?

Enter Lucio. 2240

Luc. Good'euen;
Frier, where's the Prouost?
Duke. Not within Sir.
Luc. Oh prettie *Isabella*, I am pale at mine heart, to
see thine eyes so red: thou must be patient; I am faine 2245
to dine and sup with water and bran: I dare not for my
head fill my belly. One fruitful Meale would set mee
too't: but they say the Duke will be heere to Morrow.

2239–43 *Lines ending* even! . . . sir. v1793-v1821, SING, KNT, COL, WH1, STAU, KTLY, ARD2; here? . . . sir. HAL; here? . . . provost? . . . sir. DYCE, CAM, GLO, DEL4, HUD2-PEL1, PEN2, EVNS
2239 peruert] prevert ROWE2
2240 SCENE XI. POPE, HAN1, WARB, JOHN
2242 where's] where is HAN1, CAP-v1821, SING, KNT, COL, WH1, KTLY, DEL4, ARD1
2245 thine] thy v1778-RANN

2237 **fretting**] *OED* (*ppl. a.* 1a): "Corroding, consuming."
2239 **peruert**] SCHMIDT (1875): "Lead astray." See *OED* (*v.* 2a): "Turn aside from justice."
2241 **Good'euen**] LEVER (ed. 1965; cf. pp. xxii–iii): "Conflicting with the Duke's 'Good morning', [2200]." See n. 1700.
2241–2 The two lines of prose set as verse might indicate a pause between them (see n. 514–15), but cf. 2257–8.
2244 **pale at mine heart**] SCHMIDT (1875): Cf. *pale-hearted Feare* in *Mac.* 4.1.85 (1626). WINNY (ed. 1959): "Full of fear."
2245 **thou**] BYRNE (1936, p. 97): "Lucio says a familiar yet compassionate *thou* to Isabella" [see n. 887], then "flippant, rude, *thou*" to the Duke as Friar, 2254, but *you* in 2269.
   faine] JOHNSON (1755): "Forced; obliged; compelled." See *OED* (*a.* 2): "Glad under the circumstances . . . as the lesser of two evils." So in 2264.
2246 **water and bran**] THIRLBY (1723–33): Cf. *LLL* 1.1.303 (296). HART (ed. 1905): "So Nashe, *Summers Last Will* [3:260], 1592: '. . . branne and water (fit for dogs)'."
2246–7 **for my head**] LEVER (ed. 1965): "To save my head (from the fate of Claudio's)."
2247 **fruitful**] *OED* (*a.* 3): "Abundant, copious. Chiefly in Shaks."
2247–8 **set mee too't**] SCHMIDT (1875, p. 1033): *Set,* "To incite, to instigate." See n. 2480. PARTRIDGE (1947, p. 186): "Render a person lustful." LEVER (ed. 1965): "Cf. 'past it', [1667–8]." Also *too't* 679: see n.

By my troth *Isabell* I lou'd thy brother, if the olde fantastical Duke of darke corners had bene at home, he had   2250
liued.

   Duke. Sir, the Duke is marueilous little beholding
to your reports, but the best is, he liues not in them.

   Luc. Friar, thou knowest not the Duke so wel as I
do: he's a better woodman then thou tak'st him for.   2255

   Duke. Well: you'l answer this one day. Fare ye well.

   Luc. Nay tarrie, Ile go along with thee,
I can tel thee pretty tales of the Duke.

   Duke. You haue told me too many of him already sir
if they be true: if not true, none were enough.   2260

   Lucio. I was once before him for getting a Wench
with childe.

   Duke. Did you such a thing?

2249 thy] your CAP
2251 *Ex.* Isabella. THEO, WARB+
2253 reports] report v1778, v1785
2257-8 *Prose* POPE1+
2260 not true] not ROWE, POPE, HAN1

   2249-50 **olde fantastical**] CLARKE (1879, p. 573): *Old,* "used to imply familiarity, without implying age" (*OED, a.* 8). HART (ed. 1905): "Pleasantly whimsical."
See n. 877-8.

   2250 **Duke of darke corners**] MALONE (1780, 1:102): "This duke who meets
his mistresses in by-places." [Cf. *2 Return from Parnassus* (1606), ed. Leishman,
1233-4, "an old knight may haue his wench in a corner," and Jonson, *Discoveries,* 59,
"making a little winter-love in a darke corner."] See n. 1663.

   he had] He would have. See n. 188.

   2252 **beholding**] SCHMIDT (1874): "Obliged" (*OED, ppl. a.* 1).

   2253 **he . . . them**] STEEVENS (Var. 1778): "His character depends not on
them." HALLIWELL (ed. 1854): "He exists not in the kind of life indicated by your
slanders." HUNTER (ed. 1873): "His life does not answer to them." LEVER (ed.
1965): He "is not to be found" in them.

   2255 **woodman**] THIRLBY (1733-47): "Sportsman." See *Wiv.* 5.5.30 (2508).
JOHNSON (ed. 1765): "*Huntsman,* here taken for a *hunter of girls.*" REED (in Var.
1785) quotes *The Chances,* 1.9 (Beaumont & Fletcher, ed. Glover & Waller, 4:187):
"I see ye are a wood-man, and can chuse Your dear, though it be i'th'dark." HAL-
LIWELL (ed. 1854) adds *The Faithfull Shepheardesse* (Beaumont & Fletcher, ed. Bow-
ers, 1.2.131), and HART (ed. 1905) quotes two examples from Greene, 1590. See
OED (Woodman[1] 1b).

   2256 **answer**] See n. 848.

   2257-8 Prose set as verse by Compositor B.

   2260 **were**] Would be. See n. 40.

Luc. Yes marrie did I; but I was faine to forswear it,
They would else haue married me to the rotten Medler.   2265
    Duke. Sir your company is fairer then honest, rest you
well.
    Lucio. By my troth Ile go with thee to the lanes end:
if baudy talke offend you, we'el haue very litle of it: nay
Friar, I am a kind of Burre, I shal sticke.   *Exeunt*   2270

Scena Quarta.   4.4

Enter Angelo & Escalus.

Esc. Euery Letter he hath writ, hath disuouch'd other.

2264 I was] was v1793, v1813, v1821, SING, KTLY
2266 your] you F2
2269 it] *Om.* F2
2270 of] of a F2-F4
2271 *Scena Quarta*] SCENE III ROWE; SCENE XII POPE, HAN1, WARB, JOHN
  The Palace. ROWE1-JOHN2, v1773-RANN; *A Room in* Angelo's *House.* CAP, MAL-
SIS (*subst.*); *In Vienna* ARD2
2273 other] the other THEO4, JOHN, WH1

2264 **faine**] See n. 2245.
2265 **else**] See n. 281.
    Medler] ONIONS (1911): "Fruit which is like a small brown-skinned apple
and is eaten when decayed to a soft pulpy state; always with quibble on 'meddler'."
BALD (ed. 1956): "A pear that rotted as it ripened (here, a prostitute)." Cf. TILLEY
(M863) and WILSON (p. 523): "Medlars are never good till they be rotten."
    2266 **fairer**] HART (ed. 1905): "More friendly, or agreeable." See *OED* (Fair
a. 5): "Attractive or pleasing at the first sight or hearing; specious." SAUNDERS (ed.
1971): "Lucio is 'a fantastic' and hence dressed very ostentatiously."
    rest you] SCHMIDT (1875): "A salutation in meeting, and oftener in parting
(the word *God* mostly omitted)." See *OED* (*v.*¹ 3b, 7b, 8c).
    2270 **Burre**] HART (ed. 1905): " 'They cleave together like burrs' occurs in John
Heywood" (*Prouerbes,* 1546, ed. Milligan, 2.5.207; TILLEY, B723). LEVER (ed.
1965): A closer parallel is TILLEY (B724): "To stick like burrs." Cf. *Tro.* 3.2.119-20
(1742-3).
    2273 **Euery Letter**] HART (ed. 1905): "There is an interesting parallelism be-
tween the opening of this scene and that of the fifth scene of the last act of Jonson's
Sejanus" (1605, 5:293-5). Sejanus says: "A *Senate* warn'd without my knowledge?

An. In most vneuen and distracted manner, his actions   (G4⁴
show much like to madnesse, pray heauen his wisedome   2275
bee not tainted: and why meet him at the gates and re-
liuer our authorities there?

Esc. I ghesse not.

Ang. And why should wee proclaime it in an howre
before his entring, that if any craue redresse of iniustice,   2280
they should exhibit their petitions in the street?

Esc. He showes his reason for that: to haue a dispatch
of Complaints, and to deliuer vs from deuices heereafter, which shall then haue no power to stand against
vs.   2285

2274–7 *Verse lines ending* manner. . . . heaven, . . . tainted! . . . re-deliver . . . there?
COL1, COL2, COL4; manner. . . . pray . . . tainted! . . . re-deliver . . . there? COL3
2276–7 reliuer] F1, IRV, PEN2; deliver F2-JOHN2, HAL, SIS; re-deliver mTBY1
conj., CAP *etc.*
2279–81 *Verse lines ending* we . . . ent'ring, . . . injustice, . . . petitions . . . street?
COL
2279 in] *Om.* mTBY1 *conj.,* RANN, CAM3
2282 reason] reasons v1785
2284–5 which . . . vs.] *One verse line* COL1, COL2, COL3

And on this sodaine? Senators by letters Required to be there!" "The machinery of
the letters in both cases leads immediately to the catastrophe of the play. Later again
[2361–4] our duke professes public honour to Angelo, whom he is about to destroy,
as Tiberius does (by Macro as proxy)." Jonson's *Workes* (1616) names Sh. as an actor
in *Seianus* in 1603.

    disuouch'd] JOHNSON (1755): "To destroy the credit of; to contradict." *OED*
(v.): "*Disavouch*, *Disavow*," only quotation.

    2274 **In . . . manner**] COLLIER (ed. 1842): "This is a complete line, and although
not so printed, it seems clear that the author meant this brief interview between two
such principal personages to be r[h]ythmical. Some of the lines are rugged and
irregular." All other eds. line as prose.

    vneuen] *OED* (*a.* 4, 4c): "Irregular," *fig.* sense first in Sh.

    2276 **tainted**] SCHMIDT (1875): "Infected," "Applied to diseases of the mind."
Cf. 2407.

    2276–7 **reliuer**] SCHMIDT (1875): "To give back." STONE (1884, p. 116*): Cf.
COTGRAVE (1611), "Relivrer. *To redeliuer*," and Ducange [*Glossarium Mediæ et Infimæ
Latinitatis*] on *reliberare. OED* (*v.*): "To give up again, restore." A legal term, which
has wrongly been changed to *redeliver.*

    2279 **in an howre**] THIRLBY (1747–53): *In,* "within." LEVER (ed. 1965):
"'Leaving a clear hour', so that petitioners may not find access obstructed."

    2281 **exhibit**] JOHNSON (1755): "Offer or propose in a formal or publick man-
ner." SCHMIDT (1874): "To present, to offer officially" (*OED, v.* 5a).

    2282 **dispatch**] ONIONS (1911): "Settlement." LEISI (ed. 1964): "'Prompt
settlement' (OED 5 [or rather 6])." See n. 1486.

    2283 **deuices**] HARDING (ed. 1954): "Cunning plots" (*OED,* 6). BALD (ed.
1956): "Contrived complaints."

Ang. Well: I beseech you let it bee proclaim'd be-
times i'th' morne, Ile call you at your house: giue notice
to such men of sort and suite as are to meete him.
   Esc. I shall sir: fareyouwell.   *Exit.*
   Ang. Good night.   2290
This deede vnshapes me quite, makes me vnpregnant
And dull to all proceedings. A deflowred maid,
And by an eminent body, that enforc'd
The Law against it? But that her tender shame

2286–9 *Verse lines ending* proclaim'd: . . . house: . . . suit . . . him. . . . well. mTBY1
conj., CAP-MAL; proclaim'd: . . . house: . . . suit . . . well. v1793-DYCE1, COL3, STAU,
DYCE2-HUD2, IRV, BUL, ARD1, CAM3-PEN2
   2286 proclaim'd⌃] ~ : CAP-STAU (−RANN), DYCE2-PEN2 (−WH2, CAM2,
NLSN, ARD2)
   2289 *Exit.*] *After* 2290 CAP, HAL, DYCE, STAU-GLO, HUD2+ (−NLSN)
   2290–2 *Lines ending* deed . . . unpregnant, dull . . . maid, HAN1
   2292 proceedings] proceeding SING1

2286–8 LEVER (ed. 1965, p. xxviii): "Not more than about a dozen lines [of verse
set as prose in *MM*] can be clearly distinguished. . . . The reasons for confusion are
nearly always the same—unexpected variations from verse to prose or difficulty in
arranging half-lines."
   2286–7 **betimes**] See n. 2124.
   2287 **call**] SCHMIDT (1874): "To seek, to come for." ONIONS (1911): " 'Call
upon', to visit," used only by Sh., here and in *TN* 3.2.56 (1431). So *OED* (*v.* 4e).
Cf. *OED* (23g), *call upon,* first used in *Ham.* 3.3.34 (2309).
   2288 **sort and suite**] JOHNSON (ed. 1765): "Figure and rank." CAPELL (1780,
2:3:55): "Men of rank and condition, and men owing *suit,* or (in language of law)
suit and service, which bound them to such attendance." *OED* (*sb.* ² 2b): "*Of sort,* of
(high) quality or rank," first use in this sense. LEVER (ed. 1965): "Men of rank with
a retinue" (*OED,* Suit *sb.* 16).
   2289 **fareyouwell**] Sometimes printed as one word, like *farewell.* Cf. 1488 and
p. 278.
   Exit.] This should follow 2290.
   2291 **vnshapes**] DYCE (1867): "Confounds." SCHMIDT (1875): "To deprive of
shape, to derange." Cf. *vnshaped* in *Ham.* 4.5.8 (2753). *OED:* "To deform, to destroy," first fig. use.
   vnpregnant] JOHNSON (1755): "Not prolifick." IDEM (1773): "Not quick
of wit." STEEVENS (Var. 1778): *"Unready, unprepared."* Cf. *pregnant* 14. BECKET
(1815, 1:234): "Without ideas, barren of project." SCHMIDT (1875): "Unapt for
business." Cf. *Ham.* 2.2.595 (1608).
   2293 **eminent**] *OED* (*a.* 2): "Exalted, dignified in rank or station," first use of
a person. See n. 257.
   body] JOHNSON (1755): "Person" (*OED,* 13). So in *any body* 1786.
   enforc'd] See n. 74.

Will not proclaime against her maiden losse,   2295
How might she tongue me? yet reason dares her no,
For my Authority beares of a credent bulke,

2296 dares her no,] dares her: POPE, THEO; dares her: no, HAN1; dares her No.
WARB, JOHN, v1773, v1778, KNT; dares her—No: UPTON *conj.*, RANN; dares her?
no; CAP, v1785, MAL-SING1, COL1; dares her not; STEEVENS (v1773) *conj.*, COL4;
dares her on; MASON (1785) *conj.*, WH; says her, No; KTLY

2297 beares of a credent bulke] bears off a credent bulk F4, ROWE, MAL, v1821,
HAL, PEL1; bears off all credence POPE, HAN1; bears a credent Bulk THEO, WARB-
RANN, v1793-v1813, SING1, KTLY, DEL4, COL4, WH2, BUL, NLSN, CAM3, PEN2;
bears such a credent bulk COLNE, COL2, COL3; bears so credent bulk LETTSOM (*N&Q*
1853) *conj.*, DYCE, HUD2, OXF1, KIT1, SIS, ARD2; here's of a credent bulk SING2;
bears up a credent bulk WH1; rears of a credent bulk STAU; bears a so credent bulk
HENL, ALEX

2295 **proclaime**] *OED* (*v.* 5): "Make proclamation or public announcement."
Cf. *1 Promos*, 4.2 (p. 328 below): "Hir preuie maime, hir open cryes will staye."
   against] See *OED (prep.* 3 *fig.)*: "In regard to."
   maiden losse] Loss of virginity.
2296 **tongue**] JOHNSON (1755): "To chide; to scold." *OED* (*v.* 1): "To assail
with words; to reproach, scold." PARROTT (ed. 1938): "I.e., accuse."
   reason dares her no] THEOBALD (ed. 1733): "Perhaps, *dares her* Note: i. e.
stifles her Voice; frights her from speaking." UPTON (1746, p. 182): "dares her. No:
. . . Yet (you'll say) she has reason on her side, and that will make her dare to do
it. I think not." WARBURTON (ed. 1747): "She will never venture to contradict me:
dares her to reply *No* to me, whatever I say." STEEVENS (Var. 1778): "I would read:
—yet reason dares her *not.*" HENLEY (1780, p. 22): "Reason defies her to do it."
ANON. (1786, p. 86): "Reason, or reflection, is, we conceive, personified by Shakspeare, and represented as *daring* or *over-awing* Isabella, and crying No, to her,
whenever she finds herself prompted to 'tongue' Angelo." MALONE (ed. 1790):
"Yet does not reason *challenge* or *incite her* to accuse me?—no, (answers the speaker).
. . . To *dare*, in this sense, is yet a school-phrase: Shakspeare probably learnt it there."
HALLIWELL (ed. 1854): "*No* is here used for *not.* . . . Her reason or reflection does
not challenge or prompt her to tongue me, will not make her dare to do it." SCHMIDT
(1874, p. 276): "Reason defies her denial of my assertions." THISELTON (1901, p.
36): " 'Reason defies her to refuse compliance with its dictates'." HART (ed. 1905):
"Reason taunts her, or defies her with no. . . . Craig suggests the sense of dare
(frighten) in the fowling expression 'daring larks'." PARROTT (ed. 1938): "Frightens
her into saying no." NEILSON & HILL (ed. 1942): "Forbids her to dare." See p. 290.
2297 **beares of**] STEEVENS (Var. 1778): "I suppose for—bears *off*, i. e., carries
along with it." MALONE (ed. 1790): "Perhaps Angelo means, that his authority will
ward off or set aside the weightiest and most probable charge that can be brought
against him." HALLIWELL (ed. 1854): "In the first folio, *off* is spelled *of*, but these
two words were often interchangeable." DYCE (ed. 1857): "Is not the 'of a' of the
folio a corruption of '*soe*'?" HART (ed. 1905): "Bears so much of, or such a kind of."
See p. 290.
   credent] JOHNSON (1755): "Having credit; not to be questioned." CLARKE
(ed. 1864): " 'Credent bulk' means large-sized credit, credit of large amount or

That no particular scandall once can touch
But it confounds the breather. He should haue liu'd,
Saue that his riotous youth with dangerous sence   2300
Might in the times to come haue ta'ne reuenge
By so receiuing a dishonor'd life
With ransome of such shame: would yet he had liued.
Alack, when once our grace we haue forgot,
Nothing goes right, we would, and we would not.   *Exit.*   2305

2302 By] For JOHN, v1773
2305 *Exit.*] *Om.* CAP

---

weight." *OED* (*a.* 2a): "Having credit or repute," only quotation in this sense. ONIONS (1911): "Credible." LEVER (ed. 1965): "Plausible; cf. *Wint.,* I. ii. [142–3 (218–19)]." *Credent bulk,* "great capacity to induce belief."

bulke] HALLIWELL (ed. 1854): "Body." SCHMIDT (1874): "Especially largeness of the body, great size" (cf. *OED, sb.* 1 4).

2298 **particular**] THIRLBY (1723–33): "Private, that is by a private person" (*OED, a.* 3). JOHNSON (ed. 1765): *"Private,* a *French* sense. No scandal from any *private* mouth can reach a man in my authority." LEISI (ed. 1964): "Sh. often uses *particular* in the sense of 'whatever'; *each particular* clearly means 'every single' in [2620]."

2299 **confounds**] SCHMIDT (1874): "To destroy, to ruin." See also *OED* (*v.* 3b): "Silence, confute."

breather] *OED* (4): "One who breathes forth, speaks, proclaims."

should] LEISI (ed. 1964): "Probably 'would' i. e. the conditional." See FRANZ §612.

2300 **riotous**] SCHMIDT (1875): "Tumultuous" (*OED, a.* 4). EMPSON (1951, p. 277): "Sensual."

sence] JOHNSON (1755): "Sensibility; quickness or keenness of perception." SCHMIDT (1875): "Faculty of thinking and feeling." EMPSON (1951, pp. 276–7): "I think 'sensuality' is the idea that comes first in his mind, and acts as chief meaning of the word; if you had to choose only one meaning, what the logic of the passage requires is 'sensibility', but it is regarded as a consequence." BALD (ed. 1956): "Reason." LEVER (ed. 1965): "Passion, as in [901] and elsewhere." NOSWORTHY (ed. 1969): "Intention."

2301 . **ta'ne**] See n. 1808.

2302 **By**] Because of. See ABBOTT §146 and *OED* (*prep.* 36).

2303 **would**] I wish. See n. 1664.

he had] KÖNIG (1888, p. 57): Pronounced *he'd.*

2304–5 NOBLE (1935, p. 228) quotes Rom. 7:15, 16; Gal. 5:17. Cf. 777.

2304 **grace**] SCHMIDT (1874): "Virtue." See n. 1403.

2305 JOHNSON (ed. 1765): "Here undoubtedly the act should end, and was ended by the poet; for here is properly a cessation of action, and a night intervenes, and the place is changed, between the passages of this scene and those of the next. The next act beginning with the following scene, proceeds without any interruption of time or change of place." See n. 950.

Scena Quinta. 4.5

Enter Duke and Frier Peter.

Duke. These Letters at fit time deliuer me.
The Prouost knowes our purpose and our plot,
The matter being a foote, keepe your instruction 2310
And hold you euer to our speciall drift,
Though sometimes you doe blench from this to that
As cause doth minister: Goe call at *Flauia*'s house,

2306 *Scena Quinta*] SCENE IV ROWE; SCENE XIII POPE, HAN1, WARB, JOHN;
ACT V. SCENE I JOHN1 *conj.*, RANN   *The Fields without the Town.* ROWE1-SIS
(*subst.*); *A Friar's Cell.* ARD2
    2307 *Enter . . .*] *Enter* Duke *in his own Habit, and Friar* Peter. ROWE1+ (−CAP)
    2308 *Giving letters.* JOHN1-ALEX (−CAP, WH1), EVNS
    2311 our] your WALKER (1860, 2:9) *conj.*, DEL4
    2313 Goe] *Om.* HAN1   *Flauia*'s] *Flauius*'s ROWE1, ROWE2; *Flavius* ROWE3;
Flavius' POPE1-PEN2; Flavio's mTHEO *conj.*, EVNS

2308 **These Letters**] JOHNSON (ed. 1765): "*Peter* never delivers the letters, but
tells his story without any credentials. The poet forgot the plot which he had formed."
HALLIWELL (ed. 1854): "The pronoun *me* is redundant, as in numerous other cases.
These letters do not necessarily refer to the introduction of Peter in the next act."
WILSON (ed. 1922): "The Duke's letters are very puzzling, and we are not told for
whom these particular ones were intended; in any case 'deliver me' may mean 'deliver
for me' and not 'to me'." LEVER (ed. 1965): "The letters would be the Friar's
credentials to Flavius, Valencius, etc."
    2311 **drift**] SCHMIDT (1874): "Aim, intention, meaning, scheme" (*OED, sb.* 4,
5).
    2312 **blench**] JOHNSON (1755): "To shrink; to start back; to fly off." *OED*
(*v.* 1 2): "Swerve." HART (ed. 1905): "Turn aside."
    2313 **As . . . minister**] *OED* (*v.* 2c): "Prompt, suggest," only use in this sense.
LEISI (ed. 1964): " 'As the matter occasions it'." See n. 331.
    Flauia's] Apparently a misreading of *Flauius;* cf. 2317. ERLER (1913, p. 81):
Sh. chose Latin instead of Italian names for a number of persons in 4.5. Perhaps he
wished by these names to characterize the bearers as belonging to the high nobility.
LAW (1951, p. 64): "Shakespeare's mind seems to be still dwelling on the men he
has been reading of" in North's Plutarch. Flavius is a tribune in *JC* and a steward
in *Tim.;* the life of Crassus is in Plutarch; and Varrius in Plutarch was a drinking

And tell him where I stay: giue the like notice
To *Valencius*, *Rowland*, and to *Crassus*,   2315
And bid them bring the Trumpets to the gate:
But send me *Flauius* first.
  Peter. It shall be speeded well.

                          Enter Varrius.

  Duke. I thank thee *Varrius*, thou hast made good hast,   2320
Come, we will walke: There's other of our friends
Will greet vs heere anon: my gentle *Varrius.*   *Exeunt.*

2315 To *Valencius*] Unto *Valentius* POPE1-JOHN2, v1773-RANN, COL3, COL4;
To *Valentinus* mTBY1 *conj.*, CAP, v1793-v1821, SING, KNT, HAL, STAU, GLO, DYCE2,
DYCE3, HUD2, WH2, NLSN-SIS   *Rowland*] to Rowland KTLY
2317–18 *One line* v1793+ (−IRV)
2318 *Exit* Friar. THEO1+ (*subst.*)

---

companion of Antony. GREG (1955, p. 355): "A Flavius is sent for but does not
appear, and a Valencius, a Rowland, and a Crassus are mentioned. The object, of
course, is to give a background." LEVER (ed. 1965): "Mention of these figures
without speaking parts adds 'depth', suggesting a ducal court."
    2315 *Valencius*] WILSON (ed. 1922): "This error, together with 'Flauia's' above,
suggests dictation." But there is no proof that *Valencius* is an error. Sh. uses *Valentio*
in *Rom.* 1.2.72 (318) as well as *Valentine* in *Rom.* 1.2.70 (317), *Tit.* 5.2.151 (2438),
and *TGV* (*Valentinus* in 1.3.67 [369]).
    Crassus] NOSWORTHY (ed. 1969): "Shakespeare evidently picked up the
name from Whetstone's *Heptameron* which alludes to 'the two brave Romanes, Marcus
Crassus, and Marius' [see p. 374 below]." But Sh. mentions Plutarch's Crassus in
Ant. 3.1.2 (1497).
    2316 **Trumpets**] SCHMIDT (1875): "Trumpeter" (*OED, sb.* 4). LEVER (ed.
1965) thinks it "may mean the instruments," but this is less likely. *Trumpet* means
"trumpeter" in *Tro.* 4.5.6 (2555) and elsewhere in Sh.
    2318 **speeded**] SCHMIDT (1875): "Hastened." LEVER (ed. 1965): "Accom-
plished, expedited" (*OED, v.* 8, 11b).
    2319 *Enter Varrius*] WILSON (ed. 1922): "This mysterious personage does not
appear in 'The Names of all the Actors', and though given a second entry at the head
of 5. 1., has nothing to say either there or here." RIDLEY (ed. 1935): "*Enter Varrius;*
and who, in the name of all that is oddest, is he? He appears without warning, says
nothing, and apparently walks on for the purpose of immediately walking off. . . . Is
it just that the Provost once had, or has here suddenly acquired, a name?" LEVER (ed.
1965, pp. 123, xlv): "There is a messenger called Varrius in *Ant.*, II. i. The chief
function of Varrius here is to escort the Duke, now in his proper person, off and on
the stage." The name is "apparently a recollection of the Varius mentioned [by Sir
Thomas Elyot] as the father of Severus." But Sh. could also have found it in Plutarch:
see n. 2313. He has *Varrus* in *JC* 4.3.244 ff. (2252 ff.).
    2321 **walke**] SCHMIDT (1875): "To go away, to come away, to withdraw."
WILSON (ed. 1922): "Walk about, while waiting for 'other of our friends'." See n.
1833.

Scena Sexta.   4.6

Enter Isabella and Mariana.

Isab. To speak so indirectly I am loath,   2325
I would say the truth, but to accuse him so
That is your part, yet I am aduis'd to doe it,
He saies, to vaile full purpose.
     Mar. Be rul'd by him.
     Isab. Besides he tells me, that if peraduenture   2330   (G4ᵛ
He speake against me on the aduerse side,
I should not thinke it strange, for 'tis a physicke

2323 *Scena Sexta*] SCENE V ROWE; SCENE XIV POPE, HAN1, WARB, JOHN;
SCENE II v1778; ACT V. SCENE II RANN   *Street near the Gate.* CAP, MAL-SIS;
In Vienna. ARD2
     2328 to vaile full] t'availful THEO; to 'vailful mTBY1 *conj.*, HAN1, CAP, RANN,
SING, COLNE, DYCE, COL3, DEL4-HUD2, BUL; to veil his full KTLY

2325 **indirectly**] SEYMOUR (1805, 1:101): *"Deviating from the direct course of
truth."* OED (*adv.* 1c): *"Evasively."*
     2326 **would**] See n. 17.
     2327 **part**] Role (*OED, sb.* 9). See n. 1031.
     2328 **to vaile full purpose**] THEOBALD (ed. 1733) reads *t'availful purpose:* "to
a Purpose that will stand us in stead, that will profit us." WARBURTON (ed. 1747):
"Yet the common reading is right. . . . *To hide a beneficial purpose, that must not yet be
revealed."* JOHNSON (ed. 1765): *"To vail full purpose,* may, with very little force on
the words, mean *to hide the whole extent of our design,* and therefore the reading may
stand; yet I cannot but think Mr. *Theobald*'s alteration either lucky or ingenious."
KELLNER (1931, p. 263): To further (*vail,* cf. *OED,* Avail *v.* 3) the full attainment
of the goal, namely the conviction of Angelo. HARDING (ed. 1954): "Conceal our
full plan" (*OED,* Veil *v.* 4).
     2331 **He**] THIRLBY (1747–53): "This should be the Duke in disguise, I think.
But though he is rough with her as Duke and takes Angelo's part, he does not so as
a frier. To what purpose then is this put in? Is Frier Peter meant? He speaks against
her" (in 2508 ff.).
     2332-3 TILLEY (M558, P327) and WILSON (p. 63): "Men take bitter potions for
sweet health"; "Bitter pills may have wholesome effects."

That's bitter, to sweet end.

Enter Peter.

Mar. I would *Frier Peter*   2335
Isab. Oh peace, the *Frier* is come.
Peter. Come I haue found you out a stand most fit,
Where you may haue such vantage on the *Duke*
He shall not passe you:
Twice haue the Trumpets sounded.   2340
The generous, and grauest Citizens
Haue hent the gates, and very neere vpon
The *Duke* is entring:
Therefore hence away.   *Exeunt.*

2333–6 *Lines ending* end. . . . come. v1793-PEL1, PEN2, EVNS; Peter— . . . come.
ARD2
2334 *Enter Peter.*] *After* 2336 POPE1-CAM3 (−NLSN); *after* 2335 ALEX-PEL1,
PEN2
2335 *Peter*ᴧ] ∼ .— F2, F3; ∼ — F4+
2339–40, 2343–4 *One line* POPE1+
2341 generous] most generous KTLY
2342 upon] upon this time KTLY

2334 Peter enters after 2335 or 2336: see textual notes.
2335 **would**] See n. 817.
    *Peter*ᴧ] An unfinished sentence: see n. 140.
2336 **peace**] Be silent (*OED, v.* 1).
2337 **stand**] JOHNSON (1755): "A station; a place where one waits standing."
OED (*sb.* 1 11): "A place of standing, position, station." WILSON (ed. 1922): Literally
"a sheltered position or covert for shooting at game" (*OED, sb.* 13).
2338 **vantage**] DURHAM (ed. 1926): "Advantage of position" (*OED,* 4).
2339–40, 2343–4 Each is one line of verse set as two half lines.
    2341 **generous**] STEEVENS (Var. 1778): "*Most noble,* &c. *Generous* is here used
in its Latin sense" (*OED, a.* 1, "High-born"). So in *Oth.* 3.3.280 (1913). DELIUS (ed.
1860): The superlative in *gravest* is also to be applied to *generous.* See ABBOTT §398.
    2342 **hent**] GILDON (1710, glossary, p. lxx): "Took hold of." HANMER (ed.
1743, 6, glossary): "To *Hend,* to seize, to lay hold of: also, to hem in, to surround."
RICHARDSON (1836): "To seize, to occupy." *OED* (*v.* 3b): "Arrive at, reach, occupy." BALD (ed. 1956): "Taken up positions at."
    neere vpon] SCHMIDT (1875): Near in time. ONIONS (1911): "Close at
hand." PARROTT (ed. 1938): "Soon." BALD (ed. 1956): "Almost at once."

Actus Quintus. Scæna Prima. 5.1

Enter Duke, Varrius, Lords, Angelo, Esculus, Lucio, 2346
Citizens at seuerall doores.

Duk. My very worthy Cosen, fairely met,
Our old, and faithfull friend, we are glad to see you.
Ang. Esc. Happy returne be to your royall grace. 2350
Duk. Many and harty thankings to you both:
We haue made enquiry of you, and we heare
Such goodnesse of your Iustice, that our soule

2345 *Scæna Prima.*] *Om.* THEO, CAP, HAL; SCENE III. RANN *the Street.*
ROWE, POPE, HAN1; *a publick Place near the City.* THEO, WARB, JOHN, v1773-RANN;
The City Gate. CAP, MAL-SIS, ARD2 (*subst.*)
2346 *Enter* . . .] *A State with Chairs under it: Crowds of Citizens,* LUCIO, Provost,
Officers, &c. *attending:* MARIANA *veil'd,* ISABELL, *and Friar* Peter, *at their Stand. Enter,*
at opposite Doors, Duke, VARRIUS; ANGELO, ESCALUS; *and their Trains.* CAP;
MARIANA (*veil'd*), ISABELLA, *and* PETER, *at a distance. Enter at opposite Doors,* Duke,
VARRIUS, Lords; ANGELO, ESCALUS, LUCIO, Provost, *Officers, and Citizens.* MAL-
ARD1, CAM3, SIS (*subst.*)
2351 thankings] thankings be F2, F3, ROWE1, ROWE2; thinkings be F4; thanks
be ROWE3-v1773 (−CAP)

2346-7 WILSON (ed. 1922): "F. gives a stage-entry for Peter and Isabella at
[2367], and for Mariana at [2540], but they are clearly supposed to be at their 'stand'
from the beginning."
2348 **Cosen**] SCHMIDT (1874): "A title given by princes to other princes and
distinguished noblemen" (*OED, sb.* 5a).
2349 **we are**] Pronounced *we're.*
2350 **Happy**] SCHMIDT (1874): "Fortunate" (*OED, a.* 2). Cf. 83.
2352 **We haue**] KÖNIG (1888, p. 57): Pronounced *we've.*
2352-3 **we heare . . . Iustice**] HALLIWELL (ed. 1854): Cf. *2 Promos,* 1.9 (p. 345
below): "*Promos,* the good report, of your good gouernment I heare. . . ."
2353 **soule**] See n. 20.

Cannot but yeeld you forth to publique thankes
Forerunning more requitall. 2355
 Ang. You make my bonds still greater.
 Duk. Oh your desert speaks loud, & I should wrong it
To locke it in the wards of couert bosome
When it deserues with characters of brasse
A forted residence 'gainst the tooth of time, 2360
And razure of obliuion: Giue we your hand
And let the Subiect see, to make them know
That outward curtesies would faine proclaime
Fauours that keepe within: Come *Escalus*,
You must walke by vs, on our other hand: 2365
And good supporters are you.

2354 you forth to] forth to you WH1, HUD2
2355–6 *One line* v1793+ (−ARD2)
2357 Oh] O, but ARD2 it] *Om.* F2-POPE2
2361 we your] me your F3-PEL1, PEN2, EVNS; we our ARD2
2362 Subiect] subjects POPE2-MAL (−CAP)

2354 **yeeld you forth to**] SCHMIDT (1875): "Give . . . to you." ROLFE (ed. 1882): "Call you forth to give you."
2356 **bonds**] SCHMIDT (1874): "Obligation" (*OED, sb.* [1] 6).
2358 **wards**] HART (ed. 1905): "Prison-cells." WILSON (ed. 1922): "Bolts, locks, cf. *Son.* 48." Neither is right: see n. 2142.
 couert bosome] SCHMIDT (1874): The heart, "the receptacle of secrets" (*OED, sb.* 6a). LEVER (ed. 1965): "Undisclosed affection."
2359–61 TYRWHITT (1766, pp. 46–7): Cf. *Tro.* 1.3.64 (523). LEVER (ed. 1965): "The inspiration is Horace, *Odes*, III. xxx: '*Exegi monumentum aere perennius* [I have built a monument more lasting than brass]' and Ovid, *Metam.*, XV. 871 ff.; a Renaissance commonplace for eternal fame."
2360 **forted**] JOHNSON (1755): "Furnished or guarded by forts." CAPELL (1779, 1:glossary, 26): "Strong, seated as in a Fort." DELIUS (ed. 1860): *Forted*, fortified, seems a word invented by Sh. (cf. *OED*, Fort).
 residence] *OED* (*sb.* [1] 5b): "Dwelling," "mansion," first use in this sense. Two syllables: see n. 331.
 the tooth of time] ANDERS (1904, p. 285): Cf. Ovid's *tempus edax rerum*, *Metam.*, 15.234, and *Son.* 19. *OED* (*sb.* 2b): "Denoting a . . . destructive, or devouring agency."
2361 **razure**] JOHNSON (1755): "Act of erasing." *OED* (Rasure[1] 3b): "Obliteration, effacement," first use in this sense. HARRIS (1909, pp. 44–5): Cf. *Son.* 122.7, *raz'd obliuion.* See n. 1192.
 we] F3 reads *me*, followed by all later eds. except LEVER (ed. 1965).
2362 **Subiect**] See n. 1030.
2363 **outward curtesies**] Cf. "outward showes" in *2 Promos*, 1.9 (p. 345 below).
2364 **keepe**] See n. 300.
2366 **supporters**] SCHMIDT (1875): "Prop," as in *TN* 1.5.158 (442). *OED*

Enter Peter and Isabella.

Peter. Now is your time
Speake loud, and kneele before him.
   Isab. Iustice, O royall *Duke*, vaile your regard   2370
Vpon a wrong'd (I would faine haue said a Maid)
Oh worthy Prince, dishonor not your eye
By throwing it on any other obiect,
Till you haue heard me, in my true complaint,
And giuen me Iustice, Iustice, Iustice, Iustice.   2375
   Duk. Relate your wrongs;
In what, by whom? be briefe:
Here is Lord *Angelo* shall giue you Iustice,
Reueale your selfe to him.
   Isab. Oh worthy *Duke*,   2380

2367 SCENE II. POPE, HAN1, WARB, JOHN   *Enter . . .*] Peter, *and* ISABELLA,
come forward. CAP, MAL-ARD1, CAM3, SIS
   2368–9, 2376–7 *One line* POPE1 +
   2375 giuen] give F4-POPE2, HAN1, v1785   Iustice, . . . Iustice.] Justice, Justice, Justice. ROWE2; justice. Justice! justice! justice! WH1, ARD2

---

quotes this passage under 5, "an attendant, as in a procession," and suggests possible
allusion to 4, in heraldry, "A figure . . . represented as holding up or standing beside
the shield."

   2368 **Now . . . time**] These four syllables complete a pentameter line with either
2366 or 2369.

   2370 ff. BALDWIN (1944, 2:325–6): Sh. uses directly or indirectly all the tech-
nicalities of *restructio* [an argument in refutation] in Aphthonius (*Progymnasmata*,
1555). The argument pivots on the technical terms "unlike" *(incredibilis)* and "impossible" *(impossibilis)*.

   2370–5 **Iustice . . . Iustice**] HALLIWELL (ed. 1854, 3:439): Cf. *Err.* 5.1.190–4
(1666–70). LEVER (ed. 1965): "So Kyd's Hieronimo seeks to intercept the king in
The Spanish Tragedy, III. xii: 'Iustice, O, iustice to *Hieronimo* . . . Iustice, O, iustice,
iustice, gentle King. . . . Iustice, O iustice'. Angelo's imputation that Isabella's 'wits
. . . are not firm' [2386] may also have been suggested by Lorenzo's comments in
this scene."

   2370 **vaile your regard**] JOHNSON (ed. 1765): "That is, withdraw your
thoughts from higher things; let your notice descend upon a wronged woman. To
vail, is to lower" (*OED, v.*[2] 1c). STEEVENS (Var. 1773): "This is one of the few
expressions which might have been borrowed from the old play . . . 'Vaile thou thine
eares' " (*1 Promos*, 2.3 [p. 314 below]; cf. *2 Promos*, 1.8 [p. 344 below]). DYCE
(1867): "*Regard*, a look" (*OED, sb.* 2).

   2376–7, 2384–5 Each is one verse line set as two half lines.

   2378 **shall**] Who shall. See n. 758.

   2379 **Reueale your selfe**] SCHMIDT (1875): "Lay open: . . . expound your case."
LEVER (ed. 1965): " 'Disclose your complaint'."

You bid me seeke redemption of the diuell,
Heare me your selfe: for that which I must speake
Must either punish me, not being beleeu'd,
Or wring redresse from you:
Heare me: oh heare me, heere.   2385
   Ang. My Lord, her wits I feare me are not firme:
She hath bin a suitor to me, for her Brother
Cut off by course of Iustice.
   Isab. By course of Iustice.
   Ang. And she will speake most bitterly, and strange.   2390
   Isab. Most strange: but yet most truely wil I speake,   (G4va)
That *Angelo's* forsworne, is it not strange?
That *Angelo's* a murtherer, is't not strange?
That *Angelo* is an adulterous thiefe,
An hypocrite, a virgin violator,   2395
Is it not strange? and strange?
   Duke. Nay it is ten times strange?

2384–5 *One line* POPE1+ (−ARD2)
2385 Heare . . . heere.] oh hear me here. POPE, HAN1; oh, hear me, hear me.
THEO, WARB; Hear me, O, hear me! CAPN (V. R.) *conj.,* COL4, HUD2; Hear me, O,
hear me, hear! KEIGHTLEY (1867) *conj.,* RLTR, KIT1, ARD2, PEN2
2387 She hath] Sh' 'ath POPE, HAN1   a] *Om.* v1785
2388 Iustice.] ∼ ; CAP, DYCE, STAU-KTLY, DEL4, HUD2+ (−SIS, ARD2)
2389 By] *Om.* POPE1-CAP (−JOHN)   Iustice.] F1; ∼ ? SIS; ∼ ! F2 *etc.*
2390 and strange] *Om.* F2-POPE2; and strangely COLNE, COL2
2391 strange: but] strangely, yet COLNE, COL2
2396–7 *One line* v1793+ (−ARD2)
2397 it is] *Om.* POPE, HAN1, v1803-SING1, HUD2   strange?] F1-F3; ∼ !
CAM3, KIT1, ARD2; ∼ . F4 *etc.*

2383 **not being**] See n. 1077.
2388 **by course of**] *OED* (*sb.* 33c): "According to the customary course or
procedure of (the law, etc.)."
2390 **bitterly, and strange**] ABBOTT (§474; cf. §§1, 397): "The adverbial
inflection *ly* does duty for two adverbs." So again in next line. SMITH (1904, p. 115):
"The ending is usually added to the adverb nearest the verb." See FRANZ §§244a,
705.
2392–4 HART (ed. 1905): "This device of repetition is very frequent in early
plays, particularly Shakespeare, for the enforcing of a thought or point." Puttenham
deals with it in *The Arte of English Poesie* (1589, 3.19), under the name of "Anaphora,
or the Figure of Repetition." FRANZ §761 stresses the emotional effect of the mysterious and strongly suggestive *strange.*
2395 **virgin violator**] BUTLER (1886, p. 16): "No one class of once-used words
is more conspicuous in Shakespeare than *alliterative compounds.*"
2396 **strange? and strange?**] LEVER (ed. 1965): "Intensive; cf. [2234]." See n.
2234.

Isa. It is not truer he is *Angelo*,
Then this is all as true, as it is strange;
Nay, it is ten times true, for truth is truth   2400
To th'end of reckning.
  Duke. Away with her: poore soule
She speakes this, in th'infirmity of sence.
  Isa. Oh Prince, I coniure thee, as thou beleeu'st
There is another comfort, then this world,   2405
That thou neglect me not, with that opinion
That I am touch'd with madnesse: make not impossible
That which but seemes vnlike, 'tis not impossible
But one, the wickedst caitiffe on the ground
May seeme as shie, as graue, as iust, as absolute: 2410

2400 true] truer THEO2, WARB-JOHN2
2404 Oh . . . thee] Oh I coniure thee, Prince POPE, HAN1; O prince, I do coniure thee CAP

2399 **Then**] LEISI (ed. 1964): " 'Than that'." See n. 1145.

    as true . . . strange] TILLEY (S914) and WILSON (p. 779): "No more strange than true." Cf. *MND* 5.1.2 (1794).

    2400–1 **truth is . . . reckning**] JOHNSON (ed. 1765): "That is, Truth has no gradations; nothing which admits of encrease can be so much what it is, as *truth* is *truth.* There may be a *strange* thing, and a thing *more strange,* but if a proposition be *true* there can be none *more true.*" HART (ed. 1905): Cf. Nashe, *Haue with You* (1596, 3:64): "Truth is truth, and will out at one time or other." CARTER (1905, p. 413) and NOBLE (1935, p. 228) quote 3 Esdras 4:38, "As for the trueth it endureth, and is alway strong, it liueth, and conquereth for euermore world without ende" (Bishops' Bible, 1585; 1 Esdras in Geneva). JENTE (1926, p. 438), TILLEY (T581), and WILSON (p. 844): "Truth is truth."

    2403 **sence**] SCHMIDT (1875): "Understanding, power of sound reasoning." EMPSON (1951, pp. 277–8): "The Duke is teasing Angelo, and a double meaning would be in order:" "strong feeling" and "mere reason."

    2404 **coniure**] SCHMIDT (1874): "Call on with solemnity." Sh. usually accents the first syllable. See *OED* (*v.* 4): "Appeal solemnly or earnestly to."

    thee] BYRNE (1936, p. 97): "Isabella says *you* to the Duke, then [*thee* and *thou*] in burning appeal."

    2407 **touch'd**] *OED* (*v.* 23): "To affect mentally"; (23b) "To be deranged mentally in a slight degree." See nn. 41, 2007.

    make] SCHMIDT (1875, p. 686): "Consider as" (*OED, v.* 51).

    2408 **vnlike**] JOHNSON (1755): "Improbable; unlikely" (*OED, a.* 5). See n. 2472.

    2409 **But**] But that (*OED, conj.* 16).

    caitiffe] See n. 624.

    2410 JOHNSON (ed. 1765): "*As shy;* as reserved, as abstracted: *as just;* as nice, as exact: as *absolute;* as complete in all the round of duty." DELIUS (ed. 1860): The four adjs. from *shy* to *absolute* form a climax. *OED* (Absolute *a.* 4): "Free from all

As *Angelo*, euen so may *Angelo*
In all his dressings, caracts, titles, formes,
Be an arch-villaine: Beleeue it, royall Prince
If he be lesse, he's nothing, but he's more,
Had I more name for badnesse.   2415
   Duke. By mine honesty
If she be mad, as I beleeue no other,
Her madnesse hath the oddest frame of sense,
Such a dependancy of thing, on thing,
As ere I heard in madnesse.   2420
   Isab. Oh gracious *Duke*
Harpe not on that; nor do not banish reason

2413 Beleeue it] trust me POPE, HAN1
2416 honesty] honour HAN1
2420 ere] ne'er mTBY1 *conj.,* JOHN, KTLY, DYCE2, DYCE3, HUD2
2421 Oh] *Om.* POPE1-MAL (—CAP)
2422 nor] and POPE, HAN1

---

imperfection . . . ; perfect, consummate." Cf. *OED* (Just *a.* 2): "Upright and impar-
tial," and *Ham.* 3.2.59 (1904), "as iust a man." HART (ed. 1905): *"Shy*] demure.
Shy must have a good sense here, something like reserved, dignified, grave." See n.
1618.

   2412 **In . . . dressings**] JOHNSON (ed. 1765): "In all his semblance of virtue,
in all his habiliments of office." M. S. (1795, p. 647): Cf. Matt. 23:5 on the scribes
and Pharisees. HARRISON (ed. 1948): "Outward shows."

   caracts] HANMER (ed. 1743, 6, glossary): "Characters." RANN (ed. 1786):
"Ensigns of office." NARES (1822): *Charact,* "A distinctive mark, as in arms." *OED*
(*sb.* 1): "A mark, sign, or *Character*." BALD (ed. 1956): "Insignia of office." According to HART (ed. 1905) and WILSON (ed. 1922) some copies of F1 read *characts,*
but HINMAN (1963, 1:257) finds no such variant.

   2413 **arch-villaine**] *OED:* "Chief villain," first use. Also in *Tim.* 5.1.111 (2333).

   2417–20 MORE (1815, p. 294): Cf. *Lr.* 4.6.178–9 (2616–17) and *Ham.*
2.2.207–8 (1243–4).

   2418 **frame**] SCHMIDT (1874): "Shape, form" (*OED, sb.* 5).

   sense] SCHMIDT (1875): "Rational meaning, reason" (*OED, sb.* 27). EMPSON
(1951, p. 278): "If she has reason it is of a queer kind, not common sense but the
obscure wisdom that Shakespeare expected in clowns and the half-mad."

   2419 **dependancy**] JOHNSON (1755): *Dependency,* "Concatenation; connexion;
rise of consequents from premises." *OED* (1): "Contingent logical or causal connexion," quoting only Hooker for earlier use in this sense. See n. 2794. CRAIG (ed.
1951): "Coherence."

   2420 **ere**] Ever, as in 2737, 2758.

   2421 **gracious**] See *OED* (*a.* 4b): "Used as a courteous epithet in referring to
kings, queens, or dukes."

   2422 **Harpe**] JOHNSON (1755): "To touch any passion, as the harper touches a
string; to dwell on a subject," quoting this, *Mac.* 4.1.74 (1613), and *Ant.* 3.13.142

For inequality, but let your reason serue
To make the truth appeare, where it seemes hid,
And hide the false seemes true.   2425
    Duk. Many that are not mad
Haue sure more lacke of reason:
What would you say?
    Isab. I am the Sister of one *Claudio*,
Condemnd vpon the Act of Fornication   2430
To loose his head, condemn'd by *Angelo*,
I, (in probation of a Sisterhood)
Was sent to by my Brother; one *Lucio*
As then the Messenger.

2423–4 *Lines ending* reason . . . hid, (*om.* the) POPE, HAN1
2423 inequality] incredulity COLNE, COL2, COL3
2425–8 *Lines ending* true. . . . mad . . . say? HAN1, CAP-MAL; mad . . . say?
v1793+
2425 And] Not mTBY1 *conj.*, THEO1-v1785 (−CAP), HUD2   seemes true]
seems-true SING2, HENL
2426 that are] *Om.* HAN1
2433 *Lucio*] *Lucio* being HAN1
2434 As] WasmTBY3*conj.*, JOHN,v1773-RANN   Messenger.]~,—ROWE2+
(−COL3, KIT1, ARD2)

(2322) (*OED, v.* 3). TILLEY (S934, 936) and WILSON (p. 355): "Harp no more on
that string"; "To harp upon one string." Cf. *R3* 4.4.364–5 (3149–50).
    nor] See n. 42.
    2423 **inequality**] THIRLBY (1723–33): Cf. 2407–8. JOHNSON (ed. 1765): "Let
not the high quality of my adversary prejudice you against me." MALONE (1780,
1:102): *"Do not* suppose I am mad, because I speak passionately and *unequally."*
MASON (1785, p. 43): "Apparent inconsistency." HUNTER (ed. 1873): "Partiality."
SCHMIDT (1874): "Incongruity," "improbability." HART (ed. 1905): "Injustice."
LEVER (ed. 1965): "Johnson's 'inequality of rank' (*O.E.D.* 1b) suits the context."
EVANS (ed. 1974): "Discrepancy (between her report of Angelo and the general
report)."
    2425 RANN (ed. 1786): "Disregard, discountenance the hypocritical *Angelo."*
DOUCE (1807, 1:144): *"Suppress* falsehood *where it* has the semblance of truth."
HORNE (ed. 1840, 1:212): "Hide, or dismiss from your mind, the false which seems
true." See n. 758 on omission of the relative. WILSON (ed. 1922): "We take 'hide'
with 'truth', which is to burst forth like the sun and eclipse the seeming truth." LEVER
(ed. 1965): *"Hide*] put out of sight."
    2427–8 One verse line set as two half lines.
    2428 **would**] See n. 17.
    2430 **Act**] See n. 263.
    2432 **probation**] SCHMIDT (1875): "Trial . . . (= the year of noviciate)." So
OED (*sb.* 2a). SPEAIGHT (1954, p. 92): "Isabella might have been a *postulant."* See
n. 1021.
    2434 **As then**] ABBOTT (§114): "Perhaps it means *'as far as regards* that occa-

Luc. That's I, and't like your Grace: 2435
I came to her from *Claudio*, and desir'd her,
To try her gracious fortune with Lord *Angelo*,
For her poore Brothers pardon.
Isab. That's he indeede.
Duk. You were not bid to speake.   2440
Luc. No, my good Lord,
Nor wish'd to hold my peace.
Duk. I wish you now then,
Pray you take note of it: and when you haue
A businesse for your selfe: pray heauen you then   2445
Be perfect.
Luc. I warrant your honor.
Duk. The warrant's for your selfe: take heede to't.
Isab. This Gentleman told somewhat of my Tale.
Luc. Right.   2450
Duk. It may be right, but you are i'the wrong
To speake before your time: proceed.

2440–3 *Lines ending* speak. . . . peace. . . . then; POPE1-JOHN2, v1773; lord;
. . . then; v1793+
2442 wish'd] wish WARB
2444–7 *Lines ending* it: . . . yourself, . . . perfect. CAP; have . . . then . . . honour.
v1793-CAM2, ARD1-KIT1, PEL1, PEN2, EVNS; it; . . . yourself, . . . honour. ARD2
2447 honor] honour, Sir HAN1
2448 take] be sure take HAN1   to't] to it CAP-STAU (−HAL), KTLY-HUD2,
ARD1, CAM3, KIT1
2449 somewhat] something F2-POPE2, HAN1   Tale.] ~ : CAP, DYCE, STAU-
GLO, DEL4, HUD2-NLSN, PEL1, EVNS
2450–1 *One verse line* CAM3
2451 i'the] in the POPE1-v1821, SING, KNT, COL, KTLY, DEL4, HUD2, ARD1

---

sion'." Cf. FRANZ §584. LEVER (ed. 1965): "Being at that time ('as' with adv. of
time, *O.E.D.* 34a)."
2435 **and't like**] If it please. See nn. 486, 612.
2437 **gracious**] SCHMIDT (1874): "Happy, fortunate, prosperous." So *OED, a.*
7.
2442 **wish'd**] *OED* (*v.* 5): "To bid, command," (5b) "a person *to do* something."
2446 **perfect**] *OED* (*a.* 2c): "Having learnt one's lesson or part thoroughly."
ONIONS (1911): "Fully prepared." LEVER (ed. 1965): " 'Correct (in stating your
case)'."
2447 **warrant**] Assure: see n. 128.
2448 **The warrant's . . . selfe**] LEVER (ed. 1965): "Quibbles on 'warrant': 'The
warrant is against you'. Cf. [2469]."
2451 **i'the wrong**] *OED* (Wrong *sb.*2 8b): "The fact or position of acting un-
justly."

241

Isab. I went
To this pernicious Caitiffe Deputie.
   Duk. That's somewhat madly spoken.   2455
   Isab. Pardon it,
The phrase is to the matter.   (G4vb
   Duke. Mended againe: the matter: proceed.
   Isab. In briefe, to set the needlesse processe by:
How I perswaded, how I praid, and kneel'd,   2460
How he refeld me, and how I replide
(For this was of much length) the vild conclusion
I now begin with griefe, and shame to vtter.
He would not, but by gift of my chaste body
To his concupiscible intemperate lust   2465
Release my brother; and after much debatement,
My sisterly remorse, confutes mine honour,
And I did yeeld to him: But the next morne betimes,

2454 Deputie.] ∼ : CAP, DYCE, STAU-KTLY, COL4-BUL, NLSN, PEL1, PEN2, EVNS
2458 the matter:] the matter then: HAN1; *om.* CAP, RANN; ∼ ∼ ? COL, SING2,
WH1   proceed] Now proceed COL3, COL4
2459 processe] *Om.* F2-POPE2
2461 refeld] repell'd POPE1-JOHN2
2465 concupiscible] concupiscent POPE1-JOHN2
2466 and] *Om.* POPE, HAN1
2467 mine] my v1773-RANN
2468 But the] *Om.* POPE, HAN1

2454 **Caitiffe**] See n. 624.
2457 **matter**] See n. 778.
2458 **Mended**] Set right (*OED, v.* 5c).
2459 **processe**] ONIONS (1911): "Narrative" (*OED, sb.* 4). BALDWIN (1944,
2:372): Sh. knows the technical terms of the "process" or "debatement" in school
disputations.
2461 **refeld**] STEEVENS (Var. 1773): "To *refel* is to refute." HALLIWELL (ed.
1854): "Denied, put away, repelled." WILSON (ed. 1922): "Repelled, refused to
admit my plea (v. N.E.D. 'refel' 2, 3)." LEVER (ed. 1965): " 'Rejected my request'."
   2462 **vild**] See *OED (a.):* "Variant of *Vile* . . . the form is extremely common
from *c* 1580 to 1650."
2465 **concupiscible**] WALKER (1860, 1:183): "Adjectives in *able* and *ible* . . .
are frequently used by old writers in an *active* sense." *OED (a.* 2): "Vehemently
desirous." HART (ed. 1905): "The word is four-syllabled here, the 'ci' being slurred
over."
   2467 **remorse**] Pity. See n. 803.
     confutes] SCHMIDT (1874): "To refute, to put to silence" (*OED, v.* 1). HART
(ed. 1905): "Overcomes." WILSON (ed. 1922): *"(a)* render futile, *(b)* silence in
argument (cf. 'debatement')." LEVER (ed. 1965): "Confounds, brings to nought."
   2468 **betimes**] Early. See n. 2124.

His purpose surfetting, he sends a warrant
For my poore brothers head.   2470
   Duke. This is most likely.
   Isab. Oh that it were as like as it is true.
   Duk. By heauen (fond wretch) yᵘ knowst not what thou speak'st,
Or else thou art suborn'd against his honor
In hatefull practise: first his Integritie   2475
Stands without blemish: next it imports no reason,
That with such vehemency he should pursue
Faults proper to himselfe: if he had so offended
He would haue waigh'd thy brother by himselfe,
And not haue cut him off: some one hath set you on: 2480

2469 surfetting] forfeiting F4-POPE2, HAN1, CAP
2471 likely] like LETTSOM *conj. in* DYCE2, HUD2
2473 wretch] wench F4
2475 first] *Om.* POPE, HAN1
2476 next] *Om.* POPE, HAN1
2477 vehemency] vehemence POPE1-v1773 (−CAP)
2478–81 *Lines ending* so . . . by . . . one . . . say HAN1

2469 **surfetting**] HALLIWELL (ed. 1854): "His purpose being satiated." Cf.
1 Promos, 4.3 (p. 329 below): "hauing wonne what they did wish, for othes nor Lady
care." "Or the meaning may simply be,—his purpose of releasing my brother now
cooling." See *OED* (*v.* 3b, 4b).

2472 **like**] WARBURTON (ed. 1747): "*Like* is not here used for *probable,* but for
seemly." EDWARDS (1758, p. 144): "She wishes it were equally *probable,* or *credible,*
as it was true." JOHNSON (ed. 1765): "I do not see why *like* may not stand here for
probable, or why the Lady should not wish that since her tale is true it may obtain
belief." MALONE (1780, 1:103): "O that it had as much of the *appearance* as it has
of the *reality* of truth!" WHITE (ed. 1857): " 'As likely to be believed'." *OED* (*a.*
8): "Probable, likely." See n. 2408.

2473 **fond**] STEEVENS (Var. 1778): "*Foolish*" (*OED, a.* 2).

   yᵘ] LEISI (ed. 1964): " 'Thou', a common abbreviation, *y* being the letter that
most closely resembles the OE sign for *th;* cf. [yᵉ 862]." See n. 862.

2474 **suborn'd**] JOHNSON (1755): "To procure privately; to procure by secret
collusion." *OED* (*v.* 2): "To bribe or unlawfully procure (a person) *to* make accusations or give evidence; to induce *to* give false testimony."

2475 **practise**] JOHNSON (ed. 1765): "*Practice* was used by the old writers for
any unlawful or insidious stratagem." See n. 1759.

2476 **imports**] SCHMIDT (1874): "To carry with it, to have in it" (*OED, v.* 5a),
as in 2934.

2477 **pursue**] SCHMIDT (1875): "Persecute." *OED* (*v.* 1b): "Follow with punishment."

2478 **proper**] See n. 36.

2479 **waigh'd**] See n. 884.

2480 **set . . . on**] SCHMIDT (1875): "To incite, to instigate" (*OED, v.* 148c
[*b*]). Cf. 2247–8.

Confesse the truth, and say by whose aduice
Thou cam'st heere to complaine.
   Isab. And is this all?
Then oh you blessed Ministers aboue
Keepe me in patience, and with ripened time   2485
Vnfold the euill, which is heere wrapt vp
In countenance: heauen shield your Grace from woe,
As I thus wrong'd, hence vnbeleeued goe.
   Duke. I know you'ld faine be gone: An Officer:
To prison with her: Shall we thus permit   2490
A blasting and a scandalous breath to fall,
On him so neere vs? This needs must be a practise;
Who knew of your intent and comming hither?
   Isa. One that I would were heere, *Frier Lodowick.*

2491 breath] name CAP
2492 needs must] must POPE, HAN1; must needs v1773   a] *Om.* F4, JOHN, DYCE2, DYCE3-HUD2
2493 your] our ROWE2-POPE2, HAN1
2494 *Exit guarded.* ARD2

2484 **Ministers**] SCHMIDT (1875): "A servant and messenger of God, an angel" (*OED, sb.* 2), as in *Ham.* 1.4.39 (624).
2486 **Vnfold**] SCHMIDT (1875): "Bring to light" (*OED, v.* ¹ 3).
2487 **In countenance**] WARBURTON (ed. 1747): "In partial favour." JOHNSON (1755): "Superficial appearance; show; resemblance." MASON (1785, p. 43): "False appearance—hypocrisy." SCHMIDT (1874): "Authority, credit, patronage." WILSON (ed. 1922): "Confidence of mien, hypocrisy, worldly credit. All these meanings are possible and 'wrapt up' suggests that Shakespeare had more than one meaning in mind. Isabella, we suppose, points at Angelo, as she utters the word." HARRISON (ed. 1948): "Favoritism." CAMPBELL (ed. 1949): "Reputation (of Angelo)." WINNY (ed. 1959): "A remarkable ambiguity": Angelo's virtuous face, his composure, his partiality, and his authority. "The context allows all four senses to be exploited."
2491 **blasting**] *OED (ppl. a.):* "Blighting, . . . defaming," and see *v.* 8b, quoting Drayton, "to blast Me with Defame."
2492 **practise**] See n. 2475.
2494 **would**] See n. 17.
    Lodowick] Cf. *Lodowicke* in *AWW* 4.3.186 (2269) and *Lodouico* in *Oth.* IZARD (1942, p. 63) thinks the name suggests Giraldi's Vico (Lodovico). Sh. was familiar with the English form from Lodowick Greville (ECCLES, 1961, pp. 76–7) and from characters in *The Jew of Malta, The True Tragedie of Richard the Third,* and *Edward III.* The name has three syllables here, two in 2514 and prob. in 2496.
    WILSON (ed. 1922) inserts after this line the SD *"At a motion of the DUKE, the officer and ISABELLA withdraw to a distance."* "We thus attempt to deal with an insoluble difficulty. The F. gives no exit for Isabella, though the Duke describes her as 'gone' [2619] and she has a re-entry at [2656]. Capell fixed her exit at [2534],

Duk. A ghostly Father, belike: 2495
Who knowes that *Lodowicke?*
Luc. My Lord, I know him, 'tis a medling Fryer,
I doe not like the man: had he been Lay my Lord,
For certaine words he spake against your Grace
In your retirment, I had swing'd him soundly.   2500
Duke. Words against mee? this 'a good Fryer belike
And to set on this wretched woman here
Against our Substitute: Let this Fryer be found.
Luc. But yesternight my Lord, she and that Fryer
I saw them at the prison: a sawcy Fryar,   2505
A very scuruy fellow.
Peter. Blessed be your Royall Grace:
I haue stood by my Lord, and I haue heard
Your royall eare abus'd: first hath this woman

2495–6 *One line* mTBY1 *conj.,* HAN1, JOHN1+
2501 this 'a] this a F4, SING, COL, STAU, KTLY; This is a ROWE1-JOHN2, KNT2,
GLO; this's a CAM1, CAM2, ARD1, NLSN, ALEX; 'tis a HUD2; That's a N&H
2505 saw] say ROWE2, ROWE3   them] him v1785
2506–7 *One line* v1793-HUD2, IRV, BUL, ARD, ALEX, SIS
2507 Royall] *Om.* HAN1

---

and all mod. edd. follow; but it is absurd to take her off immediately after Friar Peter's declaration that she shall be 'disproved to her eyes, Till she her self confess it'."

2495 **ghostly**] NOSWORTHY (ed. 1969): "Since the title *Friar Lodowick* signifies that he is a ghostly, or spiritual, father, the Duke must intend an ironical pun. Hence *ghostly* here means 'non-existent'." But no such meaning exists in *OED*. See n. 2127–8.

2495, 2501 **belike**] See *OED (adv.):* "In all likelihood."

2495–6 One verse line set as two half lines.

2497 **'tis**] See n. 1938.

2500 **retirment**] SCHMIDT (1875): "The act of withdrawing from company . . . (= during your absence)." *OED* (3): "The state or condition of being withdrawn from society," first use in this sense.

   swing'd] DYCE (1867): "Whipped, beaten, chastised" (*OED*, Swinge *v.*¹ 1).

2501 **this 'a**] ABBOTT (§461): " 'This is' " a. Cf. n. 1964. SCHMIDT (1875): So in *Shr.* 1.2.46 (612) and *Lr.* 4.6.187 (2625). LEVER (ed. 1965): "Shakespeare's own spelling omitted the apostrophe, as in *More, M.S.R.,* Add. II (D), 212: 'nay this a sound fellowe'."

2504 **she**] FRANZ (§287g): Colloquial for *her,* as in 2924. See nn. 529, 1434.

2504–5 **she . . . them**] SMITH (1904, p. 114): Cf. *Ham.* 3.2.251-2 (2109-10).

2506, 2516 **scuruy**] JOHNSON (1755): "Vile; bad; sorry; worthless; contemptible; offensive" (*OED, a.* 2).

2509 **abus'd**] LEVER (ed. 1965): "Imposed upon" (*OED, v.* 4). See nn. 2577, 2624. Ears are "abused" also in *AWW* 5.3.295 (3028), *Ham.* 1.5.36–8 (723-5), *Oth.* 1.3.401 (741), and *Lr.* 2.4.310 (1611).

Most wrongfully accus'd your Substitute,   2510
Who is as free from touch, or soyle with her
As she from one vngot.
    Duke. We did beleeue no lesse.
Know you that Frier *Lodowick* that she speakes of?
    Peter. I know him for a man diuine and holy,   2515
Not scuruy, nor a temporary medler
As he's reported by this Gentleman:
And on my trust, a man that neuer yet
Did (as he vouches) mis-report your Grace.
    Luc. My Lord, most villanously, beleeue it.   2520
    Peter. Well: he in time may come to cleere himselfe;
But at this instant he is sicke, my Lord:
Of a strange Feauor: vpon his meere request   (G5ᵃ
Being come to knowledge, that there was complaint
Intended 'gainst Lord *Angelo*, came I hether   2525
To speake as from his mouth, what he doth know

2513–14 *Lines ending* believe . . . Lodowick? HAN1
2514 that she speakes of] which she speakes of F2-THEO2, WARB-RANN; *om.*
HAN1
2518 trust] truth mTBY3 *conj.,* COLNE, COL2
2520 My . . . villanously,] My lord, most villainously he did; HAN1; He did, my
lord, most villainously; KTLY
2523 vpon] On POPE1-JOHN2
2525 'gainst] against F2-ROWE3

2511 **touch**] *OED* (*sb.* 1b): "Sexual contact." See n. 1513.
2512 **vngot**] See JOHNSON (1755): "Not begotten." *OED* (*ppl. a.* 2): Only
quotation in this sense.
2516 **scuruy**] M. S. (1795, p. 647): Sh. may have recollected Acts 24:5, "a
pestilent fellowe, and a mouer of sedition."
    temporary] JOHNSON (ed. 1765): "It may stand for *temporal:* the sense will
then be, *I know him for a holy man, one that meddles not with* secular *affairs:* It may mean
temporising." *OED* (*a.* 2): "= *Temporal,"* " 'not a meddler with temporal or secular
affairs'," first use in this sense.
2519 **vouches**] *OED* (*v.* 4): "To allege, assert," quoting 2705. See n. 1170.
2523 **strange Feauor**] WILLIAMS (1862, 1:442, 849): "Allusions to new, *i.e.*
strange, diseases, are not unfrequent in early writers." Cf. "tis a strange Feauer" in
Beaumont & Fletcher, *A King and No King* (4.2.106–7). See 1227 and n., 2060 and
n. SCHMIDT (1875): "Extraordinary." See *OED* (*a.* 7) "Unknown" and (9) "Excep-
tionally great."
    his meere request] STEEVENS (Var. 1778): "His *absolute* request." MALONE
(ed. 1790): *"Solely, entirely* upon his request" (*OED, a.* ² 2). CLARKE (ed. 1864):
" 'Particular request'."

Is true, and false: And what he with his oath
And all probation will make vp full cleare
Whensoeuer he's conuented: First for this woman,
To iustifie this worthy Noble man   2530
So vulgarly and personally accus'd,
Her shall you heare disproued to her eyes,
Till she her selfe confesse it.
   Duk. Good Frier, let's heare it:
Doe you not smile at this, Lord *Angelo?*   2535
Oh heauen, the vanity of wretched fooles.
Giue vs some seates, Come cosen *Angelo*,
In this I'll be impartiall: be you Iudge

2527 and] or HAN1   what he with] he with ROWE2, ROWE3; he upon POPE,
HAN1
   2528 And] By POPE1-v1773 (−CAP)
   2529 Whensoeuer] Whenever POPE1-RANN (−CAP)   conuented] convened
ROWE3; conven'd POPE, THEO, HAN1
   2530 Noble man] Nobleman F2+
   2534 *Officers bear off* ISABELLA; *and* MARIANA *comes forward.* CAP, MAL-WH2,
CAM2-ARD1 (*subst.*); *Exit Isabella, guarded.* IRV, NLSN, KIT1, ALEX, EVNS (*subst.*);
[*Isabella withdraws, guarded.*] *Enter Mariana.* PEL1, PEN2
   2536 Oh] Ah F4-ROWE2
   2538 I'll be impartiall] I will be partial mTBY1 *and* THEOBALD (1729) *conj.*,
THEO, HAN1, JOHN1-v1773

   2528 **probation**] SCHMIDT (1875): "Proof" (*OED, sb.* 4).
   make vp] See *OED* (*v.* [1] 96c [*a*]): "Fill up what is wanting to."
   2529 **Whensoeuer**] KÖKERITZ (1953, p. 324): Pronounced whensoe'er.
   conuented] WARBURTON (ed. 1747): "To cite, or summons" (*OED, v.* 3,
"Summon").
   2531 **vulgarly**] THIRLBY (1733-47): "Perhaps it means, openly." JOHNSON
(ed. 1765): "Meaning either, so *grosly,* with such *indecency* of invective, or by so *mean*
and inadequate witnesses." STEEVENS (Var. 1778): *"Publickly."* CLARKE (ed. 1864):
"Used here in its sense of publicly (Latin, *vulgo*), and in that of coarsely. An instance
of Shakespeare's way of combining varied meanings in one word." *OED* (*adv.* 3):
"Publicly; in the eyes of the world," quoting in this sense only *MM* and Jonson's
Poetaster, 3.3.21.
   2532 **to her eyes**] THIRLBY (1747-53): Cf. 2233: see n. JOHNSON (1755): *Eye,*
"front; face." SCHMIDT (1874): "To the face," as in *2H4* 3.1.64 (1482).
   2538 **impartiall**] THEOBALD (1729, in NICHOLS, 1817, 2:291): "Surely this
Duke had odd notions of impartiality, to commit the decision of a cause to the person
accused of being criminal. . . . Sure, it should be,—In this I will be *partial."* SEYMOUR
(1805, 1:103-4): " 'I'll be indifferent, I'll take no part in the cause'." This has been
generally accepted, as by Collier, Halliwell, Dyce, Schmidt, Onions, Leisi, and Lever.
   2538-9 **Iudge . . . Cause**] TILLEY (M341) and WILSON (p. 415): "No man
ought to be judge in his own cause." Cf. *TN* 5.1.362-3 (2524-5); *Oth.* 1.3.67-9
(404-6). See n. 2214.

Of your owne Cause: Is this the Witnes Frier?

               Enter Mariana.   2540

First, let her shew your face, and after, speake.
  Mar. Pardon my Lord, I will not shew my face
Vntill my husband bid me.
  Duke. What, are you married?
  Mar. No my Lord.   2545
  Duke. Are you a Maid?
  Mar. No my Lord.
  Duk. A Widow then?
  Mar. Neither, my Lord.
  Duk. Why you are nothing then: neither Maid, Wi- 2550
dow, nor Wife?
  Luc. My Lord, she may be a Puncke: for many of
them, are neither Maid, Widow, nor Wife.
  Duk. Silence that fellow: I would he had some cause
to prattle for himselfe.   2555

2539 Isabella *is carried off, guarded.* THEO1-RANN (−CAP), RLTR
    2540 SCENE III. POPE, HAN1, WARB, JOHN   *Enter Mariana.*] *Enter* Mariana
veil'd. ROWE1-RANN (−CAP), RLTR, NLSN, KIT1, ALEX, ARD2, EVNS; *Mariana advances, veiled.* IRV, CAM3, SIS (*subst.*)
    2541 your] her F2+
    2543–4 *One verse line* v1793-STAU (−SING), KTLY-HUD2, CAM3, ARD2
    2545–51 *Verse lines ending* lord. . . . you . . . wife? v1793-v1821, SING, KNT, COL, HAL, DYCE, WH1, KTLY, DEL4, HUD2; lord. . . . lord. . . . wife? STAU
    2546 Maid] maid then KTLY
    2548 A] *Om.* CAP
    2550–3 *Verse lines ending* then? . . . wife? . . . them . . . wife. CAP-RANN
    2550 Why] What, CAP   you are] are you F2-v1773   then:] ∼ ? F4-v1773
    2551, 2553 nor] or JOHN2
    2551 Wife?] ∼ . JOHN, v1773, ALEX; ∼ ! ARD2
    2554–5 *Verse lines ending* cause . . . himself. mTBY1 *conj.*, CAP+ (−ARD2)

    2541 your] F2 corrects to *her.*
    2550–1 **neither . . . Wife**] THIRLBY (1733–47) quotes Ray's *Proverbs:* "She is neither wife, widow, nor maid" (1678, p. 90). See also TILLEY (M26) and WILSON (p. 499). HART (ed. 1905): Cf. *1 Promos,* 4.3 (p. 329 below): "I monster now, no mayde nor wife, haue stoupte to *Promos* lust." FELVER (1960, pp. 385–7): Cf. Robert Armin, *Quips upon Questions* (1600; ed. 1875, sig. E1ᵛ): "Nor mayde, wife, widdow, but a common whore."
    2552 **Puncke**] *OED* (*sb.*¹): "Harlot," first recorded in 1596. Lucio objects in 2921 to "Marrying a punke."
    2554 **would**] See n. 17.

Luc. Well my Lord.

Mar. My Lord, I doe confesse I nere was married,
And I confesse besides, I am no Maid,
I haue known my husband, yet my husband
Knowes not, that euer he knew me.   2560
Luc. He was drunk then, my Lord, it can be no better.
Duk. For the benefit of silence, would thou wert so to.
Luc. Well, my Lord.
Duk. This is no witnesse for Lord *Angelo.*
Mar. Now I come to't, my Lord.   2565
Shee that accuses him of Fornication,
In selfe-same manner, doth accuse my husband,
And charges him, my Lord, with such a time,
When I'le depose I had him in mine Armes
With all th'effect of Loue.   2570
Ang. Charges she moe then me?
Mar. Not that I know.
Duk. No? you say your husband.
Mar. Why iust, my Lord, and that is *Angelo*,
Who thinkes he knowes, that he nere knew my body,   2575
But knowes, he thinkes, that he knowes *Isabels.*

2559–60 *Lines ending* not . . . me. POPE1-ARD1 (−CAM1, GLO, WH2, CAM2),
CAM3, KIT1, SIS
    2570–3 *Lines ending* love. . . . more . . . me? . . . know. . . . husband. HAN1; me?
. . . husband. v1793-STAU, KTLY; love. . . . know. . . . husband. CAM, GLO, DYCE2,
DYCE3, HUD2 +
    2571 moe] more ROWE1-IRV, ARD1, PEN2
    2572 know] know of CAP, KTLY
    2573 No?] *Om.* HAN1   husband.] — ? WH1, PEL1, PEN2
    2576 knowes, he thinkes,] — ˄ ∼ — ∼ ˄ KNT, DYCE, STAU-GLO, HUD2-ALEX
(−CAM3), PEL1, EVNS; ∼ , ∼ — ∼ ˄ HAL   he knowes] he knew mTBY1 *conj.*,
HAN1, SING, KTLY, DYCE2, DYCE3, HUD2

    2559 **known**] SCHMIDT (1874): "To have sexual commerce with" (*OED, v.* 7,
which quotes 2575).
    2560 **Knowes not**] HUNTER (1959, p. 142): Cf. *AWW* 5.3.291-2 (3024-5).
      euer] Pronounced *e'er.* Cf. 2420.
    2561 **no**] See *OED* (*adv.* ²): "With comparatives: Not any, not at all (better,
etc.)."
    2562 **would**] See n. 1664.
    2564 **witnesse**] See *OED* (*sb.* 2): "Testimony, evidence."
    2570 **effect**] SCHMIDT (1874): "Manifestation" (*OED, sb.* 3). See n. 1227.
    2571 **moe**] See *OED* (Mo quasi-*sb.* 3): "Other persons."
    2574 **iust**] HART (ed. 1905): "True, as in [1279]." EVANS (ed. 1974): "Just so,
exactly" (*OED, adv.* 3).
    2575 **knew**] See n. 2559.

Ang. This is a strange abuse: Let's see thy face.

Mar. My husband bids me, now I will vnmaske.

This is that face, thou cruell *Angelo*

Which once thou sworst, was worth the looking on: 2580

This is the hand, which with a vowd contract

Was fast belockt in thine: This is the body

That tooke away the match from *Isabell*,

And did supply thee at thy garden-house

In her Imagin'd person.   2585

Duke. Know you this woman?

Luc. Carnallie she saies.

Duk. Sirha, no more.   (G5

Luc. Enough my Lord.

Ang. My Lord, I must confesse, I know this woman,   2590

And fiue yeres since there was some speech of marriage

Betwixt my selfe, and her: which was broke off,

Partly for that her promis'd proportions

Came short of Composition: But in chiefe

2578 *Unveiling.* ROWE1+ (−CAP, WH1)

2589 my Lord] *Om.* HAN1

2593 promis'd] promised ROWE1+ (−HAL)

2594 Came] Come F4

2577 **abuse**] JOHNSON (ed. 1765): *"Deception,* or *puzzle.* So in *Macbeth"* (3.4.142 [1425]). CLARKE (ed. 1864): "Delusion; attempted abusion of our belief " (*OED, sb.* 4, "Imposture, deceit; delusion"). See nn. 2509, 2624.

2582 **fast**] See n. 239.

     belockt] JOHNSON (1755): "To fasten, as with a lock." *OED (v.):* Intensive for *lock,* only quotation.

2583 **match**] RANN (ed. 1786): "Assignation." See *OED (sb.* 1 11): "Appointment."

2584 **supply**] DELIUS (ed. 1860): Cf. *Oth.* 4.1.28 (2401). *OED (v.* 1 8): "Satisfy."

     garden-house] MALONE (1783, p. 6): "A *garden-house* in the time of our author was usually appropriated to purposes of intrigue. So, in [Guilpin,] *Skialetheia,* 1598 [sig. B8ᵛ]; *The London Prodigall,* 1605 [*Sh. Apoc.,* 5.1.86]." REED (in Var. 1785): "See . . . *Stubbes's Anatomie of Abuses,* 4to, 1597, p. 57" (and *N.S.S.* ed., p. 88, with notes). NARES (1822) and HALLIWELL (ed. 1854) quote many instances. *OED* (1): "Any small building in a garden; a summer-house."

2593, 2595 **for that**] Because (*OED,* For that *conj.* 1).

2593–4 **her . . . Composition**] JOHNSON (ed. 1765): "Her fortune which was promised *proportionate* to mine, fell short of the *composition,* that is, contract or bargain" (*OED,* 22). DELIUS (ed. 1860): Perhaps Sh. uses *proportions* simply for *portion,* dowry (*OED, sb.* 1). LEVER (ed. 1965): Her "marriage portion . . . proved insufficient for the agreement to be confirmed." See n. 98.

For that her reputation was dis-valued   2595
In leuitie: Since which time of fiue yeres
I neuer spake with her, saw her, nor heard from her
Vpon my faith, and honor.
   Mar. Noble Prince,
As there comes light from heauen, and words frō breath,   2600
As there is sence in truth, and truth in vertue,
I am affianced this mans wife, as strongly
As words could make vp vowes: And my good Lord,
But Tuesday night last gon, in's garden house,
He knew me as a wife. As this is true,   2605
Let me in safety raise me from my knees,
Or else for euer be confixed here
A Marble Monument.
   Ang. I did but smile till now,
Now, good my Lord, giue me the scope of Iustice,   2610
My patience here is touch'd: I doe perceiue
These poore informall women, are no more

2597 with her, saw her, nor] with, saw, or HAN1
2599 *Kneeling.* COL3, IRV, CAM3
2612 informall] informing GIL, HAN1

2595 **dis-valued**] JOHNSON (1755): "To undervalue; to set a low price upon."
CAPELL (1779, 1:glossary, 20): "Lessen'd in Value." *OED (v.):* "Depreciate, dispar-
age," first use; the noun is first recorded from *Seianus,* 3.403.
   2596 **leuitie**] See *OED* (Levity[1] 3c): "Unbecoming freedom of conduct (said esp.
of women)," a sense first recorded in 1601. See nn. 933, 2658-9.
   of] During, for (*OED, prep.* 53).
   2597 **neuer**] See n. 868.
   2600 **frō**] From, so printed because the line is full. Cf. 170.
   2601 **sence**] *OED* (*sb.* 28): "What is wise or reasonable." EMPSON (1951, p.
278): "There is meaning in a true statement. . . . The kind of truth that is in virtue
seems rather to be constancy or correspondence to natural law." LEVER (ed. 1965):
"Meaning, significance."
   2607 **confixed**] JOHNSON (1755): "To fix down; to fasten." *OED (v.):* "Fix
firmly, fasten," first quotation.
   2609 **smile**] NOSWORTHY (ed. 1969): "Angelo's smile has already been mentioned at [950; and see 2535]." Cf. *Ham.* 1.5.108 (793) and *Lr.* 2.2.79-88 (1146-
55).
   2610 **scope**] JOHNSON (ed. 1765): "Full extent." See n. 73.
   2611 **touch'd**] SCHMIDT (1875): "To move, to rouse" (*OED, v.* 24). LEVER (ed.
1965): "Injured, hurt."
   2612 **informall**] THIRLBY (1723-33): Cf. *formall* in *Err.* 5.1.105 (1574). WAR-
BURTON (ed. 1747): "Out of method, ill concerted." JOHNSON (1755): "Offering
an information; accusing." IDEM (ed. 1765, 8:Ii1): "I think, upon further enquiry,

But instruments of some more mightier member
That sets them on. Let me haue way, my Lord
To finde this practise out.   2615
    Duke. I, with my heart,
And punish them to your height of pleasure.
Thou foolish Frier, and thou pernicious woman
Compact with her that's gone: thinkst thou, thy oathes,
Though they would swear downe each particular Saint,   2620
Were testimonies against his worth, and credit
That's seald in approbation? you, Lord *Escalus*
Sit with my Cozen, lend him your kinde paines
To finde out this abuse, whence 'tis deriu'd.
There is another Frier that set them on,   2625
Let him be sent for.
    Peter. Would he were here, my Lord, for he indeed
Hath set the women on to this Complaint;
Your Prouost knowes the place where he abides,

2613 mightier] mighty POPE, HAN1
2617 to] unto POPE1-JOHN2, v1773-v1821, SING, KNT, WH, COL3, KTLY, DYCE2, DYCE3, HUD2, NLSN, KIT1; even to CAP
2621 against] gainst F2-v1773 (−CAP), DYCE2, DYCE3, HUD2, KIT1

---

that *informal* signifies *incompetent, not qualified to give testimony."* STEEVENS (Var. 1773): *"Out of their senses."* Cf. *formall* in *Ant.* 2.5.41 (1074). *OED* (*a.* 2): "? Disordered in mind," only use in this sense. BALD (ed. 1956): "Rash, turbulent."
    2613 **more mightier**] See n. 756.
        member] *OED* (*sb.* 4b): "Person." LEVER (ed. 1965): "Participant in a cause: cf. *2H4,* IV. i. 171 [2037]. Angelo claims to suspect a political intrigue. Cf. [2474–5]."
    2615 **practise**] See n. 2475.
    2619 **Compact**] JOHNSON (1755): "To league with." SCHMIDT (1874): "Confederated, leagued," as in *Lr.* (F) 2.2.125 (1194); accented on second syllable. *OED* (*ppl. a.* [2]): "Leagued," quoting only Samuel Daniel and this.
    2620 STEEVENS (Var. 1793): Cf. *Ant.* 1.3.28 (335).
        each particular] See n. 2298.
    2622 **seald**] JOHNSON (ed. 1765): "When any thing subject to counterfeits is tried by the proper officers and approved, a stamp or *seal* is put upon it, as among us on plate, weights and measures. So the Duke says that *Angelo's* faith has been tried, *approved* and *seal'd* in testimony of that *approbation,* and, like other things so *sealed,* is no more to be called in question." HUDSON (ed. 1880): "Having *a ratified approval* or *a certified attestation;* or as *being proved beyond question.* The sealing of a bond or contract is that which *finishes* it, or gives it full force and validity." See nn. 271, 1775.
    2623 **lend**] See n. 22.
    2624 **abuse**] SCHMIDT (1874): "Offence, insult, injury." More likely "imposture, deceit": see nn. 2509, 2577.
    2627 **Would**] See n. 1664.

And he may fetch him.   2630
   Duke. Goe, doe it instantly:
And you, my noble and well-warranted Cosen
Whom it concernes to heare this matter forth,
Doe with your iniuries as seemes you best
In any chastisement; I for a while   2635
Will leaue you; but stir not you till you haue
Well determin'd vpon these Slanderers.   *Exit.*
   Esc. My Lord, wee'll doe it throughly: Signior *Lu-*
cio, did not you say you knew that Frier *Lodowick* to be a
dishonest person?   2640
   Luc. Cucullus non facit Monachum, honest in nothing
but in his Clothes, and one that hath spoke most villa-
nous speeches of the Duke.
   Esc. We shall intreat you to abide heere till he come,

2630–1 *One line* DYCE1, STAU+
  2631 Goe,] *Om.* POPE, HAN1   *Exit* Provost. CAP, MAL-PEL1, PEN2, EVNS;
Exit an Attendant. ARD2
  2635–7 *Lines ending* while . . . well . . . slanderers. THEO, WARB-SING1, COL,
SING2-STAU, KTLY, WH2, PEN2; leave you; . . . determined . . . slanderers. mTBY1
and SPEDDING *in* CAM1 *conj.*, CAM1, GLO, CAM2, ARD1, NLSN, SIS; leave you;
. . . determin'd . . . throughly. (*including part of* 2638 *as verse*) DYCE2, DEL4, DYCE3,
HUD2, IRV, BUL, CAM3-ALEX, ARD2, EVNS
  2636 leaue you] leave PEN2   but] *Om.* JOHN, v1773, v1778
  2637 Well determin'd] Determin'd well HAN1   *Exit.*] *Exit* Duke. *after*
throughly. (2638) CAP, MAL+
  2638 SCENE IV. POPE, HAN1, WARB   throughly] thoroughly v1778-v1821
(−MAL), SING, KNT, COL, KTLY, DEL4, IRV, ARD1   Escalus, *and* Angelo, *seat*
themselves. CAP, IRV, CAM3
  2642 hath] has JOHN2

  2632 **well-warranted**] *OED* (*ppl. a.*): "Approved by good warrant," first use.
See n. 1630.
  2633 **to . . . forth**] JOHNSON (1755): *Forth*, "Throughly; from beginning to
end." IDEM (ed. 1765): "To hear it to the end; to search it to the bottom" (*OED*,
Forth *adv.* 8).
  2634 **seemes you**] It seems to you (*OED*, *v.* [2] 8c, e).
  2637 **determin'd**] SCHMIDT (1874): "To decide" (*OED*, 5).
  2638 **throughly**] Thoroughly (*OED*, *adv.* 1).
  2640 **dishonest**] SCHMIDT (1874): "Dishonourable." See n. 1358.
  2641 *Cucullus . . . monachum*] THEOBALD (MS n. in F2): Cf. *TN* 1.5.62 (347–8)
and *H8* 3.1.23 (1643). GREY (1754, 2:81) also cites *TN.* WHITE (ed. 1857): "The
cowl does not make the monk." SYMONS (in IRVING & MARSHALL, ed. 1889): Cf.
1 Promos, 3.6 (p. 326 below): "A holie Hoode, makes not a Frier deuoute." See
TILLEY (H586) and WILSON (p. 152). LEVER (ed. 1965): "There is irony, for the
hood of the Duke's disguise does not make him the friar Lucio takes him to be."
  2641–2 **honest . . . Clothes**] Honorable in nothing but in his friar's habit.

and inforce them against him: we shall finde this Frier a   2645
notable fellow.
  Luc. As any in *Vienna*, on my word.
  Esc. Call that same *Isabell* here once againe, I would
speake with her: pray you, my Lord, giue mee leaue to
question, you shall see how Ile handle her.   2650
  Luc. Not better then he, by her owne report.
  Esc. Say you?
  Luc. Marry sir, I thinke, if you handled her priuately
She would sooner confesse, perchance publikely she'll be   (G5ᵛ
asham'd.   2655

                    Enter Duke, Prouost, Isabella.

  Esc. I will goe darkely to worke with her.
  Luc. That's the way: for women are light at midnight.

  2649 *Exit an Attendant. (after* her:) DYCE, STAU-GLO, DEL4, HUD2+ (−CAM3,
SIS)
  2654 would] should F2-RANN (−CAP)   she'll] she'ld F4, ROWE, POPE, HAN1
  2656 SCENE V. JOHN   *Enter . . .*] *Enter* Duke *in the Friar's Habit,* Provost
and Isabella. ROWE1-SING2, WH1, COL3, KTLY, KNT3, COL4, NLSN, KIT1, ALEX,
PEL1+ (*subst.*); *the same after* 2659 CAM1, GLO, WH2, CAM2; *after* 2659 *Re-enter*
Officers *with* ISABELLA. DYCE, STAU, DEL4, HUD2, IRV, BUL, ARD1 (*subst.*); *after*
2661 *The* PROVOST *approaches, with the* DUKE *in his friar's habit* CAM3, SIS; *after* 2666
Re-enter Duke *disguised as a friar, and* Provost. DYCE, STAU, DEL4, HUD2, IRV, BUL,
ARD1

  2645 **inforce**] DYCE (1867): *"Enforce,* to press, to urge strongly" (*OED, v.* 4).
  2646 **notable**] SCHMIDT (1875): "Remarkable, egregious (oftener in a bad than
in a good sense)." WHITE (ed. 1883): "Notorious." *OED* (*a.* 1) quotes Dekker,
2 Honest Whore, 1.1.65: "This *Lodouico,* is a notable tounged fellow."
  2648 **would**] See n. 17.
  2650 **handle**] JOHNSON (1755): "To practise upon; to do with." SCHMIDT
(1874): "Treat" (*OED, v.*¹ 5b, "Deal with, treat").
  2653 **handled**] COLMAN (1974, p. 197): "To fondle." Lucio's double meanings
are obvious.
  2657 **darkely**] SCHMIDT (1874): "Obscurely." CAMPBELL (ed. 1949): "Secretly." See n. 1663.
  2658-9 **women . . . midnight**] SCHMIDT (1874): Play on *light* "bright" and
light "wanton." See nn. 933, 2596. ROLFE (ed. 1882): Cf. *MV* 5.1.129 (2551).
DAVENPORT (1954, p. 20): Cf. Lyly, *Campaspe,* 4.1.20-1. LEVER (ed. 1965): "Apparently a stock adage, though not in Tilley; e.g. Marston, *Antonio and Mellida*
[2.1.151-4]; Middleton, *A Mad World My Masters* [5.1.81-2]; Webster, *Appius and
Virginia* [3.1.13-14; and *Dutchesse of Malfy,* 4.1.48-50]."

Esc. Come on Mistris, here's a Gentlewoman,   2660
Denies all that you haue said.
   Luc. My Lord, here comes the rascall I spoke of,
'Here, with the *Prouost*.
   Esc. In very good time: speake not you to him, till
we call vpon you.   2665
   Luc. Mum.
   Esc. Come Sir, did you set these women on to slan-
der Lord *Angelo?* they haue confes'd you did.
   Duk. 'Tis false.
   Esc. How? Know you where you are?   2670
   Duk. Respect to your great place; and let the diuell
Be sometime honour'd, for his burning throne.
Where is the *Duke?* 'tis he should heare me speake.
   Esc. The *Duke's* in vs: and we will heare you speake,
Looke you speake iustly.   2675

2660–1 *Prose* F2+
2662–3 *Prose* POPE1+ (−CAM3)
2663–5 *Verse lines ending* time: . . . upon you. CAM3
2671 and] then, COL3
2672 sometime] sometimes MAL, SING, KTLY
2674 we] he SING1
2675–6 *One line* v1793-v1821, KNT, COL, HAL, WH1, DEL4, ARD1, CAM3

2660–3 Prose set as verse.
2661 **Denies**] Who denies. See n. 758.
2664 **In . . . time**] At just the right moment (*OED,* Time *sb.* 42c [*c*]).
2666 **Mum**] JENTE (1926, p. 428) and TILLEY (N279, W767): "I will say nothing (nought) but mum," "No word but mum."
2671–2 MALONE (1783, p. 6): "I believe a line preceding this has been lost." HALLIWELL (ed. 1854): "This is spoken in great indignation. Respect to your high dignity or position indeed!—you might as well respect the devil for his burning throne!" ROLFE (ed. 1882): "This seems to be spoken with a touch of irony. Malone suspected that a line had been lost before this; but the connection is clear enough: yes, I know where I am, and the respect due to your *office* at least."
2672 **sometime**] Occasionally (*OED, adv.* 1).
   for] LEISI (ed. 1964): "F1 does not always distinguish between *for* and *'fore* 'afore', 'in front of' "; cf. *AWW* 4.4.3 (2443) *for whose throne,* "where modern editions have *'fore.*"
   burning throne] EBSWORTH (1886, 6:556): Cf. "his burning throne" in Marlowe, *Hero and Leander* (1598), 1.7. WILLCOCK (1915, pp. 27–8): Cf. Jude 8–9.
2673 **should**] Who should. See n. 758.
2675 **Looke**] See n. 715.

255

Duk. Boldly, at least. But oh poore soules,
Come you to seeke the Lamb here of the Fox;
Good night to your redresse: Is the *Duke* gone?
Then is your cause gone too: The *Duke's* vniust,
Thus to retort your manifest Appeale,   2680
And put your triall in the villaines mouth,
Which here you come to accuse.
   Luc. This is the rascall: this is he I spoke of.
   Esc. Why thou vnreuerend, and vnhallowed Fryer:
Is't not enough thou hast suborn'd these women,   2685
To accuse this worthy man? but in foule mouth,
And in the witnesse of his proper eare,

2676 at least] at least I'll speak HAN1
2677 Fox;] F1; ⁓ , HAL, DYCE1, ALEX, EVNS; ⁓ ? F2 *etc.*
2679 gone] *Om.* ROWE
2680 retort] reject mTBY2 *conj.,* COLNE, COL2
2686 in] with THEO, WARB, JOHN

   2677 LEVER (ed. 1965): "Proverbial, from Erasmus' adage 'ovem lupo com-misisti [you have entrusted the sheep to the wolf]' (Tilley W 602). Shakespeare substitutes 'fox' for the usual 'wolf' (cf. *2H6,* III. i. 253 [1555], *Gent.,* IV. iv. [97 (1911)]." WILSON (1970, p. 907) notes that the Latin is from Terence, *Eunuchus,* 5.1.16.
   2678 **Good night**] SCHMIDT (1875, p. 772): "Farewell for ever."
   2679 **cause**] See n. 2214.
   2680 **retort**] JOHNSON (ed. 1765): "To *refer back* to *Angelo* the cause in which you *appealed* from *Angelo* to the *Duke.*" CLARKE (ed. 1864): "Answer by throwing back, casting into other jurisdiction." *OED* (*v.*¹ 7a): "Reject or refuse," only use in this sense. WILSON (ed. 1922): "N.E.D. explains as 'reject', but the Duke had not rejected the appeal. The meaning clearly is the etymological one, i.e. 'to twist or turn back' (from himself to Angelo)."
   manifest] SCHMIDT (1875): "Public." LEVER (ed. 1965): "Obvious (in its justice)" (*OED, a.* 1).
   Appeale] JOHNSON (1755): "Accusation" (*OED, sb.* 1c). SCHMIDT (1874): "Reference to a superior judge" (*OED, sb.* 3).
   2682 **Which**] Whom (ABBOTT §265).
   2684 **vnreuerend, and vnhallowed**] SCHMIDT (1875): *"Unreverend* or *Unrever-ent* (used indiscriminately . . .) irreverent." *Unhallowed,* "unholy, impious, wicked." [Cf. Montaigne (1603), bk. 2, ch. 12 (Everyman's ed., 2:234): "Note how some prevaile with this kinde of unreverent and unhallowed speech."]
   2687 **witnesse**] See n. 2564.
   proper] See n. 220.

To call him villaine; and then to glance from him,
To th'*Duke* himselfe, to taxe him with Iniustice?
Take him hence; to th'racke with him: we'll towze you   2690
Ioynt by ioynt, but we will know his purpose:
What? vniust?
    Duk. Be not so hot: the *Duke* dare
No more stretch this finger of mine, then he
Dare racke his owne: his Subiect am I not,   2695
Nor here Prouinciall: My businesse in this State
Made me a looker on here in *Vienna*,
Where I haue seene corruption boyle and bubble,

2688–95 *Lines ending as* F1, *then* unjust? . . . stretch . . . own: . . . not, POPE, THEO,
WARB; *as* F1, *then* unjust? . . . Duke . . . he . . . not, HAN1; villain; . . . himself,
. . . hence; . . . by joint, . . . unjust? . . . stretch . . . own: . . . not, JOHN; *as* JOHN,
then duke . . . he . . . not, CAP-SING1, DEL4, ARD1, CAM3; *as* F1, *then* duke . . . he
. . . not, KNT, CAM1, GLO, DYCE2, DYCE3, HUD2-BUL, NLSN, KIT1+; *as* F1, *then*
dare . . . he . . . not, DYCE1, WH1; him . . . injustice? . . . by joint, . . . unjust?
. . . duke . . . he . . . not, HAL; him . . . injustice? . . . you . . . What! . . . dare
. . . he . . . not, KTLY
    2688 to glance] glance POPE1-THEO4
    2690 we'll] Well ROWE2-POPE1   you] him. BLACKSTONE *conj. in* v1785,
WH2
    2691 Ioynt] Ev'n joint HAN1   his] this HAN1, CAP, v1778-SING1; your JOHN,
v1773, COL2, COL3, KTLY, DYCE2, DYCE3-HUD2
    2692 What?] What? He HAN1, HUD2   vniust] *In quotation marks* CAM, GLO,
WH2, BUL, NLSN-ALEX, EVNS
    2693 hot] hot, sir KTLY
    2695 am I] I am v1773-RANN

    2688 **glance**] SCHMIDT (1874): "Dart aside from the object first aimed at." *OED*
(*v.* ¹ 3): "Pass quickly *over, glide from.*" HART (ed. 1905): "To hit obliquely, to glide
off from something and hit." LEISI (ed. 1964): "A fine example of a 'full' meaning:
it contains not only the elements 'look' and 'hint' but also the image of an arrow which
ricochets from the first and hits the second person."
    2689 **taxe**] See n. 1087.
    2690 **towze**] JOHNSON (1755): "To pull; to tear; to haul; to drag." *OED* (*v.* 1b):
"To pull out of joint, to rack," only use in this sense.
    2691 **his purpose**] BOSWELL (Var. 1821): "I see no necessity for altering the old
reading. Escalus says to the supposed Friar, 'We'll touze you joint by joint', and
addresses the close of the sentence not to him, but the by-standers."
    2696 **Prouinciall**] JOHNSON (1755): "Relating to a province." IDEM (ed.
1765): "*Accountable.* The meaning seems to be, I am not one of his natural subjects,
nor of any dependent province." MASON (1785, p. 43): "The Duke . . . could not
punish him by his own authority, as he was not his subject, nor through that of the
superior, as he was not of that province." DYCE (1867): "Subject to the ecclesiastical
authorities of this province" (*OED, a.* 1).
    2698–9 **boyle . . . Stew**] STEEVENS (Var. 1793): "I fear that, in the present

Till it ore-run the Stew: Lawes, for all faults,
But faults so countenanc'd, that the strong Statutes 2700
Stand like the forfeites in a Barbers shop,
As much in mocke, as marke.

2702–8 *Lines ending* mark. . . . prison. . . . *Lucio?* . . . of ? . . . baldpate: . . . me?
POPE1-v1773 (− CAP), CAM3; *the same* 2702–6, *then prose* v1778-WH2, CAM2-NLSN,
KIT1-PEL1, PEN2; mark. . . . prison! *then prose* IRV; state! . . . prison! . . . Lucio?
. . . of ? *then prose* ARD2; state! . . . vouch . . . man . . . lord. . . . me? EVNS

---

instance, our author's metaphor is from the kitchen. So, in *Macbeth*" (4.1.19 [1546]).
HUDSON (ed. 1880): *Stew,* "a brothel or house of prostitution. And there is a
comparison implied between such a house and a cauldron, like that of the Weird
Sisters in *Macbeth,* in which the hell-broth or devil-soup of corruption bubbles and
foams, till the cauldron *boils over,* and floods the surroundings." *OED* (Stew *sb.* 2 1):
"A vessel for boiling, a caldron."

    2701 **forfeites**] WARBURTON (in HANMER, ed. 1743): *"It is a custom in the shops
of all mechanicks to make it a forfeiture for any stranger to use or take up the tools of their trade:
In a Barber's shop especially, when heretofore Barbers practis'd the under parts of Surgery, their
instruments being of a nice kind and their shops generally full of idle people, there was hung
up a table shewing what particular forfeiture was required for meddling with each instrument."*
KENRICK (1765, pp. 42–3): "Tables of forfeits, hung up in barbers shops, are still
extant in some parts of England; at least I remember to have seen one. . . . These
statutes were in Rhime, and were entitled, *Rules for Seemly Behaviour.* [Quotes rhymes
such as] Who checks the barber in his tale, Must pay for each a pot of ale." MASON
(1785, p. 44): "We see, even at this day, displayed in the shops of barbers, cups full
of blood, and strings of drawn teeth, to shew both the nature and the extent of their
business: These are, I apprehend, what Shakespeare means by the forfeits in a barber's
shop, considering them as mulcts paid by those who have had recourse to him for
relief." Cf. Beaumont, *The Knight of the Burning Pestle,* 3.4. This conjecture misled
many editors. HENLEY (in Var. 1793): "The barber's prohibited implements were
principally his razors. . . . These forfeits were as much in *mock* as *mark,* both because
the barber had no authority of himself to enforce them, and also as they were of a
ludicrous nature. I perfectly remember to have seen them in Devonshire (printed like
King Charles's Rules)." CROFT (1810, p. 5): "The custom still prevails, and the
table-board of the articles hangs behind the door, and are, viz.—To talk of cutting
throats; to weave a piece of hair; to call powder flour; or to meddle with any thing
on the shop board: are held as forfeits." MOOR (1823, p. 133): "Upwards of forty
years ago, I saw a string of such rules at the tonsor's of Alderton." FORBY (1830,
1:119): "They exist to this day in some, perhaps in many village shops. They are
penalties for handling the razors, &c." *OED* (*sb.* 3): "A trivial mulct or fine imposed,"
first example in this sense, quoting Fuller, *Holy and Profane State* (1642), 5.10.78–80:
"No more than the forfeits in a barbers shop, where a Gentlemans pleasure is all the
obligation to pay." HART (ed. 1905) devotes an appendix to arguing that "there is
not an iota of support for the above hypothesis," but in 1908 (p. 64) he finally settles
the matter by finding an earlier reference to the custom in Richard Harvey, *Plaine
Perceuall* (1590, p. 11): "Speake a bloody word in a Barbors shop, you make a
forfet."

    2702 **in mocke, as marke**] JOHNSON (1773): *Mark,* "Notice taken" (*OED,*
sb. 1 20). Cf. 317, "More mock'd, then fear'd."

Esc. Slander to th'State:
Away with him to prison.
Ang. What can you vouch against him Signior *Lucio*?   2705
Is this the man that you did tell vs of?
Luc. 'Tis he, my Lord: come hither goodman bald-
pate, doe you know me?
Duk. I remember you Sir, by the sound of your voice,
I met you at the Prison, in the absence of the *Duke.*   2710
Luc. Oh, did you so? and do you remember what you
said of the *Duke.*
Duk. Most notedly Sir.
Luc. Do you so Sir: And was the *Duke* a flesh-mon-
ger, a foole, and a coward, as you then reported him   2715
to be?
Duk. You must (Sir) change persons with me, ere you
make that my report: you indeede spoke so of him, and
much more, much worse.   (G5vb)
Luc. Oh thou damnable fellow: did not I plucke thee   2720

2709–10 *Verse lines ending* voice: . . . *Duke.* F4, KTLY
2714 Sir:] ∼ ? F4+ (−JOHN2)
2718 indeede] *Om.* POPE2-JOHN2 (−HAN1)

2705 **vouch**] See n. 2519.
2707–8 **goodman baldpate**] LEVER (ed. 1965): " 'Goodman' was a prefix, often ironical, for persons below the rank of gentleman [*OED,* 3b]. 'Baldpate' alludes to the Duke's supposed tonsure as friar (cf. [2733])."
2709 LEVER (ed. 1965): "The Duke is heavily hooded and cannot see or be seen clearly."
2713 **notedly**] SCHMIDT (1875): "With good perception and remembrance, exactly." *OED (adv.):* "Especially, particularly," first quotation.
2714–15 **flesh-monger**] JOHNSON (1755): "One who deals in flesh; a pimp." *OED* (2): "Fornicator," first quotation in this sense.
2715 **coward**] JOHNSON (ed. 1765): "So again afterwards [2899]. . . . But *Lucio* had not, in the former conversation, mentioned *cowardice* among the faults of the *Duke.* —Such failures of memory, are incident to writers more diligent than this poet." HALLIWELL (ed. 1854): "But some such discourse may be supposed to have taken place, when he insists upon walking with him to the lane's end." HART (ed. 1905): "Lucio's accusations against the duke . . . do not include that of cowardice, at least obviously. But what did Lucio mean when he said, 'a shy fellow was the duke; and I believe I know the cause of his withdrawing [1618–20] . . .'? Perhaps this was a hidden reference to his timidity, or to his lack of resolution, in leaving it to a deputy to enforce the laws he had let fall into contempt."
2717 **change**] See n. 397.
2720 **damnable**] JOHNSON (1755): "It is sometimes indecently used in a low and ludicrous sense; odious; pernicious" (*OED, a.* 4).
2720–1 **plucke . . . nose**] See n. 319.

by the nose, for thy speeches?

Duk. I protest, I loue the *Duke*, as I loue my selfe.

Ang. Harke how the villaine would close now, after
his treasonable abuses.

Esc. Such a fellow is not to be talk'd withall: Away   2725
with him to prison: Where is the *Prouost*? away with
him to prison: lay bolts enough vpon him: let him speak
no more: away with those Giglets too, and with the o-
ther confederate companion.

Duk. Stay Sir, stay a while.   2730

Ang. What, resists he? helpe him *Lucio.*

Luc. Come sir, come sir, come sir: foh sir, why you
bald-pated lying rascall: you must be hooded must you?
show your knaues visage with a poxe to you: show your
sheepe-biting face, and be hang'd an houre: will't   2735

2723 close] glose WARBURTON *and* DENT MS *in* HAL *and* WHITE *conj.,* SING2,
DYCE, WH, COL3, KTLY, COL4, HUD2

2729 *The* Provost *lays hands on the* Duke. JOHN1+ (−CAP, CAM1, GLO, CAM2,
BUL, KIT1, SIS)

2730 [*to the* Provost. CAP, CAM1, GLO, IRV-BUL, KIT1, SIS

2735 hang'd^ an houre:] ∼ ; ∼ ∼ ? HAN1   will't] wilt F3, SING1

2723 **would**] See n. 17.

    close] WARBURTON conjectures *glose* in a MS n. in JOHNSON (ed. 1765) at
Folger. HALLIWELL (ed. 1850 and ed. 1854) cites *gloze* from a MS n. in the Dent
copy of F3. WHITE (1854, p. 172) also conjectures *glose*. COLLIER does not mention
it in 1852 or 1853 but in his 1858 ed. asserts that *gloze* is in the Perkins F2. CLARK
& WRIGHT (ed. 1893) cite *glose* from a MS n. in the Long copy of F2 at Pembroke
College, Cambridge. HALLIWELL (ed. 1854): "The meaning of the original seems
to be,—see how the villain would conclude his speeches." CLARKE (ed. 1864.) "This
has been changed to 'gloze'; but Shakespeare here, and elsewhere, uses 'close' to
express 'agree with', 'come round to the same opinion with'." SCHMIDT (1874):
"Come to an agreement . . . (= make his peace, make reparation)." *OED* (*v.* 14):
"Come to terms or agreement." ONIONS (1911): "Take a lower stand, 'climb
down'."

    after] See n. 161.

2724 **abuses**] *OED* (*sb.* 7): "Injurious speech, reviling."

2725 **withall**] See n. 2232.

2728 **Giglets**] HANMER (ed. 1743, 6, glossary): "Wanton Women, Strumpets."
OED (1a): "A lewd, wanton woman."

2729 **companion**] ROLFE (ed. 1882): "Used contemptuously (= fellow)"
(*OED, sb.* ¹ 4).

2732 **foh**] SCHMIDT (1874): "An exclamation of contempt" (*OED,* Faugh
int.).

2734 **a poxe**] See n. 2102.

2735 **sheepe-biting**] JOHNSON (1755): "To use petty thefts." IDEM (ed. 1765):

not off ?

Duk. Thou art the first knaue, that ere mad'st a *Duke.*
First *Prouost*, let me bayle these gentle three:
Sneake not away Sir, for the Fryer, and you,
Must haue a word anon: lay hold on him.   2740

Luc. This may proue worse then hanging.

Duk. What you haue spoke, I pardon: sit you downe,
We'll borrow place of him; Sir, by your leaue:
Ha'st thou or word, or wit, or impudence,
That yet can doe thee office? If thou ha'st   2745

2736 *Pulls off the* Friars *Hood, and discovers the* Duke. ROWE1+
2737 mad'st] made CAP, MAL-HUD2 (−HAL, WH1, CAM1, GLO), ARD1
2742 [*To* Escalus. ROWE1+
2743 [*To* Angelo. HAN1, JOHN1+ (−CAP, WH, NLSN, CAM3, EVNS)   *thrusts*
Angelo *from his Chair, and seats himself in it.* CAP, WH, IRV, RLTR, NLSN, CAM3, EVNS
(*subst.*)
2744 or word] a word THEO4, JOHN
2745 thee] the MAL

"This is intended to be the common language of vulgar indignation." *OED: "Fig.*
thieving, sneaking," first quotation. BALD (ed. 1956): "Currish." LEVER (ed. 1965):
" 'Sheep-biter', i.e. a dog or wolf that attacked sheep, was a common epithet for a
dangerous rogue, especially a sanctimonious one." Cf. *TN* 2.5.6 (1021). EVANS (ed.
1974): "Probably alluding to the fable of the wolf in sheep's clothing."

   be hang'd an houre] FARMER (in Var. 1773, 10:Oo6): "In the *Alchemist*
[5.1.36–7] we meet with 'a man that has been *strangled an hour*'. 'What, Piper, ho!
be *hang'd a-while*', is a line of an old madrigal" [by Thomas Morley: *English Madrigal*
School, ed. Fellowes, 2:89]. HENLEY (1780, p. 22): "The Poet evidently refers to the
ancient mode of punishing by the collistrigium, or the original pillory." GIFFORD
(1816; 1875, 4:153–4): "*Strangled an hour* . . . has no reference to duration of time,
but means simply suffocated. . . . A similar mode of expression occurs in [*MM*]
. . . it is merely a vulgar imprecation—'shew—and be hanged!' " See n. 2098. HART
(ed. 1905): "Go be hanged for a while." LEISI (ed. 1964): " 'A little', probably a
standing joke." See also *Mucedorus* (1598, *Sh. Apoc.*), 3.1.26: "*Clo[wn]*. Euen goe
hang thy selfe halfe an hower."

   2737 **ere**] Ever. See n. 2420.

   2738 **these gentle three**] LEVER (ed. 1965): "Isabella, Mariana, and Friar
Peter."

   2742 **you**] Escalus.

   2743 **him**] Angelo.

   Sir, by your leaue] ABBOTT (§233): "In addressing Angelo, whose seat he
occupies, the Duke . . . begins with ironical politeness, but passes into open contempt"
(with *thou, thee*).

   2744 **Ha'st**] HOWARD-HILL (1972, p. 89): The redundant apostrophes here and
in the next line are characteristic of Crane. See n. 1523 and *was't* in 114, 2758.

   or word, or] See *OED* (Or *conj.*² 3): "*Either . . or.*" See n. 1235.

   2745 **office**] STEEVENS (Var. 1793): "Service" (*OED, sb.* 1).

Rely vpon it, till my tale be heard,
And hold no longer out.
　Ang. Oh, my dread Lord,
I should be guiltier then my guiltinesse,
To thinke I can be vndiscerneable,　　　　　　　　　　　　2750
When I perceiue your grace, like powre diuine,
Hath look'd vpon my passes. Then good Prince,
No longer Session hold vpon my shame,
But let my Triall, be mine owne Confession:
Immediate sentence then, and sequent death,　　　　　　　2755
Is all the grace I beg.
　Duk. Come hither *Mariana*,
Say: was't thou ere contracted to this woman?
　Ang. I was my Lord.
　Duk. Goe take her hence, and marry her instantly.　　　2760

2756–8 *Lines ending* beg. . . . thou . . . woman? (*om.* ere) HAN1; Mariana:—
. . . woman? v1793+
2758 to] with v1785

2747 **hold . . . out**] SCHMIDT (1874, p. 546): "Continue, . . . play your part no longer." ONIONS (1911): "Remain unsubdued, continue or persist" (*OED, v.* 41j).

2750 **vndiscerneable**] JOHNSON (1755): "Invisible." SCHMIDT (1875): "Undiscoverable, not to be seen through." Early uses in *OED* are all from Hooker or other divines.

2751–2 **like . . . passes**] Cf. Gen. 16:13, "Thou God lookest on me."

2752 **passes**] GENTLEMAN (ed. 1773): "Ways." STEEVENS (Var. 1778): "What has past in my administration." CAPELL (1779, 1:glossary, 48): "Goings, Actions, Passages." LUCIUS (1786, p. 359) "Artful devices, deceitful contrivances." SINGER (ed. 1826): "Probably put for *trespasses;* or it may mean *courses* from *passées,* Fr." KNIGHT (ed. 1854, 2:91): "Transactions." HALLIWELL (ed. 1854): "Conditions; or, possibly, though no instance of the word occurs in that sense, faults." CLARKE (ed. 1864): " 'Passages of misconduct', 'evil courses'." SCHMIDT (1875): "Act, proceeding, course." LEE (ed. 1907): "The word here is almost equivalent to 'trespass'. But there is an allusion to the passes (*i. e.,* tricks) of jugglery." *OED* (*sb.* [2] 2): "(?) course of action." WILSON (ed. 1922): " 'Tricks, devices'." WINNY (ed. 1959): "Suggests rather an image from fencing." But Capell and *OED* are prob. right. Cf. Job 34:21: "For his eies are vpon the waies of man, and he seeth all his goings," and Webster, *Dutchesse of Malfy* (1623, 5.3.42–3): "Make scruteny throughout the passes Of your owne life."

2754 HALLIWELL (ed. 1854) quotes *2 Promos,* 3.3 (p. 356 below): "I doe confesse this tale is true, and I deserue thy wrath."

2755 **sequent**] JOHNSON (1755): "Following; succeeding." *OED* (*a.* 2): "That follows as a result."

2756 **Is**] On sing. verb after two nouns see ABBOTT §336.

2758 **was't**] See n. 114.
　ere] Ever. See n. 2420.

Doe you the office (*Fryer*) which consummate,
Returne him here againe: goe with him *Prouost.*   *Exit.*
   Esc. My Lord, I am more amaz'd at his dishonor,
Then at the strangenesse of it.
   Duk. Come hither *Isabell*,   2765
Your *Frier* is now your Prince: As I was then
Aduertysing, and holy to your businesse,
(Not changing heart with habit) I am still,
Atturnied at your seruice.
   Isab. Oh giue me pardon   2770
That I, your vassaile, haue imploid, and pain'd
Your vnknowne Soueraigntie.
   Duk. You are pardon'd *Isabell*:
And now, deere Maide, be you as free to vs.
Your Brothers death I know sits at your heart: 2775

2762 *Exit.*] *Exeunt* Angelo, Mariana *and* Provost. ROWE; *Exeunt* Angelo, Mariana, Peter, *and* Provost. POPE1+
2763 SCENE V. POPE, HAN1, WARB; SCENE VI. JOHN
2764 of it.] of— CAP
2767 and] all HAN1

2761 **office**] See n. 2745.
    consummate] MALONE (1780, 1:103): *"Being* consummated." Cf. *OED (a.* as *pa. pple.):* "Completed."
2767 **Aduertysing**] JOHNSON (1755): "Active in giving intelligence; monitory." IDEM (ed. 1765): "Attentive." HUDSON (ed. 1880): *"Instructing* or *counselling."* Cf. *aduertise* (47). *OED* (*ppl. a.* 1): "Adverting, attending, attentive," only quotation in this sense. See n. 46–7.
    holy] JOHNSON (ed. 1765): "Faithful." SCHMIDT (1874): "Reverend . . . (i. e. in the character of a priest)." HART (ed. 1905): "Devoted." WILSON (ed. 1922): "Dedicated." LEISI (ed. 1964): "The prevailing sense, apart from the religious meaning, is 'virtuous', 'of integrity', as in [1747]. There may be a connotation of 'dedicated to' (OED 3a, 3b)."
2769 **Atturnied**] JOHNSON (1755): "To employ as a proxy." HALLIWELL (ed. 1854): "The Duke merely means to say he is still Isabella's spokesman and agent. A person attorneyed, when he delegated or appointed some other character to act instead of him. The verb is here used in an active sense." HART (ed. 1905): "Employed as your attorney. The verb occurs in a different sense (performed by proxy) in [*WT* 1.1.30 (30)]. . . . This passage has escaped the *New Eng. Dict.,* which gives the [*WT*] reference as the solitary example of the verb."
2771 **vassaile**] SCHMIDT (1875): "Subject."
    pain'd] SCHMIDT (1875): "Put to labour and trouble." *OED* overlooks this sense (cf. *v.* 4 *refl.*).
2774 **free**] JOHNSON (ed. 1765): *"Generous"* (*OED, a.* 21).
2775 **sits**] JOHNSON (1755): "To rest as a weight or burthen." SCHMIDT (1875): "To bear on, to be felt." *OED* (*v.* 14a): "To affect one deeply."

And you may maruaile, why I obscur'd my selfe,
Labouring to saue his life: and would not rather
Make rash remonstrance of my hidden powre,
Then let him so be lost: oh most kinde Maid,
It was the swift celeritie of his death,   2780
Which I did thinke, with slower foot came on,
That brain'd my purpose: but peace be with him,
That life is better life past fearing death,
Then that which liues to feare: make it your comfort,
So happy is your Brother.   2785   (G6

Enter Angelo, Maria, Peter, Prouost.

Isab. I doe my Lord.
Duk. For this new-maried man, approaching here,
Whose salt imagination yet hath wrong'd
Your well defended honor: you must pardon   2790

2778 remonstrance] demonstrance MALONE *conj.,* COL3, STAU, COL4
2779 so be] be so F4-RANN (−CAP)
2780 swift] quick CAP
2782 brain'd] bain'd WARB   but] but now HAN1, DYCE2, DYCE3; but, God's
WALKER (1860, 1:263) *conj.,* HUD2; but, all COL4
2785 So‸] ~ , THEO, WARB-v1785 (−CAP)
2786 SCENE VI. POPE, HAN1, WARB; SCENE VII. JOHN   *Enter . . .*] *After*
2787 DYCE, STAU-ARD2 (−KTLY, KNT3, NLSN, PEL1)   *Maria*] Mariana
ROWE2+
2790 pardon] pardon him HAN1, JOHN1-RANN (−CAP), KTLY

2776 **maruaile**] HARDING (ed. 1954): "Probably to be read 'mar'l'." See
KÖKERITZ (1953), p. 326.
2778 **rash remonstrance**] THIRLBY (1747–53): "Shewing again after conceal-
ment." JOHNSON (1755): "Show; discovery." MASON (1785, p. 44): "A premature
discovery." HUDSON (ed. 1851): "Perhaps we should read *de*monstrance; but the
word may be formed from *remonstrer,* French, *to show again."* DYCE (1867): "A
demonstration, a manifestation, a discovery." Cf. *OED* (*sb.* 2): "Demonstration,
proof, evidence . . . (common in 17th c.)."
2780 **celeritie**] See n. 1974.
2782 **brain'd**] JOHNSON (ed. 1765): "We now use in conversation a like phrase.
This it was that knocked my design on the head." DYCE (1867): "Defeated." *OED* (*v.*
1): "To kill by dashing out the brains," only quotation in fig. sense.
2783–4 **That . . . feare**] THEOBALD (MS n. in F2): Cf. *JC* 2.2.32–3 (1020–1).
Cf. TILLEY (D27): "Better pass a danger once than be always in fear." See nn.
1242–4, 1291.
2785 WILSON (ed. 1922): "That your brother is thus happy." SCHMIDT (1874)
explains *happy* as "contented," but it may mean "fortunate," as in 2350.
2789 **salt**] JOHNSON (1755) and *OED* (*a.*² b): "Lecherous; salacious."

For *Mariana*'s sake: But as he adiudg'd your Brother,
Being criminall, in double violation
Of sacred Chastitie, and of promise-breach,
Thereon dependant for your Brothers life,
The very mercy of the Law cries out   2795
Most audible, euen from his proper tongue.
An *Angelo* for *Claudio*, death for death:
Haste still paies haste, and leasure, answers leasure;
Like doth quit like, and *Measure* still for *Measure*:

2791 he adiudg'd your Brother] a judge HAN1
2792 criminall, in double] doubly criminal, in mTBY1 *conj.,* HAN1
2793 and of] and in HAN1, JOHN1-v1773, HUD2
2796 tongue.] ～ , F2+
2797 *Marked as quotation* MAL+ (−KNT, HAL, SIS); 2797-9 *marked* ARD2
An] And ROWE2, ROWE3
2799 *Measure:*] ～ ? SING, KTLY

2791 See n. 2231.
    adiudg'd] SCHMIDT (1874): "Condemn" (*OED, v.* 5).
2792 **criminall, in double**] HART (ed. 1905): "Doubly criminal. Shakespeare freely transposes adjectives from their normal position. Double cannot refer here to violation, since violation cannot refer to promise-breach. Double refers to the two crimes of which Angelo was guilty." Cf. *1 Promos,* 4.2 (p. 328 below): "But double wrong, I so should do *Cassandra.*"
2794 **dependant**] SCHMIDT (1874): "Relating to and occasioned by something previous" (*OED, a.* 2). See n. 2419. LAWRENCE (1931, p. 115) suggests changing the punctuation to *"dependent, —"* and omitting the comma after *life.*
2795 **The very mercy**] The mercy, properly so called (*OED,* Very *a.* 1).
2796 **audible**] SCHMIDT (1874): "Loud; adverbially." Not in *OED.*
    proper] See n. 220.
2797 **death for death**] JENTE (1926, p. 403), TILLEY (B458), and WILSON (p. 69): "Blood will have blood." Cf. Gen. 9:6 and *1 Promos,* 2.7 (p. 319 below): "Blood, axeth blood." WHITING (D91): "Death for death," quoting Lydgate in *Troy Book* and *Fall of Princes.*
2798 **still**] "Always," as in 214 and often.
    paies] *OED* (*v.* 1 4): "To give a recompense for . . . in a good or bad sense."
    leasure] SCHMIDT (1874): *Leisure,* "Freedom from hurry, the contrary to haste" (*OED,* 4, "Leisureliness, deliberation").
    answers] SCHMIDT (1874): "To agree with, to correspond." *OED* (*v.* 24): "Repeat the action of, correspond to," quoting only this and *H5* 4. Prol. 8 (1797).
2799 **Like . . . like**] JENTE (1926, p. 424), TILLEY (L286), and WILSON (p. 465): "Like will to like."
    quit] SCHMIDT (1875): "To requite, to repay, to pay for." ONIONS (1911): "Repay, reward, requite" (*OED, v.* 10). See n. 2895.
    Measure . . . Measure] See n. 0.1-0.2.

Then *Angelo*, thy fault's thus manifested; 2800
Which though thou would'st deny, denies thee vantage.
We doe condemne thee to the very Blocke
Where *Claudio* stoop'd to death, and with like haste.
Away with him.
    Mar. Oh my most gracious Lord, 2805
I hope you will not mocke me with a husband?
    Duk. It is your husband mock't you with a husband,
Consenting to the safe-guard of your honor,
I thought your marriage fit: else Imputation,
For that he knew you, might reproach your life, 2810
And choake your good to come: For his Possessions,
Although by confutation they are ours;
We doe en-state, and widow you with all,

2800 fault's thus manifested] Faults are manifested ROWE1-THEO2, WARB-JOHN2; faults are manifest HAN1; faults thus manifested mTBY1 *conj.*, v1785, KTLY, PEN2; fault thus manifested mTBY1 *conj.*, DYCE, STAU, KNT3, DEL4, HUD2, BUL
    2801 deny, denies] deny 'em, deny HAN1; deny, deny WARB, JOHN, v1773
    2812 confutation] confiscation F2+ (−IRV)
    2813 with all] withall F2-SIS (−CAM3)

2801 **denies thee vantage**] MALONE (ed. 1790): "The denial of which will avail thee nothing." Cf. *WT* 3.2.87 (1264). CLARKE (ed. 1864): "Forbids thy deriving advantage from its confession." LEVER (ed. 1965): " 'Denies you the right to claim superior treatment'. Angelo has already confessed his 'fault' [2748–56]: what he might still hypothetically 'deny' is that he deserves the identical treatment decreed for Claudio." Cf. *OED* (*sb.* 1): "Advantage, benefit," and n. 826.
    2805 **gracious**] See n. 2421.
    2807 **mock't**] Who mocked. See n. 758.
    2808 **safe-guard**] See *OED* (*sb.* 1): "Protection."
    2809 **else**] See n. 281.
    Imputation] SCHMIDT (1874): "Censure." Cf. *OED* (1): "The action of imputing or attributing something, usually a fault, crime, etc., to a person."
    2810 **For that**] See n. 2593.
    knew] See n. 2559.
    2812 **confutation**] MALONE (ed. 1790): "*Confutation* . . . may be right:—by his being confuted, or proved guilty of the fact which he had denied." STONE (1884, pp. 116*–17*): "Conviction" or "overcoming." So SYMONS (in IRVING & MARSHALL, ed. 1889). LEE (ed. 1907): "No example of this usage of 'confutation' has been discovered." HARDING (ed. 1954): "The Folio reading, however, can be defended." But F2 is almost certainly right in emending to *confiscation.*
    2813 **en-state**] JOHNSON (1755): *Instate,* "invest." SCHMIDT (1874): "Put in possession." *OED* (*v.* 2): "To endow or invest (a person) *with,*" first quotation.
    widow] JOHNSON (1755): "Endow with a widow-right." ONIONS (1911): "Settle a jointure upon." *OED* (*v.* 3): "Endow with a widow's right," only use in this sense; cf. *widdow-hood* in *Shr.* 2.1.125 (989), the only instance of the meaning "An estate settled on a widow, a widow's right." CLARKSON & WARREN (1942, pp.

To buy you a better husband.

    Mar. Oh my deere Lord, 2815
I craue no other, nor no better man.
    Duke. Neuer craue him, we are definitiue.
    Mar. Gentle my Liege.
    Duke. You doe but loose your labour.
Away with him to death: Now Sir, to you. 2820
    Mar. Oh my good Lord, sweet *Isabell*, take my part,
Lend me your knees, and all my life to come,
I'll lend you all my life to doe you seruice.
    Duke. Against all sence you doe importune her,
Should she kneele downe, in mercie of this fact, 2825
Her Brothers ghost, his paued bed would breake,

2818 Liege.] ～ — POPE1 +   *Kneeling.* JOHN1-SIS, EVNS; *before* 2821 ARD2
2820 [*To* Lucio. JOHN1 +
2822–3 come, . . . lend you‸] Ff., SING, WH1, KTLY, PEL1, PEN2; ～ ‸ . . . ～
～ , ROWE, POPE, HAN1, CAP, v1778-v1821, COL, DEL4; ～ ‸ . . . ～ ～ ‸ THEO1
etc.

204–6) think it means "to make a widow out of."
    with all] SCHMIDT (1875): *Withal* or *Withall*, "with this, with it." On the other hand, the Duke may emphasize *all*, as CLARKSON & WARREN argue. See n. 714.
    2816 **nor**] See n. 42.
    2817 **definitiue**] SCHMIDT (1874): "Resolved, free from hesitation." *OED* (*a.* 1b): "Decisive," first use as applied to a person. ONIONS (1911): "Resolute." Cf. *Definitiuely* in *R3* 3.7.153 (2374).
    2818 **Gentle my Liege**] SCHMIDT (1874): *Liege,* "sovereign." See nn. 54, 357.
    2819 TILLEY (L9) and WILSON (p. 485): "You lose your labour," as in the title of *LLL* and often in Sh.
    2821 *Isabell*] See n. 818.
    2822, 2823, 2834 **Lend**] See n. 22.
    2824 **Against all sence**] WARBURTON (ed. 1747): "The meaning required is, against all reason and natural affection; *Shakespear,* therefore, judiciously uses a single word that implies both." SCHMIDT (1875): "Reason," as in 900, 2403, 2601. *OED* (*sb.* 28): "What is wise or reasonable." EMPSON (1951, pp. 279–80): "The final use of *sense* can carry a good deal of meaning, though if you suppose the Duke meant all of it he is not likely to have married her afterwards. 'Against all reason'—'all normal decent feeling'—'all depth or delicacy of feeling'; whatever kind of *sense* is meant here, she lacks it. . . . This is certainly not what the Duke thinks."
    importune] JOHNSON (1755): "Accented anciently on the second syllable," quoting this. See n. 64.
    2825 **fact**] See n. 2002.
    2826 **paued**] HART (ed. 1905): "Does this imply that the condemned man was buried in the precincts of the gaol, as was the custom? Excepting in such circumstances, 'paved' is not a usual term to apply to a common grave." HARRISON (ed. 1948): "Persons of rank were buried inside the church beneath the pavement."

And take her hence in horror.
   Mar. Isabell:
Sweet *Isabel*, doe yet but kneele by me,
Hold vp your hands, say nothing: I'll speake all.   2830
They say best men are moulded out of faults,
And for the most, become much more the better
For being a little bad: So may my husband.
Oh *Isabel*: will you not lend a knee?
   Duke. He dies for *Claudio's* death.   2835
   Isab. Most bounteous Sir.

2836 *Kneeling.* ROWE1 +

HARDING (ed. 1954): It seems likely "that the Duke is alluding to the family crypt or vault."

2829 **yet**] SCHMIDT (1875): "At least; though nothing else."

2831 HUDSON (ed. 1851): "On the principle that Nature or Providence often uses our vices to scourge down our pride." So in *AWW* 4.3.84-5 (2178-9): "Our vertues would bee proud, if our faults whipt them not." IDEM (ed. 1880): "Hooker has a like thought in one of his sermons" (quoted). JENTE (1926, p. 415), TILLEY (M116), and WILSON (p. 229): "Every man has his faults" (Erasmus). Cf. *Ant.* 5.1.32-3 (3148-9).

2832 **for the most**] *OED* (Most *a.* 6b): "For the most part," one of two quotations.

2835 **death**] DAVID (1951, p. 137): At Stratford in 1950 "The climax of the play was breath-taking. . . . 'He dies for Claudio'. The pause that followed must have been among the longest in theatre history. Then hesitantly, still silent, Isabella moved across the stage and knelt before the Duke. Her words came quiet and level, and as their full import of mercy reached Angelo, a sob broke from him. It was perfectly calculated and perfectly timed."

2836-46 JOHNSON (ed. 1765): "The *Duke* has justly observed that *Isabel* is *importuned against all sense* to solicit for *Angelo,* yet here *against all sense* she solicits for him. Her argument is extraordinary. . . . That *Angelo* had committed all the crimes charged against him, as far as he could commit them, is evident. The only *intent* which *his act did not overtake,* was the defilement of *Isabel.* Of this *Angelo* was only intentionally guilty. *Angelo's* crimes were such, as must sufficiently justify punishment, whether its end be to secure the innocent from wrong, or to deter guilt by example; and I believe every reader feels some indignation when he finds him spared. From what extenuation of his crime can *Isabel,* who yet supposes her brother dead, form any plea in his favour? *Since he was good 'till he looked on me, let him not die.* I am afraid our Varlet Poet intended to inculcate, that women think ill of nothing that raises the credit of their beauty, and are ready, however virtuous, to pardon any act which they think incited by their own charms." KENRICK (1765, pp. 46-8): It is not "out of character for Isabel, after repeated solicitations, to be moved to oblige Mariana, who had already obliged her. . . . From a principle of philosophy, she must be very conscious that the death of Angelo could not bring her brother to life again; and if to this reflection we suppose her religion might add the suggestion of Christian charity and forgiveness, I do not see any impropriety in Isabel's soliciting Angelo's pardon." The

Looke if it please you, on this man condemn'd,
As if my Brother liu'd: I partly thinke,
A due sinceritie gouerned his deedes,
Till he did looke on me: Since it is so,   2840
Let him not die: my Brother had but Iustice,
In that he did the thing for which he dide.
For *Angelo*, his Act did not ore-take his bad intent,
And must be buried but as an intent
That perish'd by the way: thoughts are no subiects   2845

2839–43 *Lines ending* he . . . die. . . . did . . . Angelo, . . . intent; KTLY
2843–6 *Lines ending* o'ertake . . . but . . . way: . . . thoughts. HAN1
2843 For *Angelo*,] *Separate line* mTBY1 *conj.,* JOHN1+ (−KTLY)

---

reader "must perceive the propriety of doing poetical justice to the injured Mariana;
which would not be the case, if her new-made husband were to be immediately
punished with the severity due to his wicked designs." There is no "covert satire on
the fair sex." RITSON (in *Var.* 1793): "It is evident that Isabella condescends to
Mariana's importunate solicitation, with great reluctance. Bad as her argument might
be, it is the best that the guilt of Angelo would admit. The sacrifice that she makes
of her revenge to her friendship, scarcely merits to be considered in so harsh a light."
HORNE (ed. 1840, 1:212): "*I partly think.* . . . This was not only true, but it is a
beautiful trait in the character of Isabel that she should be so forgiving as to admit
the fact; and, at the passionate intercession of Mariana, make it a plea for the sparing
of Angelo's life. Dr. Johnson is shocked at this forgiving disposition in Isabel . . .
saying, 'I am afraid, our *varlet poet* intended to inculcate, that women', &c. . . . It is
one of the most marked characteristics of Shakspere, that he never 'inculcates' anything; he leaves people to find what they can." WILSON (ed. 1922): "Dr Johnson
rightly stigmatised Isabella's argument as 'extraordinary'." MAXWELL (1947, p. 55):
"She is pushing a manifestly weak case as far as she dare. . . . She is doing just the
same for Angelo as she had done for Claudio." LASCELLES (1953, pp. 132–3): "Into
this plea for Angelo, as into that for Claudio, Isabel has been precipitated by the
passion of pity—stirred, now, by Mariana; and this, like that, is a piece of improvisa-
tion: she is thinking out her case as she speaks, seeking for a plea that will prevail.
Johnson was, in this instance, wrong. There is no coquetry in her reference to herself.
. . . It is the *benefit* of the law she now demands, the benefit of doubt, even of quibble,
and the only echo of her first plea to be heard in her second is the appeal for
forbearance in the exercise of power. . . . Mercy forgoes advantage."
    2843 STEEVENS (*Var.* 1778): "So in *Macbeth*" (4.1.145–6 [1698–9]).
    2844 **buried**] THEOBALD (1729, in NICHOLS, 1817, 2:291): "What does she
mean by *buried?* forgot, buried in silence?" STEEVENS (*Var.* 1793): "Like the traveller, who dies on his journey, is obscurely interred, and thought of no more."
    2845 **subiects**] THEOBALD (1729, in NICHOLS, 1817, 2:291): "And how is
subjects to be understood, as with the Philosophers?" THIRLBY (1733–47) cites RAY
(who in *Proverbs*, 1670, p. 148, gives this explanation: "Humane laws can take no
cognizance of thoughts, unless they discover themselves by some overt actions"). Cf.
TILLEY (T244) and WILSON (pp. 814–15); *TN* 1.3.73 (183); *Tmp.* 3.2.132 (1479).
HALLIWELL (ed. 1854): "Subjects for punishment? Or, possibly,—our thoughts are

Intents, but meerely thoughts.

Mar. Meerely my Lord.

Duk. Your suite's vnprofitable: stand vp I say:
I haue bethought me of another fault.

Prouost, how came it *Claudio* was beheaded   2850
At an vnusuall howre?   (G6b)

Pro. It was commanded so.

Duke. Had you a speciall warrant for the deed?

Pro. No my good Lord: it was by priuate message.

Duk. For which I doe discharge you of your office,   2855
Giue vp your keyes.

Pro. Pardon me, noble Lord,
I thought it was a fault, but knew it not,
Yet did repent me after more aduice,
For testimony whereof, one in the prison   2860
That should by priuate order else haue dide,
I haue reseru'd aliue.

Duk. What's he?

Pro. His name is *Barnardine.*

Duke. I would thou hadst done so by *Claudio*:   2865
Goe fetch him hither, let me looke vpon him.

2846 but] *Om.* HAN1
2852 It . . . so] 'Twas so commanded HAN1
2862-4 *One verse line* v1793+
2863 What's] And what is HAN1
2865 would] wouldst F2-F4; wish CAP (would *in* CAPN)   hadst] hast F4
2866 *Exit* Prov. HAN1, JOHN1+

---

no subjects, not always subject to our will, and intentions are merely thoughts.
Intentions, therefore, are frequently involuntary." SCHMIDT (1875): "Real, existing
things." *OED* (*sb.* 6b): "A thing having real independent existence," only quotation
in this sense. RUSHTON (1907, p. 38): "An evil intention is not punishable equally
with the fact. . . . So Ulpian says: 'Cogitationis pœnam nemo patitur [No one suffers
punishment for thought]'."

2846 **meerely**] *OED* (*adv.*² 3): "Only . . . and nothing more." WILSON (ed.
1922): "Nothing but." Cf. 1214, 1233 and nn.

2848 **vnprofitable**] SCHMIDT (1875): "Useless."

2849 **bethought**] See n. 841.

2859 **after more aduice**] STEEVENS (Var. 1778): "After more mature consideration" (*OED*, 4). SINGER (ed. 1826): Cf. *H5* 2.2.43 (672).

2861 **should**] Was to. See n. 270.

   else] See n. 281.

2865 **would**] See n. 17.

   by] SCHMIDT (1874, p. 160): "In the case of" (*OED, prep.* 26).

2866 THEOBALD (ed. 1733): "The introducing *Barnardine* here, is, seemingly a

Esc. I am sorry, one so learned, and so wise
As you, Lord *Angelo*, haue stil appear'd,
Should slip so grosselie, both in the heat of bloud
And lacke of temper'd iudgement afterward.   2870
    Ang. I am sorrie, that such sorrow I procure,
And so deepe sticks it in my penitent heart,
That I craue death more willingly then mercy,
'Tis my deseruing, and I doe entreat it.

       Enter Barnardine and Prouost, Claudio, Iulietta.   2875

Duke. Which is that *Barnardine?*
Pro. This my Lord.
Duke. There was a Friar told me of this man.
Sirha, thou art said to haue a stubborne soule
That apprehends no further then this world,   2880
And squar'st thy life according: Thou'rt condemn'd,
But for those earthly faults, I quit them all,

2869 the] *Om.* POPE1-JOHN2
2875 SCENE VII. POPE, HAN1, WARB; SCENE VIII. JOHN
2877 This] 'Tis this, JOHN; This is, KTLY   Lord] good lord HAN1, CAP
2880 further] farther COL, WH1
2881 according] accordingly F4-JOHN2

---

matter of no Consequence . . . but, to our Poet's Praise, let me observe, that it is not done without double Art; it gives a Handle for the Discovery of *Claudio* being alive, and so heightens the Surprize; and, at the same time, by the Pardon of *Barnardine,* gives a fine Opportunity of making the *Duke*'s Character more amiable, both for Mercy, and Virtue."

2867, 2871 **I am**] One syllable, as in *I'm sorry, Ham.* (F) 1.5.134 (826).

2868 **stil**] Always. See n. 728.

2869 **slip**] See n. 814.

    bloud] See n. 463.

2871 **procure**] SCHMIDT (1875): "To bring about, to effect, to cause" (*OED, v.* 4a).

2878 **told**] Who told. See n. 758.

2879 **thou art**] See n. 1222.

2880 **apprehends**] See n. 2008.

2881 **squar'st**] JOHNSON (1755): "To adjust; to regulate; to mould; to shape." HART (ed. 1905): Craig sends a parallel from Montaigne (1603), bk. 2, ch.12 (Everyman's ed., 2:130): "conforme his behaviors and square his life unto it" (doctrine). *OED* (*v.* 4): "To regulate, frame, arrange, or direct, *by, according to,* or *on* some standard or principle of action."

2882 JOHNSON (ed. 1765): "Thy faults, so far as they are punishable on earth, so far as they are cognisable by temporal power, I forgive."

    quit] DYCE (1867): "Acquit." SCHMIDT (1875): "Remit" (*OED, v.* 4, *rare*).

And pray thee take this mercie to prouide
For better times to come: Frier aduise him,
I leaue him to your hand. What muffeld fellow's that?   2885
　　Pro. This is another prisoner that I sau'd,
Who should haue di'd when *Claudio* lost his head,
As like almost to *Claudio*, as himselfe.
　　Duke. If he be like your brother, for his sake
Is he pardon'd, and for your louelie sake   2890
Giue me your hand, and say you will be mine,
He is my brother too: But fitter time for that:
By this Lord *Angelo* perceiues he's safe,
Methinkes I see a quickning in his eye:
Well *Angelo*, your euill quits you well.   2895

2883 And] I F2-RANN (−CAP)

2885 your hand] you HAN1　　*Exeunt Barnardine and Friar into the city. (after* hand.) IRV, RLTR

2887 Who] That v1793-COL3 (−DYCE1), KTLY, KNT3, DEL4, COL4

2888 *Uncovers him.* HAN1, CAP, MAL+ *(subst.)*

2889 [*To* Isab. THEO2+　　Claudio *and* Isabella *embrace.* COL2, COL3; *after* pardon'd,— (2890) IRV

2890 Is he] He's mTBY1 *conj.,* HAN1; Is he too CAP; Then is he DYCE2, DYCE3, HUD2; Is he now COL4　　sake⌃] ~ ; IRV; ~ — NLSN, PEL1

2891-2 and . . . is] say you'll be mine, and he's HAN1

2891 mine,] ~ ; F4, KNT, HAL, WH1; ~ — NLSN, SIS, PEL1; ~ . ARD2, PEN2

ROLFE (ed. 1882): "Forgive."

2883-4 MATTHEWS (1962, p. 116): "He is given the chance of repentance as Claudio and Angelo were, so that the nature of the crime is seen to be irrelevant. *All* have sinned and come short."

2883 **mercie**] *OED* (*sb.* 6): "Act of mercy."

2885 **muffeld**] HART (ed. 1905): "The muffler over the lower parts of the face was a common method of disguising one's self." See *Wiv.* 4.2.77 (1962).

2887 **should**] Was to. See n. 270.

2888 SEYMOUR (1805, 1:105): "The same comparison is attempted in *Hamlet*" (1.1.58–9 [74–5]).

2889 JOHNSON (ed. 1765): "It is somewhat strange, that *Isabel* is not made to express either gratitude, wonder or joy at the sight of her brother." BOSWELL (Var. 1821): "Shakspeare, it should be recollected, wrote for the stage, on which Isabel might express her feelings by action." COLLIER (ed. 1858): "It would have been strange, if she had not been so lost in her gratitude, wonder, and joy, as to be unable to express the state of her mind in words: she probably rushed into Claudio's arms, and fell upon his neck in silent delight and astonishment." MUIR (1960, p. 95): "The silent reunion of Isabella and Claudio is a little-recognized master-stroke."

2891 **Giue me**] HUNTER (ed. 1873): "If you give me."

2894 **quickning**] LEVER (ed. 1965): "Return of life" (*OED, v.* 6, "To recover life, to revive").

2895 **quits**] JOHNSON (ed. 1765): "Recompenses, requites." See n. 2799.

Looke that you loue your wife: her worth, worth yours.
I finde an apt remission in my selfe:
And yet heere's one in place I cannot pardon,
You sirha, that knew me for a foole, a Coward,
One all of Luxurie, an asse, a mad man: 2900
Wherein haue I so deseru'd of you
That you extoll me thus?
  Luc. 'Faith my Lord, I spoke it but according to the

2896 her worth, worth yours.] her worth works yours. mTBY2 *conj.,* HAN1,
WARB; her worth's worth yours. HEATH *conj.,* KTLY; her worth work yours! WALKER
conj. in DYCE1 (*and* 1860, 1:295), HUD2
  2899 *To* Lucio. ROWE1+
  2900 all of] of all POPE2, THEO, WARB-v1773 (−CAP)
  2901 so deseru'd] deserved so POPE1-RANN, STAU, KTLY, DYCE2, DYCE3,
HUD2, CAM3, KIT1; so well deserv'd COL3, COL4

2896 **Looke . . . wife**] STEEVENS (Var. 1778): So in *2 Promos,* 5.6 (p. 369
below): "Be louing to good *Cassandra,* thy Wife." See n. 715.
  her . . . yours] JOHNSON (ed. 1765): "The words are, as they are too frequently, an affected gingle, but the sense is plain. . . . Her value is equal to your value,
the match is not unworthy of you." WILSON (ed. 1922, p. 176): "Her personal
qualities are worthy of your standing." LEVER (ed. 1965): " '(Look that) to her worth
yours be equal'."
  2897 **apt remission**] HUDSON (ed. 1880): *"Aptness* or inclination to *remit*
offences; that is, to pardon them." *OED* (Remission 2d): "An inclination towards
pardon," only use in this sense. Cf. 1048 *remit,* "pardon," and n. 398 on *apt.*
  2898 **in place**] See *OED* (Place *sb.* 19b): "In presence, present." Cf. *1 Promos,*
3.2 (p. 320 below): "See, as I wisht, Lord *Promos* is in place."
  I cannot pardon] JOHNSON (ed. 1765): "After the pardon of two murderers
Lucio might be treated by the good *Duke* with less harshness; but perhaps the Poet
intended to show, what is too often seen, *that men easily forgive wrongs which are not
committed against themselves."* STEEVENS (Var. 1778): "The Duke only meant to
frighten *Lucio,* whose final sentence is to marry the woman whom he had wronged,
on which all his other punishments are remitted." SCHANZER (1963, p. 125): "The
sentence initially imposed upon Lucio . . . comes as a shock. . . . It becomes much
more comprehensible in the light of James's notorious sensitiveness to slander, which
led to the passing of a Scottish Act of Parliament in 1585 that made slander of the
King a treasonable offence, punishable with death."
  2900 **Luxurie**] DYCE (1867): "Lasciviousness (its only sense in Shakespeare)"
(*OED,* 1).
  2901 LEVER (ed. 1965): "The speech stress makes a trochaic pentameter."
  2903 **'Faith**] See n. 712.
  2903-4 **according to the trick**] EDWARDS (1748, p. 62): *"The trick* signifies
habit, custom, as he has got a trick of doing so or so." JOHNSON (ed. 1765): "To
my custom, my habitual practice." MASON (1785, p. 44): "According to *the* trick and
practice of the times." MALONE (ed. 1790, 10:568): "According to the fashion of
thoughtless youth." KNIGHT (ed. 1840): "After the fashion of banter and exaggeration." PARROTT (ed. 1938): "In character (as a jest)." See n. 1541.

trick: if you will hang me for it you may: but I had ra-
ther it would please you, I might be whipt.   2905
   Duke. Whipt first, sir, and hang'd after.
Proclaime it Prouost round about the Citie,
If any woman wrong'd by this lewd fellow
(As I haue heard him sweare himselfe there's one
Whom he begot with childe) let her appeare,   2910
And he shall marry her: the nuptiall finish'd,
Let him be whipt and hang'd.
   Luc. I beseech your Highnesse doe not marry me to
a Whore: your Highnesse said euen now I made you a
Duke, good my Lord do not recompence me, in making   2915
me a Cuckold.
   Duke. Vpon mine honor thou shalt marrie her.   (G6va)
Thy slanders I forgiue, and therewithall
Remit thy other forfeits: take him to prison,
And see our pleasure herein executed.   2920
   Luc. Marrying a punke my Lord, is pressing to death,

2908 If] Is CAM1, GLO, DYCE2, DYCE3, WH2, ARD1, NLSN   woman] woman's
mTBY1 *conj.,* HAN1, JOHN, v1773-STAU, KTLY, KNT3, DEL4, COL4, HUD2, IRV,
CAM3, KIT1
   2920 executed] execute HAN1
   2921-2 *Prose* POPE1+ (−CAP, CAM3, ARD2); *verse lines ending* death, . . . it.
(*including* 2923) CAM3, ARD2

   2908 **If any woman wrong'd**] SISSON (1956, 1:87): "Hanmer's *woman's* for
woman is generally accepted. . . . The Folio reading . . . could well bear the meaning
'If there is any woman wronged'." LEISI (ed. 1964): "Sh. may have intended something like: *If any woman, wrong'd . . . , appears,* and then changed his thought." LEVER
(ed. 1965): "But the sentence may be elliptical, due to the intrusion of the parenthesis."
   2918 **therewithall**] SCHMIDT (1875): "With it, with that; at the same time."
LEISI (ed. 1964): " 'Moreover' (OED 1)." LEVER (ed. 1965): "Therewith."
   2919 **Remit**] HARDING (ed. 1954): "Cancel" (*OED, v.* 3b, "To refrain from
inflicting . . . ; to withdraw, cancel").
      forfeits] JOHNSON (1755): "Something paid for expiation of a crime." IDEM
(ed. 1765): "Punishments." SCHMIDT (1874): "Penalty incurred by a trespass"
(*OED, sb.* 2).
   2921 **pressing to death**] HALLIWELL (ed. 1854): "The pressing to death was the
popular name of the *peine forte et dure,* inflicted upon prisoners who refused to plead.
Harrison, in his *Description of England,* p. 185, says,—'Such fellons as stand mute, and
speake not at their arraignement, are pressed to death by huge weights laid upon a
boord that lieth over their brest, and a sharpe stone under their backs'." HART (ed.
1905) notes that Sh. uses this metaphor also in *Tro.* 3.2.217–18 (1843–4), *Ado* 3.1.76
(1166), and *R2* 3.4.72 (1884). ECCLES (1961, p. 77): Lodowick Greville of Milcote
near Stratford-on-Avon was pressed to death in 1589 at the Tower.

Whipping and hanging.
  Duke. Slandering a Prince deserues it.
She *Claudio* that you wrong'd, looke you restore.
Ioy to you *Mariana*, loue her *Angelo*:   2925
I haue confes'd her, and I know her vertue.
Thanks good friend, *Escalus*, for thy much goodnesse,
There's more behinde that is more gratulate.   (G6vb)
Thanks *Prouost* for thy care, and secrecie,
We shall imploy thee in a worthier place.   2930
Forgiue him *Angelo*, that brought you home
The head of *Ragozine* for *Claudio's*,
Th'offence pardons it selfe. Deere *Isabell*,
I haue a motion much imports your good,
Whereto if you'll a willing eare incline;   2935
What's mine is yours, and what is yours is mine.

2923 *Exeunt Officers with Lucio.* DYCE, STAU-GLO, HUD2+ (−CAM3, SIS, ARD2)
2924 She] Her HAN1
2928, 2932-3 *After* 2931 *in this order:* The head . . . Claudio's. *Ang.* Th'offence
pardons itself. *Duke.* There's more behind That is more gratulate.—Dear Isabel,
JOHN1 *conj.,* RANN, HENL
2932 *Ragozine*] *Rogozine* F4, ROWE

2922 **Whipping**] HOWARD-HILL (1972, p. 36): Initial *w* in Crane's transcripts
can often be read as either capital or lowercase.
  2924 **She**] See nn. 1434, 2504.
  looke] See n. 715.
  2928 **behinde**] *OED (adv.* 4 *fig.):* "In reserve," "still to come," quoting 2938.
  gratulate] HANMER (ed. 1743, 6, glossary): "Fit for Gratulation." STEEVENS
(Var. 1778): *"To be more rejoiced in;*—meaning, I suppose, that there is another world,
where he [Escalus] will find yet greater reason to rejoice in consequence of his upright
ministry." MASON (1785, pp. 44–5): "The Duke . . . tells him that he had some other
reward in store for him, more acceptable than thanks, which agrees with what he said
before [2355] . . . 'Forerunning more requital'." *OED (a):* "To be rejoiced at;
pleasing, gratifying," only quotation.
  2934 **motion**] SCHMIDT (1875): "Proposal, offer, request" (*OED, sb.* 7). LEISI
(ed. 1964): "Obviously, the Duke's formal proposal is still to come; the words *and
say you will be mine* [2891] were both private and unofficial; cf. *But fitter time for that*
[2892]."
  much] That much. See n. 758.
  imports] See n. 2476.
  2936 TILLEY (M980) and WILSON (p. 533). BYRNE (1936, p. 97): "It is note-
worthy that in conferring his love on Isabella, the Duke yet never moves to the
intimate *thee,* probably because of reverence for her position and reserve. This would
support the opinion that Shakespeare did not intend the Duke to marry Isabella."
KITTREDGE (ed 1936): "The conclusion of the play leaves the audience guessing—
as was doubtless Shakespeare's intent." EDWARDS (1968, pp. 116–17): "Isabella does

So bring vs to our Pallace, where wee'll show   2937
What's yet behinde, that meete you all should know.

FINIS.

2938 that] thats F2; that's F3+   *Exeunt.* ROWE1+ (−COL3); *Curtain drawn*
COLNE, COL2, COL3

---

not reply. The suggestion of betrothal is as far as Shakespeare wished to go." LAVIN (1972, p. 109): Isabella may "be seen as successfully undergoing a test which proves her worthy of marriage to the Duke. . . . Seen against the tradition to which Isabella belongs, her marriage to the Duke is inevitable from the start." KIRSCH (1975, p. 100): "The Duke's proposal offers the promise that in marriage Isabella can fully express her newborn awareness of herself as a woman." BERRY (1977, p. 103) quotes Robin Phillips, who directed a Canadian production in 1975: "The almost unbearable bewilderment at the end is that of decision. . . . But she doesn't say anything, so we are left to make up our own minds."

2937 **bring**] Accompany. See n. 70.

2938 **behinde**] See n. 2928.

    that] F2 reads *thats.*

    LEVER (ed. 1965): "A processional exit in pairs seems to be indicated by the dialogue; led by the Duke and Isabella; then Claudio and Juliet; Angelo and Mariana; Escalus and the Provost; Friar Peter and Barnardine; with Lucio under guard bringing up the rear."

APPENDIX

Emendations of Accidentals in F1

As noted in the Plan of the Work (pp. xi–xxvii), the Variorum text does not attempt to reproduce all the typographical features of F1. Obvious defects such as the misalignment of types, printing space-types, and occasional wrong-font letters have been corrected silently, as has irregular spacing when no true word was created thereby (e.g., 2277 ou rauthorities). The following list records emendations of other F1 accidentals that clearly seem errors or the compositors' responses to mechanical exigencies (as, for example, the turning over of a line or the omission of punctuation for lack of space). F1 typographical errors which have influenced later texts (as in 353) are recorded in the textual notes.

In each note the lemma is the reading of the Variorum text as emended. The first siglum to the right of the bracket is that of the edition from which the emendation is drawn, F2 in all instances. This is followed by the rejected F1 reading. Typographical rearrangements are not traced to a source in an early edition.

    6   vnfold,] vn-| (fold, *(turnover)* F1
   41   touch'd] F2; tonch'd F1
  103   conclud'st] F2; eonclud'st F1
  215   restraint.] re-| (straint. *(turnover)* F1
  356   *Isa.*] F2; *Isa:* F1
  393   teeming] F2; teemiug F1
  724   remedie.] F2; ─ : F1
  769   your will?] your| (will? *(turnover)* F1
  787   Actor.] F2; ─ : F1
  845   slept:] F2; ─ ₍ *(full line)* F1
  852   hatch'd] F2; hatc'hd F1
  961   needfull.] F2; ─ ₍ *(full line)* F1
  981   offencefull] F2; offence full F1
 1036   please me,] please| (me, *(turnover)* F1
 1172   report] F2; reporr F1
 1272   twaine.] F2; ─ : F1

1422 the angry] F2; theangry F1
1488 fare you well] F2; fare youwell F1
1627 fellow.] F2; ~ ˌ *(full line)* F1
1692 vs.] F2; ~ , F1
1722 merrie] F2 (merry); merrrie F1
1859 if] F2; is (long *s*) F1
2109 *Clo.*] F2; *Clo*: F1
2175 *Angelo.*] F2; ~ ˌ *(full line)* F1
2222 wisdome,] wis-| (dome, *(turnover)* F1
2350 your] F2; yonr F1
2452 proceed.] F2; ~ , F1
2456 *Isab.*] F2; *Isab*: F1
2473 thou speak'st,] thou| (speak'st, *(turnover)* F1
2588 *Duk.*] F2; ~ ˌ F1
2589 Enough] F2; Enoug F1
2732 foh sir] F2; foh fir F1
2857 me] F2; mc (?) F1
2896 yours.] F2; ~ ˌ *(full line)* F1
2910 Whom] F2; whom F1

Conjectural Emendations

The following is a list of conjectural readings that are not recorded in either the textual or the commentary notes. The reasons why no editor has adopted these orphans are usually obvious. As Johnson writes in a note on *MM* 1667, "It were to be wished, that we all explained more, and amended less."

4 *Escalus.*] Now hear our purpose, Escalus. SEYMOUR
8 put] let *or* but mTBY3; but ARD1
  put to know] not to learn mF2FL; put to avow LLOYD (1883)
9–11 Exceeds the lists of all, advice can give you; And thus no more remains, but add my strength To your sufficiency—your worth is able!—LEO (1884)
11 But that to your Sufficiency you add Due Diligency, as your Worth is able; THEO1; But that you put to your sufficiency (*then* And let it) mTBY1; But that to your sufficiency and worth (*then* I leave the work.) mTBY3; But that to your sufficiency you put A zeal as willing as your worth is able, TYRWHITT (*in* v1773); Your sufficiency as your worth is able, STEEVENS (v1773); But that your sufficiency, as your worth is able, MASON (1785); But your sufficiency as worth is able, FARMER *in* CAM1; But task to your sufficience, as your worth is able, DENT MS *in* HAL; To your sufficiency, as your worth is able (*then* But that you let) WHELER MS *in* HAL; To your

sufficiency your worth is able, HULL MS *in* HAL; But that sufficiency, as worth is able, *or* But your sufficiency as your worth is able, *or* But that sufficiency to your worth is abled, STEEVENS (v1803); But to your sufficiency your worth be added, SEYMOUR; But that your sufficiency be, as your worth is stable, BECKET; But state to your sufficiency, as your worth is able, JACKSON (1819); Put that to your sufficiency, as able, (*then* And let that) MITFORD; Put that to your sufficiency, as your worth is able, ANON. *in* QUINCY, ARD1; But that (as your sufficiency to your worth is equal) (*then* You let that) LETTSOM (*Blackwood's,* 1853); But that, [*Tendering his Commission.*] to your sufficiency, And, as your worth is able, (*then* let them) STAU; But that to your sufficiency I add Commission ample as your worth is able, SPEDDING *in* CAM1; But that to your sufficiency you add worth as ample, BAILEY (1866); But that to your sufficiency your worth is able, KNT3; But that to your sufficiency I add A power as mighty (*or* forceful) as your worth is able, FURNIVALL (1874); But that to your sufficiency you take This your Commission, as your worth is able, JABEZ; To that, but your sufficiency as your worth is able, HICKS; But t'add sufficiency, as your worth is ample, HUD2; But that to your sufficiency add your worth as able, KINNEAR; But your sufficiency, as your worth, I able, SPENCE; But that to add to your sufficiency; And, as your worth is able, MARSHALL *in* IRV; But that to your sufficiency I yield Our laws' enforcement, as your worth is able, MORRIS (ed. 1912); But that to your sufficiency you add Such execution as your worth is able, CUNINGHAM (1924); But that: To your sufficience add your worth as noble, KELLNER (1931); But that to your sufficiency I lend Powers as ample as your worth is able, MUNRO (ed. 1957); But that, to your sufficiency, as your worth is able, You add the talents of succeeding years LEISI (ed. 1964)

12   And] I mTBY3, CHALMERS (p. 405)

13   Termes] Formes mTHEO, mTBY2; laws KELLNER (1931)

15   As any, most enrich'd by art and practice, SEYMOUR

16   our] your mTBY3, WAGNER (ed. 1880)

20   soule] seal JOHN1; zeal TERRELL; rule ORGER

22   loue] mercy mTBY1; awe mTBY3; lore TERRELL

33–4   Character . . . history] history . . . character mTBY3, MASON (1785)

33   life] look JOHN1; lefe ("love") BECKET; lines WAGNER (ed. 1880)

34   history] heart's history KINNEAR

41   As if we had] We had SEYMOUR; As we'd KELLNER (1931)

45   glory] guerdon BAILEY (1866); duty TERRELL

47   my . . . aduertise] my part to him advertise JOHN1; in him, my part advertise BECKET; my part extemporize KELLNER (1931)

51   Liue] Lye mTBY1 (DAWSON)

52   first in question] put in quorum TERRELL; first in gresson (see *OED,* Grecing, "steps") KELLNER (1931)

54   Now] No, WAGNER (ed. 1880)

58   No more euasion] No, no more evasions KELLNER (1931)

59   leauen'd] level'd *or* level *or* unleaven'd *or* even'd mTBY1; un-leaven'd HEATH; levin'd ("confidential") BECKET

64   importune] import mTBY3

75   soule] zeal TERRELL

78   it doe well] I do well mTBY3, STAUNTON (1872, p. 666); I do meet KELLNER (1931)

80   safe] sane mTBY3, mF2FL

85   *Om.* SEYMOUR

87   and] as mTBY3, SEYMOUR

90   instructed] instructed, and would learn SEYMOUR

111   before] for KELLNER (1931)

118   *Luc.*] 2 *Gent.* HEATH

138   *Mitigation*] Midnight *or* Multiplication mTBY3; initiation KELL-NER (1931)

139   I haue] You have *or* Thou hast mTBY3

161   *Luc.* Tut, after all, this is fooling? I would but haue it so. KELLNER (1931)

165   *Luc.*] 2 *Gent.* KELLNER (1931)

174   *Ad. after* Custom-shrunke. Exit Bawd. Enter a second Bawd with Thomas Tapster. KELLNER (1931)

185   howses] ale-houses *or* hot-houses mTBY1

212   waight] right. TERRELL

213   The words] Th' Awards mTHEO, NICHOLSON *in* CAM2; The word's BECKET; The works JACKSON (1819); The award ORGER

216   (my *Lucio*) Liberty] my Lucio, mSTAU; wi' Julia's love KELLNER (1931)

218   euery Scope] liberty WHELER MS *in* HAL

221   thirsty] thirsted SPEDDING *in* CAM1

222–6   *Lines ending* arrest . . . creditors; . . . truth, . . . freedom . . . imprisonment. . . . Claudio YOUNG (p. 201); wise under arrest, . . . creditors. . . . lief *(then reading)* To have the sop of freedom as the mort Of prison. What is thy offence, friend Claudio? KELLNER (1931)

224   foppery] frippery TERRELL

225   mortality] reality TERRELL

237   vpon] on mTBY3; 'pon KELLNER (1931)

240   denunciation] consummation mF2FL; vindication KELLNER (1931)

242   propogation] propugnation mTBY3, STAU; propriation CAM3
        a] her KEIGHTLEY (1867)

243   Coffer] coffers KEIGHTLEY (1867)

251   fault] foil T. WHITE MS *(withdrawn),* THOMPSON *in* CAM3; faust ("fortunate state") BECKET; gilt *or* heat BAILEY (1866); vaunt WAGNER (ed. 1880); guilt *or* gilt GOULD (1887, p. 67)
        fault and] faulting KELLNER (1931)

glimpse] gloss mTBY3, BAILEY (1866); guise mTBY3, MASON
(1785)

newnes] highness KELLNER (1931)

257 Eminence] enmitie KELLNER (1931)

264 name] ware KELLNER (1931)

273 voice] name mF2FL, WHELER MS *in* HAL

275 youth] zenith JOHN1; youth, Her beauty, and her maiden modesty, WALKER (1860, 1:76)

276 prone] pow'r *or* prompt JOHN1; proue ("sufficiently powerful")
BECKET; proved KELLNER (1931); pure SISSON (1956)

and] all KELLNER (1931)

281 the] thy ARD2

282–3 who . . . should] which . . . should *or* who . . . shou'dst
SEYMOUR

291 dribling] dribbing SCHMIDT (1874)

300 witlesse] with witless CAM1

309 biting] hitting KELLNER (1931)

310 weedes] deeds mSTAU, PERRING (1885); evils ORGER

312 ore-growne] old-grown mTBY3, KELLNER (1931)

Caue] case ("cage") ORGER

315 to] do DENT MS *in* HAL

316 to] for mTBY3, JOICEY (1891)

in time the] will find in time The BADHAM (p. 279); in time thus
make The JOICEY (1891)

334 yet, my] let my mTBY1 (DAWSON); yet by BULLOCH; put my LEO
(1884)

nature neuer in] nature never come in mTBY3; nature ever in
JACKSON (1819); nature never win STAU; nature's never in SEAGER *in*
CAM2; name be never in KINNEAR; nature ne'er be in MOORE (1888)

334–5 fight To do in] sight, So doing JOHNSON *in* v1773; sight To
draw in DENT MS *in* HAL; fight To dole in JACKSON (1819); light To do it
SINGER (1853); light To do him SING2; fight To die in STAU; fight To do
with SEAGER *in* CAM2; plight To draw on BULLOCH; sight To do me LEO
(1884); fight To go in HIRSCHBERG

335 slander] slandered JOHNSON *in* v1773

And] or JACKSON (1819)

338 instruct me] instruct KELLNER (1931)

339 beare] bear it mSTAU, THISELTON (1901, p. 11)

342 one] now STAUNTON (1872, p. 666)

343 Enuie] sinne GOULD (1884, p. 55); engin KELLNER (1931)

364–5 *Lucio.* Peace and prosperity! *Fran.* He calls again. I pray you
answer him. *Isab.* Who is't that calls? STAUNTON (1872, pp. 666–7)

380 storie] mockery GOULD (1884, p. 10); stale ORGER

391 as blossoming Time] at blossoming time JOHN1

392 from the seednes,] forms the seed, next WAGNER (ed. 1880);

from the leannes LEO (1880); from the seeddues ("what is due from the seed") GOULD (1884, p. 10)

404   and] with JOHN1; on KELLNER (1925, p. 36)

414   vse] vice mTBY1

424–5   *Isa.* Doth he so? seek his life? CAM1

426   censur'd] censure in DENT MS *in* HAL

457   fall] fell WARB; foil KELLNER (1931)

466   him] in JACKSON (1819)

470   passing] panneled TERRELL

472   Guiltier than he they try; what's ope to justice SEYMOUR

472–3   to . . . ceizes] To justice, justice eyes SPENCE

473   What knowes the Lawes] what! know we the laws BULLOCH; what use the law LEO (1888); what's known to law KELLNER (1931)

491   heauen] God ADEE

493   run . . . Ice] ransom breaks of vice JOICEY (1891); range in brakes of vice JOICEY (1892); furr'd on backes of vice CUNINGHAM (1907)

from brakes of Ice] from brakes, off ice KNT1; through brakes of ice CARTWRIGHT; from pranks of Iceland BULLOCH; from banks of vice GOULD (1881, p. 13); from brakes of law HERR; from blackest vice LEO (1888); from brakes of Iron THISELTON (1901, p. 14); through brakes o' fire SKEAT (1910); from rank offence *(plural)* KELLNER (1925, p. 124)

and answere] answering BULLOCH

494   And some] Some are SEAGER *in* CAM2

alone] atone RID

518   parcell] pareil ("likewise") BECKET

520–1   a hot-house] an ale-house GOULD (1884, p. 11)

536   the] this DENT MS *in* HAL

580   chaire, Sir] chamber ANON. *in* CAM1

583   open] oven KELLNER (1925, p. 92)

606   supposd] subpoened TERRELL; sworn GOULD (1884, p. 11)

650   by] be ANON. *in* CAM2

653   hang] hang on HEATH

738   Sects] sorts WALKER *in* DYCE1 (*and* 1860, 3:17)

Ages] age *(plural)* KELLNER (1931)

738–42   smack . . . Now, what's . . . Is it] Smack . . . Now What is . . . Is't WALKER (1860, 3:17)

776   that] yet mTBY3

782   graces] grace WALKER (1860, 1:248)

786   the] his TERRELL

in] on mTBY1

797   Yes: I] Yet I KELLNER (1925, p. 104)

798   heauen] God mTBY1

822   of] to mTBY1, SEYMOUR

831   man] May KELLNER (1931)

847   If the first he that did the edict infringe SPEDDING *in* CAM1; If he that did the edict first infringe ANON. *in* CAM2

851   new] now mTBY3

853   degrees] decrees mTBY3; egress KELLNER (1931)

867   great men] great man STAUNTON (1872, p. 667); gnat men KELLNER (1931)

868   *Ioue . . . Ioue*] God . . . God mTBY3

871   Nothing] Nought KELLNER (1931)

      heauen] God mTBY3

874   man, proud] man, weak, proud MAL; a man, proud HUD2

875–80   Of what he is most ignorant. Most assur'd, Drest in a little brief authority,—(His glassy essence) angry, like an ape Plays . . . All mortal, —would laugh themselves. BECKET

877   glassie] grassy J. LLOYD *in* CAM1, BAILEY (1866); glossy FERNOW *in* WAGNER (ed. 1880); ghostly GOULD (1884, p. 11)

880   all themselues laugh] laugh themselves all KEIGHTLEY (1867)

884   cannot] can but ANON. *in* CAM1

885   Saints] sins ANON. *in* CAM1

901   breeds] bends THEOBALD (1729) *in* NICHOLS (2:287); brees ("becomes alarmed") BECKET; prides KELLNER (1931)

908   fond] round mTBY3; foul KELLNER (1931)

      Sickles] cycles COL1

      the tested-gold] detested gold JACKSON (1819), KELLNER (1931)

912   preserued] reserved mTBY1, mSTAU, DANIEL (1870); professed ORGER

920   Where] Which your JOHN1

943   Saint] soule GOULD (1887, p. 67)

949   Euer] Even from youth COLNE

959   crimes, that I may] several crimes, that I May SEYMOUR

963   mine] mien mTHEO; name STAUNTON (1872, p. 667); means KELLNER (1931)

965   blisterd] blasted mTBY1

980   wrong'd] has wrong'd KELLNER (1931)

986   least] I fear DENT MS *in* HAL; is't STAUNTON (1872, p. 769)

988   Which sorrow] World-sorrow TERRELL

989   we would not spare] we'd not appease SING2; we would not share STAUNTON (1872, p. 769)

996   Grace goe] So Grace be mF2FL; All grace go SEYMOUR

999   still] full KELLNER (1931)

1004   empty] *Om.* SEYMOUR

1008   swelling] smelling mTBY3, SEYMOUR

1009   studied] steadied TERRELL

1011   feard] froid mTHEO; stale ANON. *in* CAM1; hard GOULD (1884, p. 11)

1012 take] took mTBY3, SEYMOUR
1014 beats,] ⁓ , ORGER
vaine: oh place] vane o' the place MALONE (1783, p. 5); O vain
place MITFORD
1016 and tye] yea, tie SEYMOUR
1017 Blood] Blood, blood WALKER *in* DYCE1 (*and* 1860, 2:142)
1019 not] yet JOHN1; now CAM3
1023 my bloud] the blood ANON. *in* CAM2
1026 fitnesse] fullness KELLNER (1931)
1030 generall subiect] gentle subjects STEEVENS (v1773)
1050 all as easie] as offensive KELLNER (1925, p. 102)
1052 restrained meanes] restrained moulds MALONE (1780, 1:97);
reserved wombs KELLNER (1931)
1055 Say] Yea, say WALKER (1854, p. 23)
1056–7 had . . . tooke] would . . . take SEYMOUR
1062 compel'd] corporal KELLNER (1931)
1065–6 for I . . . say] for it . . . 'say ("assay") KELLNER (1931)
1067 I (now] If now CAM3
1077 you] your mTBY1
1079 of] are DENT MS *in* HAL
1080 your] yours JOHN1
1087 these] those TANNENBAUM (1931)
1088 an en-shield] an enshrined ANON. *in* LEE (ed. 1907); a conceal'd
BAILEY (1866); an inshealed ("inhusked") HAINES
louder] lovelier BAILEY (1866)
1089 beauty] itself KEIGHTLEY (1867)
could displaied] broad-displayed BAILEY (1866)
me] me now KEIGHTLEY (1867)
1097 that] this SEYMOUR; to that JACKSON (1819)
1098 But in the losse of] Put in the loss in JACKSON (1819)
losse] list HEATH; case WHITE (1854, pp. 153–6, *withdrawn*
1857); top WELLESLEY
1102 all-building-Law] thrall-holding law BULLOCH; all-beilding-Law
("impregnable") THISELTON (1901, p. 22); all-wielding law PERRING
(1907), KELLNER (1925, p. 43)
and] an mTBY3
1111 longing haue bin sicke] being sick I had long'd mTBY3
1115 at] for JOHN1
1119 so] *Om.* SEYMOUR
1121 houses] opposed houses CAM1
1128 not what vve] what we not WAGNER (ed. 1880)
1132 Else] I'se KELLNER (1931)
1133–4 I'm not a fedary, not one that owes And does succeed thy
weakness. KELLNER (1931)
1133 fedarie] feodary of Heaven KTLY; federary TERRELL

1134　O we are weak and succeed all thy weakness. TIECK (ed. 1831, 5:382)

　　　　Owe] Love MASON (1785)

　　　　and] or LEO (1888)

　　　　succeed thy] succumb to th' GOULD (1884, p. 11); succeed man's LAMBRECHTS

1137　make] take JOHN1

1138　their] thy CAM1

1139　profiting] propagating CAPN; procreating LAMBRECHTS

1150　on] off TERRELL

1157　vertue] office GOULD (1884, p. 56)

　　　　hath a licence in't] hates all licence out KELLNER (1931)

1158–9　Which feins a little—fowler that it is—To pluck in others. KELLNER (1931)

1162　to be] too, too KELLNER (1931)

1166　aloud] SD GOULD (1884, p. 56)

1174　race] rage WAGNER (ed. 1880), GOULD (1884, p. 11); rut(t) KELLNER (1925, p. 39)

1186　perilous] pernicious mTBY3, WALKER (1860, 3:18–19)

1193　minde] mine mTBY3, JACKSON (1819)

1211　keepe] weep BAILEY (1866)

　　　　a breath thou art] Life, thou art a breath BECKET

1212　influences] influence WH1

1214　afflict] assail BECKET

　　　　Meerely] verily KELLNER (1925, p. 79)

1222　not] nought WAGNER (ed. 1880)

1232　bowels] barnes GOULD (1884, p. 56)

1233　meere] verie KELLNER (1925, p. 79)

1234　Sapego] vertigo WRAY in CAM2 (1895 *Additions,* 9:756)

1235–6　nor age But as it were] Nor age, but, as 'twere, ELZE (1886)

1237　blessed] blasted JOHN1; best of T. WHITE MS

1238　Becomes as aged] Beholding is to age KINNEAR; By curbs is anger'd KELLNER (1925, p. 124)

　　　　as aged] unaged *or* non-aged SMITH *in* GREY; enag'd T. WHITE MS; assieged BECKET; abased CAM1; as gaged *or* an abject KEIGHTLEY (1867); assailed BULLOCH

1240　neither] not *or* nor CAM3

1241–3　what's . . . deaths;] What's in this That . . . life, when in this life . . . deaths? LLOYD (1884)

1242　life? Yet] life? but mTBY1; life when KELLNER (1931); life but MAXWELL (1968)

1243　moe] near KELLNER (1931)

1260–1　*Duke.* Bring them to speak, where I may hear them speak Yet be conceal'd; MITFORD

1264   As comforts all are good, most good indeed. CAM1
        As all comforts] as all Our comforts HUD2; As comforts KELL-
NER (1931)
1280   vastiditie] vast empery WAGNER (ed. 1880)
        had] adde DENT MS *in* HAL
1290   die] not die LLOYD (1884)
1294   As doth a giant dying. SEYMOUR
1296–7   can . . . From] cannot resolution fetch For DANIEL (1870); can
in resolution faint From LLOYD (1884)
1305   head] bud mTBY3, GREY
        emmew] correct LEO (1888)
1306   Falcon] faulconer GREY
1307–8   filth . . . pond] pond . . . filth UPTON (1748, p. 239)
1309, 1312   prenzie] preenzie ("trim") BECKET; pensive LEGES;
saintly HICKSON (1851); printsy ("in print, precise") TAYLOR (1851);
phrenzied W. G. M.; frenzy! KNIGHT (ed. 1854 *in* 1309 *only*); pensie BUL-
LOCH *in* CAM1 (*withdrawn* 1878); frippery TERRELL; proxy BULLOCH;
priest-like KINNEAR; preuzie (*from Fr. preux*) ADEE, SKEAT (1896); 'prentice
LEO (1888, *in* 1309 *only*); praised THISELTON (1901, p. 25); seemly
HUTCHINSON; queazie TANNENBAUM (1931, *in* 1309 *only*), CRUNDELL;
peregrin ("falcon") BARRETT; prenez (garde) STOPES; puisne DREW; pol-
lency ("power") HULME
1310   Liuerie] knavery *or* mockery *or* witchery STAUNTON (1872, p.
769; *withdrawn* 1873, p. 535)
1312   prenzie gardes] frippery gauds TERRELL; prenzie garb *or* robes
STAUNTON (1872, p. 769); pharisee garbs JOICEY (1891); prosne *or* prozne
("homily") guards CAM3
1316   giu't] quit mTBY3, STAUNTON (1872, p. 770), ORGER (*adding
as next line*) And give thee licence from thy sister's shame
1317   him still] himself mTBY1, STAUNTON (1872, p. 770)
1324   deere] *Om.* WAGNER (ed. 1880)
1326   Yes. Has] Yet, yet, has KELLNER (1931)
1338   obstruction] destruction BAILEY (1866); abstraction CART-
WRIGHT; obstriction GOULD (1884, p. 56); astriction KELLNER
(1931)
1340   kneaded] leaded KELLNER (1931)
        delighted] delinquent mTBY2, UPTON (1746, pp. 245–6, *with-
drawn* 1748, p. 217), KELLNER (1931); benighted mTBY3, JOHN1; delated
ANON. (1780), JACKSON (1819); delivered HUTCHESSON; belighted
BECKET; alighted ANON. *in* CAM1; dislodged BULLOCH; ill-guided WAGNER
(ed. 1880); deleted *or* delited ("destroyed") ANON. *in* WHEATLEY
1342   thrilling] chilling CARTWRIGHT
1346–7   that . . . Imagine] whom . . . thought Imagines HEATH; that
termless ay in torture thole With rage and KELLNER (1931)
1347   Imagine] Immerge in WAGNER (ed. 1880)

1362 shield] yield mTBY3, WAGNER (ed. 1880); shield's! KELLNER (1931)

faire] foul KELLNER (1931)

1363 wildernesse] wildness *or* wiliness GREY

1365 perish] perish, wretch CARTWRIGHT; perish thou HUD2

1385 with] in KELLNER (1931)

1389 satisfie] fortify LAMBRECHTS

1389–90 resolution] irresolution CARTWRIGHT

1398 minde] mien mTBY2, KELLNER (1931)

1401 hand] lord KELLNER (1931)

1441 portion] virtue KELLNER (1931)

1449 her on her owne] on her her own mTBY3, CAPN (V. R.), MALONE (1780, 1:99); on her her gown of *or* on her a lamentation gown STAUNTON (1872, p. 770)

1450 a] as *or* all WAGNER (ed. 1880)

1466 referre your selfe to] reserve to yourself mTBY1, JOHN1; reserve yourself to JOHN1

1475 scaled] sealed STAU; stale'd KELLNER (1925, p. 47)

1492 we] *Clown.* We KELLNER (1931)

1498 and] over mTBY3

1502 Father] *Om.* JOHN1; *Elb.* Father—*Duke.* STEEVENS (v1773)

1528 From all faults, or at least from seeming, free! mTBY2; Free from all faults, as, faults from, seeming free! MASON (1785); Free from our faults, as from fault-seeming free! DENT MS *in* HAL; From all our faults, as faults from seeming, free SEAGER *in* CAM2; From overt faults assoilzied ("assoiled"), from seeming free! BULLOCH *in* CAM2; Free from our faults; our faults from seeming free! KINNEAR; Free from our faults, as from false seeming, free! GOLLANCZ (ed. 1894)

1537–8 this . . . not] this tune? Matter and method, is't not? mTBY3; this? tune, matter, and method,—is't not? JOHN1

1538–9 Is't . . . raine?] It's not down i' th' last reign. WARB

1540 few] of few KELLNER (1931)

1548–9 Euer . . . so.] *Verse lines ending* bawd; . . . so. WALKER (1860, 1:18)

1564 not . . . mettle] but . . . merit GOULD (1884, p. 11)

1587 harme in him:] harm. In him's KELLNER (1931)

1588 general] genteel GREY *(withdrawn in errata)*

1590 but] tut, KELLNER (1931)

1599–1600 he is a motion generatiue] he is a notion generative UPTON (1746, p. 224); he is a mule ungenerative ANON. *in* CAM1; he is a'most ungenerative BULLOCH; he has a motion generative TIESSEN; he's not a motion generative WAGNER (ed. 1880); he is a motion generated SEAGER *in* CAM2; his is a motion ungenerative SPENCE; his is a motion generative MOORE (1888); he is a mote ("mannikin") ungenerative KELLNER (1925, p. 137)

1627   vnweighing] and weening KELLNER (1931)

1630   neede] meed GOULD (1884, p. 11)

1652   I] tho' I WAGNER (ed. 1880)

1665   this͵] — : CAM1

1674   tie the gall vp] rid up the gall KELLNER (1931)

1681   sweare] severe FARMER (v1773, 10:Oo6r)

1690   abuse] reimburse mTBY3

1696   wrought] were wrought KELLNER (1931)

1704   time] turne mTHEO, GOULD (1884, p. 11); inne mTBY3

1705   Sea] Holy See KEIGHTLEY (1867)

1710   is onely] only is STAUNTON (1872, p. 867)

1710–12 as it . . . constant] as it is dangerous . . . so it is . . . inconstant STAUNTON (1872, p. 867)

1711   vertuous] perilous KELLNER (1931)

1732   leisure] lectures mTBY1; lecture CAPN (V. R.)

1748–9 Pattern in himself to shew, Grace . . . go; mTBY1; Pattern . . . In grace . . . go; MASON (1785); Pattern in himself, to show Grace and virtue. Stand or go; BECKET; Patterning . . . stand, virtue to go; HARN; Pattern . . . stand and undergo; WELLESLEY; Pattern . . . show Grace . . . go; STAU; Pattern . . . show Grace withstanding virtue's foe; BULLOCH; Pattern . . . show, . . . owe; KINNEAR; Pattern . . . show Of grace . . . go; LLOYD (1884); Pattern . . . know Place to stand on, way to go; LEO (1884)

1751   Then] Them CAM3

1758   How may likenesse made] Now may likeness made MITFORD; How, made likeness may NICHOLSON (1866); To have my likeness trade BULLOCH; How many likewise wade JOICEY (1894), KELLNER (1925, p. 86); How my likeness made ARD1

        likenesse made in] likeness hiding mTBY3; such likeness trade in HEATH; likeness, mate in LEO (1859); weakness wade in JERVIS (1860, *withdrawn* 1861), GOULD (1887, p. 67); lewdness trade in WELLESLEY; likeness masking BAILEY (1866); lightness made in SEAGER *in* CAM2; lightness make in LLOYD (1884)

        crimes] crime KEIGHTLEY (1867)

1759   Making] Make sin JACKSON (1819); (Making) FIELD; Make ill NICHOLSON (1866); Magic LLOYD (1884)

        on the Times,] on the times! FIELD; oftentimes WELLESLEY; on the time KEIGHTLEY (1867)

1760   To draw] So draw STAU; And draw NICHOLSON (1866); Drawing BULLOCH *in* CAM2

        Spiders strings] spider-strings BAILEY (1866), NICHOLSON (1866)

1761   things?] — , FIELD

1764   but] but now mSTAU

1765   disguise shall by] disguise shall buy BADHAM (p. 286); shall disguise buy BULLOCH

1783 displeas'd] displac'd WAGNER (ed. 1880)

1786 body] lady STAUNTON (1872, p. 867), KELLNER (1931)

1787 much] for much mF2FL; who *or* whom much WAGNER (ed. 1880)

here] her STAUNTON (1872, p. 867)

1792 constantly] confidently KELLNER (1931)

time] same STAUNTON (1872, p. 867)

1805–6 There I've my heavy promise made to call, Upon the middle of the night, on him. BULLOCH

1807 you] she STAUNTON (1872, p. 667)

1810 action] accent mTHEO

1828 haue] have oft STAU; here have *or* have here WALKER (1860, 2:262)

1835 volumes of report] millions of reporters KELLNER (1931)

1836 Quest] gest ("lampoon") KELLNER (1931)

1838 father] fable KELLNER (1931)

1849 Nor] No, KELLNER (1931)

1854 Our tythe's to reap not yet; our corn's to sow. WARBURTON MS *in* JOHN1; Our tythe's to reap, for yet our corn's to sow. CAPN; Nor, corn to reap, forget our time to sow. ORGER

for yet our Tithes to sow] for that our tilth's to sow JERVIS (1860, *withdrawn* 1861); though yet our tithe's to sow WAGNER (ed. 1880); afore our tithe's to stow KELLNER (1931)

1896 *Abh.*] *Om.* J. LLOYD *in* CAM1

1900 Theefe] hangman KINNEAR

1926 spirits] spirit WALKER (1860, 1:248)

1931–2 *Lines ending* Provost. . . . rung. FLEAY (1881, p. 84); here . . . rung. ELZE (1886)

1935 They] There CAPN (V. R.)

1949 Wounds th'unresisting Posterne with these strokes mTHEO; That wounds the postern with these insisting strokes. BECKET

vnsisting] unfeeling mTBY3, JOHN1; unlistening JOHN1 (8:Ii^r); unyielding GOULD (1884, p. 12); unfensive ("defenseless") KELLNER (1931); unsensing LAMBRECHTS

1973 Pardoner] pardonéd LAMBRECHTS

2008 A man] As a man KEIGHTLEY (1867)

2041 tie] clip mTBY3; rid KELLNER (1925, p. 110)

2068 writ] right COL3, STAUNTON (1872, p. 867)

2095 are now] cry now ANON. *in* CAM1; are now here WAGNER (ed. 1880); ure ("practise") now KELLNER (1931)

Lords] law's JACKSON (1819)

2149 is] is in KEIGHTLEY (1867)

2155 omit] remit KELLNER (1931)

2162 sent] send LAMBRECHTS

2166 continue] continue to keep KEIGHTLEY (1867)

2172   yond generation] yon degenerate one JOICEY (1891)

2175   Quicke] Be quick WAGNER (ed. 1880)

2176   write Letters] letters write KELLNER (1925, p. 152)

2183   cold] slow GOULD (1884, p. 12); old KELLNER (1931)

2203   Deputie] depute KELLNER (1931)

2208   Show your close wisdom, daughter, in your patience. WAGNER (ed. 1880)

2216   By] In mF2FL; To KELLNER (1931)

2119   instance] notice GOULD (1884, p. 12)

2224   And] There KINNEAR; *om.* GOULD (1884, p. 12)

2235   combined] constrained R. S. WHITE MS, KEIGHTLEY (1867); commanded ORGER; convened KELLNER (1925, p. 43); convented KELLNER (1931)

2295   against] at large *or* to th' world *or* aloud STAUNTON (1872, p. 867)

2296   reason dares her no] her reason dares not mF2FL, W. W. WILLIAMS in COL3; no reason dares her STEEVENS (v1793); treason dares her? —No JACKSON (1819); reason, dare she not ORGER

         dares her no] dares her to it MASON (1785); warns her not HARN; fears her not CARTWRIGHT; dares her mo STAUNTON (1872, p. 867); dares her do't WAGNER (ed. 1880)

2297   beares of a credent bulke] bears off a credence ANON. MS *in* QUINCY; boasts of a credent bulk ORGER; leans of a credent bulk KELLNER (1931)

2302   By] For SEYMOUR

         receiuing] reviving TERRELL

2315   *Valencius*] Varrius and to mF2FL

2326   so] soundly GOULD (1884, p. 56)

2342   hent] hemm'd ANON. *in* THEO1

2359   with] in ANON. MS *in* HAL

2362   see] see't mTBY3, KELLNER (1931)

2371   Upon a wronged—I would fain say maid. *or* Upon a wrong'd— I fain would have said maid. SEYMOUR

2396   strange? and] strange on KELLNER (1931)

2415   name] names mTBY1, KELLNER (1931)

2416   honesty] honor ANON. MS *in* QUINCY

2420   As] That SEYMOUR

         madnesse] sanity *or* saneness STAUNTON (1872, p. 867)

2425   And hide] And hid, PHELPS *in* CAM2; And chide JERVIS (1860); Unhid JERVIS (1861)

         seemes true] *Om.* MITFORD

2447   I] Ay, I ANON. *in* CAM2

2458   Mended againe:] Mend it again—MALONE (1780, 1:102); Wei(gh) again KELLNER (1931)

         matter:] matter? pray ARD1

2469   purpose surfetting] promise forfeiting mTBY3, WH2

2471   likely] unlikely LONG MS *in* CAM2

2472   like] unlike GOULD (1884, p. 12)

2516   temporary] tamperer and JOHN1; temporal WALKER (1860, 1:65)

2518   trust] troth SINGER (1853, p. 14)

2523   strange] strong mTBY2, DENT MS *in* HAL, WALKER *in* DYCE1
(*and* 1860, 3:23)

2568   such a] such, a CAM1; such, at CAM2

2583   match] murch *or* murck ("defilement") GOULD (1884, p. 12)

2612   informall] infernall LONG MS *in* CAM2

2616   with] with all LONG MS *in* CAM2

2617   to] too to mTBY3, WAGNER (ed. 1880)

2690   Take] Go take HUD2

2696   here] his TERRELL

2701   forfeites] forceps R.S. WHITE MS, JACKSON (1818, pp. 16–17)

2728   and with] and *or* with GOULD (1884, p. 12)

2735   hang'd an houre:] hanged—an' how? JOHN1; hanged anon! J.
LLOYD *in* CAM1

2752   passes] trespasses MALONE (1783, p. 6); lapses STAU

2757   *Mariana*] Marian mSTAU, ELZE (1886)

2767   Aduertysing] Administring mTBY3; Advantaging GOULD
(1884, p. 12)

         holy] wholly WAGNER (ed. 1880)

2782   purpose] purposes mTBY1, COL1

2791   *Mariana's*] Marian's mSTAU, ELZE (1886)

         adiudg'd] judg'd mTBY3; 'djudged KELLNER (1931)

2798   Loss still pays loss, and treasure answers treasure. KELLNER
(1931)

2812   confutation] computation ANON. *in* CAM2

2813   widow] endow mTBY1, TERRELL, WAGNER (ed. 1880)

2862–4   *Two lines ending* name . . . Barnardine. CAM1

2891–2   He . . . that;—Give . . . mine. JOICEY (1891)

2896   worth, worth yours] worth weighs yours BAILEY (1866);
worth's your life WAGNER (ed. 1880)

2901   so deseru'd] so undeserv'd WALKER *in* DYCE1 (*and* 1860,
1:151); sir, so deserv'd CARTWRIGHT; so ill deserv'd WAGNER (ed. 1880)

2925   *Mariana*] Marian mSTAU

2928   gratulate] gratulatory mTBY3; gratulating KEIGHTLEY (1867)

The Text

The text of *Measure for Measure* has long been a mystery to editors.
JOHNSON wrote in 1765, "There is perhaps not one of *Shakespear's* plays
more darkened than this by the peculiarities of its Authour, and the unskilful-

ness of its Editors, by distortions of phrase, or negligence of transcription." WHITE remarked in 1857 that "the text of this play is generally well printed in the folio; but it contains several passages which give more trouble to the editor and the reader than any others which occur in that volume." ROLFE commented with a lighter touch (1881, p. 352) that the text reminded him of the little girl with the curl on her forehead: "When it is good, it is very good indeed; And when it is bad, it is horrid." He agreed with White that "the play is in the main well printed in the folio (the only early text), but here and there we come across corrupt passages of the most exasperating sort; like, for instance, the famous *crux* in ii. 1. 39: 'Some run from brakes of ice, and answer none'—a textual conundrum to which Echo replies, 'And answer none'."

Conflicting views have been held about the copy for the play. KNIGHT (ed. 1840) is sure that the play was printed from the author's MS, HERFORD (ed. 1899) that "it was doubtless printed from the theatre-copy," and WILSON (ed. 1922) that the copy "was prompt-copy made up, seemingly, in places at least if not entirely, of players' parts." GREG, however, gives strong evidence for his conclusion (1955, p. 356) that "we may fairly assume that the copy for F was an edited transcript, possibly by Crane," from "foul papers that had been left in a rather rough state." LEVER (ed. 1965, p. xi) writes that "it is generally accepted that the copy" for *MM* "was the work of Ralph Crane" and (p. xxxi) that Crane transcribed his MS from "Shakespeare's own rough draft, in reasonably good condition." Recent advances in bibliography now help us to understand better the transmission of the text from MS to print.

The printers of the First Folio (1623) set *MM* from a transcript written by Ralph Crane. We have to consider, therefore, the handwriting and other characteristics of Sh.'s MSS, the scribal habits of Crane, and the different ways in which several compositors set the text.

The three pages of Addition II to *Sir Thomas More* (Harleian MS 7368, fols. 8–9r) are almost certainly in Sh.'s hand. As EVANS writes (ed. 1974, p. 1684), "They afford us a unique view of what Shakespeare's 'foul papers' may have looked like and of the kinds of problems which such copy posed for a scribe." Most lines have no punctuation at all; there are a few commas and semicolons and one doubtful colon, but not a single question mark or exclamation point. Lack of punctuation led a playhouse scribe to cancel lines 112–14, which he could not understand, and substitute four words of his own. He had to add SDs (the only one in the Shn. Hand D is incomplete, omitting More and others) and change SPs that were vague or wrong ("other," "all," and "Sher," which the scribe changed once to "Maior" and once to "Williamson," since the speakers were clearly not the same). Sh. himself, if Hand D is his, corrected miswritings such as "ar" for "or," "But" for "what," "theise" for "the," "in" for "no," and "their" for "yor," but he overlooked other errors such as "ordered" for "ordere," and he crowded more than one line of verse into lines 94, 95, 114, and 147 in the MS. Such a MS would have made poor printer's copy, and if the version of *MM* available to the Folio editors was in similar condition, it is not surprising that they chose to substitute for it a more legible text. Yet critics may have assumed too readily that the manuscript from which Crane worked was a rough draft in Sh.'s hand throughout. It may have been an intermediate transcript containing authorial revisions, of the sort which apparently underlies *JC,* and the fact that Crane prepared the printer's copy for the first four Folio plays *(Tmp., TGV, Wiv.,* and *MM)* suggests that initial editorial policy called for scribal transcripts to be given to the printer if quartos were not available. If so, one cannot be sure just what Crane was handed to copy, especially as "his influence was so strong that it obscures evidence of the kind of manuscript which he transcribed" (HOWARD-HILL, 1972, p. 138).

LEVER (ed. 1965, pp. xi–xii) and HOWARD-HILL (1972, pp. 99–102, 122–8) demonstrate many ways in which Crane's scribal habits "show through" in the Folio text of *MM.* Characteristic spellings in his transcripts of dramatic MSS which appear also in *MM,* they note, include *ceizes, coheard, confes'd, creadit, encrease, flowre, happely, masques, midle* (nowhere else in F), *misterie* (5 times, nowhere else in F), and *sirha* (for references see *Oxford Shakespeare Concordances: MM* [1969]). I find many other spellings in common between Crane's transcripts and *MM: bath* as a verb (1341 and *Barnavelt* 4.3), *beleeue* (24 times in verb forms in *MM,* never *belieue*), *choake, cleere, compleat, coyne, daies, deere, easie, feauor(ous), imploy* and *imploid, loose* (5 times as a verb, never *lose*), *medler* and *medling, meere(ly), Mistris* (11 times), *neere, paies, pallace, peece, plaid* and *plaies, practise* (6 times), *prouoake, saies* and *saist, sence* (11 times, *sense* twice), *sillable, sodaine, thether, tirant* and *tirran(n)y, tyde, vnhappely, vertue* and *vertuous, waies, waight,* and *yong* (never *young*). Many of these appear elsewhere in F, but in *MM* they were printed from Crane's MS. Crane's *-nes* was usually changed by the printers to *-nesse,* but in *MM* they kept it in *boldnes, doublenes, fewnes, goodnes* (thrice), *greatnes, newnes, seednes, sweetnes,* and *witnes.* These eleven *-nes* spellings are more than in any other Folio comedy, though there are nine in *Tmp.,* which also seems to have been printed from a transcript by Crane.

Punctuation in the Folio text of the play is mainly Crane's, somewhat modified by the compositors. Crane preferred colons to semicolons: according to HOWARD-HILL (1972, pp. 32, 82), his dramatic MSS average one colon for every 27 words (*MM* has one for every 34) and one semicolon for every 123 words (*MM* has one for every 135). He preferred question marks to exclamation marks: his MSS average one question mark for every 56 words (*MM* has one for every 66) and contain only five exclamation marks, all in 1619 in *Barnavelt* (*MM* has none). Apostrophes in his MSS average one for every 30 words, in *MM* one for every 44, with forms characteristic of Crane such as *I'haue* 1206, *ha'st* 2744 and 2745, *do'st* 207, *'Faith* 712 and 2903, *'fore-noone* 923, *Good'euen* 1700 and 2241, *'Saue* 768 and 924, *'blesse* 1500, *'Please* 771, *'Pray* 735, and *pray'thee* 155. *MM* has 93 hyphens, fewer than in the other comedies set from copy written by Crane, but including hyphenated compounds of different kinds such as *en-skied* 384, *run-by* 415, *Sister-hood* 761, *tested-gold* 908, *all-building-Law* 1102, and *vnpre-par'd* 2148. Parentheses are printed 75 times, less often than in the other Crane comedies but much oftener than in Folio comedies set from other copy. The frequency of commas and periods hardly varies from one comedy to another, so that their use seems to have been decided mainly by the compositors (Howard-Hill, pp. 85–6). Of 176 uses of a full stop within a speech in *MM,* I find that Compositor B set 77, averaging 12 to a page, while the other three compositors set 99, averaging 5½ to a page.

Crane probably added *"The Scene Vienna"* on the last page, which is paralleled in F only by "The Scene, an vn-inhabited Island" in *Tmp.* His transcript of Middleton's *Witch* has *"The Sceane Rauenna"* above the list of characters. "The names of all the Actors" (see n. 2940) lists and describes characters as in the other Folio plays printed from Crane's transcripts except *Wiv.,* where no room was left for dramatis personae. This list is the only authority for the name of the Duke, Vincentio, but it calls Pompey "Clowne" and omits the mute Varrius and all unnamed characters except the Provost and two Gentlemen.

All the five comedies printed from Crane's transcripts are divided into acts and scenes, though seven of the nine other Folio comedies are divided merely into acts and only *A YL* and *TN* into both. Howard-Hill (p. 19) finds that "acts and scenes are correctly marked in all Crane's transcripts of plays." As GREG (1955, p. 356) explains, F marks a new scene at 205 (see n.) because there is a clear stage, but Rowe and most editors continue 1.2 because Pompey had mentioned that Claudio, Provost, and Juliet were coming, and the place does not change. On the other hand, Pope and most editors mark a new scene, 3.2, at 1490 (see n.), where the Duke remains on stage. Johnson (see n. 2305) believes that Act 5 should begin after 4.4, since "a night intervenes, and the place is changed," but Rann is the only editor who agrees.

Stage-directions in *MM* are sparse, as they probably were in the MS that Crane transcribed. Entrances are usually marked, except after 365 (which follows *"Lucio within"* at 354) and 756 (where the servant returns from the door). *"Enter Isabella"* at 1248 should read *"Isabella within,"* with her entry after 1252 or 1254, and *"Enter Lucio"* at 1529 is a line too early, as is *"Exit"* at 84 (cf. Howard-Hill, pp. 24–5). Of the twenty-one exits not marked, most are obvious from commands or farewells to minor characters and only five involve major figures (924, 1926, 2251?, 2494 or 2534?, and 2938 at the end). Only one SD mentions sound, *"Enter Mariana, and Boy singing"* (1769), and only one says that persons enter *"at seuerall doores"* (2357). Greg remarks (p. 354) that not even a flourish of trumpets is indicated and that "centred directions of so-and-so 'within', followed by an entrance, are unusual and perhaps confined to this play." Howard-Hill (p. 124), noting that Compositor B set *"Cry within"* on I1ᵛ (5.1.182 [1657]) of *Err.* and also

"Barnardine within" on G3 (2101) and *"Isabell within"* on G3ᵛ (2191), though not *"Lucio within"* on F2ᵛ (354), concludes that "the compositors were almost certainly responsible" for centering these directions, since Crane's practise was to write "within" either after the SP or in the right margin. GREG (1942, p. 146) suggests that Sh. wrote the SD at 348 naming *"Francisca a Nun"* and LEVER (ed. 1965, pp. xxiv–v) that he wrote this name and *"Frier Thomas"* (289) at the head of the scenes in case he should later decide to use them. Neither name now appears in the dialogue. Lever adds that "the placing of *'Iustice'* after *'seruants'* in II. i [450] could be due to its absence from the stage directions in the draft and represent a last-minute addition taken from the speech-prefixes." I find no other evidence that Crane changed any of Sh.'s directions, though he could have, as he later changed Middleton's directions in *A Game at Chesse* (see Howard-Hill, pp. 21–4). SDs as they now stand do not suggest that he used a promptbook, since they contain none of the language characteristic of a prompter's notations.

Lever observes (p. xii) that "the absence of oaths or references to the deity where such might have been expected" may be explained by the use of a Crane transcript. Howard-Hill writes (p. 134) that "it cannot be decided whether the language had been incompletely reformed in the manuscripts Crane was given to transcribe, or whether he was instructed to remove offensive expressions." Whoever was responsible, the play seems to have been carefully purged of oaths, so that none is left stronger than *By heauen* or *Oh heauen(s).* It is especially striking that *God* is not printed even once, while *heauen* or *heauens* occurs forty-four times. THIRLBY (1747–53) in a MS note and WHITE (1854, p. 153) conjecture that *God* was changed to *heauen* in 1006, and Noble and Lever agree (see n. and cf. n. 1316–17). Thirlby and WALKER (1860, 1:214, 263) would add *God* before *'Saue your Honour* in 768 and 924, and many editors make the emendation, but either form is possible. Walker also adds *God's* before *grace* in 996 and *peace* in 2782 to improve the meter. No editor has adopted Thirlby's conjectures of *God* for *heauen* in 798 and 871 or for *Ioue* in 868, or ADEE's (1885) of *God* for *heauen* in 491, but NOSWORTHY (ed. 1969) reads *God's* for *heauens* in 1049. *Heauen* is used nine times before *forgiue, giue, grant, keepe,* or *shield* and three times in *Pray heauen,* and in all these either *God* or *heauen* is possible. The name of the Christian God is not printed in any of the Folio comedies derived from Crane transcripts except *Wiv.* (which has *the feare of God, Gods patience, Got,* and *od's*) or in *The Dutchesse of Malfy* (ed. BROWN, 1964, p. lxviii), which was also printed from Crane's transcript in 1623.

The fourth play in the Folio, *MM* fits neatly into two quires, signed F1–[G6ᵛ] and paged from 61 through 84. HINMAN (1963, 2:376–87) demonstrates that four compositors set type for the play, casting off copy and using two skeletons in regular alternation. Though evidence from distinctive types does not help here in identifying compositors, Hinman shows that a compositor new to the Folio, D, began work in *MM* and that B set five pages, F5ᵛ, F6, G2ᵛ, G3, and G3ᵛ, where he usually changed Crane's spellings *doe, goe, here* to *do, go, heere,* whereas the other three usually followed copy. CAIRNCROSS (1971, 1972) proposes further criteria and assigns many pages to C, but his arguments have rarely convinced other scholars. HOWARD-HILL (1973) gives good evidence for assigning most of the pages, proving that often one compositor set the first column and another the second. He shows that C was the only one of the four compositors who often inserted a space before a comma at the end of a line. O'CONNOR (1975, p. 101) calls quires F and G "the most vexing and challenging in the Comedies." Still, he agrees with Howard-Hill in assigning forty-one of the forty-eight columns and differs only on F1^b, F1^{va}, F2^v, F6^{va}, G1^b, and G2^a. Howard-Hill writes in a letter on 18 Sept. 1975 that he still thinks D somewhat more likely than C to have set F1^b and F1^{va} but that he accepts O'Connor's attributions of F2^v to D, F6^{va} and probably G1^b to C, and G2^a to F. If Howard-Hill's attributions in his letter prove correct, then B set thirteen columns, C set twenty-one, D set eight, and F set six.

Hinman established the order of the printing of quires, and I add the compositor most likely, on present evidence, to have set each page or column:

C C	D C	D C D	C D B	D? C B	C D? C
F3^v:4	F3:4^v	F2^v:5^a 5^b	F2^a 2^b:5^v	F1^{va} 1vb:6	F1^a 1^b:6^v

B C F	B F C	B C	F C F	B F C	B C? C
G3^v:4^a 4^b	G3:4va 4vb	G2^v:5	G2^a 2^b:5^v	G1^v:6^a 6^b	G1^a 1^b:6^v

In the first copies of F1 (about fifty) that he collated HINMAN (1963, 1:257, 265–6) found only one press variant in *MM:* in 2477 on G4^{vb} *That* is unevenly inked in Folger copies 10 and 18 but evenly inked in all others examined. He concluded that "we almost certainly have evidence here of stopping the press for the correction of a single typographical imperfection" and that the main aim of the proofreader, probably Isaac Jaggard, was "rather to remove non-substantive blemishes than to ensure the accuracy of the text." In the introduction to his facsimile of F1 (1968, p. xxi), Hinman added a second press variant: in 1760 on G1^{vb} *stings* appears in the Elizabethan Club copy at Yale but has been corrected to *strings* in all Folger copies. These two variants contrast with at least ten certain or reasonably certain variants that he found in *Tmp.,* twenty-four in *TGV,* and four in *Wiv.* COLLIER (1841, p. 4) claimed to have found a press variant *sear'd* at 1011 (see n.) in the Bridgewater F1, but INGLEBY (1861, p. 24) showed that the cross of the *f* had merely been erased and that the same change had been made in *fire* at 1232 in Collier's F2. HART (ed. 1905) notes on *caracts* at 2412 "*characts* Ff." and WILSON (ed. 1922) says "Some copies (F.) 'characts'," but HINMAN (1963, 1:257) finds no such variant, nor does he find *Tunner-dish,* which TANNENBAUM (1933, p. 107) says "occurs in some copies" of F1 for *Tunne-dish* at 1658.

Casting off copy to divide it among compositors, HINMAN (1955, p.

265) proves, led to crowding F1ᵛ, which has a narrow box for *"Scena Tertia"* followed by an entry squeezed into one line and unleaded. To save five more lines on this page, C set two other entries on the same lines with dialogue (137, 175), shortened *Gent.* to *Gen.* in 135 and -on to -ō in 170, and turned over 215. LEVER (ed. 1965, p. xx) conjectures that 176–82 "were not meant to be printed" and that the compositor set "six or seven lines which the caster-off had not taken into account."

The only wrong catchword in the play is *That* for *Then* on F5, set by D after he had set *That* in 1108 and 1111 (see n. 1113). The catchword is a SP on two pages set by B (G2ᵛ, G3ᵛ) and one possibly set by C (G1), but it is a SP and the first word on four pages set by C (F4ᵛ, F6ᵛ, G2, G6), two by D (F3, F5), and one by F (G4). B never indents the second line of a verse that overflows one line but always runs on the second line without indenting (1207, 1250, 1252, 1257, 1261, 2201). The only indentings are the *nesse* of *happinesse* set perhaps by D in 84, where there is no room to turn over or under, and the *night* of *midnight* set by F in 2659 in prose misprinted as verse. C prefers to finish a line with a turnover (6, 215, 769, 1036, 2473), and B does the same in 2222 to save a line on a crowded page. Literal errors include three confusions of *n* with *u,* two of *c* with *e,* two of *f* with long *s,* and one *r* for *t* (see pp. 277–8).

Comparison of substantive verbal errors shows that Compositor B made more numerous and more serious errors in setting 6½ pages than the other compositors did in setting 17½ pages. Probable errors by B include *fire* (1232) on F5ᵛ; *Bring them to heare me* (1260), *Through* (1280), *emmew* (1305), *prenzie* (1309, 1312), and *periury* (1349) on F6; *eate away* (1514) and *From our faults* (1528) on G1ᵃ; *deare* (1638) and *as it is as* (1710) on G1ᵛ; *y'are* (1912), *vnsisting* (1949), and *Lords* (1964) on G2ᵛ; *Forthlight* (2092) on G3; and *yond generation* (2172) and *weale-ballanc'd* (2183) on G3ᵛ, while many more are possible. Probable errors by C include *feard* (1011) on F5ᵃ; *beares of a* (2297) on G4ᵃ; *your face* (2541) on G5; and *that meete* (2938) on G6ᵛ; by D, *the rod* (316) on F2ᵇ; *Sisterstood* (353), *giuing-out* (406), and *our blood* (463) on F2ᵛ; *and to redeeme* (1057), *crafty* (1083), *Let be* (1084), *all-building-Law* (1102), *longing haue* (1111), and catchword *That* (1113) on F5ᵇ; and by F, *Giue we your hand* (2361) on G4ᵇ and *confutation* (2812) on G6ᵃ. Even if some of these are not compositorial errors, the differing degree of accuracy of the different compositors is striking. It follows that an editor should think twice before emending text set by C or F, who made very few substantive errors, and should be less reluctant to emend text set by B, who made at least one substantive error on every page he set and six on F6, or by D, who made six probable errors on F5ᵇ.

Another habit of B is to set many lines of prose as verse. LEVER (ed. 1965, p. xxviii) notes this and lists 37 such lines in the play, but I find 53, of which B set 42. C may have set 139–40, 1858–60, and F 2658–63, but B set all the rest: 1517–18, 1718–19, 1740–1, 1966–70, 1979–83, 1996–7, 2001, 2034–9, 2098, 2104–5, 2107–8, 2117–18, 2121–2, 2130–1, 2136–7,

2241-2 (which Lever prints as verse), and 2264-5. B probably followed Crane's MS, since Crane "did not extend lines of prose uniformly to the right-hand margins of his transcripts" (HOWARD-HILL, 1972, p. 36). Only nine lines of verse are printed as prose: one by D in 590-1 and the rest by C in 699-700, 2286-8 (four verse lines), and 2554-5, since all these lines scan. Lever adds five lines in 3.1, but these seem to me verse lines carried on to the next line (1206, 1249, 1251, 1256, 1260).

Apparent mislining is sometimes only apparent: Sh. may have intended a pause followed by a new line in 514-15, 1565-6, 1574-5, and 2384-5. Either he or Crane seems often to have begun a new line after a colon, since in F1 a verse line is divided into two lines after a colon at 233, 235, 2339, 2343, 2384, 2427, 2495, and 2703. Other lines were either written irregularly by Sh. or by a scribe or misread by a compositor. Different editors arrange lines differently; the best arrangement generally seems to me that of EVANS (ed. 1974). One cannot be certain, but F1 appears to divide lines wrongly in 233-6, 381, 424-30, 813, 836-7, 870-1, 900-1, 1127-8, 1206-7, 1263-4, 1517-18, 1805-6, 2339-40, 2343-4, 2376-7, 2427-8, 2495-6, 2559-60, 2693-4, and 2843. I do not think it necessary to assume mislining, as Lever does, in 472, 2169-70, 2444-6, or 2635-7, or omission before 2320, but something may have dropped out in line 11 and before 1760. The textual and commentary notes show how editors have treated these passages.

William and Isaac Jaggard printed *MM* early in 1622 from one of Crane's "reasonably accurate scribal transcripts of foul papers" (HINMAN, 1968, p. xv). Crane was evidently one of the best professional scribes of his time, since Jonson chose him in 1618 to copy *Pleasure Reconciled to Virtue,* the King's men in 1619 to prepare the promptbook of *Barnavelt,* Webster in 1623 to transcribe *The Dutchesse of Malfy* for printing, and Middleton about 1624 to copy *The Witch* and make three copies of *A Game at Chesse.* HOWARD-HILL (1972, pp. 60, 133) has shown that "the number of errors affecting the sense of the text in Crane's transcripts is relatively small, but . . . the cumulative effect of his orthographical alterations is great. . . . The general level of Crane's accuracy was high, but he was not reluctant to interfere with his text, consciously or unconsciously, when its meaning was obscure to him." The spelling and punctuation of *MM* are certainly more Crane's than Sh.'s, and he probably regularized the speech-prefixes and the division into acts and scenes.

Compositor analysis helps to explain why the text of *MM* is sometimes "very good indeed" and sometimes "horrid." An expert workman, C, set almost half the play, providing careful texts of 2.2-3 and half of 5, while another expert, F, set most of 4.1 and the other half of 5. An inexperienced workman, D, made frequent errors in 1.5 and 2.4, and B made even more in setting most of 3 and 4, especially in the great scene between Claudio and Isabel. The four compositors are almost, as Isabel puts it, "of two houses," but they are not alike in dignity.

The Date of Composition

The first record of *MM* dates the court performance before King James 26 Dec. 1604, but the play had probably been acted at the Globe earlier in the year. TYRWHITT (1766, pp. 36–7) sees allusions to James I being "impatient of the crowds that flocked to see him, especially upon his first coming" to England, quoting 76–81 (see n.) and 1030–3, and in 1773 (Var., 10:Ll4v) he finds in 1087 ff. (see n.) "ground for supposing that the play was written to be acted at court." MALONE (in Var. 1778, 1: < 319–20 >) dates the play 1603 from the same passages and adds that it was written before 1607 because 1027–9 (see n.) are imitated in that year by William Barksted in his poem *Mirrha*. CAPELL (1780, 2:3:34) suggests that references in 1.2 to war, peace, and plague (see n. 172) give "a picture of the situation of England, and of her sentiments also, in the latter end of 1603." MALONE (ed. 1790, 1.1.346) believes that 97–101 and 172 "almost decisively prove [*MM*] to have been written in 1603; when the war was not yet ended . . . and when there was some *prospect* of peace" with Spain, a peace which was proclaimed on 19 Aug. 1604. He notes (p. 347) that Parliament enacted a statute against stabbing in 1604 and that of ten prisoners named in 2078–95 "four are stabbers, or duellists." HURDIS (1792, p. 11) agrees that the play was probably produced in the first year of James (1603–4), unless the allusions already mentioned were added later. According to CHALMERS (1799, pp. 412–13) *MM* "appears to have been written" in 1604, but his only evidence for 1604 is a mistaken identification of "the Act of Fornication" (2430) with a 1604 statute which revived an act of 1 Edw. VI against bigamy.

TIECK (ed. 1831, 5:379) dates the play about 1611–12 because of the style, and ULRICI (1839, tr. 1846, p. 309 n.) thinks that "it did not precede 1609." Guessing equally wildly, LLOYD (in SINGER, ed. 1856, 1:439–42) and MATHEW (1922, pp. 66, 301–5) consider it an early play revised under James, and SAINTSBURY (1898, p. 323, and 1910, 5:214) thinks it early but left half-finished. JUNG (1904, pp. 22–5) dates it before *Blurt Master-Constable* (1602), but his parallels are too slight to prove anything. As CHAMBERS (1930, 1:453) observes, "The only marked early echo, which has been traced," is Barksted's in *Mirrha* (1607). MALONE (ed. 1790, 1.1.348 n.) points out that Barksted acted in Jonson's *Silent Woman*, produced late in 1609 under the auspices of the Queen's Revels, and "might therefore have performed a part in [*MM*], or have seen the copy before it was printed." Barksted is not known to have acted with the King's men, but he may have heard the lines spoken on the stage.

CUNNINGHAM (1842, p. 204) published the Revels Account entry in the Audit Office of the 1604 performance at Whitehall, transcribing it as follows (cf. the transcript on p. 467): "By his Matis plaiers. On St. Stiuens Night in the Hall A Play called Mesur for Mesur. Shaxberd." The Revels Account for 1604–5 was later wrongly supposed a forgery, but HAL-

LIWELL-PHILLIPPS (1880, pp. 9–10; 1885, p. 609; 1887, 2:161–7) found that Malone MS 29, which has been at the Bodleian since 1821, is "a faithful abridgement, sent most probably to Malone from the Audit Office, of the list which was printed in 1842" (1887, 2:163). LAW (1911) proved that the Revels Account is genuine, and though TANNENBAUM (1928) tried to discredit it, STAMP (1930) established its authenticity beyond further question. See also CHAMBERS (1923, 4:136–9; 1930, 2:330–1), and KELLIHER (1977, pp. 7–12), who finds Sh.'s name spelled "Shackesbeare" in 1605.

COLLIER (ed. 1842, 2:5), citing the Revels entry, concludes that *MM* was "written either at the close of 1603, or in the beginning of 1604." Since metrical tests prove useless in deciding whether a play was written in 1603 or in 1604, FLEAY dates *MM* 1603 in 1874 (p. 10) and in 1881 (in INGLEBY, p. 59), but in 1886 (p. 234) argues that all the allusions suit 1604 and that it was written in rivalry to Marston's *Fawne.* LAW (1910, p. 10) suggests that it was written in 1603 and acted at the Globe in the late spring or early summer of 1604, and ALBRECHT (1914, pp. 222–31) dates its composition between February and July 1604 because James was then negotiating peace with Spain. WILSON (ed. 1922, p. 105) conjectures that "the play was cut down shortly before Dec. 26, 1604" and "was lengthened sometime after Nov. 11, 1606," but his speculations are castles in the air, incapable of proof. WENTERSDORF (1951, pp. 175–6) thinks it "not unlikely that *MM* was written as the first new piece of James' reign for the Christmas and New Year's festivities of 1603–04," when the King's men acted at court eight times, though the plays are not named. Most scholars now agree with CHAMBERS (1930, 1:453) that "the style of the play is not inconsistent with 1604" and with KITTREDGE (ed. 1936) that "1604 is a reasonable date for its composition."

LEVER (1959, pp. 384–5) and STEVENSON (1959, pp. 192–3) support this date by quoting *The Time Triumphant* (1604), published under the name of Gilbert Dugdale and first compared with *MM* by FIRTH (1903, p. xii), which reports that King James not long before 15 Mar. 1604 "discommended the rudenes of the Multitude, who regardles of time place or person will be so troublesome." The author asks the people, "Will you in loue prease vppon your Soueraigne thereby to offend him, your Soueraigne perchance mistake your loue, and punnish it as an offence"? This is very like what Angelo says in 1030–3. Agreeing with Malone and Albrecht that the play was composed before the peace with Spain, and noting that *The Time Triumphant* was entered on the Stationers' Register 27 Mar. 1604, Lever concludes (ed. 1965, p. xxxv) that "there are good grounds for supposing that *Measure for Measure* was written between May and August 1604." This dating is possible but somewhat too precise, since the allusions are not certain enough to be conclusive.

MM seems most likely to have been written in 1604. The Paul's boys acted before the King, probably on 20 Feb. 1604 (CHAMBERS, 1923,

3:439), *The Phoenix* by Middleton, where a prince pretends to travel but remains in disguise to discover wrongs and redress them. The Blackfriars boys produced in 1604 *The Malcontent* and perhaps *The Fawne,* both by Marston and with disguised dukes. Prince Henry's men staged another disguise play in 1604, *When You See Me, You Know Me* by Samuel Rowley. Sh. and his fellow actors, now the King's men, probably expected *MM* to appeal especially to the interests of King James, like *Mac.* in 1605–6. If they followed theatrical custom, they would try out the play at the Globe, which reopened on 9 April, before they presented it at court.

Sources, Analogues, and Influences

I. Sources

Sh. could have found the plot of *MM* in one or more of these sources: George Whetstone's play *Promos and Cassandra,* his novella in *An Heptameron of Ciuill Discourses,* Cinthio Giraldi's novella in *Hecatommithi,* and his play *Epitia.*

The main source for *MM* was a two-part play by George Whetstone, *The Right Excellent and Famous Historye, of Promos and Cassandra: Deuided into Two Commical Discourses* (1578). This play was never acted, but Whetstone sent it to the printer Richard Jones before he sailed for America on a voyage with "the aduenturous Captaine, Syr *Humfrey Gylbert.*" The full text was reprinted by STEEVENS & NICHOLS (1779, 1:1–108), HALLIWELL (ed. 1854, 3:237–91), HAZLITT (1875, 6:202–304), FARMER (facsimile, 1910), BULLOUGH (1958, 2:442–513), and AMOS (1969).

Whetstone was a young man when he wrote his play, for while searching parish registers in 1930 I found the record of his baptism on 27 July 1550 at St. Lawrence Jewry, London (see *Harleian Soc. Registers* 70 [1940], 5). He was in the English army in the Netherlands when he was killed in a duel in 1587 at Bergen-op-Zoom (ECCLES, 1931, p. 648; IZARD, 1942, pp. 28–30).

THEOBALD (ed. 1733) writes that he "could prove to Demonstration, that *Shakespeare* had perus'd" *Promos and Cassandra,* but describes it as "execrable mean Stuff." WARBURTON (ed. 1747), LENNOX (1753), and JOHNSON (ed. 1765) do not even mention the play. STEEVENS (Var. 1773) remarks on its "barren insipidity" but adds that it "exhibits an almost complete embryo" of *MM* and that Sh. "took the fable of this play" from Whetstone. The first full comparison was made by SKOTTOWE (1824, 2:54–68), who notes that "Whetstone saves the culprit by producing the head of another person" (p. 56), finds many verbal parallels, and contrasts Whetstone's Rosko with Sh.'s Clown. COLLIER (1831, 3:66 n.) suggests that Sh. may have taken the title of his play from *Promos,* but his claim (ed. 1842) that Sh. "was not indebted to Whetstone for a single thought, nor for a casual expression" is disproved by HALLIWELL (ed. 1854), WHITE (ed. 1857), and SANDMANN (1882). FOTH (1878) and Sandmann also compare the characters in the two plays, and Sandmann (p. 293) concludes that *Promos* does not deserve such harsh judgments as that of Steevens. ALBRECHT (1914, pp. 41–2) thinks that Sh. may have been influenced by a soliloquy by Promos on the sudden change caused by Cassandra's modest words and another before he sees her again, "Do what I can, no reason cooles desire" (3.1). KITTREDGE (ed. 1936) emphasizes the low comedy that illustrates the corruption of society and regards Rosko as "certainly a foreshadowing of Pompey." For TILLYARD (1949, pp. 137–8) *Promos* kindled Sh.'s imagination by its "simple and basic human passions and conflicts: Promos's dilemma between justice and lust; Andrugio's instinct to save his life at almost any cost; Cassandra's dilemma between the desires to save her brother's life and to save her honour." BULLOUGH (1958, 2:407) comments that Sh. took over from Whetstone "his division of the play into scenes from high and low life and his linking of them by a common theme of sexual license and social abuse." LEVER (ed. 1965, pp. xlii–iii) points out that "most of the plot-sequence of Shakespeare's first two acts was based on" *Promos,* as were the preparations for the Duke's reentry into Vienna, and NOSWORTHY (1965, p. 130) that "Whetstone's play supplies the main plot, a fair proportion of the background and practically the whole of the governing morality." HAMILTON (1968, pp. 69–102) carefully compares and contrasts the comic elements in *Promos* and *MM.*

The following notes comment on similarities of situation and of language between the two plays: 0.1–0.2, 52, 98, 310, 534, 810, 811, 885–6, 935, 939–40, 997–9, 1011, 1040, 1062–3, 1075, 1096, 1117, 1131, 1157–9, 1321–3, 1355, 1495, 1667, 1912, 1996, 2295, 2352–3, 2363, 2370, 2469, 2550–1, 2641, 2754, 2792, 2797, 2896, and 2898.

Whetstone retold in prose "The rare Historie of Promos and Cassandra, reported by Madam Isabella" and published it as a Christmas tale in *An Heptameron of Ciuill Discourses* (1582, rpt. as *Aurelia* in 1593). This is not, as COLLIER (1831, 3:64) and others wrongly call it, a translation from Cinthio Giraldi. It condenses the main plot of Whetstone's play, with few changes. The tale was reprinted by COLLIER (1843, 2:53–62), HALLIWELL (ed. 1854, 3:11–16), HAZLITT (1875, 3:155–66), O'BRIEN (1937, pp. 154–65), SPENCER (1968, pp. 119–27), and SHKLANKA (1977).

FARMER (1767, p. 15), who doubted that Sh. could read Italian, thought that "probably all he knew of the matter was from Madam *Isabella* in the *Heptameron* of *Whetstone.*" After Steevens everyone agreed that the chief source is *Promos,* but Collier and many others believed that Sh. took the name Isabella from *Heptameron,* a conjecture incapable of proof. HEBLER (1874, p. 156) remarks that Andrugio's disguise as a hermit in *Heptameron* may have suggested that of the Duke, and ALBRECHT (1914, pp. 88–90) that Andrugio before pleading with his sister is torn between shame and fear of death in *Heptameron* but not in *Promos*. TILLYARD (1949, pp. 136–7) concludes that Sh. was indebted to both but that the way he "deals with the theme of the principles of justice is nearer the narrative." LASCELLES (1953, p. 19) argues that the climax is better handled in *Heptameron* than in *Promos,* and BENNETT (1966, p. 16) that Sh. "might well have turned through this attractive little book and found all that he actually took from the old plot." Others have agreed with LEVER (ed. 1965, p. xxxv n.) that Whetstone's story "adds nothing to the material of his play." There are no clear verbal echoes, and I find no convincing proof that Sh. used *Heptameron*. Nevertheless, the story is reprinted here so that readers may compare it with *Promos and Cassandra*. It is alluded to in notes 2955, 2127–8, and 2315.

Whetstone's source, which Sh. probably read since he used it for *Oth.,* was *Hecatommithi,* or *Cento Novelle* (Monreale, 1565) by Giovanni Battista Giraldi, who also called himself Cinthio Giraldi. This book proved so popular that it was reprinted at Venice in 1566, 1574, 1580, 1584, and 1593, and translated into French by Gabriel Chappuys in 1583–4 and into Spanish in 1590. Novella 85 may be read in Italian in HALLIWELL (ed. 1854, 3:4–11) and HAZLITT (1875, 3:169*–84*) and in English translation in LENNOX (1753, 1:1–20), BULLOUGH (1958, 2:420–30), and LEVER (ed. 1965, pp. 155–65). I have compared the English versions and made my own translation. Giraldi's "Massimiano" is not the Roman emperor Maximian, as supposed by LASCELLES (1953, p. 10) and Bullough (2:410 n.), but the famous Maximilian I, 1459–1519 (BUDD, 1931, p. 720; HORNE, 1962, p. 111).

LANGBAINE (1691, p. 459) lists *"Measure for Measure,* a Comedy, founded on a Novel in *Cynthio Giraldi: viz. Deca Ottava, Novella 5ª."* POPE (ed. 1723) abbreviates the reference to *"Dec. 8. Nov. 5."* and WARBURTON (ed. 1747) absurdly expands this to *"December 8. November 5."* THEOBALD (ed. 1733) remarks "with how much Judgment *Shakespeare* has given Turns to this Story, from what he found it in *Cinthio Giraldi*'s Novel," saving the brother's life and his sister's honor by inventing Mariana and making the Duke remain incognito to observe his deputy, but LENNOX (1753, 1:37) objects that "what he has altered from *Cinthio,* is altered greatly for the worse." JOHNSON (ed. 1765) suspects "that *Cinthio* was not the authour whom *Shakespear* immediately followed" and DOUCE (1807, 1:157–8) doubts whether he "ever saw the story as related by Cinthio," but HALLIWELL (ed. 1854, 3:16) thinks it "by no means improbable" that he knew it. HART (ed. 1905, p. xix) suggests that he met the story in Cinthio while writing *Oth.* and then looked up Whetstone's play, whereas ADAMS (1923, pp. 362–3) and LASCELLES (1953, p. 161) conjecture that he read *Promos* first and then *Hecatommithi*. ALBRECHT (1914, pp. 47–81), in a full and valuable comparison, finds Cinthio's influence important, from the fine dramatic opening to the Emperor's sentence of death for death. Sh.'s indebtedness to *Hecatommithi* seems possible to LAWRENCE (1931, p. 89) and DORAN

(1954, pp. 385–9), probable to BUDD (1931, p. 721), Lascelles (pp. 32–6), MUIR (1957, pp. 101–5), and BULLOUGH (1958, 2:401–2, 406), and certain to SISSON (ed. 1954), SCHANZER (1963, pp. 84–6, 103), and LEVER (ed. 1965, p. xxxix). See also nn. 1199, 2494.

Giraldi dramatized the story in the last play he wrote before his death in 1573: *Epitia,* published in 1583. BULLOUGH (1958, 2:430–42) summarizes the play and translates some speeches. A Magistrate urges Juriste, Governor of Innsbruck, to execute strict justice on Vico, who had been condemned to death for ravishing a virgin, whereas a Secretary argues for equity and mercy, since Vico would marry the girl to save his life. Juriste promises Vico's sister Epitia that if she will lie with him he will spare her brother and marry her, but after enjoying her he orders Vico put to death and sends the head to her. A Messenger tells how Vico was executed: the Captain of the Prison had expected a reprieve but had to obey the letter from Juriste signed with his seal. After Epitia convinces the Emperor that her complaint is "More true than truth," he orders Juriste to marry her, after which he will be put to death. Though Juriste's sister Angela pleads for his life, Epitia seeks revenge, until the Captain reveals that he has saved Vico and instead sent the head of a murderer who looked just like him. Epitia then forgives Juriste, begs mercy for him, and secures his pardon as well as her brother's.

HALLIWELL (ed. 1854, 3:16) finds "a few minor indications" that Sh. read *Epitia.* This seems unlikely to KLEIN (1874, 5:353–5), ANDERS (1904, pp. 71, 136), CUNLIFFE (1907, pp. 599 f.), and LASCELLES (1953, pp. 12–13, 17–18), but likely to GARNETT (1898, p. 227), LEE (1898, pp. 237–8), WOLFF (1910, p. 18), DOCCIOLI (1914, pp. 155 ff.), ADAMS (1923, pp. 362–3), LAWRENCE (1931, p. 89), PRAZ (ed. 1939, pp. xvi–xxvi), and CAVALCHINI (1968, pp. 59–69). ALBRECHT (1914, pp. 94–111) argues for it by noting wordplay on the names of Angela and Angelo, parallels in the messenger, letter, and seal and in the wishes of Angela and Isabella to "pluck out his eyes," the close resemblance between brother and criminal, and the insistence by the Magistrate and Angelo on rigorous justice. BUDD (1931, pp. 722–6) concludes that Sh. must have known the play well and that "practically every opinion on Justice expressed in [*MM*] is canvassed at greater length in *Epitia.*" BALL (1945, pp. 143–6) compares Angela with Mariana, each "a woman who loves the deputy, who is deceived by him, and who, when his guilt is brought to light, nevertheless pleads for his life," and finds the final scenes of the plays similar. DORAN (1954, pp. 385–9) observes many significant correspondences, emphasizing the full treatment of the themes of justice and mercy, power and authority. HORNE (1962, pp. 112–13) compares *Epitia,* 5.7, "Vico is saved, Iuriste is saved, Epitia's honour is saved," with *MM* 1473–5, "by this is your brother saued, your honor vntainted, the poore *Mariana* aduantaged." *Epitia* has been accepted as an important source by MUIR (1957, pp. 102–5, and 1977, pp. 176–7), who cites other verbal parallels; BULLOUGH (1958, 2:402–3, 406), who calls it "a problem-play about Justice and Mercy"; SCHANZER (1963, p. 86), who considers it a strong influence on Angelo and his dialogue with Escalus; and LEVER (ed. 1965, pp. xl–i), who writes that "as a whole, Cinthio's drama, with its neoclassical structure and formal characterization, bears little obvious resemblance to Shakespeare's; but the high intellectual tone of *Epitia,* its serious treatment of judicial issues, its example of a potential tragedy steered to a happy conclusion, place it on an artistic level nearer to that of Shakespeare's play than any other version of the story."

Sh. based *MM* chiefly on *Promos and Cassandra,* but there is some evidence that he also read *Hecatommithi* and *Epitia.* Since the influence of *Epitia* seems to have been more general than specific, that play is not reprinted here. Following are the texts of *Promos and Cassandra,* of Whetstone's story from the *Heptameron* for purposes of comparison with his play, and of the novella from *Hecatommithi.*

GEORGE WHETSTONE, *PROMOS AND CASSANDRA* (1578)

The copy of "the famous historie of Promos and Cassandra, devided into twoe comicall discourses, compiled by George Whetstone" (Greg, *Bibliography,* no. 73–4) was entered on the Stationers' Register to Richard Jones on 31 July 1578. A quarto of the two-part play was issued in August, probably from the press of John Charlewood. There was no subsequent edition during the 16th or 17th c.

In the 1578 quarto the Epistle and the Argument are printed in roman with incidental italic and "The Printer to the Reader" and the text of the play in black letter with incidental roman and italic. Here the Epistle and the Argument are reprinted in Q's roman and italic. In the rest of the text black letter is converted to roman, and italic is used incidentally according to the conventions usually observed by Elizabethan printers. Except for a few turnovers, Q's verse lineation is retained but prose is relined. Ornamental initials and display capitals have been replaced by regular capitals, and the capitals which conventionally follow display letters have been reduced. Flowerets and other typographical ornaments have been removed. Q's occasional *vv*'s have been replaced by *w*'s, its abbreviations and contractions expanded, and its incorrect or badly misleading punctuation emended after Q's own style, which punctuates to mark caesuras and other pauses. The TLNs which occasionally appear refer to the text of *MM.*

The text is based on the Folger Shakespeare Library's complete copy of the quarto (STC 25347, copy 1).

THE RIGHT EXCEL-   [A1ʳ]

lent and famous Historye, of

Promos and *Cassandra* :

Deuided into two Commicall
Discourses.

In the fyrste parte is showne, the
vnsufferable abuse, of a lewde Magistrate:

The vertuous behauiours of a chaste Ladye:

The vncontrowled leawdenes of a fauoured
Curtisan.

And the vndeserued estimation of a pernicious Parasyte.

In the second parte is discoursed,
the perfect magnanimitye of a noble Kinge,
in checking Vice and fauouringe Vertue:

Wherein is showne, the Ruyne and ouer-
throwe, of dishonest practises: with the ad-
uauncement of vpright dealing.

The worke of George
Whetstones Gent.

Formæ nulla fides.

TO HIS WORSHIPFVLL   [A2ʳ]
friende, and Kinseman, *William*
Fleetewoode Esquier, Recorder
of London.

Syr, (desirous, to acquite your tryed frendships, with some token of good
will:) of late I perused diuers of my vnperfect workes, fully minded to bestowe
on you, the trauell of some of my forepassed time. But (resolued to accompanye,
the aduenturous Captaine, Syr *Humfrey Gylbert*, in his honorable voiadge,) I found
my leysure too littel, to correct the errors in my sayd workes. So that (inforced) I
lefte them disparsed, amonge my learned freendes, at theyr leasure, to polish, if I
faild to returne: spoyling (by this meanes) my studdy of his necessarye furnyture.
Amonge other vnregarded papers, I fownde this Discource of *Promos* and *Cassandra*: which, for the rarenesse, (and the needeful knowledge) of the necessary matter contained therein (to make the actions appeare more liuely,) I deuided the
whole history into two Commedies: for that, *Decorum* vsed, it would not be con-
uayde in one. The effects of both, are good and bad: vertue intermyxt with vice,
vnlawfull desyres (yf it were posible) queancht with chaste denyals: al needeful
actions (I thinke) for publike vewe. For by the rewarde of the good, the good
are encouraged in wel doinge: and with the scowrge of the lewde, the lewde are
feared from euill attempts: mainetayning this my oppinion with *Platoes* auctority.

Nawghtinesse, commes of the corruption of nature, and not by readinge or hearinge the liues of the good or lewde (for such publication is necessarye,) but goodnesse (sayth he) is beawtifyed by either action. And to [A2ᵛ] these endes: *Menander*, *Plautus*, and *Terence*, them selues many yeares since intombed, (by their Commedies) in honour, liue at this daye. The auncient *Romanes*, heald these showes of suche prise, that they not onely allowde the publike exercise of them, but the graue Senators themselues countenaunced the Actors with their presence: who from these trifles wonne morallytye, as the Bee suckes honny from weedes. But the aduised deuises of auncient Poets, discredited, with the tryfels of yonge, vnaduised, and rashe witted wryters, hath brought this commendable exercise in mislike. For at this daye, the *Italian* is so lasciuious in his commedies, that honest hearers are greeued at his actions: the *Frenchman* and *Spaniarde* folowes the *Italians* humor: the *Germaine* is too holye: for he presentes on euerye common Stage, what Preachers should pronounce in Pulpets. The *Englishman* in this quallitie, is most vaine, indiscreete, and out of order: he fyrst groundes his worke, on impossibilities: then in three howers ronnes he throwe the worlde: marryes, gets Children, makes Children men, men to conquer kingdomes, murder Monsters, and bringeth Gods from Heauen, and fetcheth Diuels from Hel. And (that which is worst) their ground is not so vnperfect, as their workinge indiscreete: not waying, so the people laugh, though they laugh them (for theyr follyes) to scorne: Manye tymes (to make mirthe) they make a Clowne companion with a Kinge: in theyr graue Counsels, they allow the aduise of fooles: yea they vse one order of speach for all persons: a grose *Indecorum*, for a Crowe, wyll yll counterfet the Nightingales sweete voice: euen so, affected speeche doth misbecome a Clowne. For to worke a Commedie kindly, graue olde men, should instruct: yonge men, should showe the imperfections of youth: Strumpets should be lasciuious: Boyes vnhappy: and Clownes, should speake disorderlye: entermingling all these actions, in such sorte, as the graue matter, may instruct: and the pleasant, delight: for without this chaunge, the [A3ʳ] attention, would be small: and the likinge, lesse.

But leaue I this rehearsall, of the vse, and abuse of Commedies: least that, I checke that in others, which I cannot amend in my selfe. But this I am assured, what actions so euer passeth in this History, either merry, or morneful: graue, or lasciuious: the conclusion showes, the confusion of Vice, and the cherising of Vertue. And sythe the end tends to this good, although the worke (because of euel handlinge) be vnworthy your learned Censure, allowe (I beseeche you) of my good wyll, vntyl leasure serues me, to perfect, some labour of more worthe. No more, but that, almightye God be your protector, and preserue me from dainger, in this voiadge, the xxix. of Iuly. 1578.

Your Kinsman to vse,
George Whetstone.

The Printer to the Reader. [A3ᵛ]

Gentle Reader, this labour of Maister *Whetstons*, came into my handes, in his fyrst coppy, whose leasure was so lyttle (being then readie to depart his country) that he had no time to worke it a new, nor to geue apt instructions, to prynte so difficult a worke, beyng full of variety, both matter, speache, and verse: for that euery sundry Actor, hath in all these a sundry grace: so that, if I commit an error, without blaming the Auctor, amend my amisse: and if by chaunce, thou light of some speache that seemeth dark, consider of it with iudgement, before thou condemne the worke: for in many places he is driuen, both to praise, and blame, with one breath, which in readinge wil seeme hard, and in action, appeare plaine. Vsing this courtesy, I hould my paynes wel satisfyed, and Maister *Whetston* vniniured: and for my owne part, I wil not faile to procure such bookes, as may profit thee with delight.

Thy friend. R. I.

The Argument of the whole   [A4ʳ]
Historye.

In the Cyttie of *Iulio* (sometimes vnder the dominion of *Coruinus* Kinge of *Hungarie*, and *Boemia*) there was a law, that what man so euer commited Adultery, should lose his head, and the woman offender, should weare some disguised apparrel, during her life, to make her infamouslye noted. This seuere lawe, by the fauour of some mercifull magistrate, became little regarded, vntill the time of Lord *Promos* auctority: who conuicting, a yong Gentleman named *Andrugio* of incontinency, condemned, both him, and his minion to the execution of this statute. *Andrugio* had a very vertuous, and beawtiful Gentlewoman to his Sister, named *Cassandra*: *Cassandra* to enlarge her brothers life, submitted an humble petition to the Lord *Promos*: *Promos* regarding her good behauiours, and fantasyng her great beawtie, was much delighted with the sweete order of her talke: and doyng good, that euill might come thereof: for a time, he repryu'd her brother: but wicked man, tourning his liking vnto vnlawfull lust, he set downe the spoile of her honour, raunsome for her Brothers life: Chaste *Cassandra*, abhorring both him and his sute, by no perswasion would yeald to this raunsome. But in fine, wonne with the importunitye of hir brother (pleading for life:) vpon these conditions, she agreede to *Promos*. First that he should pardon her brother, and after marry her. *Promos* as feareles in promisse, as carelesse in performance, with sollemne vowe, sygned her conditions: but worse then any Infydel, his will satisfyed, he performed neither the one nor the other: for to keepe his aucthoritye, vnspotted with fauour, and to preuent *Cassandraes* clamors, he commaunded the Gayler secretly, to present *Cassandra* with her brothers head. The Gayler, with the outcryes of *Andrugio*, (abhorryng *Promos* lewdenes,) by the prouidence of God, prouided thus for his safety. He presented *Cassandra* with a Felons head newlie executed, who (being mangled, knew it not from her brothers, by the Gayler, who was set at libertie) was so agree-[A4ᵛ]ued at this trecherye, that at the pointe to kyl her selfe, she spared that stroke, to be auenged of *Promos.* And deuisyng a way, she concluded, to make her fortunes knowne vnto the kinge. She (executinge this resolution) was so highly fauoured of the King, that forthwith he hasted to do Iustice on *Promos*: whose iudgement was, to marrye *Cassandra*, to repaire her crased Honour: which donne, for his hainous offence he should lose his head. This maryage solempnised, *Cassandra* tyed in the greatest bondes of affection to her husband, became an earnest suter for his life: the Kinge (tendringe the generall benefit of the common weale, before her special ease, although he fauoured her much) would not graunt her sute. *Andrugio* (disguised amonge the company) sorrowing the griefe of his sister, bewrayde his safetye, and craued pardon. The Kinge, to renowne the vertues of *Cassandra*, pardoned both him, and *Promos.* The circumstances of this rare Historye, in action lyuelye foloweth.

The Historie, of *Promos* and *Cassandra*.

Actus. 1.*Scena.* 1.

Promos, Mayor, Shirife, Sworde bearer: One with a
bunche of keyes: Phallax, *Promos man.*

[*Promos.*] You Officers which now in *Iulio* staye,
Know you our leadge, the King of *Hungarie*:
Sent me, *Promos*, to ioyne with you in sway:
That styll we may to *Iustice* haue an eye.
And now to show, my rule and power at lardge,
Attentiuelie, his Letters Pattents heare:
Phallax, reade out my Soueraines chardge.
   Phal. As you commaunde, I wyll: giue heedefull eare.

Phallax *readeth the Kinges Letters Patents, which must be
fayre written in parchment, with some great counterfeat seale.* *

   Pro. Loe, here you see what is our Soueraignes wyl,
Loe, heare his wish, that right, not might, beare swaye:
Loe, heare his care, to weede from good the yll,
To scoorge the wights, good Lawes that disobay.
Such zeale he beares, vnto the Common weale,
(How so he byds, the ignoraunt to saue)
As he commaundes, the lewde doo rigor feele.
Such is his wish, such is my wyll to haue:
And such a Iudge, here *Promos* vowes to be.
No wylfull wrong, sharpe punishment shall mysse,
The simple thrall, shalbe iudgde with mercie,
Each shall be doombde, euen as his merite is: *Loue, hate*
Loue shall not staye, nor hate reuenge procure,   *and gaine,*
Ne yet shall Coyne, corrupt or foster wrong: *the causes*
I doo protest, whylste that my charge indure,   *of Iniu-*
For friende nor foe, to singe a partiall song.   *stice.*
   Thus haue you heard, howe my Commission goes,
He absent, I present our Soueraigne styll:
It aunsweres then, each one his dutie showes,
To mee, as him, what I commaunde and wyll.
   Ma. Worthy Deputie, at thy chardge we ioye,   [B1ᵛ]
We doe submitte our selues, to worke thy heast:
Receyue the sword of *Iustice* to destroy,   [TLN 810]
The wicked impes, and to defend the rest.
   Shri. Our Citty keyes, take wisht Liftenaunt heare,
We doe committe our safetie to thy head:
Thy wyse foresight, will keepe vs voyde of feare,
Yet wyll we be assistant still at neede.

seale] *zeale* Q

Pro. Both Swoorde and Keies, vnto my Princes vse,
I doo receyue and gladlie take my chardge.
It resteth nowe, for to reforme abuse,
We poynt a tyme, of Councell more at lardge,
To treate of which, a whyle we wyll depart.
   Al speake. To worke your wyll, we yeelde a wylling hart.   *Exeunt.*

Actus. 1.*Scena.* 2.

Lamia, *a Curtizane*, entreth synging.

Al a flaunt now vaunt it, braue wenche cast away care,   *The Song.*
With Layes of Loue chaunt it, for no cost see thou spare:

Sith Nature hath made thee, with bewty most braue,
Sith Fortune doth lade thee, with what thou wouldst haue.
Ere Pleasure doth vade thee, thy selfe set to sale:
All wantons wyll trade thee, and stowpe to thy stale.
   All a flaunt, Vt Supra.

Yong Ruflers maintaines thee, defends thee and thine,
Olde Dottrels retaines thee, thy Beuties so shine:
Though many disdaynes thee, yet none maye thee tuch:
Thus Enuie refraynes thee, thy countenaunce is such.
   All a flaunt, Vt Supra.

Triumphe fayre *Lamia* now, thy wanton flag aduaunce,   *Shee speaketh.* [B2ʳ]
Set foorth thy selfe to brauest show, bost thou of happy chaunce:
Gyrle, accompt thou thy selfe the cheefe, of Lady Pleasures traine,
Thy face is faire, thy forme content, thy Fortunes both doth staine.
Euen as thou wouldst, thy house doth stande, thy furniture is gay,
Thy weedes are braue, thy face is fine, and who for this doth paye?
Thou thy self? no, the rushing* Youthes, that bathe in wanton blisse,
Yea, olde and dooting fooles sometimes, doo helpe to paye for this.
Free cost betweene them both I haue, all this for my behoue,
I am the sterne, that gides their thoughts, looke what I like, they loue.
Few of them sturre, that I byd staie, if I bid go, they flye:
If I on foe pursue reuenge, *Alarme* a hundred crye.
The brauest I their harts, their handes, their purses holde at wyl,
Ioynde with the credite of the best, to bowlster mee in yll.
But see wher as my trustie man, doth run, what newes brings he?

Actus. 1.*Scena.* 3.

Rosko (Lamias man) *Lamia.*

*rushing] *read* rufling?

Ros. Good people, did none of you, my mistresse *Lamia* see?
La. *Rosko,* what newes, that in such haste you come blowing?*
Ros. Mistresse, you must shut vp your shops, and leaue your
    occupying.
La. What so they be, foolish knaue, tell mee true?
Ros. Oh yll, for thirtie? besydes you.
La. For mee good fellowe, I praye thee why so?
Ros. Be patient Mistresse, and you shall knowe.
La. Go too, saye on.
Ros. Marrie, right nowe at the Sessions I was,
And thirtie must to *Trussum corde** go.
Among the which (I weepe to showe) alas:
La. Why, what's the matter man?
Ros. O *Andrugio*,
For louing too kindlie, must loose his heade,
And his sweete hart, must weare the shamefull weedes:
Ordainde for Dames, that fall through fleshly deedes.
La. Is this offence, in question come againe?   [B2ᵛ]
Tell, tell, no more, 'tys tyme this tale were done:
See, see, howe soone, my triumphe turnes to paine.
Ros. Mistresse, you promised to be quiet,
For Gods sake, for your own sake, be so.
La. Alas poore *Rosko*, our dayntie dyet,
Our brauerie and all we must forgo.
Ros. I am sorie.
La. Yea, but out alas, sorrowe wyll not serue:
Rosko, thou must needes prouide thee else where,
My gaynes are past, yea, I my selfe might starue:
Saue that, I did prouide for a deare yeare.
Ros. They rewarde fayre (their haruest in the stacke,)
When winter coms, that byd their seruaunts packe.
Alas Mistresse, if you turne mee off now,
Better then a Roge, none wyll me allowe.
La. Thou shalt haue a Pasporte.
Ros. Yea, but after what sorte?
La. Why, that thou wart my man.
Ros. O the Iudge, sylde showes the fauour,
To let one theefe, bayle another:
Tush I know, ere long you so wyll slyp awrye,*
As you, for your selfe, must seeke some testimony
Of your good lyfe.
La. Neuer feare: honestly
Lamia nowe meanes to lyue, euen tyll she dye.
Ros. As iumpe as Apes, in vewe of Nuttes to daunce,
Kytte wyll to kinde, of custome, or by chaunce:
Well, howe so you stande vpon this holy poynt,
For the thing you knowe, you wyll ieobarde a ioynt.
La. Admitte I woulde, my hazarde were in vaine.
Ros. Perhappes I know, to turne the same to gaine.
La. Thou comforts mee, good *Rosko*, tell mee howe?

---

*blowing] *read* flying *for rhyme?*
* *Trussum corde*] i.e., hanging (pun on *sursum corda*, lift up your hearts)
*awrye] awaye Q

Ros. You wyl be honest, 'twere syn to hinder you.
La. I dyd but ieast, good sweete seruaunt tell mee.
Ros. Sweete seruaunt now, and late, pack syr, god bwy ye.
La. Tush, to trye thy vnwillingnesse, I dyd but ieast. [B3ʳ]
Ros. And I doo but trye, how long you woulde be honest.
La. I thought thy talke was too sweete to be true.
Ros. Yea, but meant you, to byd honestie adue?
La. No, I dyd so long since, but inforste by neede,
To byd him welcome home againe, I was decreede.
Ros. Verie good, Mistresse, I know your minde,
And for your ease, this remedie I finde:
Prying abroade, for playe fellowes and such,
For you Mistresse, I hearde of one *Phallax*,
A man esteemde, of *Promos* verie much:
Of whose Nature, I was so bolde to axe,
And I smealt, he lou'd lase mutton well. [TLN 1667]
    La. And what of this?
    Ros. Marry of this, if you the waye can tell
To towle him home, he of you wyll be fayne:
Whose countenaunce, wyll so excuse your faultes,
As none for life, dare of your lyfe complaine.
    La. A good deuice, God graunt vs good successe:
But I praye thee, what trade doth he professe?
    Ros. He is a paltrie petyfogger.
    La. All the better, suspition wyll be the lesse.
Well, go thy wayes, and if thou him espye,
Tell him from mee, that I a case* or two,
Woulde put to him, at leysure wyllinglie.
    Ros. Hir case is so common, that smal pleading wyl serue:
I go (nay ronne) your commaundement to obserue.
    La. Aye me alas, lesse *Phallax* helpe, poore wench vndone I am:
My foes nowe in the winde wyll lye, to worke my open shame:
Now enuious eyes will prie abroade, offenders to intrap, *The scurge*
Of force now *Lamia*, must be chaste, to shun a more mishap. *of lawe*
And wanton girle, how wilt thou shift, for garments fine and gay? *(and not*
For dainty fare, can crusts content? who shal thy houserent pay? *zeale)*
And that delights thee most of all, thou must thy daliaunce leaue? *keepeth*
And can then force* of lawe, or death, thy minde of loue bereaue? *the lewde*
In good faith, no: the wight that once, hath tast the fruits of loue, *in awe.*
Vntill hir dying daye will long, Sir *Chaucers* iests to proue.

Actus. 1.*Sce.* 4. [B3ᵛ]

Lamias mayde, *Lamia.*

May. Forsooth Mistris your thraule stayes for you at home.
La. Were you borne in a myll, curtole? you prate so hye.
May. The gentelman, that came the last day with Captain *Prie*:

*case] cause Q
*then force] then the force Q

La. What young *Hipolito*?
May. Euen he.
La. Least he be gone, home hye:
And will *Dalia* pop him in the neather roome,
And keepe the falling doore close tyll I come:
And tell my thraule his fortune wyll not staye.
   May. Wyll you ought else?   *Exet.*
   La. Pratyng vixen away.
Gallants adue, I venter must *Hipolito* to see,
He is both young and welthy yet, the better spoyle for mee.
My hassard for his sake I trowe, shall make him pray and pay: *Note*
He: he: shal pranck me in my plumes, and deck mee braue and gay.
Of Curtisie, I praye you yet, if *Phallax* come this waye,
Report to put a case with him, heare *Lamia* long dyd stay.

                                               Exet.

Actus. 2.Scena. 1.

Cassandra, a Mayde.

   Cass. Aye mee, vnhappy wenche, that I must liue the day,
To see *Andrugio* tymeles dye, my brother and my stay.
The onely meane, God wot, that should our house aduaunce,
Who in the hope of his good hap, must dy through wanton chance:
O blynde affectes in loue, whose tormentes none can tell,   *The force*
Yet wantons wyll byde fyre, and frost, yea hassard death, nay hell: *of loue.*
To taste thy sowre sweete frutes, digested styll with care,
Fowle fall thee loue, thy lightning ioyes, hath blasted my welfare.
Thou fyerst* affection fyrst, within my brothers brest.
Thou mad'st *Polina* graunt him (earst) euen what he would request: [B4ʳ]
Thou mad'st him craue and haue, a proofe of *Venus* meede,
For which foule act he is adiudgd, eare long to lose his heade.
The lawe is so seuere, in scourging fleshly sinne,
As marriage to worke after mends doth seldome fauor win.
A law first made of zeale, but wrested much amis.   *A good*
Faults should be measured by desart, but all is one in this,   *lawe yll*
The lecher fyerd with lust, is punished no more,   *executed.*
Then he which fel through force of loue, whose mariage salues his
       sore:
So that poore I dispayre, of my *Andrugios* lyfe,
O would my dayes myght end with his, for to appease my stryfe.

Actus. 2.Scena. 2.

Andrugio in prison, *Cassandra.*

*fyerst] *read* fyerdst?

313

An. My good Syster *Cassandra?*

Cass. Who calleth *Cassandra?*

An. Thy wofull brother *Andrugio.*

Cas. Andrugio, O dismall day, what greefes, doe mee assayle?
Condempned wretch to see thee here, fast fettered now in Iayle,
How haps thy wits were witched so, that knowing death was meede
Thou wouldest commit (to slay vs both) this vile laciuious deede.

An. O good *Cassandra*, leaue to check, and chide me, thraule therfore.
If late repentaunce wrought me helpe, I would doe so no more.
But out alas, I wretch, too late, doe sorrowe my amys,
Vnles Lord *Promos* graunt me grace: in vayne is hadywist,
Wherfore sweete sister, whylst in hope, my dampned lyfe yet weares,*
Assaulte his hart, in my behalfe, with battering tyre of teares.
If thou by sute doest saue my lyfe, it both our ioyes will be,
If not it may suffice thou soughtst,* to set thy brother free:
Wherefore speede to proroge my dayes, to morrowe else I dye.

Cas. I wyll not fayle to pleade and praye, to purchase the mercye,
Farewell awhyle, God graunte mee well to speede.

An. Syster adew, tyl thy returne, I lyue, twene hope, and dreede.

Cas. Oh happy tyme, see where Lord *Promos* coms? [B4v]
Now tongue addresse thy selfe, my minde to wray.
And yet least haste worke waste, I hold it best,
In couert, for some aduauntage, to stay.

Actus. 2.Scena. 3.

Promos with the *Shriefe* and their Officers.

Pro. Tis strange to thinke, what swarms of vnthrifts liue,
Within this towne, by rapine spoyle and theft:
That were it not, that *Iustice* ofte them greeue,
The iust mans goods, by Ruflers should be reft.
At this our Syse, are thirty iudgde to dye,
Whose falles I see, their fellowes smally feare:
So that the way, is by seuerity [TLN 310]
Such wicked weedes, euen by the rootes to teare:
Wherefore *Shriefe*, execute with speedy pace,
The dampned wightes, to cutte of hope of Grace.

Shriefe. It shalbe done.

Cas. O cruell words, they make my hart to bleede,   Cassandra
Now, now, I must, this dome seeke to reuoke,   *to hir selfe.*
Least grace come short, when starued is the steede:
    Most mighty Lord, and worthy Iudge, thy iudgement sharpe   *She kneeling*
      abate,   *speakes to*
Vaile thou thine eares, to heare the plaint, that wretched I   Promos.
    relate,   [TLN 2370]
Behold the wofull Syster here, of poore *Andrugio*,
Whom though that lawe awardeth death, yet mercy do him show:

*weares] were Q
*soughtst] soughst Q

314

Way his yong yeares, the force of loue, which forced his amis,
Way, way, that Mariage, works amends, for what committed is,
He hath defilde no nuptial bed, nor forced rape hath mou'd,
He fel through loue, who neuer ment, but wiue the wight he lou'd.
And wantons sure, to keepe in awe, these statutes first were made,
Or none but lustfull leachers, should, with rygrous law be payd.
And yet to adde intent thereto, is farre from my pretence,
I sue with teares, to wyn him grace, that sorrows his offence.
Wherefore herein, renowned Lorde, Iustice with pitie payse: [TLN 1075] [C1ʳ]
Which two in equal ballance waide, to heauen your fame will raise.
   Pro. Cassandra, leaue thy* bootlesse sute, by law he hath bene tride,
Lawe founde his faulte, Lawe iudgde him death.
   Cas. Yet this maye be replide,
That law a mischiefe oft permits, to keepe due forme of lawe,
That lawe small faultes, with greatest doomes, to keepe men styl in awe:
Yet Kings, or such as execute, regall authoritie:
If mends be made, may ouer rule, the force of lawe with mercie.
Here is no wylful murder wrought, which axeth blood againe,
Andrugios faulte may salued* be, Mariage wipes out his stayne.
   Pro. Faire Dame, I see the naturall zeale, thou bearest to *Andrugio*,
And for thy sake (not his desart) this fauour wyll I showe:
I wyll repriue him yet a whyle, and on the matter pawse,
To morrowe you shall lycence haue, a fresh to pleade his cause:
Shriefe execute my chardge, but staye *Andrugio*,
Vntill that you in this behalfe, more of my pleasure knowe.
   Shri. I wyll performe your wyll.
   Cas. O most worthy Magistrate, my selfe thy thrall I binde,*
Euen for this lytle lightning hope, which at thy handes I finde.
Now wyl I go and comfort him, which hangs twixt death and life.   *Exit.*
   Pro. Happie is the man, that inioyes the loue of such a wife,
I do protest, hir modest wordes, hath wrought in me a maze.*
Though she be faire, she is not deackt, with garish shewes for gaze,
Hir bewtie lures, hir lookes cut off, fond sutes with chast disdain.
O God I feele a sodaine change, that doth my freedome chayne.
What didst thou say? fie *Promos* fie: of hir auoide the thought,   [TLN 935]
And so I will, my other cares wyll cure what loue hath wrought.
Come awaye.   *Exeunt.*

Actus. 2.Scena. 4.

Phallax, Promos offycer, *Gripax*, and *Rapax* Promoters.

   Phal. My trusty friendes about your businesse straight,
With symple showes, your subtile meanings bayte:
Promote all faults, vp into my office,   [C1ᵛ]
Then turne me lose, the offenders to fleece.

*leaue thy] leaue of thy Q
*salued] valued Q
*binde] finde Q
*a maze] i.e., amaze

315

Gri. Tush, to finde lawe breakers let me alone,
I haue eyes, will looke into a Mylstone.
Phal. God a mercy *Gripax.*
Ra. And I am so subtyll sighted I trowe,
As I the very thoughts of men doo know.
Gri. I fayth *Rapax*, what thought thy wife when she.
To lye with the preest, by night stole from thee?
Ra. Marry she knew, you and I were at square,
And least we fell to blowes, she did prepare
To arme my head, to match thy horned browe.
Gri. Goe and a knaue with thee.
Ra. I stay for you.
Phal. No harme is done, here is but blow for blow,
Byrds of a fether, best flye together,
Then like partners, about your market goe,
Marrowes adew, God send* you fayre wether.
Gri. Fare you well, for vs take no care,
With vs this brode speeche sildome breedeth square.   *Exeunt.*
                                                                        Phallax
Phal. Marry syr, welfare an office, what some euer it be,   *alone.*
The very countenaunce, is great, though slender be the fee,
I thanke my good Lord *Promos* now, I am an officer made,   *Offices.*
In sooth more by hap then desart, in secret be it sayde:
No force for that, each shyft for one, for *Phallax* will doo so,
Well fare a head can take his tyme, nay watch for time I trow.
I smyle to thinke of my fellowes, how some braue it, some
                weight,
And thinke reward, there seruice iust, with offred shifts wyl
                bayght   *A note*
When they (poore soules) in troth do falle a myle vpon account,   *for way-*
For flattery and feruent plesing, are meanes to make men mount: *ters.*
I speake on proofe, Lord *Promos*, I haue pleased many a day,
Yet am I neither learned, true, nor honest any way.
What skyls for that, by wit or wyle, I haue an office got,
By force wherof euery lycence, warrant, pattent, pasport,
Leace, fyne, fee, *et cetera*, pas and repas, through *Phallax* hands,
Disordred persons brybe me wel, to escape from *Iustice* bands,
And welthy churles for to promote, I now haue set a worke,   [C2ʳ]
Such hungry lads, as soone will smell, where statute breakers lurk,
And if they come, within our Grype, we meane to stripe them so,
As (if they scape from open shame) their bagges with vs shall goe.
And trust me this, we officers, of this mylde mould are wrought,
Agree with vs, and sure your shame by vs shal not be sought:
But soft a whyle, I see my Lord, what makes him lowre so?
I wyll intrude into his sight, perhaps his greefe to know.

*Actus. 2.Scena. 5.**

Phallax, Promos.

*send] sent Q
**Scena. 5.*] *Scena.* 4. Q

Pro. Well mette *Phallax*, I long haue wysht to showe,
A cause to thee which none but I yet know.

Phal. Say on my Lord, a happy man weare I,
If any way, your wish I could supply.

Pro. Faine would I speake, but oh, a chylling feare,
(The case is such) makes mee from speech forbeare.

Phal. These wordes my Lord (whome euer haue bene iust)
Now makes me thinke, that you my truth mistrust.
But cease suspect, my wyll with yours shall gree,
What so (or against whome) your dealing be.

Pro. Against a wight of small account it is,
And yet I feare, I shall my purpose mys.

Phal. Feare not my Lorde, the olde Prouerbe doth saye,
Faynt harts doth steale fayre Ladyes seld away.

Pro. Fayre Ladyes O, no Lady is my loue,
And yet she sure, as coye as they wyl proue.

Phal. I thought as much, loue dyd torment you so.
But what is she that dare saye *Promos* noe?

Pro. Doe what one can, fyre wyll breake forth I see,
My words vnwares, hath showen what greeueth mee:
My wound is such, as loue must be my leache,
Which cure wyll bryng, my Grauity in speeche,   [TLN 1011]
For what maye be, a folly of more note,   [C2ᵛ]
Then for to see, a man gray heard* to dote.

Phal. No my Lorde, *Amor omnia vincit*,
And *Ouid* sayth, *Forma numen habet*.
And for to proue, loues seruice seemes the wise,
Set *Sallamon* and *Sampson*, before your eyes,
For wyt, and strength, who wonne the cheefest prise,
And both lyu'd by the lawes loue did deuise,
Which proues in loue, a certaine godhed lyes.
And Goddes rule yearely,* by wisdome from the skyes:
Whose wyls (thinke I) are wrought best by the wise.

[*Pro.*] In deede deuine, I thinke loues working is,
From reasons vse, in that my sences swarue,
In pleasure paine, in payne I fynde a blysse,
On woe I feede, in sight of foode I stearue:
These strange effects, by loue are lodgd in mee,
My thoughts are bound, yet I my selfe am free.

Phal. Well my Good Lord, I axe (with pardon sought)
Who she may be, that hath your thrauldome wrought?

Pro. The example is such, as I sygh to showe,
Syster she is, to dampned *Andrugio.*

Phal. All the better for you the game doth goe.
The prouerbe sayth, that kyt wyll vnto kinde,
If it be true, this comfort then I fynde:
Cassandras flesh is as her brothers, frayle,   [TLN 1131]
Then wyll shee stoupe, (in cheefe) when Lords assayle.

Pro. The contrary (through feare) doth worke my payne,
For in her face, such modesty doth raigne,
As cuttes of louing sutes, with chaste disdayne.

*heard] i.e., hair'd
*yearely] i.e., yarely

Phal. What loue wyll not, necessity shall gayne,
Her brothers lyfe, will make her glad and fayne.
    Pro. What, is it best, *Andrugio* free to set,
Ere I am sure, his systers loue to gette?
    Phal. My louyng Lord, your seruaunt meanes not so,
But if you will, else where in secret goe:
To worke your wyll, a shift I hope to showe.
    Pro. With ryght good wyll, for such my sicknes is,   [C3ʳ]
As I shall dye, if her good will I mys.   *Exeunt.*

Actus. 2. Scena. 6. *

The *Hangman*, with a greate many ropes abought his necke.

[*Han.*] The wynd is yl, blowes no mans gaine, for cold I neede not
    care,
Here is nyne and twenty sutes of apparrell for my share:
And some berlady very good, for so standeth the case,
As neyther gentelman, nor other, Lord *Promos* sheweth Grace.
But I maruell much, poore slaues, that they are hanged so soone,
They were wont to staye a day or two, now scarce an after noone:
All the better for the hangman, I pardons dreaded sore,
Would cutters* saue, whose clothes are good, I neuer feard the poore.
Let mee see, I must be dapper in this my facultie,   [TLN 1912]
Heare are new ropes, how are my knots, I faith syr slippery.
At fast or loose, with my *Giptian*, I meane to haue a cast:
Tenne to one I read his fortune by the Marymas fast.
    Serg. A way, what a stur is this, to see men goe to hanging?
    Han. Harke, god bwy ye, I must begone, the prisners are a comming.   *Exet.*

Actus. 2. Scena. 7. *

Sixe prisoners bounde with cordes, Two *Hacksters*, one *Woman*, one
lyke a *Giptian*, the rest poore *Roges*, a *Preacher*, with other Offycers.

> *With harte and voyce to thee O Lorde,*   *They sing.*
> *At latter gaspe, for grace we crie:*
> *Vnto our sutes, good God accorde,*
> *Which thus appeale, to thy mercie.*
> *Forsake vs not, in this distresse,*   [C3ᵛ]
> *Which vnto thee, our sinnes confesse:*
> *Forsake vs not, in this distresse,*
> *Which vnto thee, our sinnes confesse.*

*Scena. 6.] Scena. 5. Q
*cutters] i.e., cutthroats
*Scena. 7.] Scena. 6. Q

Hac. Al sorts of men beware by vs, whom present death   *First Hackster.*
     assaults,
Looke in your conscience what you find, and sorow for your faults:
Example take by our fresh harmes, see here the fruites of pride,
I for my part deserued death, long ere my theft was spide.
O careles youth, lead, lead* awrie, with euerie pleasing toy,
Note well my words, they are of woorth, the cause though my annoy.
Shun to be pranckt, in peacocks plumes, for gaze which only are,
Hate, hate, the dyce, euen as the diuell, of wanton Dames beware:
These, these, wer they, that suckt my welth, what folowed then in need?
I was intist by lawles men, on theeuish spoyles to feede.
And nusled once in wicked deedes, I feard not to offende,
From bad, to worse, and worst I fell, I would at leysure mende.
But oh presuming ouer much, styll to escape in hope,
My faultes were found, and I adiudgde, to totter in a rope:
To which I go with these my mates, likewise for breach of lawes,
For murder some, for theeuerie some, and some for litle cause.
     [*Hac.*] Beware deere frends of quarelling, thirst spoile of   *Second Hackster.*
     no mans breath,
Blood, axeth blood, I sheeding blood, vntimelie catch my   [TLN 2797]
     death.
     Wo. Maides and women, shun pride, and sloth, the rootes of   *A woman.*
     euery vice,
My death ere long, wil shew their ends, God graunt it make you
     wise.
     Ca. How now *Giptian? All a mort knaue*, for want of   *A scoffing catchpole.*
     company?
Be crustie man, the *Hangman* straight, wil reade Fortunes with thee.
     Prea. With this thy scoffing speach, good friend offend him not,   *The preacher.*
His faults are scorged, thine scape (perhaps) that do deserue his
     lot?
     Rog. Iesus saue me, I am cast, for a purse with three halfepence.   *A poore Roge.*
     Of. Dispatch prating knaue, and be hangd, that we were   *A churlish officer.*
     iogging hence.

They leysurablie depart synging. The *Preacher* whispering
some one or other of the Prisoners styll in the eare.

Our secrete thoughts, thou Christ dost knowe,   *They sing.* [C4ʳ]
Whome the worlde, doth hate in thrall.
Yet hope we that, thou wilt not soe,
On whome alone, we thus do call.
Forsake vs not, in this distresse,
Which vnto thee, our sinnes confesse,
Forsake vs not, etc.

Actus. 3. *Scena.* 1.

Promos, alone.

*lead, lead] i.e., led

319

Pro. Do what I can, no reason cooles desire,
The more I striue, my fonde affectes to tame:
The hotter (oh) I feele, a burning fire
Within my breast, vaine thoughts to forge and frame.
O straynge* effectes, of blinde affected Loue,
From wisdomes pathes, which doth astraye our wittes:
Which makes vs haunt, that which our harmes doth moue,
A sickness lyke, the Feuer Etticke* fittes:
Which shakes with colde, when we do burne like fire.
Euen so in Loue, we freese, through chilling feare,
When as our hartes, doth frye with hote desire:
What saide I? lyke to Etticke fittes? nothing neare:
In sowrest Loue, some sweete is euer suckt.
The Louer findeth peace, in wrangling strife,
So that if paine, were from his pleasure pluckt,
There were no Heauen, like to the Louers life.
But why stande I, to pleade their ioye or woe,
And rest vnsure, of hir I wish to haue?
I knowe not if *Cassandra* loue, or no?
But yet admytte, she graunt not what I craue,
If I be nyce, to hir brother lyfe to giue:
Hir brothers life, too much wyll make hir yeelde: [C4ᵛ]
A promise then, to let hir brother lyue,   *Might*
Hath force inough, to make hir flie the fielde.   *masters*
Thus though sute fayle, necessitie shall wyn,   *right.*
Of Lordlie rule, the conquering power is such:
But (oh sweete sight) see where she enters in,
Both hope and dreade, at once my harte doth tuch.

Actus. 3. Scena. 2.

Cassandra, Promos.

Cass. I see to* thralles, sweete seemes a lytle ioye,   Cassandra
For fancies free, *Andrugios* breast hath scope: *Speakes to*
But least detract, doth rayse a new annoye,   *her selfe.*
I nowe will seeke, to turne to happe his hope.
See, as I wisht, Lord *Promos* is in place,   [TLN 2898]
Nowe in my sute, God graunt I maye finde grace.
      Renowned Lorde, whylst life in me doth last,   *Shee*
In homage bondes, I binde my selfe to thee: *kneeling*
And though I did thy goodnesse latelie taste,   *speaks to*
Yet once againe, on knees I mercie seeke,   Promos.
In his behalfe, that hanges twene death and life,
Who styll is preast, if you the mendes do leeke,
His lawles loue, to make his lawfull wife.
      Pro. Faire Dame, I wel haue wayd thy sute, and wish to do thee good,

*straynge] straying Q
*Etticke] i.e., hectic
*to] two Q

320

But all in vaine, al things conclude, to haue thy brothers blood:
The stricknes of the lawe condempnes, an ignoraunt abuse,
Then wylfull faultes are hardlie helpt, or cloked with excuse:
And what maye be more wylfull, then a Maide to violate?

 Cas. The force was smal, when with hir wyl, he wretch the conquest
  gate.*

 Pro. Lawe euer at the worst, doth conster euyl intent.

 Cas. And lawe euen with the worst, awardes them punishment:
And sith that rigorous lawe adiudged* him to dye,
Your glorie will be much the more, in showing him mercie.
The world wil think, how that you do but graunt him grace on cause,   [D1ʳ]
And where cause is, there mercy should abate the force of lawes.

 Pro. Cassandra in thy brothers halfe, thou hast sayde what may be
And for thy sake, it is, if I doe set *Andrugio* free:
Short tale to make, thy beauty hath surprysed mee with loue,
That maugre wit, I turne my thoughts, as blynd affections moue.
And quite subdude by *Cupids* might, neede makes mee sue for grace
To thee *Cassandra*, which doest holde my freedome in a lace.
Yeelde to my will, and then commaund, euen what thou wilt of mee,
Thy brothers life, and all that else, may with thy liking gree.

 Cas. And may it be, a Iudge himself, the selfe   [TLN 939–40] Cassandra
  same fault should vse,   *to hir self.*
For which he domes an others death, O crime without excuse.
Renowned Lorde, you vse this speach (I hope) your   [TLN 1157–9]
  thrall to trye,
If otherwise, my brothers life, so deare I will not bye.

 Pro. Faire Dame my outward looks, my inward thoughts bewray,
If you mistrust, to search my harte, would God you had a kaye.

 Cas. If that you loue (as you saye) the force of loue you know,
Which fealt, in conscience you should, my brother fauour show.

 Pro. In doubtfull warre, one prisoner still, doth set another free.

 Cas. What so warre seekes, loue vnto warre, contrary is, you see.
Hate fostreth warre, loue cannot hate, then maye it couet force?

 Pro. The Louer ofte sues to his foe, and findeth no remorse:
Then if he hap to haue a helpe, to wyn his frowarde foe,
Too kinde a foole, I will him holde, that lets such vantage goe.

 Cas. Well, to be short, my selfe wyll dye, ere I my honor staine,
You know my minde, leaue off to tempt, your offers are in vaine.

 Pro. Bethink your self, at price inough I purchase sweet your loue,
Andrugios life suffis'd alone, your straungenes to remoue:
The which I graunt, with any wealth that else you wyll require,
Who buyeth loue at such a rate, payes well for his desire.

 Cas. No *Promos*, no, honor neuer at value maye be solde,
Honor farre dearer is then life, which passeth price of golde.

 Pro. To buie this Iuell at the full, my wife I may thee make.

 Cas. For vnsure hope, that peereles pearle, I neuer will forsake.

 Pro. These sutes seemes strange at first I see, wher modesty   *To himself.*
  beares sway,
I therfore wil set down my wyll, and for hir answer staye.

  Fayre Cassandra, *the iuell of my ioye,*   [D1ᵛ]
  Howe so in showe, my tale seemes straunge to thee:

---

*gate] i.e., got
*adiudged] adiudgd Q

> *The same well waide, thou need'st not be so coye,*
> *Yet for to giue thee respite to agree,*
> *I wyll two daies hope styll of thy consent,*
> *Which if thou graunt (to cleare my clowdes of care)*
> *Cloth'd like a Page (suspect for to preuent,)*
> *Vnto my Court, some night, sweet wenche repaire.*

Tyl then adue, thou these my words, in works perform'd shalt find.

    Cas. Farewel my Lord, but in this sute, you bootles wast your wind.

Cassandra, O most vnhappy, subiect to euerie woe,

What tongue can tel, what thought conceiue, what pen thy griefe can show?

Whom to scurge, Nature, heauen and earth, do heapes of thral ordain,

Whose words in waste, whose works are lost, whose wishes are in vain.

That which to others comfort yeelds, doth cause my heuy cheer,

I meane my beautie breedes my bale, which many hold so deere.

I woulde to God that kinde else where, bestowed had this blase,

My vertues then had wrought regard, my shape now giues the gase:

This forme so *Promos* fiers with Loue, as wisdom can not quench,

His hote desire, tyll he lust,* in *Venus* seas hath drencht.

    At these wordes *Ganio* must be readie to speake.

Actus. 3. Scena. 3.

Ganio, Andrugios boye. Cassandra.

    Ga. Mistres *Cassandra*, my Master longs to heare of your good speed.

    Cas. Poore *Ganio* his death alas, fierce Fortune hath decreed.

    Ga. His death: God forbyd, all his hope should turne to such successe,

For Gods sake, go and comfort him, I sorrowe his distresse.

    Cas. I needes must go, although with heauy cheere.

    Ga. Sir, your syster *Cassandra* is here.   *Exit.*

Actus. 3. Scena. 4.   [D2ʳ]

Andrugio *out of prison.* Cassandra *on the stage.*

    An. My *Cassandra* what newes, good sister showe?

    Cas. All thinges conclude thy death *Andrugio*:

Prepare thy selfe, to hope it ware in vaine.

    An. My death, alas what raysed this new disdayne?

    Cas. Not Iustice zeale, in wicked *Promos* sure.

    An. Sweete, show the cause, I must this doome indure?

    Cas. If thou dost liue I must my honor lose,

Thy raunsome is, to *Promos* fleshly wyll

That I do yelde: then which I rather chose,

*he lust] *read* he his lust?

322

With torments sharpe, my selfe he first should kyll:
Thus am I bent, thou seest thy death at hand.
O would my life, would satisfie his yre,   [TLN 1321–3]
Cassandra then, would cancell soone thy band.
   An. And may it be a Iudge of his account,
Can spot his minde, with lawles loue or lust?
But more, may he doome any fault with death,
When in such faute, he findes himself iniust?
Syster, that wise men loue we often see,
And where loue rules, gainst thornes doth reason spurne.
But who so loues, if he reiected be,
His passing loue, to peeuish hate will turne.
Deare sister then, note how my fortune stands,
That *Promos* loue, the like is oft in vse:
And sith he craue, this kindnesse at your hands,
Thinke this, if you his pleasure do refuse,
I in his rage (poore wretch) shall sing *Peccaui.*
Here are two euyls, the best harde to digest,
But where as things are driuen vnto necessity,
There are we byd, of both euyls choose the least.
   Cas. And of these euils, the least, I hold, is death,   [D2ᵛ]
To shun whose dart, we can no meane deuise,
Yet honor lyues, when death hath done his worst,
Thus fame then lyfe is of farre more emprise.
   An. Nay *Cassandra*, if thou thy selfe submyt,
To saue my life, to *Promos* fleashly wyll,
Iustice wyll say, thou dost no cryme commit: [TLN 1062–3]
For in forst faultes is no intent of yll.
   Cass. How so th'intent, is construed in offence,
The Prouerbe saies, that tenne good turnes lye dead,
And one yll deede, tenne tymes beyonde pretence,
By enuious tongues, report abrode doth spread:
Andrugio so, my fame, shall vallewed bee;
Dispite wyll blase my crime, but not the cause:
And thus although I fayne would set thee free,
Poore wench I feare, the grype of slaunders pawes.
   An. Nay sweete sister, more slaunder would infame,
Your spotles lyfe, to reaue your brothers breath:
When you haue powre, for to enlarge the same,
Once in your handes, doth lye my lyfe, and death.
Way that I am, the selfe same flesh you are,
Thinke I once gone, our house will goe to wrack:
Knowe forced faultes, for slaunder neede not care:
Looke you for blame, if I quaile through your lack.
Consider well, my great extremitie:
If other wise, this doome I could reuoke,
I would not spare, for any ieberdye,
To free thee wench, from this same heauy yoke.
But ah I see, else, no way saues my life.
And yet his hope, may further thy consent,
He sayde, he maye percase make thee his wife,
And t'is likelie, he can not be content
With one nights ioye: if loue he after seekes,

And I dischargd, if thou aloofe then be,
Before he lose thy selfe, that so he leekes,
No dought but he, to marryage, wyll agree.

   Cas. And shall I sticke to stoupe, to *Promos* wyll,   [D3ʳ]
Since my brother inioyeth lyfe thereby?
No, although it doth my credit kyll,
Ere that he should, my selfe would chuse to dye.
My *Andrugio*, take comfort in distresse,
Cassandra is wonne, thy raunsome great to paye:
Such care she hath, thy thraldome to releace,
As she consentes, her honor for to slay.
Farewell, I must, my virgins weedes forsake: *Exit.*
And lyke a page, to *Promos* lewde repayre.

   An. My good sister to God I thee betake,
To whome I pray, that comforte change thy care.

Actus. 3. Scena. 5.

Phallax alone.

   Phal. Tis more then straunge, to see Lord *Promos* plight,
He fryskes abought, as byrdes ware in his breech.
Euen now he seemes (through hope) to taste delight,
And straight (through feare) where he clawes it doth not ytch.
He museth now, strayght wayes the man doth sing,
(A sight in sooth, vnseemely for his age:)
He longing lookes, when any newes shal bring,
To speake with him, without there waytes a page.
O worthy wit (fyt for a *Iudges* head)
Vnto a man to chaunge a shiftles mayde,
Wyncke not on me, twas his, and not my deede:
His, nay, his rule, this *Metamorphos* made.
But *Holla* tongue, no more of this I pray,
Non bonus est, ludere cum sanctis.   [TLN 885–6]
The quietest, and the thryftiest course they say,
Is, not to checke, but prayse great mens amys.
I finde it true, for soothing *Promos* vaine,
None lyke my selfe, is lykte in his conceyte:
While fauour last, then good, I fish for gaine: [D3ᵛ]
(For Grace wyll not byte alwayes at my bayte)
And as I wish, at hande good Fortune see:
Here coms *Rapax*,* and *Gripax*, but what's this,
As good as fayre handsell, God graunt it bee:
The knaues bring a Woman, *Coram nobis.*

Rapax] Phallax Q

Actus. 3. Scena. 6.

Phallax, *Gripax*, *Rapax*, a *Bedell*, and one with a browne Byll,
bring in *Lamia*, and *Rosko* hir man.

La. Teare not my clothes my friends, they cost more then you are a ware.
Be. Tush, soon you shal haue a blew gown, for these take you no care.
Ro. If she tooke thy offer poore knaue, thy wife would starue with cold.
Gri. Well syr, whipping shall keepe you warme.
Phal. What meanes these knaues to scolde.
Ra. Maister *Phallax*, we finde you in good time,
A *Woman* here, we haue brought afore you:
One to be chargde with many a wanton crime,
Which tryall will, with proofe inough finde true:
A knaue of hirs, we haue stayed likewise,
Both to be vs'd, as you shall vs aduise.
Phal. What call you hir name?
Ra. Lamia.
Phal. Faire Dame, hereto what do you saye?
La. Worshipfull Sir, my selfe I happy reake,
With patience that my aunswer you will heare:
These naughtie men, these wordes on mallice speake,
And for this cause, yll wyll to me they beare:
I scornde to keepe, their mindes with money playe,
I meane to keepe, my life from open shame,
Yea, if I lyu'd, as lewdlie as they saye:
But I that knewe, my selfe vnworthy blame,
Shrunk not, to come vnto my triall nowe.
My tale is tolde, conceyue as lyketh you.
Phal. My friends, what proofe haue you against this dame?   [D4r]
Speake on sure ground, least that you reape the shame:
The wrong is great, and craues great recompence,
To touch her honest name, without offence.
Gri. All *Iulio* Syr doth ryng of her lewd lyfe.
Byl. In deede she is knowne for an ydle huswife.
Ros. He lyes, she is occupied day and night.
Phal. To sweare against her is there any wight?
Ra. No, not present, but if you do detayne her,
There wilbe found by oth, some that wyll stayne her.
Phal. I see she is then on suspition stayde,
Whose faultes to search, vpon my charge is layde:
From charge of her I therfore set* you free,
My selfe will search her faultes if any be.
A Gods name you may depart.
2 or .3. speake. God bwy Syr.
Gri. In such shares as this, henceforth I will begin,
For all is his, in his clawes that commeth in.   *Exeunt.*
Phal. Fayre *Lamia*, since that we are alone,
I plainely wyll discourse to you my minde.
I thinke you not to be so chast a one,
As that your lyfe, this fauor ought to fynde:

*therfore set] therfore will set Q

325

No force for that, since that you scot free goe,
Vnpunished, whose life is iudged yll:
Yet thinke (through loue) this grace the Iudge doth show,
And loue with loue ought to be answered styll.
   La. Indeede I graunt (although I could reproue,
Their lewde Complayntes, with goodnesse of my lyfe)
Your curtesy, your detter doth me proue,
In that you tooke (my honest fame in stryfe,)
My aunswere for discharge of their report:
For which good turne, I at your pleasure rest,
To worke amends, in any honest sort.
   Phal. Away with honesty, your answeare then in sooth,
Fyts me as iumpe as a pudding a Friars mouth.
   Ros. He is a craftie childe, dally, but do not.   [D4ᵛ]
   La. Tush, I warrant thee, I am not so whot.
Your wordes are too harde Sir, for me to conster.
   Phal. Then to be short, your rare bewtie my hart hath wounded so,
As (saue your loue, become my leach) I sure shall die with woe.
   La. I see no signe of death, in your face to appeare,
Tis but some vsuall qualme you haue, pitifull Dames to feare.
   Phal. Faire *Lamia*, trust me I faine not, betimes bestow som grace.
   La. Well, I admit it so, onelie to argue in your case.   [TLN 1096]
I am maried, so that to set your loue on me were vaine.
   Phal. It suffiseth me, that I may your secrete friend remaine.
   Ros. A holie Hoode, makes not a Frier deuoute,   [TLN 2641]
He will playe at small game, or* he sitte out.
   La. Though for pleasure, or to proue me, these profers you do moue,
You are to wise, to hassarde life, vpon my yeelding loue:
The man is painde with present death, that vseth wanton pleasure.
   Phal. To scape such paine, wise men, these ioyes, without suspect can
       measure.
Furthermore, I haue ben (my Girle) a Lawier to too long,
If at a pinche, I cannot wrest the Law from right to wrong.
   La. If lawe you do professe, I gladlie craue,
In a cause or two, your aduise to haue.
   Phal. To resolue you, you shall commaunde my skyll,
Wherfore like friendes, lets common in good wyll.
   La. You are a merie man, but leaue to ieast,
To morrowe night, if you will be my Geast,
At my poore house, you shall my causes knowe,
For good cause, which I meane not here to showe.
   Phal. Willinglie, and for that haste calles me hence,
My sute tyll then, shall remaine in suspence:
Farewell Clyent, to morrow looke for me.   *Exit.*
   La. Your good welcome Sir, your best cheere will be.
   Ros. I tolde you earst, the nature of *Phallax*,
Money, or faire Women, workes him as waxe:
And yet I must commend your sober cheere,
You tolde your tale, as if a Saint you were.
   La. Well (in secreete, be it sayde) how so I seemd diuine,   [E1ʳ]
I feared once, a blew gowne, would haue bene my shrine.
But nowe that paine is flead, and pleasure keepes his holde,

*or] i.e., ere

I knowe that *Phallax* will, my Fame henceforth vpholde:
To entertaine which Geast, I will some dayntie cheere
       prepare,
Yet ere I go, in pleasant Song, I meane to purge my care.

> *Adue poore care, adue,*   *The Song.*
> *Go, cloye some helples wretche:*
> *My life, to make me rue,*
> *Thy forces do not stretche.*
>
> *Thy harbor, is the harte,*
> *Whom wrong, hath wrapt in woe:*
> *But wrong, doth take my parte,*
> *With cloke of right in shoe.* *
>
> *My faultes, inquirie scape,*
> *At them the Iudges winke:*
> *Those for my fall that gape,*
> *To showe my lewdnesse shrinke.*
>
> *Then silly care go packe,*
> *Thou art no Geast for mee:*
> *I haue, and haue no lacke,*
> *And lacke, is shrowde for thee.*

                                          Exeunt.

Actus. 3. Scena. 7.

Cassandra, apparelled like a Page.

Cas. Vnhappy wretche, I blush my selfe to see,
Apparelled thus monstrous to my kinde:
But oh, my weedes, wyll with my fault agree,
When I haue pleasde, lewde *Promos* fleshlie minde.
What shall I doo, go proffer what he sought?   [E1ᵛ]
Or on more sute, shall I giue my consent?
The best is sure, since this must needes be wrought:
I go, and showe, neede makes me to his bent.
My fluddes of teares, from true intent which floe,
Maye quenche his lust, or ope his mufled eyen,
To see that I deserue to be his wife,
Though now constrainde to be his Concubine.
But so, or no, I must the venter giue,
No daunger feares the wight, prickt foorth by neede:
And thus lyke one more glad to dye, then lyue,
I forewarde set, God graunt me well to speede.   *Exit.*

---

*shoe] i.e., show

327

Actus 4.*Scena.* 1.

Dalia, *Lamias* Maide, going to market.

Da. With my Mistresse, the worlde is chaunged well,
She fearde of late, of whipping cheere to smell:
And nowe againe, both gallant, fresh and gaye,
Who in *Iulio* flauntes it out, lyke *Lamia*?
A luckie friende (yea, one that beareth swaye)
Is nowe become a proppe, of such a staye
To hir good name, as who is he dare saye,
That *Lamia* doeth offende, nowe any waye?
This, hir good friende, wyll be hir Geast this night,
And that he maye in his welcome delyght,
To market I, in haste, am sent to buye,
The best cheare, that I fasten on my eye.   *Exit.*

Actus. 4.*Scena.* 2.   [E2ʳ]

Promos alone.

Pro. By proofe I finde, no reason cooles desire,
Cassandraes sute, suffised to remoue
My lewde request, but contrarie, the fire,
Hir teares inflam'd, of lust and filthy Loue.
And hauing thus, the conquest in my handes,
No prayer seru'de to worke restraint in mee:
But needes I woulde vntye the precious bandes,
Of this fayre Dames spotles Virginitie.
The spoyle was sweete, and wonne euen as I woulde,
And yet vngainde, tyll I had giuen my trothe,
To marie hir, and that hir brother shoulde
Be free from death, all which I bounde with oathe:
It resteth nowe (vnlesse I wrong hir much)
I keepe my vowe: and shall *Andrugio* lyue?*
Such grace woulde mee, with vnindifferencie tuch,
To pardon him, that dyd commit a Rape.
To set him free, I to *Cassandra* sware:
But no man else, is priuie to the same,
And rage of Loue, for thousande oathes nyll spare,
More then are kept, when gotten is the game.
Well, what I sayde, then Louer like I sayde,
Nowe reason sayes, vnto thy credite looke:
And hauing well, the circumstaunces wayde,
I finde I must, vnsweare the oathe I tooke:
But double wrong, I so should do *Cassandra*.   [TLN 2792]
No force for that, my might, commaundeth right,
Hir preuie maime, hir open cryes will staye: [TLN 2295]

*lyue] read scape for rhyme?

328

Or if not so, my frowning will hir fright,
And thus shall rule, conceale my filthy deede.
Nowe foorthwith, I wyll to the Gayler sende,
That secretelie *Andrugio* he behead,
Whose head he shall, with these same wordes commend:
To Cassandra, *as* Promos *promist thee,*   [E2ᵛ]
From prison loe, he sendes thy Brother free.

Actus. 4. *Scena.* 3.

Cassandra.

Cas. Fayne would I wretch conceale, the spoyle of my virginity,
But O my gilt doth make mee blush, chast virgins here to see:
I monster now, no mayde nor wife, haue stoupte to *Promos* lust,   [TLN 2550–1]
The cause was nether sute nor teares, could quench his wanton thurst.
What cloke wyl scuse my crime? my selfe, my conscience doth accuse
And shall *Cassandra* now be termed, in common speeche, a stewes?
Shall she, whose vertues bare the bell, be calld a vicious dame?
O cruell death, nay hell to her, that was constraynd to shame:
Alas few wyll giue foorth I synd,* to saue my brothers lyfe:
And fayntly I through *Promos* othes, doo hope to be his wife.
For louers feare not how they sweare, to wyn a Lady fayre,
And hauing wonne what they did wish, for othes nor Lady care.   [TLN 2469]
But be he iust or no, I ioy *Andrugio* yet shall lyue,
But ah, I see a sight, that doth my hart a sunder ryue.

Actus. 4. *Scena.* 4.

Gaylar, *with a dead mans head in a charger.* Cassandra.

Gay. This present wilbe Galle I know, to fayre *Cassandra,*
Yet if she knewe as much as I, most swete I dare well say.
In good tyme, see where she doth come, to whome my arrand is.
    Cas. Alas his hasty pace to me, showes some what is amys.
    Gay. Fayre *Cassandra* my Lord *Promos,* commends him vnto thee,
To keepe his word, who sayes from prison he sends thy brother free.
    Cas. Is my *Andrugio* done to death? fye, fye of faythles trust.
    Gay. Be quiet Lady, law found his fault, then was his iudgement iust.
    Cas. Wel my good friend, show *Promos* this: since law hath don this   [E3ʳ]
        deed.
I thank him yet, he would vouchsaf on me my brothers head,
Loe this is all, now geue me leaue to rew his losse alone.
    Gay. I wyll performe your will, and wish you cease your mone.
    Cass. Fare well.
    Gay. I sure had showen what I had done, her teares I pittied so,

*synd] fynd Q

329

But that I wayde, that women syld do dye with greefe and woe,
And it behoues me to be secret or else my neck verse cun.
Well now to pack my dead man hence, it is hye tyme I run.
   Cas. Is he past sight? then haue I time to wayle my woes alone,
Andrugio, let mee kis thy lippes, yet ere I fall to mone.
O would that I could wast to teares, to wash this bloddy face,
Which fortune farre beyond desart hath followed with disgrace.
O *Promos* falce, and most vnkinde, both spoyld of loue and ruth,
O *Promos* thou dost wound my hart, to thinke on thy vntruth,
Whose plyghted fayth, is tournd to frawd, and words to works
      vniust.
Why doe I lyue vnhappy wench, syth treason quites my trust?
O death deuorse me wretch at once, from this same worldly lyfe.
But why do I not slay my selfe, for to appease thys stryfe?
Perhaps within this wombe of myne, an other *Promos* is:
I so by death shalbe auengd of him in murthring his.
And ere I am assured that I haue reuengd this deede,
Shall I dispatch my lothed life? that hast, weare* more then speede.
So *Promos* would triumphe that none his Tiranny should know.
No, no this wicked fact of his so slightly shall not goe:
The king is iust and mercyfull, he doth both heare and see:
See mens desarts, heare their complaynts, to Iudge with equity.
My wofull case with speede I wyll vnto his grace addresse,
And from the first vnto the last, the truth I wyll confesse.
So *Promos* thou, by that same lawe shalt lose thy hated breth,
Through breach wherof, thou didst condemne *Andrugio* vnto death.
So doing yet, the world will say I broke *Dianas* lawes,
But what of that? no shame is myne, when truth hath showne my
      cause.
I am resolued, the king shall knowe of *Promos* iniury,
Yet ere I goe, my brothers head, I wyll ingraued see.   *Exit.*

Actus. 4. Scena. 5.   [E3ᵛ]

Gayler, Andrugio.

   Gay. Andrugio, as you loue our liues, forthwith post you away.
For Gods sake to no lyuing friend, your safety yet bewraye:
The prouerbe sayth, two may keepe counsell if that one be gone.
   An. Assure thy selfe, most faithful friend, I wylbe knowne to none:
To none? alas, I see my scape yeeldes mee but small releefe,
Cassandra, and *Polina* wyll destroye themselues, with greefe,
Through thought that I am dead: they dead, to liue what helpeth me?
   Gay. Leaue of these plaints of smal auaile, thank God that you are
      free,
For God it was, within my mind, that did your safety moue,
And that same God, no doubt wyl worke for your and their behoue.
   An. Most faithful friend, I hope that God wyl worke as you do say,
And therfore, to some place vnknowne, I wyl my selfe conuaye.

*hast, weare] i.e., haste were

330

Gayler, fare wel: for thy good deede, I must remayne thy debter,
In meane whyle yet receyue this gyft, tyll fortune sends a better.
   Gay. God bwy syr, but kepe your mony, your need you do not
      know.
   An. I pas not now for fortuns threats, yea though hir force she
      show,
And therefore styck not to receyue this smale reward in part.
   Gay. I wyll not sure, such proffers leaue, tys time you doe depart.
   An. Since so thou wilt, I wylbe gone, adue tyl fortune smile.   *Exit.*
   Gay. Syr, fare you wel, I wyl not fayle to pray for you the while.
Well, I am glad that I haue sent him gone,
For by my fayth, I lyu'd in perlous feare:
And yet God wot, to see his bytter mone,
When he should dye, would force a man forbeare,
From harming him, if pitty might beare sway:
But see how God hath wrought for his safety?
A dead mans head, that suffered th'other day,
Makes him thou'ht dead, through out the citie.
Such a iust, good and righteous God is he:
Although awhyle he let the wicked raygne,
Yet he releeues, the wretch in misery,
And in his pryde, he throwes the tyraunt downe.   [E4ʳ]
I vse these wordes, vpon this onely thought,
That *Promos* long his rod can not escape:
Who hath in thought, a wylfull murder wrought,
Who hath in act performd a wicked rape.
Gods wyll be done, who well *Andrugio* speede.
Once well I hope, to heare of his good lucke,
For God thou knowest my conscience dyd this deede,
And no desire of any worldly muck.   *Exit.*

Actus. 4. Scena. 6.

Dalia *from Market.*

   Da. In good sweete sooth, I feare I shalbe shent,
It is so long since I to market went,
But trust me, wyldfowle are such costly geare,
Specially, woodcoks, out of reason deare,
That this houre, I haue the market bett,*
To driue a bargayne to my most profyt:
And in the end I chaunst to light on one,
Hyt me as pat, as a pudding *Pope Ione.*
Other market maydes pay downe for their meate,
But that I haue bought, on my score is set.
Well fare credit when mony runneth low,
Marry yet, Butchers, the which do credit so,
(As much Good meate, as they kyll) may perchaunce,
Be glad and fayne at heryng cobs to daunce.

*the market bett] i.e., beaten down the price

331

What force I that? euery man shyft for one,
For if I starue, let none my fortune mone.

She faynes to goe out.

Grimball, *Dalia*, eyther of them a Basket.

Gri. Softe *Dalia*, a woorde with you, I praye.
Da. What, friend *Grimbal*, welcome as I maye saye.
Gri. Sayst thou me so, then kysse me for acquaintaunce.
Da. If I lyke your manhoode, I may do so perchaunce.

She faynes to looke in his basket.

Gri. Bate me an ase, quoth *Boulton*, Tush, your minde I know:
Ah syr, you would, be like, let my Cocke Sparrowes goe.
Da. I warrant thee *Grimball*.

She takes out a white pudding.

Gri. Laye off handes *Dalia*.
You powte me,* if that you got my Pudding awaye.
Da. Nay good sweete, honny *Grimball*, this Pudding giue mee.
Gri. Iche were as good geete* hir, for she wyll hate,* I see.
Well, my nown good harte roote, I freelie giue thee this,
Vpon condition, that thou giue me a kys.
Da. Nay, but first wash your lippes, with sweete water you shall.
Gri. Why ych was ryte now, for my Pudding, hony sweet *Grimbal*:
Well *Dalia*, you will floute so long, tyll (though I saye)
With kindnesse you wyll cast a proper handsome man away,
Wherfore soote Conny, euen a lyttle spurte:
Da. Laye off handes Sir:
Gri. Good do not byte, for ych meane thee no hurte:
Come off Pyggesnie, prefarre* me not a iote.
Da. What woulde the good foole haue?
Gri. Why, you woot whote.*
Hearke in your eare:
Da. You shall commaunde, so proper a man ye are,
That for your sake, I wyll not sticke to ware
A blew Cassocke, during my lyfe forsoothe.
Mary for my sake, I woulde be verie lothe
So goodlie a handsome man, should lose his head.
Gri. Nay, for my head, care not a Tinkers torde,   [F1ʳ]

*powte me] i.e., make me pout
*geete] i.e., give it
*hate] i.e., have it
*prefarre] i.e., defer
*woot whote] i.e., know what

For so God iudge me, and at one bare worde:
Yle lose my death, yea, and my great browne Cowe,
I loue you so filthilie: law ye nowe.
   Da. Thou sayest valiantlie, nowe sing aswell too:
And thou shalt quicklie knowe, what I meane to doo.
   Gri. Yes by Gogs foote, to pleasure thee, ych shall,
Both syng, spring, fight and playe, the dewl and all.
   Da. O lustilie.

The Song.

   Gri. Come smack me, come smack me, I long for a smouch.
   Da. Go pack thee, go pack thee, thou filthie fine slouch.

   Gri. Leard howe I loue thee.
   Da. This can not moue mee.
   Gri. Why pretie Pygsney, my harte, and my honny?
   Da. Because goodman Hogsface, you woe without mony.
   Gri. I lacke mony, chy graunt.
   Da. Then *Grimball* auaunt.
   Gri. Cham yong, sweete hart, and feate, come kysse me for loue.
   Da. Crokeshanke, your Iowle is to great, such lyking to moue.
   Gri. What meane you by this?
   Da. To leaue thee by gys.

   Gri. First smack me, first smack me*, I dye for a smouch.
   Da. Go pack thee, go pack thee, thou filthy fine slouch.   *Exit.*

   Gri. Dalia, arte thou gone? what, wolt serue me soe?
O God, cham readie to raye my selfe for woe.
Be valiaunt *Grimball*, kyll thy selfe man?
Nay, bum Ladie, I will not by Saint *Anne*.
Ich haue hearde my great Grandsier saye:
Maide will saye naye, and take it: and so she maye,
And therfore chyll, to Mistresse *Lamia*,
With these Puddings, and Cock Sparowes, by and by:
And in the darke, againe, ych wyll hir trye.   *Exit.*

Actus. 5. Scena. 1.   [F1ᵛ]

Phallax *alone.*

   Phal. I maruell much what worketh so my Lord *Promos* vnrest,
He fares as if a thousand Deuils, were gnawing in his brest:
There is sure some worme of griefe, that doth his conscience nip,
For since *Andrugio* lost his head, he hath hung downe the lippe.
And truth to say, his fault is such as well may greue his mynd,
The Deuill himselfe could not haue vsde, a practise more vnkind.
This is once, I loue a woman, for my life, as well as he,

---

*first smack me] *first smack* Q

But (fayre dames) with her that loues mee, I deale well with, trust mee.
Well, leaue I now my Lord *Promos*, his owne deedes to aunswere,
Lamia I know lookes, and double lookes, when I come to supper:
I thought as much: see, to seeke mee, heare coms her Aple squier.

Actus. 5. Scena. 2.

Rosko. Phallax.

Ros. O that I could find Master *Phallax*, the meat burnes at the fire:
And by your leaue, *Andrugios* death, doth make my mistris sweate.
Phal. How now *Rosko*?
Ros. Ist you syr? my Mistris doth intreate,
That with all speede, your worship will come away to supper:
The meate and all is ready to set vpon the borde syr.
Phal. Gramercy for thy paynes, I was euen comming to her.
Ros. You are the welcomst man alyue to her I know,
And trust mee at your commaundement remayneth poore *Rosko*.
Phal. It is honestly sayd, but now tell mee,
What quality hast, that I may vse thee.
Ros. I am a Barbour, and when you please syr,
Call (and spare not) for a cast of rose water.
Phal. But heare me, canst thou heale a greene wound well?
Ros. Yea, greene and ould.
Phal. Then thy best were to dwel,
In some vsuall place or streete, where, through frayes,   [F2ʳ]
Thou mayst be set a worke with wounds alwayes.
Ros. I thanke my Mistris I haue my hands full,
To trym gentelmen of her acquayntaunce:
And I trust Syr, if that your worship chaunce,
To haue neede of my helpe, I shall earne your mony,
Afore an other.
Phal. That thou shalt truly:
But syrra, where dwels *Lamia*?
Ros. Euen heare syr, enter I pray.
Phal. That I wyl sure, if that my way be cleare.
Ros. Yes sir, her doores be open all the yeare.   *Exeunt.*

Actus. 5. Scena. 3.

Polina, *(the mayde, that* Andrugio *lou'd) in a blew gowne.*

Po. Polina curst, what dame a lyue hath cause of griefe lyke thee?
Who (wonne by loue) hast yeeld the spoyle of thy virginity?
And he for to repayre thy fame, to marry thee, that vowde,
Is done to death for first offence, the second mends not lowde.*

*mends not lowde] i.e., amends not allowed

334

,Great shame redounds to thee, O *Loue*, in leauing vs in thrall: [TLN 997–9]
Andrugio and *Polina* both, in honoryng thee did fall.
Thou so dydst witch our wits, as we from reason strayed quight,
Prouockt by thee, we dyd refuse no vauntage of delight:
Delight, what did I say? nay death, by rash and fowle abuse,
Alas I shame to tell thus much, though loue doe worke excuse.
So that (fayre dames) from such consent, my accydents of harme,
Forewarneth you, to keepe aloofe, though loue your harts do arme.
But ah *Polina*, whether* runnes thy words into aduise,
When others harmes, inforst by loue, could neuer make thee wise?
The cause is plaine, for that in loue, no reason stands in steede,
And reason is the onely meane, that others harmes we dreade.
Then, that the world hereafter may, to loue inferre my yll,
Andrugios Tombe with dayly teares, *Polina* worship wyll.
And further more I vowe,* whylst life in mee doth foster breth,   [F2ᵛ]
No one shall vaunt of conquered loue, by my *Andrugios* death.
These shameful weedes, which forst I were* that men my fault may know,
Whilst that I liue, shall show I morne for my *Andrugio*.
I wyll not byde the sharpe assaultes, from sugred words isent,*
I wyll not trust to careles othes, which often wyn consent:
I wyll cut off occasions all, which hope of myrth may moue,
With ceaseles teares yle quench each cause, that kindleth coles of loue:
And thus tyl death *Polina* wyll estraunge her selfe from ioy,
Andrugio, to reward thy loue which dyd thy life destroy.   *Exit.*

Act. 5. Scena. 4.

Rosko *alone.*

Ros. A Syr, in fayth, the case is altred quight:
My mistris, late that liued in wretched plight,
Byds care adue and euery cause of woe,
The feare is fled, which made her sorrow so.
Master *Phallax* so vnder props her fame,
As none for lyfe dare now her lewdnes blame.
I feare (nay hope) she hath bewicht him so,
As haulfe his brybes, vnto her share will goe:
No force for that, who others doth deceyue,   [TLN 0.1-0.2]
Deserues himselfe, lyke measure to receyue.
Well, leaue I *Lamia*, for her selfe to pray,
Better then I can showe, who knowes the way.
It stands me on, for my poore selfe to shyfte,
And I haue founde a helpe at a dead lyfte:
My ould friende *Grimbals* purce, with pence is full,
And if I empty it not, *Dalia* wull.
The slauering foole, what he can rap and rend,

*whether] i.e., whither
*vowe] vowde Q
*were] i.e., wear
*isent] I sent Q

335

(He loues her so) vpon the fylth wyll spend:
But bye your leaue, yle barre her of this match,
My net and all is set, the foole to catch.
Forsooth before his amorous sute he moue,   [F3^r]
He must be trimd to make her more to loue.
And in good sooth, the world shal hardly fall,
But that he shalbe washt, pould, shau'd and all:
And see the luck, the foole is fast I know,
In that with *Rowke* he doth so sadly goe.

[*Act.* 5.] *Scena.* 5.

Grymball, Rowke, Rosko.

Grym. God bores, as sayst, when somewhat handsome ch'am,
I fayth she wyll come off for very shame.
   Row. Yea without doubt for I sweare by saynt *Anne*:
My selfe loues you, you are so cleane a youngman.
   Grim. Nay, thou woult say so, when my face is fayre washt.
   Ros. Good luck a Gods name, the wodcocke is masht.
   Row. And who Barbes ye *Grimball?*
   Grim. A dapper knaue, one *Rosko.*
   Ros. Well letherface, we shall haue you Asse ere you goe.
   Row. I know him not, is he a deaft barber?
   Grim. O, yea, why he is Mistris *Lamias* powler.
And looke syrra, yen is the lyttell knaue.
How dost *Rosko?*
   Ros. Whope, my eye sight God saue,
What ould *Grimball*, welcome, sit you downe heare.
Boye?
   Boy. Anon.   *Boy in the house.*
   Ros. Bay leaues in warme water, quick, bring cleane geare.
   Boy. Strayght.
   Row. As thou sayd'st *Grymball*, this is a feate knaue indeede.
   Ros. How say'syr? oyntments for a scab, do you neede?
   Row. Scab, scuruy Iack, ile set you a worke Syr.
   Grym. Nay gogs foote, good nowe, no more of this stur.
   Row. I fayth Barber, I wyll pyck your teeth straight.
   Ros. Nay, to pick my purse, I feare thou dost wayght.
   Row. Yea, gogs hart.
   Grym. Nay, gogs foote.
   Ros. Nowe come Ruffen.   [F3^v]
   Grim. Leaue, if you be men.
Heare ye me nowe? be friendes, and by my trothe,
Chill spende a whole quarte of Ale on you bothe.
   Ros. Well, masse *Grimball*, I lytle thought Iwus,
You woulde a brought a knaue, to vse mee thus.
   Grim. Why, knowest him not? why it is lustie *Rowke.*
   Ros. A strong theefe, I warrant him by his looke.
   Row. Go to Barber, no more, least Copper you catch.

Grim. What? wilt giue thy nose a waye? beware that match.
For chy see no Copper, vnlest be theare.   *Boy brings water.*
  Boy. Master, here is delicate water, and cleane geare.   *Exit.*
  Ros. Well, to quiet my house, and for *Grimbals* sake,
If it pleaseth you, as friendes, we handes will shake.
  Grim. I, I, do so.
  Row. And for his sake I agree.
  Grim. Well then: that we may drinke, straight wayes wash mee.
  Ros. Good syr, here's water as sweete as a Rose,
Nowe whyles I wash, your eyes harde you must close.
  Grim. Thus?
  Ros. Harder yet:
  Grim. O, thus.
  Ros. Yea marry, so.
Howe syrra, you knowe what you haue to doe.

Rowke cuttes *Grimbals* purse.

  Ros. Winke harde, *Grimball.*
  Grim. Yes, yes, I shall.
  Row. Heare's the toothpick, and all.   *Exit.*
  Ros. Departe then tyll I call?
Verie well syr, your face, is gayly cleane,
Were your teeth nowe pickt, you maye kisse a queane?
  Grim. Sayst thou mee so? Good nowe dispatch and awaye?
I euen fyssell,* vntyll I smouch *Dalia.*
  Ros. O doo you so? I am right glad you tell.
I else had thought, tad bene your teethe dyd smell.
  Grim. O Lorde, gogs foote, you picke me to the quicke.   [F4r]
  Ros. Quiet your selfe, your teeth are furred thicke.
  Grim. O, oh no more, O God, I spattell blood.
  Ros. I haue done, spyt out, this doth you much good.
Boye?
  Boy. Anon.   *Boy within.*
  Ros. Bring the drinke in the Porringer,
To gargalis his teeth.
  Boy. It is here syr.   *Exit.*
  Ros. Wash your teeth with this, good maister *Grimball.*
  Grim. I am poysoned, ah, it is bytter gall.
  Ros. Eate these Comfyts, to sweeten your mouth with all.
  Grim. Yea mary syr, these are gay sugred geare.
  Ros. Their sweetnesse straight wyll make you stinke I feare.
  Grim. Well nowe, what must I paye, that chy were gone?
  Ros. What you wyll.
  Grim. Sayest me so? O cham vndone.
  Ros. Howe nowe *Grimball*?
  Grim. O Leard, my Purse is cutte.
  Ros. When? where?
  Grim. Nowe, here.
  Ros. *Boye*, let the doore be shutte:
If it be here, we wyll straight wayes see.
Where's he, that came with you?

*fyssell] i.e., fizzle, quietly break wind

Grim. I can not tell.

Ros. What is hee?

Grim. I knowe not.

Ros. Where doth he dwell?

Grim. O Leard, I ken not I.

Ros. You haue done well.

This knaue, your pence, in his pocket hath purst:

Let's seeke him out.

Grim. Nay harke, I must neades first:

O Learde, Learde, cham sicke, my belly akes, too, too:

Ros. Thou lookst yll: well, yle tell thee what to doo.

Since thou art so sicke, straight wayes, get thee home.   [F4ᵛ]

To finde this Iacke, my selfe abroade wyll rome,

The rather, for that he playde the knaue with mee.

Gri. Cham sicke in deede, and therfore ych thanke thee.

Ros. I see sometime, the blinde man hits a Crowe,

He maye thanke me, that he is plagued soe.

Gri. Well, well, *Dalia*, the Loue ych bare to thee,

Hath made me sicke, and pickt my purse from mee.   *Exit.*

Ros. A, is he gone? a foole company him.

In good soothe Sir, this match fadged trim:

Well, I wyll trudge, to finde my fellewe *Rowke*,

To share the price, that my deuise hath tooke.   *Exit.*

Actus. 5.Scena. 6.

Cassandra, in blacke.

Cas. The heauy chardge, that Nature bindes me too,

I haue perform'd, ingrau'd my Brother is:

O woulde to God (to ease my ceaseles woo)

My wretched bones, intombed were with his.

But O in vaine, this bootelesse wish I vse,

I, poore I must lyue in sorrowe, ioynde with shame:

And shall he lyue? that dyd vs both abuse?

And quench through rule, the coles of iust reuenge?

O: no, I wyll nowe hye me to the King:

To whome, I wyll recount my wretched state,

Lewde *Promos* rape, my Brothers death and all:

And (though with shame, I maye this tale relate)

To prooue that force, enforced me to fall:

When I haue showne, Lorde *Promos* fowle misdeedes,

This knife foorthwith, shall ende my woe and shame,

My gored harte, which at his feete then bleedes,

To scorge his faultes, the King wyll more inflame.

In deedes to doo, that I in woordes pretende,   [G1ʳ]

I nowe aduise, my iourney to the King:

Yet ere I go, as Swans sing at their ende,

In solemne Song, I meane my knell to ryng.

338

Cassandraes Song.

Sith fortune thwart, doth crosse my ioyes with care,
Sith that my blisse, is chaungde to bale by fate:
Sith frowarde chaunce, my dayes in woe doth weare,
Sith I alas, must mone without a mate:
I wretch haue vowde, to sing both daye and night,
O sorrowe slaye, all motions of delight.

Come grieslie griefe, torment this harte of mine,
Come deepe dispaire, and stoppe my loathed breath:
Come wretched woe, my thought of hope to pine:
Come cruell care, preferre my sute to death.
Death, ende my wo, which sing both daye and night,
O sorrowe slaye, all motions of delight.

Exit.

FINIS.   G. W.

The seconde part   [G2ʳ]

of the Famous Historie

of *Promos* and *Cassandra.*

Set forth in a Comi-
call Discourse, by George
Whetstone Gent.

Formæ nulla fides.

The seconde parte of the Historie   [G3ʳ]
of *Promos* and *Cassandra.*

Actus. 1.*Scena.* 1.

Polina in a blewe Gowne, shadowed with a blacke Sarcenet,
going to the Temple to praye, vpon *Andrugios* Tombe.

[*Pol.*] Promise is debt, and I my vowe haue past,

339

Andrugios Tombe, to wash with daylie teares:
Which Sacrifice (although God wot in waste)
I wyll performe: my Alter is of cares,
Of fuming sighes, my offring incense is,
My pittious playntes, in steede of Prayers are:
Yea, woulde to God in penaunce of my mys,
I with the rest, my loathed lyfe might share.*
But O in vaine, I wish this welcomde ende,
Death is to slowe, to slaye the wretched wight:
And all to soone, he doth his forces bende,
To wounde their hartes, which wallowe in delight.
Yet in my eare,* styll goes my passing Bell,
So ofte as I, *Andrugios* death doo minde:
So ofte as men, with poynted fingers tell,
Their friendes, my faultes, which by my weedes they finde.
But O the cause, with Death, which threates me most,
I wysh to dye, I dye through wretched woe,
My dying harte, desires to yeelde the ghost,
My traunces straunge, a present death foreshowe.
But as the reede doth bow at euery blast,
To breake the same, when rowghest stormes lackes might,
So wretched I, with euery woe doe waste,
Yet care wants force, to kyll my hart out ryght.
O gratious God, and is my gilt so great,
As you the same, with thousand deathes must wreake?
You will it so, else care I could intreate,
With halfe these woes, my thryd of lyfe to breake.
But what meanst thou *Polina*, most accurst,   [G3ᵛ]
To muse, why God, this pennaunce ioynes thee to?
Whose correction, although we take at worst,
To our great good he doth the same bestow.
So that, syth greefe can not relyue my friend,
Syth scorching syghes my sorrowes cannot drye:
Syth care himselfe, lackes force my lyfe to ende,
Syth styll I lyue that euery howre doe dye:
Syth mighty God appoyntes my pennaunce so,
In mornefull song I wyll my patience show.

Polinas Song.

> *Amyd my bale, the lightning ioy, that pyning care doth bring,*
> *With patience cheares my heauy hart, as in my woes I sing,*
> *I know my Gilt, I feele my scurge: my ease is death I see:*
> *And care (I fynde) by peecemeale weares, my hart to set mee free.*
> *O care, my comfort and refuge, feare not to worke thy wyll,*
> *With patience I thy corsiues byde, feede on my life thy fyll.*
> *Thy appetyte with syghes and teares, I dayly wyl procure,*
> *And wretched I wil vaile to death, throw when thou wilt thy Lure.*

Exit. Polina.

*share] i.e., shear, cut off
*eare] care Q

Actus. 1.Scena. 2.

Enter a Messenger from the King.

[*Mess.*] I haue at length (though weery come in troth)
Obtaynd a sight of *Iulios* stately walles.
A Kings message, can not be done with sloth:
Whome he bids goe, must runne through myre and dyrt,
And I am sent, to Lord *Promos* in post,
To tel him that the king wyll see him strayght.
But much I feare that *Promos* needes not bost
Of any gayne by his soueraygnes receyte.
But *Holla* tongue, of lauysh speeche beware,   [G4r]
Though subiects oft in Princes meaning prye,
They must their words, and not their myndes declare,
Vnto which course I wyll my tongue apply,
Lord *Promos* shall my princes comming know,
My prince himselfe, the cause thereof shall show.   *Exit.*

Actus. 1.Scena. 3.

Rosko Lamias man.

Ros. Ist possible that my Mistris *Lamia*,
Ouer the shooes should b'yn loue with *Phallax*?
Why by Iesus (as she her selfe doth saye,)
With pure good wyll, her harte doth melt lyke waxe:
And this I am sure, euery howre they themselues,
By their sweete selues, or by their letters greete.
But the sporte is to see the louing elues,
Byll together when they in secret meete.
She lowres, he lauffes, she syghes throwe pure loue:
Nay, nay, sayes he (good pugges) no more of this:
Well, sayes shee, and weepes, my griefe you do not proue.   *The strumpets*
Then strayght this storme is cleared* with a kys,   *and Crocodiles*
And then aboth sides, three wordes and a smouch: *teares alyke.*
Within hir eare, then whispereth this slouch,
And by the way he stumbleth on her lyppes.
Thus eyther stryues most louing signes to show,
Much good doo it them, syth they are both content.
Once I am sure: how so the game doth goe,
I haue no cause their lyking to repent:
I syldome doe betweene them message beare,
But that I haue an Item in the hande.
Well, I must trudge to doe a certaine chare,
Which, take I tyme, cocke for my gayne doth stand.

*cleared] cheared Q

341

Actus. 1.*Scena.* 4.   [G4ᵛ]

Phallax. Dowson a Carpenter.

Phal. Dispatch *Dowson*, vp with the frame quickly.
So space your roomes, as the nyne worthyes may
Be so instauld, as best may please the eye.
　Dow. Very good, I shall.
　Phal. Nay soft *Dowson*, stay:
Let your man at saynt *Annes* crosse, out of hande,
Ereckt a stage, that the Wayghts in sight may stande.
　Dow. Wyll you ought else?
　Phal. Soft awhyle, let me see.
On Iesus gate, the fowre vertues, I trow,
Appoynted are to stand.
　Dow. I syr, they are so.
　Phal. Wel, then about your charge. I wyll fore see,
The Consort of Musick, well plast to be.
　Dow. I am gone syr.   *Exit.*

Actus 1.*Scena.* 5.

The *Bedell* of the Taylers, *Phallax.*

Be. Heare you maister *Phallax?*
The Wardens of the Marchantaylers axe,
Where (with themselues) they shall their Pageaunt place?
　Phal. With what strange showes, doo they their Pageaunt grace?
　Be. They haue *Hercules*, of Monsters conqueryng,
Huge great *Giants*, in a forest fighting,
With *Lyons*, *Beares*, *Wolues*, *Apes*, *Foxes*, and *Grayes*,
Baiards, *Brockes*, *etc.*
　Phal. O wondrous frayes.
Marry syr, since they are prouided thus,
Out of their wayes, God keepe Maister *Pediculus.*
　Be. You are plesaunt syr, but with speede I pray,   [H1ʳ]
You aunswere mee, I was charged not to stay.
　Phal. Because I know, you haue all things currant,
They shall stand where they shal no viewers want:
How say you to the ende of Ducke Alley?
　Be. There all the beggers in the towne wilbe.
　Phal. O, most attendaunce is, where beggers are,
Farewell, away.
　Be. I wyll your wyll declare.   *Exit.*

Actus. 1.*Scena.* 6.

Phallax, Two men, apparrelled, lyke greene men
at the Mayors feast, with clubbes of fyre worke.

Phal. This geare fadgeth, now that these fellowes peare.
Friendes where waight you?
First. In Iesus streete to keepe a passadge cleare,
That the King and his trayne, may passe with ease.
Phal. O, very good.
Second. Ought else Syr, do you please?
Phal. No, no: about your charge.
Both. We are gone.   *Exeunt.*
Phal. A syr, heare is short knowledge, to entertayne a kyng,
But O, O, *quid non pecunia?* yea, at a dayes warning?
The king in prouision that thought to take vs tardy,
As if we had a yeare bene warnd, shall by his welcome see:
I haue yet one chare to do: but soft, heare is *Rosko,*
I must needes delyuer him a messadge before I goe.

Actus. 1.*Scena.* 7.

Rosko, Phallax.

Ros. I fayth, I haue noble newes for *Lamia.*
Phal. Nay soft, friend *Rosko*, take myne in your way.
Ros. Mayster *Phallax*, O syr I cry you mercy.   [H1ᵛ]
Phal. Rosko with speede tell thy Mistris from mee,
The King straight wayes wyll come to the Cytie:
In whose great trayne there is a company,
Within her house with mee shall mery be.
Therefore, for my sake, wyll her to foresee,
To welcome them, that nothing wanting be.
This is all I wyll, for want of leysure.   *Exit.*
Ros. I wyll not fayle syr, to show your pleasure:
Mary, in fayth, these newes falles iumpe with the rest,
They shalbe welcome and fare of the best:
But although they well fyll their bodyes thus,
Their purses will be dryuen to a *non plus*:
No force a whyt, each pleasure hath his payne,
Better the purce then body starue of twayne.
Well, I wyll trudge, my welcome newes to tell,
And then abroade, good company to smell.   *Exit.*

Actus. 1.*Scena.* 8.

Coruinus the King, *Cassandra*, two counsellers.
And *Vdislao*,* a young noble man.

Kyng. Cassandra, we draw neare vnto the Towne,
So that I wyll that you from vs depart,
Tyll further of our pleasure you doe heare.
Yet rest assur'd, that wycked *Promos*,
Shall abide such punishment, as the world,
Shal hould mee iust, and cleare thee of offence.
    Cas. Dread soueraigne, as you wyl, *Cassandra* goeth hence.   *Exit.*
    King. I playnely see, it tendes to great behoue,
That Prynces oft doo vayle their eares to heare,   [TLN 2370]
The Misers* playnt: for though they doe appoynt,
Such as they thynke will Iustice execute,
Aucthority is such a commaunder,
As, where as men by office beareth sway,   [H2r]
If they their rule by conscience measure not,
The poore mans ryght is ouercome by might.
If loue or hate from Iustice leade the Iudge,
Then money sure may ouerrule the case.
Thus one abuse is cause of many moe:
And therefore none in Iudges ought to be.
How Rulers wrong, fewe tales are tould the King:
The reason is, their power keepes in awe
Such men as haue great cause for to complayne.
If *Cassandra* her goodes, nay, lyfe preferd,
Before reuenge of *Promos* trechery:
I had not knowne, his detestable rape,
The which he forst to saue her brothers lyfe.
And furthermore, *Andrugios* raunsome payde,
I had not knowne he put him vnto death:
For when (good soule) she had this treason tould,
Through very shame her honour so was spoyld,
She drewe her knyfe to wound her selfe to death.
Whose pytious plyght, my hart prouockt to wrath,
At *Promos* wyles:
So that to vse indifferency to both,
Euen in the place where all these wronges were done,
My selfe am come, to syt vpon the cause.
But see where *Promos* and the Mayor waight,
To welcome mee with great solemnity:
With cheereful showe I shadowe wyll the hate,
I beare to him for his insolency:
Perhaps I may learne more of his abuse,
Whereby the more his punishment may be.
Come my Lords, to the Towne haste we apace.
    All speake. We all are prest, to wayght vpon your Grace.

*Udislao (Vladislao in Painter, *Palace of Pleasure*) is a Hungarian baron in Whetstone's *Rocke of Regard* (1576).
*Misers] i.e., wretch's

Actus. 1.*Scena.* 9.   [H2ᵛ]

Promos, *Maior*, three *Aldermen*, in red Gownes, with a
Sworde bearer, awayghtes the *Kinges* comming.

Promos, his briefe Oration.

Pro. Renowned *King*, lo here your faithful subiects preast to show
The loyall duetie, which (in ryght) they to your highnesse owe.
Your presence, cheares all sorts of vs: yet ten times more we ioye,
You thinke vs stoarde, our warning short, for to receyue a Roye.
Our wyll, is such, as shall supplie, I trust in vs all want,
And where good wyll the welcome geues, prouision syld is scant.
Loe, this is all: yea, for vs all, that I in wordes bestowe,
Your Maiestie, our further zeale, in ready deedes shall knowe.
And first, dreade King, I render you, the swoorde of Iustice heare,
Which as your Liuetenant I trust, vprightlie I dyd beare.

The *King* delyuers the Sworde, to one of his Counsell.

King. Promos, the good report, of your good gouernment I   [TLN 2352-3]
　　heare,
Or at the least, the good conceyte, that towards you I beare:
To incourage you the more, in Iustice to perseauer,
Is the cheefe cause, I dyd addresse, my Progresse heather.
　Pro. I thanke your Highnesse.

The *Maior* presentes the *King*, with a fayre Purse.

Ma. Renowned King, our ready wylles to showe,
In your behalfe, our goodes (nay lyues) to spende:
In all our names, I freelie here bestowe
On your Highnes, this Purse: vnto this ende,
To possesse your most Royall Maiestie,
In all our wealth, therto bounde by duetie.
　Kin. Your great good wyls, and gyfts with thanks I take:
But keepe you styll, your goodes, to do you good.
It is inough, and all that I do craue,   [H3ʳ]
If needes compels for your and our safety,
That you in part your proffers large performe:
And for this time as outward showes make proofe,   [TLN 2363]
It is inough (and all that I desire)
That your harts and tongues (alyke) byd me welcome.
　All. Lord preserue your Maiesty.

　　Fiue or sixe, the one halfe men, the other women, neare vnto
　　the Musick, singing on some stage, erected from the ground:
　　　During the first parte of the song, the King faineth
　　　　to talke sadlie with some of his Counsell.

The Kings Gentleman Vsher. Forewards my Lordes.

They all go out leysurablie while the rest
of the Song is made an ende.

Actus. 2.Scena. 1.

Lamia the Curtizan.

La. The match goes harde, which rayseth no mans gaine,
The vertue rare, that none to vice maye wreast:
And sure, the Lawe, that made me late complaine,
Allureth me, many a wanton geast:
Dames of my Trade, shutte vp their shoppes for feare,
Their stuffe prou'd *Contra formam Statuti*,
Then I, which lycenst am to sell fine ware,
Am lyke to be well customed perdy:
And nowe Tyme serues, least custome after fayle,
At hyest rate, my Toyes I vallue must:
Let me alone, to set my Toyes to sale:
Yong Ruflers I, in faith, wyll serue of trust.
Who wayes me not, him wyll I fayne to loue,   [H3ᵛ]
Who loues me once, is lymed to my heast:
My cullers some, and some shall weare my gloue,
And he my harte, whose payment lykes me best.
And here at hande are customers I trowe,
These are the friendes of *Phallax*, my sweete friende:
Nowe wyll I go, and set my wares to showe,
But let them laugh, that wynneth in the ende.   *Exit.*

Actus. 2.Scena. 2.

Apio and *Bruno.* Two Gentlemen straungers, with *Rosko.*

Apio. Come on good friende: where dwels Lady *Lamia?*
Ros. Euen by Syr.
Apio. Well then, go thy waye,
Showe who sent vs, and what our meaning is:
Least she not knowing vs, doo take amys,
That thus boldlye we come to visite hir.
Ros. No bolder then welcome, I warrant you Sir.
Bruno. Well, thy Message doo.
Ros. I go.   *Exit.*

Fowre *Women* brauelie apparelled, sitting singing in
Lamiaes windowe, with wrought Smockes, and Cawles,
in their hands, as if they were a working.

346

The Quyre.　　*If pleasure, be treasure,*

Apio. Harke.

[The Quyre.]　*The golden worlde is here, the golden worlde is here.*
　　　　　　Refuse you, or chuse you:
　　　　　　But welcome who drawes neare, but welcome who drawes neare.

Bruno. They be the *Muses*, sure.
Apio. Naye, *Syrens* lure.

First sings.　　*Here lyues delyght,*　　　　　　　　　　　　[H4ʳ]
Second sin.　　*Here dyes despight:*
Thei both.　　　　*Desyre here hath his wyll.*

Third sin.　　*Here Loues reliefe,*
Fourth sin.　　*Destroyeth griefe:*
Last two.　　　　*Which carefull hartes doth kyll.*

Bruno. Attende them styll.
Apio. That, as you wyll.

First sings.　　*Here wysh in wyll, doth care destroye,*
Second sin.　　*Playe here your fyll, we are not coye:*
Third sin.　　　*Which breedes much yll, we purge annoy,*
Fourth sin.　　*Our lyues here styll, we leade in ioye.*

The Quyre.　　*If Pleasure, be treasure,*
　　　　　　　The golden worlde is here, the golden worlde is here:
　　　　　　　Refuse you, or chuse you,
　　　　　　　But welcome, who coms neare, but welcome, who coms neare.

First.　　　　*Wantons drawe neare.*
Second.　　　*Taste of our cheare:*
Both.　　　　　*Our Cates are fine and sweete.*

Thirde.　　　*Come be not coye,*
Fowrth.　　　*To worke your ioye:*
The last two.　　*We fall wyll at your feete.*

Bruno. A, good kinde wormes:
Apio. Harke.

First.　　　　*Loe, here we be, good wyll which moue,*
Seconde.　　　*We lyue you see, for your behoue:*
Thirde.　　　*Come we agree, to let you proue,*
Fowrth.　　　*Without a fee, the fruites of Loue.*

The quire all. *If pleasure, be treasure, the golden worlde is here, etc.*

Bruno. Vpon this large warrant, we maye venter,　　　　[H4ᵛ]
　　　　The doore opes alone, come, let vs enter.
Apio. Agreede.

[*Actus. 2.Scena. 3.*]

Enter a *Sergeaunt* bearing a Mace, another *Offycer*, with a
Paper, lyke a Proclamation: and with them the *Cryer*.

Officer. Cryer, Make a noyse.
Cry. O yes.* *And so thrise.*
Off. All manner of personnes, here present,
Cry. All manner of personnes, here present,
Off. Be sylent, on payne, of imprisonment.
Cry. Be sylent, on payne, of imprisonment.

The *Offycer* reades the Proclamation.

Coruinus, the hye, and mightie King, of *Hungarie*, and *Boemia*:   [TLN 1966]
Vnto all his louing Subiects of *Iulio*, sendeth greeting. And therwithall,
giueth knowledge, of his Princelie fauour, towards euery sort of them.

First, if any person, Officer, or other: hath wronged any of his true subiects, by
the corruption of brybes, affecting or not fauoring, of the person: through Vsurie, extortion, wrong imprisonment: or with any other vniust practise: His Maiestie wylles the partie so grieued, to repayre to Syr *Vlrico*, one of his highnesse priuie Counsell: who (finding his, or their iniuries) is commaunded, to certifie them,
and their proofe, vnto the Kings maiestie: where incontinentlie, he wyll order the
controuersie, to the releafe* of the partie grieued, and the punishment of the
offenders.

Further, if any of his faithfull subiectes, can charge any person, Officer, or
other, with any notable or haynous of-[I1r]fence: as Treason, Murder, Sacriledge,
sedicion: or with any such notorious cryme: for the safetie of his Royal person,
benefyte and quiet of his Realme, and subiectes, on Fridaye next, his most excellent Maiestie (with the aduise of his honorable Counsell) wyl in open Court syt,
to heare and determine, all such offences. Therfore he strayghtlie chargeth all
and euerie of his subiectes, that knowe any such haynous offenders: one the fore-
named daye, that he present, both the offender, and his faulte. Dated at his
Royall Court, in *Iulio*, the *.6.* of *Februarie.*

God saue the King.   *Exeunt.*

Actus. 2.Scena. 4.

Rosko.

Ros. See howe we are crost: we thought the King for pleasure,
Came to visite vs: when to his paine,
And our plagues, I feare, he bestowes his leysure,
To heare the wronges, of such as wyll complaine
Of any man: But the sport is to see
Vs Officers, one looke of another:

*O yes] i.e., Oyez
*releafe] release Q

I at Lorde *Promos*, Lorde *Promos* at mee,
The *Lawiers*, at the *Shriefe* and *Maior*,
They gase asmuch on the ruling *Lawier*.
For to be plaine, the clearest of all,
Peccaui syng, to heare the grieuous call,
Against Vsurie, brybrie, and barrating,
Suborning, extorcion, and boulstring.
Some faultes are hearde, some by Proclamation staye,
Before the King, to be hearde on Fridaye.
I yet haue scapte, and hope to go scotfree:
But so, or no, whylst leysure serues mee,
To haue my aunswers fresh if I be cauld,   [I1ᵛ]
Of merry mates, I haue a meetyng stauld,
To whome, my sences to refresh, I wend.
Who gets a pace as meryly may spend.   *Exit.*

Actus. 2.Scena. 5.

Sir *Vlrico*, with diuers papers in his hand, two
poore Citysens, soliciting* complayntes.

Vl. As thou complaynst, agaynst all equity,
Houldes *Phallax* thy house, by this extremity?
First. Yea sure, and he hath bound me so subtylly,
As lesse you helpe, lawe yeeldes mee no remidy.
Vl. Well, what say you? is *Phallax* mony payd?
Se. Saue fyue pound Syr.
Vl. For which your bond is stayde.
Se. Nay mary, the same I would gladly pay,
But my bonde for the forfeyt he doth stay.
Vl. Summum Ius, I see, is *Summa Iniuria*:
So these wronges must be salued some other way.
First. Yea, more then this, most men say:
Vl. What?
First. To be playne, he keepes Mistris *Lamia*.
Vl. Admyt he doe, what helpe haue you by this?
Se. Yes mary, it prooues, a double knaue he is: [TLN 1495]
A couetous churle, and a lecher too.
Vl. Well, well, honest men, for your witnesse go,
And as on proofe, I fynde your iniuries,
So I wyl moue, the king for remedyes.
Both. We thanke your honour.   *Exeunt.*
Vl. Tys more then straunge, to see with honest show,
What fowle deceytes, lewde officers can hyde:
In euery case, their crafte, they collour so,
As styll they haue stryckt lawe vpon their side.
These cunning Theeues, with lawe, can Lordships steale,   [I2ʳ]
When for a sheepe, the ignoraunt are trust:*

*soliciting] soliting Q
*trust] i.e., trussed, hanged

349

Yea, who more rough, with small offenders deale,
Then these false men, to make themselues seeme iust?
The tirant *Phallaris*, was praysed in this:
When *Perillus* the brasen torment made,
He founde the wretch, strayght wayes in some amys,
And made him first, the scourge thereof taste:
A iust reward for such as doe present
An others fault, himselfe, the guiltyest man.
Well, to our weale, our gratious king is bent,
To taste these theeues, to vse what meanes he can.
But as at Cheastes, though skylfull players play,
Skyllesse vewers, may see what they omyt:
So though our king, in searching Iudgement may,
Gesse at their faultes, which secret wronges commit:
Yet for to iudge, by trueth, and not by ame,
My selfe in cheefe, his highnesse doth auctorise,
On proofe for to returne who meryts blame,
And as I fynde, so he himselfe will punish:
So that to vse, my charge indyfferently,
My Clyents wronges, I wyll with wytnesse trye.

As he is going out, *Pimos*, a young gentelman speakes to him.

Actus. 2.Scena. 6.

Pi. Sir *Vlrico*, I humbly craue to know,
What good successe, my honest sute ensues?
Vl. Master *Pimos*, in breefe, the same to showe,
I feare, you both, my order wyll refuse:
Lyros, that thinkes he geues more then he should,
And you, for that, you haue not, what you would.
Pi. It shall goe hard, if that your award mislikes mee.
Vl. Wel, goe with mee, and you the same shall see.
Pi. I waight on you.   *Exeunt.*

Actus 3.Scena. 1.   [I2ᵛ]

Phallax.

Phal. My troubled hart with guiltynesse agreu'd,
Lyke fyre doth make my eares and cheekes to glow:
God Graunt I scape this blacke day vnrepreu'd,
I care not how the game goe to morrow.
Well, I wyll set a face of brasse on it,
And with the rest, vpon the King attend:
Who euen anon wyll heare in Iudgement syt,
To heauen or hel some officers to send.

But soft, a pryze, *Gripax* and *Rapax* I see.
A share of their venture belonges to mee.

Actus. 3.Scena. 2.

Gripax, *Rapax*, Promoters, *Iohn Adroynes*, A Clowne, *Phallax*.

Iohn. Nay, good honest *Promoters* let mee go.
Gri. Tush *Iohn Adroines*, we must not leaue you so:
What? an ould hobclunch a wanton knaue?
You shal to the King.
Iohn. Marry *Iohn Adroynes* God saue:
The king? why he wyll not looke of poore men.
Ra. Yes, yes, and wyll spye a knaue in your face.
Iohn. Wyll he so? then, good you be gone apace.
Gri. And why?
Iohn. Least in my face, he spye you two.*
Phal. Haue you seene a dawe, bebob two crowes so?
Ra. Well, come awaye syr patch.
Iohn. Leaue, or by God yle scratch.

They fawle a fightyng. [I3^r]

Gri. What wilt thou so?
Iohn. Yea, and byte too.
Gri. Helpe *Rapax*, play the man.
Iohn. Nay, do both what you can.
Phal. If that in bobs, theyr bargayne be,
In fayth they share alone for mee.
Ra. What bytest thou hobclunch?
Iohn. Yea, that chull, and punch.
Gri. O Lorde God, my hart.
Iohn. Knaues, ile make you fart.
Ra. Hould thy hands Lob.
Iohn. Fyrst, take this bob.
Phal. To parte this fraye, it is hye time, I can tell,
My *Promoters* else of the roste wyll smell.
Ra. O, my neck thou wylt breake.
Iohn. Yea, Gods ames,* cryst thou creake?*
Phal. How now my friends? why what a stur is this?
Gri. Marry.
Phal. What?
Iohn. Eare they part, yle make them pys.
Phal. Houlde, no more blowes.
Iohn. Knaues, this honest man thanke,
That you scape so well.

*two] too Q
*ames] i.e., arms
*cryst thou creake?] i.e., do you give up?

Phal. Friend be not to cranke,*
I am an officer, and meane to know
The cause, why you brauld thus, before I goe:
Your bobs show, that the same, you best can tell.
    Ra. I would your worship, felt the same as well,
I then am sure, this blockhedded slaue,
For both his faultes, double punishment should haue.
    Phal. What faultes?
    Ra. Marry,
    Iohn. He wyll lye lyke a dogge.
    Phal. How now you churle, your tongue, would haue a clog.
Say on.
    Ra. To showe his first, and chiefest faughte: [13ᵛ]
His Fathers maide, and he are naught.
    Iohn. What I?
    Ra. I.
    Iohn. By my Grandsires soule, you lye.
    Phal. Peace:
Friende, for this faulte, thou must dye.
    Iohn. Dye, Learde saue vs: you sqawde* knaue, yle bum yee,
For reforming a lye, thus against mee.
    Phal. Tush, tush, it helpeth not: if they can proue this.
    Gri. For some proofe, I sawe him and the Maide kys.
    Iohn. Can not foke kys, but they are naught by and by?
    Phal. This presumption friende, wyll touch thee shrowdlie:
If thou scape with life, be thou sure of this,
Thou shalt be terriblie whypped, for this kys.
    Iohn. Whypt, mary God shielde, chy had rather be hangde.
    Ra. Growte nowle, come to the King.
    Iohn. Arte not well bangde?
    Phal. Well, good fellowes, lets take vp this matter.
    Gri. Nay, first *Iohn Adroines*, shalbe trust in a halter.
    Phal. Why? helpes it you, to see the poore man whypt?
I praye you friendes, for this tyme let him go.
    Iohn. Stande styll, and chull, whether they wyll or no.
    Ra. Nay, but we charge him, in the Kings name, staye thee.
    Phal. Harke honest man, I warrant thee set free:
Grease them well, in their handes, and speake them fayre.
    Iohn. O Leard God, our tallowe potte is not here.
    Phal. Tush, clawe them with money.
    Iohn. Why so, my nayles are sharpe.
    Phal. I see, for Clownes, *Pans* Pype, is meeter, then *Apollos* Harpe:
They can skyll of no Musicke, but plaine Song.
    Gri. I praye lets goe, we tryfle tyme too long.
    Phal. Strayght.
Cockes soule knaue, stoppe his mouth with money.
    Iohn. O, I ken you nowe syr, chy crie you mercie.
    Ra. Come on slouch, wylt please you be iogging hence?
    Iohn. Here is all, tenne shyllinges, and thyrtene pence.
    Phal. Harke ye my friendes.   [14ʳ]
    Gri. We must not let him goe.

*to cranke] i.e., too cocky
*sqawde] i.e., scald, scabby

Phal. Harke once more.
Iohn. Giue them the money.
Phal. It shall be so.
Ra. Well, although he deserues great punishment,
For your sake, for this tyme we are content:
Iohn Adroines farewell, henceforth be honest,
And for this faulte, wyll* passe it ore in ieast.   *Exeunt.*
   Iohn. Then giues our money.
   Phal. Why?
   Iohn. Why, they dyd but ieast.
   Phal. Yea, but they tooke thy money in earnest.   *Exit.*
   Iohn. Art gone? nowe the Dewle choake you all with it:
Howe chy kisse againe, the knaues hae taught me wyt.
But by Saint *Anne*, chy do see burlady:
Men maye do what them woll, that haue money.
Ich surely had bene whipt, but for my golde,
But chull no more, with smouches be so bolde.
Yea, and ych wysh all Louers to be wyse,
There be learing knaues abroade, haue Cattes eyes:
Why, by Gods bores*, they can bothe see and marke,
If a man steale, but a smouch in the darke.
And nowe the worlde is growne, to such iollie spye:
As if foke doo kysse, the'are naught by and by.
Well, ych wyll home, and tell my Father *Droyne*:
Howe that two theeues robd mee of my Coyne.   *Exit.*

[*Actus. 3.Scena. 3.*]

Enter the *King*, *Promos*, *Vlrico*, *Maior*, *Gonsago*,
Phallax, with two other attendantes.

King. Sir *Gonsago*, if that we henceforth heare,
With will, or wealth, you doe our subiects wrong:
Looke not agayne, this fauour for to fynde.
We vse this grace, to wyn you to amende:
If not, our wrath shall feare you to offende.
God speede you.

Gonsago, doth reuerence and departeth.

Kyng. I see by proofe, that true the prouerbe is,   [I4ᵛ]
Myght maisters right, wealth is such a canker,
As woundes the conscience, of his Maister,
And deuoures the hart of his poore neyghbour.
To cure which sore, Iustice his pryde must pyne,
Which Iustice ought in Princes most to shine:
And syth subiects lyue by their princes law,
Whose lawes in cheefe, the rytch should keepe in awe:

*wyll] i.e., we'll
*bores] i.e., wounds

353

The poore in wronges, but sildome doth delyght,
They haue inuffe, for to defende their right:
It much behoues the maker of these lawes,
(This mony findes in them, so many flawes)
To see his lawes obser[u]'d, as they are ment:
Or else good lawes, wyll turne to euyll intent.
Well, ere I leaue, my poorest subiects shall,
Both lyue, and lyke: and by the richest stawll.
   Pro. Regarded and most mightie Prince, your clemency herein,
Those harts, your rule commands through feare, to faithful loue shal win.
   Vl. Renowmed king, I am for to complaine,
Of *Phallax*, Lord *Promos* secondary,   [TLN 52]
Whose hainous wronges many poore men doth paine,
By me, who pray your highnes remedy.
   King. My Lord *Promos*, it seemes you rule at large,
When as your clarkes are officers vniust.
   Pro. Dread king, I thinke, he can these wronges* discharge.
   Kyng. Doe you but thinke syr: a sure speare to trust?
A dum, deafe,* and blynde Iudge, can do as much:
Well, well, God graunt, your owne lyfe, byde the tutch.
Syr *Vlrico*, your complaynt continew.
   Vl. Gratious King, his wronges be these insew:
Fyrst *Phallax*, is a common Barriter,
In office, a lewd extortioner:
The crafty man, oft puts these wronges in vre,
If poore men haue, that lykes his searching eye,
He showeth gould, the needy soules to lure:
Which if they take, so fast he doth them tye,
That by some bonde, or couenaunt forfayted,   [K1r]
They are inforst (farre beneath the vallew)
To let him haue what his eye coueyted:
And for to proue, that this report is true,
I showe no more, then witnesse prou'd by oth,
Whose names and handes, defends it heare as troth.

Vlrico deliuers the King a writing with names at it.

   King. How now *Promos*? how thinke you of your man?
Vse both your wyttes, to cleare him if you can
   Pro. Dread King, my hart to heare his faultes doth bleede.
   King. Howe far'de it then, to suffer it indeede?
It dyde, I trowe, or now you speake in iest:
Thy Master's mute *Phallax*, I hould it best
That thou speake, for thy selfe.
   Phal. I humbly craue,
Of your grace, for aunswere, respyt to haue.
   King. Why? to deuise a cloke to hyde a knaue?
Friend, *veritas non querit angulos*,
And if your selfe, you on your truth repose,
You may be bould, these faultes for to deny.

---

*wronges] wrong Q
*deafe] death Q

Some, lyttel care, vpon their othes to lye:
See if any in your behalfe will sweare.
    Phal. O Lord God, is there no knyghtes of the poste heare?
Well, then of force, I must sing *Peccaui*,
And crye out ryght, to the king for mercy.
        O King, I am in faulte, I must confesse,
        The which I wyll with repentaunce redresse.
    King. Thy confession, doth meryt some fauour,
But repentaunce payes not thy poore neyghbour:
Wherefore, Syr *Vlrico*, his goods sease you,
And those, he wrong'd, restore you to their due.
    Vl. Looke what he gettes, most thinke, he wastes straight waye,
Vpon a leawde harlot, named *Lamia*:
So that his goods, wyll scarse pay euery wight.
    King. Where naught is left, the king must lose his right.
Pay as you may, I hould it no offence,   [K1ᵛ]
If eache pay somewhat for experience:
But by the way, you rule the citty well,
That suffer, by your nose, such dames to dwell.
And now *Phallax*, thy further pennaunce ys,
That forthwith, thou do resigne thy office.
Vlrico, to his account lykewise, see.
    Vl. It shalbe done.
    King. Phallax, further heare mee:
Because thou didst, thy faultes at first confesse,
From punishment, thy person I release.
    Phal. I most humbly, do thanke your maiesty.
    Pro. Ah, out alas, *Cassandra* heare I see.

      Cassandra in a blewe gowne, shadowed with black.

    Cas. O would that teares, myght tel my tale, I shame so much my fall,
Or else, Lord *Promos* lewdnes showen, would death would ende my thrall.
    Pro. Welcome my sweete *Cassandra.*
    Cas. Murdrous varlet, away.
Renowmed King, I pardon craue, for this my bould attempt,
In preasing thus so neare your grace, my sorrow to present:
And least my foe, false *Promos* heare, doe interrupt my tale,
Graunt gratious King, that vncontrould, I may report my bale.
    King. How now *Promos*? how lyke you, of this song?
Say on fayre dame, I long to heare thy wrong.
    Cas. Then knowe dread souerayne, that he this doome did geue,
That my Brother, for wantonnesse should lose his head:
And that the mayde, which sind, should euer after lyue
In some religious house, to sorrowe her misdeede:
To saue my brother iug'd to dye, with teares I sought to moue
Lord *Promos* hart, to showe him grace: but he with lawles loue,
Was fyred by and by: and knowing necessity,
To saue my brothers lyfe, would make me yeeld to much,
He crau'd this raunsome, to haue my virginitie:
No teares could worke restraynt, his wicked lust was such.
Two euils here were, one must I chuse, though bad were very best,

355

To see my brother put to death, or graunt his lewde request: [K2ʳ]
In fyne, subdude with naturall loue, I did agree,
Vpon these two poyntes: that marry mee he should,
And that from prison vyle, he should my brother free.
All this with monstrous othes, he promised he would.
But O this periurd *Promos*, when he had wrought his wyll,
Fyrst cast mee of: and after causd the Gailer for to kill
My brother, raunsomde with the spoyle of my good name:
So that for companing, with such a hellish feende,
I haue condemnde my selfe to weare these weedes of shame:
Whose cognisance doth showe, that I haue (fleshly) sind.
Loe thus, hie and renowned king, *Cassandra* endes her tale,
And this is wicked *Promos* that hath wrought her endles bale.
    King. If this be true, so fowle a deede, shall not vnpunisht goe.
How sayst thou *Promos*, to her playnte? arte giltye? yea, or noe?
Why speakst thou not? a faulty harte, thy scilence sure doth showe.
    Pro. My gilty hart commaunds my tongue, O king, to tell a troth,
I doe confesse this tale is true, and I deserue thy wrath.   [TLN 2754]
    King. And is it so? this wicked deede, thou shalt ere long buy deare.
Cassandra, take comfort in care, be of good cheere:
Thy forced fault, was free from euill intent,
So long, no shame, can blot thee any way.
And though at ful, I hardly can content thee,
Yet as I may, assure thy selfe I wyl.
Thou wycked man, might it not thee suffice,
By worse then force, to spoyle her chastitie,
But heaping sinne on sinne, against thy oth,
Haste cruelly, her brother done to death.
This ouert* proofe, ne can but make me thinke,
That many waies thou hast my subiectes wrongd:
For how canst thou with Iustice vse thy swaie,
When thou thy selfe dost make thy will a lawe?
Thy tyrranny made mee, this progresse make,
(How so, for sport tyll nowe I colloured it)
Vnto this ende, that I might learne at large,
What other wronges by power, thou hast wrought,
And heere, I heare: the Ritche suppresse the poore: [K2ᵛ]
So that it seemes, the best and thou art friendes:
I plaste thee not, to be a partiall Iudge.
Thy Offycers are couetous I finde,
By whose reportes, thou ouer rulest sutes:
Then who that geues, an Item in the hande,
In ryght, and wrong, is sure of good successe.
Well, Varlet, well: too slowe I hether came,
To scourge thy faultes, and salue the sores thou mad'st.
On thee vyle wretche, this sentence I pronounce:
That foorthwith, thou shalt marrie *Cassandra*,
For to repayre hir honour, thou dydst waste:
The next daye thou shalt lose thy hated lyfe,
In penaunce, that thou mad'st hir Brother dye.
    Pro. My faultes were great, O king, yet graunt me mercie,
That nowe with bloody sighes, lament my sinnes too late.

*ouert] ouer Q

King. Hoc facias alteri, quod tibi vis fieri.
Pittie was no plee Syr, when you in iudgement sate.
Prepare your selfe to dye, in vaine you hope for lyfe.
My Lordes, bring him with mee: *Cassandra* come you in like case:
Myselfe wyll see, thy honour salu'd, in making thee his Wife,
The sooner to shorten his dayes.
All the company. We wayte vpon your Grace.

As the King is going out, a Poore man shall kneele in his waye.

Kyng. Syr *Vlrico*, I wyld, Commission should be made,
To Syr *Anthony Alberto*, and *Iustice Diron*,
To heare and determine, all sutes to be had
Betwene Maister *Prostro*, and this poore man: is it done?
Vlrico. Renowned King, it is ready.
King. Repayre to Syr *Vlrico*, for thy Commission.
All. God preserue your Maiestie.

They all depart, saue the *Clowne.*

Clow. Bones of me, a man were better speak to great Lords, chy see,   [K3ʳ]
Then to our proude Iustlers of peace, that byn in the cuntry:
He that is rytch, as my dame sayth, goes away with the Hare.
This two yeere, they haue hard* my matter, and yet cham nere the neere,
And at first dash, a good fatte Lorde, God in heauen saue his life,
Fayth, for nothing, teld the King of Mas *Prostros*, and my strife.
O Leard, ych thought the King could not bide, on poore men to looke,
But God saue his Grace, at fyrst dash, my Supplycation he tooke:
And you hard, how gently, he called mee poore man, and wild me goe,
For my Pasport, I kenne not what, to good syr *Vlrico*.
Well, chull goe fort, and hope to be with Master *Prostros* to bring:*
But ere ych goe, chul my Ballat, of good King *Coruine* sing.

The Clownes Song.

You Barrons bolde, and lustie Lads,
  Prepare to welcome, our good King:
Whose comming so, his Subiectes glads,
  As they for ioye, the Belles doo ryng.
    They fryske, and skippe, in euerie place,
    And happy he, can see his face:
    Who checks the rytch, that wrong by might,
    And helpes the poore, vnto his right.

The loue that rygour gettes through feare,
  With grace and mercie, he doth wyn:
For which we praye thus, euerie where,
  Good Lorde preserue, our King Coruin.
    His fauour raignes, in euerie place:
    And happy he, can see his face.   *Exit.*

*hard] i.e., heard
*be with . . . to bring] i.e., get the better of

Actus 4.*Scena*. 1. [K3ᵛ]

Gresco, a good substantiall Offycer, Two *Beadelles*
in blew Coates, with Typestaues.

Gresco. Come loytring knaues, speede about your businesse.
Fetche mee in, all ydle vacaboundes.
   First. Yes syr, yes.
   Gres. Searche Ducke alley, Cocke lane, and Scouldes corner.
About your charge, lets see, howe you can sturre.
   Sec. Yes, I haue winges in my heeles to flee.
   First. Who giues two pence, a straunge Monster to see?
   Sec. What Monster?
   First. A horned Beast, with winges vpon his heeles.
   Sec. Out dronken dreule?
   Gres. What? runnes your heades a wheeles?
Be packing bothe, and that betymes, you are best.
   First. We are gone Syr, we dyd but speake in ieast.   *Exeunt. Beadelles.*
   Gres. The King, I fayth, hath set vs all a worke,
To searche odde holes, where ydle varlettes lurke.
He so nypped, our *Maior* for yll rule:
As euer since, he hath bene lyke to whule.*
And in a rage, the man is nowe so whotte,
As lewde personnes, tagge and ragge, goes to potte,
But in chiefe, he stormes, at fine Mistrisse *Lamia.*
She drinkes for all, come she once in his waye,
And least she scape, my selfe forsooth he wylles,
Worshipfullie to fetche hir, with fortie Bylles.
Well, I must goe, and worke our *Maiors* heast.
No force, for once, she wyll neuer be honest.   *Exit.*

Actus. 4.*Scena.* 2. [K4ʳ]

Andrugio, as out of the wooddes, with Bowe
and Arrowes, and a Cony at his gyrdle.

An. This sauage life, were hard to brooke, if hope no comfort gaue:
But I (whose life, from Tyrants wrath, Gods prouidence did saue),
Do take in worth this misery, as penaunce for my mys:
Stil fed with hope to chaunge this state, when Gods good pleasure is.
A hollow Caue for house, and bed, in worth *Andrugio* takes,
Such sorie foode, as fortune sendes, he syldome nowe forsakes.
I am my selfe forsoothe, nowe Butcher, Cooke, Cater and all:
Yea, often tymes I fall to sleepe, with none, or supper small.
Then in my Denne, I call to minde, the lyfe I lyu'de in blisse:
And by the want I freedome iudge, the greatest ioye that is:
The freeman is in viewe of friendes, to haue releafe* in neede:

*whule] i.e., howl
*releafe] release Q

358

The exyle, though he haue no lacke, yet lyues he styll in dreede
That his mysdeedes, wyll hardly scape, the punishment of lawe:
And lyuing, he were better dead, that lyueth in this awe,
Besides this feare, which neuer fayles, the banisht man in want,
As ofte he is, is sure to finde his succor's verie scant.
Then who is he so mad, that friendes, and freedome doth enioye,
That wyll aduenture breach of lawe, to lyue in this annoye?
And not annoye to him alone, but to his friendes and kyn:
Great be the cares, *Cassandra*, and *Polina* lyueth in,
Through thought of me, whom long agone, beheaded they suppose,
For my offence, thus are they scorgde, yet dare I not disclose
My safetie, for their helpe: but harke, who commeth here?
This chaunce seemes strange: God graunt good newes: I hope, and yet I
    feare.

Iohn Adroynes a Clowne, *Andrugio.*   [K4ᵛ]

Iohn. If che could finde my Mare, che would be rusty* by the rood,
And cham sure the hoorechup, is peaking in this wood.
Chy wyl seeke euery corner, but che wyll find her.

He whistlyng lookes vp and downe the stage.

An. This clowne can hardly mee bewray, and yet such dunghyll churles,
Such newes, as is in market tounes, about the country whorles.
What seekes thou good fellow?
Iohn. My sqawde Mare, dost her know?
An. No.
Iohn. Then scummer* mee not, in haste ych goe,
Seeke my Mare, to see the sport at *Iulio.*
An. What sport?
Iohn. A lyttel sport.
An. What?
Iohn. Nay skyl not a whit?
An. What meanes this Asse?
Iohn. T'wyll teache the hoorecup wyt.
H'yll* hang, handsome young men for the soote sinne of loue,
When so his knauery, himselfe, a bawdy iack doth proue.
An. His wordes seemeth straunge, somwhat is a wry.
Iohn. Well, chyll see his shoulders, from's iowle to flye.
An. Whose shoulders friend?
Iohn. As though you dyd not know.*
An. Whome?
Iohn. Lord *Promos.*
An. Yes: my most accursed foe:
But what of him?
Iohn. Thou kenst.
An. No.
Iohn. Sayst not, yes?

*rusty] *read* lusty, i.e., joyful?
*scummer] i.e., cumber, bother
*H'yll] i.e., he'll
*dyd not know] dyd know Q

359

An. Yes.

Iohn. So.

An. But friend thou took'st my wordes amys,　　　　　　　　[L1ʳ]
I know nothing, in what state *Promos* is.

Iohn. Thou knowst, and thou knowest not: out horson foole,
Leaue stealing Cunnyes, and get thee to scoole.
Farewell.

An. Soft.

Iohn. O th'arte no foole good theefe:
Saue my mony take my life.

An. Tush be breefe.
Some newes, of lewde Lord *Promos* tell mee,
And wyth lyfe and mony, yle set thee free.

Iohn. I wyll: thou knowst the King now at *Iulio.*

An. Very well.

Iohn. Thou canst tel as wel as I.
Let me goe.

An. Nay yle see if thou dost lye.
If thou dost, yle whip thee, when thou hast done.

Iohn. Kissyng and lying, ich see is all one:
And chaue no mony, chul tell true therfore.

An. Dispatch then.

Iohn. Then, lying Promoter, this more:
Casgandra scusde, *Promos* of honestie:　　　　　　　　[TLN 534]
And killyng *Ramstrugio* for baudry.

An. What more?

Iohn. The king at *Promos*, great pleasure did take,
And *Casgandra*, an honest woman to make:
The King maunded him, her strayght to marry,
And for killyng her brother, he must dye.

An. Is this true?

Iohn. Why? how say you? doe I lye?

An. Well, so or noe, for thy newes haue this connie.

Iohn. Gods boores, geue it me, to be swete, tis to cheape,
Bur Lady yet, tyll sunday it will keepe:
Well, now god bwye, Mas lying Promoter,
Wees see at the sport.

An. I, peraduenture.

Iohn. Since can not finde my Mare, on foote chull goe:　　　[L1ᵛ]
Ych thinke, each daye a nowre,* to be at *Iulio.*　　　　　　　*Exit.*

An. Straunge are the newes, the Clowne hath showne to me:
Not straunge a whyt, if they well scanned be.
For God we see, styll throwes the Tyrant downe:
Euen in the heyght, and pride of his renowne.
Lorde *Promos* rule, nay, tyranny in deede,
For Iudges is a mirror, worthy heede.
The wretched man, with showe of Iustice zeale,
Throughly dyd, with poore offenders deale.
The wicked man, both knewe, and iudg'd, abuse:
And none so much as he, her faultes dyd vse.
He fellons hang'd, yet by extorcion, stoale:

---

*a nowre] i.e., an hour

He wantons plag'd, himselfe a doating foole.
He others checkt, for suing for their right:
And he himselfe, mayntained wrongs by might.
But see the rule of mischiefe, in his pride:
He headlong falles, when least he thought to slide.
Well, by his fall, I maye perhaps aryse:
Andrugio yet, in clyming be thou wyse.
What? styll vnknowne, shall I liue in this wood?
Not so.
Go wraye these newes, no doubt, vnto my good.
Yet ere I go, I wyll my selfe disguise,
As in the Towne, in spyte of *Linxes* eyes,
I wyll vnknowne, learne howe the game doth go.
But ere I go, syth eased is my woe,
My thankes to God, I first in song wyll shoe.

Andrugios Song.

To thee O Lorde, with harte and voyce I syng,
 Whose mercie great, from mone to sweete delight:
From griefe to ioye, my troubled soule doest bring,
 Yea more, thy wrath, hath foylde my foe in syght.
Who sought my lyfe (which thou O God didst saue) [L2ʳ]
 Thy scorge hath brought, vntimelie to his graue.

Whose griefe wyll gawle, a thousande Iudges moe,
 And wyll them see them selues, and sentence iust:
When blacke reproche, this thundring shame shall shoe,
 A Iudge condemde for murder, thefte, and luste.
This scorge, O God, the lewde in feare wyll bring,
 The iust for ioye, thy prayses lowde wyll syng. *Exit.*

[*Actus. 4.Scena.* 3.]

Gresco, with three other, with bylles, bringing in *Lamia* prisoner.

Gres. Come on faire Dame, since faire words, works no heede,
Now fowle meanes shall, in you repentaunce breede.
 La. Maister *Gresco*, where you maye helpe, hurt not.
 Gres. And nothing but chastment, wyll helpe you to amende.
Well, I wyll not hurt you, your lewdnes to defende.
 La. My lewdnes Syr: what is the difference,
Betwixt wantons, and hoorders of pence?
 Gres. Thou hast winde at wyll, but in thy eyes no water:
Tho'arte full of Grace, howe she blusheth at the matter.
 La. Howe sample* I your wyfe and daughter Syr?
 Gres. Axe mee, when whypping hath chaung'd thy Nature.
 La. What, whypping? why? am I a Horse or a Mare?
 Gres. No, but a beast, that meetelie well wyll bare.

*sample] i.e., match

La. In deede (as)* nowe, perforce, I beare this flowt:
But vse me well, else I fayth, gette I out,
Looke for quittaunce.
    Byl. Binde hir to the Peace Syr.   *First Bilm.*
So maye your Worship be out of daunger.
    Gres. Bring hir awaye, I knowe howe to tame hir.
    La. Perhaps Syr, no: the worst is but shame hir.
    Byl. Come ye drab.   *Second Bilm.*
    La. Howe nowe scab? handes of my Gowne.
    Byl. Care not for this, yuse haue a blew one soone.   *Exeunt.*   *Third Bil.*

[*Actus.* 4. *Scena.* 4.]   [L2v]

Cassandra.

Cas. Vnhappy Wench, the more I seeke, for to abandone griefe,
The furder off, I wretched finde, both comfort and reliefe.
My Brother first, for wanton faultes, condempned was to dye:
To saue whose life, my sute, wrought hope of Grace, but haples I,
By such request, my honor spoyld, and gayned not his breath:
For which deceyte, I haue pursude, Lorde *Promos* vnto death.
Who is my Husbande nowe become, it pleasd our Soueraigne so,
For to repayre, my crased Fame: but that nowe workes my wo.
This day, he must (oh) leese his head, my Brothers death to quite,
And therin Fortune hath alas, showne me hir greatest spyte.
Nature wyld mee, my Brother loue, now dutie commaunds mee,   [TLN 1355]
To preferre before kyn, or friend, my Husbands safetie.
But O, aye mee, by Fortune, I am made his chiefest foe:
T'was I al[a]s, euen onely I, that wrought his ouerthroe.
What shall I doo, to worke amends, for this my haynous deede?
The tyme is short, my power small, his succors axeth speede.
And shall I seeke, to saue his blood, that lately sought his lyfe?
O yea, I then was sworne his foe: but nowe as faithfull Wife,
I must and wyll, preferre his health, God sende me good successe:
For nowe vnto the King I wyll, my chaunged minde to expresse.   *Exit.*

[*Actus.* 4. *Scena.* 5.]

Phallax.

Phal. Was euer man, set more freer then I?
First went my goodes, then my Office dyd flye?
But had the King, set me free from flattrie,
The next deare yeare, I might haue staru'd, perdie.

*(as)] i.e., like an ass

But Lorde *Promos*, hath a farre more freer chaunce:
He free from Landes, goodes, and Office doth daunce:
And shalbe free from life, ere long, with a Launce.
The Officers, and chiefe men of *Iulio*:
Vengeaunce lyberall, themselues lykewise shoe.
Poore knaues, and queanes that vp and downe do goe,
These horesen kinde crustes, in houses bestoe.
But yet, poore cheere they haue: marry, for heate,   [L3ʳ]
They whyp them, vntyll verie blood they sweate.
But see, their cost bestowde of fyne *Lamia*,
To saue hir feete, from harde stones, and colde waye,
Into a Carte, they dyd the queane conuaye,
Apparelled, in collours verie gaye:
Both Hoode, and Gowne, of greene, and yellowe Saye.
Hir Garde, weare* Typstaues, all in blewe arraye.
Before hir, a noyse of Basons dyd playe,
In this triumphe, she ryd well nye a daye.
Fie, fie, the Citie is so purged nowe,
As they of none, but honest men allowe,
So that farewell my parte, of thriuing there:
But the best is, flattrers lyue euerie where.
Set cocke on hoope, *Domini est terra*.
If thou can not where thou wouldst, lyue where thou maye.
Yes, yes *Phallax*, knoweth whether* to go.
Nowe, God bwy ye all, honest men of *Iulio*.
As the Deuilles lykes, the company of Friers,
So flattrers loues as lyfe, to ioyne with lyers.

Actus. 5. Scena. 1.

Andrugio, disguised in some long blacke Cloake.

An. These two dayes, I haue bene in Court disguis'd:
Where I haue learnd, the scorge that is deuis'd,
For *Promos* faulte: he my Syster spowsed hath,
To salue hir Fame, crackt by his breache of fayth,
And shortlie, he must lose his subtyll head,
For murdring me, whome no man thinkes but dead.
His wyll was good: and therfore beshrewe mee,
If (mou'd with ruthe) I seeke, to set him free.
But softlie, with some newes, these fellowes come:
I wyll stande close, and heare both all and some.

*weare] i.e., were
*whether] i.e., whither

363

Actus 5.*Scena.* 2.

Enter *Vlrico*, *Marshall.*

Vl. Marshall, heare your* warrant is: with speede,
The king commaundes, that *Promos* you behead.
   Mar. Sir, his highnesse wyll, shalbe forthwith done.   *Exit. Marshall.*
   Vl. The king welnye to pardon him was wonne,
His heauy wyfe, such stormes of teares did showre,
As myght, with rueth, haue moyst a stony hart.
But *Promos* guylt, dyd soone this grace deuoure.
Our gratious king, before hir wretched smart,
Preferd the helth, of this our common weale:
But see againe, to sue for him she comes.
Her ruthfull lookes, her greefe doth force mee feele.
With hope, I must hir sorrowes needes delay:
Tyll *Promos* be dispacht out of the way.

Actus. 5.*Scena.* 3.

Cassandra.

   Cas. Syr *Vlrico*, if that my vnknowne greefe,
May moue good mindes, to helpe mee to releefe,
Or bytter syghes, of comfort cleane dismayde,
May moue a man, a shiftlesse dame to ayde:
Rue of my teares, from true intent which flowe,
Vnto the king, with me, yet once more goe.
See if his grace, my husbands lyfe wyll saue,
If not, with his, death shall my corps ingraue.
   Vl. What shall I doe, her sorrowes to decreace?
Feede her with hope: fayre dame, this mone surcease,
I see the king to grace is somewhat bent,
We once agayne thy sorrowes wyll present:
Come we wyl wayght for tyme, thy sute to show.
   Cas. Good knight, for time, doe not my sute foreslowe.
Whylst grasse doth growe, ofte sterues the seely steede.
   Vl. Feare not, your Lorde, shal not dye with such speede.   *Exeunt.*

[*Actus.* 5.*Scena.* 4.]

Enter *Andrugio.*

*your] you Q

An. Lord God, how am I tormented in thought?
My sisters woe, such rueth in me doth graue:
As fayne I would (if ought saue death I caught)
Bewray my selfe, Lord *Promos* life to saue.
But lyfe is sweete, and naught but death I eye,
If that I should, my safety now disclose:
So that I chuse, of both the euels, he dye:
Time wyll appease, no dought, *Cassandras* woes.
And shal I thus acquite *Cassandras* loue?
To worke her ioy, and shall I feare to dye?
Whylst that she lyue, no comforte may remoue
Care from her harte, if that hir husband dye.
Then shall I stycke, to hasard lym? nay life?
To salue hir greefe, since in my cure it rests?
Nay fyrst, I wilbe spoyld, with blooddy knife,
Before I fayle her, plunged in distres.
Death, is but death, and all in fyne shall dye.   [TLN 1040]
Thus (being dead) my fame, shall liue alway:
Well, to the king, *Andrugio* now wyll hye,
Hap lyfe, hap death, his safety to bewray.   *Exit.*

Actus. 5. Scena. 5.*

The *Marshall*, three or fowre with halbards,
Leading *Promos* to execution.

Byl. Roome friends, what meane you thus to gase on vs?   *A Bylman.*
A comes behinde, makes all the sport I wus.
  Pro. Farewell, my friendes, take warning by my fall,   [L4ᵛ]
Disdaine my life, but lysten to my ende.
Fresh harmes, they say, the viewers so apall,
As oft they win, the wicked to amend.
I neede not heare, my faultes at large resyte,
Vntimely death, doth witnesse what I was:
A wicked man, which made eache wrong seeme right,
Euen as I would, was wrested euery case.
And thus long tyme, I liu'd and rul'd* by wyl,
Where as I lou'd, their faultes, I would not see:
Those I did hate, tenne tymes beyond there yll
I did persue, vyle wretch, with cruelty.
Yea dayly I, from bad, to worse did slyde,
The reason was, none durst, controule my lyfe:
But see the fall, of mischeeue, in his pride,

---

*Scena. 5.] Scena. 4. Q
*rul'd] rule Q

365

My faultes, were knowne, and loe with bloddy Axe,
The headseman strayght, my wronges with death wyll quite:
The which, in worth I take, acknowledging,
The doome was geuen on cause, and not on spyte,
Wishing my ende, might serue for a warning,
For such as rule, and make their will a lawe.
If to such good, my faynting tale might tend,
Wretched *Promos*, the same would lenger draw:
But if that wordes preuayle, my wofull ende
From my huge faultes, then tenne times more wyll warne.
Forgeuenesse now, of all the world I craue,
Therewith that you, in zealous prayer, wyll
Beseeche of God, that I the grace may haue,
At latter gaspe, the feare of death to kyll.
    Mar. Forwards my Lord, me thinkes you fayntly goe.
    Pro. O syr, in my case, your selfe would be as slowe.

*Actus. 5. Scena. 6.**   [M1ʳ]

Enter *Cassandra*, *Polina*, and one mayde.

    Cas. Aye me, alas: my hope is vntimely.
Whether goes my good Lord?
    Pro. Sweete wife, to dye.
    Cas. O wretched wench, where may I first complayne?
When heauen, and earth, agrees vpon my payne?
    Pro. This mone good wife, for Chrystes sake, forsake:
I, late resolu'd, through feare of death, now quake.
Not so much, for my haynous sinnes forepast:
As for the greefe that present thou dost tast.
    Cas. Nay, I vile wretch, should most agreeued be,
Before thy time, thy death which hastened haue:
But (O swete husband) my fault forgeue mee,
And for amends, Ile helpe to fyll thy graue.
    Pro. Forgeue thee, ah: nay, for my soules releefe,
Forget sweete wyfe, this thy most guyltles greefe.
    Mar. My Lord *Promos*, these playntes, but moue hir mone,
And your more greefe, it is best you ware gone:
Good Maddame, way, by lawe, your Lord doth dye,
Wherefore make vertue of necessity:
Delay, but workes your sorrowes, and our blames,
So that now, to the comfort of these dames,
And your wisdome, inforced, we leaue you:
My Lord *Promos*, byd your wife and friends adew.
    Pro. Farewell, farewell, be of good cheare, deare wyfe:
With ioy for woe, I shall exchange this life.
Andrugios death, *Polina* forgeue mee.
    Poli. I doe, and pray the Lord, to releeue yee.

**Scena. 6.*] *Scena. 5.* Q

Cas. Yet ere we part, sweete husband, let vs kis.
O, at his lyppes, why fayleth not my breath?
Pro. Leaue mone, swete wife, I doe deserue this death.
Farewell, farewell.

They all depart, saue *Polina*, *Cassandra*, and her woman.   [M1ᵛ]

Cas. My louing Lorde, farewell,
I hope ere long, my soule with thine shall dwell.
Po. Now, good Madame, leaue of this bootelesse griefe.
Cas. O *Polina*, sorrowe is my reliefe.
Wherfore, sweete wenche, helpe me to rue my woe,
With me vyle wretche, thy bytter plaintes bestowe,
To hasten lyngring death, who wanteth might,
I see, alone, to sley the wretched wight.
Po. Nay, first powre foorth your playnts, to the powers Diuine,
When hate doth clowde all worldly grace, whose mercies styll do shine.
Cas. O, so or no, thy motion doeth well,
Swan lyke, in song, to towle my passing Bell.

The Song of *Cassandra*.

Deare Dames, diuorse your minds from ioy, helpe to bewayle my wo,
Condole with me, whose heauy sighes, * the pangs of death do shoe:*
Rend heairs, shed teares, poore wench distrest, to hast the means to dye,
Whose ioye, annoy: reliefe, whose griefe, hath spoyld with crueltie.

My brother slaine, my husband ah, at poynt to lose his head,
Why lyue I then vnhappy wench, my suckers being dead?
O time, O cryme, O cause, O lawes, that Iudgd them thus to dye:
I blame you all, my shame, my thrall, you hate that harmelesse trye.

This Tragidy they haue begun, conclude I wretched must,
O welcome care, consume the thread, whereto * my life doth trust:*
Sound bell, my knell, away delaie, and geue mee leaue to dye,
Les hope, haue scope, vnto my hart, a fresh for ayde to flye.

Enter *Ganio* sometime *Andrugios* Boye.   [M2ʳ]

Ga. O sweete newes, for *Polina* and *Cassandra*.
Andrugio lyues.
Po. What doth poore *Ganio* saye?
Ga. Andrugio lyues: and *Promos* is repriu'd.
Cas. Vaine is thy hope, I sawe *Andrugio* dead.
Ga. Well, then from death, he is againe reuyu'd.
Euen nowe, I sawe him, in the market stead.
Po. His wordes are straunge.
Cas. Too sweete, God wot, for true.
Ga. I praye you, who are these here in your view?
Cas. The King.

*sighes] *sights* Q
*whereto] *thereto* Q

Ga. Who more?
Po. O, I see *Andrugio.*
Cas. And I my Lorde *Promos*, adue sorrowe.

Enter the *King*, *Andrugio*, *Promos*, *Vlrico*, the *Marshall.*

Po. My good *Andrugio*?
An. My sweete *Polina.*
Cas. Lyues *Andrugio*? welcome sweete brother.
An. Cassandra?
Cas. I.
An. Howe fare, my deare Syster?
King. Andrugio, you shall haue more leysure,
To greete one another: it is our pleasure,
That you forthwith, your Fortunes here declare,
And by what meanes, you thus preserued weare.
An. My faull, through loue, and iudgement for my faulte,
Lorde *Promos* wronges, vnto my Sister done,
My death supposde, dreade King, were vaine to tell.
Cassandra heare, those dealinges all hath showne.
The rest are these.
When I should dye, the Gayler mou'd to ruth,   [M2^v]
Declard to mee, what *Promos* pleasure was:
Amazde wherat, I tolde him all the trueth,
What, betwene *Cassandra*, and him dyd passe.
He, much agrieu'd, Lorde *Promos* guylt to heare,
Was verie lothe, mee (wofull man) to harme:
At length, iust God, to set me (wretched) cleare,
With this defence, his wylling minde dyd arme.
Two dayes afore, to death, were diuers done,
For seuerall faultes, by them committed:
So that of them, he tooke the head from one,
And to *Cassandra*, the same presented:
Affirming it to be hir brothers head.
Which done, by night, he sent me post away,
None but supposed, that I in deede was dead:
When as in trueth, in vncouth hauntes I laye.
In fine, a Clowne, came peaking through the wood,
Wherin I lyu'd: your Graces being here,
And *Promos* death, by whome I vnderstood.
Glad of which newes, howe so I lyud in feare,
I ventured to see his wretched fall:
To free suspect, yet straunger lyke arayde,
I hether came: but loe, the inwarde thrall
Of *Cassandra*, the hate so sore dismayde,
Which I conceyued agaynst my brother *Promos*,
That loe, I chews'd, to yeeld my selfe to death,
To set him free: for otherwyse I knew,
His death, ere long, would sure haue stopt her breath.
Loe gratious king, in breefe I here haue showne,
Such aduentures, as wretched I haue past:
Beseeching you with grace to thinke vpon,
The wight that wayles, his follyes at the last.

King. A strange discourse, as straungely come to light.
Gods pleasure is, that thou should'st pardoned be:
To salue the fault, thou with *Polina* mad'st,
But marry her, and heare I set thee free.
   An. Most gratious Prince, thereto I gladly gree.   [M3^r]
   Poli. Polina, the happiest newes of all for thee.
   Cas. Most gratious King, with these my ioye to match,
Vouchsafe, to geue my dampned husbande lyfe.
   King. If I doo so, let him thanke thee his Wife:
Cassandra, I haue noted thy distresse,
Thy vertues eke, from first, vnto the last:
And glad I am, without offence it lyes,
In me to ease thy griefe, and heauines.
Andrugio sau'd, the iuell of thy ioye,
And for thy sake, I pardon *Promos* faulte.
Yea let them both, thy vertues rare commende:
In that their woes, with this delyght doth ende.
   Company. God preserue your Maiestie.
   Pro. Cassandra, howe shall I discharge thy due?
   Cas. I dyd, but what a Wife, shoulde do for you.
   King. Well, since all partes are pleased, as they woulde,
Before I parte, yet *Promos*, this to thee:
Henceforth, forethinke, of thy forepassed faultes,
And measure Grace, with Iustice euermore.
Vnto the poore, haue euermore an eye,
And let not might, out countenaunce their right:
Thy Officers, trust not in euery tale,
In chiefe, when they are meanes, in strifes and sutes.
Though thou be iust, yet coyne maye them corrupt.
And if by them, thou dost vniustice showe,
Tys thou shalt beare, the burden of their faultes.
Be louing to good *Cassandra*, thy Wife: [TLN 2896]
And friendlie to thy brother *Andrugio*,
Whome I commaund, as faythfull for to be
To thee, as beseemes the duety of a brother.
And now agayne, thy gouernment receyue,
Inioye it so, as thou in Iustice ioye.
If thou be wyse, thy fall maye make thee ryse.
The lost sheepe founde, for ioye, the feast was made.   [M3^v]
Well, here an ende, of my aduise I make,
As I haue sayde, be good vnto the poore,
And Iustice ioyne, with mercie euermore.
   Pro. Most gratious King, I wyll not fayle my best,
In these preceptes, to followe your beheast.

     FINIS.   *G. Whetstone.*

Imprinted at London by Richarde Ihones, and are to be solde
ouer agaynst Saint Sepulchres Church, without Newgate.
August.20. 1578.

GEORGE WHETSTONE, *AN HEPTAMERON OF CIVILL DISCOVRSES* (1582)

Entered on the Stationers' Register to Richard Jones on 11 Jan. 1582 (Arber, *Transcript,* 2:404), Whetstone's *Heptameron* was published by Jones, according to its title page on 3 Feb. The first edition's black letter is here reproduced as roman and its roman as italic (except for 1582's first line of type, which is in roman). The prose is relined. Abbreviations have been expanded and a few errors corrected. The TLNs which occasionally appear refer to the text of *MM*.

The text of the *Historie,* told on the fourth day in the *Heptameron*, is based on the Huntington Library copy (STC 25337).

The rare Historie of Promos and Cassandra,   [N
reported by Madam ISABELLA.

This Historie for rarenes ther-of, is liuely set out in a Comme-die, by the Re-porter of the whole worke, but yet neuer presented vpon stage.

A hard Lawe for incontinent persons.

At what time *Coruinus* the scourge of the *Turkes*, rayned as Kinge of *Bohemia*: for to well gouerne the free Cities of his Realme, hee sent diuers worthy Maiestrates. Among the rest, he gaue the Lorde *Promos* the Lieutennauntship of *Iulio*: who in the beginning of his gouerment, purged the Cittie of many ancient vices, and seuerely punished new offenders.

In this Cittie, there was an olde custome (by the suffering of some Maiestrates, growne out of vse) that what man so euer committed Adulterie, should lose his head: And the woman offender should euer after be infamously noted, by the wear-ing of some disguised apparrell: For the man was helde to bee the greatest offender, and therefore had the seuerest punish-ment.

Lorde *Promos*, with a rough execution, reuiued this Stat-ute, and in the hyest degree of iniurie, brake it hym-[N3ʳ] selfe, as shall appeare by the sequell of *Andrugioes* aduen-tures.

This *Andrugio* by the yeelding fauour of fayre *Polina*, trespassed against this ordinaunce, who through enuie, was accused, and by Lorde *Promos* condemned, to suffer execu-tion.

The wofull *Cassandra*, *Andrugioes* Sister, prostrates her selfe at Lorde *Promos* Feete, and with more teares then wordes, thus pleaded for her Brothers lyfe.

Most noble Lorde, and worthy Iudge, voutchsafe, mee the fauour to speake, whose case is so desperate, as vnlesse you beholde mee with the eyes of mercie, the frayle trespasse, of condemned *Andrugio* my Brother, will bee the death of sorrowfull *Cassandra*, his innocent Sister. I wil not presume, to excuse his offence, or reproche the Lawe of rigor: for in the generall construction, hee hath done most euill, and the Law hath iudged but what is right: But (reuerent Iudge,) pardon that necessitie maketh mee here tel, that your wisdome already knoweth. The most Soueraigne Iustice, is crowned with Laurell, although shee bee gyrt with a Sword: And this priueledge shee giueth vnto her Administrators: that they shall mitigate the seueretie of the Law, according to the quallyty of the offence. Then, that Iustice be not robbed of her gratious pitty, listen Good Lorde *Promos*, to the nature of my Brothers offence, and his able meanes to repayre the iniurie. Hee hath defyled, no Nuptiall Bed, the stayne wherof dishonoureth the guyltlesse Husband: Hee hath committed no violent Rape, in which Act the iniuried Mayde can haue no amends. But with yeelding consent of his Mistresse, *Andrugio* hath onlye sinned through Loue, and neuer ment but with Marriage to make amendes.

I humbly beseeche you to accept his satisfaction, and by this Example, you shall be as much beloued for your clemencye, as feared for your seueritie. *Andrugio* shalbe well warned, and hee with his Sister wofull *Cassandra*, shall euer remayne, your Lordships true Seruantes.

[N3ᵛ] *Promos* eares were not so attentiue, to heare *Cassandras* ruethful tale, as his eyes were settled to regarde her excellent Beautie. And Loue, that was the appoincted Headsman of *Andrugio*, became now the Soueraigne of his Iudges thought. But because he would seeme to bridle his passions, he aunswered: fayre Damsell, haue patience, you importune me with an impossybylytie: he is condempned by Lawe, then without iniurie to Lawe, he can not be saued.

Princes and their Deputies Prerogatiues (quoth she) are aboue the Lawe. Besides, Lawe, truelie construed, is but the amends of Iniurie: and where, the faulte may bee salued,* and amendes had, the Breache of Lawe is sufficiently repayred.

Quoth Lorde *Promos*, your passions mooueth more then your proofes: and for your sake, I wyll repriue *Andrugio,* and studie how to do you ease, without apparant breache of Lawe.

Cassandra, recomforted, with humble thankes receyued his fauoure, and in great haste goeth too participate this hope, with her dying Brother: But oh, that Aucthorytie, should haue

*salued] valued 1582

euyll Maiestra-
tes, is a Scourge
vnto the good.

power, to make the vertuous to doo amisse, as well, as
throughe Correction, to enforce the vicious to fall vnto goodnesse.

Promos, is a witnes of this Priuiledge: who not able to
subdue his incontinent loue, and (withal) resolued, that *Cas-*
sandra would neuer be ouercome, with fayre wordes, large

A monstrous re-
quest.

promises, or riche rewardes: demaunded the spoyle of her
Virginitie, for raunsome of her Brothers lybertie.

Cassandra, ymagynyng* at the first, that Lorde *Promos*,

Vnlesse they be
reprobate, good
Examples, may
refourme the
wicked.

vsed this speache, but to trie her behauiour: Aunswered hym
so wisely, as if he had not ben the Ryuall of Vertue, he could
not but haue suppressed his lewde Affection, and haue sub-
scribed to her iust petition: But to leaue circumstaunces, *Promos*
was fiered with a vicious desyre, which must be quenched with
Cassandraes yeldyng loue, or *Andrugio* must dye.

Cassandra, mooued with a chaste disdayne, departed,
[N4r] with the resolution, rather to dye her selfe, then to
stayne her honour: And with this heauie newes, greeted her
condemned Brother: poore man, alas, what should he do? Life
was sweete: but to be redeemed with his Sisters Infamie, could
not, but be alwayes vnsauerie.

To perswade her to consente, was vnnaturall: too yealde
to Death, was more greeuous.

A hard choice of
two euyls.

To choose the leaste of these euylles, was difficult: to
studie long was daungerous.

Fayne would he lyue, but Shame cloased his mouth, when
he attempted to perswade his Sister.

The force of Ne-
cessytie.

But Necessytie, that maistereth both Shame and feare,
brake a passadge for his imprysoned intent.

The force of
Loue.

Sweete *Cassandra*, (quoth he) that men loue, is vsuall, but
to subdue Affection, is impossyble: and so thornie are the
motions of incontinent Desire, as to finde ease, the tongue is
only occupied to perswade. The Purse, is euer open to entice,
and wheare neither words nor Giftes can corrupt (with the
mightie) force shall constrayne, or dispight, auenge. That
Promos do loue, is but iust, thy Beautie commaundes hym. That
Promos be refused, is more iust, because Consent is thy Shame.

Thou maiste refuse and lyue: but he beynge reiected, I
die: For wantyng his wyll in thee, he wyll wreake his teene on
mee.

A hard
Fortune.

This is my hard estate: *My life, lieth in thy Infamie, and thy*
honour in my death. Which of these euylles be leaste, I leaue for
thee to iudge.

*ymagynyng] ymagyned 1582

Death is to be preferred, before dishonorable lyfe.

The wofull *Cassandra*, answered: that Death, was the leaste: whose Darte, we can not shunne: when Honour, in Deathes dispight, outlyueth tyme.

It is true (quoth *Andrugio*,) but thy Trespasse, wyll be in the leaste degree of blame: For, in forced Faultes, Iustice sayth, there is no intent of euyll.

Oh *Andrugio*, (quoth she) Intent, is now adayes, lytle considred: thou art not condemned by the intent, but by [N4ᵛ] the strickt worde of the Law: so shall my crime bee

The venemous nature of Enuy.

reproched, and the forced cause passe vnexcused: and such is the venome of Enuye, one euill deede shall disgrace ten good turnes: and in this yeelding, so shall I be valued: Enuye, Disdaine, Spight, Mallice, Sclaunder, and many moe furies will

The vertuous are assured of many enemies, and incertaine of any friendes.

endeuour to shame mee, and the meanest vertue, wyll blush to help to support my honour: so that I see no lybertie for thee but Death, nor no ease for mee but to hasten my ende.

O yes (quoth *Andrugio*), for if this offence be known, thy fame will bee enlarged, because it will lykewise bee knowne,

A cause that may excuse the breach of honour.

that thou receauedst dishonor to giue thy Brother lyfe: If it be secreat, thy Conscience wyl be without scruple of guiltinesse. Thus, knowne, or vnknowne, thou shalt be deflowred, but not dishonested, and for amends wee both shall lyue.

This further hope remaineth, that as the Gilliflower, both pleaseth the eye and feedeth the sence: euen so the vertue of thy chast behauiour may so grace thy bewty, as *Promos* filthie lust, may bee turned into faithfull loue: and so moue him, to

A faint hope.

salue thy honour in making thee hys wife. Or for conscience, forbeare to doe so heynous an iniurie.

Soueraigne Maddame, and you faire Gentlewomen, (quoth *Isabella*) I intreate you in *Cassandras* behalfe, these reasons well wayed, to iudge her yeelding a constrainte, and no consent: who werie of her owne life, and tender ouer her brothers, with the teares of her louely eyes, bathed his Cheekes, with this comfortable sentence.

A louyng kys.

Lyue Andrugio, and make much of this kisse, which breatheth my honour into thy bowels: and draweth the infamie of thy first trespasse into my bosome.

The sharpe incounters betweene life and death, so occupied *Andrugio* sences, that his tongue had not the vertue, to bid her fare well. To greeue you with the hearing of *Cassandras* secreate plaints, were an iniurie: vertuous [O1ʳ] Ladies, for they concluded with their good fortune, and euerlasting fame:

A good consideration in Cassandra.

But for that her offence grew neyther of frayltie, free wyl, or any motion of a Woman, but by the meere inforcement of a man, because she would not staine the modest weedes of her kynde, shee attired her selfe in the habit of a Page, and with the bashfull grace of a pure Virgin, shee presented wicked *Promos*, Andrugioes precious ransome.

This Deuill, in humaine shape, more vicious then *Hyliogabalus* of *Rome*: and withall, as cruell as *Denis* of *Sicyll*: receaued this Iuell with a thousande protestations of fauour. But what should I say? In the beginnyng of his loue, *Promos* was *metamorphosed* into *Priapus*: and of a Feende what may we expect? but vengeaunce heaped upon villany. And therefore, let it not seeme straunge, that after this Helhound, had dishonoured *Cassandra*, hee sent his warrant, to the Gayler pryuely, to execute *Andrugio*, and with his head crowned with these two Breefes, in *Promos* name, to present *Cassandra*:

A damnable offence.

Fayre Cassandra, as Promos promist thee:
From Pryson loe, he sendes thy Brother free.

A villanous Ingratitude.

This was his Charge, whose cursed wyll had ben executed, had not God by an especiall prouidence, at the howre of his Death, possessed *Andrugio* with the vertues of the two braue *Romanes*, *Marcus Crassus* [TLN 2315], and *Marius*, the one of whiche, by the force of his tongue, and the other by the motions of his eyes, caused the Axe to fall out of the Headsmans hand, and mollyfyed his cruell mynde.

An especiall prouidence of God.

With lyke compassion, the Gayler (in hearinge *Andrugios* hard aduenture) left his resolution: And vppon a solempne othe, to liue vnknowne, yea to his deare Sister, he gaue him life, and in the dead of the night, betooke him to God, and to good fortune: which done this good Gayler tooke the head of a yonge man newe executed, who somewhat resembled *Andrugio*: and according to lewde *Promos* commaundement made a present thereof to *Cassan*-[O1ᵛ]*dra*. How vnwelcome this Present was, the testimonie of her former sorowes somewhat discouer: but to giue her present passion a true grace, were the taske of *Prometheus*, or such a one as hath had experience of the anguishes of hell.

A signe of an honest nature.

An vnwelcome present.

O quoth shee, sweete *Andrugio*, whether shall I firste lament thy death? exclaime of *Promos* iniurie? or bemone my owne estate, depriued of honour? and which is worse, cannot die, but by the violence of my owne hands. Alas, the least of these greefes, are to heauie a burden for a man, then all ioyned in one poore womans hearte, can not be eased but by death: and to be auenged of iniurious Fortune, I wil forthwith cut my Fillet of life. But so shall

Promos lewdnesse escape vnpunished: what remedie? I am
not of power to reuenge: to complayne, I expresse my
owne infamie, but withal, proclaime his vilanie: and to
heare his lewdnes reproued, woulde take away the bitter-
nesse of my death. I will goe vnto the King, who is iust
and mercifull, hee shall heare the ruthfull euents of *Promos*
Tyrannie: and to giue him example of vengeaunce, I will
seale my complaintes with my dearest bloode.

Continuing this determination, *Cassandra* buried her
imagined brothers heade, and with speed iornyed vnto King
Coruinus Court: Before whose presence when shee arriued,
her mourninge Attyre, but especially her modest countenaunce moued him to beholde her with an especiall regarde.

Cassandra (vppon the graunt of audience) with her eyes
ouercharged with teares, reported, the alreadie discoursed Ac-
cidentes, with suche an apparaunce of greefe, as the King and
his Attendants were astonied to heare her: and sure had shee
not been happily preuented, shee had concluded her determination, with chast *Lucretias* destiny. The King comforted her
with many gratious words and promised to take such order,
that (although he could not be reuiued) her brothers death
should fully be reuenged, [O2^r] and her crased honour, repayred, withoute blemysh of her former reputation.

Cassandra, vpon these comfortable wordes, a lytell suc-
coured her afflicted hart, and with patience, attended the Iustice of the King: who with a chosen companie, made a Progresse to *Iulio*, and entred the Town, with a semblaunce of
great fauour towardes *Promos*: by that colour, to learne what
other corrupte Maiestrates, ruled in the Cittie: for well he
knewe, that Byrdes of a feather, would flie together, and
wicked men would ioyne in Affection to boulster each others
euil.

After this gratious King, had by heedfull intelligence
vnderstoode the factions* of the people, vnlooked for of the
Magistrates, he caused a proclamation to be published: in
which was a clause, that if anie person coulde charge anie
Magistrate or Officer, with anie notable or haynous offence,
Treason, Murder, Rape, Sedition, or with any such notorious
Crime: where they were the Iudges of the multitude, hee
woulde himselfe bee the Iudge of them, and doe iustice vnto
the meanest.

Vppon this Proclamation it was a hell to heare, the excla-

A mischiefe well
preuented.

A noble fauour.

A necessarie pol-
ly[cy]e.

A Ryal grace.

The clamors of
the poore, and

*factions] facions (?)

375

the consciences of the rich, like Hell.

mations of the poore, and the festered consciences of the rich, appeared as lothsome, as the Riuer of *Stix*.

Among manie that complayned, and receiued iudgement of comfort, *Cassandras* Processe was presented, who lead betweene sorrow and shame, accused *Promos* to his face.

Sorrowe and Shame, the Attendantes of Cassandra.

The euidence was so playne, as the horrour of a guiltie conscience reaued *Promos* of all motions of excuse: so that holding vp his hande, among the worst degree of theeues, the litle hope that was leaft, moued him to confesse the crime, and with repentance to sue for mercy.

An vnusual place for a Iudge.

O (quoth the King) such espetial mercy were tyrannie to a common wealth. No *Promos* no, *Hoc facias alteri, quod tibi vis fieri:* You shall be measured with the grace you bestowed on *Andrugio.*

A necessarie regarde in a Prince.

[O2v] O God (quoth hee) if men durst bark as Dogges, manie a Iudge in the world would be bewrayed for a theefe: It behoueth a Prince to know to whom hee committeth Authoritie, least the Sword of Iustice, appointed to chasten the lewde, wound the good: and where good subiects are wronged, euill Officers receaue the benefit, and their Soueraignes beareth the blame.

Princes beres the blame of euyll Officers extortion.

A iust Iudgement.

Well, wicked *Promos*, to scourge thy impious offences, I heere giue sentence, that thou foorthwith marry *Cassandra*, to repayre her honour by thee violated, and that the next day thou lose thy head, to make satisfaction for her Brothers death.

The good protect the lewde.

This iust Iudgement of the good Kinge, in the first point, was foorthwith executed: But sacred is the Authoritie, that the vertues of the good, are a Sheelde vnto the lewde: So sweete *Cassandra*, who (simply) by vertue ouercame the spight of Fortune: In this marriadge was charged with a new assault of sorrow: and preferring the dutie of a wife, before the naturall zeale of a Sister, where she before prosecuted, the reuenge of her Brothers death, shee now was an humble suter to the Kinge for her Husbands lyfe.

The duetie of a wyfe, truely showen.

The comon weale, is to be regarded before priuate fauour.

The gracious Kinge, sought to appease her with good words, but hee could not do her this priuate fauour, without iniurie vnto the publyke weale: for though (quoth he) your sute be iust, and the bounden dutie of a wife, yet I in fulfillyng the same should do iniustly, and (generally) iniure my Subiects: and therfore, good Gentlewoman, haue patience, and no doubt vertue in the ende will giue you power ouer all your afflictions.

There was no remedie, *Cassandra* must departe, out of hope, to obtayne her sute. But as the experience, is in dayly vse, the dooinges of Princes post through the world on PE-GASVS backe: And as theyr actions are good or badde, so is their fame. With the lyke speede, the Kynges Iustice, and PROMOS execution was spred abroad: and by the tonge of a Clowne, was blowen into [O3ʳ] *Andrugioes* eares, who tyll then lyued lyke an Outlawe in the Desart wooddes.

But vpon these Newes, couertly, in the Habyt of an Hermyt, by the Diuine motion of the sowle, who directes vs in thinges that be good, and the Flesshe in Actions of euyll, *Andrugio*, goes to see the Death of his Capitall enemie: But on the other parte, regardyng the sorrow of his Sister, he wisshed hym lyfe, as a friende.

To conclude, as well to geue terrour to the lewde, as comfort to his good Subiectes, the Kyng (personallie) came to see the execution of *Promos*, who, garded with Officers, and strengthened with the comfortable perswasions of his Ghostly Fathers [TLN 2127–8]: Among whom, *Andrugio* was, meekely offered his lyfe, as a satisfaction for his offences, which were many more, then the Lawe tooke knowledge of: And yet, to say the trueth, suche was his Repentance, as the multitude did both forgeue and pittie him: yea, the King wondred that his lyfe was gouerned with no more vertue, consideryng the grace he showed at his death.

Andrugio, behouldyng this ruethfull Spectackle, was so ouercome with loue towardes his Sister, as to giue her comfort, he franckly consented anew to emperill his own life: And followinge this Resolution, in his Hermyts weede, vpon his knees, he humblye desired the Kinge too giue hym leaue to speake. The Kyng (gratiously) graunted hym Audience. Whervpon (quoth he) regarded Soueraigne, if Lawe may (possibly) be satisfied: *Promos* true Repentance, meritteth pardon.

Good Father (quoth the King) he can not liue, and the Lawe satisfied, vnlesse (by Miracle) *Andrugio* be reuiued.

Then (quoth the Hermyt,) if *Andrugio* lyue, the Law is satisfied, and *Promos* discharged.

I (quoth the King,) if your Praier can reuiue the one, my mercie shall acquite the other.

I humbly thanke your Maiestie (quoth *Andrugio*) and discoueryng himselfe, shewed the Prouidence of God and the meane of his escape: and tendrynge his Sisters [O3ᵛ] comfort, aboue his owne safetie, hee prostrated him selfe at his Maiesties Feete: humblye to obay the sentence of his pleasure. The Kinge vppon the reporte of this straunge Aduenture: after good deliberation, pardoned *Promos*, to keepe his worde, and

Siue bonum, siue malum, Fama est.

Good motions, proceede from the soule, and euyll from the flesh.

A gratefull parte.

Murther asketh death, and no other Satisfaction.

Princes are bounde to their word.

Of two, the least
euill is least
daungerous.

withall, houldyng an opinyon, that it was more benefitiall for the Citezens, to be ruled by their olde euell gouernour, new refourmed, then to aduenture vppon an newe, whose behauiours were vnknowne: And to perfect *Cassandras* ioye, he pardoned her Brother *Andrugio*, with condition, that he should marrie *Polina*. Thus, from betweene the teethe of daunger, euery partie was preserued, and in the ende establyshed in their hartes desire.

CINTHIO GIRALDI, *HECATOMMITHI* (1565)

The following excerpt from *Hecatommithi* has been translated by Mark Eccles from a copy in the Folger Shakespeare Library.

Deca Ottava, Novella V.   [2:416

. . . And when everyone was silent, Fulvia said: The lords who are appointed by God to govern the world ought to punish ingratitude, whenever they learn of it, no less than they punish murders, adulteries, and robberies, which, although they are serious crimes, perhaps deserve lesser penalty than ingratitude. For this reason Maximilian, the great and most worthy Emperor, wished at one stroke to punish the ingratitude and injustice of one of his officers and would have done so if the goodness of the lady against whom the ungrateful man had shown himself most unjust had not by her generosity saved him from punishment, as I am ready to show you.

While this great lord, who was a rare example of courtesy, magnanimity, and remarkable justice, ruled the Roman empire with great success, he used to send his officers to govern the states that flourished under his power. And among the rest he sent to govern Innsbruck a close friend, very dear to him, called Juriste. And before he sent him there he said to him: "Juriste, the good opinion I have formed of you while you have been in my service causes me to send you as governor of so noble a city as Innsbruck is. I could give you many commands about ruling there, but I want to limit them all to only one command: which is that you keep justice without violating it, even if [*417*] you have to give sentence against me myself, your lord. And I warn you that I could forgive you all other faults, whether committed through ignorance or negligence (though I want you to guard yourself from these as much as you can), but anything done against justice would find no pardon from me. And if perhaps you do not feel it your duty to be such a man as I desire (since no man is good for everything), keep yourself from taking this responsibility and instead stay here at court, where I hold you dear, in your usual duties, rather than lead me, by being governor of this city, to act against you as I should most unwillingly have to act by my obligation to justice, if you should not uphold justice." And here he ended.

Juriste, more pleased with the office to which the Emperor called him than rightly knowing himself, thanked his lord for this sign of love and said that he was himself eager to uphold justice, but that he would now uphold it all the more because those words were like a torch that had fired him still more to do so, and that he meant to succeed so well in this office that his majesty would only have reason to praise him. His words pleased the Emperor, who said to him: "Indeed I shall have reason to praise you if your deeds are as good as your words." And he gave him the letters patent that were already prepared and sent him to that place.

Juriste began to rule the city very prudently and diligently, taking great care and pains that both scales of justice should be even, no less in decisions than in assigning offices, and in rewarding virtue and punishing vices. And he continued for a long time with such moderation that he won greater favor from his lord and earned the good will of all that people. And he might have been considered fortunate among all others if he had kept on governing in such manner.

It happened that a young man [*418*] of the region whose name was Vico* forced a young woman, a citizen of Innsbruck, for which complaint was made to Juriste. He at once had the young man arrested, and on his confessing that he had done violence to the virgin, sentenced him according to the law of that city, which provided that such men be condemned to beheading even if they were willing to take the woman to wife.

This young man had a sister, a maiden of not more than eighteen, who was adorned with unusual beauty and had a very sweet way of speaking and a lovely presence, together with womanly virtue. This lady, whose name was Epitia, on hearing that her brother was condemned to death, was overcome with deep grief and resolved to try to see whether she could, if not free her brother, at least soften his punishment; for she had been educated with her brother by an old man whom their father had kept in the house to teach them both philosophy, though the brother had made poor use of it. She went to Juriste and begged him to have pity on her brother, both because of his youth, for he was only sixteen, which made him deserving of pardon, and because of his inexperience and the spur of love in his side. She argued that wise men were of opinion that adultery committed through force of love, and not to wrong the lady's husband, deserved lesser punishment than that which did such wrong, and that the same should be said in the case of her brother, who had done that for which he was condemned not to wrong a husband but driven by ardent love; that to make amends for his fault he would take the young woman as his wife; and that although the law required that this would not save those who violated virgins, nevertheless Juriste, being the wise man he was, had power to mitigate that severity which brought

*Vico] 1580; Vieo 1565

with it harm rather than justice, since he was [*419*] the living law in that place by the authority he held from the Emperor, who, she believed, had given him this authority so that he might show himself by equity merciful rather than harsh. And that if such moderation ought to be used in any case, he ought to use it in cases of love, especially when the honor of the violated lady remained safe, as it would in the case of her brother, who was very ready to marry her. And that she believed that the law had been drawn up in this way more to strike terror than to be observed, for it seemed to her cruelty to wish to punish with death a sin that could be atoned for honorably and religiously by making amends for the offense. And with many other arguments she sought to persuade Juriste to pardon that unhappy man.

Juriste, whose ears were no less delighted by Epitia's sweet way of talking than his eyes were by her great beauty, in his eagerness to see and hear her urged her to repeat her speech once again. The lady, taking this as a good omen, spoke again to him with even greater effect than before. Overcome by Epitia's grace in speaking and her rare beauty, and struck by lustful appetite, he turned his mind to committing against her the same fault for which he had condemned Vico to death. And he said to her: "Epitia, your arguments have helped your brother so much that, whereas his head should have been cut off tomorrow, the execution will be put off until I have considered the arguments you have given me, and if I find them such that they can free your brother, I shall give him to you the more willingly because it would grieve me to see him led to death through the rigor of the harsh law that has so provided."

Epitia took good hope from these words and thanked him greatly for showing himself so courteous, saying that she would be obliged to him forever; thinking to find him no less courteous [*420*] in freeing her brother than she had found him in prolonging the term of his life. And she added that she hoped firmly that if he thought over what she had said he would make her completely happy by freeing her brother. He told her that he would think it over and that, if he could do it without offending justice, he would not fail to grant her wish.

Full of hope, Epitia left and went to her brother and told him all that she had done with Juriste and how much hope she had conceived from her first conversation. This was very welcome to Vico in his desperate situation, and he begged her not to fail to plead for his freedom, and she promised him all her help. Juriste, who had imprinted the lady's image in his mind, turned all his thoughts, lascivious as he was, to being able to enjoy Epitia, and for that reason waited for her to come again and speak to him. After three days she returned and asked him courteously what he had decided. As soon as he saw her, Juriste felt himself all on fire and said to her: "Fair young woman, you are welcome. I have not failed to look diligently into what your arguments could do in favor of your brother, and I have searched for still others, so that you might remain happy. But I find that everything points to his death; for it is a universal law that when one sins not through ignorance but brutishly, his sin can have no excuse, because he ought to know what all men everywhere must know to live well, and whoever sins by ignoring this deserves neither pardon nor pity. Your brother, in this situation, ought to have known very well that the law required that whoever violated a virgin deserved death, and so he must die and I cannot with reason grant mercy. To be sure, as for you, whom I wish to please, if you (since you love your [421] brother so much) are willing to let me take my pleasure of you, I am ready to spare his life and change the death penalty into one less severe."

Epitia's face became red as fire at these words, and she said to him: "My brother's life is very dear to me, but even dearer to me is my honor, and I would rather seek to save him by losing my life than by losing my honor. Give up this dishonorable idea of yours; but if I can get back my brother by any other way than by giving myself to you, I shall do it very willingly." "There is no other way," said Juriste, "but what I have told you, and you ought not to show such shame, since it may easily come about that our first encounters may be such that you will become my wife." "I do not wish," said Epitia, "to put my honor in danger." "And why in danger?" said Juriste. "Perhaps you are the kind of person who cannot believe that this could be. Think it over well, and I shall wait all tomorrow for your answer." "I give you my answer right now," she said, "that if you want my brother's freedom to depend on that, without taking me to wife, you are throwing words to the wind." Juriste replied that she should think it over and bring him back the answer after considering carefully who he was, what power he held in that city, and how useful he could be not only to her but to anyone else who was her friend, since in that place he held in his hands both right and might.

Epitia, deeply troubled, went from him to her brother and told him what had happened between her and Juriste, ending by saying that she had no wish to lose her honor to save his life. And with tears she begged him to prepare himself to endure patiently that lot which either the necessity of fate or his ill fortune was bringing him. At this Vico began to weep and to beg his sister not to consent to his death, since she had power to free him in the way that Juriste had proposed. "Can it be that you wish," he said, "Epitia, to see me with the ax on my neck and my head cut off, I who was born of the same womb as you [422] and begotten by the same father, who grew up with you till now and was educated with you, to see my head thrown to the ground by the executioner? Ah, sister, may the arguments of nature, of blood, and of the affection that has always been between us have such power over you that you will free me, as you can, from so shameful and wretched an end. I have done wrong, I confess. You, my sister, who can atone for my fault, do not be miserly of your help. Juriste has said that he may marry you, and why should you not think that it would be so? You are very beautiful, adorned with all those graces that Nature can give a noble lady. You are noble and charming; you have a wonderful way of speaking; so that not only all these things, but each by itself, can make you dear, not only to Juriste, but to the emperor of the world. You have no reason at all to doubt that Juriste will take you as his wife, and thus you will save your honor and at the same time your brother's life."

Vico wept as he spoke these words, and Epitia wept with him. Embracing her by the neck, Vico did not leave her until she was constrained (overcome by her brother's laments) to promise him that she would give herself to Juriste, if he would save Vico's life and support her in the hope that he would take her to wife.

When this was settled between them, next day the young woman went to Juriste and told him that the hope he had given her of marrying her after their first encounters, and her desire to free her brother not only from death but from any other penalty he had deserved for the fault he had committed, had led her to put herself wholly at his disposal, and that for these two reasons she was content to give herself to him, but above everything she wanted him to promise her the safety and liberty of her brother.

Juriste thought himself fortunate above any other man because he was to enjoy so beautiful and lovely a young woman, and said to her that he gave her that same hope he had given her before and that he would grant her her brother free from prison the morning after he had been with her. [*423*] So after dining together Juriste and Epitia went to bed, and the wicked man took his full pleasure of the lady. But before he went to lie with the maiden, instead of freeing Vico, he ordered him beheaded at once. The lady, longing to see her brother free, waited for day to break, and it seemed to her that never had the sun been so slow to bring in day as on that night. When morning came, Epitia released herself from Juriste's arms and begged him in the sweetest way that he would be pleased to fulfil the hope of marriage he had given her, and that meanwhile he would send her her brother free. And he answered that he had been very happy to have been with her, that it pleased him that she had entertained the hope he had given her, and that he would send her brother home. So saying, he called for the jailer and said to him, "Go to the prison and bring out this lady's brother and take him home to her."

Epitia, hearing this, went home full of great joy, to wait for her brother. The jailer had Vico's body placed on a bier, set the head at its feet, and had it carried, covered with black cloth and himself going before, to Epitia. Entering the house, he called the young woman and said: "This is your brother, whom the lord governor sends you freed from prison." So saying, he had the bier uncovered and presented her with her brother in such manner as you have heard.

I do not think that tongue could tell or human mind comprehend of what kind and how great were the sorrow and grief of Epitia when she saw her brother presented to her dead when she was expecting with the greatest joy to see him alive and released from all penalty. I am sure, ladies, that you are convinced that such was the unhappy lady's grief that it went beyond every kind of anguish. But she hid it in her heart, and whereas any other lady would have begun to weep and cry out, she, whom philosophy had taught what [*424*] the human mind should be like in every kind of fortune, pretended to be satisfied. She said to the jailer: "You will tell your lord and mine that I accept my brother as he is pleased to send him to me; and that since he has not been willing to fulfil my will, I remain satisfied that he has fulfilled his own, and thus I make his will mine, thinking that what he has done he has done justly; and you will commend me to him, presenting myself always most ready to please him."

The jailer reported to Juriste what Epitia had said, telling him that she had given no sign of displeasure at so horrible a spectacle. Juriste was happy to hear this and reflected that he was able to have the young woman as much at his will as if she had been his wife and he had given her Vico alive.

Epitia, when the jailer had gone, immediately wept long and grievingly over her dead brother, cursing Juriste's cruelty and her simplicity that she had given herself to him before he had freed her brother. And after many tears she had the body buried. Then shutting herself up alone in her room, urged on by just anger, she began to say to herself: "Will you endure it, Epitia, that this rascal has robbed you of your honor by promising to give you back your brother free and alive and then has presented him to you dead in so pitiful a state? Will you endure it that he should be able to boast of two such deceptions practised on your innocence, without having from you the punishment that is due?" Firing herself to vengeance with such words, she said: "My simplicity has opened the way for this criminal to achieve his dishonorable desire. I intend that his lust shall give me the means of avenging myself, and though revenge will not give me back my brother alive, yet it will take away my vexation." In such disturbance of mind she came to this decision. Expecting that Juriste would send for her again to ask her to lie with him, [*425*] she determined to take with her a hidden knife and stab him, sleeping or waking, at the first chance, and if she saw opportunity, to cut off his head, take it to her brother's grave, and consecrate it to his shade. But on thinking it over more maturely, she saw that even if she managed to kill the deceiver it might easily be assumed that she, as a woman dishonored and so kindled to any evil, had done that through anger and scorn rather than because he had failed to keep his word. Having heard of the great justice of the Emperor, who was then at Villach, she resolved to go and find him and complain to his majesty of the ingratitude and injustice shown to her by Juriste, believing firmly that that best and justest of emperors would bring justest punishment upon that wicked man for his injustice and ingratitude.

So she put on mourning, set out all alone in secret on the journey, and went to Maximilian. After she had asked for a hearing and obtained it, she threw herself at his feet and said to him, suiting her mourning dress with a sad voice: "Most sacred Emperor, I have been driven to appear before your majesty by the cruel ingratitude and unbelievable injustice with which I have been treated by Juriste, your imperial majesty's governor in Innsbruck. I hope that justice will be done in such fashion that no other wretch will ever have to suffer such infinite grief as I have suffered from Juriste through the wrong he has done me, than which no greater was ever heard of, and that no proud man will do what he has done to me, miserably assassinated me (if I may use that word before your majesty), so that even harsh punishment would not equal the cruel and unheard-of shame that this bad man has done to me, proving that he is at the same time most unjust and most ungrateful." And here, weeping and [426] sighing, she told his majesty how Juriste, giving hope that he would marry her and free her brother, had taken away her virginity and then sent her her brother dead on a bier with his head at his feet. Here she gave so great a cry and her eyes so filled with tears that the Emperor and the other lords with him were so moved that they stood like men pale as ghosts for pity.

But though Maximilian felt great compassion for her, yet after giving one ear to Epitia (whom at the end of her speech he made rise to her feet), he kept the other ear for Juriste. Sending the lady to rest, at once he summoned Juriste, bidding the messenger and all the others who were there, as they held his favor dear, to say not a word of it to Juriste.

Juriste, who would have thought anything possible rather than that Epitia would go to the Emperor, came quite gladly, and on reaching his majesty's presence bowed and asked what was wanted of him. "You will know that this very moment," said Maximilian, and at once had Epitia summoned. Juriste, when he saw there the one whom he knew he had grievously wronged, was so overcome by conscience and dismay that his vital spirits left him and he began to tremble all over. When Maximilian saw this he was sure that the lady had told him nothing but the truth. Turning toward Juriste with that severity fitting such an atrocious case, he said: "Hear what this young woman complains about you." And he ordered Epitia to say why she was complaining. She told the whole story from the beginning and at the end, weeping as before, called on the Emperor for justice.

When Juriste heard the accusation, he tried to flatter the lady by saying: "I should never have believed that you, whom I so much love, would have come to accuse me thus before his majesty." But Maximilian did not let him cajole her, and said: "This is no time to play [427] the lover; just answer the charge she has made against you." Juriste now gave up what could only harm him. "It is true," he said, "that I had her brother beheaded for having carried off and raped a virgin, and I did this so as not to violate the sanctity of the laws and in order to preserve that justice which your majesty urged on me so strongly, for without wrong to justice he could not remain alive."

Here Epitia spoke: "If you thought justice required that, why did you promise me to give him back alive, and why, under that promise and giving me hope that you would marry me, did you rob me of my virginity? If my brother deserved to feel the severity of justice for only one sin, you deserve even more than he for two sins." Juriste stood there like a dumb man. Then the Emperor said: "Does it seem to you, Juriste, that this has been to serve justice, or only to wrong it so greatly that you almost killed it? Have you not treated this noble young woman with greater ingratitude than any criminal ever did? But you will not go away rejoicing, believe me."

Juriste now began to ask for mercy and Epitia on the other hand to ask for justice. Maximilian, recognizing the young lady's innocence and Juriste's wickedness, suddenly thought how he could both preserve her honor and preserve justice, and when he decided what to do, his will was that Juriste should marry Epitia. The lady did not want to consent, saying that she could not believe she would ever get anything from him but crimes and betrayals. But Maximilian's will was that she should be satisfied with what he had decided.

After marrying the lady Juriste supposed that his troubles were ended, but it turned out otherwise. As soon as Maximilian had given the lady leave to return to her inn, he turned to Juriste, who was still there, and said: "Your crimes have been two, both very serious: one in having dishonored this young woman [428] by such deception that it must be said that you raped her; the other in having killed her brother contrary to the promise you gave her, which has also deserved death. Since you were prepared to violate justice, it would have been more worthy to keep faith with his sister, after your unbridled lust brought you so low as to promise him to her on your word, rather than after disgracing her to send him to her dead, as you did. Since I have provided for your first sin by having you marry the lady you violated, to make amends for the second it is my will that your head be cut off, as you had her brother's head cut off."

How deep was Juriste's grief when he heard the Emperor's sentence can be imagined rather than fully described. He was given to sergeants to be put to death next morning according to the sentence. From now on Juriste was fully prepared to die and expected nothing but that the executioner would end his life.

But now Epitia, who had been so inflamed against him, when she heard of the Emperor's sentence was moved by her natural kindness and decided that it would be unworthy of her, since the Emperor had ordered Juriste to be her husband and she had accepted him as such, to consent to his being put to death because of her. It seemed to her that it could be attributed to craving for revenge and to cruelty rather than to desire for justice. Turning all her thoughts for that reason to saving the unhappy man, she went to the Emperor and, having had leave to speak, said thus: "Most sacred Emperor, the injustice and ingratitude with which Juriste treated me led me to ask your majesty for justice against him. Most just as you are, you have provided most justly for the two crimes that he committed; for one, that he robbed my virginity by deception, by making him [429] take me as his wife; for the other, that he killed my brother contrary to the promise he gave me, by condemning him to death. But just as, before I was his wife, I had to desire that your majesty should condemn him to death, as you have done very justly, so now, since it has pleased you to bind me to Juriste by the holy bond of marriage, if I should consent to his death I should consider myself to deserve the reputation of a pitiless and cruel lady, with perpetual infamy. The result would be contrary to your majesty's intention, which sought my honor as well as justice. But, most sacred Emperor, in order that your majesty's good intention should achieve its end and my honor remain unstained, I beg you most humbly and reverently not to require that by your majesty's sentence the sword of justice should miserably cut that knot by which it has pleased you to bind me to Juriste. And whereas your majesty's sentence has given clear proof of your justice by condemning him to death, so now may it please you, as I earnestly beg once again, to manifest your mercy by giving him back to me alive. Most sacred Emperor, it is no less praise for one who holds the government of the world, as your majesty now holds it most worthily, to show mercy than to show justice. For whereas justice demonstrates that vices are hated and therefore punished, mercy makes a ruler most resemble the immortal gods. And if I obtain this special favor from your kindness by your kind act towards me, your majesty's most humble servant, I shall always pray to God devoutly that he may preserve your majesty to long and happy years, so that you may long exercise your justice and mercy for the benefit of mortals and to your own honor and immortal glory." And here Epitia put an end to her speech.

It seemed a wonderful thing to Maximilian [430] that she should thrust into oblivion the deep wrong she had received from Juriste, for whom she entreated so warmly. And he thought that so much goodness as he saw in that lady deserved that he by his grace should grant her the life of the man who had been sentenced to death by justice. So calling Juriste before him, at the very hour when he was expecting to be led to death, he said to him: "Epitia's goodness, guilty man, has prevailed on me so much that, whereas your crime deserved to be punished not with one death only but with two, she has moved me to pardon your life. This life, I want you to know, comes from her; and since she is willing to live with you, joined by that bond with which I willed you to be bound, I am willing that you should live with her. If I ever hear that you treat her as less than a most loving and generous wife, I shall make you feel what great displeasure that will cause me."

With these words the Emperor took Epitia by the hand and gave her to Juriste. She and Juriste both thanked his majesty for the grace and favor granted them. And Juriste, realizing how generous Epitia had been to him, always held her most dear, so that she lived with him very happily for the rest of her life.

Novella VI. [2:431]

I should find it hard to say whether the ladies were more pleased by Maximilian's justice or by his mercy. At first it seemed that they would have been happy that the grave outrage done with such ingratitude to the virtuous young woman should have been punished as it deserved. But it seemed to them no less praiseworthy that, since it had pleased his majesty that Juriste should marry the lady whose honor he had stained, the Emperor had yielded to her pleadings so that he turned justice into mercy. The more experienced said that mercy is a very worthy companion to royal justice, because it tempers punishment; and for that reason we read that it is most fitting for princes, since it leads to a certain moderation in their minds that causes them to be kind towards their subjects. And they concluded that Maximilian had shown himself, in justice and in mercy, truly worthy of empire. "And so he is indeed," said Lucretia.

II. Analogues

Many other stories were told of promise-breach like Angelo's, but there is no proof that Sh. knew any of them. They will therefore be mentioned only briefly. For references see DOUCE (1807, 1:152–60, 2:273), OESTERLEY (1869, 5:152–3), BOLTE (1902, p. 65 n.; 1910, pp. xii–xv), BUDD (1930, 1931), BULLOUGH (1958, 2:537–8), and J. H. SMITH (1972).

St. Augustine discusses a remote analogue, with no deaths, in *On the Lord's Sermon on the Mount,* which has been compared with *MM* by DU-PORT (1828, 2:190), SIMROCK (1870, 1:156–7), KITTREDGE (ed. 1936), and LASCELLES (1953, pp. 6–7) and translated in Bullough (2:418–19). Luther in *On Secular Authority* (1523, *Werke,* 11 [1900]: 279–80, *Works,* 45 [1962]:128–9), cited by SEHRT (1952, p. 165) and SMITH (1972, pp. 388–93), tells a more relevant exemplum from oral tradition ("Man sagt," "The story is told") of how Duke Charles of Burgundy justly punished a nobleman who promised a wife to free her husband from prison if she lay with him but next day sent her the husband's body. When she complained, the Duke made him marry her to restore her honor, cut off the head of the nobleman as he had done her husband's, and gave her the man's property. Luther relates the same tale in a sermon of 1522, published from notes in 1846; Melanchthon uses it in lectures at Wittenberg, also unpublished in the 16th c.; and it is repeated in later books such as Andreas Hondorff's *Promtuarium Exemplorum* in 1572 (Oesterley, 5:22, 152; Smith). Hans Folz of Nuremberg (c. 1450–1513), in a song copied in MS by Hans Sachs in 1517, attributes this just judgment to a Duke of Burgundy about 1450; an anonymous *meisterlied* printed in the 1520s names Duke Charles; and Sachs repeats the story, "which the true chronicle tells us," in three poems and in a tragedy written in 1552 and printed in 1558, *The Two Knights of Burgundy* (MINOR, 1888; BOLTE, 1910; Smith). The same story, in some version, was acted by English players in Germany in 1604 and 1606 under the title *Of the Wise Judgment of Charles, Duke of Burgundy, against Two Knights* (CREIZENACH, 1889, p. lxiii; TRAUTMANN, 1894, pp. 60–2; CHAMBERS, 1923, 2:283–4). Sebastian Franck in *Germaniae Chronicon* (1538: Frankfurt ed., f. 99ᵛ; Augsburg ed., sig. q2) assigns the judgment to Charlemagne but echoes Luther's comment that independent reason is above the law in all the books (Oesterley; Bolte, 1902, 1910; Smith). Christian Zyrl transfers Luther's story to Solomon in *Urteil Salomons* (Strassburg, 1592), acted in 1587 by townsmen of Weissenburg on the Rhine (ODINGA, 1889).

Le jugement du duc Charles, a lost "jeu et moralité," was acted at Besançon in 1548 (Bolte, 1902; Budd, 1931, p. 718). Charles the Bold in 1469 executed a nobleman who broke his promise and put to death a prisoner in order to enjoy his wife, according to the chronicler Pontus Heuter in 1584 (LANCASTER, 1911, pp. 163–4; Smith). No punishment is mentioned for a Provost la Voulte who seduced a wife by promising to give back her husband but sent her the hanged body, according to Henri Estienne in 1566 and Simon Goulart in 1601 (Douce, 1:155–6; LIEBRECHT, 1851, pp. 278–9; Lancaster; Budd, 1931). Thomas Lupton has a wicked judge married and executed and his goods given to the widow, as in Luther, in *The Second Part of Too Good to be True* (1581), discussed by Douce (1:155), Budd (1931), LASCELLES (1953, pp. 21–4), Bullough (2:405; cf. 514–24), and LEVER (ed. 1965, pp. xxxvi–vii). Thomas Danett (1596) records that Louis XI's Flemish favorite Oliver le Dain broke his promise and had the husband drowned, but Oliver was not hanged until 1484, after Louis died (Douce, 1:154; Budd, 1931).

An important series of analogues is set not in Burgundy or France but in northern Italy. In 1547 a Hungarian student in Vienna, Joseph Macarius, wrote in a letter that the emperor's deputy in Milan, Ferrando de Gonzaga (1507–57, brother of the first Duke of Mantua), had recently compelled a Spanish count in a town near Milan to marry the citizen's wife he had seduced and deceived and pay her a dowry, then to lose his head in return for her husband's (L. L. K., 1893; LAWRENCE, 1931, pp. 86–7; LEVER, ed. 1965, pp. xxxvi, 151–4). "This story," he reports, "is now being told in various versions." It has been argued that it is folklore rather than fact (CAVALCHINI, 1968; Smith). Georg Lauterbeck in his *Regentenbuch* (Leipzig, 1559, bk. 2, ch. 15, sigs. P2–3) tells the same story about "Gonzago, Duke of Ferrara" (an error for Ferrando or Ferrante Gonzaga), and adds that he made the Spanish captain repay 200 ducats that he had demanded from the wronged woman, the beautiful wife of a citizen of Como who had consented to his wife's sacrifice of her honor (as the husband had in Augustine and Luther). Lauterbeck compares the similar stories told by Luther and Augustine and the punishment by Cambyses of his deputy Sisamnes (see p. 390). Gonzaga is rightly described as deputy in Milan for the Emperor Charles V by Hans Wilhelm Kirchhof, *Wendunmuth* (Frankfurt, 1603, ed. Oesterley, 4:186–7) and by Andreas Hoppenrod, "Wider den Huren Teuffel," in Sigmund Feyerabend's *Theatrum Diabolorum* (Frankfurt, 1569; 1575, f. 305v). Henning Grosse's *Tragica* (Eisleben, 1597), Thomas Beard's *Theatre of Gods Iudgements* (London, 1597), and Simon Goulart's *Histoires admirables* (Paris, 1601) all mention the Duke of Ferrara, like Lauterbeck, but agree with Hoppenrod that the tragedy at Como took place in 1547 (Douce, 1:155; Liebrecht, p. 493; Oesterley; Bolte, 1902; Lancaster; Budd, 1931).

Budd (1930) argues that this crime at Como provided the basis for Claude Rouillet's Latin tragedy *Philanira* (in *Claudii Roilleti Belnensis Varia Poemata,* Paris, 1556, French tr. 1563). The parallel had been noted by Liebrecht in 1867 and Simrock in 1870. Rouillet sets his tragedy in Piedmont and makes the King of France's deputy punish the judge Severus. Cambridge students acted *Philanira* in 1564 or 1565 (MSC 2.2.165), Edward Mychelborne of Oxford owned a copy in 1586, and Budd suggests that Whetstone used the play for *Promos and Cassandra* in addition to *Hecatommithi.* François de Belleforest in *Histoires tragiques* (Paris, 1582, 6:173v–201v) also places his story in Piedmont and attributes a similar judgment to the Maréchal de Brissac, viceroy for Henri II from 1550 to 1559 (Douce, 1:154; Lancaster; Budd, 1931). Davenant names the same city, Turin, in his adaptation of *MM* in 1662.

A Spanish *Comedia del Degollado (The Beheaded)* by Juan de la Cueva, acted in 1579 and printed in 1583, changes Giraldi's tale to end happily when a Moorish prince spares two lovers because they prefer death to dishonor (CRAWFORD, 1920). Three Italian *commedie dell'arte* on the unjust judge, with tragic endings, were written down in the 17th c. (W. SMITH, 1922; Budd, 1931; KAUFMAN, 1957), but as LEA observes (1934, 2:431), "the sources in 'novelle' and literary drama have the stronger claim. The production of the corresponding plots in the collections of scenari is interesting for contrast rather than for comparison." In the 19th c. ballads such as "La povera Cecilia" were still sung in Italy, Spain, Strassburg, and Hungary (WOLF, 1864, pp. 321–2, 365–6; SIM-ROCK, 1870, 1:158–60; NIGRA, 1888, pp. 43–50; Bolte, 1902, pp. 64–5; ANCONA, 1906, pp. 140–6), and Slovaks in Hungary told how King Matthias (see n. 98) made a judge marry a sister who had sacrificed her honor for her brother, though no one was put to death (OSZTOYA, 1894). All these analogues except Augustine's and Cueva's and the Slovak tale end tragically, with no forgiveness, and in all but Cueva's, the Hungarian ballad, and the Slovak tale the victims are husband and wife, unlike the brother and sister in Giraldi, Whetstone, and *MM.*

Two analogues in Giraldi's *Hecatommithi* end happily after a wife refuses, like Isabel, to be seduced. In novella 52 the governor of Constantinople under Constantine falsely accuses a merchant but fails to blackmail his wife Dorothea and finally dies confessing that the charge was false. In 56 Gratiosa, a tailor's wife, foils the judge by appealing to Alfonso I, Duke of Ferrara, who pardons the husband and orders the judge hanged, though the end leaves it possible that he may be forgiven. LASCELLES (1953, pp. 32–6) suggests that Sh. read these tales, which emphasize a ruler's duty to temper law with mercy. BULLOUGH (1976) believes that novella 56 provided hints for Isabel and Lucio and (p. 115) that Sh. may have "decided to combine the two conceptions, the woman who steadfastly refuses to surrender her virtue and the romantic plot by which Vico and Andrugio are saved" in *Epitia* and *Promos.*

The disguised ruler had long been a favorite in English ballads and plays, and Sh. had already brought him on the stage in *H5.* He became still more popular after James I succeeded Elizabeth in 1603. *The Phoenix* by Middleton, a compliment to the new king, who was called a "second Phoenix," was acted before him probably in Feb. 1604 (CHAMBERS, 1923, 3:439), as *MM* was in Dec. 1604. Pretending to travel abroad, but remaining in Ferrara, Prince Phoenix in disguise finds out abuses and in the end pardons all offenders except Proditor, whom he banishes (see LASCELLES, 1953, pp. 26–7, 102–3, 125–6). HAZLITT (1820; 1931, 6:226–8) observes that the disguised Duke of Ferrara in Marston's *Fawne* (written in 1604?) has "a sort of family likeness to the Duke" in *MM,* and contrasts Malevole in *The Malcontent* (1604). The Duke of Genoa in John Day's *Law-Trickes* (written in 1604?) leaves his son to govern and returning disguised finds him prodigal; and Henry VIII in Samuel Rowley's *When You See Me, You Know Me* (written in 1604?) disguises himself one night to "see our Cities gouernment," meeting foolish constables, a murderer, and unhappy prisoners (CREIZENACH, 1909, 4:253–4, tr. 1916, pp. 221–2; FREEBURG, 1915, pp. 160–72, who also notes how many plays use disguise as a friar). ANDERS (1904, p. 137) compares Thomas Preston's *Cambises* (1569, mentioned in *1H4*), which opens with the King deputing Sisamnes as governor while he is absent and shows

Cambises on his return executing the "corrupt judge." BENNETT (1966, p. 97) points out that James I's grandfather James V "was famous for going among his people incognito." As LEVER (ed. 1965, pp. xlix–l) remarks, King James "could not walk the streets of London disguised as a merchant; but his would-be secret visit to the Exchange in March 1604, with the object of watching the merchants while remaining unobserved, was an adventure in much the same spirit."

A king who does disguise himself as a merchant is Leonarchus of Epirus in a romance by Barnaby Riche, *The Adventures of Brusanus, Prince of Hungaria,* 1592 (BULLOUGH, 1958, 2:411–13, 524–30). Sh. need not have known this analogue, but he could have, and there are some parallels. Leonarchus, "secretly rejoysing to heare him selfe so praised," tells Brusanus that some come to court "to satisfie their youthful humors with a little foolish bravery" in new fashions, so that the court is "a nursse of vice to suche as measure their wils with witlesse affection" (cf. *MM* 300). News of the king's absence, "straunge, yet not so straunge as true" (cf. *MM* 2391), causes many conjectures, "some immagininge him to bee privily murthered, some thinking him secretly vowed to some monastery or other religious house" (cf. *MM* 2066–8). Leonarchus is accused of speaking treason by Gloriosus, a courtier who claims to know the king well, and after he is cleared and discloses himself, "sitting himselfe downe in the seate of majestie," he describes the vices of his country and banishes Gloriosus. LEVER (ed. 1965, p. li) concludes that "Lucio may well have been suggested by Riche's slanderous courtier." Sh. had used Riche's *Apolonius and Silla* as his main source for *TN* (Bullough, 2:275–8).

Sir Thomas Elyot in *The Image of Governaunce* (1541), following Antonio de Guevara, pictures the emperor Alexander Severus as a model of justice, who "vsed many tymes to disguise hym selfe in dyvers straunge facions, as sometyme in the habite of a scholer of philosophie . . . oftentimes like a marchaunt . . . to see the state of the people, with the industrie or negligence of theym that were officers" (sig. M3r–v; LASCELLES, 1953, p. 101; LEVER, ed. 1965, pp. xliv–v). Whetstone repeats this account in *A Mirour for Magestrates of Cyties* (1584), "Representing the Ordinaunces, Policies, and Diligence, of the Noble Emperour, Alexander (surnamed) Severus, to suppresse and chastise the notorious Vices noorished in Rome, by the superfluous nomber of Dicing-houses, Tauarns, and common Stewes: Suffred and cherished, by his beastlye Predecessour, Helyogabalus."

James I's *Basilicon Doron,* written for his son Henry and privately printed at Edinburgh in 1599, was reprinted at London in 1603 in over a dozen editions (BENNETT, 1966, pp. 82–3). CHALMERS in 1799 (pp. 404–5) suggested that Sh. used it, and the case has been argued more fully by ALBRECHT (1914, pp. 129–63), STEVENSON (1959, pp. 195 ff.), and Bennett. As SCHANZER (1963, pp. 122–3) puts it, "That Shakespeare had read the *Basilikon Doron* before writing *Measure for Measure* is inherently probable," since Bacon wrote of this book "falling into every man's hand," but though many of James's views "find fairly exact parallels in Shakespeare's play, these are of too commonplace a nature to prove indebtedness in the absence of close verbal echoes." He agrees that *MM,* like *Mac.,* "was deliberately made to turn upon themes which were of special interest to James" and that the Duke is an idealized image of the King, "made up of the qualities in a ruler which James in his writings had particularly praised; and that it is yet sufficiently particularized, and endowed with traits peculiar to the King, to enable Shakespeare's audience and James himself to recognize the likeness." Lever (p. xlviii) believes that "the case for some measure of identification is too strong to be discounted," but the influence of James is rejected by LAWRENCE (p. 108), LASCELLES (p. 109), and LEVIN (1974, *Clio*).

The substitution of Mariana for Isabel in Angelo's bed has an early analogue in Gen. 29:23–5, where Jacob married the woman he thought was Rachel and "in the morning, behold, it was Leah." In *AWW* Sh. dramatized Boccaccio's novella in the *Decameron,* which he could have read in the French translation of 1545 or the English version of 1566 in William Painter, *The Palace of Pleasure* (1575 ed. rpt. by Bullough, 2:389–96). After comparing analogues from India to Iceland, LAWRENCE (1931, p. 49) concludes that in the sources of *AWW* "we recognize a Virtue Story, exalting the devotion of a woman to the man who so far forgets his duty as to treat her cruelly." The same is true in *Blurt Master-Constable* (1602, attributed to Middleton but probably by Dekker), where Violetta takes the place of the courtesan Imperia in her husband's bed. FRIPP (1938, 2:601) and HUNTER (1959, p. xliv) cite Francis Osborne's story of the Earl of Oxford, who against his will was married to Burghley's daughter Anne in 1571 and "whose *Lady* was brought to his bed under the notion of his *Mistris,*" which Osborne terms "a virtuous deceit." As BOWDEN (1969, p. 120) observes, in *MM* "the bed trick provides a way of escaping the impossible dilemma." On the religious and legal justifications for the bed trick see n. 1850.

III. Influences

INFLUENCE OF THE BIBLE

Sh.'s use of the Bible in *MM* has been observed since the 18th c. The commentary notes give chapter and verse, which need not be repeated here, but a brief review will show how many writers have pointed out biblical influence. THIRLBY (d. 1753) set down parallels in MS, GREY (1754) found a biblical phrase echoed in 1680, STEEVENS (Var. 1773) observed that *die the death* (1179) is "a phrase taken from scripture," HENLEY (1780) identified *The words of heauen* in 213, WHITER (1794) showed that 39–42 echo the Gospel of Mark, and M. S. (1795) first compared the title and 38–9 with the Sermon on the Mount and 42–6 with the parable of the talents. ULRICI (1839, tr. 1846, pp. 309–16) declared that the whole play rests on the prime Christian truth that we are all sinners and need mercy, quoting the Lord's Prayer on forgiving our sins as we forgive others. PRICE (1839) quoted biblical sources for 825–31, WATSON (1843) for 1746–7, and BIRCH (1848) for 894–9. BROWN (1864) added parallels with 894–9, 1018–19, 1246–7, and 1429, WORDSWORTH (1864) with 894–9, 1231, 1246–7, and 1746–7, and HERAUD (1865) and a writer in *The Congregationalist* (1872) discussed the play's use of the Sermon on the Mount and the parables of the vineyard, the talents, and the unfaithful steward. REES (1876) cited Matt. on 1006, BURGESS (1903) Rom. on 2304–5, and ANDERS (1904) Gal. on 534–5. Quoting the Geneva Bible, CARTER (1905) suggested parallels with 345, 1307–8, 1637–8, 1921–2, 2400–1, and others less to the point. WILL-COCK (1915) compared Jude with 2671–2. The fullest source study, by NOBLE (1935), showed clearly that Sh. used both the Bishops' Bible and the Geneva version. LEVER (ed. 1965) added other parallels, and SIMS (1966) compared Jas. 3:10 with 1186–8.

Twentieth-century writers have been less concerned with finding sources than with studying the ethics of the play in the light of the New Testament. KNIGHT (1930, p. 106) calls *MM* a parable which inverts the plot of the parable of the unmerciful servant (Matt. 18:23–35) and ends with forgiveness as in that of the two debtors (Luke 7:41–3). Sh.'s use of the Gospels and especially of the Sermon on the Mount has been emphasized in different ways by R. W. CHAMBERS (1937; 1939), BATTENHOUSE (1946), POPE (1949), COGHILL (1955), BRYANT (1961), and S. C. VELZ (1972), and his use of Paul's letter to the Romans by Battenhouse, Bryant, BERMAN (1967), FISCH (1974), and HASKIN (1977).

OTHER INFLUENCES

Possible influence of Montaigne on *MM* is discussed by KÖNIG (1875, p. 236), ROBERTSON (1897, pp. 52–64; 1909, pp. 86–95), HOOKER (1902, pp. 326–47, 358–62), UPHAM (1908, pp. 284, 531–3), TAYLOR (1925, pp. 22, 38–42), HARMON (1942), and ELLRODT (1975, pp. 48–50). See n. 1208 ff. This and other notes mention suggested sources in Seneca and other authors. Among less likely borrowings that have been suggested are passages from Augustine (LIVERMORE, 1965, p. 190), Juan de Flores (PEROTT, 1909, pp. 153–5), Castiglione (GENT, 1972, pp. 252–6; SCOTT, 1972, p. 128), Gentillet (HOLLAND, 1959, pp. 16–20), Bruno (KÖNIG, 1876, pp. 108–9), Sylvain (NOWOTTNY, 1965, pp. 814–24), Goslicki (GOLLANCZ, 1916, p. 177; TESLAR, 1960, pp. 27–9, 34–5), and Mush (KAULA, 1970; 1975, pp. 60–73).

Criticism

I. General Comments

DRYDEN (1672, p. 163): "Poetry was then, if not in its infancy among us, at least not arriv'd to its vigor and maturity: witness the lameness of their Plots. . . . I suppose I need not name *Pericles Prince* of *Tyre,* nor the historical plays of *Shakespear.* Besides many of the rest as the *Winters Tale, Love's labour lost, Measure for Measure,* which were either grounded on impossibilities, or at least, so meanly written that the comedy neither caus'd your mirth, nor the serious part your concernment."

GILDON (1710, pp. 292–3): "The Unities of Action and Place are pretty well observed in this Play, especially as they are in the Modern Acceptation. The Design of the Play [*293*] carries an excellent Moral, and a just Satire against our present Reformers; who wou'd alter their Course of Nature and bring us to a Perfection, Mankind never knew since the World was half Peopled. . . . The Scene betwixt *Isabella* and *Angelo* in the second Act is very fine. . . . Allowing for some *Peccadillos* the last Act is wonderful, and moving to such a Degree, that he must have very little Sense of Things, and Nature, who finds himself Calm in the reading it. . . . I shall proceed to the fine Moral Reflections and Topics of it."

UPTON (1746, p. 72): "The unity of action is very visible in *Measure for Measure.* That reflection of Horace, *Quid leges sine moribus Vanae proficiunt?* [What good are empty laws without morals?] is the chief moral of the play. How knowing in the characters of men is our poet, to make the severe and inexorable Angelo incur the penalty of that sanguinary law, which he was so forward to revive?"

LENNOX (1753, 1:27–8, 36–7): "Since the Fable in *Cinthio* is so much better contrived than that of *Measure for Measure,* on which it is founded, the Poet sure cannot be defended, for having altered it so much for the worse; and it would be but a poor Excuse, for his want of Judgment, to say, that had he followed the Novelist closer, his Play would have been a Tragedy, and to make a Comedy, he was under a Necessity of winding up the Catastrophe as he has done. . . .

[*28*] "That *Shakespear* made a wrong Choice of his Subject, since he was resolved to torture it into a Comedy, appears by the low Contrivance, absurd Intrigue, and improbable Incidents, he was obliged to introduce, in order to bring about three or four Weddings, instead of one good Beheading, which was the Consequence naturally expected. . . .

[*36*] "This Play therefore being absolutely defective in a due Distribution of Rewards and [*37*] Punishments; *Measure for Measure* ought not to be the Title, since Justice is not the Virtue it inculcates; nor can *Shakespear's* Invention in the Fable be praised; for what he has altered from *Cinthio,* is altered greatly for the worse."

JOHNSON (ed. 1765, 1:382): "Of this play the light or comick part is very natural and pleasing, but the grave scenes, if a few passages be excepted, have more labour than elegance. The plot is rather intricate than artful. The time of the action is indefinite; some time, we know not how much, must have elapsed between the recess of the *Duke* and the imprisonment of *Claudio;* for he must have learned the story of *Mariana* in his disguise, or he delegated his power to a man already known to be corrupted. The unities of action and place are sufficiently preserved."

PYE (1807, pp. 33–4): "Though there are several striking passages in *Measure for Measure,* there are more faults in it, as a whole, than in any of the plays that are undoubtedly written by Shakespear. How much stronger would the interest be if the friar was not known to be the duke till he suddenly broke forth, which should have been while Angelo was treating the remonstrance of Isabella (which might be made to Escalus) with insult, and just as he was saying, 'Away to prison with her' [2490]. The death of Angelo should be respited by the unexpected appearance of Claudio, and not by the preposterous interference of Isabella, which . . . is a gross violation of consistency of character, only to be equalled by the offer of Valentine of his mistress to Protheus, in the *Two Gentlemen of Verona.* Such faults as these . . . [*34*] are mortal sins against the probability of the drama. There is a great impropriety (not to mention the gross indecency of their language) in the impurity of such a character as Lucio; and the lenity with which Pompey and the bawd are treated, at a time when the interest of the drama turns on fornication being punished with death. There seems also justice in the remark of Johnson, that it is strange Isabella should not express either gratitude, joy, or wonder, at the sight of her brother; but perhaps they were supplied by the action. Shakespear was a player as well as a poet, and probably was more anxious for stage effect than the perfection of his drama as a composition."

SCHLEGEL (1809–11, tr. 1846, pp. 387–8): "The most beautiful embellishment of the composition is the character of Isabella . . . : in the humble robes of the novice she is a very angel of light. When the cold and stern Angelo . . . is even himself tempted by the virgin charms of Isabella, supplicating for the pardon of her brother Claudio, condemned to death for a youthful indiscretion; when at first, in timid and obscure language, he insinuates, but at last impudently avouches his readiness to grant Claudio's life to the sacrifice of her honour; when Isabella repulses his offer with a noble scorn; in her account of the interview to her brother, when the latter at first applauds her conduct, but at length, overcome by the fear of death, strives to persuade her to consent to dishonour;—in these masterly scenes, Shakespeare [*388*] has sounded the depths of the human heart."

HAZLITT (1817, pp. 320–3): "This is a play as full of genius as it is of wisdom. Yet there is an original sin in the nature of the subject, which prevents us from taking a cordial interest in it. 'The height of moral argument' which the author has maintained in the intervals of passion or blended with the more powerful impulses of nature, is hardly surpassed in any of his plays. But there is in general a want of passion; the affections are at a stand; our sympathies are repulsed and defeated in all directions. The only passion which influences the story is that of Angelo; and yet he seems to have a much greater passion for hypocrisy than for his mistress. . . . [*321*] As to the Duke, who makes a very imposing and mysterious stage-character, he is more absorbed in his own plots and gravity than anxious for the welfare of the state; more tenacious of his own character than attentive to the feelings and apprehensions of others. Claudio is the only person who feels naturally; and yet he is placed in circumstances of distress which almost preclude the wish for his deliverance. Mariana is also in love with Angelo, whom we hate. In this respect, there may be said to be a general system of cross-purposes between the feelings of the different characters and the sympathy of the reader or the audience. This principle of repugnance seems to have reached its height in the character of Master Barnardine, who not only sets at defiance the opinions of others, but has even thrown off all self-regard. . . . He is a fine antithesis to the morality and the hypocrisy of the other characters of the play. . . . [*322*] We do not understand why the philosophical German critic, Schlegel, should be so severe on those pleasant persons, Lucio, Pompey, and Master Froth, as to call them 'wretches'. They appear all mighty comfortable in their occupations, and determined to pursue them, 'as the flesh and fortune should serve'. A very good exposure of the want of self-knowledge and contempt for others, which is so common in the world, is put into the mouth of Abhorson, the jailor, when the Provost proposes to associate Pompey with him in his office—'A bawd, sir? Fie upon him, he will discredit our mystery' [1881–2]. And the same answer would serve in nine instances out of ten to the same kind of remark, 'Go to, sir, you weigh equally; a feather will turn the scale' [1883–4]. Shakespear was in one sense the least moral of all writers; for morality (commonly so called) is made up of antipathies; and his talent consisted in sympathy with human nature, in all its shapes, degrees, depressions, and elevations. The object of the pedantic moralist is to find out the bad in every thing: his was to shew that 'there is some soul of goodness in things evil'. Even Master Barnardine is not left to the mercy of what others think of him; but when he comes in, speaks for himself, and pleads his own cause, [*323*] as well as if counsel had been assigned him. In one sense, Shakespear was no moralist at all: in another, he was the greatest of all moralists. He was a moralist in the same sense in which nature is one. He taught what he had learnt from her. He shewed the greatest knowledge of humanity with the greatest fellow-feeling for it."

COLERIDGE (before 1834; ed. Raysor, 1960, 1:102–3): "This play, which is Shakespeare's throughout, is to me the most painful—say rather, the only painful—part of his genuine works. The comic and tragic parts equally border on the μισητόν [hateful], the one disgusting, the other horrible; and the pardon and marriage of Angelo not merely baffles the strong indignant claim of justice (for cruelty, with lust and damnable baseness, cannot be forgiven, because we cannot conceive them as being *morally* repented of) but it is likewise degrading to the character of woman. . . . Of the counterbalancing beauties of the *Measure for Measure* I need [*103*] say nothing, for I have already said that it is Shakespeare's throughout."

HALLAM (1839, 3:564–5): "*Measure for Measure,* commonly referred to the end of 1603, is perhaps, after *Hamlet, Lear* and *Macbeth,* the play in which Shakspeare struggles, as it were, most with the over-mastering power of his own mind; the depths and intricacies of being which he has searched and sounded with intense reflection, perplex and harass him; his personages arrest their course of action to pour forth, in language the most remote from common use, thoughts which few could grasp in the clearest expression; and thus he loses something of dramatic excellence in that of his contemplative philosophy. The Duke is designed as the representative of this philosophical character. . . . The virtue of Isabella, inflexible and independent of circumstance, has something very grand and elevated; yet one is disposed to ask, whether, if Claudio had been really executed, the spectator would not have gone away with no great affection for her; and at [*565*] least we now feel that her reproaches against her miserable brother when he clings to life like a frail and guilty being, are too harsh. There is great skill in the invention of Mariana, and without this the story could not have had any thing like a satisfactory termination; yet it is never explained how the Duke had become acquainted with this secret, and being acquainted with it, how he had preserved his esteem and confidence in Angelo. . . . In dramatic effect *Measure for Measure* ranks high; the two scenes between Isabella and Angelo, that between her and Claudio, those where the Duke appears in disguise, and the catastrophe in the fifth act are admirably written and very interesting."

MÉZIÈRES (1860, pp. 478–9): "The moral elevation of the sentiments and the abundance of philosophic ideas make up the true beauty of *Measure for Measure.* Its plot is involved, complicated and improbable. . . . It is better to read the play than to see it acted. Indeed, it is more like a novel than a play. Walter Scott, who knew the sixteenth-century drama so well, doubtless remembered the most pathetic situation in this play [*479*] when he wrote *The Heart of Mid-Lothian.* He puts his Jeanie Deans, as Shakespeare had already put Isabella, in the dilemma of committing a mortal sin or of allowing a dearly-loved sister to die." In French.

PATER (1874; 1889, pp. 188–91): "As Shakspere in *Measure for Measure* has refashioned, after a nobler pattern, materials already at hand, so that the relics of other men's poetry are incorporated into his perfect work, so traces of the old 'morality', that early form of dramatic composition which had for its function the inculcating of some moral theme, survive in it also, and give it a peculiar ethical interest. . . . [*189*] Here the very intricacy and subtlety of the moral world itself, the difficulty of seizing the true relations of so complex a material, the difficulty of just judgment, of judgment that shall not be unjust, are the lessons conveyed. . . . [*190*] As sympathy alone can discover that which really is in matters of feeling and thought, true justice is in its essence a finer knowledge through love. [Quotes 474–7.] It is for this finer justice, a justice based on a more delicate appreciation of the true conditions of men and things, a true respect of persons in our estimate of actions, that the people in *Measure for Measure* cry out as they pass before us; and as the poetry of this play is full of the peculiarities of Shakspere's poetry, so in its ethics it is an epitome of Shakspere's moral judgments. They are the moral judgments of an observer, of one who sits as a spectator, and knows how the threads in the design before him hold together under the surface: they are the judgments of the humourist also, who follows with a half-amused but always pitiful sympathy, the various ways of human disposition, and sees less distance than ordinary men between what are called respec-[*191*]tively great and little things."

DOWDEN (1875, p. 82): "Shakspere was evidently bidding farewell to mirth; its [*MM*'s] significance is grave and earnest; the humorous scenes would be altogether repulsive were it not that they are needed to present without disguise or extenuation the world of moral licence and corruption out of and above which rise the virginal strength and severity and beauty of Isabella."

SYMONS (1889; 1920, pp. 48–9): "It is part of the irony of things that the worst complication, the deepest tragedy in all this tortuous action, comes about by the innocent means of the stainless Isabella; who also, by her steadfast heroism, brings about the final peace. But for Isabella, Claudio would simply have died, perhaps meeting his fate, when it came, with a desperate flash of his father's courage; Angelo might have lived securely to his last hour, unconscious of his own weakness, of the fire that lurked in so impenetrable a flint. . . . [*49*] Angelo, let us remember, is not a hypocrite: he has no dishonourable intention in his mind; he conceives himself to be firmly grounded on a broad basis of rectitude, and in condemning Claudio he condemns a sin which he sincerely abhors. His treatment of the betrothed Mariana would probably be in his own eyes an act of frigid justice; it certainly shows a man not sensually-minded, but cold, calculating, likely to err, if he errs at all, rather on the side of the miserly virtues than of the generous sins. It is thus the nobility of Isabella that attracts him; her freedom from the tenderest signs of frailty, her unbiassed intellect, her regard for justice, her religious sanctity; and it is on his noblest side first, the side of him that can respond to these qualities, that he is tempted. I know of nothing more consummate than the way in which his mind is led on, step by step, towards the trap still hidden from him, the trap prepared by the merciless foresight of the chance that tries the professions and the thoughts of men."

ROBINSON (1894; 1947, p. 136): "This morning I read two acts of *Measure for Measure* and was thunderstruck. . . . It is a comedy of the flesh and a tragedy of the soul. . . . Dark as the subject is, there is a rich vein of a rather broad humor running through the play which lends to the whole thing that wonderfully human effect which is a synonym for Shakspere."

SAINTSBURY (1898, p. 323): "Even in that unequal medley, *Measure for Measure,* the great scene between Isabel and Claudio so far transcends anything that English, anything that European, drama had had to show for nearly two thousand years, that in this special point of view it remains perhaps the most wonderful in Shakespeare. Marlowe has nothing like it; his greatest passages, psychologically speaking, are always monologues; he cannot even attempt the clash and play of soul with soul that is so miraculously given here."

SHAW (1898, 1:xxi): "Shakespear, unsurpassed as poet, storyteller, character draughtsman, humorist, and rhetorician, has left us no intellectually coherent drama, and could not afford to pursue a genuinely scientific method in his studies of character and society, though in such unpopular plays as *All's Well, Measure for Measure,* and *Troilus and Cressida,* we find him ready and willing to start at the twentieth century if the seventeenth would only let him."

MOULTON (1903; 1907, pp. 148–9, 156–7): "We find in *Measure for Measure* perhaps the purest example in poetry of a moral experiment. This is no case of a crisis arising of itself in the course of human events; the Duke, in his withdrawal from Vienna, is designedly contriving [*149*] special conditions in which he will be able to study the workings of human nature. . . .

[*156*] "Thus the complication of this exquisite plot has reached its adequate resolution; the moral problem has been fully solved, and the reconciling force emerges as Mercy in its many-sidedness. . . . [*157*] Surveying from all its sides this drama of Justice we catch a majestic presentation of Mercy, not as diluted and weakened Justice, but as something transcending Justice, holding allegiance equally to the law and the individual."

BRADLEY (1904, pp. 78, 275 n.): "We know well enough what Shakespeare is doing when at the end of *Measure for Measure* he marries Isabella to the Duke—and a scandalous proceeding it is; but who can ever feel sure that the doubts which vex him as to some not unimportant points in *Hamlet* are due to his own want of eyesight or to Shakespeare's want of care? . . .

[*275* n.] "He wrote also in these years [after *TN*] (probably in the earlier of them) certain 'comedies', *Measure for Measure* and *Troilus and Cressida* and perhaps *All's Well.* But about these comedies there is a peculiar air of coldness; there is humour, of course, but little mirth; in *Measure for Measure* perhaps, certainly in *Troilus and Cressida,* a spirit of bitterness and contempt seems to pervade an intellectual atmosphere of an intense but hard clearness."

E. K. CHAMBERS (ed. 1906; 1925, pp. 210–11): "Whatever the explanation, the fact remains that for a period in Shakespeare's history near the beginning of the seventeenth century the rose-red vision gave place to the grey, and that, if he still wrote as an idealist, it was as an idealist into whose imagination had passed the ferment of doubt and the bitterness of disillusion. And so *Measure for Measure* wears the rue of comedy with a difference. [*211*] Lucio is of the tribe of Mercutio, just without Mercutio's saving grace of the readiness to throw away his life for the sake of the game. The *milieu* of Mistress Overdone is the *milieu* of Mistress Quickly, and you may catch a veritable echo of the talk of mine hostess of Eastcheap in Pompey's description of the stewed prunes. . . . The change is not in the puppets, but in their observer and interpreter. Sin, which was human, has become devilish. Here are the forms of comedy, the by-play of jest and the ending of reconciliation. But the limits of comedy, which may be serious but must be suave, are sorely strained. There is a cruel hint in the laughter, and the engineer of the reconciliation is surely a cynic."

BRIDGES (in BULLEN, ed. 1907, 10:326–7): "This drama was written in the height of Shakespeare's attainment, and if he had left not a record beside, we should know him from Isabella's three great scenes [2.2, 2.4, 3.1] to have been by far the most gifted dramatist of all time. Even the short scene [2.3], between the Duke and Julietta,—where the Duke, graciously playing the confessor's role, finds himself at every professional move baffled and checkmated by the briefest possible replies of a loving, modest, and true heart, till he is rebuffed into a Christ-like sympathy,— appears to me a masterpiece which in its kind no other dramatist has equalled. How strange then is this blurred outline of Angelo, and how incomprehensible the neglect of Isabella at the close, [*327*] when her brother, whom she thought worse than dead, is restored to her [see n. 2889]. The actress is not denied a fine opportunity, but the situation passes without a word, and it must be concluded that the audience took no interest in Isabella's religious character."

RALEIGH (1907, pp. 165–73): "In criticisms of *Measure for Measure,* we are commonly [*166*] presented with a picture of Vienna as a black pit of seething wickedness; and against this background there rises the dazzling, white, and saintly figure of Isabella. The picture makes a good enough Christmas card, but it is not Shakespeare. If the humorous scenes are needed only, as Professor Dowden says, 'to present without disguise or extenuation a world of moral licence and corruption', why are they humorous? The wretches who inhabit the purlieus of the city are live men, pleasant to Shakespeare. Abhorson, the public executioner, is infamous by his profession, and is redeemed from infamy by his pride in it. . . . Pompey himself, the irrelevant, talkative clown, half a wit and half a dunce, is one of those humble, cheerful beings, willing to help in anything that is going forward, who are the mainstay of human affairs. . . . Elbow, the thick-witted constable, own cousin to Dogberry, is no less dutiful. Froth is an amiable, feather-headed young gentleman—to dislike him would argue an ill nature, and a small one. Even Lucio has his uses; nor is it very plain that in his conversations with the Duke he forfeits Shakespeare's sympathy. He has a taste for scandal, but it is a mere luxury of idleness; though his tongue is loose, his heart is simply affectionate, and he is eager to help his friend. Lastly, to omit none of the figures who make up the background, Mistress Overdone pays a strict attention to business, and is carried to prison in due course of law. This world of Vienna, as Shakespeare paints it, [*167*] is not a black world; it is a weak world, full of little vanities and stupidities, regardful of custom, fond of pleasure, idle, and abundantly human. No one need go far to find it. . . .

[*169*] "Of all Shakespeare's plays, this one comes nearest to the direct treatment of a moral problem. What did he think of it all? He condemns no one, high or low. The meaning of the play is missed by those who forget that Claudio is not wicked, merely human, and fails only from sudden terror of the dark. Angelo himself is considerately and mildly treated; his hypocrisy is self-deception, not cold and calculated wickedness. Like many another man, he has a lofty, fanciful idea of himself, and his public acts belong to this imaginary person. At a crisis, the real man surprises the play-actor, and pushes him aside. Angelo had underestimated the possibilities of temptation. . . .

[*171*] "In this play there is thus no single character through whose eyes we can see the questions at issue as Shakespeare saw them. His own thought is interwoven in every part of it; his care is to maintain the balance, [*172*] and to show us every side. He stands between the gallants of the playhouse and the puritans of the city; speaking of charity and mercy to these; to those asserting the reality of virtue in the direst straits, when charity and mercy seem to be in league against it. Even virtue, answering to a sudden challenge, alarmed, and glowing with indignation, though it is a beautiful thing, is not the exponent of his ultimate judgment. His attitude is critical and ironical, expressed in reminders, and questions, and comparisons. When we seem to be committed to one party, he calls us back to a feeling of kinship with the other. He pleads for his creatures, as he pleads in the Sonnets for his friend. . . .

[*173*] "This wonderful sympathy, which, more than any other of his qualities, is the secret of Shakespeare's greatness, answers at once to any human appeal."

MASEFIELD (1911, p. 179): "The play is a marvellous piece of unflinching thought. Like all the greatest of the plays, it is so full of illustration of the main idea that it gives an illusion of an infinity like that of life. It is constructed closely and subtly for the stage. It is more full of the ingenuities of play-writing than any of the plays. The verse and the prose have that smoothness of happy ease which makes one think of Shakespeare not as a poet writing, but as a sun shining. . . . The thought of the play is penetrating rather than impassioned. The poetry follows the thought. There are cold lines like Death laying a hand on the blood."

MATTHEWS (1913, p. 229): "The play has many fine lines—passages such as only Shakspere could pen. It contains certain of his most significant ethical judgments on sin and mercy and death. But it is as painful as it is ill-shaped; and at the core of it is a distasteful device. What lingers in the memory after its performance is the figure of Isabella, nobly conceived, even if inconsistently presented. And it is due solely to the histrionic opportunities of the part of Isabella that the piece is still seen at rare intervals on the stage, from which *All's Well* and *Troilus and Cressida* have long been banished. Even when it now emerges before the footlights its stay is but brief, for it gives the playgoer neither the purging pleasure of true tragedy nor the sparkling joy of genuine comedy."

WINTER (1913, 1:389): "The grim and painful play of *Measure for Measure,* powerful, pathetic, and wonderfully eloquent though it is, and abounding in knowledge of human nature, is one that might well be spared from the Stage. Its treatment of a dark subject is superb. Its language is frequently magnificent. Its discriminative delineations of character are transcendently able and true. It is peculiarly felicitous in its searching inspection of the human heart and its truthful exposition of the motives of human conduct. . . . Its effect when represented has, however, always been gloomy and depressing, and if acquaintance is to be made with it at all, it is better to be read than to be seen, for it is unfit for the modern Theatre."

QUILLER-COUCH (in WILSON, ed. 1922, pp. xiii, xxvii, xli): "What is wrong with this play? Evidently *something* is wrong, since the critics so tangle themselves in apologies and interpretations. . . .

[*xxvii*] "We submit that in *Measure for Measure,* as we have it, the idea is not thoroughly clear, has not been thoroughly realised. We take as our test Isabella; the 'heroine' and mainspring of the whole action. Isabella, more than any other character in the play, should carry our sympathy with her, or, at the least, our understanding. But does she? On the contrary the critics can make nothing of her or—which is worse—they make two opposite women of her, and praise or blame her accordingly. . . .

[*xli*] "*Measure for Measure* is a great play—in parts, and in despite that its parts do not fit. It arrests—it impresses while it puzzles—every reader. It does not, in our experience, gain new votes when transferred from the library to the stage. . . . But no play of Shakespeare's carries a stronger conviction that, although the goods may be 'mixed', we are trafficking with genius."

KNIGHT (1930; 1949, p. 96): "The play must be read, not as a picture of normal human affairs, but as a parable, like the parables of Jesus. The plot is, in fact, an inversion of one of those parables—that of the Unmerciful Servant (Matthew, xviii); and the universal and level forgiveness at the end, where all alike meet pardon, is one with the forgiveness of the Parable of the Two Debtors (Luke, vii). Much has been said about the difficulties of

Measure for Measure. But, in truth, no play of Shakespeare shows more thoughtful care, more deliberate purpose, more consummate skill in structural technique, and, finally, more penetrating ethical and psychological insight. None shows a more exquisitely inwoven pattern. And, if ever the thought at first sight seems strange, or the action unreasonable, it will be found to reflect the sublime strangeness and unreason of Jesus' teaching."

LAWRENCE (1931, pp. 119–20): "The essentially realistic character of the main plot, which deals with the fortunes of Claudio, Angelo and Isabella, a plot apparently based upon an episode from real life, was emphasized by Shakespeare's vivid and sympathetic treatment, and its realism was further heightened by the portrayal of the low-comedy characters. . . . The elements added to the main plot by Shakespeare, which most affect the Duke and Mariana, offer a striking contrast, since those elements were drawn from conventional story-telling, and are thoroughly artificial. By his art in making them plausible, Shakespeare preserved, to a large extent, the illusion of reality produced by the play as a whole. . . .

"The ruse suggested by the Duke, agreed to by Isabella, and accepted by Mariana, has been shown to have involved, in the eyes of an Elizabethan audience, no moral laxity in any of those characters, mainly for the reason that Mariana [*120*] had earlier been betrothed to Angelo, and that such a betrothal was held to confer the exercise of marital rights. . . . The frequency of this episode in popular story, and the clear evidence that it was there held not only to be entirely worthy of a heroine, but praiseworthy as well, must also be taken into consideration. The marriage of Isabella to the Duke, which appears to be impending at the close of the play, must be accepted as proper, since she had not yet taken vows, and since the retirement of a novice from an order and her subsequent marriage was, and still is, in complete accord with Roman Catholic custom.

"The machinations of the Duke, his deceptions that good may result, must be judged in the light of romantic and dramatic tradition, which may be studied in other Shakespearean plays. . . . Neither his character nor his actions can be judged on a realistic basis."

BRECHT (1932; 1962, p. 162): *"Measure for Measure* is considered by many as the most philosophic of all Shakespeare's works; it is undoubtedly his most progressive. He demands of those in high places that they not measure according to a different measure from that by which they themselves are willing to be measured. And it becomes evident that they have no right to demand from their subjects a moral attitude which they themselves do not assume." In German.

WILSON (1932, p. 117): *"Measure for Measure* is written in much the same key as *Point Counter Point* and others of Mr. Aldous Huxley's novels. The hatred of sentimentalism and romance, the savage determination to tear aside all veils, to expose reality in its crudity and hideousness, the self-laceration, weariness, discord, cynicism and disgust of our modern 'literature of negation' all belonged to Shakespeare about 1603; and he would well have understood Mr. T. S. Eliot's *The Waste Land.''*

SISSON (1934, p. 59): *"Measure for Measure* with its superb dramatic poetry, diversified by comic force, and its absorbing theme, is one of Shakespeare's finest acting plays."

ELLIS-FERMOR (1936, pp. 260-1): "In *Measure for Measure* the lowest depths of Jacobean negation are touched. Cynicism has taken on a kind of diabolic vigilance; with the exception of the kindly, timid Provost, there is no character who is not suspect, and those whose claims to goodness or decency seem most vigorous are precisely those in whom meanness, self-regard and hypocrisy root deepest. The theme of the main plot is Isabella's triumphant preservation of physical chastity against Angelo's cunning and at the risk of [*261*] Claudio's life; that of the underplot, the shifts of a company of brothel-keepers to maintain their trade. Before the end of the play we prefer the company of the second group to that of the first."

R. W. CHAMBERS (1937; 1939, pp. 304, 309–10): *"Measure for Measure* is a play of forgiveness, more distinctly even than *The Tempest.* Isabel forgives in her moment of direst loss: Prospero only when he has recovered his Dukedom. Isabel urges forgiveness because a Christian must forgive: Prospero forgives because he does not condescend to torment his enemies further. . . .

[*309*] "I submit that *Measure for Measure,* whilst it is akin to the tragedies with which it is contemporary, has also a likeness to those 'Romances' with which Shakespeare crowned his work. It is, indeed, for the continuity of Shakespeare that I am pleading. 'Shakespeare's career is the career of an artist'. Let us study his plays as the works of art which we know them to be, rather than weave baseless conjectures concerning details of a biography which we can never know. No one formula can summarize Shakespeare's life for us. Yet instead of always seeing him as suddenly plunged into the Depths, then raised by some convulsion to the Heights, might we not sometimes think of his career as a continuous progress to the Heights? We can trace the steady advance of Shakespeare's art from *Henry VI . . .* to *The Tempest.* We can also trace, I believe, the growth of a faith in the power of goodness. . . .

"I deprecate attempts to define Shakespeare's theological beliefs or unbeliefs. But from his earliest plays to his latest, he shows a belief in forgiveness as the virtue by which human goodness draws nearest to the divine: [*310*] Who by repentance is not satisfied Is nor of heaven nor earth, for these are pleased [*TGV* 5.4.79 (2203–4)]. And so far from agreeing that when he wrote *Measure for Measure* 'he quite obviously believed in nothing' [WILSON, 1932, p. 122], I submit that it is precisely the depth of his belief in forgiveness which has puzzled, in their judgement of that play, so many of his greatest critics, from Coleridge and Hazlitt and Swinburne, down to the present day."

CHARLTON (1938, pp. 257–8): "Is it not therefore palpably an error to take *Measure for Measure* as a cynic's play? The most loathsome creature in it is Abhorson, the man whose profession it is to cut life off. Even its most fallible mortals, like Lucio, and Pompey, and Mistress Overdone, somehow creep into our sympathy if not into our affection. And in those whose lot brings them into closest touch with the erring there grows a benevolent sense of human kindness: the governor of the prison, the Provost as he is called, is one of the most humane figures in the play. The mere bulk of evil which is spread across the scene of *Measure for Measure* is in itself no indication of the mood of the author. The greater the evil, the greater the author's faith in the goodness which can overcome it. And the evil in the play is nominally vanquished by the forces of virtue which the Duke and Isabella bring against it. That their conquest is more nominal than real simply means that Shakespeare's dramatic art has not welded his matter into an imaginative organism. But the [*258*] intention seems patent. There is virtue in man to make life well worth the living."

KNIGHTS (1942, pp. 222–3, 228, 232): "Like many other Elizabethan plays, *Measure for Measure* has an obvious relation to the old Moralities. It is too lively and dramatic—too Elizabethan—to be considered merely as a homiletic debate, but it turns, in its own way, on certain moral problems, the nature of which is indicated by the recurrent use of the words 'scope', 'liberty', and 'restraint'. What, Shakespeare seems to ask, is the relation between natural impulse and individual [*223*] liberty on the one hand, and self-restraint and public law on the other? . . .

[*228*] "The play of course is only 'about' Claudio to the extent that he is the central figure of the plot; he is not consistently *created*, and he only lives in the intensity of his plea for life. But I think it is the slight uncertainty of attitude in Shakespeare's handling of him that explains some part, at least, of the play's disturbing effect. . . . [*232*] Angelo's temptation and fall finely enforces the need for self-knowledge and sympathy which seems to be the central 'moral' of the play, and which certainly has a very direct bearing on the problems of law and statecraft involved in any attempt to produce order in an imperfect society. But the problems remain."

LEAVIS (1942; 1952, pp. 160–62, 166): "Re-reading, both of L. C. Knights's essay and of *Measure for Measure,* has only heightened my first surprise that such an argument about what seems to me one of the very greatest of the plays, and most consummate and convincing of Shakespeare's achievements, should have come from the author of *How Many Children Had Lady Macbeth?* For I cannot see that the 'discomfort' he sets out to explain is other in kind than that which, in the bad prepotent tradition, has placed *Measure for Measure* both among the 'unpleasant' ('cynical') plays and among the unconscionable compromises of the artist with the botcher, the tragic poet with the slick provider of bespoke comedy. . . . [*161*] Knights finds it disconcerting that Claudio should express vehe-[*162*]ment self-condemnation and self-disgust. But Claudio has committed a serious offence, not only in the eyes of the law, but in his own eyes. No doubt he doesn't feel that the offence deserves death; nor does anyone in the play, except Angelo (it is characteristic of Isabella that she should be not quite certain about it). On the other hand, is it difficult to grant his acquiescence in the moral conventions that, barring Lucio and the professionals, everyone about him accepts? A Claudio who took an advanced twentieth-century line in these matters might have made a more interesting 'character'; but such an emancipated Claudio was no part of Shakespeare's conception of his theme. . . . [*166*] It is Shakespeare's great triumph in *Measure for Measure* to have achieved so inclusive and delicate a complexity, and to have shown us complexity distinguished from contradiction, conflict and uncertainty, with so sure and subtle a touch. The quality of the whole, in fact, answers to the promise of the poetic texture."

CAMPBELL (ed. 1949, p. 655): *"Measure for Measure* thus proves to be a highly original work, different in method and in tone from any other of Shakespeare's dramas. The poet's main interest was to present a subtly conceived problem of conduct which he treats in the spirit of satire. Since Angelo is more knave than fool, the poet mixes his ridicule with scorn. Isabella, whose principal function is to accomplish the unmasking of Angelo, in joining the chorus of censure becomes the eloquent mouthpiece of the most exalted form of Christian ethics. Judged by her white purity and noble idealism, Angelo's sin seems as black as night. Her sublime utterances give her heroic stature and bring to the drama a strong religious atmosphere. The striking contrast between the divine air that Isabella breathes and the foul breath rising from the stews of Vienna is calculated. It renders the dramatic conflicts more striking and produces much of the sinewy strength which makes *Measure for Measure* both masterfully adapted to the stage and a work of deep psychological subtlety—'one of the greatest works of the greatest English mind' [MASEFIELD, 1911, p. 175]."

TILLYARD (1949, pp. 129–33): "The simple and ineluctable fact is that the tone in the first half of the play is frankly, acutely human and quite hostile to the tone of allegory or symbol. And, however much the tone changes in the second half, nothing in the world can make an allegorical interpretation poetically valid throughout. Recent critics, in their anxiety to correct old errors, [*130*] have in fact gone too far in the other direction and ignored one of the prime facts from which those old errors had their origin: namely that the play is not of a piece but changes its nature half-way through. It was partly through their correct perception of something being wrong that some earlier critics felt justified in making the Isabella of the first half of the play the scapegoat of the play's imperfections.

"The above inconsistency has long been noted, but since of late it has been so strongly denied, I had better assert it once more, and if possible not quite in the old terms. Briefly, the inconsistency is the most serious and complete possible, being one of literary style. Up to III. 1. 151 [1375], when the Duke enters to interrupt the passionate conversation between Claudio and Isabella on the conflicting claims of his life and her chastity, the play is predominantly poetical, the poetry being, it is true, set off by passages of animated prose. And the poetry is of that kind of which Shakespeare is the great master, the kind that seems extremely close to the business of living, to the problem of how to function as a human being. One character after another is pictured in a difficult, a critical, position, and yet one which all of us can imagine ourselves to share; and the poetry answers magnificently to this penetrating sense of human intimacy. Up to the above point the Duke, far from being guide and controller, has been a mere conventional piece of dramatic convenience for creating the setting for the human conflicts. Beyond that he is just an onlooker. And, as pointed out above, any symbolic potentialities the characters may possess are obscured by the tumult of passions their minds present to us. From the Duke's entry at III. 1. 151 to the end of the play there is little poetry of any kind [*131*] and scarcely any of the kind just described. . . .

[*132*] "A similar inconsistency extends to some of the characters. From being a minor character in the first half, with no influence on the way human motives are presented, the Duke becomes the dominant character in the second half and the one through whose mind human motives are judged. In the first half of the play we are in the very thick of action, where different human beings have their own special and different problems and are concerned [*133*] with how to settle them. . . . Reality is too urgent to allow of reflection. In the second half the Duke is in charge. He has his plans, and, knowing they will come to fruition, we can watch their workings. Reflection has encroached on reality."

DAVID (1951, p. 136): "The great duets largely play themselves. It is they that make the play memorable, and such tense and moving writing is found elsewhere in Shakespeare only in the great tragedies. There is of course the notorious danger that to a modern audience Isabella may appear unbearably self-centred and priggish. Isabella knows, and a Jacobean audience took for granted, that there can be no compromise with evil, that, though the only road to right may appear to lie through wrong, the taking of it can do no one any good. Claudio acknowledges it, when not blinded by his panic, for he finally begs his sister's pardon for suggesting otherwise; and we know it, too. But we are shy of being dogmatic about it in the manner of the Jacobeans; though we may admit Isabella's reasons we find it hard to swallow her matter-of-fact schematization of them—'More than our brother is our chastity' [1199]."

H. S. WILSON (1953, pp. 381–3): "The play is not a parable or an allegory, unless we regard it in only one aspect, its symbolic aspect; it is an action, a drama of men and women lusting and hating, loving and suffering, as well. But it has great dramatic suspense and a most happy ending, and the Duke's conduct, until the end, seems very mysterious and arbitrary; and all this makes the play seem something like a fairy tale too. It is this mingling of effects of successful realism with the more obvious artifice of the Duke's role that apparently sits so ill with some critics; though the same mingling of 'art' and 'artifice'—to use Professor Stoll's distinction—is to be found in *The Tempest.* . . .

[*382*] "When we reflect upon it, we cannot help noticing how close the parallel is with *Measure for Measure.* In each play, the action is set going and guided throughout by its duke; yet neither Duke Vincentio nor Prospero controls anyone else's choice; rather, they prepare the conditions in which others choose while taking precautions that no one shall give effect to a choice injurious to others. As Vincentio guides Claudio and Angelo to choose penitence and Isabella to prefer mercy to revenge or justice, so Prospero guides Alonso to choose penitence, Ferdinand to choose the love of Miranda, while he himself forgoes revenge or even justice in favor of mercy; and even Caliban shows signs of amendment at the end. As Barnardine and Lucio in *Measure for Measure* are given the chance to repent, though they remain unmoved, so with Antonio and Sebastian; but though all four are pardoned, they are also curbed of their evil propensities. . . . [*383*] Duke Vincentio and Duke Prospero are both temporal rulers; that is, to a sixteenth-century way of thought, they are divinely constituted authorities whose duty it is to rule and judge other men, according to the precept and example of Scripture, with justice and mercy. This is precisely the problem with which *Measure for Measure* deals, how to do this; and it is likewise the difficulty that confronts Prospero. Each of them solves the problem, though by different means."

COGHILL (1955, pp. 19–20): "Of course the Duke knows, before the play begins, that there is some reason to suspect Angelo's integrity; indeed he gives him the strongest possible hint that he knows of his not wholly creditable past when he tells him that one who has observed his history could unfold his character. The hint wears a polite veil of ambiguity, but it is a warning to him none the less. . . .

"Angelo's mettle is to be tested. Of course he falls at the first fence, though I believe the point has not been noted. He falls at the test of his faithfulness in elementary matters of justice, when he is to adjudicate in the case of Mr Froth and Pompey Bum; instead of doing his duty he exhibits the insolence of office, refuses the tedium of sifting evidence and departs with a pun and a flick of cruelty, leaving the patient Escalus to do his work for him. . . .

[*20*] "Then comes the greater testing when he is confronted by the pleading beauty of Isabella, and the anguish of his spirit expresses itself in two soliloquies of a quality not inferior to those of Hamlet. From then on

he continues to fail and fall under successive test, more and more hideously up to the instant of discovery.

"It was the action of the devious Lucio in persuading Isabella to intercede for her brother with Angelo that had brought him to this pass; it also brought Isabella to the test of her chastity. The fact that she resisted in that brought her to the further test of her courage: she had to tell her condemned brother that he must die. She could easily have lied to him, need never have told him of the one condition upon which life had been promised to him. But she preferred to tell the truth. In these two tests she is seen to triumph. . . . She has still, as Chambers has so well noted, to be searched for charity of heart. When the time comes, she is found to have that also; perhaps she learnt it during the play."

BUSH (1956, pp. 39–40): "The persons of *Measure for Measure* propose ideals of behavior. The Duke, or so he says, would have Claudio absolute for death; Angelo is absolute for justice; and Isabella, a maid whose mind is dedicate to nothing temporal, would be absolute for heaven. But a perfect image of conduct is not possible; the persons of the play are educated in natural fact. The Duke is put out of countenance by the prisoner Barnardine, a voice of dissent who refuses to be silent. Barnardine is absolute for life: 'I will not consent to die this day, that's certain' [2134–5]. . . . Angelo is absolute for justice and Isabella for heaven: they also learn that their judgments are too precise. They are instructed in nature, like the characters of the comedies; but they cry out at their discovery of natural frailty. . . .

[*40*] "In every play there is a moment of discovery and *anagnorisis,* when character and event stand self-exposed. . . . The problem plays accept as their explicit theme the contradiction between . . . two aspects of experience: Ulysses and Hector and the Duke and Isabella are made to know and confront the fact of common natural weakness. At their most dramatic moments, they find themselves in a double situation, addressed by the world both as it is and as it ought to be. These are moments of intellectual anguish, when Angelo is torn between would and would not, and Isabella is at war ''twixt will and will not' [777]."

MAHOOD (1957, pp. 99–100): "*Measure for Measure* seems to me a great but unsatisfactory play for the same reason that Sonnet 94 is, on its own scale, a great but unsatisfactory poem: in each case Shakespeare is emotionally too involved in the situation to achieve a dramatic clarification of its issues. He was perhaps drawn to the existing versions of the *Measure for Measure* story by the dramatic potentialities in the character he calls Angelo: the self-centred, self-sufficient man who makes a tragic discovery of his own weakness. The story, however, compelled Shakespeare to make the centre of interest the clash between Angelo's hypocrisy and Isabella's integrity whereas the play's fundamental conflict is less a moral than a psychic one, and is summed up in the confrontation of the Duke's Innocent-the-Third asceticism in the 'Be absolute [*100*] for death' speech with the affirmation of life in Claudio's outcry: 'I, but to die, and go we know not where!' [1337] A play can quite well embody a psychic alongside a moral conflict, but here the two issues do not correspond. Shakespeare is on Isabella's side in the moral conflict, since he and his audience believe the soul matters more than the body; but he cannot side with her in the psychic conflict because virginity could never seem to him the positive good it appeared to Spenser and Milton. For Shakespeare there could be no doubt that it was better to live and give life than to die, or to live in a way that amounted to a refusal of life.''

ORNSTEIN (1957; 1960, p. 258): "The ending of the play is unsatisfactory in that it disappoints our longing for a more perfect justice than the world affords and because it avoids the very moral problems which lend reality and meaning to a contrived *novella* fable. The conflict between divine commandment and human frailty, between the high ethic of the Gospel and the necessity of punitive law, is brushed aside, not resolved. To the final scene Angelo's legalistic conception of justice remains valid in the eyes of his fellow citizens and even triumphs in Isabella's 'mercy'.''

BULLOUGH (1958, 2:416–17): *"Measure for Measure* is not a 'Morality' but a romance interwoven with threads of sociology and ethics. The romance dominates in the plot, which gathers energy as it advances because the Duke is in full charge to bring about a happy ending. But as the events occur they excite reflections in the dramatist in which moral and religious ideas support each other. Mr Wilson Knight's comparison of the Duke with Prospero [see p. 431] is just; Vincentio tests the other characters (indeed he is tested himself) and the last scene with its elaborate preparation and teasing suspense is conceived as a climactic test of Isabella's goodness. Can she bring herself to forgive her enemy (not her husband as in the sources) while still believing that he murdered Claudio? The Duke puts every obstacle in her way, raising objections and exclaiming in pretended horror at Mariana's plea. But Isabella yields (and thereby proves herself too valuable to the world to immure herself in a convent). . . . Isabella responds to Mariana's desperate prayer, but the terms she herself uses are rational and earthly. She pardons; . . . but this is not full Christian forgiveness. She does not love her [417] enemy; nor should we wish it. . . .

"Shakespeare here shows himself rather the *anima naturaliter Christiana* than the exponent of particular Christian doctrines, though it is wrong to limit his religious ideas to wellings up from an unconscious heritage, in view of the treatment of Barnardine and pervasive references to Christian teaching. Rather the Christian heritage is blended in a wide pattern of humane ethics which allows of inconsistencies, touches of pagan feeling, bawdiness, delight in crooked ways. Like most believers Shakespeare is the incomplete Christian, and the Duke is not Christ but a good Duke. . . . The play is one of justice, severity, mercy, restitution and pardon, conceived not as allegory but in terms of individual human beings.''

ROSSITER (1961, pp. 168, 170): "I believe that *Measure for Measure* was *intended* to finish as a play of a higher ethic, and that ethic 'Christian'. But this remains largely an aim. . . .

[*170*] "I can imagine *Measure for Measure* being read, for its humanity, its keen and subtle inquisition into man's nature (into justice and truth, sex and love), by humans in a remote future to whom all the Gospel references belong to a bygone myth—'a local faith called Christianity'—no nearer to them than the gods in Euripides. And I can imagine it holding them none the less, as *we* can be held by the human tangles of the Greek problem-playwright."

FRYE (1965, pp. 12–13, 64–5): *"Measure for Measure,* whatever else it is, is not an attempt at socially significant realism: it is much more disturbing fantasy than a Johann Strauss opera, but its relation to any actual Vienna is equally remote. We note in passing a fact discovered by Thomas Rymer and at intervals by other critics since: that it is easy to make a Shakespeare play look ridiculous by refusing to accept its convention. . . . But Shakespeare . . . does not ask his audience to accept an illusion: he asks them to listen to the story. Everything we are told in that story is of equal authority. In discussing any difficulties of plausibility in Shakespeare, we [*13*] are often presented with the Elizabethan audience as a kind of censor principle. We are assured that the Elizabethan audience would think very differently about the behavior of Isabella in *Measure for Measure* from anyone today who was expecting a problem play. But it seems clear that no audience of Shakespeare, whether Elizabethan or modern, is allowed to think at all. They have the power to like or dislike the play, but no right to raise questions, as long as the action is going on, about the plausibility of the incidents or their correspondence with their habitual view of life. . . .

[*64*] "The problems of the problem comedies have to be looked at first of all as conventional descendants of myths. . . . The problem in *Measure for Measure* is how Isabella's chastity, always a magical force in romance, is going to rescue both the violated Julietta and the jilted Mariana as a result of being exposed to the solicitations of Angelo. . . . Isabella is unlikely to be our favorite Shakespearean [*65*] heroine, but militant chastity, which is seldom likable, is her dramatic role, and the condition of her quest."

HUNTER (1965, pp. 213, 217–18, 221–2): "Shakespeare first casts in the role of Justice a contemporary type that his audience would have recognized—the Puritan. Furthermore, he gives his Justice figure a legal instrument—a law punishing offenses against the seventh commandment with death—which was precisely the weapon that the Puritans had been demanding for the reform of what appeared to them the excessive sexual immorality of the time. And he proceeds to demonstrate that a ruler who, like the duke, intrusts such power to such a figure would be allowing a man ignorant of human nature (including his own) to impose a dangerously unrealistic sexual ethic upon his fellow humans. . . .

[*217*] "As the advocate of Mercy, Isabella has spoken with the tongue

of men and of angels, but in the role of Justice she has proved notably lacking in charity. She has ruthlessly condemned her brother for falling short of her own heroic ideal. That ideal and the ethic from which it springs is certainly not being attacked in *Measure for Measure,* at least not so vehemently as the rigidly repressive Puritanical ethic of Angelo is being attacked. Isabella, I think, in some degree stands for the monastic ideal which predates Puritanism as an attempt to repress the human impulses with which *Measure for Measure* is concerned. . . . Shakespeare seems to find it more sympathetic and to handle it more gently. He by no means allows it to go uncriticized, however. His play demonstrates, through Isabella, that when forced to deal with the world of ordinary men, those who are devoted to the monastic ideal may respond to human perplexities with a notable [*218*] lack of charity. . . .

[*221*] "Both Angelo and Isabella entered the tawdry but very human world of Vienna encased in an armor of unyielding righteousness. Both of them have been impelled by the play's action to surrender an unrealistic ethic which they had thought to impose on themselves and others. Both have been forced to recognize their membership in the human race. . . . [*222*] Just as Angelo is forced to surrender his pharisaical Puritanism, Isabella is persuaded to leave behind the cloistered virtue of the votarists of St. Clare and become the wife of Vienna's ruler."

For surveys of criticism on *MM* see DURHAM (1929, pp. 111–32), R. M. SMITH (1950, pp. 208–18), MORRIS (1957), LEVER (ed. 1965, pp. lv–viii), GECKLE (1966), STEVENSON (1966, pp. 63–92), PRICE (1969, pp. 179–204), JAMIESON (1972, pp. 1–10), and MILES (1976, pp. 13–122).

Critics who emphasize strengths in *MM* include, besides those quoted, MURPHY (1757, p. 215, and 1758, p. 367), TIECK (c. 1794; 1920, p. 233), DRAKE (1817, 2:454–6), DANIEL (1826, pp. 5–7), HORN (1827, 4:220–48), DUPORT (1828, 2:141–91), ULRICI (1839, tr. 1846, pp. 309–16), GERVINUS (1849–50, tr. 1875, pp. 485–504), VEHSE (1851, 1:348–50), KREYSSIG (1862; 1877, 2:443–62), GENÉE (1872, pp. 328–9, and 1905, pp. 304–8), HERFORD (ed. 1899, 3:238–40), ARMSTRONG (1913, pp. 78–9), LANDAUER (1920, 2:1–4), BAKER (1923, pp. 18–23), SCHELLING (1925, p. 149), HEARN (1928, 2:117–19), SPURGEON (1935, pp. 287–90), STOESSL (1935, pp. 302–6), BELGION (1938, pp. 18–28), ALEXANDER (1939, pp. 188–91), SPENCER (1940, pp. 299–304), WEBSTER (1942; 1957, pp. 248–52), FERGUSSON (1952; 1957, pp. 126–43), STEVENSON (1956, *ELH,* pp. 256–78, and 1966, pp. 121–33), HENNINGS (1958, pp. 1–24), GILBERT (1964, pp. 45–62), WILES (1964, pp. 181–93), BENNETT (1966, pp. 153–9), HAMILTON (1969), HETRICK (1970), DURRANT (1972, pp. 21–39), and BROCKBANK (1976, pp. 1470–1).

Others who emphasize faults and improbabilities in *MM* include INCHBALD (ed. 1808, pp. 3–5), P. P. (ed. 1822, pp. iii–vi), HUNTER (1845, 1:221), GRILLPARZER (1849, tr. 1963, pp. 137–9), LLOYD (in SINGER, ed. 1856, 1:439–49), HART (ed. 1905, pp. xxii–viii), SAINTSBURY (1910,

5:213–15), CHAMBERS (1911), FIGGIS (1911, pp. 227–8, 265–6), ARCHER (1912, pp. 340–2), MORRIS (ed. 1912, pp. xiii–xiv), BROOKE (1913, pp. 139–64), CROCE (1920, p. 294), CHAPMAN (1922, p. 88), SCHÜCKING (1922, pp. 196–9), ROBERTSON (1923, pp. 158–211), MACKENZIE (1924, pp. 225–43), AGATE (1925, pp. 51–5), ECKHARDT (1928, pp. 188–90), BAILEY (1929, pp. 159–63), C. WILLIAMS (1932, pp. 63–5), RIDLEY (1937, pp. 153–7), WEST (1947, pp. 136–41), CRAIG (1948, pp. 228–36), PETTET (1949, pp. 156–60), LEECH (1950, pp. 66–73), WHITAKER (1951, pp. 351–4), NICOLL (1952, pp. 116–20), WEST (1957, pp. 44–9), MARSH (1963, pp. 31–8), BANHAM (1964, pp. 28–31), MUSGROVE (1964, pp. 67–74), CALLAHAN (1966, pp. 31–52), LEIGHTON (1969, pp. 31–9), CHAMPION (1970, pp. 152–3), EVANS (1971, pp. 74–84), FOAKES (1971, pp. 17–31), GELB (1971, pp. 25–34), HAWKINS (1972, pp. 51–77), and BARTON (in EVANS, ed. 1974, pp. 545–9).

Others who balance the virtues of *MM* with its faults include HUDSON (1872, 1:398–420), LASCELLES (1953, pp. 139–64), DORAN (1954, pp. 363, 366–9), GRIVELET (ed. 1957, pp. 7–81), URE (1961, pp. 18–32), SCHANZER (1963, pp. 71–131), LEVER (ed. 1965, pp. xci–viii), and MAXWELL (1974, pp. 199–218).

Others who praise the first half of *MM,* but not the second, include DUPORT (1828, 2:141–91), COURTHOPE (1903, 4:135–9), RALEIGH (1907, p. 169), WOLFF (1907, 2:140), LEGOUIS (1909–10, pp. 267–72), LEGOUIS & CAZAMIAN (1924, tr. 1929, pp. 431–2), C. WILLIAMS (1932, pp. 63–5), PARROTT (ed. 1938, pp. 590–2), CRAIG (1951, pp. 26–7, and 1964, pp. 123–5), BALD (ed. 1956, pp. 20–1), LAWLOR (1960, pp. 62–5), O'CONNOR (1960, pp. 150–69), ROSSITER (1961, pp. 164–9), HARBAGE (1964, pp. 8–9), WAIN (1964, pp. 92–9), EDWARDS (1968, pp. 110, 115–19), FLY (1976, pp. 53–83), and MILES (1976, pp. 255–63).

Other writers on *MM* include KNIGHT (ed. 1840; 1849, pp. 314–20), FRIESEN (1876, 3:376–400), O'BRIEN (1888, pp. 264–77), BRANDES (1895–6, tr. 1898, 2:70–80), SIMPSON (in BOWDEN, 1899, p. 359), COSENTINO (1906, pp. 198–221), SMEATON (1911, pp. 385–95), BRANDL (1922, pp. 350–5), POURTALÈS (1924, pp. 42–6), GUNDOLF (1928, 2:156–87), MACKAIL (1930, p. 24), RAPIN (1930, pp. 42–51), WAGNER (1934, pp. 1–17), SMIRNOV (1934, tr. 1936, pp. 81–2), STAUFFER (1949, pp. 141–62), POGSON (1950, pp. 58–69), RUEGG (1951, pp. 271–6), MAXWELL (1955, pp. 220–3), D. G. SMITH (1956), BIANCOTTI (1957, pp. 266–9), BROWN (1957, pp. 183–5, 192–7), KREHAYN (1958, pp. 904–16), SLACK (1958, pp. 19–35, and 1966, pp. 53–4), FINKELSTEIN (1961, pp. 35–42, and 1973, pp. 149–57), CHUNG (1962, pp. 95–125), CARD (1964, pp. 61–9), HYMAN (1964, pp. 123–7, and 1975, pp. 3–20), JANES (1964, pp. 47–50), KUCKHOFF (1964, pp. 278–98), LONGO (1964), SRINIVASA IYENGAR (1964, pp. 430–40), TOOLE (1966, pp. 158–97), BACHE (1969, pp. 1–66), SCHLÖSSER (1970, pp. 100–26), MARDER (1971, p. 16), RICH-

MOND (1971, pp. 153–8), GOLDMAN (1972), LYNCH (1972), J. SPENCER (1972), and LONG (1976, pp. 79–101).

MM has been compared with the *Antigone* of Sophocles by COLLINS (1880; 1904, p. 78), SHELDON (1892, pp. 609–12), MAXWELL (1949, pp. 32–6), and HAWKINS (1972, p. 54); with Dante by RANKIN (1841, p. 32), DYCE (1853, p. 25), KÖNIG (1872, pp. 192, 208), STONE (1879, pp. 286–7), BARING (1936, p. 109), DWYER (1955, pp. 33–4), and FERGUSSON (1968, pp. 116–24); with Spenser by WATKINS (1950, pp. 47–51, 87) and POTTS (1958, pp. 150–73); with Donne by PRAZ (1945, pp. 23–5), COOK (1953, pp. 122–7), STEVENSON (1956, *ELH,* p. 262), ROSSITER (1961, p. 128), and H. M. WILLIAMS (1965, pp. 39–43); with Jonson by KRIEGER (1951, pp. 778–84), NOSWORTHY (ed. 1969, pp. 34–9), DONALDSON (1970, pp. 5, 76–7), and NELSON (1973, pp. 253–63); with Molière by PUSHKIN (1837, tr. 1941, p. 121), HUGO (ed. 1862, p. 23), CHASLES (1867, 2:75), BRANDES (1895–6, tr. 1898, 2:80), MATTHEWS (1910, pp. 157, 170–1), and STOLL (1944, *RR*); with Goethe by WOLFF (1907, 2:143); with Kleist by CORSSEN (1930, pp. 29–40, 66–72, 142–3) and KRUMPELMANN (1951, pp. 13–21); with Keats by GRADMAN (1975, pp. 177–82) and GRENNAN (1975, pp. 272–92); with Scott's *Heart of Mid-Lothian* by DUPORT (1828, 2:190), HÜLSMANN (1856, p. 84), MÉZIÈRES (1860, pp. 478–9), BREWER (1925, pp. 273–8), TILLYARD (1949, pp. 125–6, 134–5), LASCELLES (1953, pp. 84–8), and BIGGINS (1961, pp. 193–205); with Cooper's *Spy* by GATES (1952, p. 718); with Manzoni's *I Promessi Sposi* by GETTO (1967, pp. 210–11); with Pushkin's *Angelo* by LIRONDELLE (1912, pp. 145–6), SIMMONS (1937, p. 97), GIBIAN (1951, pp. 426–31), WOLFF (1952, p. 102), ALEXEJEW (1968, pp. 170–3), and URNOW (1969, pp. 140–57); with Hawthorne by PEARCE (1973, pp. 11–15); with Melville's *Billy Budd* by HAWKINS (1972, p. 67); with James's *Portrait of a Lady* by SALE (1968, p. 61); with Gilbert's *Mikado* by ARMSTRONG (1913, p. 79) and BENNETT (1966, pp. 19, 158); with Lawrence by CRAIG (1964; 1973, pp. 17–38); with Kafka by BELGION (1938, pp. 18–28); with Brecht by MITTENZWEI (1962, pp. 154–65), WEISSTEIN (1968, pp. 24–39), FLUDAS (1970), SYMINGTON (1970, pp. 126–36), KUSSMAUL (1974, pp. 95–104), COHN (1976, pp. 341–56), and PACHE (1976, pp. 173–96).

II. Genre

COMEDY

PALMER (1914, pp. 19–20): "These plays, far from being a fit of temper, are Shakespeare's effort to achieve a fit of detachment. He is trying, against the grain of his nature, to stand apart from his creatures, to play the absolute just judge of Molière, to see them in the light of simple intelligence.

Measure for Measure opens with a promise of comedy as comedy is understood by one who weighs and pictures men with unemotional discretion. Shakespeare puts himself with Molière in the safe way of a golden mean, and brings life to the touch of reason. . . . [20] In Claudio we are offered a comedy of the over-sanguine man, to which is opposed, for a judicial contrast, the comedy of Angelo the precisian. But Shakespeare was too eagerly sympathetic, too easily touched into emotion, too quickly prompted into a perfect understanding of his creatures, too speedily pricked into fellow-feeling, to sustain the detachment of a purely comic writer. Shakespeare was imaginatively too great to write the comedy of pure reason. *Measure for Measure* breaks gradually down as a comedy. Emotion surges upon the barriers erected to keep it out. They break utterly down at last. Shakespeare becomes ever more at one with the people he has created; and, at last, in a play wherein he intended to stand aloof and critically to laugh, there intrudes that most bitter cry of all flesh—a speech at the top of tragedy: 'Ay, but to die, and go we know not where . . .' [1337]."

KRIEGER (1951, pp. 781–3): "It seems likely that the two conflicting varieties of Elizabethan comedy, that of Jonson and that of Greene, are combined in *Measure for Measure,* and that their incompatibility has caused the critical confusion which still exists about the play. . . . Isabella's development is not so much an accident or loss of control during playwriting as it is a manifestation of a clearly defined variety of romantic comedy which had its hold on Shake-[782]speare and which he could not or would not shake off even as he was introducing the currently popular Jonsonian characteristics. . . .

[783] "The Duke and Lucio seem to have more consistently Jonsonian functions than the others. From the outset the Duke has determined to test Angelo. And once Angelo has committed himself, the Duke directs all his efforts toward exposing him. . . . The explanation would seem to lie solely in the realm of dramatic convention. For it is the essence of the comedy of ridicule to push the gull, by means of intrigue, as far as possible until his self-exposure is most painful. It should be noted that the Duke's continuous and assuring presence, demanded by his function as intriguer, does prevent the romantic element from involving too dangerous a situation; we see here how a Jonsonian device helps maintain the play as comedy."

BENNETT (1966, pp. 158–9): "The play is, from beginning to end, pure comedy, based on absurdity, like *The Mikado,* full of topical allusions to a current best seller [*Basilicon Doron* by James I], and every situation exaggerated into patent theatricality. The great emotional scenes, first Isabella's, then Angelo's, and then Claudio's, each in a different way keep the emotions in check, as they must be kept in check in a comedy, because we cannot be amused when our sympathies are deeply involved. We must feel superior to the foolish people in the play, must know [159] more than they know (or feel that we do), and must be confident that everything will come out right in the end.

415

"The understanding of this multifaceted play restores to us much of the fun of Shakespeare's other comedies. It is not the simple guffaw of the unsophisticated, but the complex enjoyment of many things at once, of the actor as well as of the part he is playing, and here especially of the playwright as the creator of illusions and modulator of emotions."

STEVENSON (1966, pp. 128, 133): *"Measure for Measure* achieves its comic power over us by dramatizing its events with the seriousness of tragedy, but without the harsh, unyielding 'reality' of tragedy. Perhaps we could best identify *Measure for Measure* as a comedy wholly in an ironic mode: it suggests no serious, realizable solution to the moral dilemmas it has dramatized, but it comes to an end by implicating all of us in the perception that moral dilemma is a part of the human situation. I choose, then, to call Shakespeare's *Measure for Measure* his greatest comedy (though obviously not his greatest play). . . .

[*133*] *"Measure for Measure,* finally, is a comedy which unlocks our most profound awareness of the nature of an ineluctable evil in man. It is not evil as defined by prohibitions of church and state, not a postlapsarian and expected evil. It is the evil in man contingent upon his human predicament. . . . The play achieves its great penetrating power, its great moral intensity, because it allows us to win for ourselves this knowledge even of ourselves."

Others who discuss *MM* as a comedy include ULRICI (1839, tr. 1846, pp. 314–15), CHAMBERS (ed. 1906; 1925, pp. 210–11), RALEIGH (1907, p. 165), BELGION (1938, pp. 19–26), CAMPBELL (1943, pp. 124–41, and ed. 1949, pp. 651–5), COGHILL (1950, pp. 13, 18, 28, and 1955, pp. 14–27), SHEDD (1953), GRIVELET (ed. 1957, pp. 66–72, and 1968, pp. 69–72), BIRRELL (1958, pp. 100–1), EVANS (1960, pp. 186–219), SEHRT (1961, pp. 42–7), URE (1961, pp. 18–32), WILES (1964, pp. 181–93), WEIL (1965, and 1970, pp. 55–72), SCHWARTZ (1967), SALE (1968, pp. 55–61), SIEGEL (1968, pp. 190–8), HAMILTON (1969), NOSWORTHY (ed. 1969, pp. 20, 27–46), CHAMPION (1970, pp. 137–53), HETRICK (1970), LAVIN (1972, pp. 109–13), PARTEE (1973, pp. 274–97), and REDMAN (1974).

TRAGEDY

GILDON (1710, p. 293): "The Main Story or Fable of the Play is truly *Tragical* for it is Adapted to move Terror, and Compassion, and the Action is one. Its having a Fortunate *Catastrophe,* is nothing to the purpose for that is in many of the Greek Tragedies; tho' *Aristotle* indeed makes the Unfortunate Ending the most beautiful and perfect."

SWINBURNE (1880, pp. 203–4): "That this play is in its very inmost essence a tragedy, and that no sleight of hand or force of hand could give it even a tolerable show of coherence or consistency when clipped and docked of its proper and rightful end, the mere tone of style prevalent throughout all its better parts to the absolute exclusion of any other would of itself most amply suffice to show. Almost all that is here worthy of [*204*] Shakespeare at any time is worthy of Shakespeare at his highest: and of this every touch, every line, every incident, every syllable, belongs to pure and simple tragedy. The evasion of a tragic end by the invention and intromission of Mariana has deserved and received high praise for its ingenuity: but ingenious evasion of a natural and proper end is usually the distinctive quality which denotes a workman of a very much lower school than the school of Shakespeare."

SITWELL (1948, p. 122): "I place this play among the Tragedies."

TOSCANO (1976, p. 288) calls it "a tragedy within a divine comic structure."

TRAGICOMEDY

PARROTT (1949, p. 362): *"Measure for Measure . . .* is in effect a tragicomedy; in Fletcher's well-known definition [*The Faithfull Shepheardesse,* "To the Reader"]: 'it wants deaths, which is enough to make it no tragedy, yet brings some near it, which is enough to make it no comedy'. It employs in the main action all the conventional devices of this genre: disguise, mistaken identity, complex intrigue, and the surprise ending. There is no more striking instance of the *coup-de-théâtre* in Elizabethan drama than the discovery of the Duke when his friar's hood is pulled off by the jesting Lucio and the guilty Angelo beholds his master face to face. And this discovery is purely for theatrical effect; the Duke could have passed an earlier sentence upon his deputy while sitting on the judgment seat *in propria persona;* but, then, of course, the suspense which Shakespeare has been so artfully building up would have been destroyed. The free pardon of Angelo, which 'baffles the strong indignant claim of justice' [see Coleridge, p. 396], is in the strict convention of tragi-comedy; there can hardly be a case in Elizabethan tragicomedy where the villain gets his due reward."

LEVER (ed. 1965, pp. lx–ii): "The form here is a close blend of tragic and comic elements, so carefully patterned as to suggest a conscious experiment in the new medium of tragicomedy. Limited precedents for this treatment were to be found in the dramas of Cinthio and Whetstone. . . .

[*lxi*] "Guarini's *Compendio della Poesia Tragicomica* (1601) set forth a closely reasoned defence of 'true' tragicomedy, as distinguished from tragedy twisted to a happy ending or the loose medley of English tradition. The form was defined as a close blend or fusion of seeming disparates; taking from tragedy 'its great characters, but not its great action; a likely story, but not a true one; . . . delight, not sadness; danger, not death'; and from comedy 'laughter that was not dissolute, modest attractions, a well-tied knot, a happy reversal, and, above all, the comic order of things'. . . . [*lxii*] The new theory

was widely influential, and the term tragicomedy, previously fallen into disrepute, soon took on new dignity. Whether or not Shakespeare had read Guarini's treatise, its ideas were in the air after 1602 and may well have prompted the design of *Measure for Measure*, with its blend of serious and comic, extreme peril and happy solution, mixed characters and 'well-tied knot'."

EDWARDS (1968, p. 119): *"The Tempest* shows just where Shakespeare fails in *Measure for Measure*. It is not that he has included subjects too grave to be solved in terms of a comic or tragicomic structure, or that the idea of a *dramatis persona* controlling events with more than human power is too much for a play which meets good and evil head on. . . . *The Tempest* has unity, but *Measure for Measure* is a hybrid. The great idea of deepening comedy, of trying to make the comic form contain the facts of tragedy, is not achieved by the graft of comedy on to tragedy half-way through a play. The comedy-fabric, as Shakespeare has woven it in *All's Well* and *Measure for Measure*, is simply not strong enough to bear the weight of the human problems pressed on to it, nor the weight of their religious solution."

Others who discuss *MM* as a tragicomedy or a mixture of tragic with comic include LENNOX (1753, 1:27–8), ULRICI (1869, tr. 1876, 2:154), BRANDES (1895–6, tr. 1898, 2:71–2), BRINK (1895, p. 88), BROOKE (1913, pp. 143, 148), CROCE (1920, pp. 197–8, 294), WILSON (1932, pp. 116–17), STOLL (1944, *From Sh. to Joyce,* pp. 249–68), ROSSITER (1950, pp. 146–7, and 1961, pp. 122–5), LASCELLES (1953, pp. 135–8, 157–9), DORAN (1954, pp. 212, 366–9), WEST (1957, pp. 44–9), HOY (1964, pp. 6–7), MEHL (1964, pp. 166–7), NAGARAJAN (ed. 1964, pp. xxx f.), STOCKHOLDER (1965), GHOSH (1966, pp. 63–77), BECKERMAN (1970, p. 132), GELB (1971, pp. 25–34), KIRCHHEIM (1971, pp. 125–87), HUNTER (1973, pp. 123–48), BABULA (1975, pp. 106–10), KIRSCH (1975, pp. 104–5), TARSITANO (1975), and TROMBETTA (1976, pp. 60, 73–4).

PROBLEM PLAY

BOAS (1896, pp. 345, 357–8): "Most of the plays which with more or less warrant may be assigned to the last three years of Elizabeth's reign, contain painful studies of the weakness, levity, and unbridled passion of young men. This is especially the case with *All's Well that Ends Well, Measure for Measure, Troilus and Cressida,* and *Hamlet.* . . . All these dramas introduce us into highly artificial societies, whose civilization is ripe unto rottenness. Amidst such media abnormal conditions of brain and of emotion are generated, and intricate cases of conscience demand a solution by unprecedented methods. Thus throughout these plays we move along dim untrodden paths, and at the close our feeling is neither of simple joy nor pain; we are excited, fascinated, perplexed, for the issues raised preclude a completely satisfactory outcome, even when, as in *All's Well* and *Measure for Measure,* the complications are outwardly adjusted in the fifth act. . . . Dramas so singular in theme and temper cannot be strictly called comedies or tragedies. We may therefore borrow a convenient phrase from the theatre of to-day and class them together as Shakspere's problem-plays. . . . [357] With *Hamlet* the play is linked by its deeply reflective tone, its brooding sense of the pollution spread by lust in the single soul and in society at large, and the shivering recoil of the man of phantasies from the mystery of the unknown hereafter. Claudio's gloomy meditations on death sound like an echo from the soliloquies of the Danish Prince. It is this wealth of philosophic thought, this concern with the deepest issues of life here and beyond the grave, that give the [358] play a massive weight which the original framework of plot might well have seemed too slight to bear."

LAWRENCE (1931, pp. 3–5): "These three comedies [*AWW, MM,* and *Tro.*] mark one of the most striking developments of Shakespeare's genius. . . . The settings and the plots are still those of romance, but the treatment is in the main serious and realistic. They are concerned, not with the pleasant and fantastic aspects of life, but with painful experiences and with the darker complexities of human nature. . . . [4] The essential characteristic of a problem play, I take it, is that a perplexing and distressing complication in human life is presented in a spirit of high seriousness. This special treatment distinguishes such a play from other kinds of drama, in that the theme is handled so as to arouse not merely interest or excitement, or pity or amusement, but to probe the complicated interrelations of character and action, in a situation admitting of different ethical interpretations. . . .

[5] "The term 'problem play', then, is particularly useful to apply to those productions which clearly do not fall into the category of tragedy, and yet are too serious and analytic to fit the commonly accepted conception of comedy."

SCHANZER (1963, pp. 106, 130–1): "*Measure for Measure* is thus seen to conform to the definition of the Problem Play given in the Introduction (p. 6). We have found in it 'a concern with a moral problem which is central to it, presented in such a manner that we are unsure of our moral bearings, so that uncertain and divided responses to it in the minds of the audience are possible or even probable'. This view of the play is supported by Raleigh when he writes of it: 'Of all Shakespeare's plays, this one comes nearest to the direct treatment of a moral problem' [see p. 401]. It finds its sharpest opponent in E. E. Stoll [1944, p. 259], who declares that *Measure for Measure* is 'a tragicomedy, still less than *All's Well* a problem play. No question is raised, no "casuistry" is engaged in, no "dilemma," whether intolerable or tolerable, is put'. . . .

[130] "Considered as a problem play, *Measure for Measure* reveals a marked though unobtrusive likeness to *Julius Caesar*. In Isabel's choice between the death of her brother and the loss of her virginity, as in Brutus's

choice between the death of Caesar and what he believes to be the loss of his country's liberty, personal ties, human loyalties and affections, are made to clash with high ideals and moral principles which, if adhered to, involve the death of the loved person. In both plays the protagonists choose to sacrifice these human loyalties and ties to what they consider [*131*] their higher loyalties. And in both plays, by the orientation of his material and the manipulation of our responses, Shakespeare seems to me to suggest, strongly but not compulsively, his siding against the choice which is made."

Others who discuss *MM* as a problem play include MOULTON (1903; 1907, pp. 143–57, 353), BRADBROOK (1941, p. 398), FLUCHÈRE (1948, tr. 1953, pp. 216–23), STAUFFER (1949, p. 142), TILLYARD (1949, pp. 3–13, 124–45), DORAN (1954, pp. 366–9), BUSH (1956, pp. 49–50), LACY (1956), WASSON (1960, p. 262), ROSSITER (1961, pp. 108–28), ACKERMAN (1969), MURRAY (1969, pp. 95–6), VROONLAND (1969), EVANS (1971, pp. 56–62), FELPERIN (1972, pp. 71–4, 84–96), SALINGAR (1974, pp. 301–3, 319–22), ALEXANDER (1975, pp. 9–10), and MARSH (1976, pp. 29–35).

III. *Characters*

ANGELO

LENNOX (1753, 1:31): "As the Character of the Duke is absurd and ridiculous, that of *Angelo* is inconsistent to the last Degree; his Baseness to *Mariana,* his wicked Attempts on the Chastity of *Isabella,* his villainous Breach of Promise, and Cruelty to *Claudio,* prove him to be a very bad Man, long practised in Wickedness; yet when he finds himself struck with the Beauty of *Isabella,* he starts at the Temptation; reasons on his Frailty; asks Assistance from Heaven to overcome it; resolves against it, and seems carried away by the Violence of his Passion, to commit what his better Judgment abhors.

"Are these the Manners of a sanctified Hypocrite, such as *Angelo* is represented to be? Are they not rather those of a good Man, overcome by a powerful Temptation?"

JOHNSON (ed. 1765, 1:378): *"Angelo's crimes were such, as must sufficiently justify punishment, whether its end be to secure the innocent from wrong, or to deter guilt by example; and I believe every reader feels some indignation when he finds him spared."*

PUSHKIN (1837, tr. 1941, p. 120): "The characters portrayed by Shakspere are not, like Molière's, types of this particular passion or that particular vice, but are living beings filled with many passions, many vices; the circumstances unfold before the spectator their variety and their complex aspects. . . . In Shakspere the hypocrite pronounces a court verdict with conceited austerity, but with equity; he justifies his heartlessness with the thoughtful considerations of a statesman; he courts innocence with captivating sophistry and not with ludicrous concoctions of devotion and gallantry. *Angelo* is a hypocrite because his known actions contradict his secret passions! And what depth in this character!''

GERVINUS (1849–50, tr. 1875, pp. 500–1): "The poet, in this character, has designed a new variation of his favourite theme of *show.* The task in Angelo is a worthy sequel for the actor who represented the gross hypocrisy arising from the systematic selfishness of a villain like Richard, and the regardless contempt of all show, based as in Prince Henry on the absence of all selfishness. The actor is here required to represent a man who is too little for the great, bold, and dangerous projects of an ambitious selfishness; too noble for the weak errors of a vain self-love, who wavers negatively between the two, who aspires after honour, who would be a master in his political vocation, a saint in his moral life, but who, in the hour of temptation, is found as false and tyrannical in the one as he is hypocritical and base in the other. The task demands that the actor should not allow the mental endowments and the germ of good in this character utterly to be lost sight of in the midst of his fall; that he should let the original nobility of this nature appear through all its immoderate errors, and thus leave open the sure prospect of a radical reformation and repentance. Or could it be true, as Coleridge was of opinion, that sincere repentance on the part of Angelo was impossible? Certainly, after this deed, there was no more *show* for this man. The [*501*] eyes of the tester would no more leave him; he would deceive no one again. He has henceforth only the prospect of becoming a great criminal or of raising himself to lasting virtue and honour. Isabella—she who has most to complain against him—petitions for him, and seems to trust in the germ of good within him. Mariana—she who takes the greatest interest in him— will keep him with all his faults. . . . She speaks in the sense of the prince in Whetstone's play, who says at last to the pardoned judge: ['If thou be wyse, thy fall maye make thee ryse. The lost sheepe founde, for ioye, the feast was made', *2 Promos,* p. 369 above]."

BAGEHOT (1853; 1965, 1:205): "Now the entire character of Angelo, which is the expressive feature of the piece, is nothing but a successful embodiment of the pleasure, the malevolent pleasure, which a warm-blooded and expansive man takes in watching the rare, the dangerous and inanimate excesses of the constrained and cold-blooded. One seems to see Shakespeare, with his bright eyes and his large lips and buoyant face, watching with a pleasant excitement the excesses of his thin-lipped and calculating creation, as though they were the excesses of a real person. It is the complete picture of a natural hypocrite, who does not consciously disguise strong impulses, but whose very passions seem of their own accord to have disguised themselves and retreated into the recesses of the character, yet only to recur even more dangerously when their proper period is expired, when the will is cheated into security by their absence, and the world (and, it may be, the 'judicious person' himself) is impressed with a sure reliance in his chilling and remarkable rectitude."

PATER (1874; 1889, p. 183): "Of Angelo we may feel at first sight inclined to say only *guarda e passa!* or to ask whether he is indeed psychologically possible. In the old story, he figures as an embodiment of pure and unmodified evil, like 'Hyliogabalus of Rome or Denis of Sicyll' [Whetstone, *Heptameron*, p. 374 above]. But the embodiment of pure evil is no proper subject of art, and Shakspere, in the spirit of a philosophy which dwells much on the complications of outward circumstance with men's inclinations, turns into a subtle study in casuistry this incident of the austere judge fallen suddenly into utmost corruption by a momentary contact with supreme purity."

BRIDGES (in BULLEN, ed. 1907, 10:325–6): "Angelo, as introduced to us, is not a hypocrite, meaning by that term an unprincipled man who wears a mask. He is rather a Pharisee, a hard, cold, austere professor of virtue, with an introspective, logical mind of considerable intelligence and ambition. His most marked and consistently maintained characteristics are heartlessness and over-regard for his reputation: he is therefore unholy, and yet he deems himself a saint: he is consequently a self-deceiver, and presumably a sincere one. He sets out on his main course in the drama stiff with the pride and self-confidence of his saintly reputation; then meeting with a strange experience, which something hitherto unsuspected or repressed within him converts into a temptation, he commits horrible crimes. His fall works his salvation, for he is thereby undeceived, and, knowing himself, repents, and is pardoned, and, we suppose, reformed. . . .

[*326*] "The situation might be satisfied either with an unprincipled or with a passionate man. Angelo is neither: there is no passion in his calculating lust. He seems to have been purposely constructed incapable of the required reaction. His temperament does not, I think, tally with the notion of the sudden outburst of an uncontrollable animal instinct which had been artificially repressed. . . . Again his self-knowledge began with his temptation, and was complete at his fall: yet this unmelting man shows no remorse until he is publicly discovered. . . .

"Reminded, as we are at this juncture, of his conduct to Mariana, we believe that he has been a solid hypocrite all along; that, having no virtue to fall from, he never fell; that the spiritual conflict of his 'temptation' could not have occurred: and, as there was nothing in his first character to respond to the call to crime, so now, in the revelation of his second phase, there is, —except his demoniacal passion for Isabella,—nothing left of him to be pardoned and married to Mariana."

KNIGHT (1930; 1949, pp. 85–9): "Angelo, indeed, does not know himself: no one receives so great a shock as he himself when temptation overthrows his virtue. He is no hypocrite. He cannot, however, be acquitted of Pharisaical pride: his reputation means much to him. . . . [*86*] Angelo is, however, sincere: terribly sincere. . . .

"Angelo's arguments are rationally conclusive. A thing irrational breaks them, however: his passion for Isabella. . . . [*87*] The violent struggle is short. He surrenders—his ideals all toppled over like ninepins. . . . He has no moral values left. [*88*] . . . Angelo has not been overcome with evil. He has been ensnared by good—by his own love of sanctity, exquisitely [*89*] symbolized in his love of Isabella: the hook is baited with a saint, and the saint is caught. The cause of his fall is this and this only. The coin of his moral purity, which flashed so brilliantly, when tested does not ring true. Angelo is the symbol of a false intellectualized ethic divorced from the deeper springs of human instinct."

FAIRCHILD (1931, p. 59): "We cannot say that Angelo is a good man who succumbs to temptation, nor can we say that he is a hypocritical villain. There are two Angelos. The first is a characteristically Shakespearian development of Whetstone's Promos. The second is merely the result of the introduction of the Mariana plot."

LAWRENCE (1931, p. 113): "Did Shakespeare mean Angelo to be regarded as a good, though narrow, man, suddenly gone wrong through an overmastering sexual temptation? . . . Or was Angelo a villain from the start, who deceived the Duke as to his real character? I do not imagine that there is any way of settling this point. It is even possible that Shakespeare had not made up his mind about the virtue of Angelo, any more than Thackeray had —in a different sense—about the virtue of Becky Sharp. But it seems more likely that Angelo is to be regarded as having been a smooth rascal, who had been successful in concealing his baseness."

R. W. CHAMBERS (1937; 1939, pp. 283, 287): "The deputy, Angelo, is not so called for nothing. He *is* 'angel on the outward side' [1757]—an ascetic saint in the judgment of his fellow citizens, and despite the meanness of his spirit, nay, because of it, a saint in his own esteem. His soliloquies prove this, and Isabel at the end gives him some credit for sincerity. . . . [*287*] The plot is rather like that of Calderon's *Magician,* where the scholarly, austere Cipriano is overthrown by speaking with the saintly Justina."

SPENCER (1940, p. 302): "In Angelo we have one of Shakespeare's most fascinating portraits. His self-analysis, the contrast between his uncontrollable desires and the gravity of his aspect, 'Wherein (let no man hear me) I take pride' [1210], and the acid-etched delineation in him of a too common type of the successful man, would put this play, even if it were not preoccupied with sex, into the category of the more realistic comedies. Angelo has every appearance of being studied from the life. . . . It is a type of character frequently advanced to executive positions, where it enjoys tyrannizing over less successful, more decent men. For natures like Angelo's are subject to a powerful emotional drive, though such a man tries to conceal it or attempts to turn his passions into the sole channel of ambition. The mask of gravity often impresses and deceives trustees and other appointing officials. Shakespeare is deceived by no one; he has Angelo's number—that is, he sees through men of his stamp."

KNIGHTS (1942, p. 223): "The figure of Angelo, although a sketch rather than a developed character study, is the admitted success of the play. In few but firm lines we are made aware that his boasted self-control is not only a matter of conscious will ('What I will not, that I cannot do' [801]), but of a will taut and strained. . . . It is the unnaturalness and rigidity of his ideal that is insisted on."

DODDS (1946, p. 255): "It is possible to regard *Measure for Measure* as an experiment by Shakespeare: an attempt to handle, in a comedy, a character comparable to the characters of the tragedies. . . . Angelo, like any ordinary character in a comedy, is made to see himself in a new light by the impact of an external accident—in his case, the accident of meeting Isabel. But, unlike the ordinary characters of comedy, he bears the marks of having been imagined intensely in all his complexity and capacity for suffering, just as Shakespeare's tragic characters are imagined, though his suffering is not fully bodied forth."

HARBAGE (1947, pp. 89–91): *"Indictment . . . Angelo is mercenary, a vow-breaker, a hypocrite, cruel, and slanderous. . . .*

[*90*] *"Defense* The charges above would be valid only if Angelo were a corporeal person whose dreams were realities and whose career was followed chronologically. In the play his initial mistreatment of Mariana is presented to us only after he [*91*] has become in our eyes a wicked man. It is, so to speak, a projection of his impure present into his pure past. It does not alter the fact that he was in his own eyes and ours a righteous man acting upon principle at the time he condemned Claudio. His proposal to Isabella is the first offense of a chaste man assailed in his weakest spot. Her very purity incites him, because he values purity so much. . . . The sum of Angelo's guilt is wayward intentions, for which he is publicly humiliated, and which he sincerely repents. . . . The play has a logical ending. Angelo's pardon and marriage to Mariana would have been impossible, however, if Shakespeare had abandoned his method of keeping ethical issues suspended. If he had put one canting phrase into Angelo's mouth—as he puts many into Falstaff's,— if he had made Angelo not *precise* but a *precisian,* there would have been no enigma."

MAXWELL (1949, p. 34): "Sophocles and Shakespeare have in many ways conceived curiously similar figures to face their heroines, and both have received less than justice. Creon [in *Antigone*] is not a conventional tyrant, nor is Angelo a mere self-righteous prig, still less a covert villain who only waits to be exposed. . . . In *Measure for Measure* problems of law and its enforcement are less in the centre of Shakespeare's mind than has sometimes been supposed, but it is essential that Angelo should have a passion which we can respect for the enforcement of justice, and that the conflict should take place over a real offence, though it is one which no one else in the play thinks ought to be a capital one."

SEWELL (1951, pp. 70–1): "The implied agony and the moral seriousness of Angelo's case are such that they cannot be sustained unless he is seen —unless in Shakespeare's vision [*71*] he has been apprehended—as a human soul. For we refuse to accept him either as a study in morbid psychology or as a canting hypocrite. We must conclude, then, that in Angelo Shakespeare has introduced a situation, a case, and a character, intractable to the working out of the comprehensive vision of the play."

BRYANT (1961, pp. 102–3): "The thing that makes Angelo salvageable is that when he comes really to know his lord, he does not try to lie to him. . . . [Quotes 2748–56.] From this point on, Angelo is all contrition and obedience. To make what amends he can, he marries Mariana, he accepts the [*103*] sentence of death imposed upon him, and he confesses his faults to his brother deputy, Escalus [2871–4]. His completeness at what he presumes to be the end of his life merits for him the renewal of his life, not as a matter of right but as a gift of mercy. The dissolution of Angelo's 'goodness' thus has cured the evil that made that goodness accursed. 'Well, Angelo', says the Duke, 'your evil quits you well' [2895]. In him the ancient paradox of the fortunate fall has been proved once more; and if we reject that, we must also reject Shakespeare's play."

MACKAY (1963, p. 113): "There seems no reason, in the text, for presenting Angelo as a sinister, inhibited, creeping, black figure, and every reason to suppose him young and good-looking. Mariana is in love with him and seems even fonder of him in Act V. . . . Only a very young man could take himself so seriously, and the younger he is the more easily we can forgive his original selfish jilting of Mariana. For he is undoubtedly meant to appear as a noble character at the beginning of the play, a noble character who is tempted and who falls. . . . He descends steeply from lust to blackmail and treachery, but he is Lucifer redeemed."

SCHANZER (1963, pp. 85, 92–3): "Angelo's lack of self-knowledge, revealed above all in his first soliloquy [925 ff.], is basic to Shakespeare's conception of his character. Except for the short time at the end of the play in which he dissembles in order to save his skin, he is not a hypocrite, but is rather living up to the ideal of inhumanity which he has set himself. There is therefore nothing incongruous in the fact that even after his treatment of Mariana . . . Angelo can refer to himself in soliloquy as a 'saint' [943]. He is a self-deceiver rather than a deceiver of others. In this he is the opposite of the Duke, who takes pleasure in deceiving others (for good ends), but whose search for self-knowledge is, according to Escalus, his most notable characteristic. . . . The hint for Angelo's lack of self-knowledge seems to have come from Cinthio's *novella,* where Iuriste is described as being 'vie più lieto dell' vfficio, a che il chiamaua lo Imperadore, che buon conoscitore di se stesso [more pleased with the office to which the

Emperor called him than rightly knowing himself (p. 379 above)]'. [*92*]
His ruling attribute is inhumanity in its most literal sense, a total absence of
normal human feelings and desires. . . .

"That Angelo is thus a compendium of the human qualities which
Shakespeare most disliked seems to me undeniable. [*93*] Cruelty, ingratitude, perfidy, judicial tyranny, calculated cunning, Pharisaism, humourless-
ness—the list could easily be prolonged. That in spite of all this we feel a
measure of sympathy towards him even before his repentance at the end
seems largely due to the way in which, in his three soliloquies, we are allowed
to see him suffer and struggle, so that we feel towards him more as we do
towards Macbeth and Claudius than towards Iago and Edmund."

Others who consider Angelo a hypocrite from the first include
INCHBALD (ed. 1808, pp. 4–5), HAZLITT (1817, p. 320), COLERIDGE
(before 1834; ed. Raysor, 1960, 1:102), P. P. (ed. 1822, pp. iv–v),
DANIEL (ed. 1826, pp. 5–7), ULRICI (1839, tr. 1846, pp. 310, 314),
HUGO (ed. 1862, pp. 22–39), HEBLER (1865; 1874, p. 153), WILKES
(1876; 1882, pp. 114–17), JONES (1885, p. 163), THOMPSON (1920,
pp. 235–7), WILSON (1932, p. 116), CAMPBELL (1943, pp. 124–35, and
ed. 1949, pp. 651–5), ELLIS-FERMOR (1945, p. 50), CRAIG (1948, pp.
230–2), FLUCHÈRE (1948, tr. 1953, pp. 217–19), FLIESS (1957, pp. 109–
10), and WEST (1957, pp. 44–8).

Others who consider Angelo a sincere self-deceiver include ULRICI
(1839, tr. 1876, 2:256–63), HUDSON (1848; 1872, 1:410–13), BRAE
(1851, p. 63), SYMONS (1889; 1920, p. 49), CURTIUS (1891, pp. 57–
67), HERFORD (ed. 1899, 3:238–9), COURTHOPE (1903, 4:137–9),
MOULTON (1903; 1907, pp. 146–57), RALEIGH (1907, pp. 167–70),
WOLFF (1907, 2:140–3), ALBRECHT (1914, pp. 247–55), GOULD
(1923, p. 241), GUNDOLF (1928, 2:160–8), RICHTER (1930, pp. 112–
14), SLEETH (1935, pp. 106–7), STOESSL (1935, pp. 303–5), MURRY
(1936, pp. 306–10), REIMER (1937, pp. 7–11), DURHAM (1941, pp.
168–9), KREIDER (1941, pp. 26, 74–5), LEAVIS (1942; 1952, pp. 171–
2), TRAVERSI (1942; 1969, pp. 368–9), RADBRUCH (1944, pp. 41–2),
STEWART (1949, pp. 27–9), SEHRT (1952, pp. 147–58), WEILGART
(1952, pp. 48–50), LASCELLES (1953, pp. 70–4), FLATTER (1956, pp.
137–8), ÉMERY (1957, pp. 40, 72), WASSON (1960, pp. 262–75), URE
(1961, pp. 21–31), KUCKHOFF (1964, pp. 282–98), GROSS (1965, pp.
39–58), LEVER (ed. 1965, pp. xcii–v), MARTIN (1966, pp. 227–44),
TOOLE (1966, pp. 178–80, 189–97, and 1970–1, pp. 21–34), VAN
KAAM & HEALY (1967, pp. 139–67), EDWARDS (1968, pp. 115–18),
FITCH (1969, p. 100), CHAMPION (1970, pp. 128–37), CLEMEN (1972,
pp. 174–5), PARTEE (1973, pp. 275, 281), McCANLES (1975, pp. 200–
6), and MILES (1976, pp. 198–214, 268–9).

Others who consider Angelo a Puritan include BIRCH (1848, pp. 353,
370), LLOYD (in SINGER, ed. 1856, 1:443–4), KREYSSIG (1858–62; 1877,

2:448–52), CHASLES (1867, 2:75), WILKES (1876; 1882, p. 117), BRANDES (1895–6, tr. 1898, 2:70–80), LEVI (1901, 2:120–1), COSENTINO (1906, pp. 205–6, 217), SUDDARD (1909; 1912, pp. 136–52), ALBRECHT (1914, pp. 247–53), THOMPSON (1920, pp. 235–7), QUILLER-COUCH (ed. WILSON, 1922, pp. xli–ii), ABERCROMBIE (1930, p. 146), SMIRNOV (1934, tr. 1936, pp. 81–2), MESSIAEN (1937, pp. 425–7), DANIELS (1938, pp. 40–53), McGINN (1948, pp. 129–39), GRIVELET (ed. 1957, p. 47), SCHANZER (1963, pp. 86–7), HUNTER (1965, pp. 207–26), SIEGEL (1968, pp. 195–8), NOSWORTHY (ed. 1969, pp. 37–9), FISCH (1974, pp. 81–92), and SYPHER (1976, pp. 58–62).

Others who consider Angelo potentially tragic include WENDELL (1894, p. 265), QUILLER-COUCH (ed. WILSON, 1922, p. xlii), RAPIN (1930, pp. 43–5), MESSIAEN (1937, pp. 426–7), RIDLEY (1937, p. 157), SITWELL (1948, pp. 124–5), HALLIDAY (1954, p. 145), LACY (1956), URE (1961, pp. 21–31), HOWARTH (1970, p. 140), KIRCHHEIM (1971, pp. 125–35), VELIE (1972, pp. 38, 56), and BAYLEY (1976, pp. 244–8).

Others who express different views on Angelo include DOUCE (1807, 1:157–60), THÜMMEL (1884, pp. 62–3), RANK (1912; 1926, p. 394), NEWBOLT (1917, pp. 198–9), AINSLIE (1918, pp. 117–18), HERFORD (1921, pp. 39–40), CHAPMAN (1922, p. 83), MATHEW (1922, p. 304), BAKER (1923, pp. 18–23), BRADBROOK (1941, pp. 385–96), SACHS (1942, pp. 63–99), WEBSTER (1942; 1957, pp. 250–1), POPE (1949, pp. 76–80), FRICKER (1951, pp. 98–100), MUTSCHMANN & WENTERSDORF (1952, pp. 286–9), CRUTTWELL (1954, pp. 25, 30–2), COGHILL (1955, pp. 19–20), MIKKELSEN (1958, pp. 261–75), ORNSTEIN (1960, pp. 250–60), KIRSCHBAUM (1962, pp. 119–26), HART (1964, pp. 79–80), GROSS (1965, pp. 39–58), BENNETT (1966, pp. 20–1, 126, 153), MANSELL (1966, pp. 270–84), DONOVAN (1968), NUTTALL (1968, pp. 233–7, 242–8), TOOLE (1970–1, pp. 21–34), ARONSON (1972, pp. 126–50), SIEMON (1972, pp. 438–42), SOELLNER (1972, pp. 215–36), HOY (1974, pp. 89–93), KAULA (1975, pp. 62–73), PATRICK (1976), and VAN LAAN (1978, pp. 85–8).

BARNARDINE

HAZLITT (1817, pp. 321–2): "Barnardine is Caliban transported from Prospero's wizard island to the forests of Bohemia or the prisons of Vienna. He is the creature of bad habits as Caliban is of gross instincts. He has, however, a strong notion of the natural fitness of things, according to his own sensations—'He [*322*] has been drinking hard all night, and he will not be hanged that day' [2121]—and Shakespear has let him off at last."

RALEIGH (1907, pp. 148–9): "All arrangements are made for the substitution, and Barnardine is called forth to his death. Then a strange thing happens. Barnardine, a mere detail of the machinery, comes alive, and so endears himself to his maker, that his execution is felt to be impossible. Even the murderer of Antigonus [in *WT*] has not the heart to put Barnardine to death. A way [*149*] out must be found; the disguised Duke suggests that Barnardine is unfit to die, and the Provost comes in with the timely news that a pirate called Ragozine, who exactly resembles Claudio, has just died in the prison of a fever. So Barnardine, who was born to be hanged, is left useless in his cell, until at the close of the play he is kindly remembered and pardoned. The plot is managed without him; yet, if he were omitted, he would be sadly missed. . . . It is a wonderful portrait of the gentleman vagabond, and is presented by Shakespeare to his audience, a perfect gratuity."

LASCELLES (1953, pp. 111–13): "If Barnardine was really created for no other purpose than to do Claudio *a present and a dangerous courtesy* [2027], it is surely odd that the whole resources of authority in the prison should be engaged in obtaining his compliance; odder still that it should prove unobtainable, and that a character called into being only to die, should survive. . . . Suppose we consider Barnardine as created for survival. Would not that first audience, who *knew their Shakespeare* in the double sense in which we can never know him, receive the fooling between Pompey and Abhorson as an assurance that the happy ending was to be complete? Even if they were momentarily disconcerted by the Duke's [*112*] insistence that Barnardine is to die as soon as he is fit for death, they might recollect that, no sooner was the Duke satisfied of Claudio's readiness for death, than he began to take measures for preserving his life. . . . [*113*] That Barnardine was never intended to die in the play, I am certain. But whether the qualities that have made him deathless in the imagination of many readers were part of Shakespeare's design, or came from that bounty which he could hardly deny any of his creatures—here lies no certainty, nor the hope of any."

LEVER (ed. 1965, p. xc): "The basic need for Barnardine's existence on the stage was surely that he might assert the major truth, that no man's life was so worthless as to be sacrificed to another's convenience. For a vivid moment the Duke, elsewhere the paragon of rulers, is revealed in his fallibility and exposed to the laughter of comedy. Barnardine's appearance and survival demonstrate that, at the level of the individual's right to live, authority must accept its limits."

Others who discuss Barnardine include HAZLITT (1816; 1930, 5:283), CROCE (1920, pp. 265–6), GAW (1933, pp. 93–5), CHARLTON (1938, p. 216), GODDARD (1951, p. 451), BALDINI (1953, pp. 324–30), MCPEEK (1969, pp. 79, 271–3), MAHOOD (1972, p. 174), POWELL (1972, pp. 199–204), and DODGE (1975, pp. 50–2).

CLAUDIO

PATER (1874; 1889, pp. 187–8): "The many veins of thought which render the poetry of this play so weighty and impressive unite in the image of Claudio, a flowerlike young man, whom, prompted by a few hints from Shakspere, the imagination easily clothes with all the bravery of youth, as he crosses the stage before us on his way to death, coming so hastily to the end of his pilgrimage. Set in the horrible blackness of the prison, with its various forms of unsightly death, this flower seems the braver. Fallen by 'prompture of the blood', the victim of a suddenly revived law against the common fault of youth like his, he finds his life forfeited as if by the chance of a lottery. With that instinctive clinging to life, which breaks through the subtlest casuistries of monk or sage apologising for an early death, he welcomes for a moment the chance of life through his sister's shame, though he revolts hardly less from the notion of perpetual im-[*188*]prisonment so repulsive to the buoyant energy of youth. Familiarised, by the words alike of friends and the indifferent, to the thought of death, he becomes gentle and subdued indeed, yet more perhaps through pride than real resignation, and would go down to darkness at last hard and unblinded. Called upon suddenly to encounter his fate, looking with keen and resolute profile straight before him, he gives utterance to some of the central truths of human feeling, the sincere, concentrated expression of the recoiling flesh. Thoughts as profound and poetical as Hamlet's arise in him; and but for the accidental arrest of sentence he would descend into the dust, a mere gilded, idle flower of youth indeed, but with what are perhaps the most eloquent of all Shakspere's words upon his lips."

SCHANZER (1963, p. 80): "Claudio is portrayed by Shakespeare with unfailing sympathy and affection. It is astonishing to find Coleridge describe him as 'detestable' and to hear other critics join in the chorus of abuse. The provost, himself upright and kindly, knows better than they when he calls him 'the most gentle Claudio' [1928], an epithet which Shakespeare never bestows upon characters whom he wishes us to detest. . . . He first reduced the gravity of Claudio's transgression as far as was compatible with his need to make him subject to the death-penalty, and then further increased our sympathies for him by showing his remorse for what he had done."

Others who discuss Claudio include SYMONS (1889; 1920, pp. 45, 48–51), HERFORD (ed. 1899, 3:239), COURTHOPE (1903, 4:137–9), KNIGHTS (1942, pp. 223–8), LEAVIS (1942; 1952, pp. 161–5), LACY (1956), HOLMES (1960, pp. 172–3, and 1972, p. 14), W. D. SMITH (1962, pp. 315–17), LEVER (ed. 1965, pp. lxvii f., lxxv f., lxxix–lxxxii), and KIRCHHEIM (1971, pp. 153–60).

THE DUKE

LENNOX (1753, 1:28–31): "The Duke, who it must be confess'd, has an excellent plotting Brain, gives it out that he is going *incog.* to *Poland,* upon weighty Affairs of State, and substitutes *Angelo* to govern till his Return; to Friar *Thomas* his Confidant, however, he imparts his true Design, which is, in his Absence, to have some severe Laws revived, that had been long disused: Methinks this Conduct is very unworthy of a good Prince; if he thought it fit and necessary to revive those Laws, why does he commit that to another, which it was his Duty to perform? . . .

[*29*] "How comes it to pass, that the Duke is so well acquainted with the Story of *Mariana,* [*30*] to whom *Angelo* was betrothed, but abandoned by him on Account of the Loss of her Fortune? She speaks of the Duke as of a Person she had been long acquainted with. [Quotes 1778–9.] Yet this could only happen while he assumed the Character of a Friar, which was but for two or three Days at most; he could not possibly have been acquainted with her Story before; if he had, the Character of *Angelo* would have been also known to him; and consequently it was unnecessary to make him his Deputy, in order to try him further, which was one of his Reasons, as he tells Friar *Thomas,* for concealing himself. . . . [*31*] The Character of the Duke is absurd and ridiculous."

SCHLEGEL (1809–11, tr. 1846, p. 388): "The Duke acts the part of the Monk naturally, even to deception; he unites in his person the wisdom of the priest and the prince. Only in his wisdom he is too fond of round-about ways; his vanity is flattered with acting invisibly like an earthly providence; he takes more pleasure in overhearing his subjects than governing them in the customary way of princes. As he ultimately extends a free pardon to all the guilty, we do not see how his original purpose, in committing the execution of the laws to other hands, of restoring their strictness, has in any wise been accomplished. The poet might have had this irony in view, that of the numberless slanders of the Duke, told him by the petulant Lucio, in ignorance of the person whom he is addressing, that at least which regarded his singularities and whims was not wholly without foundation."

PORTER (ed. PORTER & CLARKE, 1909, pp. xiii–xiv): "Like a *Deus ex machina,* he sets a crucial test of Angelo that leaves him at liberty to take his own course, and gives him a final chance, moreover, to free or to incriminate himself yet more deeply when he consti-[*xiv*]tutes him his own Judge. The Duke watches the test in all of its effects and cross-relations and forbears to come into the plot to do justice until the critical moment. Meanwhile, he is a very present help in time of trouble. He devises the honest cheat of substituting Mariana for Isabella, repellant to those who dislike a bad name more than a bad thing, as an undeniable proof of the Precisian's lewd iniquity. Isabella's continued denial of Angelo's infamous desires could otherwise never have convicted him. It is part of the dramatic interest of the plot, adroitly made one with its wise ethical purpose, that he institutes the trial of Isabella and Mariana as false witnesses, in order not alone to bring out all intricacies clearly, but generously to give Angelo all the rope he justly needed wherewith to save or hang himself. And so, only when he is irredeemably noosed does the Duke appear openly before him. Like the gods of the drama of Euripides, he comes into the conclusion to bring about the good in an unsuspected manner.

"His dignity and ardor of soul as an independent character is obscured to the unpenetrating by his long-continued disguise and the strictness of his duty to his prescribed rôle of divine inquisitor."

KNIGHT (1930; 1949, p. 79): "The Duke's sense of human responsibility is delightful throughout: he is like a kindly father, and all the rest are his children. Thus he now performs the experiment of handing the reins of government to a man of ascetic purity who has an hitherto invulnerable faith in the rightness and justice of his own ideals—a man of spotless reputation and self-conscious integrity, who will have no fears as to the 'justice' of enforcing precise obedience. The scheme is a plot, or trap: a scientific experiment to see if extreme ascetic righteousness can stand the test of power.

"The Duke, disguised as the Friar, moves through the play, a dark figure, directing, watching, moralizing on the actions of the other persons. As the play progresses and his plot on Angelo works he assumes an ever-increasing mysterious dignity, his original purpose seems to become more and more profound in human insight, the action marches with measured pace to its appointed and logical end. We have ceased altogether to think of the Duke as merely a studious and unpractical governor, incapable of office. Rather he holds, within the dramatic universe, the dignity and power of a Prospero, to whom he is strangely similar. With both, their plot and plan is the plot and plan of the play: they make and forge the play, and thus are automatically to be equated in a unique sense with the poet himself—since both are symbols of the poet's controlling, purposeful, combined, movement of the chess-men of the drama. Like Prospero, the Duke tends to assume proportions evidently divine."

LAWRENCE (1931, pp. 103–6): "The Duke in *Measure for Measure* combines the functions both of State and Church in his person. As Duke, he is supreme ruler of Vienna, who returns at the end to straighten out the tangles of the action, and dispense justice to all. In his disguise as Friar, he represents the wisdom [*104*] and adroitness of the Church, in directing courses of action and advising stratagems so that good may come out of evil. But the plots which he sets in motion and the justice which he dispenses are the stuff of story; they cannot be judged as if they were historical occurrences. And the Duke's character cannot be estimated on a rationalistic basis. . . . No, he knows what is expected of him as a stage Duke, and makes the most of his part. Similarly, in *All's Well,* the King, assisted by Diana, squeezes the last drop of theatrical effectiveness out of the complications at the end of the play.

Of course, as Hart [ed. 1905, p. xxii] complains, the Duke's way of bringing Angelo to justice is 'shifty', and not a straight prosecution. But it is just these shifts which keep the audience alert and interested. Of course the Duke 'plunges into a vortex of scheming and intrigue'; it is this which makes the play. . . . [*105*] Of course he lies when he tells Claudio that as confessor to Angelo he knows that Angelo's purpose is only to try Isabella's virtue; the plot requires that Claudio should believe that he is going to lose his life. It really does seem a little absurd to accuse the Duke of 'transgressing against the confessional'. . . . The Duke, in his capacity as Friar, was telling a falsehood to Claudio in order that the ends of justice (and of effective drama) might be served. He lies for a good purpose again and again. . . . The counsels of a stage friar are, however, *ipso facto* holy and [*106*] just, and to be obeyed without question."

R. W. CHAMBERS (1937; 1939, p. 282): "Shakespeare puts into the Duke's mouth a speech on Death which might have been uttered by Hamlet; and Shakespeare seems to have meant us to regard him as a man of Hamlet's thoughtful, scholarly type, but older, with much experience of government and of war: no longer 'courtier, soldier, scholar', but 'statesman, soldier, scholar'; yet still rather melancholy and distrustful of himself. Shakespeare, however, did not depict him with that intensity which makes his greatest characters come alive. The Duke remains somewhat impersonal, a controlling force; we never think of him by his name, Vincentio. . . . Very truly he has been described [ANON., 1931, p. 554] as rather a power than a character. So far from 'shirking his proper responsibility' [QUILLER-COUCH in WILSON, ed. 1922, p. xxxiv], he controls the fate of all the characters in the play."

WEBSTER (1942; 1957, pp. 249–50): "Shakespeare knew, and no doubt counted upon, the interpretative possibilities of silence. The Duke does quite a lot of listening and quite a lot of learning as he listens; there is, further, much ironic humour implicit in his actual lines. He is dispassionate; he has the power to end all the threatened evils of the play or, rather, to resolve its immediate problems in terms of a pattern roughly just. . . . [*250*] He is, supremely, a part for an actor of imagination who has the ability to project unspoken thought."

BATTENHOUSE (1946, pp. 1054–5): "In *Measure for Measure* the key personage is Vincentio, and there are two stands from which to estimate his character: one natural, the other supernatural. From the natural point of view Escalus calls him 'a gentleman of all temperance' [1723]: he seems to have the golden mean. . . . Supernaturally viewed, he fulfils the portrait of the ideal prince, described by Isaiah as the prince of four names: Wonderful Counsellor, Mighty God, Everlasting Father, Prince of Peace. For we see him offering counsel to the distressed, exercising just power like a mighty God, disciplining and car-[*1055*]ing for his kingdom like a father, and blessing his kingdom with peace. . . . In Shakespeare's play, so it seems to me, justice, charity, and wisdom are all present, centered in the Duke and richly exhibited in the plotted peace and merciful comedy which he effects. The happy ending is one which may be not inaptly described by borrowing words from Isaiah and St. Luke: there is release for the captive Claudio, a recovering of sight for the blind Angelo, a setting at liberty the bruised Mariana, and a proclaiming of the acceptable year of the lord Vincentio. The mysterious 'star' mentioned in the play [2069] has called up a 'shepherd' who has brought all his sheep safely home; and at the same time the great leviathan has been caught."

STAUFFER (1949, pp. 142, 160): "With the exception of *The Tempest,* this is Shakespeare's only play in which a character is allowed to play God. The Duke Vincentio is in complete control, directing all events, knowing the consequences of each person's actions, meting out deserts, and aware, like divinity, of unspoken thoughts and instincts. His rôle as an omniscient and unerring force keeps him from being convincing as a character, and tends to turn the drama into a morality play. Or into a 'problem' play in which this Duke of dark corners sets a number of problems as experiments which various characters must work out for their own salvation. . . .

[*160*] "Vincentio, then, is more than a human Duke of Vienna. . . . He speaks of what he represents in the third person, as if he himself were a mere instrument. He is grace beyond the reach of dramatic art, a hint of the Christian mystery which makes 'heavenly comforts of despair when it is least expected' [2196–7]. When he says to Isabella, 'for your lovely sake, Give me your hand and say you will be mine' [2891–2], we are not witnessing the perfunctory happy ending of a bitter comedy, but the acceptance of a pure human aspiration by a more than mortal power."

EMPSON (1951, pp. 280–3): "The pomposity of the man he [Sh.] probably found natural, but the touchiness, the confidence in error, the self-indulgence of his incessant lying, must I think always have been absurd. . . .

[*281*] "It seems hard not to regard him as a comic character. Indeed the play gives us a sufficiently memorable phrase to sum him up; he is 'the old fantastical Duke of Dark Corners' [2249–50]. . . . [*282*] What makes the Duke ridiculous on the stage is the fuss he makes about the backbiting of Lucio. . . . In the final scene, the mutual petty accusations of Lucio and the Duke, working up to 'yet here's one in place I cannot pardon' [2898], are good farce and nothing else. . . .

[*283*] "What is really offensive about the Duke is . . . that he should treat his subjects as puppets for the fun of making them twitch. But here, I suppose, the Character is saved by the Plot. It seems a peculiarly brutal flippancy that he should not only trick Isabella about Claudio unnecessarily but take pains to thrust the imagined death of Claudio upon her mind. . . . He is playing at being God."

GODDARD (1951, pp. 438, 444): "The Duke is as introspective as

Hamlet, 'one that, above all other strifes, contended especially to know himself' [1718–19], and his theatrical instinct also reminds us of the Prince of Denmark, though in his fondness for dazzling his audience he is more like Hal. In spite of his professed love of retirement and hatred of crowds and applause, he is the very reverse of a hermit, and intends (though he doesn't announce the fact in advance and may even be unconscious of it) to burst forth out of the clouds of disguise in full dramatic glory, as he does in the fifth act. His whole plan may be viewed as a sort of play within a play to catch the conscience of his deputy—and of the city. . . . It is as if the Duke were saying to himself: 'Granted that my dispensation has been too lenient; I'll show you what will happen under a paragon of strictness. See how you like it then!' . . .

[*444*] "The only way to make the Duke morally acceptable is frankly to take the whole piece as a morality play with the Duke in the role of God, omniscient and unseen, looking down on the world. . . . If Shakespeare wants us to take it so, the execution of his intention is not especially successful. But we may at any rate say there is a morality play lurking behind *Measure for Measure.*"

EVANS (1960, pp. 200, 218): "A benevolent power, becoming ever more godlike, the Duke is concerned for Isabella and Angelo as for the rest of Vienna. Were he to give up the masquerade, neither would be saved. Isabella would withdraw to the nunnery, where an enduring rage at Angelo and Claudio would remain her only human indulgence. As for Angelo, arrested in his course, his blood would again congeal. The Duke's task is grander than merely the saving of Claudio's life: it is the salvation of Angelo and Isabella, and that, in these cases, amounts to the humanization of two 'saints'.

"To carry out the purpose he must continue the masquerade. His use of the abandoned Mariana would be an absurdly inefficient method which would hardly occur to him if his purpose were only to free Claudio. The direct way to accomplish that end would be to take off his hood and speak to the Provost. *But Mariana provides a way for the salvation of everyone in need of salvation.* Much is in the Duke's mind when he tells Isabella of Mariana's plight. From his suggestion that she will at least be able to do 'uprighteously' what she is asked to do, he advances gingerly in the education of Isabella's humanity. . . .

[*218*] "It has taken much time, shrewd deception, and sharp nudging at the last moment, but the proof is won on the Duke's uncompromising terms. Working in mysterious ways, he has transformed an erstwhile 'saint' into a creature of human sympathies and forced her to demonstrate them against odds. She who had once shrieked refusal—'Might but my bending down'—to save her brother's life has at last humbly knelt to beg mercy for one who, she believes, has done her terrible wrong."

URE (1961, p. 30): "When the Duke withdraws from Vienna in order to put Angelo to the test, his action accords with his role as deputy of heaven, until we learn that after all he was fully informed about Angelo's entanglement with Mariana from the beginning; and then his action begins to look more consistent with that of a man who wishes to set off a story. When he tells Claudio that he must in any case die, or refrains from telling Isabella that Claudio is living still, it is foolish to blame him for cruelty, but proper to note that the reasons for his actions may include both power's prerogative to subject brother and sister to a final trial and the dramatist's need for a fine *dénouement* and a striking *coup de théâtre.* When he spares Barnardine, the condemned and dissolute felon in Claudio's prison, he does so as a merciful ruler who believes him unfit for death, and yet is at the same time acting as the guardian of comedy, by whose laws it would outrage us that any man (especially so vivid a one as Barnardine) should die. In all this, it is difficult to declare whether Shakespeare is saying that Providence is a kind of story-teller, or that a storyteller is a kind of Providence."

W. D. SMITH (1962, pp. 319–21): "Shakespeare's duke is more than a Renaissance stereotype, just as he is more interesting than merely an 'omniscient and unerring force' [STAUFFER, 1949, p. 142]. Neither puppet nor supernatural being, Vincentio is a living man who—while effecting the changes for the better in Isabella, Claudio, and Angelo—himself undergoes a more subtle but equally unmistakable alteration in perspective. . . . [*320*] The duke, to be sure, is in no need of the kind of over-all reformation undergone by Angelo, Isabella, and Claudio; but at the end of the play he too changes somewhat. . . . The change in Vincentio seems to be purposeful, revealing growth in [*321*] stature from the 'shy' duke of the early scenes to the masterful public leader at the close."

FREEDMAN (1964, pp. 33–4, 37): "The Duke's extraordinary consciousness of and concern for reputation, his own and that of others, is first made clear in Act I, Scene 3. . . . [*34*] In the first place, . . . the Duke seems to regret his current reputation, but at the same time is concerned that his name not be stained in the process of restoring order to his city. Secondly, he is interested in discovering whether Angelo's reputation for staunch rectitude, so much stronger than his own, be truly deserved. If we keep in mind the Duke's dissatisfaction with the public image he has thus far created of himself along with his desire to restore order without injuring his name, we may have a key to many of his otherwise quite puzzling actions. . . . [*37*] A public device, such as the final scene is, represents the Duke's attempt to restore order to his subjects on the basis of an increased respect for their sovereign as well as an increased understanding of the nature of true justice."

BENNETT (1966, p. 126): "The Duke's is a great part, and a difficult one to act. The action is kept firmly on the human level. He is no Prospero, no wizard. He is neither omnipotent nor omniscient, since he is sometimes mistaken; and he saves the situation by his cleverness, not by his power. On the other hand, the whole play, and especially the last act, provides the actor of this part with magnificent opportunity for a display of his skill."

HAMILTON (1970, p. 175): "Contrary to the most widely accepted critical views, the Duke is neither a *deus ex machina* nor an omnipotent power who brings mercy and grace to his people. While he plans the activities of the last scene, his plan is not carried out; and he must learn along with the other citizens of Vienna the meaning of mercy and the kinds of demands which mercy makes. Shakespeare's Duke, a more complex character than many have admitted, functions structurally to repeat the actions and extend the implications of the main issues raised throughout the play. When the Duke's actions are considered in these terms, there will be little difficulty in accepting the ending as both morally and aesthetically satisfying."

Others who consider the Duke a wise ruler include ULRICI (1839, tr. 1876, 2:155–8), GERVINUS (1849–50, tr. 1875, pp. 487–90, 501–4), BRANDES (1895–6, tr. 1898, 2:72–80), GENÉE (1905, pp. 307–8), COSENTINO (1906, pp. 207–16), ALBRECHT (1914, pp. 256–73), CRAIG (1948, pp. 230, 235), POPE (1949, pp. 66–82), POGSON (1950, pp. 58–69), SCHIEDER (1951, pp. 163–5), SEHRT (1952, pp. 175–92), H. S. WILSON (1953, pp. 375–84), HOLMES (1960, pp. 175–7), WASSON (1960, pp. 262–75), GROSS (1965, pp. 59–146), LEVER (ed. 1965, pp. lxx–xcvii), GRUDIN (1970), TOOLE (1970–1, pp. 31–5), MORGAN (1972), ROSENHEIM (1976), and WEISER (1977, pp. 335–45).

Others who consider the Duke a manipulator or experimenter include KNIGHT (ed. 1840; 1849, p. 319), HUDSON (1872, 1:416–19), MOULTON (1903; 1907, pp. 148–57), THALER (1929, pp. 86–90), VAN DOREN (1939, pp. 217–19), LEAVIS (1942; 1952, pp. 163–70), CAMPBELL (1943, pp. 125–35, and ed. 1949, pp. 651–5), SEN GUPTA (1950, pp. 187–90), FRICKER (1951, pp. 60–4), FERGUSSON (1952; 1957, pp. 132–43), LASCELLES (1953, pp. 142–8), H. S. WILSON (1953, pp. 381–3), LÜTHI (1957, p. 264), DUNKEL (1962, pp. 280–5), RIGHTER (1962, pp. 176–80), HOLLAND (1964, pp. 218, 230–1), HUNTER (1965, pp. 206–25), COURSEN (1966), D'AMICO (1966), WELLS (1966, pp. 114–18), LEIGHTON (1969, pp. 36–7), MURRAY (1969, p. 133), CHAMPION (1970, pp. 146–52), FLOWER (1971), RICHMOND (1971, p. 156), THOMPSON (1971, pp. 115–16), DURRANT (1972, pp. 26–7), HAWKINS (1972, pp. 62–77), SOELLNER (1972, pp. 227–36), SWADLEY (1972), ALLMAN (1973), BARTON (in EVANS, ed. 1974, pp. 547–9), BILTON (1974, pp. 131–7), HUBBUCH (1974), KIRSCH (1975, pp. 103–5), SIEMON (1975, pp. 105–23), STEGE (1975), TARSITANO (1975), VINCENT (1975), HAILEY (1976), HAMILL (1976), SYPHER (1976, pp. 57–62), VELZ (1976, p. 33), and VAN LAAN (1978, pp. 89, 94–101).

Others who consider the Duke an inconsistent character include HART (ed. 1905, pp. xxii–iii), QUILLER-COUCH (in WILSON, ed. 1922, pp.

xxxiii f.), DURHAM (1941, p. 171), TILLYARD (1949, pp. 132–6), NUT-
TALL (1968, pp. 231–51), and MILES (1976, pp. 167, 172–96).

Others who suggest that the Duke represents Providence include HE-
RAUD (1865, pp. 280–92), KOHLER (1883–4; 1919, pp. 163–4), SYMONS
(1889; 1920, pp. 44–5), CHAMBERS (ed. 1906; 1925, pp. 215–16), GUN-
DOLF (1928, 2:170–7), ANON. (1931, p. 554), REIMER (1937, pp. 11–12,
96–9), BRADBROOK (1941, pp. 385–99), LEAVIS (1942; 1952, p. 170),
F. P. WILSON (1945, p. 118), POPE (1949, p. 71), PARKER (1955, pp.
117–19), SPEAIGHT (1960, pp. 70–8), URE (1961, pp. 29–32), HOLLAND
(1964, pp. 218, 229), TOOLE (1966, pp. 181–97), MURRAY (1969, pp.
26–8), OWEN (1974, pp. 20–32), and BABULA (1975, p. 99).

Others who suggest that the Duke resembles James I include CHALMERS
(1799, p. 404), KNIGHT (ed. 1840; 1849, p. 319), LLOYD (in SINGER, ed.
1856, 1:439–49), GARNETT (1889, p. 564), GENÉE (1905, pp. 307–8),
ALBRECHT (1914, pp. 164–216), KELLER (1918, pp. xxiv–vi), THOMPSON
(1920, p. 232), WINSTANLEY (1921, pp. 99 f.), BRANDL (1922, p. 354),
ECKHARDT (1928, p. 189), BRADBROOK (1941, p. 386), LEFRANC (1945,
2:77–84), POPE (1949, pp. 70–80), SHEDD (1953), NATHAN (1956, pp.
43–5), STEVENSON (1959, pp. 188–208), SCHANZER (1963, pp. 120–6),
ALEXANDER (1964, p. 152, and 1967, pp. 478–88), GROSS (1965, pp.
59–146), HOWARTH (1965; 1970, pp. 120–37), LEVER (ed. 1965, pp.
xlviii–l), BENNETT (1966, pp. 79–103), MINCOFF (1966, p. 149), ROSE
(1966, pp. 72–82), DRAPER (1969, pp. 5–9), and HAMBURGER (1969, pp.
158–67). This view is opposed by LASCELLES (1953, pp. 108–9) and LEVIN
(1974, *Clio,* pp. 129–63, and *PMLA,* pp. 302–11).

Others who think that the Duke changes and learns during the play
include SNIDER (1875, pp. 313–25), SPALDING (1953, pp. 128–9), HETH-
MON (1962, pp. 270–7), RIGHTER (1962, p. 180), M. B. SMITH (1966, pp.
154–5), KAUFMANN (1967, pp. 87, 93–6), NOSWORTHY (ed. 1969, pp.
21–3), BECKERMAN (1970, pp. 116–32), POWELL (1972, pp. 183–6, 196–
209), and PARTEE (1973, p. 274).

Others who express different views on the Duke include HAZLITT
(1817, p. 321), P. P. (ed. 1822, pp. iii–iv), HORN (1827, 4:222–4, and
1831, 5:258–62), SNIDER (1875, pp. 313–25), RALEIGH (1907, p. 167),
HARRIS (1909, pp. 36–46), RAPIN (1930, pp. 44–6), MURRY (1936, pp.
306–10), BRADBROOK (1941, pp. 385–99), WATSON (1941, pp. 33–41),
TRAVERSI (1942; 1969, pp. 375–81), BETHELL (1944, p. 107), LEECH
(1950, pp. 67–71, and 1964, pp. 101–14), FRYE (1953, pp. 275–6),
NAGARAJAN (1953, pp. 1–9), AXELRAD (1955, pp. 231–2), COGHILL
(1955, p. 21), BROWN (1957, pp. 193–4), GRIVELET (ed. 1957, pp. 48–
54), HOLLAND (1959, pp. 16–20), ORNSTEIN (1960, pp. 255–9), ROS-
SITER (1961, pp. 156, 164–8), HETHMON (1962, pp. 269–71), MARSH
(1963, pp. 31–8), WAIN (1964, pp. 96–8), COLE (1965, pp. 425–51),
FERGUSSON (1968, pp. 117–20), SALE (1968, pp. 55–61), BOND (1970,

pp. 43–5), GELB (1971, pp. 25–34), ROSENBERG (1972, pp. 51–72), ANTALOCY (1976), and WOLF (1976, p. 33).

ELBOW

WHITE (1854, pp. 117–18): "I cannot agree with those who find in *Elbow* only a feeble imitation of *Dogberry.* He has nothing in common with the guardian of Messina, except his ignorance. . . . [*118*] *Elbow* lacks the force and self-possession of *Dogberry.* Feeble-minded, modest, and well meaning, as well as ignorant, he is rather the type of 'goodman *Verges'* [in *Ado*] in his youth."

Others who discuss Elbow include LATHAM (1896, p. 146), FRASURE (1934, pp. 388–9), G. R. SMITH (1965, pp. 75–7), EVANS (1969, pp. 427–33), KIRCHHEIM (1971, pp. 167–8), and ROBERTS (1975, pp. 133–4).

ESCALUS

ULRICI (1839, tr. 1846, p. 312): "Æscalus stands by the side of Angelo like the mild, peaceful, and aged sage, by impetuous and energetic manhood: his long years have taught and purified him, and he no longer mistakes proud pretension for virtue, nor rigour for justice. His part is indispensable as an organic counterpoise to Angelo; and partly as a mean between him and the Duke. For the Duke and Isabella stand far higher than he does; they have the grace of God with them, while he possesses nothing more than human experience and compassion."

SCHANZER (1963, pp. 116–17): "It is Escalus who in this play illustrates the *via media* between the two excesses in the administration of justice. He possesses the proper mixture of severity and mercy which marks the ideal judge. He is 'accounted a merciful man', as Mrs. Overdone tells him, but in this very scene he shows that he can also be severe: 'Away with her to prison. Go to; no more words' [1692–3]. The Elbow-Pompey-Froth scene, excellent comedy though it is, seems to have been introduced mainly to show the ideal judge at work. Escalus is full of patience, humanity, and tolerance, in sharp contrast to Angelo. . . . [*117*] Escalus's true mercy is contrasted both with the 'devilish mercy' of Angelo and the dangerous mercy formerly exercised by the Duke."

BECKERMAN (1970, pp. 118–19, 131): "In his decision on Pompey, Escalus illustrates the very thing the Duke had always done: sticking 'the threatening twigs of birch' in his subjects' sight, but not using them. Though made to look a fool by Pompey, Escalus is certainly not a fool. He realizes his failure at the end of the scene when a figure called Justice echoes Escalus' plea for moderation by asserting, 'Lord Angelo is severe' [725]. [*119*] Why the Duke chose Angelo over Escalus is now apparent. Escalus is too much like him. Although Escalus can see the need for rigour, he vacillates, lamenting, 'yet poor Claudio'. Escalus clearly embodies the lenient way, which the Duke now rejects. . . .

[*131*] "Escalus says of Isabel, 'I will go darkly to work with her' [2657]. In taking this tack, he is a throwback to the Duke who would have dark things darkly answered. . . . Escalus, as substitute Duke in the passage just cited, suggests the Duke investigating himself."

Others who discuss Escalus include THÜMMEL (1883, p. 139), MOULTON (1903; 1907, pp. 148, 150, 155), SLEETH (1935, p. 107), DICKINSON (1962, pp. 294–7), and ALTIERI (1974, pp. 15–16).

FROTH

The only writer to say much about Froth is CLARKE (1863, pp. 507–9).

ISABEL

LENNOX (1753, 1:32): "The Character of *Isabella* in the Play seems to be an Improvement upon that of *Epitia* in the Novel; for *Isabella* absolutely refuses, and persists in her Refusal, to give up her Honour to save her Brother's Life; whereas *Epitia,* overcome by her own Tenderness of Nature, and the affecting Prayers of the unhappy Youth, yields to what her Soul abhors, to redeem him from a shameful Death. It is certain however, that *Isabella* is a mere Vixen in her Virtue; how she rates her wretched Brother, who gently urges her to save him!"

MURPHY (1757, p. 215): "In Isabella's Character there is a fine Variety of Passions, and a beautiful Struggle between her Virtue and her tender Sentiments for her Brother."

JOHNSON (ed. 1765, 1:321): "In *Isabella's* declamation [to Claudio] there is something harsh, and something forced and far-fetched. But her indignation cannot be thought violent when we consider her not only as a virgin but as a nun."

RICHARDSON (1788; 1789, pp. 66–7, 69–70): "Isabella is represented . . . blameless, amiable, and affectionate: she is particularly distinguished by intellectual ability. Her understanding and good-sense are conspicuous: her arguments are well-applied, and her pleading persuasive. Yet her abilities do not offend by appearing too masculine: they are mitigated and finely blended with female softness. If she venture to argue, it is to save the life of a brother. [*67*] Even then, it is with such reluctance, hesitation, and diffidence, as need to be urged and encouraged. . . .

[*69*] "Isabella is not only sensible and persuasive, but sagacious, and capable of becoming address. In communicating to her brother the unworthy designs of Angelo, she seems aware of his weakness; she is not rash nor incautious, but gives her intimation by degrees, and with studied dexterity. . . .

439

[*70*] "Neither is it incongruous, but a fine tint in the character, that she feels indignation, and expresses it strongly. But it is not indignation against an adversary; it is not on account of injury; it is a disinterested emotion: it is against a brother who does not respect himself; who expresses pusillanimous sentiments; and would have her act in an unworthy manner.—Such is the amiable, pious, sensible, resolute, determined, and eloquent Isabella."

DRAKE (1817, 2:454): "Of *Measure for Measure,* independent of the comic characters which afford a rich fund of entertainment, the great charm springs from the lovely example of female excellence in the person of Isabella. Piety, spotless purity, tenderness combined with firmness, and an eloquence most persuasive, unite to render her singularly interesting and attractive."

HAZLITT (1817, pp. 320–1): "Neither are we greatly enamoured of Isabella's rigid chastity, though she could not act otherwise than she did. We do not feel the same confidence in the virtue that is 'sublimely good' at another's expense, [*321*] as if it had been put to some less disinterested trial."

JAMESON (1832; 1879, pp. 65, 73): "Isabella is distinguished from Portia, and strongly individualized by a certain moral grandeur, a saintly grace, something of vestal dignity and purity, which render her less attractive and more imposing. . . .

[*73*] "Nor should we fail to remark the deeper interest which is thrown round Isabella, by one part of her character. . . . It is the strong undercurrent of passion and enthusiasm flowing beneath this calm and saintly self-possession, it is the capacity for high feeling and generous and strong indignation veiled beneath the sweet austere composure of the religious recluse, which, by the very force of contrast, powerfully impress the imagination. As we see in real life that where, from some external or habitual cause, a strong controul is exercised over naturally quick feelings and an impetuous temper, they display themselves with a proportionate vehemence when that restraint is removed; so the very violence with which her passion bursts forth, when opposed or under the influence of strong excitement, is admirably characteristic."

COLERIDGE (before 1834; ed. Raysor, 1936, p. 49): "I confess that Isabella, of all Shakespeare's female characters, interests me the least."

WHITE (1854, pp. 135, 149–50): "The poet has given us one marvellously faithful, and yet ideal portrait of the woman sometimes, and, heaven be thanked, but rarely, seen, who is compounded solely of intellect and a sense of propriety. This woman makes piety her employment, and chastity her profession. . . . She is a pietist in her religion, a pedant in her talk, a prude in her notions, and a prig in her conduct. This is the sort of woman which alone could furnish a proper companion portrait to *Angelo.* . . .

[*149*] "*Isabella* is a woman with too much brain or too little heart. A woman cannot have too fine an intellect, or one too large, if, only, her affections be finer and larger; but [*150*] the moment that she shows an excess

of the first, she becomes unfeminine, repulsive, monstrous. Shakespeare has given us an ideal of every type of man and womankind; and he could not pass by this. . . . He drew an *Iago* and an *Angelo* among men; among women, why should he withhold his hand from a *Lady Macbeth* and an *Isabella?*"

HUDSON (1872, 1:409, 414): "Her reproaches were indeed too harsh, if they sprang from want of love; but such is evidently not the case. The truth is, she is in a very hard struggle between affection and principle: she needs, and she hopes, to have the strain upon her womanly fortitude lightened by the manly fortitude of her brother; and her harshness of reproof discovers the natural workings of a tender and deep affection, in an agony of disappointment at being urged, by one for whom she would die, to an act which she shrinks from with noble horror, and justly considers worse than death. So that we here have the keen anguish of conflicting feelings venting itself in a severity which, though unmerited, serves to disclose the more impressively her nobleness of character. . . . [*414*] With great strength of intellect and depth of feeling she unites an equal power of imagination, the whole being pervaded, quickened, and guided by a still, intense religious enthusiasm. . . . Accordingly her character appears to me among the finest, in some respects the very finest, in Shakespeare's matchless cabinet of female excellence."

PATER (1874; 1889, pp. 184–6): "At first Isabella comes upon the scene as a tranquillising influence in it. But Shakspere, in the development of the action, brings quite different and unexpected qualities out of her. It is his characteristic poetry to expose this cold, chastened personality, respected even by the worldly Lucio . . . , to two sharp, shameful trials, and [w]ring out of her a fiery, revealing eloquence. Thrown into the terrible dilemma of the piece, called upon to sacrifice that cloistral whiteness to sisterly affection, become in a moment the ground of strong, contending passions, she developes a new character and shows herself suddenly of kindred with those strangely conceived women, like Webster's Vittoria, who unite to a seductive sweetness something of a dangerous and tigerlike changefulness of feeling. The swift, vindictive anger leaps, like a white flame, into this white spirit, and, stripped in a moment of all convention, she stands before us clear, detached, columnar. . . . [*185*] The stream of ardent natural affection, poured as sudden hatred upon the youth condemned to die, adds an additional note of expression to the horror of the prison where so much of the [*186*] scene takes place. It is not here only that Shakspere has conceived of such extreme anger and pity as putting a sort of genius into simple women, so that their 'lips drop eloquence', and their intuitions interpret that which is often too hard or fine for manlier reason; and it is Isabella with her grand imaginative diction, and that poetry laid upon the 'prone and speechless dialect' [276] there is in mere youth itself, who gives utterance to the equity, the finer judgments of the piece on men and things."

DOWDEN (1875, pp. 82–4): "At the entrance to the dark and dangerous tragic world into which Shakspere was now about to pass stand the figures of Isabella and of Helena,—one the embodiment of conscience, the other the embodiment of will. Isabella is the only one of Shakspere's women whose heart and eye are fixed upon an impersonal ideal, to whom something abstract is more, in the ardour and energy of youth, than any human personality. . . . Isabella's saintliness is not of the passive, timorous, or merely meditative kind. It is an active pursuit of holiness through exercise and discipline. . . . [*83*] And as she has strength to accept pain and death for herself rather than dishonour, so she can resolutely accept pain and death for those who are dearest to her. . . . [*84*] She accepts her place as Duchess of Vienna. In this there is no dropping away, through love of pleasure or through supineness, from her ideal; it is entirely meet and right. She has learned that in the world may be found a discipline more strict, more awful than the discipline of the convent; she has learned that the world has need of her."

RUSKIN (1882; 1906, 25:416): "Isabel. All earthly love, and the possibilities of it, held in absolute subjection to the laws of God, and the judgments of His will. She is Shakespeare's only 'Saint'. "

RALEIGH (1907, pp. 170–71): "Is the meaning of the play centred in the part of Isabella? She is severe, and beautiful, and white with an absolute whiteness. Yet it seems that even she is touched now and again by Shakespeare's irony. She stands apart, and loses sympathy as an angel might lose it, by seeming to have too little stake in humanity. . . . [*171*] She is an ascetic by nature, and some of the Duke's remarks on the vanity of self-regarding virtue, though they are addressed to Angelo, seem to glance delicately at her. . . . It is not by accident that Shakespeare calls Isabella back from the threshold of the nunnery, and after passing her through the furnace of trial, marries her to the Duke. She too, like Angelo, is redeemed for worldly uses."

QUILLER-COUCH (in WILSON, ed. 1922, pp. xxx f.): "We grant . . . that hers (as opposed to Cassandra's in the original) was the righteous choice. Still, it has to be admitted that she is something rancid in her chastity; and, on top of this, not by any means such a saint as she looks. To put it nakedly, she is all for saving her own soul, and she saves it by turning, of a sudden, into a bare procuress. . . . [*xxxi*] We have no doubt that it lay within Shakespeare's power, at its best, to create an Isabella who should make the refusal and yet keep our sympathy along with our admiration. In the play, as we have it, he has not done this; and the trouble, to our thinking, lies *in his failure to make Isabella a consistent character.*"

KNIGHT (1930; 1949, pp. 92–3): "Isabella lacks human feeling. . . . Lucio has to urge her on continually. We begin to feel that Isabella has no real affection for Claudio; has stifled all human love in pursuit of sanctity. . . . The Shakespearian satire here [1198–9] strikes once, and deep: there is no need to point it further. But now we know our Isabel. We are not surprised that she behaves to Claudio, who hints for her sacrifice, like a fiend [quotes 1364–8]. [*93*] Is her fall any less than Angelo's? Deeper, I think. . . . Her sex inhibitions have been horribly shown her as they are, naked.

. . . In a way, it is not her fault. Chastity is hardly a sin—but neither, as the play emphasizes, is it the whole of virtue. And she, like the rest, has to find a new wisdom. Mariana in the last act prays for Angelo's life. Confronted by that warm, potent, forgiving, human love, Isabella herself suddenly shows a softening, a sweet humanity. . . . Isabella, like Angelo, has progressed far during the play's action: from sanctity to humanity."

SISSON (1934, pp. 58–9): "Let there be no mistake about this; Shakespeare sets up Isabella as a heroine, who represents something in womanhood which Shakespeare, no less than Lucio in this play, reveres with all his heart. Nothing but a pseudo-romantic sentimentalism, utterly alien to the spirit of Shakespeare and of Elizabethan England, could fail to understand the rightness of Isabella and the reality of her dilemma. What we are pleased to call enlightenment to-day seeks to evade the embarrassing notion of sin, and is naturally anxious to enrol Shakespeare among its adepts. But sin, and deadly sin at that, is fundamental in Christian thought. . . . [59] And Isabella was a novice of St. Clare. She could plead for mercy for Claudio, both from temporal and eternal justice, but could not pray for herself in like case. We must not pick and choose with Shakespeare's characters or with Christianity. We must not, for example, applaud Isabella's heavenly plea to Angelo on behalf of Claudio, because we approve of the Christian promise of mercy, and in the same breath condemn her faithfulness to what is no less integral a part of Christianity, though less fashionable to-day. In a word, it is Isabella's soul that is at stake. Her life she makes nothing of, and would be ready to sacrifice it for her brother 'as frankly as a pin' [1323]. To describe her, as does Professor Abercrombie [1930, p. 146], as a type of 'true puritanism', is to confuse puritanism with virtue, a confusion which Sir Toby indignantly reprehended. Change 'puritanism' to 'purity', and we are nearer the truth. The very rake Lucio in this play, who so deeply offends prudish refinement, is the most loyal of friends, and also venerates true virtue. Far from being rotten, the play is sound to the core, and profoundly Christian in spirit. Isabella is one of Shakespeare's greatest creations, hardly to be excelled among his characters of women even by Cleopatra."

ELLIS-FERMOR (1936, p. 262): "What seals our impression of a world-order ineradicably corrupted and given over to evil is the character of Isabella, where the same method is followed as in that of Angelo, but with a mingling of the elements so much deeper as to call in question the sanctity of religion, sex, marriage and even 'the holiness of the heart's affections'. . . . Hard as an icicle she visits Claudio in prison and lays before him the terms and her decision. She does right to 'fear' him, for primitive humanity is at all times stronger in him than in her. But because of her very inhumanity she can watch unmoved while he faces the awful realization of immediate death, her pitilessness only growing with his pleading. Weak as he is, his self-indulgence cannot stand comparison with hers, with the pitiless, unimaginative, self-absorbed virtue which sustains her."

R. W. CHAMBERS (1937; 1939, pp. 286–7, 290, 292, 307): "Never does Shakespeare seem more passionately to identify himself with any of his characters than he does with Isabel, as she pleads for mercy against strict justice. . . . [*287*] If we fail to see the nobility of Isabel, we cannot see the story as we should. . . .

[*290*] "Isabel then, as Shakespeare sees her and asks us to see her, would frankly, joyously, give her life to save Claudio: and *'greater love hath no man than this'.* And now Claudio is asking for what she cannot give, and she bursts out in agony. Have the critics never seen a human soul or a human body in the extremity of torment? Physical torture Isabel thinks she could have stood without flinching. She has said so to Angelo [quotes 1109–12]. . . . To suppose that Shakespeare gave these burning words to Isabel so that we should perceive her to be selfish and cold, is to suppose that he did not know his job. The honour of her family and her religion are more to her than mere life, her own or Claudio's. . . .

[*292*] "The fierceness of Isabel's words is the measure of the agony of her soul. . . . And it is our fault if we don't see that Isabel is suffering martyrdom none the less because her torment is mental, not physical. . . .

[*307*] "No woman in Shakespeare is more individual than Isabel: silent yet eloquent, sternly righteous yet capable of infinite forgiveness, a very saint and a very vixen. But, first and last, she 'stands for' mercy."

TRAVERSI (1942; 1969, pp. 370–1): "Isabella's virtue, though standing at the other extreme from Angelo's, is related to it by a common foundation in inexperience. When the play opens, she is about to take her vows of profession as a nun. The fact is in itself significant. Virtue in *Measure for Measure* is habitually on its guard, defending itself by withdrawal against the temptations that so insistently beset it. . . . [*371*] If Isabella's virtue does not fully satisfy, that is not primarily through any obvious moral deficiency in her own nature . . . but simply because the state of simple virtue does not exist in *Measure for Measure.* Chastity there is surrounded by reservations not of its own making, flaws related to the flesh and inherent in the human situation. If Isabella has any fault, it is that she is unaware of these flaws and reservations. Her retirement is too simple, her virtue too little grounded in experience to correspond to the spirit in which this play is conceived."

MAXWELL (1947, p. 50): "The critics of Isabella admit that the final summing-up is in her favour—the balance is somehow redressed in the last act. . . . Isabella, who has unsuccessfully pleaded with Angelo for her brother's life, is now asked, when she still believes that Angelo's breaking of his word has resulted in the death of her brother, to plead for Angelo's life. This is surely trial enough, without any need to suppose that there is any question of her having learnt or not learnt a lesson—it is a supreme test of her capacity for Christian forgiveness, and she proves equal to it. . . . What she obviously did need—what anyone whether 'self-centred saint' or loving sister would have needed—was almost superhuman charity."

CAMPBELL (ed. 1949, pp. 653–4): "One of the important changes which Shakespeare made in the Italianate story was to make the wronged woman a kind of saint. He gives us our first view of Isabella at the moment she is about to become a votaress of St. Clare. Even the wanton Lucio holds her 'as a thing enskied and sainted' [384]. A woman of her austere purity cannot be imagined as selling herself to sexual sin under any circumstances whatever, even though her yielding might buy her brother's life. This fact enables the poet to state her dilemma in extreme terms in order to magnify the test of her virtue. This is both a relic of the archaic plotting of the mediaeval virtue story and a foretaste of the melodramatic situations in the dramatic romances of Beaumont and Fletcher. Her two great scenes with Angelo, the first in which she begs him to spare her brother's life (II, ii), the second in which she gradually understands and finally violently rejects Angelo's offer to save Claudio at the expense of her honor (II, iv), are among the most effective Shakespeare ever wrote. Each mounts with a relentless crescendo to a thrilling climax. Moreover, in the give and take of these dialogues, Isabella, in some of Shakespeare's most eloquent lines, utters inspired pleas for the Christian virtue of mercy. It is these heroic declamations which throw the spotlight upon Isabella and have misled many critics into thinking that her problem forms the real center of the drama.

"Her interview with Claudio (III, i), which ends with her violent attack on him for asking that she sin to save a brother's life, is another scene constructed with consummate theatrical skill. The hardness which leads her to hurl such epithets at the distracted Claudio as 'O you beast, O faithless coward! O dishonest wretch!' [1357–8] has caused the critics to call her self-righteousness cruel and her purity rancid. But as the trial of her virtue is extreme, so is the language immoderate in which she spurns Angelo's offer. The moral rigidity with which [654] she meets the test renders her unsympathetic to a modern audience. Yet, granted Isabella's understanding of the issues involved in her choice, we must accept her conclusion [1115–17]."

TILLYARD (1949, pp. 134–6): "There is no more independent character in Shakespeare than the Isabella of the first half of the play: and independent in two senses. The essence of her disposition is decision and the acute sense of her own independent and inviolate personality. . . . At the beginning of the third act, when she has learnt Angelo's full villainy, her nature is working at the very height of its accustomed freedom. She enters almost choked with bitter fury at Angelo, in the mood for martyrdom and feeling that Claudio's mere life is a trifle before the mighty issues of right and wrong. Her scorn of Claudio's weakness is dramatically definitive and perfect. To his pathetic pleas, 'Sweet sister, let me live' etc., the lines Scott prefixed to the twentieth chapter of *The Heart of Mid-Lothian,* comes, as it must, her own, spontaneous retort from the depth of her being [quotes 1357–68]. That is the true Isabella, and whether or not we like that kind of woman is beside the point. But immediately after her speech, at line [1375], the Duke takes charge and she proceeds to exchange her native ferocity for the hushed [*135*] and submissive tones of a well-trained confidential secretary. . . . In the last scene she does indeed bear some part in the action; but her freedom of utterance is so hampered by [*136*] misunderstanding and mystification that she never speaks with her full voice: she is not, dramatically, the same Isabella."

ROSCELLI (1962, p. 219): "We have then in Isabella a very complex, if not paradoxical, character. Were she simply a cold-blooded moralist who could sacrifice her brother to preserve her virtue, she might win our admiration but she could hardly enlist our sympathy. On the other hand, were she an irresolute sentimentalist, who could abandon her principles to save Claudio, she would become for us merely a pathetic figure. But Isabella is neither. Far from being dogmatic in her approach to morality, she passionately defends the right of every man to resist, if necessary, the pressures of society and civil law in order to follow his own moral convictions. Ironically enough, this same doctrine compels her to reject Angelo's sordid proposal and thereby seal her brother's death-warrant. Her ethical philosophy thus involves her in a cruel moral dilemma which she cannot resolve by appealing either to conscience or sentiment."

BENTLEY (1964, p. 333): "In the last scene, Isabella is asked to practice all she preaches: to take the Christian message so much to heart that she will plead for mercy, not for her brother, whom she supposes dead, but for her enemy, whom she thinks her brother's killer. . . . In the beginning, she could not have done it; in the end, she can. As with Cordelia, the ice melts. The bristling virgin becomes the compassionate woman. Guilty of a rigidity that could have been as fatal as Angelo's, she, like him, learns a lesson in forgiveness—a lesson, of course, not in ethical theory, but in human, emotional practice."

Others who praise or defend Isabel include HORN (1827, 4:230–5), KNIGHT (ed. 1840; 1849, pp. 317–19), VERPLANCK (ed. 1847, vol. 2, *MM*, p. 5), GRILLPARZER (1849, tr. 1963, pp. 138–9), GERVINUS (1849–50, tr. 1875, pp. 492–9, 504), KREYSSIG (1862; 1867, 2:453–8), CLARKE (1863, pp. 497–503, and 1873, pp. 520–3), RUSKIN (1864, p. 119), ULRICI (1869, tr. 1876, 2:158–60), ANON. (1872, *Englishwoman's Mag.,* pp. 250–1), BODENSTEDT (1873; 1887, pp. 209–20), SNIDER (1875, pp. 317–25), WILKES (1876; 1882, pp. 104–5), FURNIVALL (ed. 1877, p. lxxiv), THÜMMEL (1881; 1887, 1:51–3), DOWDEN (1888, pp. 368–70), SYMONS (1889; 1920, pp. 44–52), LEWES (1893, tr. 1895, pp. 297–302), BRINK (1893, tr. 1895, pp. 88–9), HERFORD (ed. 1899, 3:239–40), BURGESS (1903, pp. 69–70), COURTHOPE (1903, 4:137–9), MOULTON (1903; 1907, pp. 146–7, 152–3, 157), COLLINS (1904, p. 78), STRACHEY (1904; 1922, p. 61), HART (ed. 1905, pp. xxii f., xxvii), GLEICHEN-RUSSWURM (1909, pp. 252–61), SWINBURNE (1909, p. 40), TEMPLE (1917, pp. 203–4), DE LORENZO (1921, pp. 247–50), FORD (1922, pp. 31, 69–73), SIMPSON (1924; 1950, pp. 42–50), GUNDOLF (1928, 2:168–

70), HEARN (1928, pp. 39–40, 118–19), THALER (1929, pp. 18–20, 86–9), RICHTER (1930, p. 114), DAVIES (1939, pp. 74–6), CAMPBELL (1943, pp. 135–9, and ed. 1949, p. 655), CRAIG (1948, pp. 230–5), JAIN (1948, pp. 19, 47, 179–81), DAVID (1951, pp. 136–7), GODDARD (1951, pp. 441–3), SEHRT (1952, pp. 158–69), WHITAKER (1953, pp. 218–21), DORAN (1954, p. 363), COGHILL (1955, p. 20), LACY (1956), HOLMES (1960, pp. 173–7), HETHMON (1962, pp. 270–6), HIGHLEY (1965), H. M. WILLIAMS (1965, pp. 33–6), MINCOFF (1966, p. 148), ALEXANDER (1967, pp. 482–3), EDWARDS (1968, pp. 117–18), GECKLE (1971, pp. 163–8), KLENE (1971), FRIEDMAN (1973), HOY (1974, p. 91), and ZEEVELD (1974, pp. 165–9).

Others who dislike or attack Isabel include P. P. (ed. 1822, p. iv), LLOYD (in SINGER, ed. 1856, 1:444–8), ELLIOTT (1885, pp. 129–46), LANG (1891, pp. 64–6), GREENWOOD (1920, pp. 535–40), GOULD (1923, p. 242), MACKENZIE (1924, pp. 225–43), FALCONER (1928, pp. 119–22), GILLET (1930, p. 72), WILSON (1932, p. 116), SITWELL (1948, pp. 123–8), NICOLL (1952, p. 119), GREEN (1966, pp. 22–3), RABKIN (1967, pp. 102–3), BOND (1970, pp. 43–5), RICHMOND (1971, pp. 153–5), VELIE (1972, pp. 46–9), SWINDEN (1973, pp. 144–7), and VAN LAAN (1978, pp. 89–94).

Others who suggest that Isabel changes and learns during the play include BATTENHOUSE (1946, pp. 1051–3), STAUFFER (1949, pp. 154–6), FLATTER (1956, pp. 153–4), MILLET (1956, p. 216), GRIVELET (ed. 1957, pp. 58–63), MAINUSCH (1959, pp. 415–16), EVANS (1960, pp. 199, 217–19), HETHMON (1962, pp. 270–7), NAGARAJAN (1962), W. D. SMITH (1962, pp. 309–15), CARD (1964, p. 67), HAWKES (1964, pp. 92–8), SEQUEIRA (1964, pp. 115–24), HUNTER (1965, pp. 214–25), BENNETT (1966, pp. 62–77), M. B. SMITH (1966, pp. 141–58), TOOLE (1966, pp. 180–1), KAUFMANN (1967, pp. 92–3), SHALVI (1967, pp. 199–201, and 1972, pp. 250–69, and 1973, pp. 19–35), NOSWORTHY (ed. 1969, pp. 29–34), CHAMPION (1970, p. 137), GRECO (1970, pp. 160–71), HERNDL (1970, pp. 257–8), KIRCHHEIM (1971, pp. 143–52), RICHMOND (1971, pp. 153–8), POWELL (1972, pp. 190–4, 205–9), SOELLNER (1972, pp. 223–32), PARTEE (1973, pp. 288–93), BARTON (in EVANS, ed. 1974, p. 546), OWEN (1974, pp. 17–32), GLESS (1975), HYMAN (1975, pp. 12–20), KIRSCH (1975, pp. 96–7), and MILES (1976, pp. 214–29).

Others who express different views on Isabel include HALLAM (1839, 3:564–5), GOULD (1923, pp. 242–3), VESSIE (1936, pp. 141–5), BRADBROOK (1941, pp. 386–96), LEAVIS (1942; 1952, pp. 167–9), STOLL (1944, *From Sh. to Joyce*, pp. 255–8), BANDEL (1951), FRICKER (1951, pp. 79–81), GODDARD (1951, pp. 440–3), LASCELLES (1953, pp. 148–53), MAHOOD (1957, p. 100), SPEAIGHT (1960, pp. 72–8, and 1977, pp. 260–4), ROSSITER (1961, pp. 159–63), SCHANZER (1963, pp. 96–112), LEVER (ed. 1965, pp. lxxv–lxxxiii, xciv), MAXWELL (1966, pp.

253–5, and 1974, pp. 214–15), LAVIN (1972, pp. 102–9), J. SMITH (1974, pp. 115–24), DUSINBERRE (1975, p. 53), SPROAT (1975), and PATRICK (1976).

JULIET

PRICE (1948, pp. 106–7): "In *Measure for Measure,* Shakespeare deals with the whole range of attitudes towards sexual passion, and to make this complete, he gives us a brief but profound study of Juliet. She is the counter-part of Claudio, the woman who has sinned, set over against the man who [*107*] has sinned, and in her attitude Shakespeare shows pure womanliness, love, repentance, patience, and entire submission."

Others who discuss Juliet include BRIDGES (in BULLEN, ed. 1907, 10:326), RIGHTER (1962, p. 179), and BECKERMAN (1970, pp. 119–20).

LUCIO

MURPHY (1758, p. 367): "The part of Lucio in this piece, an impudent, prating, coxcomb, is, as far as I can judge, both for humour and nature by many degrees superior to any character of the same stamp introduced upon the stage since."

GENTLEMAN (ed. 1773, pp. 59, 61): "*Lucio's* coxcomical forwardness has always a very pleasant effect, in representation; to give him his due, the last scene would be very flat, without him. . . .

[*61*] "*Lucio's* pert interruptions, through this scene [5.1], are very laughable and characteristic."

SHAW (1898; ed. Wilson, 1961, pp. 141–2): "Lucio, as a character study, is worth forty Benedicks [*142*] and Birons. His obscenity is not only inoffensive, but irresistibly entertaining, because it is drawn with perfect skill, offered at its true value, and given its proper interest, without any complicity of the author in its lewdness. Lucio is much more of a gentleman than Benedick, because he keeps his coarse sallies for coarse people" [but see 1602 ff.].

LAWSON (1937, pp. 263–4): "From the hurly-burly of Elizabethan street-life, Shakespeare took Lucio, who, a petty gentleman in rank, moved principally in the underworld, considered his depraved morals an indication of virility, and, in his behavior as a 'fantastic', followed the fashion of his kind by attempting, through impudence and malicious gossip, to attract attention to his own smartness, boldness, and sophistication. Lucio would be merely comic if the dramatist had not taken pains to develop his character—a charac-ter which, although unique in Shakespeare in its entirety, has parallels among others of the poet's numerous realistic figures. Falstaff has much of his morals and his bragadoccio; Roderigo is a gentleman similarly without constructive interests who has lapsed into bad company; Armado, the 'fantastical Spaniard', believing that to be a 'gentleman and gamester' is to possess the 'varnish of a complete man', could be Lucio's intimate; and Iago, the burly soldier, outdoes him in foulness of speech. Like Parolles and Falstaff, he speaks false slander and is apprehended by his intended victim. . . . [*264*] Drawn in detail from contemporary life, he takes, in the earlier acts, a natural and necessary part in the plot, and, in the latter acts, gives, through his asininities, a farcical strain to an otherwise sombre comedy; and provides also, perhaps, a piquant, timely reference to King James' fear and hatred of detractors.''

CAMPBELL (ed. 1949, pp. 654-5): "The liveliest patron of the city's organized prostitution is the gay, ribald Lucio. Sexual incontinence to him is a joke and a merry one. This is an attitude which lends all his comments a careless, cynical tone appropriate to a satirist who is also a buffoon. His talk is filled with extravagant and bawdy figures of speech, so that his observations on men and their affairs are caricatures of the truth. Lucio, despite his scurrility, lightens the tone of the play. Through him Shakespeare keeps alive [*655*] some of the traditional gaiety of comedy in a drama permeated with a severe spirit of correction. . . . Lucio's rueful last remark, 'Marrying a punk, my lord, is pressing to death, whipping and hanging' [2921-2], shows that he has not been reformed, merely ejected from the play with a smile for his incorrigibility rather than with a whip of steel. The exposure and deflation of the merry libertine is in the proper key for satiric comedy.''

PARROTT (1949, p. 364): "Lucio . . . is the type of clubman closely in touch with the underworld. . . . His peculiar quality is a zest for social scandal, which he practices to great effect by telling his disguised master 'pretty tales' [2258] of the 'old fantastical Duke of dark corners' [2249-50]; it must have especially delighted the Elizabethan groundlings to see this worldly-wise man giving himself away with every word he utters in this scene. The final sentence passed on him that he should marry his 'punk' has been denounced as 'harshness unrelieved', but nothing is more common in Elizabethan comedy than the marriage by force or fraud of a rogue to a prostitute. To Shakespeare's hearers this sentence, no doubt, seemed rather in the nature of a practical joke.''

LEECH (1950, p. 71): "Our reaction to the Duke's punishment of the one man he could not forgive is compounded of amusement at Lucio's discomfiture and astonishment at the intensity of the Duke's spite. When Lucio protests against the sentence, the Duke's reply is 'Slandering a prince deserves it' [2923]. Before that, I think, most readers and spectators have frankly enjoyed Lucio's baiting of the Friar. Not only do his words 'old fantastical duke of dark corners' [2249-50] bite shrewdly, but it is amusing to see how the Friar tries in vain to shake Lucio off when he is garrulous concerning the Duke's misdemeanours. Critics, searching for ethical formulations, are apt to forget that in the theatre the low life of Vienna and Lucio's persevering wit can arouse our sympathetic laughter.''

CAZAMIAN (1952, pp. 273–4): "Lucio, the irrepressible 'fantastic',
. . . proves a wag who can be funny, by repeating Falstaff's trick of irre-
sponsibility and cheek; but he overdoes it signally, and will be impudent
at the wrong time to the wrong person, so that the laugh is finally turned
full against him. Laugh we must, however, and it is Lucio who preserves
a comic atmosphere during the tense last act; indeed, through his per-
[*274*]sistent efforts, he adds a good deal to the amusing ingredients in a
rather grim irony."

FERGUSSON (1952; 1957, pp. 135–6): "In this nascent tragedy Lucio
is the counterpart of the Duke, and thus throws a great deal of light upon
him. Lucio has a talent for chaos as great as the Duke for wisdom or the
central order. Shakespeare uses Lucio in the first two acts as the chief reflector
of the action, to use Henry James's valuable term: it is through Lucio's
intelligent and faithless eyes that we grasp what is going on. . . . [*136*] Above
all, it is Lucio who arranges the fight between Angelo and Isabella, and
interprets it for us, blow by blow, with the most refined psychological insight.
It was his inspiration to 'bait the hook with a saint in order to catch a saint'
[943–4], as Angelo says, with terror, when he sees how he is caught. He
suggests that Lucio is more than the devil's advocate, almost the devil himself."

COGHILL (1955, pp. 23–4, 27 n.): "Amusing as he is, Lucio is a foul-
mouthed liar, and that fact should restore us to our senses; but it may not
succeed with everybody. Some of the mud will cling perhaps. 'I am a kind
of burr; I shall stick', as he says himself [2270]. Whether or not this be so,
his function is that of comic adversary to the Duke. . . . [*24*] He is never
tempted himself: . . . he is the Duke's adversary and mocker: it is hinted that
he has recognized the Duke in the Friar, and he is not afraid of him. It seems
almost too obvious what part Lucio plays in the parable of the play. Like the
Duke, he suggests an anagogical plane of meaning, on which he stands for
what Hardy would have called the Spirit Ironic or the Spirit Sinister; or Satan,
as he is called in that other play of testing, *The Book of Job*. He is very far,
of course, from Milton's Satan. . . . Lucio is not of his calibre, nor even of
that of Lucifer, though the name is suggestive; he is hardly more than a minor
fiend. . . .

[*27* n.] "Lucio has a function not unlike that of Thersites in *Troilus and
Cressida*. He is there to say the worst that can be said against people or things
we should admire."

LAWRENCE (1958, p. 452): "To return to the question whether Lucio
has penetrated the Duke's disguise, may it not be, after all, as has commonly
been assumed, that the joke is that this fellow, who fancies himself 'in the
know', is really deceived all along, until the Duke finally stands revealed?
This is an old theatrical device, which Shakespeare had already used in the
fooling of Malvolio and of Parolles. The audience, understanding more than
the self-deceiver, enjoys his deception and final discomfiture."

CAPUTI (1961, p. 434): "For all Lucio's lightheartedness, his is in many ways the low point of cynicism in the play: unlike Pompey and Barnardine, he is a man in whom we expect beliefs; yet he has none. He has no serious loyalties and no capacity for guilt or repentance because he is incapable of a serious commitment of any kind. There is, accordingly, a subtle justice in the Duke's active disapproval of him that has very little to do with the Duke's personal pique. In one sense Lucio's punishment represents the finest adjustment, though hardly the most important, that the just forces make toward the end of the play."

ROSSITER (1961, p. 155): "Lucio is an entirely human being: if very low, he is also very funny. And though he 'stands for' sex intellectualized as witty smuttiness, stripped of emotion and therefore debased, he is a mingled yarn; for there are touches in him of good sense in a 'low' mind which is denied to his betters. [Quotes 1602–4 and 1590–1.]"

SCHANZER (1963, p. 82): "It is strange that critics who profess to delight in Falstaff should sternly refuse to be amused by Lucio. He has not only a touch of Falstaff about him (compare, for instance, the excellent scene in which he slanders the Duke to his face with the very similar scene in which Falstaff slanders the Prince), but also of Hal. . . . He is a rather complex and, in some ways, contradictory character (which does not make him the less Shakespearian). Towards Claudio he shows himself to be a true and loyal friend, while towards Mrs. Overdone and Pompey he proves callous and perfidious."

Others who discuss Lucio include GILDON (1710, p. 292), HAZLITT (1817, p. 322), P. P. (ed. 1822, p. vi), CLARKE (1863, pp. 503–6), RALEIGH (1907, p. 166), KNIGHT (1930; 1949, pp. 89–91), VAN DOREN (1939, p. 222), FRYE (1953, pp. 276–7), GRIVELET (ed. 1957, pp. 63–6), ROTHE (1961, p. 302), DUNKEL (1962, p. 283), RIGHTER (1962, pp. 179–80), LEVER (ed. 1965, p. xcvi), SPENCER (1965, pp. 17–21), O'KEEFE (1966, pp. 23–9), CHAMPION (1970, pp. 142–6), EVANS (1971, pp. 80–4), KIRCHHEIM (1971, pp. 179–80), POWELL (1972, pp. 195–8), ALEXANDER (1975, pp. 57–8), BURNS (1975), KIRSCH (1975, pp. 101–2), and WEISER (1977, pp. 324–7).

MARIANA

Writers who discuss Mariana include O'BRIEN (1888, pp. 274–5), POWELL (1972, pp. 193–5), BLACK (1973, pp. 119–28), and DUSINBERRE (1975, p. 124).

MRS. OVERDONE

Mrs. Overdone is compared with Juliet's Nurse by MATHESON (1932, p. 40) and with Mrs. Quickly by DRAPER (1977, p. 9).

POMPEY

CAZAMIAN (1952, p. 273): "It may be a humbling thought that Pompey, the bawd, is the most genuine humorist in the play. Of course he is not refined; but he has verve, readiness, and that fund of first-hand observation without which mere would-be wits are thin and inefficient. At his better moments—as in IV, ii—he is not unworthy of standing for the poetry of absurdity, with a something that leaves a sting behind and reveals a hidden reason in the absurd."

Others who discuss Pompey include HAZLITT (1817, p. 322), DANIEL (ed. 1826, p. 6), CLARKE (1863, pp. 509–10), ECKHARDT (1902, pp. 279–81), RALEIGH (1907, p. 166), RICHTER (1909, p. 11), KIRCHHEIM (1971, pp. 168–73), and COLMAN (1974, p. 146).

PROVOST

Writers who discuss the Provost include CLARKE (1863, pp. 504–5), MOULTON (1903; 1907, pp. 147–8), and HAPGOOD (1964, pp. 114–15).

IV. Style

HUDSON (1872, 1:407): "The play abounds in fearless grapplings and strugglings of mind with matters too hard to consist with much facility and gracefulness of tongue. The thought is strong, and in its strength careless of appearances, and seems rather wishing than fearing to have its roughnesses seen: the style is rugged, irregular, abrupt, sometimes running into an almost forbidding sternness, but everywhere throbbing with life: often a whole page of meaning is condensed and rammed into a clause or an image, so that the force thereof beats and reverberates through the entire scene: with little of elaborate grace or finish, we have bold, deep strokes, where the want of finer softenings and shadings is more than made up by increased energy and expressiveness; the words going right to the spot, and leaving none of their work undone. . . . Hence it is perhaps, in part, that so many axioms and 'brief sententious precepts' of moral and practical wisdom from this play have wrought themselves into the currency and familiarity of household words, and live for instruction or comfort in the memory of many who know nothing of their original source."

HOFMANNSTHAL (1905, tr. 1952, pp. 253–4): "What matters is Shakespeare's music, and that again and again there must be someone to whom it is granted to hear the whole music of these poems. But it must be as a Whole.—Take *Measure for Measure,* a play full of harshness, with sombre passages, with a strange, tart blending of the high and the low; more difficult in language, its motives moving [254] us less quickly than the others—a play that begins to live only after we have heard its whole music. . . . What a wonderful composition it is! what lights thrown on darkness! what life these lights give the shadows! In the mouth of the one who has to die and is afraid of dying, what a voice, what eloquence, what language . . . ! And in the mouth of the girl who is helpless, who is betrayed, what strength, what a sword of God suddenly in her hand!"

RYLANDS (1928, pp. 198, 201–2): *"Measure for Measure,* like *All's Well* and *Troilus,* has many of the characteristics of *Hamlet,* and all these four experiment in diction, in the new use of metaphor and amplification, in Latinising the vocabulary. . . .

[*201*] "The most terrific line in the play is, of course, the famous—'to lie in cold obstruction and to rot' [1338]. What a combination of abstract and concrete! The vague formidable phrase—I have heard its exact meaning discussed with acrimony—is brought up [*202*] against a pitiless monosyllable. It is one of the best examples of a favourite Shakespearian device."

SPURGEON (1935, pp. 287–90): *"Measure for Measure* in several respects stands alone among Shakespeare's plays. There are two points which [*288*] strike one at once on examining its images. The first is that we find among them, chiefly in the speech of the duke, some of the most beautiful, as well as the most thoughtful similes in the whole of Shakespeare, . . . as well as many of the most brilliant and unusual of Shakespeare's pictures and personifications. . . .

"The second remarkable point is that out of the hundred and thirty-six images in the play, I feel I can classify eighteen only as 'poetical', because by far the largest group (twenty-seven in number) seem to fall under another category which I can only call vivid, quaint, or grotesque. . . . Often these latter ones are poetical as well, from sheer force and brilliance, as in Isabella's outburst against man [874 ff.] . . . but what strikes one first is the unusual pictures they conjure up, and their touch of grimness, grotesqueness, [*289*] or a vividness so piercing as to give one a shock almost as if from lightning. . . .

[*290*] "So these two qualities, for which the images as a whole in *Measure for Measure* are remarkable, thoughtful poetry and strange brilliance, with a touch of the bizarre, are curiously expressive of the peculiar character and mental atmosphere of the play. . . . This character, in spite of the intolerable nature of the plot, goes far, so it seems to me, to make it, of all the plays, the one which bears in it most clearly and unmistakably the impress of Shakespeare's mind and outlook."

TRAVERSI (1942; 1969, p. 364) "The linguistic power of *Measure for Measure,* far from expanding easily into lyricism or rhetoric, is subordinated to a supple bareness and concentrated most often upon an intense underlining of the value of single words. This does not mean that the effect is necessarily simple. No word in Claudio's speech [216–21] is logically superfluous, but more than one is, in its context, surprising. The verb 'ravin', for instance, suggests bestial, immoderate feeding, and so 'appetite', but the next line proceeds, through a 'thirsty evil', to transfer the metaphor to drinking; the shift of the image and the sharp focusing of impressions by which it is accompanied are characteristic of Shakespeare's mature art."

FLUCHÈRE (1948, tr. 1953, pp. 178–9): "This celebrated passage [1337–51] (which, more than any other, defies translation) achieves that perfect alliance of poetic imagination and dramatic movement precipitated by an intense emotion. Clearly Claudio is here using all his powers of persuasion, all the resources of imagination and eloquence. He wants to communicate to Isabella his own master-passion, fear: to prove to her that nothing is more terrible than this horrible unknown thing, death. . . . But death for Claudio wears the terrifying guise of a perceptible void where the threat of a frightened conscience nevertheless subsists. And it is the pangs of this conscience that Claudio tries to put into words. Let Isabella [*179*] be like him afraid, more afraid of death than of her own dishonour, and Claudio will be served.

"To imprison in words this void, the most fleeting of abstracts is caught in the concrete toils of sensual antitheses: *obstruction* is opposed to *motion*, cold to heat, the sensible to the insensible. . . . It is by the abstract words 'sensible *warm* motion' that Claudio best and most briefly expresses what is implicit in life—sensibility, heat, movement—and, by a concrete image, what becomes of the living body's remains—'a kneaded clod'. Then comes the turn of the immortal soul which delighted in the earthly life, to undergo its metamorphosis and its unknown but terrifying ordeal. Two expected aspects of hell (rivers of fire and icy solitudes) are evoked in the strange sixth line [quotes 1342]. But this does not exhaust the possibilities. . . . And finally he reaches the end of the resources of expression . . . he breaks off with the words "tis too horrible!'

"Here the function of imagery is indeed to express a dramatic reality beyond which no further expression is possible. It conveys the content of an emotion: it is an ardent idea, the inevitable language of a mind which seizes upon the only reality that passionately interests it and interests us: that of a character in a given situation. The sonorous words, the rhythms themselves are in direct accord with the gasping of the emotion, with the shades of internal meaning. Everything contributes to the total effect. It is here that blank verse, which we saw earlier so clumsy and mechanical, becomes marvellously supple and varied."

TILLYARD (1949, pp. 131–2): "Where in the first half the most intense writing was poetical, in the second half it is comic or at least prosaic. . . . Another evident sign of tension relaxed in the second half of the play is the increased use of rhyme. . . . [*132*] Most characteristic . . . are the Duke's octosyllabic couplets at the end of III. 2. . . . Far from being spurious, the Duke's couplets in their antique stiffness and formality agree with the whole trend of the play's second half in relaxing the poetical tension and preparing for a more abstract form of drama."

CRANE (1951, pp. 113–14): "The incantation-like quality of the verse [in 1746–67] (as in *A Midsummer Night's Dream*) emphasizes the quasi-supernatural character of the Duke's rôle: he is the *deus ex machina* transformed into a player of the drama, walking among the rest.

[*114*] "The prose in *Measure for Measure,* barring the comic prose and such conventional usages as Angelo's letter, centers around the Duke's disguise with its attendant complications. It is a remarkable use of prose, and the most extended example of this use in the plays. It provides an additional element of contrast in the play, rendering more complex the construction of individual scenes and elaborating the technical structure of the entire play."

EVANS (1952; 1964, pp. 132–3, 137–8): "There is a compression of the [*133*] sense, a closely packed argument, replacing the gentle, unhurried movement found, so frequently, in the earlier plays. Verse is now more closely, or possibly even more aridly conditioned to an argument from which gracious similitudes and an easy flow of language are eliminated. So from the very opening lines the play breaks into a proposition, precisely dissected. . . . [*137*] Shakespeare seems at once fascinated and disturbed by men's conduct and their real motives, by the parade of moral conformity and the actuality of sensual desire. The image of the impression of a face on a coin and the face itself . . . is only another attempt to discover the imagery that will answer the idea. But it is the mirror or glass that mainly serves as an illustration. . . .

[*138*] *"Measure for Measure . . .* marks a profound stage in the development of Shakespeare's language. Delight in the patterns of speech for their own sake has gone, and so have the more decorative of rhetorical flourishes. Instead there is argument, analysis, compression, a curious, or as Horatio might indicate, an over-curious searching."

MAHOOD (1957, p. 179): "This word *honour* has a special fascination for Shakespeare at this stage of his life's work because the tension between its shallow and deeper meanings corresponds to his own dilemma between linguistic scepticism and faith in the power of words. It is particularly effective as Isabella uses it five times over to Angelo in *Measure for Measure:* 'Heauen keepe your honor' [1038]. At first this seems a piece of direct, negative irony; Angelo's honour is merely his title as judge, and does not correspond to any real quality in his character. But if honour is a mere scutcheon to Angelo in the depths of his self-discovery, it is for Isabella the concept which preserves them both. Her conventional phrase is also a prayer which is answered when the Duke, in his Providential aspect, preserves Angelo from the seduction of Isabella and from the murder of her brother. In the second scene between Isabella and Angelo, the word is set against the word—not destructively, as in *King John,* but creatively, as in the third book of *Paradise Lost:* mercy against justice, the redemptive promise against the harshness of the law. And the play's conclusion sustains this by upholding the power of the Word; more particularly, of the Sermon on the Mount."

BECKERMAN (1970, pp. 114, 116): "The contrast of tone between the dignity of the opening verses of the Duke and the ribald wit of Lucio provides the musical key to the entire play. Until the Duke addresses Isabella in Act III, he does not speak a word of prose. Then suddenly, his lines no longer keep their measured step but turn to a more casual rhythm. After this major shift, Shakespeare gradually reintroduces poetic passages, never quite abandoning passages in prose, but allowing the poetic form to dominate. . . . At this point it is enough, I believe, to note the skilful modulation of his style. It leads me to accept the division of the play into two halves as a deliberate artistic choice. . . . [*116*] *Measure for Measure* shares not only the narrative shift common to many plays but also a tonal and verbal shift. The deliberateness of this shift in *Measure for Measure* and its repetition, more adroitly I believe, in *The Winter's Tale,* argues Shakespeare's desire to create a novel dramatic effect."

Others who discuss style in *MM* include VERPLANCK (ed. 1847, vol. 2, *MM,* pp. 5–6), WENDELL (1894, p. 268), VAN DOREN (1939, pp. 217–21), BRADBROOK (1941, pp. 397–8), DODDS (1946, pp. 248–52), SYPHER (1950, pp. 262–80), COOK (1953, pp. 122–7), HALLIDAY (1954, pp. 144–7), GRIVELET (ed. 1957, pp. 72–9), KLEINSCHMIT (1961, pp. 79–81), ROSSITER (1961, pp. 157, 163–4), NOSWORTHY (ed. 1969, pp. 40–5), POWELL (1972, pp. 182, 192–4), EAGLESON (1975), p. 208), and SIEMON (1975, p. 120).

On versification in *MM* see also BATHURST (1857, pp. 94–6), KÖNIG (1888, passim), SAINTSBURY (1908, 2:34), ELIOT (1920, p. 90, "astonishing versification"), YOUNG (1928, pp. 201–2), FRANZ (1935, passim), NESS (1941, pp. 40, 58, 60, 75, 79), CAPOCCI (1950, pp. 34–44), DRAPER (1953; 1957, pp. 94–100), and BRASHEAR (1970). On prose see also DELIUS (1870, pp. 249–50), JANSSEN (1897, pp. 34–40), BORINSKI (1955, p. 66), VICKERS (1968, pp. 314–29), and ALTIERI (1970, and 1974, pp. 6, 12–16). On images see also WHITER (1794, pp. 142–7, 254), PHILIPS (1888, pp. 22–3), LATHAM (1892, pp. 420–3), BRADBROOK (1941, pp. 397–8), DODDS (1946, pp. 248–52), DUPONT (1952, pp. 129–48), HARRISON (1954, pp. 1–10), GRIVELET (ed. 1957, pp. 73, 77–8), LEISI (ed. 1964, pp. 43, 57), LEVER (ed. 1965, pp. lxxxv f., 4–8), POWELL (1972, pp. 182, 186–9, 193), and JEWETT (1973). On rhetoric see RUSHTON (1868, 2:48, 50–1), MIRIAM JOSEPH (1947, pp. 81, 145–6, 153, 182–3, 201–2, 232–4), WEBER (1963, pp. 89–91), VICKERS (1968, pp. 320–8), and DENNEY (1973). On irony see WEISER (1977, pp. 323–47). On diction see also HALLIDAY (1954, pp. 146–7) and SCHÄFER (1973, pp. 111, 149, 175, 214). On wordplay see also WURTH (1895), TILLEY (1930, pp. 111–20), MUIR (1954, *SJ,* p. 65), HALIO (1956), PRAGER (1966), VICKERS (1968, pp. 315–19), and BERRY (1976–7, pp. 150–9). On proverbs see WAHL (1887–8), JENTE (1926), LEVER (1938, pp. 180–1, 232–9), and TILLEY (1950, p. 804).

V. *Technique*

KOSZUL (1927, pp. 151–2); "So this whole [first] act—which is short indeed (hardly longer than our commentary)—is a cascade, skilfully arranged, of indications that repeat themselves, in echoes carefully graduated, from the slightest to the strongest. The preparations intersect without confusion. The spectator is introduced to the action, which will be fully set in motion only in the following act, by a whole series of steps whose direction becomes apparent little by little. Here is no static 'exposition' but rather an 'induction', to revive a word used by the old English dramatists. It is an induction which proceeds much more in the manner of an 'overture' subtly orchestrated than in the manner of a wholly logical explication, whose facts would be presented to the spectator with the simplified, swift, and as it were economical rigor that the needs of the intellect alone usually require. That the action is delayed thereby is quite clear. But this delay, maintained by successive approaches, is invaluable for dramatic pleasure. Let us go back to Whetstone, whose two-part play would have been able more readily to afford the luxury of these preliminary steps. We shall be unpleasantly surprised by the hastiness, one is tempted to say the clumsiness, of the introduction to the subject. And if we reflect that all these bits of thread, so put by Shakespeare into the hands of his spectators, make up a carefully woven fabric, our admiration grows still greater. For this overture presents, on its lesser scale, the alternate contrasts that the whole play will unfold: it presents in its second scene this painfully sarcastic theme which will return at the heart of the serious and poignant motifs of which we have as yet heard only the foreshadowing. And this meditative tonality which will harmonize everything in the play, laughter as well as tears, is here already dominant, to the extent of catching our attention perhaps more than all the rest. . . .

[*152*] "It is not a matter here of clearing Shakespeare from all the charges that have been aimed at his dramatic technique. His endings are unquestionably many times, and especially in *Measure for Measure*, hurried and offhand. But his preparations are usually, if we are not mistaken, unequaled in patience, ingenuity, and delicacy of constructive thought." In French.

DURHAM (1941, pp. 167–72, 174): "Here we find in its full development Shakespeare's perception of the ironic incongruity between appearance and reality, one which Pirandello could later parallel but which he could not transcend. . . . The speech of Isabella in which this definition appears is one of the best known . . . [quotes 874–80]. . . .

[*168*] "So assured are men that they do know their essential natures that more than one competent critic has, despite this explicit warning, failed to see that it is Angelo's ignorance of his own essence which occasions his surprising behavior. . . .

[*169*] "What is true of Angelo in this respect is true of the other important personages of the play. . . .

[*171*] "The Duke's behavior, although less surprising, is no less inconsistent with his professions. . . .

[*172*] "In *Measure for Measure,* then, the presentation of the difference between what a man is and what he thinks he is was made in such a way as to convey the profoundly significant possibilities implicit in this difference. In exploring these possibilities it reaches the limits of comedy, if it does not go beyond them. . . .

[*174*] "By transforming a familiar and mechanical theatrical device [mistaken identity] into a psychological one he [Sh.] was able to present his characters from many angles. . . . We are able to see them, not—as in many excellent novels and plays—from a single point of view, but from many. We see them as this person and that person sees them; we see them as they themselves think they are today and as they thought they were yesterday. . . . Thus they have for us not merely one dimension, but three, or even four."

WATKINS (1950, p. 87): "The stripping of Angelo's surface is close to the conventional Elizabethan dramatic method; but the parallel stripping of Isabella shows how masterfully Shakespeare has worked out his new technique of psychological realism. No serious reader of the play can miss the conscious artistry with which Shakespeare prepares step by step through the First and Second Acts for the final revelation of Isabella in the first scene of the Third—not only to the audience or reader but to herself; and being beautifully prepared for, it is accomplished in a hundred lines of dialogue so subtle that even in reading it one follows exactly what is going on in Claudio's and Isabella's minds, and imagines the changing expression on their faces, the very inflections of voice."

FERGUSSON (1952; 1957, pp. 138, 140–2): "It has often been maintained that Act V is a mere perfunctory windup of the plot, in which Shakespeare himself had no real interest. I am sure that on the contrary it is composed with the utmost care, and in perfect consistency with the basis of the whole play—this quite apart from the question whether one *likes* it or not. It is indeed so beautifully composed that it could almost stand alone. Perhaps we should think of it as a play within a play, presenting the theme of justice and mercy in another story and in another and colder tone. But the new story —that of the Duke's intervention and demonstration—was implicit from the first; and the new cold, intellectual tone may be understood as underneath the more richly poetic manner of the first three acts. . . .

[*140*] "Moreover, he has written Act V with its own theatrical poetry, which one may miss if one does not think of its actual stage effects. It is not only a series of trials and a [*141*] demonstration of the Duke's wise authority; it is also a masquerade, a play of pretense and illusion. As we watch it with what I have called our 'double vision', we can see each character in turn compelled to relinquish his pretense, his public costume.

And in this respect Act V merely carries to its conclusion one of the important theater-poetic themes of the whole play, that of human life itself as a dream or masquerade. . . . In the first three acts we are in the midst of these masquerades; we are moved by their seductive passion and music. In the last act, playtime over, the music changes, the masques are put aside, and we are shown what [*142*] Shakespeare evidently regarded as the underlying truth of the human situation."

EVANS (1960, pp. 186, 190, 207): "Only *The Comedy of Errors,* which has nothing to offer besides, relies more exclusively than *Measure for Measure* on discrepancies in awareness for both action and effect. We hold advantage over all named persons except the Duke and his accomplice friars during thirteen of seventeen scenes—that is, from I.iii to the end except for IV.v, when only the Duke and Friar Peter are present. Throughout this period the gap between our awareness and the participants', like the several secondary differences in the awarenesses of participants, is not only wide but defined with unfailing clarity. Once established our main advantage remains fixed until the abrupt, spectacular denouement. . . .

[*190*] "The chasm opened between Vienna's awareness and ours by the Duke's announcement of his masquerade is the principal dramatic fact during all subsequent action. It conditions our view of every scene after I.iii. . . .

[*207*] "Dependent upon discrepancies in awareness for its very existence, the denouement of *Measure for Measure,* in both its workmanship and its effects achieved by workmanship, has few peers and no superiors in Shakespearian comedy."

CAPUTI (1961, pp. 427–8): "The structural analogy between the Escalus-Pompey scene [in 2.1] and the other interview scenes provides an important insight into the function of the low-life characters in the play. Actually, the analogy is hardly limited to this scene: throughout the play Pompey, Mistress Overdone, and Barnardine are at odds with law and morality. In other words, throughout the play they dramatize a conflict like that dramatized rather painfully in the scenes involving Angelo, Isabella, Claudio, and the Duke. . . . They represent the intractability of human nature: its refusal to submit to laws and codes, indeed, in the case of Barnardine, its contemptuous defiance of them. Moreover, these low-life offenders have their counterpart among the representatives of law and order: Elbow, with his genius for getting things wrong side to, is unmistakably a comic variation on Escalus and Angelo. The scenes involving these characters provide a comic exhibition of the precariousness of civilized foundations that counterpoints the more [*428*] serious dramatization of the other scenes. They furnish a kind of comic obbligato that prevents the feelings of distress aroused from becoming too intense, and tempers these feelings with complexity of outlook. To put the matter another way, the low-life scenes control the quality of the other interview scenes by putting them in a framework that adds comic dimensions to otherwise serious exhibitions of moral disorder;

they dramatize what must always be funny from the detached point of view of the comic muse: the hilarity of man's high designs."

BENNETT (1966, pp. 47, 131–2): "This preservation of suspense until the very last moment is one of the marvels of the play. We have only to compare Act V with the last act of the *Comedy of Errors* to see how good it is. All the elements of the Duke's little play point to the judgment of Angelo, and the deliberate ambiguity of the title, *Measure for Measure,* helps (like a false clue in a mystery story) to keep the outcome from being prematurely obvious. The ending is, therefore, more delightful in its rightness than we had been led to expect. . . .

[*131*] "The last act makes a brilliant ending to a witty comedy, providing an amazing exhibition of the actor's art for the part of the Duke. The regular, five-act structure of the play-within-a-play is too complete and clear to be accidental. . . .

[*132*] "Act V of *Measure for Measure* is a complete five-act play in miniature, directed by the Duke."

STYAN (1967, pp. 84–8): *"The Duologue Visualized.* Shakespeare's control of movement over the whole stage is seen in a concentrated way when he is working with two players [as in *JC* 4.2–3]. . . .

[*85*] "The long probative duologue between Angelo and Isabella in the second act of *Measure for Measure* guides audience response by a more complex stagecraft. It is carefully broken into two scenes (II, ii and II, iv) by the Duke's visit to Juliet in prison, a bridge scene to recall normal human sexuality as well as a device [*86*] to mark a brief passage of time. Angelo is a changed man after this break, and accordingly the second half of the duologue changes its pattern of movement too. The changes are accentuated by another device which works to striking effect. The first half is acted in the presence of two observers, Lucio and the Provost, as it were respectively representing the forces of anarchy and the law, and they regulate the protagonists and inhibit the action for the purposes of irony and suspense. When Isabella and Angelo meet again, they are alone, and the action grows increasingly overt. The first half ends with a direct confession by Angelo to the spectator, and the second, appropriately, with another by Isabella. . . .

"From the beginning, Angelo has asked the Provost to 'stay a little while' [769] and has him at his shoulder as an angel of conscience during Isabella's supplication for her brother's life. Throughout the scene, Angelo is scarcely felt to move, and his curt replies are strangely reserved, spoken almost in a growl. He moves only to turn away in dismissing her, but this, characteristically, is a frank direction for the actor to turn again to point a crucial line [quotes 902–5].

[*87*] "This one movement of Angelo's marks the idea that has been entering his mind. The situation has been pregnant with sexual overtones, and these are specially engendered by the devil's advocate, Lucio, who speaks at Isabella's shoulder. Because of his insistence, her role is less passive. Again

and again she is invited to take the offensive. . . . Increasingly she corners Angelo by her advance across the platform.

"The soliloquy with which Angelo opens II, iv seems a continuation of that with which he closes II, ii. Therefore Isabella finds him alone, once more in his former position downstage on the intimate area of the platform. . . . So the thrust and parry proceeds to the climax of argument with a last dispatching movement, when all ambiguity is finally resolved [quotes 1177–81]. [*88*] The man has cornered the woman; he has spoken out at last and he may now leave; and this he does."

On dramatic methods in *MM* see also GRANVILLE-BARKER (1931, pp. 96–100), SCHÜCKING (1947, pp. 51, 154), PRICE (1948, pp. 106–7), VENEZKY (1951, pp. 28, 73, 132), LASCELLES (1952, pp. 43–167, and 1962, pp. 175–6), MEADER (1954, pp. 208–11), GRIVELET (ed. 1957, pp. 18–31), BECKERMAN (1962, pp. 36–9, 207–12, and 1970, pp. 108–33), HETHMON (1962, pp. 261–77), OPPEL (1963, pp. 63, 80–1, 282–3, 302–3), HEYARTZ (1964), JANES (1964, pp. 47–50), REDDINGTON (1965), MEHL (1966, pp. 156–9), MUKHERJI (1966, pp. 144–8), EVANS (1971, pp. 76–9, and 1972, pp. 63–6), PAYNE (1971), HOLMES (1972, pp. 42, 195–7), POWELL (1972, pp. 181–209), SPENCER (1973, pp. 119–22), HASLER (1974, pp. 128–32), MACPHEDRAN (1974), LEECH (1975, pp. 83–5), KOLB (1976), MILES (1976, pp. 236–63), and GROSS (1978).

On the use of disguise see FREEBURG (1915, p. 160), LAWRENCE (1931, pp. 92–3, 103–12, 120), BRADBROOK (1952, pp. 159–62), LASCELLES (1953, pp. 98–103, 122–56), CURRY (1955, pp. 62–4, 152–4), STANLEY (1961), BECKERMAN (1962, pp. 197–9), GROSS (1965, pp. 100–8, 147–61), BENNETT (1966, pp. 22–4, 39–47, 95–102), FLOWER (1971), CLEMEN (1972, pp. 92–3), POWELL (1972, pp. 184, 197–206), PENDLETON (1974), SIEMON (1975, pp. 105–23), ANTALOCY (1976), and MILES (1976, pp. 125–96).

On the treatment of time see CLARKE (1879, pp. 112–17), DANIEL (1879, pp. 135–9), CLAPP (1885, pp. 400–1), BULAND (1912, pp. 113–14), WILSON (ed. 1922, pp. 157–9), HEUSER (1956, pp. 267–8), SEN GUPTA (1961, pp. 102–6), LEVER (ed. 1965, pp. xiv–xvii), and BECKERMAN (1970, pp. 108–10).

VI. Themes

ANON. (1737, pp. 558–9): *"Shakespeare* hath given us an admirable Moral . . . in one of his Plays, called *Measure for Measure . . .* [*559*] the whole Conduct of which points out an excellent Moral to the Observation of *all Princes,* how their Authority may be abused, and how They might redress it. Would *every Prince* enquire into the Conduct of their *Ministers,* and the grievances of their *People;* They might find, perhaps, the same, or more Occasion, to punish the *former,* and redress the *latter. . . .* This is so finely described in the following Passage of the *Play before mentioned,* that I conclude with recommending it to the Consideration of *all men in Power . . .* [quotes 863–5, 867–79]."

N. S. (1748, p. 503): *"Measure for Measure* contains an argument for the exercise of compassion towards offenders, the most powerful that can be thought of, *The frailty of human nature:* and this argument is exemplified in the character of the merciless *Angelo,* in such a manner that we are at once convinced of its force, and excited to a just abhorrence of that cruelly inflexible disposition in magistrates, which is often mistaken for justice."

GRIFFITH (1775, pp. 35, 48): "I cannot see what moral can be extracted from the fable of this Piece; but as the author of it seems to have thought otherwise, I shall present the reader with his idea on this subject, in his own words . . . [quotes 2798–9]. . . .

[*48*] "Shakespeare seems to have wound up the several morals of his characters and dialogue, in this place [2213–14], with an excellent Christian document, against the rage of malediction, and the passion of revenge."

SCHLEGEL (1809–11, tr. 1846, p. 387): "The piece takes improperly its name from punishment; the true significance of the whole is the triumph of mercy over strict justice; no man being himself so free from errors as to be entitled to deal it out to his equals."

ULRICI (1839, tr. 1846, p. 311): "The whole piece, accordingly, rests on the prime christian truth—we are all sinners, children of wrath, and in need of mercy; in other words, life is here contemplated in its gravest and profoundest principle of virtue and morality. But even this foundation is found to be frail, hollow, and worm-eaten, when employed exclusively in its earthly and human nature to prop up and support the human and the earthly. It is not man's moral energy, but the *divine grace,* which is the stay of human life, because it is only in and through the latter, that human virtue becomes practicable, and that it is truly and properly virtue."

GERVINUS (1849–50, tr. 1875, pp. 503–4): "But whilst our play in the first place recommends moderation in the exercise of justice, it occupies at the same time a far more general ground, and extends this doctrine to all human [*504*] relations, exhibiting, as it were, the kernel of that opinion so often expressed by Shakespeare, of a wise medium in all things. It calls us universally from all extremes, even from that of the good, because in every extreme there lies an overstraining, which avenges itself by a contrary reaction. There was good in the Duke's mildness, but it turned to the detriment of the common weal, and scattered the seeds of crime. There was good in Angelo's severity, but it erred throughout by the exaggeration of its aims, and, as in the case of Elbow, the question might have been put also with respect to him: 'Which is the wiser here? Justice or Iniquity?' [622]. There was good in Angelo's serious political studies, but the suppression of the feelings which accompanied them avenged itself by bursting asunder the unnatural restraints.

There was good in his exalted virtue, but when he prided himself in it he 'fell by virtue' [492]. . . . The single character of Angelo, with the unnaturally overstrained exaggeration of his nature, counterbalances a series of contrasts; his severity counterbalances the mildness of the Duke, his sobriety the levity of Claudio, his heartlessness the tender weakness of his faithful Mariana, and his anxious adherence to the appearance of good Lucio's indifference to the basest reputation. Between these extremes stands Isabella alone, a type of a *complete* human nature, rendering it plain that all extreme is but imperfect and fragmentary."

ANON. (*New York Times,* 7 Feb. 1888, p. 5): *"Measure for Measure* is, indeed, one of the most distinctly moral plays ever written. It teaches the same lesson that is taught in some of the chapters of the New Testament. The Pharisee who thanked God that he was not as other men might have been the counterpart of that self-sufficient deputy of the Duke who undertakes to punish his fellow-men for committing the sin to which, in the moment of his aggrandizement, he falls a victim himself. The text glows with the genius of Shakespeare; its thought is deep, and some of its language as eloquent as anything in his other plays. . . . It bears the impress of maturity, and its story conveys the reflection of a mind burdened by a sense of the injustice and intolerance that have ever marred human society; the impotency of human laws and the insufficiency of human judgment."

PORTER (ed. PORTER & CLARKE, 1909, p. vii): *"Measure for Measure* is a dramatised Sermon on the Mount of Genius, that is brother to the Sermon on the Mount.

"Thence its name manifestly draws its origin, and the whole drama its spirit. The key to the grave and noble music of the Play is there sounded and there to be sought.

"The passage in Matthew vii. 1–5 . . . finds in the mouth of the Duke a strikingly parallel statement.

"At the climax of the dramatic action, when righteous judgment, embodied in the Duke, addresses itself to the task of stripping unrighteous judgment of its false authority and scathing its hypocrisy, the speech put in his mouth has a kindred simplicity and pith. It strikes the same probing note."

BROOKE (1913, pp. 154–5): "Through the whole of this play the question of Authority and its limits, of the temptations it brings to those who possess it, and of the sins it may fall into, is debated and illustrated by Shake-[*155*]speare. It is one of three great subjects which engaged his thought, as he, musing on the world of men, wrote this play. The second is the Fear of Death, and the third is the terrible rapidity with which sin, and especially sensual sin because of its public shame, generates sin."

BRADBROOK (1941, pp. 385–6, 395): "In this play Shakespeare adopts a technique as analytic as that of Donne to something resembling the late medieval Morality. It might be named The Contention between Justice and Mercy, or False Authority unmasked by Truth and Humility; Angelo stands for Authority and for Law, usurping the place of the Duke, who is [*386*] not only the representative of Heavenly Justice but of Humility, whilst Isabel represents both Truth and Mercy. . . .

[*395*] "In the actions of Angelo, Isabel, and the Duke, the question of Truth and Seeming is stated, and they have thus a double burden of symbolism to carry. Nevertheless, the allegorical nature of *Measure for Measure* does not preclude a human interest in the characters. Though based perhaps on the Moralities, it is not a Morality. Angelo has always been recognized as a superb character study; Isabel and the Duke, though less impressive, are subtly presented. She is possibly the most intelligent of all Shakespeare's women; . . . yet she is young, and pitifully inexperienced."

POPE (1949, pp. 70–72, 80): "According to Renaissance theory, the authority of all civil rulers is derived from God. Hence, they may be called 'gods', as they are in Psalm lxxxii, 6, because they act as God's substitutes. . . . [*71*] This doctrine may very well explain why the Duke moves through so much of the action of *Measure for Measure* like an embodied Providence; why his character has such curiously allegorical overtones, yet never quite slips over the edge into actual allegory; and finally, why Roy Battenhouse's [1946] theory that Shakespeare subconsciously thought of him as the Incarnate Lord is at once so convincing and so unsatisfactory. Any Renaissance audience would have taken it for granted that the Duke did indeed 'stand for' God, but only as any good ruler 'stood for' Him; and if he behaved 'like power divine', it was because that was the way a good ruler was expected to conduct himself. . . .

[*72*] "Finally, the ruler has the privilege of using extraordinary means. . . . Hence, the Duke in *Measure for Measure* is quite justified in using disguise, applying 'craft against vice' [1762], and secretly watching Angelo much as King James advises his son in the *Basilicon Doron* to watch his own subordinates: 'Delight to haunt your Session, and spy carefully their proceedings . . . to take a sharp account of every man in his office' (pp. 90–2). . . . [*80*] He may even, to a certain extent, use retaliation in kind, or the threat of retaliation in kind, to bring malefactors to their senses: it is no accident that Angelo is paid with falsehood false exacting, or finds himself sentenced to the very block where Claudio stooped to death, and with like haste. But his primary duty is, like God, to show mercy whenever he possibly can, even when the fault is disgusting and the criminal despicable."

VYVYAN (1959, pp. 87–8): *"Measure for Measure* has sometimes been interpreted [*88*] as a sermon on the text that 'power corrupts'; but Shakespeare never says this. The real power is always retained by the duke, and in his hands it is life-giving. It is certainly a corollary of the play's main theme that power reveals: authority will display a corruption that is already there, but it will equally give scope to the love of doing good. If the seemers are exposed by it, so, also, are the true. Shakespeare was never an anarchist; and when he studies the problem of power, he does not suggest that it can be solved by abolition. His solution is an aristocracy of the spirit; his qualifications for rulership are self-realization, forgiveness and love; and his ideal is a philosopher, or perhaps a mystic king."

SCHANZER (1963, pp. 117, 126): "The main intellectual concern of *Measure for Measure* is clearly with the nature of Justice and Good Rule, a concern which is expressed at once in the opening lines . . ., an important index to the play's dominant preoccupations. The law, in Shakespeare's plays, is frequently shown to be a stalking-horse for every form of cruelty and persecution, whether by the state, as in our play and *Timon* (3.5), or by a private citizen. . . . And repeatedly, but above all in *Measure for Measure,* the poet's plea seems to be for a more humane and less literal interpretation of the law, both man-made and divine, in accordance with the circumstances of each case, and for the seasoning of Justice with Mercy. Much of this is summed up by the single word 'equity' and Aristotle's description of it in the *Nicomachean Ethics.* . . . [*126*] I do not find anything peculiarly Christian in these views. James's own references in support of them [in *Basilicon Doron*] are to ancient, pre-Christian writers, such as Aristotle, Cicero, and Seneca. They are views held by humane and enlightened men in all ages."

LEVER (ed. 1965, pp. lxiii, xcii): "In the broadest sense of the phrase, *Measure for Measure* deserves to be considered a drama of ideas. While the formal classifications 'problem play', 'allegory', 'morality', or 'satire' are misleading, there can be no doubt that the play is profoundly concerned with major intellectual issues. The following sub-sections describe the treatment of the themes of Justice and Mercy, Grace and Nature, Creation and Death. . . .

[*xcii*] "Yet the pattern of ideas, though firm and subtle, is not to be equated with the play's full dramatic truth. *Measure for Measure* is intensely concerned with the nature of authority, the workings of the psyche, and the predicament of man faced with the universal facts of procreation and death: but it is in the nature of Shakespearean drama that all such issues are taken up into the greater mystery of the actual individual."

On mercy and forgiveness in *MM* see also DANIEL (ed. 1826, p. 5), HUGO (ed. 1862, pp. 40–2), SNIDER (1875, pp. 312–25), KOHLER (1883–4; 1919, pp. 161–78), SYMONS (1889; 1920, pp. 51–2), MASSON (by 1895; 1914, p. 133), MOULTON (1903; 1907, pp. 156–7), HART (ed. 1905, p. xxv), KNIGHT (1930; 1949, pp. 73–96), CHAMBERS (1937; 1939, pp. 286–310), REIMER (1937, pp. 34 ff.), C. WILLIAMS (1942; 1950, pp. 111–14), RADBRUCH (1944, pp. 40–9), SEHRT (1952, pp. 121, 132–97), SHEDD (1953), HARDING (ed. 1954, p. 130), DAICHES (1956, pp. 11–14, and 1960, 1:292–4), BRUNNER (1957, pp. 171–3), KAUFMANN (1959, pp. 18–19), MAINUSCH (1959, pp. 416–17), WASSON (1960, pp. 262–75), MATTHEWS (1962, pp. 108–16, 123–4), HAWKES (1964, pp. 88–99), HUNTER (1965, pp. 206–26), NOSWORTHY (ed. 1969, pp. 24–6), OWEN (1974, pp. 17–32, and 1975), JONES (1975), and HASKIN (1977, pp. 348–62).

On Christian elements in *MM* see also M. S. (1795, pp. 644–7), PRICE

(1839, pp. 3, 122), BIRCH (1848, pp. 352–8), BROWN (1864, passim), WORDSWORTH (1864; 1880, passim), HERAUD (1865, pp. 280–92), ANON. (1872, *Congregationalist,* pp. 402–11), MORLEY (ed. 1889, pp. 10–11, and 1895, 11:31), COLLINS (1902, pp. 364–8), CARTER (1905, pp. 402–14), KNIGHT (1930; 1949, pp. 73–96), ANON. (1931, p. 554), SISSON (1934, pp. 58–9), NOBLE (1935, pp. 221–8), MURRY (1936, p. 307), CHAMBERS (1937; 1939, pp. 286–310), REIMER (1937, pp. 19 ff.), BATTENHOUSE (1946, pp. 1029–59), DODDS (1946, p. 247), McGINN (1948, pp. 129–39), COGHILL (1950, pp. 13, 18, 28, and 1955, pp. 16–21, 26), WHITAKER (1951, pp. 351–4), MUTSCHMANN & WENTERSDORF (1952, pp. 219–25, 277–80, 368, 379), SCHRÖDER (1952, pp. 334–7), SEHRT (1952, pp. 144–97), MILUNAS (1954), PARKER (1955, pp. 110–21), MERCHANT (1959, p. 226), CUTTS (1960, pp. 416–19), SPEAIGHT (1960, pp. 70–9), BRYANT (1961, pp. 86–108), SOUTHALL (1961, pp. 12–33), MENDL (1964, pp. 145–6), PETERSON (1964, pp. 135–7), HUXLEY (1965, pp. 168–70), M. B. SMITH (1965, pp. 7–18, and 1966, pp. 123–59), LINGS (1966, pp. 49–57), TOOLE (1966, pp. 35–8, 178–97, 231–7, and 1970–1, pp. 35–6), BERLIN (1968, pp. 214–19), NUTTALL (1968, pp. 231–51), BACHE (1969, pp. 39, 55), LYONS (1969, pp. 173–84, and 1971, pp. 127–59), MURRAY (1969, pp. 126–38), NOSWORTHY (ed. 1969, pp. 25–6), PEARLMAN (1972, pp. 232–5), S. C. VELZ (1972, pp. 37–44), DIFFEY (1974, pp. 231–7), McBRIDE (1974, pp. 264–74), BABULA (1975, pp. 93–112), KAULA (1975, pp. 65–73), KIRSCH (1975, pp. 89–105), YUCKMAN (1975), TOSCANO (1976, pp. 282–9), and HASKIN (1977, pp. 348–62).

For criticism of Christian interpretations see FRYE (1963, passim), SCHANZER (1963, pp. 126–9), STEVENSON (1966, pp. 93–120), LEVIN (1974, *PMLA,* pp. 302–11), and SCOUTEN (1975, pp. 75–84).

On justice, law, and equity see also GILDON (1710, p. 292), UPTON (1746, p. 72), KNIGHT (ed. 1840; 1849, pp. 319–20), KÖNIG (1873, pp. 122–81), PATER (1874; 1889, pp. 188–91), LEVI (1875, pp. 168–71), SNIDER (1875, pp. 312–25), FREUND (1893, pp. 60–71), ZIINO (1897, pp. 66–74), MOULTON (1903; 1907, pp. 156–7), KEETON (1930; 1968, pp. 371–93), RADBRUCH (1944, pp. 40–9), PACE (1949), TILLYARD (1949, pp. 128, 137–41), POGSON (1950, pp. 58–69), GOLDSCHMIDT (1953, pp. 3–21), POTTS (1958, pp. 150–73), WASSON (1960, pp. 262–75), DICKINSON (1962, pp. 287–97), DUNKEL (1962, pp. 275–85), McCORD (1962, pp. 63–70), SKULSKY (1964; 1976, pp. 87–119), MARTIN (1966, pp. 240–1), BERMAN (1967, pp. 141–50), EAGLETON (1967, pp. 66–97), BABULA (1970, pp. 27–33), HORTON (1971), SCHWARZE (1971, pp. 83–101), KNIGHT (1972, pp. 62–3), MORGAN (1972), LEWIS (1973), MAXWELL (1974, pp. 205–9), SEARS (1974, pp. 123–61), ZEEVELD (1974, pp. 141–84), McCANLES (1975, pp. 199–206), MALINA (1975), COOK (1976, pp. 222–3), and MILES (1976, pp. 269–74).

On other themes see also MOULTON (1903; 1907, pp. 143–57), FORD

(1922, pp. 69–74), MURRY (1922, pp. 20–4), SMIRNOV (1934, tr. 1936, pp. 81–2), DRAPER (1936, pp. 82–8, and 1969, pp. 5–9), KNIGHTS (1942, pp. 222–33), TRAVERSI (1942; 1969, pp. 363–82), HORNE (1945, pp. 119–25), STAUFFER (1949, pp. 143–60), RYLANDS (1951, pp. 105–8), FERGUS-SON (1952; 1957, pp. 127–32), SCHILLING (1953, pp. 180–1), ECKHOFF (1954, pp. 119–22), MILLET (1956, pp. 207–17), VYVYAN (1960, pp. 18–20), WATSON (1960, p. 222), ROSSITER (1961, pp. 156–8), SOUTHALL (1961, pp. 11–33), LONGO (1964), SKULSKY (1964; 1976, pp. 87–119), GHURYE (1965, pp. 158, 207, 212, 238, 246–8), HUNTER (1965, pp. 6, 206–26), GODSHALK (1970, and 1973, pp. 134–49), REID (1970, pp. 273–81), BISWAS (1971, pp. 3–6, 109–19, and 1972, pp. 18–23), PÉREZ GÁLLEGO (1971, pp. 227–42), DRISCOLL (1972), GIBSON (1972), GUHA (1972, pp. 1–2, 6–9), PEARLMAN (1972, pp. 217, 229–35), SOELLNER (1972, p. 236), J. W. VELZ (1972, pp. 89–91), MATTURRO (1973), FISCH (1974, pp. 81–92), SHANKER (1975, pp. 124–36), BARRATT (1976), HAILEY (1976), TROMBETTA (1976, pp. 60–76), DRAPER (1977, pp. 5–17), and HARDER (1977).

For criticism of the search for themes see MINCOFF (1966, pp. 141–52) and SCOUTEN (1975, pp. 68–84).

Stage History

A full stage history of *MM* would require a book. What follows is a calendar of professional productions in English-speaking countries, so far as I can trace them, with a few amateur productions of special interest. Theaters are in London unless another city is named, and opening dates are given when known. For British performances see also Frank A. Marshall in IRVING & MARSHALL (ed. 1889, 5:165–9), Harold Child in WILSON (ed. 1922, pp. 160–5), PARKER (1939, p. 1764), HARRIS (1959), WILLIAMSON (1975), and MILES (1976, pp. 298–318).

1604, Dec. 26. "The Accompte of the Office of the Reuelles" records a performance by the King's men at Whitehall: "By his Ma^tis plaiers: On St Stiuens night in the Hall A play Caled Mesur for Mesur: Shaxberd:" (Public Record Office, Audit Office 3/908/13). See CUNNINGHAM (1842, p. 204), LAW (1911), CHAMBERS (1923, 4:136–40; and 1930, 2:330–1), STAMP (1930), and comments under Date (pp. 299 f.). BALDWIN (1927, tables at p. 228) guesses at the actor of each part: Angelo, Richard Burbage; Duke, Henry Condell; Isabella, Jack Wilson; Claudio, William Sly; Escalus, John Heminge; Lucio, John Lowin; Pompey, Robert Armin; Provost, Alexander Cooke; Friar Peter, Shakespeare; Elbow, Richard Cowley; Mariana, James Sands; Juliet, John Rice; Overdone, Samuel Crosse. But there is no evidence to confirm these conjectures. Like ELZE (1888, p. 239) and FERGUSSON (1952, pp. 119–20), BENNETT (1966, p. 135) prefers to "imagine that Shakespeare himself acted the part of the Duke." It seems more likely that Burbage, who acted Hamlet and Othello, played the Duke, the fifth longest role in Sh.'s plays and one in which he could show his power to "change shapes with Proteus," as suggested by HOLMES (1960, p. 176) and MILES (1976, pp. 300–1). On possible doubling of roles see ENGELEN (1927, pp. 114–16).

1640–60? *MM* in the University of Padua copy of F1 has cuts marked for performance and prompter's notes such as "Bee ready Abhorson" and "florish," in the same hand that marks a promptbook of Shirley's *Loves Crueltie,* 1640 (EVANS, 1960–3, and 1967). *MM* in the Dent copy of F3 is not a 17th-c. promptbook (McMANAWAY, 1950), since many of its MS changes are from Hanmer or Johnson, as in *all-binding* 1102 (HALLIWELL, ed. 1854, 3:233–5; cf. G. B. EVANS, 1960, p. 16).

1660, Dec. 12. Sir William Davenant was granted a warrant to act "Measures, for Measures" and eight other plays by Sh. (Public Record Office, Lord Chamberlain 5/137, p. 343). See NICOLL (1923, p. 314).

1662, Feb. 15. The Duke's company acted Davenant's adaptation, *The Law against Lovers,* at Lincoln's Inn Fields Theater. Pepys on 18 Feb. called it "a good play and well performed, especially the Little Girle's [Viola, added by Davenant] . . . dancing and singing" (*Diary,* ed. 1970, 3:32). Evelyn on 18 Dec. saw it played at court before Charles II (*Diary,* ed. 1955, 3:347). See DAVENANT (1673), IRVING & MARSHALL (ed. 1889, 5:165–7), ILLIES (1900), WILLIAMS (1905), KILBOURNE (1906, pp. 46–53), ODELL (1920, 1:26–7), SPENCER (1927, pp. 137–51), HOTSON (1928, p. 247), STROUP (1932, pp. 309–10), SEATON (1935, pp. 334–6), EICH (1948), VAN LENNEP (1965, p. 47), and MILES (1976, pp. 97–102).

1700. Charles Gildon's adaptation, *Measure for Measure, or Beauty the Best Advocate,* was acted "this Winter" (Jan. or Feb.?) at Lincoln's Inn Fields, with prologue and epilogue by John Oldmixon. Duke, Arnold; Angelo, Betterton; Isabella, Mrs. Bracegirdle. For the music by Henry Purcell see p. 480. Though the play was printed with no author's name, Gildon's *Love's Victim* in 1701 advertises "Measure for Measure a Comedy alter'd from *Beaumont & Fletcher* [*sic*] by Mr. *Gilden.*" A promptbook in the hand of John Downes is dated 1704. See GILDON (ed. 1700), GENEST (1832, 2:221–3), KILBOURNE (1906, pp. 51–5), ODELL (1920, 1:72–4), SPENCER (1927, pp. 329–35), EICH (1948), HOGAN (1952, 1:301), MERCHANT (1959, p. 25), SHATTUCK (1965, p. 269), VAN LENNEP (1965, pp. 523–4), CAIRNS (1971), LEVISON (1973), and MILES (1976, pp. 102–6).

1701–50. HOGAN (1952, 1:461) finds *MM* acted sixty-nine times in London during these years, sixth most frequent among Sh.'s comedies and seventeenth among his plays.

1706, Apr. 26. Queen's Th. in the Haymarket. Advertised as "Written by the famous Beaumont and Fletcher." Gildon's version. See HOGAN (1952, 1:5, 301) and AVERY (1960, 1:124).

1720, Dec. 8. Lincoln's Inn Fields. Duke, Quin; Angelo, Boheme;

Isabella, Mrs. Seymour. "Not Acted these Twenty Years" (at this theater). "Written by Shakespear." Four more performances in Dec., six in 1721, one in 1722, and two in 1723. See HOGAN (1952, 1:302) and AVERY (2:603 and index). A prologue by Leonard Welstead and an epilogue by Richard Steele, written for this play but not spoken, were printed in 1721. This is the first known performance of Sh.'s *MM* since 1604. The acting version printed for Tonson in 1722 keeps all Sh.'s characters, with cuts mainly in 1.2 and 2.1, and adds only eight lines, at the end (Hogan, 1:301, and MILES, 1976, pp. 106–7).

1724, Apr. 9. Lincoln's Inn Fields. Duke, Quin; Angelo, Boheme; Isabella, Mrs. Parker. One more performance with this cast and ten with no actors' list between 1724 and 1727. See HOGAN (1952, 1:303) and AVERY (1960, 2:753 and index).

1729, Jan. 13. Lincoln's Inn Fields. Duke, Quin; Angelo, Milward; Isabella, Mrs. Buchanan. Two more performances in 1729. See HOGAN (1952, 1:303), AVERY (1960, 2:1008, 1012), and SCOUTEN (1961, 1:18).

1729, Apr. 26. Lincoln's Inn Fields. Duke, Quin; Angelo, Milward; Isabella, Mrs. Berriman. One more performance with this cast and five with no actors' list between 1730 and 1732. See HOGAN (1952, 1:303), AVERY (1960, 2:1029), and SCOUTEN (1961, 1:31 and index).

1732, Oct. 25. Lincoln's Inn Fields. Duke, Quin; Angelo, Milward; Isabella, Mrs. Hallam. See HOGAN (1952, 1:304) and SCOUTEN (1961, 1:240).

1733, Jan. 12. Covent Garden. Duke, Quin; Angelo, Milward; Isabella, Mrs. Hallam. Two more performances in 1733–4. See HOGAN (1952, 1:304) and SCOUTEN (1961, 1:263, 338, 366).

1737, Mar. 10. Drury Lane. Duke, Quin; Angelo, Milward; Isabella, Mrs. Cibber; Lucio, T. Cibber. Benefit for Quin. Four more performances in 1737–8, including benefit for Mrs. Cibber. See HOGAN (1952, 1:304–5) and SCOUTEN (1961, 2:646 and index).

1738, Mar. 16. Aungier St. Th., Dublin. First of thirty-two Dublin performances before 1837, according to HUGHES (1904, pp. 32, 39).

1740. White Swan Playhouse, Norwich. See ROSENFELD (1939, p. 59).

1742. Aungier St. Th., Dublin. Duke, Quin; Isabella, Mrs. Cibber. See HITCHCOCK (1788, 1:115).

1742, Nov. 25. Covent Garden. Duke, Quin; Angelo, Cashell; Isabella, Mrs. Cibber. Seven more performances in 1742–3. See HOGAN (1952, 1:305) and SCOUTEN (1961, 2:1015 and index).

1744, Jan. 14. Covent Garden. Duke, Quin; Angelo, Cashell; Isabella, Mrs. Pritchard. Four more performances in 1744–5. See HOGAN (1952, 1:306) and SCOUTEN (1961, 2:1083 and index).

1745, summer. Jacob's Wells Th., Bristol. Isabella, Mrs. Pritchard (?); Lucio, Woodward (his benefit). Also 1746. See ROSENFELD (1939, pp. 205, 207, 214).

1745, Aug. 31. Richmond, Surrey. Duke, Cashell; Angelo, Philips; Isabella, Mrs. Vincent. See ROSENFELD (1939, pp. 291–2).

1746, Apr. 11. Drury Lane. Duke, Berry; Angelo, Havard; Isabella, Mrs. Woffington; Lucio, Macklin. Benefit for Berry and Havard. See HOGAN (1952, 1:306–7) and SCOUTEN (1961, 2:1231).

1746, Dec. 17. Covent Garden. Duke, Quin; Angelo, Cashell; Isabella, Mrs. Cibber. George II present. See HOGAN (1952, 1:307) and SCOUTEN (1961, 2:1272).

1748, July. Tankard St. Th., Ipswich. Duke, Peterson; Angelo, Pearson; Isabella, Mrs. Bowman (Boman). Also Norwich, 1750. See ROSENFELD (1939, pp. 76, 94, 103).

1748, Nov. 26. Covent Garden. Duke, Quin; Angelo, Sparks; Isabella, Mrs. Woffington. Six more performances in 1748–50. See HOGAN (1952, 1:307–8) and STONE (1962, 1:77 and index).

1749, Jan. 9. Drury Lane. Duke, Berry; Angelo, Havard; Isabella, Mrs. Cibber; Lucio, Woodward. See HOGAN (1952, 1:308) and STONE (1962, 1:88).

1750, Dec. 10. Orchard St. Th., Bath. Benefit for Mr. and Mrs. Brookes. Also 11 Mar. 1751. See HARE (1977, p. 1).

1751–1800. HOGAN (1957, 2:718) finds *MM* acted sixty-four times in London during these years, compared with sixty-nine times between 1701 and 1750.

1754, Jan. 21. Orchard St. Th., Bath. Five more performances in 1754–5. See *N&Q* 192 (1947), 486–7, and HARE (1977, pp. 5–8, 10).

1755, Feb. 22. Drury Lane. Duke, Mossop; Angelo, Havard; Isabella, Mrs. Cibber; Lucio, Woodward. Fifteen more performances in 1755–9, once with Mrs. Pritchard and thrice with Miss Pritchard as Isabella. Prince of Wales present 30 Dec. 1756. See MURPHY (1758, p. 367), HOGAN (1957, 2:401–3), and STONE (1962, 1:470–1, 478; 2:index).

1756. Smock Alley Th., Dublin. Duke, Mossop; Isabella, Mrs. Gregory. See HITCHCOCK (1788, 1:268).

1757, July 22. Drury Lane Th., Liverpool. See BROADBENT (1908, p. 34).

1758, Mar. 18. Smock Alley Th., Dublin. Duke, Dexter; Isabella, Mrs. Fitzhenry (her benefit). Also Cork, 16 Aug. See SHELDON (1967, pp. 390, 438) and CLARK (1965, p. 332).

1758, Oct. 22. Bury St. Edmunds. The Duke, Joseph Peterson of the Norwich company, fell dead while speaking of death in 3.1.6–8 (1209–11). See ANON. (1802), BAKER (1812, 1:566), and ROSENFELD (1939, p. 92).

1759, Aug. 10. Drury Lane Th., Liverpool. See BROADBENT (1908, p. 37).

1759, Nov. Crow St. Th., Dublin. Duke, Mossop; Isabella, Mrs. Fitzhenry; Lucio, Woodward. Also Cork, 1768. See HITCHCOCK (1794, 2:17–18, 75), GENEST (1832, 10:438–9, 499), and CLARK (1965, p. 95).

1761. Smock Alley Th., Dublin. Duke, Mossop; Isabella, Mrs. Bellamy. See *MM,* Dublin, 1761.

1763, June 15. Orchard St. Th., Bath. See HARE (1977, p. 22).

1763–4. York. Duke, Frodsham; Angelo, Crisp; Isabella, Miss Phillips. See ROSENFELD (1939, p. 161).

1770, Feb. 12. Covent Garden. Duke, Bensley; Angelo, Clarke; Isabella, Mrs. Bellamy; Lucio, Woodward (his benefit). "Not acted for twenty years" at Covent Garden. Three more performances in 1770; six in 1771–2 with Mrs. Yates as Isabella. Acting version printed 1773 for John Bell (2nd ed. 1774; one Folger copy with plate of Mrs. Yates as Isabella), revised by the prompter, Joseph Younger, ed. by Francis Gentleman. See HOGAN (1957, 2:403–4) and STONE (1962, 3:1454 and index). MILES (1976, pp. 107, 332) cites a 1770 ed., with cast, which is not an acting ed. but reprints Theobald's text.

1771, Jan. 19. Salisbury. See HARE (1958, p. 111).

1775, Mar. 18. Drury Lane. Duke, Smith; Angelo, Palmer; Isabella, Mrs. Yates. Seven more performances in 1775–8. See HOGAN (1957, 2:404–6) and STONE (1962, 3:876 and index).

1777, Jan. 8. Covent Garden. Duke, Lee; Angelo, Hull (for his MS notes on the play see HULL); Isabella, Mrs. Jackson; Lucio, Woodward. See HOGAN (1957, 2:405, and 1968, 1:51).

1779, Dec. 11. Orchard St. Th., Bath. Duke, Lee; Angelo, Browne; Isabella, Mrs. Siddons. Five more performances in 1780, two in 1782. Also Bristol, 13 Dec. and in 1780, 1782. See GENEST (1832, 6:162, 164, 235, 237) and HARE (1977, pp. 68–70, 82–3).

1780, Oct. 11. Covent Garden. Duke, Henderson; Angelo, Clarke; Isabella, Mrs. Yates; Mariana, Mrs. Inchbald. Three more performances in 1781–2 with Hull as Angelo and one with Clarke as Angelo. See HOGAN (1957, 2:406–7, and 1968, 1:378, 402, 488, 495, 577).

1783, Nov. 3. Drury Lane. Duke, Smith; Angelo, Palmer; Isabella, Mrs. Siddons. Three more performances in 1783 and three in 1784–5. King and Queen present 5 Nov. 1783. Acting version printed 1784. Plate of "Mrs Siddons in Isabella" in Bell ed. 1785. See HOGAN (1957, 2:407–8, and 1968, 2:655 and index), BOADEN (1831, 2:42–7), CAMPBELL (1834, 1:198–201), and SALGADO (1975, pp. 216–17).

1792, May 29. Orchard St. Th., Bath. Also Bristol, 20 June. See *N&Q* 193 (1948), 40, and HARE (1977, pp. 138–9).

1794, Dec. 30. Drury Lane. Duke, Kemble; Angelo, Palmer; Isabella, Mrs. Siddons. Twelve more performances in 1794–8. King and Queen present 31 Dec. 1794. Acting version as altered by Kemble "to be had in the Theatre." See HOGAN (1957, 2:408–10, and 1968, 3:1716 and index), BOADEN (1825, 2:137–8), SHATTUCK (1974, 6:i–iii), and MILES (1976, pp. 108–9).

1795, May 29. Edinburgh. Isabella, Mrs. Siddons. See DIBDIN (1888, p. 228).

1795, summer. Dublin. Duke, Kemble. See HUGHES (1904, p. 39).

1797, May 31. Th. Royal, Manchester. Duke, Cooke; Isabella, Mrs. Siddons. See HODGKINSON & POGSON (1960, pp. 149–50).

1798, Oct. 27. Drury Lane. Duke, Kemble; Angelo, Barrymore; Isabella, Mrs. Siddons; Claudio, Charles Kemble. Three more performances in 1799. See HOGAN (1957, 2:410–11, and 1968, 3:2119 and index).

1803, Nov. 21. Covent Garden. Duke, Kemble; Angelo, Cooke; Isabella, Mrs. Siddons; Claudio, Charles Kemble. Acting version printed 1803. See GENEST (1832, 7:614, 624) and SHATTUCK (1974, vol. 6).

1811, Oct. 30. Covent Garden. Duke, Kemble; Angelo, Barrymore; Isabella, Mrs. Siddons (and for the last time 26 June 1812); Claudio, Charles Kemble; Pompey, Liston; Barnardine, Emery. See WILLIAMS (1812, cols. 424–6), GENEST (1832, 8:285–6, 295, 297, 306), ROBSON (1846, pp. 18, 43, 78), and SHATTUCK (1965, p. 269).

1813, Apr. Th. Royal, Bristol. See BARKER (1970, p. 68).

1816, Feb. 8. Covent Garden. Duke, Charles Mayne Young; Angelo, Daniel Terry; Isabella, Eliza O'Neill; Claudio, Charles Kemble. Acting version, ed. William Oxberry, printed 1822. See JONES (1816, pp. 83–8), HAZLITT (1818; ed. Howe, 5:281–4), GENEST (1832, 8:549), SALGADO (1975, pp. 217–18), and MILES (1976, pp. 110, 305–6).

1817, Oct. 27. Th. Royal, Liverpool. Duke, John Vandenhoff; Angelo, John Cooper; Isabella, Mrs. M'Gibbon (her benefit). Not acted in Liverpool "these many years." Playbill, Birmingham Pub. Lib., and MILES (1976, p. 305).

1818, Mar. 27. Park Th., New York. Duke, James Pritchard; Angelo, Hopkins Robertson; Isabella, Mrs. Barnes. See ODELL (1927, 2:503–4).

1820, Apr. 17. Bath. Duke, Young; Angelo, James P. Warde; Isabella, Mrs. Pope. See GENEST (1832, 9:73).

1820, July 12. Th. Royal, Liverpool. Duke, Vandenhoff; Angelo, Bass; Isabella, Mrs. Bartley. Playbill, Birmingham Pub. Lib. MILES (1976, p. 305) misprints "Bartley" as "Hartley."

1824, May 1. Drury Lane. Duke, Macready; Angelo, Terry; Isabella, Margaret Bunn. See GENEST (1832, 9:236) and MILES (1976, p. 306).

1829, Mar. 2. Drury Lane. Duke, Young; Angelo, Cooper; Isabella, Mrs. Phillips. See GENEST (1832, 9:463).

1846, Nov. 4. Sadler's Wells. Duke, Samuel Phelps; Angelo, George Bennett; Isabella, Laura Addison. See PHELPS & FORBES-ROBERTSON (1886, p. 89), SHATTUCK (1965, p. 270), and MILES (1976, p. 306).

1853, Oct. 18. Th. Royal, Birmingham. Duke, James Bennett; Angelo, H. Cooke; Isabella, Miss Edwards. Playbill, Birmingham Pub. Lib.

1854. Boston, Mass. Producer, Thomas Barry. See SHATTUCK (1965, p. 271).

1872. On tour in U.S. Isabella, Adelaide Neilson. See DE LEINE (1881, p. 37).

1876, Apr. 1. Haymarket. Duke, Henry Howe; Angelo, Charles Harcourt; Isabella, Adelaide Neilson. Also 1878 and tour in England. See DE LEINE (1881, pp. 40–3), KNIGHT (1893, pp. 110–14), and DICKINS (1907, pp. 29–30).

1880, May 24. Booth's Th., New York. Acts 2 and 3 only. Isabella, Adelaide Neilson, farewell benefit. See *NYT*, 25 May 1880, and ODELL (1939, 11:30 and plate facing p. 28).

1884, Apr. Stratford. Isabella, Miss Alleyn. Also 1885. See KEMP & TREWIN (1953, pp. 15–16).

1884. On tour in England. Isabella, Ellen Lancaster Wallis (PARKER, 1922, p. 841).

1886, Sept. 23. Brooklyn. Isabella, Celia Alsberg. See ODELL (1942, 13:385).

1887, Oct. 17. Tabor Grand Opera House, Denver. Isabella, Helena Modjeska, who played the role in sixteen more U.S. cities by 1898. See *NYT*, 7 Feb. 1888, 19 Feb. 1898, TOWSE (1916, pp. 268–70), ODELL (1949, 15:43–4, 207), COLEMAN (1969, pp. 879, 919 ff.), and SPEAIGHT (1973, p. 80).

1893, Nov. 9. Royalty. Angelo, William Poel, who produced the play with Elizabethan staging. See ARCHER (1894, pp. 260–70), POEL (1913, pp. 204–6), SPRAGUE (1947–8, pp. 31–2, and 1953, pp. 140–2), SPEAIGHT (1954, pp. 90–3), HARRIS (1963), MOORE (1972, pp. 26–7), SALGADO (1975, pp. 218–20), and STYAN (1977, pp. 57–9).

1899, Mar. 17. Manchester. Duke, John Glendinning; Angelo, Maurice Mancini; Isabella, Ellen Wallis. Also at Grand Theatre, Islington, at Kennington, and on tour. See MONTAGUE (?1900, pp. 70–5), PARKER (1922, p. 1073), and MILES (1976, p. 307).

1906, Feb. New Th., Oxford. Oxford Univ. Dramatic Soc. Duke, R. Gorell Barnes; Angelo, Gervais Rentoul; Isabella, Maud Hoffmann. Acting version by G. R. Foss, the producer, printed 1906. See *Academy*, 3 Mar., p. 207, MACKINNON (1910, pp. 248, 254–6), and RENTOUL (1944, pp. 17, 36–7).

1906, Mar. 20. Adelphi. Duke, Walter Hampden; Angelo, Oscar Asche; Isabella, Lily Brayton. Ellen Terry as Francisca 28 Apr. Acting version by Asche printed. See *Athenæum*, 24 Mar., p. 372, WALKLEY (1907, pp. 156–9), WILSON (1950, p. 107), and SHATTUCK (1965, pp. 271–2).

1908, Apr. 11. Gaiety, Manchester. Duke, James Hearn; Angelo, William Poel; Isabella, Sara Allgood; Lucio, Ben Iden Payne. Also at Stratford, Apr. 21. See YEATS (1908, Nov., p. 4), MONTAGUE (1911, pp. 242–6), SPEAIGHT (1954, pp. 94–8), *ShS* 8:77, SHATTUCK (1965, p. 272), and PAYNE (1977, pp. 86–92).

1910, Apr. 22. Birmingham. Duke, Barry Jackson; Angelo, John Drinkwater. Also 1911. See MATTHEWS (1924, pp. 19, 27, 119) and TREWIN (1963, pp. 11–12, quoting letter by Yeats).

1913. Fine Arts Th., Chicago. Chicago Theatre Soc. Producer, Iden Payne. See PAYNE (1977, pp. 117–19).

1918, Apr. 23. Birmingham. Producer, John Drinkwater. See MAT-
THEWS (1924, pp. 75, 210).

1918, Oct. 7. Old Vic. Producer, G. R. Foss. See PARKER (1939, p.
1843) and CROSSE (1953, pp. 54–5).

1923, Apr. 23. Stratford. Duke, Frank Darch; Angelo, Frank Cellier;
Isabella, Dorothy Green; Lucio, Baliol Holloway. Producer, W. Bridges-
Adams. See ELLIS (1948, p. 147).

1924, Apr. 13. Strand. Angelo, Ernest Milton; Isabella, Grizelda Her-
vey; Lucio, Holloway; Pompey, Andrew Leigh. See AGATE (1925, pp. 51–
5).

1925. Maddermarket Th., Norwich. Producer, Nugent Monck. See
RES 3:171 and *Th. Arts* 22:456.

1925, Nov. 16. Old Vic. Angelo, Holloway; Isabella, Nell Carter;
Mariana, Edith Evans. Producer, Andrew Leigh. See PARKER (1939, p.
1764) and FARJEON (1949, pp. 25–8).

1928. Carnegie Institute of Technology, Pittsburgh. Isabella, Irene Te-
drow. Producer, Payne. See PAYNE (1977, pp. 173, 176–7).

1929, Apr. 26. Haymarket. Duke, Holloway; Angelo, Cellier; Isabella,
Jean Forbes-Robertson. Producer, Robert Atkins. See PARKER (1939, p.
1764).

1929, Nov. 16. Boston Repertory. See SHATTUCK (1965, pp. 272–
3).

1930. London School of Economics Dramatic Soc. Angelo, T. H. Marshall.

1930. Festival Th., Cambridge. Angelo, Robert Donat; Isabella, Flora
Robson. Director, Anmer Hall; producer, Tyrone Guthrie. See DUNBAR
(1960, p. 97).

1931, Apr. 23. Stratford. Duke, Randle Ayrton; Angelo, Gyles Isham;
Isabella, Hilda Coxhead. Toured U.S. and Canada 1931–2. See KEMP &
TREWIN (1953, pp. 151, 156) and SPRAGUE (1953, pp. 169–70).

1931, July 6. Fortune. Duke, Henry Oscar; Angelo, Holloway; Isabella,
Jean Forbes-Robertson. See *Daily Telegraph*, 7 July, and *NYT*, 9 Aug.

1933, Dec. 4. Old Vic. Duke, Roger Livesey; Angelo, Charles Laugh-
ton; Isabella, Flora Robson; Claudio, James Mason. Producer, Guthrie. See
AGATE (1934, pp. 233–7), *Th. Arts* 18:100, WILLIAMS (1949, pp. 131–2),
and GUTHRIE (1959, p. 122).

1937, Oct. 7. Old Vic. Duke, Stephen Murray; Angelo, Emlyn Williams; Isabella, Marie Ney. Producer, Guthrie. See *PP* 72:7–9, WILLIAMSON
(1948, pp. 70–3), and FINDLATER (1956, pp. 48–9).

1940, Apr. 23. Stratford. Duke, George Skillan; Angelo, Basil Langton;
Isabella, Peggy Bryan; Lucio, Holloway. Producer, Payne. See WILLIAMSON
(1948, pp. 70–1, and 1951, p. 297), and KEMP & TREWIN (1953, pp.
193–4).

1946, Aug. 23. Stratford. Duke, David King-Wood; Angelo, Robert
Harris; Isabella, Ruth Lodge; Lucio, Paul Scofield. Producer, Frank McMul-

lan. See *NYT,* 24 Aug., WILLIAMSON (1948, pp. 70–1), and KEMP & TREWIN (1953, p. 218).

1947, Apr. 11. Stratford. Duke, Michael Golden; Angelo, Harris; Isabella, Beatrix Lehmann; Lucio, Scofield. See WILLIAMSON (1951, pp. 299 f.), CROSSE (1953, p. 86), and KEMP & TREWIN (1953, pp. 219–21).

1950, Mar. 9. Stratford. Duke, Harry Andrews; Angelo, John Gielgud; Isabella, Barbara Jefford; Claudio, Alan Badel. Producer, Peter Brook. See *ShS* 4:135–8 and plates XIII, XIV, *SQ* 2:75, TYNAN (1950, p. 151), TREWIN (1952, pp. 37–8, and 1971, pp. 53–5), WORSLEY (1952, pp. 130–2), KEMP & TREWIN (1953, p. 238), BROOK (1968, pp. 88–9), HAYMAN (1971, pp. 168–71), WEIL (1972), SPEAIGHT (1973, p. 246), WILLIAMSON (1975, pp. 150–3), and STYAN (1977, pp. 213–16).

1950. Trinity College, Toronto. Earle Grey Sh. Co. See *ShS* 4:125, 10:111–14.

1951, Aug. 2. Ashland, Oregon. Director, Angus Bowmer. See *SQ* 2:347.

1951, Sept. Maddermarket Th., Norwich. Producer, Monck. Also 1952, 1953. See *SQ* 2:347, 4:70, 5:61.

1952, Sept. 30. Bristol Old Vic. Duke, John Neville; Angelo, Robert Eddison; Isabella, Margot Vanderburgh. Producer, Basil Coleman. See *SQ* 4:70, MERCHANT (1959, pp. 222, 225 plate), and TREWIN (1961, pp. 40–1).

1954, June 29. Stratford, Ontario. Duke, Lloyd Bochner; Angelo, James Mason; Isabella, Frances Hyland; Pompey, Douglas Campbell. Director, Cecil Clarke. See *NYT,* 30 June, DAVIES (1954, pp. 61–105), *ThWN* 11:168–9, WHITTAKER (1958, pp. xvi, 16–21), and WILLIAMSON (1975, pp. 153–4).

1955. Old Globe Th., San Diego. Director, Iden Payne.

1955, May 30. Old Vic tour of Australia opened in Sydney. Angelo, Robert Helpmann; Isabella, Katharine Hepburn. Producer, Michael Benthall. See *ShS* 10:124 and SHATTUCK (1965, p. 274).

1956, June 27. Stratford, Conn. Duke, Arnold Moss; Angelo, Kent Smith; Isabella, Nina Foch; Pompey, Hiram Sherman. Director, John Houseman. Music by Virgil Thomson. Also at Phoenix Th., New York, 22 Jan. 1957, with Richard Waring as Angelo. See *NYT,* 29 June 1956, 23 Jan. 1957, *NYTCR* 18:381–5, *SQ* 7:401–2 and plate facing p. 380, 8:81, *SJ* 93:158–9, *Educational Th. Jour.* 8:218–19, *Nation,* 1957, p. 146, *ThWN* 13:164, 188, and WILLIAMSON (1975, pp. 154–5).

1956. Antioch College and Toledo, Ohio. Director, Ellis Rabb. See *SQ* 7:411–13.

1956, Aug. 14. Stratford. Duke, Anthony Nicholls; Angelo, Emlyn Williams; Isabella, Margaret Johnston; Lucio, Alan Badel. Director, Anthony Quayle. See *ThW,* Sept., pp. 39–40, *SQ* 7:408–9, BROWN (1956), and WILLIAMSON (1975, pp. 155–9).

1956, Oct. 15. Bristol Univ. Union. Producer, Nevill Coghill. See *ShS* 11:127.

1957, Nov. 19. Old Vic. Duke, Nicholls; Angelo, Neville; Isabella, Barbara Jefford. Director, Margaret Webster. See *ThW,* Dec., p. 11, TREWIN (1961, pp. 84–5), WEBSTER (1972, pp. 303–5), and WILLIAMSON (1975, pp. 156–8).

1958, Nov. 17. Little Th., Bolton. See *SQ* 11:107.

1959, July 28. Ashland, Oregon. Director, James Sandoe. See *SQ* 10:582–3, 11:107.

1960, Feb. 2. Playhouse, Oxford. Oxford Univ. Dramatic Soc. See *SQ* 12:80.

1960, Apr. 5. Wisconsin Union Th., Madison. Director, Robert Hethmon. See HETHMON (1962).

1960, July 25. Central Park, New York. Duke, Philip Bosco. Director, Alan Schneider. See *NYT,* 27 July, *SQ* 12:80, and *ThWN* 17:123.

1960, Nov. 11. Univ. of Detroit Repertory. See *SQ* 13:114.

1962, Apr. 10. Stratford. Duke, Tom Fleming; Angelo, Marius Goring; Isabella, Judi Dench; Lucio, Ian Richardson. Producer, John Blatchley. See *NYT,* 11 Apr., *ThW,* May, p. 21, *PP,* June, *SQ* 13:513–14, *Drama Survey* 2:206, 209, *ShS* 16:143–5, 147–8, GOODWIN (1964, pp. 124–7), HOBSON (ed. 1964, pp. 3–6), SPEAIGHT (1973, p. 285), and WILLIAMSON (1975, pp. 159–60, 163).

1963, Apr. 3. Old Vic. Duke, James Maxwell; Angelo, Lee Montague; Isabella, Dilys Hamlett. Producer, Michael Elliott. See *ThW,* May, p. 10, *PP,* June, pp. 32–3, *SQ* 14:422, and WILLIAMSON (1975, pp. 160–4).

1963, May 10. Maddermarket Th., Norwich. Producer, Ian Emmerson. See *ShS* 18:140.

1963. Lakewood, Ohio. See *SQ* 14:458–9.

1963, Aug. 3. Boulder, Colorado. See *SQ* 14:461–4.

1964, July 14. Old Globe Th., San Diego, and Stanford Univ. Angelo, Nicholas Kepros. See *SQ* 15:414–15, 418.

1965, Sept. 22. Nottingham. Angelo, Alan Howard; Isabella, Judi Dench. Director, John Neville. Also 1966. See *ThW,* Sept., p. 32, and MILES (1976, pp. 312–13).

1966, Mar. Bristol Old Vic. Angelo, Richard Pasco; Isabella, Barbara Leigh-Hunt. Director, Guthrie. Toured U.S. and Canada 1967. See *NYT,* 15 Feb. 1967, *SQ* 18:411, *ThWN* 23:88, HOWARTH (1970, pp. 137–42), WILLIAMSON (1975, pp. 161–5), and MILES (1976, pp. 313–14).

1966, July 12. Central Park, New York. Duke, Shepperd Strudwick. See *NYT,* 14 July, *SQ* 17:420, and *ThWN* 23:152.

1969, June 11. Stratford, Ontario. Duke, William Hutt; Angelo, Leo Ciceri; Isabella, Karin Fernald. Director, David Giles. See *NYT,* 13 and 22 June, *SQ* 20:444–6 and plates following, *ThWN* 26:164–5, *CritQ* 12:73–4, and WILLIAMSON (1975, pp. 165–7).

1970, Apr. 1. Stratford. Duke, Sebastian Shaw; Angelo, Ian Richardson;

Isabella, Estelle Kohler. Director, John Barton. See *SQ* 21:444–5, *ShS* 24:123–5, 25:63–71, and WILLIAMSON (1975, pp. 167–9).

1971. Monmouth, Maine. See *SQ* 24:391–2.

1971, Nov. 21. Victoria Th., Stoke-on-Trent.

1972, Feb. 11. Milwaukee Repertory. Duke, John Hancock; Angelo, Raye Birk; Isabella, Judith Light. Director, Nagle Jackson. See playbill.

1972, Sept. 6. Shaw Th. Duke, Albert Welling; Angelo, Jonathan Coy; Isabella, Irene Richard. See *Th. Review '73*, p. 150.

1973, June 11. Stratford, Conn. Duke, Lee Richardson; Angelo, Philip Kerr; Isabella, Christina Pickles. Director, Michael Kahn. Also Washington, 3 Sept. See *NYT*, 12 and 24 June, *SQ* 24:411–14, 448–9, and *PP*, Aug., pp. 58–9.

1973, Dec. 26. New York City Center. Director, John Houseman. See *NYT*, 27 Dec., and *ThWN* 30:31.

1974, Jan. 29. Old Vic and tour. Director, Jonathan Miller. See *PP*, Mar., pp. 44–5, and Oct., pp. 32–3.

1974, Sept. 4. Stratford. Duke, Barrie Ingham; Angelo, Michael Pennington; Isabella, Francesca Annis. See *PP*, Oct., pp. 30–3, *SQ* 25:392–3, *ShS* 28:137, 146–8, and plates V, VI, and MILES (1976, p. 315).

1975, June 11. Stratford, Ontario. Duke, William Hutt; Angelo, Brian Bedford; Isabella, Martha Henry. Director, Robin Phillips. Also 1976 with Douglas Rain as Angelo. See *NYT*, 13 June, *SQ* 27:31–2, 28:204–5, *PP*, Nov., pp. 35, 37, and BERRY (1977, pp. 22–3, 91–9, 103–4).

1975, July 9. Old Globe Th., San Diego.

1975, Aug. 12. Greenwich. Director, Jonathan Miller. See *SQ* 27:22–3, 28:204–5, and *ShN* 25:30.

1975, Oct. 5. Abbey Th., New York. CSC Repertory Co. Duke, Stuart Vaughan.

1976, Feb. 4. Guthrie Th., Minneapolis. Duke, Ken Ruta; Angelo, Nicholas Kepros; Isabella, Patricia Conolly. Director, Michael Langham. See playbill.

1976, Aug. 12. Central Park, New York. Duke, Sam Waterston; Angelo, John Cazale; Isabella, Meryl Streep. See *NYTCR* 37:133–6, *New Yorker*, 30 Aug., and *SQ* 28:215–16.

1976, Aug. 24. Assembly Hall, Edinburgh. Birmingham Repertory Co. Duke, Bernard Lloyd; Angelo, David Burke; Isabella, Anna Calder-Marshall. Director, Stuart Burge. Also Stirling, 13 Sept., Birmingham, 6 Oct., and National Th., London, 5 May 1977. See *PP*, Nov. 1976, p. 19, and playbills.

1977, June 9. St. George's Elizabethan Th. Director, Joseph O'Conor. See *PP*, June, p. 6.

1977, June 11. Ashland, Oregon. See *SQ* 29:279–80.

1977, July 22. Odessa, Texas. See *SQ* 29:249.

1977, Aug. 2. Monmouth, Maine. See *SQ* 29:226–7.

1977, Aug. 25. Berkeley, California. See *SQ* 29:274.

Music

The earliest known music for the song "Take, oh take those lips away" in 4.1 was either composed or revised by Dr. John Wilson (1595–1674). CUTTS (1959, pp. xlii–iv, 114–15, 172) suggests that Wilson adapted the music sung in 1604 for later performances of *MM* and also used it for Fletcher's *Rollo, or The Bloody Brother,* 5.2. STERNFELD (1965, pp. 201–2) thinks that Wilson composed the music for *Rollo,* perhaps about 1625. The setting was first printed in 1652 in John Playford, *Select Musicall Ayres,* 1:24, where the "first book containes ayres for a voyce alone, to the theorbo, or basse violl." Dr. Wilson, who became Professor of Music at Oxford in 1656, gave the Bodleian a MS, partly autograph, containing this setting (Mus. b.1, f. 19ᵛ). HALLIWELL (ed. 1854, 3:172) reproduces the music in facsimile. Four other MS copies are known: Christ Church, Oxford, 434, f. 1; British Library Addl. 11608, f. 56, with more complicated notation for the second stanza; and two at the New York Public Library, Drexel 4041, f. 32, and Drexel 4257.16. The setting in Playford was reprinted in *The Treasury of Musick* (1669) and in many later collections. Modern scores for this setting are in J. F. Bridge, *Songs from Shakespeare* (?1894); CUTTS (1959; rev. ed. 1971, pp. 1, 85); and STERNFELD (1965, p. 203), reprinted here. Cutts remarks that the simple version of this song possesses much charm and that it calls for all the limpidity and suppleness of the highest register of a boy's voice.

COLLIER (1845, pp. 33–6) and RIMBAULT (1846) conjecture that Dr. Wilson was the *"Iacke Wilson"* whose name is printed in the F text of *Ado* (868) as the actor who played Balthasar and sang "Sigh no more Ladies." However, Collier subsequently (1846, pp. xvii–xix) identifies *"Iacke Wilson"* with an earlier John Wilson who was born in 1585, and his argument is accepted by CHAMBERS (1923, 2:349) and BENTLEY (1941, 2:621–2).

"Take, oh take those lips away" has attracted many composers. GREEN-HILL, HARRISON, & FURNIVALL (1884, pp. xii, 26–7) list thirty settings, but at least ninety-five are now known: see HARTNOLL (1964, pp. 260–1); BOUSTEAD (1964, p. 12); and *A Shakespeare Bibliography: The Catalogue of the Birmingham Shakespeare Library* (1971, 2:794, 5:1366). The known settings are by John Alcock (1775?), H. O. Anderton (1910), T. Anderton (1863?), Luffman Atterbury (d. 1796), Frederic Ayres (1906), W. A. Barratt (1916), Augustus Barry (1810), J. Bath, J. P. Beach (1906), T. C. Sterndale-Bennett (1909), H. R. Bishop (1819), Gaston Borch (1907), W. Havergal Brian (1925), E. L. Bridgewater (1964), Geoffrey Bush, J. W. Callcott (1786, Brit. Lib. Addl. MS 27642), Mary G. Carmichael (1851–1935), Mario Castel-nuovo-Tedesco (1924), Ernest Chausson (1855–99), Thomas Chilcot (1744), Harold Clark, M. F. Coates (1924), C. E. Cover (1895), James Coward (1872), F. H. Cowen (1884), Cedric T. Davie (1913–), E. Diemer, Bernard van Dieren (1925), Christopher Dixon (c. 1760), Madeleine

Take,____ o take those lips a - way that so sweet - ly were for-sworn, and those eyes, the____ break of day, lights that do mis - lead the morn, but my kiss - es bring a - gain, seals of____ love but sealed in vain.

Playford, bars 2-3

o take those lips a way

Playford, bass, bar 3; bass, bar 7

Dring, Garth Edmundson (1943), James Elliott (c. 1811, Brit. Lib. Addl. MS 31671), William Faulkes (1920, MS), Wolfgang Fortner, A. M. Fox (1900), J. E. Galliard (1730), F. Elvira Gambogi, William Gardiner (1795?), Tommaso Giordani (1781), E. N. Grazia (1872), James Greenhill (1883), Franz Hueffer (1873), Edward Iles (1891), William Jackson (c. 1760–70), G. F. Johnson (1907), A. King (1908), Frank La Forge (1909), F. Lancelott (1858), Amelia Lehmann (1899), Egerton Letts (1915), William Linley (1816), Herbert Lumby, G. A. Macfarren (1869), Clara A. Macirone (1864?), W. H. Mellers (1944), Alfred Mellon (1864), H. S. Middleton, R. B. Montgomery (1948), E. C. Moore (1914), W. N. (1770), C. H. H. Parry (1875), F. Pascal, R. L. Pearsall (1819), H. H. Pierson, Mary Plumstead (1956), A. H. D. Prendergast (1878), Roger Quilter (1921), Samuel Reay (1869), E. D. Rubbra (1928), Henri Sauguet, B. L. Selby (1903), John Stafford Smith (c. 1812), Arthur Somervell (1898), Reginald Steggall (1919), John A. Stevenson (c. 1795), Anton Strelezki, J. A. Taylor (1905?), Virgil Thomson (1961), H. Tierney, William Tindal (1785), Donald Tovey (1875–1940), Bryceson Treharne, Ronald Tremain (1958), Thomas Tremain (1786), Peter Warlock (1916), John Weldon (c. 1702), J. A. Westrup (1948), Michael White (1961), Ralph Vaughan Williams (1926), W. Albert Williams (1956), Christopher Wilson, John Wilson (before 1652), R. W. Wood, W. B. Wordsworth, and Arthur Young (1947).

Mariana's maid instead of her boy sang "Take, oh take" in Charles Gildon's version in 1700. Henry Purcell's *Dido and Aeneas,* which had been performed by schoolgirls at Chelsea in 1689, was first acted and sung professionally as part of this production of *MM* at Lincoln's Inn Fields (WHITE, 1959). As Betterton promises in the prologue, "'Tis *Purcels* Musick, and 'tis *Shakespears* Play." Angelo listens to "the Opera," described as "The Loves of Dido and Aeneas, a Mask, in Four Musical Entertainments." But after the first he says to himself, "This Musick is no Cure for my Distemper," and after the second, "All will not do: All won't devert my Pain." Angelo and Escalus hear the third entertainment at the end of Act 3, with dances by sailors, wizards, and witches. Near the end of the play the Duke bids Isabella sit by him to hear the fourth, with dances by morris dancers and nymphs.

Richard Wagner in *My Life* (1911, 1:140–8) tells how he adapted from *MM* his opera *Das Liebesverbot (The Ban on Love),* performed at Magdeburg on 29 Mar. 1836. In his verse libretto he changed the plot so that Isabella rouses the people of Palermo to revolt against the German viceroy and free Claudio from prison. "The police at first took exception to the title of the work," Wagner writes, but when he assured the magistrate "that it was modelled upon a very serious play of Shakespeare's, the authorities contented themselves with changing the somewhat startling title" to *The Novice of Palermo.* At the first performance none of the actors knew their parts, and the opera was so unintelligible that "the story remained a complete mystery to the public." In 1866 Wagner presented the score to King Ludwig of

Bavaria with a poem apologizing for this "sin of his youth" (WAGNER, 1922; NEWMAN, 1933, 1:208–9). After the vocal score was first printed in 1922, the opera was produced in various German theaters. Wagner's changes from *MM* are discussed by KAPP (1910, pp. 142–4), REICHELT (1912, pp. 65–88), and PACHE (1977, pp. 1–16).

BIBLIOGRAPHY

The place of publication is London unless otherwise indicated. For editions of *Measure for Measure* see pp. xii ff.; for abbreviations see pp. xx ff.

Abbott, E[dwin] A. *A Shakespearian Grammar*. Rev. & enl. 1870. (Rpt. New York: Dover, 1966. 1st ed. 1869.)

Abercrombie, Lascelles. "A Plea for the Liberty of Interpreting." *PBA* 16 (1930), 137–64. (Rpt. in *Aspects of Shakespeare*, OUP, 1933, pp. 227–54.)

Ackerman, Margaret B. "Directions of Change in Shakespeare's Alterations of His Sources: The Comedies." *DA* 29 (1969), 3089A. (Berkeley.)

Adams, F. " 'Measure for Measure', [625]." 8 *N&Q* 7 (1895), 203.

Adams, Joseph Quincy. *A Life of William Shakespeare*. Boston, 1923.

Adee, Alvey A. "On 'Brakes of Ice'." *Shakespeariana* 2 (1885), 103–10.

Agate, James. *The Contemporary Theatre, 1924.* 1925.

——. *First Nights*. 1934.

Ainslie, Douglas. "Shakespeare and Croce." *EngRev* 26 (1918), 117–21.

Albrecht, Louis. *Neue Untersuchungen zu Shakespeares Mass für Mass*. Berlin, 1914. (Königsberg diss.)

Alexander, Nigel. *Shakespeare:* Measure for Measure. Stud. in Eng. Lit. 57. 1975.

Alexander, Peter. "*Measure for Measure:* A Case for the Scottish Solomon." *MLQ* 28 (1967), 478–88.

——. *Shakespeare*. OUP, 1964.

——. *Shakespeare's Life and Art*. 1939.

Alexejew, Michail P. "Shakespeare und Puschkin." *SJW* 104 (1968), 141–74.

Allman, Eileen J. "Player-King and Adversary: The Two Faces of Play in Shakespeare." *DAI* 34 (1973), 1231A. (Syracuse.)

Altieri, Joanne S. "Shakespeare's Comic Prose Style." *DAI* 31 (1970), 350A–1A. (North Carolina.)

——. "Style and Social Disorder in *Measure for Measure.*" *SQ* 25 (1974), 6–16.

Amos, George W., ed. "A Critical Edition of George Whetstone's *Promos and Cassandra.*" *DA* 29 (1969), 3089A. (Arkansas.)

Ancona, Alessandro d'. *La poesia popolare italiana*. 2nd, enl. ed. Livorno, 1906. (1st ed. 1878.)

Anders, H[enry] R. D. *Shakespeare's Books*. Schriften der Deutschen Shakespeare-Gesellschaft 1. Berlin, 1904.

Anonymous. "Authority of Princes Often Abused, Illustrated from a Play of *Shakespear.*" *Gentleman's Magazine* 7 (1737), 557–9. (1st pub. in *The Craftsman*, No. 585, 24 Sept. 1737.)

——. "A Criticism on Shakespeare's Description of the Popish Purgatory in *Measure for Measure.*" *London Museum of Politics, Miscellanies, and Literature* 1 (1770), 391–4.

——. " 'Measure for Measure'." *Congregationalist* (London) 1 (1872), 402–11.

——. "Measure for Measure." *New York Times*, 7 Feb. 1888, p. 5. (Rpt. in *The New York Times Theater Reviews, 1870–1919*, New York, 1975.)

——. "*Reed*'s Edition of Shakspeare's Plays." *Monthly Review* 75 (1786), 81–94, 161–9.

_____. "Remarks upon Some Passages of Shakespeare." *Edinburgh Magazine* 1 (1785), 34–7.

_____. "Shakespeare's Problem Plays." *TLS,* 16 July 1931, pp. 553–4.

_____. "*Steevens*'s Edition of Shakspeare." *Monthly Review* 62 (1780), 12–26, 257–70.

_____. *The Thespian Dictionary.* 1802.

_____. "The Women of Shakspeare; Isabella." *Englishwoman's Domestic Magazine* (1872), pp. 250–1.

Ansari, A. A. "*Measure for Measure* and the Masks of Death." *Aligarh Jour. of Eng. Stud.* 2 (1977), 231–46.

Antalocy, Stephanie C. "Shakespeare and the Ruler's Disguise: The Backgrounds of *Henry V* and *Measure for Measure.*" *DAI* 37 (1976), 323A–4A. (Berkeley.)

Archer, William. *Play-Making: A Manual of Craftsmanship.* Boston, 1912.

_____. *The Theatrical 'World' for 1893.* [1894.]

Armstrong, Cecil F. *Shakespeare to Shaw.* 1913. (Rpt. New York: AMS, 1969.)

Aronson, Alex. *Psyche & Symbol in Shakespeare.* Bloomington, Ind., & London, 1972.

Arrowsmith, W[illiam] R. *Shakespeare's Editors and Commentators.* 1865.

Auden, W. H. "Music in Shakespeare: Its Dramatic Use in His Plays." *Encounter* 9 (Dec. 1957), 31–44. (Rpt. in *The Dyer's Hand and Other Essays,* New York, 1962, pp. 500–27, and in *Shakespeare Criticism 1935–60,* ed. Anne Ridler, OUP, 1963, pp. 306–28.)

Avery, Emmett L., ed. *The London Stage, 1660–1800. Part 2 (1700–29).* 2 vols. Carbondale, 1960.

Axelrad, A[lbert] José. *Un Malcontent élizabéthain: John Marston (1576–1634).* Paris, 1955.

B., J. G. "'Take, O, take those lips away'." *Shakespeariana* 3 (1886), 319.

Babula, William. "Justice in *Measure for Measure.*" *The Carrell: Journal of the Friends of the Univ. of Miami Library* 11 (1970), 27–33.

_____. "*Wishes Fall Out As They're Willed*": *Shakespeare and the Tragicomic Archetype.* Salzburg Stud. in Eng. Lit., Elizabethan & Ren. Stud. Salzburg, 1975. (Berkeley diss.)

Bache, William B. *Measure for Measure as Dialectical Art.* Purdue Univ. Stud. Lafayette, Ind., 1969.

Badham, Charles. "The Text of Shakespeare." *Cambridge Essays, 1856.* 1856. Pp. 261–91.

Bagehot, Walter. "Shakespeare—The Individual." *Collected Works.* Ed. Norman St. John–Stevas. 8 vols. Cambridge, Mass., & London, 1965–74. 1:173–214. (1st pub. 1853.)

Bailey, John [C.]. *Shakespeare.* Eng. Heritage Ser. 1929.

Bailey, Samuel. *On the Received Text of Shakespeare's Dramatic Writings and Its Improvement.* 2 vols. 1862–6.

Baker, David E., Isaac Reed, & Stephen Jones. *Biographia Dramatica.* 3 vols. 1812.

Baker, Harry T. "A Shakespearean Measure of Morality." *MLN* 38 (1923), 18–23.

Baldini, Gabriele. "Atti pigri e corte parole (Un Belacqua shakespeariano)." *Belfagor* 8 (1953), 324–30.

_____. *Il dramma elisabettiano.* Milano, 1962.

Baldwin, T[homas] W. *On Act and Scene Division in the Shakspere First Folio.* Carbondale, 1965.

_____. *The Organization and Personnel of the Shakespearean Company.* Princeton, 1927. (Rpt. New York: Russell, 1961.)

_____. *William Shakspere's Small Latine & Lesse Greeke.* 2 vols. Urbana, 1944.

Ball, Robert H. "Cinthio's *Epitia* and *Measure for Measure.*" *Univ. of Colorado Stud.,* Ser. B, 2 (1945), 132–46.

Bandel, Betty. "Shakespeare's Treatment of the Social Position of Women." *Microfilm Abstracts* 11 (1951), 1030–2. (Columbia.)

Banham, Martin. "Some Notes on *Measure for Measure.*" *Ibadan* No. 20 (Oct. 1964), 28–31.

Baring, Maurice. *Have You Anything to Declare? A Note Book with Commentaries.* 1936.

Barker, Kathleen. *The Theatre Royal, Bristol.* 1970.

Barratt, Harold S. " 'The Rose Distilled': Virginity, Fertility and Marriage in Shakespeare." *DAI* 36 (1976), 5309A. (Western Ontario.)

Barrett, W[ilfred] P. " 'The Prenzie Angelo'." *TLS,* 16 Jan. 1937, p. 44.

Bartenschlager, Klaus. "Two Notes on *Measure for Measure.*" *SJH* (1976), pp. 160–3.

Barton, Anne. "Measure for Measure." *The Riverside Shakespeare.* Ed. G. Blakemore Evans et al. Boston, 1974. Pp. 545–9.

———. *See* Righter, Anne.

[Bathurst, Charles.] *Remarks on the Differences in Shakespeare's Versification in Different Periods of His Life.* 1857.

Battenhouse, Roy W. *"Measure for Measure* and Christian Doctrine of the Atonement." *PMLA* 61 (1946), 1029–59.

Bayley, John. *The Uses of Division: Unity and Disharmony in Literature.* London & New York, 1976.

Baynes, Thomas Spencer. "New Shakspearian Interpretations." *Edinburgh Review,* Oct. 1872, pp. 335–73. (Rpt. in *Shakespeare Studies and Essay on English Dictionaries,* 1894, pp. 300–57; rpt. New York: AMS, 1972.)

Beckerman, Bernard. *Shakespeare at the Globe, 1599–1609.* New York, 1962.

———. "A Shakespearean Experiment: The Dramaturgy of *Measure for Measure.*" *The Elizabethan Theatre II.* Ed. David Galloway. [Toronto,] 1970. Pp. 108–33.

Becket, Andrew. *Shakspeare's Himself Again.* 2 vols. 1815.

Belgion, Montgomery. "The Measure of Kafka." *Criterion* 18 (1938), 13–28.

Bellonci, Maria. *A Prince of Mantua: The Life and Times of Vincenzo Gonzaga.* Tr. Stuart Hood. 1956. (1st It. ed. 1947.)

Bennet, Norman. "Warburton's 'Shakespear'." 8 *N&Q* 3 (1893), 141–2.

Bennett, Josephine Waters. Measure for Measure *as Royal Entertainment.* New York & London, 1966.

Bentley, Eric. *The Life of the Drama.* New York, 1964.

Bentley, Gerald E. *The Jacobean and Caroline Stage.* 7 vols. OUP, 1941–68.

Berlin, Normand. *The Base String: The Underworld in Elizabethan Drama.* Rutherford, N.J., 1968. (Rev. from Berkeley diss.)

Berman, Ronald. "Shakespeare and the Law." *SQ* 18 (1967), 141–50.

Berry, Ralph. "Language and Structure in *Measure for Measure.*" *UTQ* 46 (1976–7), 147–61.

———. *On Directing Shakespeare: Interviews with Contemporary Directors.* London & New York, 1977.

Bertsche, Samuel. *See* Soellner, Rolf.

Bethell, S[amuel] L. *Shakespeare & the Popular Dramatic Tradition.* 1944.

Biancotti, Angiolo. *Guglielmo Shakespeare.* Torino, 1957.

Biggins, D[ennis]. " 'Measure for Measure' and 'The Heart of Mid-Lothian'." *EA* 14 (1961), 193–205.

Bilton, Peter. *Commentary and Control in Shakespeare's Plays.* Oslo & New York, 1974.

Birch, W[illiam] J. *An Inquiry into the Philosophy and Religion of Shakspere.* 1848. (Rpt. New York: Haskell, 1972.)

Birje-Patil, J. "Marriage Contracts in *Measure for Measure.*" *ShakS* 5 (1969), 106–11.

Birrell, T. A. "The Shakespearian Mixture: Recent Approaches to Shakespeare's Handling of the Comic and Tragic Kinds." *Museum* 63 (1958), 97–111.

Biswas, Dinesh Chandra. *Shakespeare's Treatment of His Sources in the Comedies.* Calcutta, 1971.

———. "Some Shakespearian Themes in the Dark Comedies." *Essays and Studies* (Jadavpur Univ.) 2 (1972), 18–26.

Black, James. "The Unfolding of 'Measure for Measure'." *ShS* 26 (1973), 119–28.

Blackstone, William (1723–80). Contributor to Malone 1780.

Blakeway, John B. (1765–1826). Contributor to v1821.

Boaden, James. *Memoirs of the Life of John Philip Kemble.* 2 vols. 1825.

———. *Memoirs of Mrs. Siddons.* 2nd ed. 2 vols. 1831. (1st ed. 1827.)

Boas, Frederick S. *Shakspere and His Predecessors.* 1896. (Rpt. New York: Greenwood, 1969.)

Bodenstedt, Friedrich. *Shakespeare's Frauencharaktere.* Vierte vermehrte Auflage. Berlin, 1887. (1st ed. 1874.)

Bolte, Johannes. *Acht Lieder aus der Reformationszeit.* Berlin, 1910.

———. "Italienische Volkslieder aus der Sammlung Hermann Kestners." *Zeitschrift des Vereins für Volkskunde* 12 (1902), 57–65.

Bond, Edward. "The Duke in *Measure for Measure.*" *Gambit* 17 (1970), 43–5.

Bond, R. Warwick, ed. *The Complete Works of John Lyly.* 3 vols. OUP, 1902.

Borinski, Ludwig. "Shakespeare's Comic Prose." *ShS* 8 (1955), 57–68.

Boustead, Alan. *Music to Shakespeare.* OUP, 1964.

Bowden, Henry S. *The Religion of Shakespeare: Chiefly from the Writings of the Late Mr. Richard Simpson.* 1899.

Bowden, William R. "The Bed Trick, 1603–1642: Its Mechanics, Ethics, and Effects." *ShakS* 5 (1969), 112–23.

Bradbrook, M[uriel] C. "Authority, Truth, and Justice in *Measure for Measure.*" *RES* 17 (1941), 385–99. (Rpt. in Ornstein, ed., 1961, pp. 78–87.)

———. "Shakespeare and the Use of Disguise in Elizabethan Drama." *EIC* 2 (1952), 159–68.

Bradley, A[ndrew] C. *Shakespearean Tragedy.* 1904.

B[rae], A[ndrew] E. " 'Cambridge Disputations' Illustrative of Shakspeare." 1 *N&Q* 6 (1852), 217.

———. " 'Prenzie' in 'Measure for Measure'." 1 *N&Q* 3 (1851), 455; 4 (1851), 63.

Brandes, Georg. *William Shakespeare: A Critical Study.* Tr. William Archer, Mary Morison, & Diana White. 2 vols. 1898. (Rpt. New York: Ungar, 1963. 1st Danish ed. 1895–6.)

Brandl, Alois. *Shakespeare: Leben—Umwelt—Kunst.* Neue Ausgabe. Berlin, 1922. (1st ed. 1894.)

Brashear, Lucy M. "Character and Prosody in Shakespeare's *Measure for Measure.*" *DAI* 30 (1970), 3424A–5A. (North Carolina.)

Brecht, Bertolt. MS written 1932, pub. Werner Mittenzwei in *Bertolt Brecht* (1962), p. 162.

Brewer, D[erek] S. "Measure for Measure, [3–11]." *N&Q* 200 (1955), 425.

Brewer, Wilmon. *Shakespeare's Influence on Sir Walter Scott.* Boston, 1925. (Harvard diss.)

Bridges, Robert. "On the Influence of the Audience." *Works of Shakespeare,* ed. A. H. Bullen. Stratford-on-Avon, 1904–7. 10:321–34. (Rpt. in *Collected Essays Papers &c.,* vol. 1, OUP, 1927.)

Brink, Bernhard ten. *Five Lectures on Shakespeare.* Tr. Julia Franklin. 1895. (1st Ger. ed. 1893.)

Brinkworth, E[dwin] R. C. *Shakespeare and the Bawdy Court of Stratford.* London & Chichester, 1972.

Broadbent, R. J. *Annals of the Liverpool Stage.* Liverpool, 1908.

Brockbank, Philip. "With a Saving Purpose." *TLS,* 26 Nov. 1976, pp. 1470–1.

Brook, G[eorge] L. *The Language of Shakespeare.* 1976.

Brook, Peter. *The Empty Space.* New York, 1968.

Brooke, Stopford A. *Ten More Plays of Shakespeare.* 1913. (Rpt. New York: Barnes & Noble, 1963.)

Brown, Ivor. [Introd.] *Shakespeare Memorial Theatre, 1954–56: A Photographic Record.* 1956. Pp. 1–19.

Brown, James [Bucham]. *Bible Truths, with Shakspearian Parallels.* 2nd ed. 1864. (1st ed. 1862. Rpt. of 1886 ed. [abridged] New York: AMS, 1975.)

Brown, John Russell. *Shakespeare and His Comedies.* 1957.

———, ed. John Webster, *The Duchess of Malfi.* 1964.

Brunner, Karl. *William Shakespeare.* Tübingen, 1957.

Bryant, J[oseph] A., Jr. *Hippolyta's View: Some Christian Aspects of Shakespeare's Plays.* Lexington, Ky., 1961.

Budd, Frederick E. "Material for a Study of the Sources of Shakespeare's *Measure for Measure.*" *RLC* 11 (1931), 711–36.

———. "Rouillet's *Philanira* and Whetstone's *Promos and Cassandra.*" *RES* 6 (1930), 31–48.

Buettner, Milton A., ed. *"A Game at Chess* by Thomas Middleton: A Textual Edition Based on the Manuscripts Written by Ralph Crane." *DAI* 33 (1972), 2317A–18A. (Michigan State.)

Buland, Mable. *The Presentation of Time in the Elizabethan Drama.* Yale Stud. in Eng. 44. New York, 1912. (Rpt. New York: Haskell, 1966.)

Bulloch, John. *Studies on the Text of Shakespeare: With Numerous Emendations.* 1878.

Bullough, Geoffrey. "Another Analogue of *Measure for Measure.*" *English Renaissance Drama: Essays in Honor of Madeleine Doran and Mark Eccles.* Ed. Standish Henning, Robert Kimbrough, & Richard Knowles. Carbondale, 1976. Pp. 108–17.

———, ed. *Narrative and Dramatic Sources of Shakespeare.* Vol. 2: *The Comedies, 1597–1603.* London & New York, 1958.

Burgess, William. *The Bible in Shakespeare.* New York, 1903.

Burns, Margie M. "The Theatrical Present in Six Shakespearean Comedies." *DAI* 36 (1975), 2214A. (Rice.)

Bush, Geoffrey. *Shakespeare and the Natural Condition.* Cambridge, Mass., 1956.

Butler, James D. " 'Measure for Measure', [1526]: 'Go a mile on his errand'." 7 *N&Q* 11 (1891), 83.

———. *The Once Used Words in Shakespeare.* Papers of the New York Sh. Soc. No. 6. New York, 1886.

Byrne, Sr. St. Geraldine. *Shakespeare's Use of the Pronoun of Address: Its Significance in Characterization and Motivation.* Washington, 1936. (Catholic Univ. diss.)

Cairncross, Andrew S. "Compositors C and D of the Shakespeare First Folio." *PBSA* 65 (1971), 41–52.

———. "Compositors E and F of the Shakespeare First Folio." *PBSA* 66 (1972), 369–406.

Cairns, Edward A., ed. "Charles Gildon's *Measure for Measure, or Beauty the Best Advocate:* A Critical Edition." *DAI* 32 (1971), 2633A. (Denver.)

Callahan, Robert D. "The Theme of 'Government' in 'Measure for Measure'." *Paunch* (Buffalo) No. 25 (Feb. 1966), pp. 31–52.

Campbell, John, Lord. *Shakespeare's Legal Acquirements Considered.* London & New York, 1859. (Rpt. New York: AMS, 1972.)

Campbell, Oscar James. "Shakespeare and the 'New' Critics." *Joseph Quincy Adams Memorial Studies.* Ed. James G. McManaway, Giles E. Dawson, & Edwin E. Willoughby. Washington, 1948. Pp. 81–100.

———. *Shakespeare's Satire.* New York: OUP, 1943.

Campbell, Thomas. *Life of Mrs. Siddons.* 2 vols. 1834.

Capocci, Valentina. *Genio e mestiere: Shakespeare e la commedia dell'arte.* Bari, 1950.

Caputi, Anthony. "Scenic Design in *Measure for Measure.*" *JEGP* 60 (1961), 423–34. (Rpt. in Geckle, ed., 1970, pp. 86–97.)

Card, James V. "In Just Proportion: Notes on the Final Scene of *Measure for Measure.*" *Topic* (Washington, Pa.) 7 (1964), 61–9.

Carter, Thomas. *Shakespeare and Holy Scripture, with the Version He Used.* 1905.

Cartwright, Robert. *New Readings in Shakspere; or, Proposed Emendations of the Text.* 1866.

Case, R[obert] H. (1857–1944). Contributor to Hart ed. 1905 and 2nd, rev. ed. 1925.

Cavalchini, Mariella. "L'*Epitia* di Giraldi Cinzio e *Measure for Measure.*" *Italica* 45 (1968), 59–69.

Cazamian, Louis. *The Development of English Humor.* Durham, 1952.

———. *L'Humour de Shakespeare.* Paris, 1945.

———. *See* Legouis, Emile.

Cebes. "Prenzie." 1 *N&Q* 3 (1851), 522.

Chalmers, George. *A Supplemental Apology for the Believers in the Shakspeare-Papers.* 1799. (Rpt. London: Cass, 1971; New York: Kelley, 1971.)

Chambers, E[dmund] K. *The Elizabethan Stage.* 4 vols. OUP, 1923.

———. [Review of Wilson ed., vols. 3–6.] *MLR* 19 (1924), 108–11.

———. *Shakespeare: A Survey.* 1925. (1st pub. in The Red Letter Shakespeare, 1904–8; *MM,* 1906.)

———. "William Shakespeare." *Encyclopaedia Britannica.* 11th ed. 1911.

———. *William Shakespeare: A Study of Facts and Problems.* 2 vols. OUP, 1930.

Chambers, R[aymond] W. "*Measure for Measure.*" *Man's Unconquerable Mind.* 1939. Pp. 277–310. (Rev. from "The Jacobean Shakespeare and *Measure for Measure,*" *PBA* 23 [1937], 135–92.)

Champion, Larry S. *The Evolution of Shakespeare's Comedy: A Study in Dramatic Perspective.* Cambridge, Mass., 1970.

Chapman, John Jay. *A Glance toward Shakespeare.* Boston, 1922.

Charlton, H[enry] B. "The Dark Comedies." *Shakespearian Comedy.* 1938. Pp. 208–65. (Delivered 1935; 1st pub. *Bull. John Rylands Lib.* 21 [1937], 78–128.)

Chasles, Philarète. *Études contemporaines.* 2 vols. Paris, 1866–7.

Chedworth, John [Howe], Lord. *Notes upon Some of the Obscure Passages in Shakespeare's Plays.* 1805.

Chung, Byung Choon. "A Study of Shakespeare's 'Measure for Measure'." *English Language and Literature* (Seoul) No. 11 (June 1962), 95–129.

Clapp, Henry A. "Time in Shakespeare's Comedies." *Atlantic Monthly* 55 (1885), 386–403.

Clark, William Smith. *The Irish Stage in the County Towns, 1720 to 1800.* OUP, 1965.

Clarke, Charles Cowden. *Shakespeare-Characters; Chiefly Those Subordinate.* 1863.

———. "Shakespeare's Women: Considered as Philosophers and Jesters." *Gentleman's Magazine* 234 (1873), 514–39.

———, & Mary Cowden Clarke. *The Shakespeare Key.* 1879.

Clarkson, Paul S., & Clyde T. Warren. *The Law of Property in Shakespeare and the Elizabethan Drama.* Baltimore, 1942. (Rpt. New York: Gordian, 1968.)

Clemen, Wolfgang. *Shakespeare's Dramatic Art: Collected Essays.* 1972.

Coghill, Nevill. "The Basis of Shakespearian Comedy." *E&S* NS 3 (1950), 1–28.

———. "Comic Form in *Measure for Measure.*" *ShS* 8 (1955), 14–27. (Rpt. in Soellner & Bertsche, eds., 1966, pp. 100–10.)

———. "Two Small Points in *Measure for Measure.*" *RES* 16 (1965), 393–5.

Cohn, Ruby. *Modern Shakespeare Offshoots.* Princeton, 1976.

Cole, Howard C. "The 'Christian' Context of *Measure for Measure.*" *JEGP* 64 (1965), 425–51.

Coleman, Marion Moore. *Fair Rosalind: The American Career of Helena Modjeska.* Cheshire, Conn., 1969.

Coleridge, Samuel Taylor. *Coleridge's Miscellaneous Criticism.* Ed. T. M. Raysor. Cambridge, Mass., 1936. (Rpt. Folcroft, Pa., 1969.)

———. *Coleridge's Shakespearean Criticism.* Ed. T. M. Raysor. 2 vols. Everyman's Lib. Rev. ed. London & New York, 1960. (1st ed., 2 vols., Cambridge, Mass., 1930.)

———. *Literary Remains.* Ed. H. N. Coleridge. 4 vols. 1836–9. (Rpt. New York: AMS, 1967.)

Collier, John Payne. *The History of English Dramatic Poetry to the Time of Shakespeare.* 3 vols. 1831. (2nd ed. 1879.)

———. "John Wilson, the Singer, in 'Much Ado about Nothing', a Musical Composer in Shakespeare's Plays." *Sh. Soc.'s Papers* 2 (1845), 33–6.

———. *Memoirs of the Principal Actors in the Plays of Shakespeare.* Sh. Soc. Pubs. 32. 1846.

———. *Notes and Emendations to the Text of Shakespeare's Plays, from Early Manuscript Corrections in a Copy of the Folio, 1632.* 2nd ed., rev. & enl. 1853. (Rpt. New York: Franklin, 1967. 1st ed. 1852.)

———. *Reasons for a New Edition of Shakespeare's Works.* 2nd, enl. ed. 1842. (Rpt. New York: AMS, 1973. 1st ed. 1841.)

———, ed. *Shakespeare's Library.* 2 vols. 1843.

Collins, John Churton. "The Religion of Shakespeare." *Ephemera Critica.* 4th ed. London & New York, 1902. (1st ed. 1901.)

———. "Shakespeare as a Prose Writer." *Studies in Shakespeare.* 1904. (Rpt. New York: AMS, 1973. 1st pub. in *Gentleman's Magazine* 249 [1880], 735–47.)

Colman, E[rnest] A. M. *The Dramatic Use of Bawdy in Shakespeare.* 1974.

Cook, Albert. "Metaphysical Poetry and 'Measure for Measure'." *Accent* (Urbana) 13 (1953), 122–7.

———. *Shakespeare's Enactment: The Dynamics of Renaissance Theatre.* Chicago, 1976.

Cooper, Thomas. *Thesaurus Linguae Romanae & Britannicae.* 1565. (Rpt. Menston: Scolar, 1969.)

Corssen, Meta. *Kleist und Shakespeare.* Forschungen zur neueren Literaturgeschichte 61. Weimar, 1930.

Cosentino, G[iuseppe]. *Le commedie di Shakespeare.* Bologna, 1906.

Cotgrave, Randle. *A Dictionarie of the French and English Tongues.* 1611. (Rpt. Columbia, S.C., 1950; Menston: Scolar, 1968.)

Coursen, Herbert R., Jr. "A Spacious Mirror: Shakespeare and the Play-Within." *DA* 26 (1966), 6693–4. (Connecticut.)

Courthope, W[illiam] J. *A History of English Poetry.* 6 vols. 1895–1910. (Rpt. New York: Russell, 1962.)

Craig, David. "Shakespeare, Lawrence, and Sexual Freedom." *The Real Foundations: Literature and Social Change.* 1973. Pp. 17–38. (Rev. from *Shakespeare in a Changing World,* ed. Arnold Kettle, 1964, pp. 195–216.)

Craig, Hardin. *An Interpretation of Shakespeare.* New York, 1948.

———. "Motivation in Shakespeare's Choice of Materials." *ShS* 4 (1951), 26–34. (Rpt. in *Shakespeare Criticism 1935–60,* ed. Anne Ridler, OUP, 1963, pp. 32–48.)

———. "When Shakespeare Altered His Sources." *Centennial Review* 8 (1964), 121–8.

Craig, W[illiam] J. (1843–1906). Contributor to Hart ed. 1905.

Craik, T[homas] W. *The Tudor Interlude: Stage, Costume, and Acting.* Leicester, 1958.

Crane, Milton. *Shakespeare's Prose.* Chicago, 1951.

Crawford, J. P. Wickersham. "A Sixteenth-Century Spanish Analogue of *Measure for Measure.*" *MLN* 35 (1920), 330–4.

Creizenach, Wilhelm. *Geschichte des neueren Dramas.* 5 vols. Halle a. S., 1893–1916. (Part tr. Cécile Hugon as *The English Drama in the Age of Shakespeare,* 1916.)

489

_____, ed. *Die Schauspiele der englischen Komödianten.* Deutsche National-Litteratur 23. Berlin & Stuttgart, [1889].

Croce, Benedetto. *Ariosto, Shakespeare and Corneille.* Tr. Douglas Ainslie. London & New York, 1920. (Rpt. New York: Russell, 1966. 1st It. ed. 1920; 2nd ed. 1929.)

Croft, John. *Annotations on Plays of Shakespear.* York, 1810.

Crosby, Joseph (1822–91). MS letter at Folger Library.

_____. MS notes in Dyce ed. 1866, vol. 1, in Univ. of Wisconsin Library, Madison.

Crosse, Gordon. *Shakespearean Playgoing, 1890–1952.* 1953.

Crundell, H. W. "The Queazie Angelo." *TLS,* 23 Apr. 1938, p. 280.

Cruttwell, Patrick. *The Shakespearean Moment and Its Place in the Poetry of the 17th Century.* 1954.

Cuming, H. Syer. "On the Beggar's Clicket." *Jour. of the British Archaeological Assn.* 35 (1879), 106–7.

Cuningham, Henry. " 'Measure for Measure'." *TLS,* 23 Oct. 1924, p. 668.

_____. " 'Measure for Measure' [493]." *Academy* 72 (1907), 162, 348–9.

Cunliffe, John W. "The Influence of Italian on Early Elizabethan Drama." *MP* 4 (1906–7), 597–604.

Cunningham, J[ames] V. " 'Essence' and the *Phoenix and Turtle."* *ELH* 19 (1952), 265–76.

Cunningham, Peter, ed. *Extracts from the Accounts of the Revels at Court, in the Reigns of Queen Elizabeth and King James I.* Sh. Soc. Pubs. 7. 1842. (Rpt. New York: AMS, 1971.)

Curry, John V. *Deception in Elizabethan Comedy.* Chicago, 1955. (Columbia diss.)

Curtius, Friedrich. "Ueber Shakespeare's 'Mass für Mass'." *Deutsche Rundschau* 66 (1891), 57–67.

Cutts, John P. *La Musique de scène de la troupe de Shakespeare, The King's Men, sous le règne de Jacques Ier.* 2nd, rev. ed. Paris, 1971. (1st ed. 1959.)

_____."Perfect Contrition: A Note on 'Measure for Measure'." *N&Q* 205 (1960), 416–19.

Daiches, David. *A Critical History of English Literature.* 2 vols. New York, 1960.

_____. "Guilt and Justice in Shakespeare." *Literary Essays.* Edinburgh & London, 1956. Pp. 1–25.

Dam. *See* Van Dam.

D'Amico, Jack P. "Symbolic Patterns of Action in Certain Shakespearean Comedies." *DA* 27 (1966), 744A. (State Univ. of New York at Buffalo.)

Daniel, P[eter] A. *Notes and Conjectural Emendations of Certain Doubtful Passages in Shakespeare's Plays.* 1870. (Rpt. New York: AMS, 1972.)

_____. "Time-Analysis of the Plots of Shakspere's Plays." *N.S.S. Trans. 1877–9.* [1879.] Pp. 117–346.

Daniels, R[obertson] Balfour. "Shakspere and the Puritans." *ShAB* 13 (1938), 40–53.

Davenant, William. *The Law against Lovers.* In *Works.* 1673. (Rpt., 2 vols., New York: Blom, 1968.)

_____. *The Law against Lovers* [with F1 text of *MM*]. Introd. by B. Frank Carpenter. Bankside-Restoration Shakespeare. Sh. Soc. of New York, 1908.

Davenport, A[rnold]. "Notes on Lyly's 'Campaspe' and Shakespeare." *N&Q* 199 (1954), 19–20.

David, Richard. "Shakespeare's Comedies and the Modern Stage." *ShS* 4 (1951), 129–38.

Davies, W[illiam] Robertson. "Measure for Measure." *Twice Have the Trumpets Sounded: A Record of the Stratford Shakespearean Festival in Canada 1954* by Tyrone Guthrie, Robertson Davies, & Grant Macdonald. Toronto, 1954. Pp. 61–105.

_____. *Shakespeare's Boy Actors.* 1939. (Rpt. New York: Russell, 1964. B.Litt. thesis Oxford.)

Davis, Cushman K. *The Law in Shakespeare.* 2nd ed. St. Paul, 1884. (Rpt. New York: AMS, 1972. 1st ed. Washington, 1883.)

Dawson, Henry (d. 1755). Emendations quoted in Thirlby's MS notes on Pope ed. 1723.

De La Mare, Walter. Introd. to *The Shakespeare Songs.* Ed. Tucker Brooke. New York, 1929. (Rpt. Folcroft, Pa., 1970.)

De Leine, M. A. *Lilian Adelaide Neilson: A Memorial Sketch, Personal and Critical.* 1881.

Delius, N[icolaus]. "Die Prosa in Shakespeare's Dramen." *SJ* 5 (1870), 227–73. (Rpt. in *Abhandlungen zu Shakspere,* Elberfeld, 1878, pp. 152–205.)

de Lorenzo, Anna Odierno. *I canti di Shakespeare.* Bari, 1933.

de Lorenzo, Giuseppe. *Shakespeare e il dolore del mondo.* Bologna, [1921].

Denney, Constance D. B. "The Dynamics of Shakespeare's Rhetoric: A Study of Judicial Debate in Four Plays." *DAI* 33 (1973), 6867A–8A. (Stanford.)

Dent, R[obert] W. [Review of Leisi ed.] *ShakS* 2 (1966), 343–50.

Derocquigny, Jules. "Comment Shakespeare est compris: *Meas.* [1375–1489]." *RAA* 4 (1926–7), 434–40.

——————."Shakespeare, Measure for Measure ([242] *propagation*)." *RAA* 4 (1926–7), 338–40.

——————." 'Wayte What' = 'Whatever'." *MLR* 3 (1907), 72.

Desai, Rupin W. "Freudian Undertones in the Isabella-Angelo Relationship of *Measure for Measure.*" *Psychoanalytic Review* 64 (1977), 487–94.

Dibdin, James C. *The Annals of the Edinburgh Stage.* Edinburgh, 1888.

Dickins, Richard. *Forty Years of Shakespeare on the English Stage: August, 1867 to August, 1907. A Student's Memories.* [1907.]

Dickinson, John W. "Renaissance Equity and *Measure for Measure.*" *SQ* 13 (1962), 287–97.

Diffey, Carole T. "The Last Judgment in *Measure for Measure.*" *Durham Univ. Jour.* 66 (1974), 231–7.

Dobson, E[ric] J. *English Pronunciation 1500–1700.* 2 vols. 2nd, rev. ed. OUP, 1968. (1st ed. 1957.)

Doccioli, Matilde. *Fonti italiane dei drammi di Guglielmo Shakespeare.* Lodi, 1914.

Dodds, W[inifred] M. T. "The Character of Angelo in *Measure for Measure.*" *MLR* 41 (1946), 246–55. (Rpt. in Ornstein, ed., 1961, pp. 88–96.)

——————. *See* Nowottny, Winifred.

Dodge, Dennis. "Life and Death in *Measure for Measure.*" *Recovering Literature* (San Diego) 4, No. 1 (1975), 43–58.

Donaldson, Ian. *The World Upside-Down: Comedy from Jonson to Fielding.* OUP, 1970.

Donovan, Richard A. "Shakespeare and the Game of Evil: A Study of Role-Playing Villains." *DA* 29 (1968), 868A. (Minnesota.)

Doran, Madeleine. *Endeavors of Art: A Study of Form in Elizabethan Drama.* Madison, 1954.

Douce, Francis (1757–1834). Contributor to v1793.

——————. *Illustrations of Shakspeare, and of Ancient Manners.* 2 vols. 1807. (Rpt. New York: Franklin, 1969.)

Dowden, Edward. *Shakspere: A Critical Study of His Mind and Art.* 1875.

——————. "Shakspere's Portraiture of Women." *Transcripts and Studies.* 1888. Pp. 338–77. (1st pub. in *Contemporary Rev.* 47 [1885], 517–35.)

Drake, Nathan. *Shakspeare and His Times.* 2 vols. 1817. (Rpt. New York: Franklin, 1969.)

Draper, John W. "King James and Shakespeare's Literary Style." *Archiv* 171 (1937), 36–48.

——————. "*Measure for Measure* and the London Stews." *West Virginia Univ. Philological Papers* 23 (1977), 5–17.

——————. "Patterns of Tempo in 'Measure for Measure'." *West Virginia Univ. Philologi-*

cal Papers 9 (1953), 11–19. (Rev. in *The Tempo-Patterns of Shakespeare's Plays,* Anglistische Forschungen 90, Heidelberg, 1957, pp. 94–100.)

———. "Political Themes in Shakespeare's Later Plays." *JEGP* 35 (1936), 61–93.

———. "Shakespeare and King James I." *Rivista di letterature moderne e comparate* 22 (1969), 5–9.

Drew, Philip. "A Suggested Reading in *Measure for Measure.*" *SQ* 9 (1958), 202–4.

Driscoll, James P. "Aspects of Identity in Shakespearean Drama." *DAI* 33 (1972), 2323A. (Wisconsin.)

Dryden, John. "Defence of the Epilogue. Or, An Essay on the Dramatique Poetry of the Last Age." *The Conquest of Granada by the Spaniards.* 1672. Pp. 160–75. (Rpt. in *Of Dramatic Poesy and Other Critical Essays,* 2 vols., ed. George Watson, Everyman's Lib., 1962.)

Dugdale, Gilbert. *The Time Triumphant.* 1604. (Rpt. in John Nichols, *The Progresses of King James the First,* 1828, 1:408–19, and in *Stuart Tracts, 1603–1693,* ed. C. H. Firth, 1903, pp. 69–82.)

Dunbar, Janet. *Flora Robson.* 1960.

Duncan-Jones, Katherine. "Stoicism in *Measure for Measure:* A New Source." *RES* NS 28 (1977), 441–6.

Dunkel, Wilbur. "Law and Equity in *Measure for Measure.*" *SQ* 13 (1962), 275–85.

Dupont, Victor. "Etude des images dans le premier acte de *Mesure pour Mesure.*" *Annales de la Faculté des Lettres de Toulouse,* Dec. 1952, pp. 129–48.

Duport, Paul. *Essais littéraires sur Shakspeare.* 2 vols. Paris, 1828.

Durham, Willard H. "Measure for Measure as Measure for Critics." *Essays in Criticism: Univ. of California Pubs. in Eng.* 1 (1929), 111–32.

———. "What Art Thou, Angelo?" *Studies in the Comic: Univ. of California Pubs. in Eng.* 8 (1941), 155–74.

Durrant, Geoffrey. "*Measure for Measure:* A Comedy." *Stratford Papers, 1968–69.* Ed. B. A. W. Jackson. Hamilton, Ont., & Shannon, Ireland, 1972. Pp. 21–39.

Dusinberre, Juliet. *Shakespeare and the Nature of Women.* 1975. (Rev. from Warwick diss.)

Dwyer, J. J. "Did Shakespeare Read Dante?" *Tablet* 206 (1955), 33–4.

Dyce, Alexander. *A Few Notes on Shakespeare; with Occasional Remarks on the Emendations of the Manuscript-Corrector in Mr. Collier's Copy of the Folio 1632.* 1853. (Rpt. New York: AMS, 1971.)

———. *A Glossary to Shakespeare.* Vol. 9 of *The Works of William Shakespeare.* 1867.

———. *Remarks on Mr. J. P. Collier's and Mr. C. Knight's Editions of Shakespeare.* 1844. (Rpt. New York: AMS, 1972.)

———. *Strictures on Mr. Collier's New Edition of Shakespeare, 1858.* 1859.

Eagleson, Robert D. "Eschatological Speculations and the Use of the Infinitive." *SQ* 26 (1975), 206–8.

Eagleton, Terence. *Shakespeare and Society: Critical Studies in Shakespearean Drama.* 1967.

Eaton, T[homas] R. *Shakespeare and the Bible.* [1860.] (Rpt. New York: AMS, 1972. 1st ed. 1858.)

Ebsworth, J. W., ed. *The Roxburghe Ballads.* Ed. William Chappell & J. W. Ebsworth. 9 vols. Ballad Soc. Hertford, 1869–99.

Eccles, Mark. "Correspondence." *SQ* 23 (1972), 461.

———. "Emendations in Whetstone's 'Promos and Cassandra'." *N&Q* 216 (1971), 12–13.

———. *Shakespeare in Warwickshire.* Madison, 1961.

———. "Shakespeare's Use of *Look How* and Similar Idioms." *JEGP* 42 (1943), 386–400.

———. "Whetstone's Death." *TLS,* 27 Aug. 1931, p. 648.

Eckhardt, Eduard. *Das englische Drama im Zeitalter der Reformation und der Hochrenaissance.* Band 1. *Vorstufen, Shakespeare und seine Zeit.* Berlin & Leipzig, 1928.

———. *Die lustige Person im älteren englischen Drama (bis 1642).* Palaestra 17. Berlin, 1902.

Eckhoff, Lorentz. *Shakespeare: Spokesman of the Third Estate.* Tr. R. I. Christophersen. Oslo Stud. in Eng. 3. Oslo & Oxford, 1954. (Rpt. New York: AMS, 1973.)

Edwards, Anthony S. G., & Anthony W. Jenkins. " 'Prenzie': *Measure for Measure* [1309, 1312]." *SQ* 27 (1976), 333–4.

Edwards, Philip. *Shakespeare and the Confines of Art.* 1968.

[Edwards, Thomas.] *A Supplement to Mr. Warburton's Edition of Shakespear. Being the Canons of Criticism, and Glossary.* 1748. (Rpt. New York: AMS, 1972. 3rd ed. 1750 as *The Canons of Criticism, and Glossary.* 6th ed. 1758. 7th ed. 1765.)

Eich, Louis M. "Alterations of Shakespeare 1660–1710." *Microfilm Abstracts* 8 (1948), 90–1. (Michigan diss. 1923.)

Eliot, T. S. "Gerontion." *Poems.* 1920.

———. "Hamlet and His Problems." *The Sacred Wood.* 1920. Pp. 87–94. (Rpt. in *Elizabethan Essays,* 1934, pp. 55–63.)

[Elliott, M(adeleine) Leigh-Noel.] *Shakspeare's Garden of Girls.* 1885.

Ellis, Ruth. *The Shakespeare Memorial Theatre.* 1948.

Ellis-Fermor, U[na] M. *The Frontiers of Drama.* 1945.

———. *The Jacobean Drama: An Interpretation.* 1936.

Ellrodt, Robert. "Self-Consciousness in Montaigne and Shakespeare." *ShS* 28 (1975), 37–50.

Elze, Karl. *Notes on Elizabethan Dramatists with Conjectural Emendations of the Text.* 3rd Ser. Halle, 1886.

———. *William Shakespeare: A Literary Biography.* Tr. L. Dora Schmitz. 1888. (Rpt. New York: AMS, 1973. 1st Ger. ed. 1876.)

Emerson, Ralph Waldo. *English Traits.* Ed. Howard M. Jones. Cambridge, Mass., 1966. (1st ed. 1856.)

Émery, Léon. *La Vision Shakespearienne du monde et de l'homme.* Lyon, [1957].

Empson, William. "Sense in *Measure for Measure.*" *The Structure of Complex Words.* London & Norfolk, Conn., 1951. Pp. 270–88. (Rpt. in Ornstein, ed., 1961, pp. 101–11. Rev. from *Southern Review* 4 [1938], 340–50.)

———. *Seven Types of Ambiguity.* 3rd, rev. ed. London & Norfolk, Conn., 1953. (1st ed. 1930.)

Engelen, Julia. "Die Schauspieler-Ökonomie in Shakespeares Dramen." *SJ* 63 (1927), 75–158.

Erler, Ernst. *Die Namengebung bei Shakespeare.* Anglistische Arbeiten 2. Heidelberg, 1913. (Enl. from Jena diss.)

Evans, [Benjamin] Ifor. *The Language of Shakespeare's Plays.* 3rd ed. 1964. (1st ed. 1952.)

Evans, Bertrand. *Shakespeare's Comedies.* OUP, 1960.

Evans, Gareth Lloyd. "Directing Problem Plays: John Barton Talks to Gareth Lloyd Evans." *ShS* 25 (1972), 63–71.

———. *Shakespeare III, 1599–1604.* Edinburgh, 1971.

Evans, G[wynne] Blakemore. "New Evidence on the Proven[i]ence of the Padua Prompt-Books of Shakespeare's *Macbeth, Measure for Measure,* and *Winter's Tale.*" *SB* 20 (1967), 239–42.

———. *Shakespearean Prompt-Books of the Seventeenth Century.* 2 vols. Charlottesville, 1960–3.

Evans, Hugh C. "Comic Constables—Fictional and Historical." *SQ* 20 (1969), 427–33.

Fairchild, Hoxie N. "The Two Angelo's." *ShAB* 6 (1931), 53–9.

Falconer, J. A. "Shakespeare's Lost Chance." *Neophilologus* 13 (1928), 117–23.

Farjeon, Herbert. *The Shakespearean Scene: Dramatic Criticisms.* [1949.]

Farmer, John S., ed. *Promos and Cassandra by George Whetstone, 1578.* Tudor Facsimile Texts. 1910.

Farmer, Richard (1735–97). Contributor to v1773, v1785.

———. *An Essay on the Learning of Shakespeare.* Cambridge, 1767. (Rpt. London: Cass, 1969.)

Felperin, Howard. *Shakespearean Romance.* Princeton, 1972.

Felver, Charles S. "A Proverb Turned Jest in *Measure for Measure.*" *SQ* 11 (1960), 385–7.

Fergusson, Francis. *"Measure for Measure." The Human Image in Dramatic Literature.* New York, 1957. Pp. 126–43. (1st pub. in *Kenyon Review* 14 [1952], 103–20. Rpt. in Geckle, ed., 1970, pp. 73–85.)

———. "Trope and Allegory: Some Themes Common to Dante and Shakespeare." *Dante Studies* 86 (1968), 113–26. (Rev. in *Trope and Allegory: Themes Common to Dante and Shakespeare,* Athens, Ga., 1977, pp. 49–70.)

Field, Barron. "Conjectures on Some of the Corrupt or Obscure Passages of Shakespeare." *Sh. Soc.'s Papers* 2 (1845), 40–61.

Figgis, Darrell. *Shakespeare: A Study.* 1911.

Findlater, Richard [Kenneth B. F. Bain]. *Emlyn Williams.* 1956.

Finkelstein, Sidney. "On Updating Shakespeare: Part II." *Mainstream* (New York), Aug. 1961, pp. 35–42.

———. *Who Needs Shakespeare?* New York, 1973.

Firth, C[harles] H. Introd. to *Stuart Tracts, 1603–1693.* In *An English Garner.* Vol. 2. 1903.

Fisch, Harold. "Shakespeare and the Puritan Dynamic." *ShS* 27 (1974), 81–92.

Fitch, Robert E. *Shakespeare: The Perspective of Value.* Philadelphia, 1969.

Flatter, Richard. *Triumph der Gnade: Shakespeare-Essays.* Wien, 1956.

Fleay, Frederick G. *A Biographical Chronicle of the English Drama, 1559–1642.* 2 vols. 1891. (Rpt. New York: Franklin, 1969.)

———. *A Chronicle History of the Life and Work of William Shakespeare.* 1886. (Rpt. New York: Franklin, 1964.)

———. "On Metrical Tests Applied to Shakespeare." In C[lement] M. Ingleby. *Occasional Papers on Shakespeare: Being the Second Part of Shakespeare the Man and the Book.* 1881. Pp. 50–141.

———. "On Metrical Tests as Applied to Dramatic Poetry. Part I. Shakspere." *N.S.S. Trans. 1874.* [1874.] Pp. 1–16.

Fleissner, Robert F. "Shakespeare's *Measure for Measure,* [1147]." *Expl* 32 (1974), item 42.

Fliess, Robert. *Erogeneity and Libido.* New York, 1957.

Florio, John. *A Worlde of Wordes, Or Most Copious, and Exact Dictionarie in Italian and English.* 1598. (Rpt. Hildesheim & New York: G. Olm, 1972. 2nd ed. as *Queen Anna's New World of Words.* 1611. Rpt. Menston: Scolar, 1968.)

Flower, Annette C. "The Disguised Prince in English Drama, 1590–1615." *DAI* 31 (1971), 6054A–5A. (Maryland.)

Fluchère, Henri. *Shakespeare.* Tr. Guy Hamilton. 1953. (1st Fr. ed. 1948.)

Fludas, John P. "Brecht's Art of Adaptation: The English Plays." *DAI* 30 (1970), 3006A–7A. (Northwestern.)

Fly, Richard. *Shakespeare's Mediated World.* Amherst, Mass., 1976.

Foakes, R[eginald] A. *Shakespeare. The Dark Comedies to the Last Plays: From Satire to Celebration.* 1971.

Forbes-Robertson, John. *See* Phelps, W. May.

Forby, Robert. *The Vocabulary of East Anglia.* 2 vols. 1830.

Ford, Harold. *Shakespeare, His Ethical Teaching.* [1922.]

Foth, K. "Shakespeare's Mass für Mass und die Geschichte von Promos und Cassandra." *SJ* 13 (1878), 163–85.

Franz, Wilhelm. *Shakespeare's Blankvers.* 2nd ed. Tübingen, 1935. (1st ed. 1932.)

―――. *Die Sprache Shakespeares in Vers und Prosa. Shakespeare-Grammatik* in 4. Auflage. Halle/Saale, 1939. (1st pub. as *Shakespeare-Grammatik* in 1898–9.)

Frasure, Louise D. "Shakespeare's Constables." *Anglia* 58 (1934), 384–91.

Freeburg, Victor O. *Disguise Plots in Elizabethan Drama.* Columbia Univ. Stud. in Eng. & Comp. Lit. New York, 1915. (Rpt. New York: Blom, 1966.)

Freedman, William A. "The Duke in *Measure for Measure:* Another Interpretation." *Tennessee Stud. in Lit.* 9 (1964), 31–8.

Freund, Fritz. "Shakespeare als Rechtsphilosoph: Kaufmann von Venedig und Mass für Mass." *SJ* 28 (1893), 54–71.

Fricker, Robert. *Kontrast und Polarität in den Charakterbildern Shakespeares.* Schweizer Anglistische Arbeiten 22. Bern, 1951.

Friedman, Simon. "Some Shakespearian Characterizations of Women and Their Traditions." *DAI* 34 (1973), 312A. (Yale.)

Friesen, Hermann, Freiherr von. *Shakspere-Studien.* 3 vols. Wien, 1874–6.

Fripp, Edgar I. *Shakespeare, Man and Artist.* 2 vols. OUP, 1938.

Frye, Northrop. *Anatomy of Criticism.* Princeton, 1957.

―――. "Characterization in Shakespearian Comedy." *SQ* 4 (1953), 271–7.

―――. *A Natural Perspective: The Development of Shakespearean Comedy and Romance.* New York & London, 1965.

Frye, Roland M. *Shakespeare and Christian Doctrine.* Princeton, 1963.

Furnivall, Frederick J. " 'Measure for Measure'." 5 *N&Q* 1 (1874), 304.

―――. *See* Greenhill, James.

Garnett, Richard. "The Date and Occasion of 'The Tempest'." *Universal Review,* Apr. 1889, pp. 556–66. (Ger. tr. in *SJ* 35 [1899], 166–79.)

―――. *A History of Italian Literature.* 1898.

Gates, W[illiam] B. "Cooper's Indebtedness to Shakespeare." *PMLA* 67 (1952), 716–31.

Gaw, J. Allison. "A Note on Barnardine in *Measure for Measure.*" *ShAB* 8 (1933), 93–5.

Geckle, George L. "Coleridge on *Measure for Measure.*" *SQ* 18 (1967), 71–3.

―――. "A History of the Literary Criticism of Shakespeare's *Measure for Measure.*" *DA* 26 (1966), 6040–1. (Virginia.)

―――. "Poetic Justice and *Measure for Measure.*" *Costerus* NS 1 (1974), 95–111.

―――. "Shakespeare's Isabella." *SQ* 22 (1971), 163–8.

―――, ed. *Twentieth Century Interpretations of* Measure for Measure: *A Collection of Critical Essays.* Englewood Cliffs, N.J., 1970.

Gelb, Hal. "Duke Vincentio and the Illusion of Comedy or All's Not Well That Ends Well." *SQ* 22 (1971), 25–34.

Genée, Rudolph. *Shakespeare: Sein Leben und seine Werke.* Hildburghausen, 1872.

―――. *William Shakespeare in seinem Werden und Wesen.* Berlin, 1905.

[Genest, John.] *Some Account of the English Stage, from the Restoration in 1660 to 1830.* 10 vols. Bath, 1832.

Gent, C. L. " 'Measure for Measure' and the Fourth Book of Castiglione's 'Il Cortegiano'." *MLR* 67 (1972), 252–6.

Gervinus, G[eorg] G. *Shakespeare Commentaries.* Tr. F. E. Bunnètt. Rev. ed. London & New York, 1875. (Rpt. New York: AMS, 1971. 1st ed. of tr., 2 vols., 1863; 1st Ger. ed. 1849–50.)

Getto, Giovanni. "Manzoni e Shakespeare." *Lettere italiane* 19 (1967), 187–236.

Ghosh, Prabodh Chandra. "Measure for Measure." *Calcutta Essays on Shakespeare.* Ed. Amalendu Bose. Calcutta, 1966.

―――. *Shakespeare's Mingled Drama.* Calcutta, 1966.

Ghurye, G[ovind] S. *Shakespeare on Conscience and Justice.* Bombay, 1965.

Gibian, George. *"Measure for Measure* and Pushkin's *Angelo." PMLA* 66 (1951), 426–31.

———. "Shakespeare in Russia." Harvard diss., 1951.

Gibson, Richard J. *"All's Well that Ends Well, Measure for Measure,* and *Pericles:* Experiments in Comic Resolution." *DAI* 32 (1972), 6974A. (North Carolina.)

Gifford, William, ed. *The Works of Ben Jonson.* 9 vols. 1875. (1st ed. 1816.)

Gilbert, Allan H. "The More Shakespeare He: *Measure for Measure." Shakespearean Essays.* Ed. Alwin Thaler & Norman Sanders. *Tennessee Stud. in Lit.* Special No. 2 (1964), 45–62.

Gildon, Charles. "Glossary." In supplementary vol. 7 (1710) added to Nicholas Rowe, ed., *The Works of Shakespear,* 6 vols., 1709. Pp. lxviii–lxxii.

———. "Remarks on the Plays of Shakespear." In supplementary vol. 7 (1710) added to Nicholas Rowe, ed., *The Works of Shakespear,* 6 vols., 1709. Pp. 257–444.

Gillet, Louis. "Shakespeare: Les Femmes de son théâtre." *Revue Hebdomadaire,* 3 May 1930, pp. 70–94.

Gillett, Peter J. "Me, U, and Non-U: Class Connotations of Two Shakespearean Idioms." *SQ* 25 (1974), 297–309.

Giraldi, Giovanni Battista (Cinthio). *Epitia.* Venezia, 1583.

———. *Hecatommithi.* 2 vols. Monreale, 1565.

Gleichen-Russwurm, Alexander, Freiherr von. *Shakespeares Frauengestalten.* Nürnberg, [1909].

Gless, Darryl J. *"Measure for Measure* and Reformation Christianity." *DAI* 36 (1975), 2218A–19A. (Princeton.)

Goddard, Harold C. *The Meaning of Shakespeare.* Chicago, 1951.

Godshalk, W[illiam] L. *"Measure for Measure:* Freedom and Restraint." *ShakS* 6 (1970), 137–50.

———. *Patterning in Shakespearean Drama.* The Hague, 1973.

Goldman, Arnold L. "The Structure of Time in Shakespearean Comedy." *DAI* 33 (1972), 2934A. (Minnesota.)

Goldschmidt, Werner. "Problemas de justicia en Medida por Medida." *Revista de Estudios Politicos,* Nov.–Dec. 1953, pp. 3–21.

Gollancz, Israel. "Bits of Timber: Some Observations on Shakespearian Names— 'Shylock'; 'Polonius'; 'Malvolio'." *A Book of Homage to Shakespeare.* 1916. Pp. 170–8.

Goodwin, John, ed. *Royal Shakespeare Theatre Company, 1960–1963.* 1964.

Gould, George. *Corrigenda and Explanations of the Text of Shakspere.* 1881.

———. *Corrigenda and Explanations of the Text of Shakspere. A New Issue* [i.e., a continuation]. 1884.

———. *Corrigenda and Explanations of the Text of Shakspere. Continuation 2.* 1887.

Gould, Gerald. "A New Reading of 'Measure for Measure'." *EngRev* 36 (1923), 232–43.

Gow, James (1854–1923). Contributor to Wright ed. 1891.

Gradman, Barry. *"Measure for Measure* and Keats's 'Nightingale' Ode." *ELN* 12 (1975), 177–82.

Granville-Barker, Harley. *On Dramatic Method.* 1931.

Gray, Arthur. "Notes on Shakspeare Lexicography." 7 *N&Q* 6 (1888), 342–3.

Greco, Anne. "A Due Sincerity." *ShakS* 6 (1970), 151–73.

Green, Henry. *Shakespeare and the Emblem Writers.* 1870. (Rpt. New York: Franklin, 1966.)

Green, J. T. "Shakespearean Women Contrasts: Cleopatra, Cordelia, and Isabella." *Fort Hare Papers* 3, No. 5 (1966), 15–23.

Greenhill, J[ames], W[illiam] A. Harrison, & F[rederick] J. Furnivall, compilers. *A List of All the Songs & Passages in Shakspere Which Have Been Set to Music.* Rev. ed.

New Shakspere Soc. Pubs., Ser. 8, No. 3. 1884. (Rpt. Folcroft, Pa., 1974.)

Greenwood, George. "Shakespeare's 'Measure for Measure'." *New World* (London) 3 (1920), 408–14, 535–40. (Part rpt. in *Shakespeare's Law,* Hartford, Conn., 1920, pp. 38–44.)

Greg, W[alter] W. (1875–1959). Contributor to Wilson ed. 1922.

——. *The Editorial Problem in Shakespeare.* OUP, 1942.

——. *The Shakespeare First Folio: Its Bibliographical and Textual History.* OUP, 1955.

Grennan, Eamon. "Keats's *Contemptus Mundi:* A Shakespearean Influence on the 'Ode to a Nightingale'." *MLQ* 36 (1975), 272–92.

Grey, Zachary. *Critical, Historical, and Explanatory Notes on Shakespeare.* 2 vols. 1754. (Rpt. New York: AMS, 1973.)

Griffin, Alice V. *See* Venezky, Alice S.

Griffith, [Elizabeth]. *The Morality of Shakespeare's Drama Illustrated.* 1775. (Rpt. New York: Kelley, 1971.)

Grillparzer, Franz. *"Measure for Measure,* 1849." Tr. LaMarr Kopp. *Shakespeare in Europe.* Ed. Oswald LeWinter. Cleveland & New York, 1963. Pp. 137–9. (Rpt. London: Penguin, 1970.)

Grivelet, Michel. " 'And measure still for measure': Sur quelques études récentes de la pièce de Shakespeare." *EA* 21 (1968), 65–72.

Gross, Gerard J. "All That Ends Well: Problems of Closure in Shakespeare's Comedies." *DAI* 38 (1978), 4179A–80A. (Case Western Reserve.)

Gross, Manfred. *Shakespeares Measure for Measure und die Politik Jakobs I.* Kieler Beiträge zur Anglistik und Amerikanistik 2. Neumünster, 1965. (Rev. from Kiel diss.)

Grove, Robin. "Shakespeare's Measure for Magistrates." *Critical Review* 19 (1977), 3–23.

Grudin, Robert. "Wisdom and Rule in *Troilus and Cressida, Measure for Measure,* and *The Tempest." DAI* 31 (1970), 2877A. (Berkeley.)

Guha, Praphulla Kumar. "How Shakespeare Handles the Sex-Problem in His Dark Comedies." *Essays and Studies* (Jadavpur Univ.) 2 (1972), 1–9.

Gundolf, Friedrich. *Shakespeare, sein Wesen und Werk.* 2 vols. Berlin, 1928.

Guthrie, Tyrone. *A Life in the Theatre.* New York, 1959.

Hailey, Jack D. "Shakespeare's Social Comedies." *DAI* 37 (1976), 331A. (Cornell.)

Haines, C[harles] R. "Emendations to Shakespeare." *N&Q* 166 (1934), 76–7.

Halio, Jay L. "Rhetorical Ambiguity as a Stylistic Device in Shakespeare's Problem Comedies." Abstracts in *ShN* 6 (1956), 39, and *DAI* 30 (1969), 1135A. (Yale.)

Hall, Lawrence S. "Isabella's Angry Ape." *SQ* 15, No. 3 (1964), 157–65.

Hallam, Henry. *Introduction to the Literature of Europe, in the Fifteenth, Sixteenth, and Seventeenth Centuries.* 4 vols. 1837–9.

Halliday, F[rank] E. *The Poetry of Shakespeare's Plays.* 1954.

Halliwell[-Phillipps], James Orchard. *A Dictionary of Archaic and Provincial Words.* 2 vols. 1847.

——. *Memoranda on Shakespeare's Comedy of Measure for Measure.* 1880. (Rpt. New York: AMS, 1974.)

——. *Outlines of the Life of Shakespeare.* 5th ed. 1885; 7th ed., 2 vols., 1887. (1st ed. 1881.)

Hamburger, Michael P. "Besonderheiten der Herzogsfigur in *Measure for Measure." SJW* 105 (1969), 158–67.

Hamill, Monica J. "Shakespeare's Recreative Comedy: A Study of *The Merchant of Venice, Measure for Measure, The Winter's Tale,* and *The Tempest." DAI* 36 (1976), 6113A. (Bryn Mawr.)

Hamilton, A. C. "On Teaching the Shakespeare Canon: The Case of *Measure for*

Measure." In *Teaching Shakespeare.* Ed. Walter Edens, Christopher Durer, Walter Eggers, Duncan Harris, & Keith Hull. Princeton, 1977. Pp. 95–113.

Hamilton, Donna B. "The Comic Vision of Shakespeare's *Measure for Measure.*" Wisconsin diss. 1968. See *DA* 29 (1969), 4456A–7A.

———. "The Duke in *Measure for Measure:* 'I Find an Apt Remission in Myself'." *ShakS* 6 (1970), 175–83.

Hankins, John E. "The Pains of the Afterworld: Fire, Wind, and Ice in Milton and Shakespeare." *PMLA* 71 (1956), 482–95.

———. *Shakespeare's Derived Imagery.* Lawrence, Kans., 1953.

Hapgood, Robert. "The Provost and Equity in *Measure for Measure.*" *SQ* 15, No. 1 (1964), 114–15.

Harbage, Alfred. *As They Liked It: An Essay on Shakespeare and Morality.* New York, 1947.

———. "Shakespeare and the Myth of Perfection." *SQ* 15, No. 2 (1964), 1–10. (Rpt. in *Conceptions of Shakespeare,* Cambridge, Mass., 1966, pp. 23–38.)

———. "Shakespeare's Ideal Man." *Joseph Quincy Adams Memorial Studies.* Ed. James G. McManaway, Giles E. Dawson, & Edwin E. Willoughby. Washington, 1948. Pp. 65–80. (Rpt. in *Conceptions of Shakespeare,* Cambridge, Mass., 1966, pp. 120–37.)

Harder, Helga I. K. "Right Self-Love as the Fulcrum of Balance in Shakespeare's Plays." *DAI* 38 (1977), 804A. (North Carolina.)

Harding, Davis P. "Elizabethan Betrothals and 'Measure for Measure'." *JEGP* 49 (1950), 139–58.

Hare, Arnold. *The Georgian Theatre in Wessex.* 1958.

———, ed. *Theatre Royal, Bath: A Calendar of Performances at the Orchard Street Theatre, 1750–1805.* Bath, 1977.

Harmon, Alice. "How Great Was Shakespeare's Debt to Montaigne?" *PMLA* 57 (1942), 988–1008.

Harris, A[rthur] J[ack]. *"Measure for Measure:* A Stage History and an Interpretation." M.A. thesis Birmingham, 1959.

———. "William Poel's Elizabethan Stage: The First Experiment." *ThN* 17 (1963), 111–14.

Harris, Frank. *The Man Shakespeare and His Tragic Life Story.* New York, 1909.

Harrison, Charles T. "The Ancient Atomists and English Literature of the Seventeenth Century." *Harvard Stud. in Classical Philology* 45 (1934), 1–79.

Harrison, John L. "The Convention of 'Heart and Tongue' and the Meaning of *Measure for Measure.*" *SQ* 5 (1954), 1–10.

Harrison, William A. *See* Greenhill, James.

Hart, Edward L. "A Mixed Consort: Leontes, Angelo, Helena." *SQ* 15, No. 1 (1964), 75–83.

Hart, H. Chichester. " 'Measure for Measure': Some Additional Notes." 10 *N&Q* 10 (1908), 63–4.

Harting, James E. *The Birds of Shakespeare.* 1871.

Hartnoll, Phyllis, ed. *Shakespeare in Music.* 1964.

Haskin, Dayton. "Mercy and the Creative Process in *Measure for Measure.*" *Texas Stud. in Lit. and Lang.* 19 (1977), 348–62.

Hasler, Jörg. *Shakespeare's Theatrical Notation: The Comedies.* Cooper Monographs on Eng. & American Lang. & Lit., Theatrical Physiognomy Ser. 21. Bern, 1974.

Hawkes, Terence. *Shakespeare and the Reason: A Study of the Tragedies and the Problem Plays.* 1964.

Hawkins, Harriett. *Likenesses of Truth in Elizabethan and Restoration Drama.* OUP, 1972.

———. "What Kind of Pre-Contract Had Angelo? A Note on Some Non-Problems in Elizabethan Drama." *College English* 36 (1974), 173–9.

Hawkins, John (1719–89). Contributor to v1778.

Hayman, Ronald. *John Gielgud.* 1971.

Hazlitt, William. *Characters of Shakespear's Plays.* 2nd ed. 1818. (1st ed. 1817.)

———. *Complete Works.* Ed. P. P. Howe. 21 vols. 1930–4.

———. *A View of the English Stage.* 1818.

[Hazlitt, William C., ed.] *Shakespeare's Library.* 6 vols. 1875.

Healy, Kathleen. *See* van Kaam, Adrian.

Hearn, Lafcadio. *Lectures on Shakespeare.* Ed. Iwao Inagaki. Tokyo, 1928. (Delivered in 1899; part pub. in *Interpretations of Literature,* ed. John Erskine, 2 vols., New York, 1915.)

[Heath, Benjamin.] *A Revisal of Shakespear's Text.* 1765.

Hebler, C[arl]. *Aufsätze über Shakespeare.* 2nd ed. Bern, 1874. (1st ed. 1865.)

Henley, Samuel (1740–1815). Contributor to Malone ed. 1790, v1793, v1821.

———. "Critical Remarks on *Shakspeare.*" *Gentleman's Magazine* 50 (1780), 21–2.

Henn, T. R. *The Living Image: Shakespearean Essays.* 1972.

Hennings, Elsa. *Shakespeares Mass für Mass.* Veröffentlichungen der Universitäts-Gesellschaft Hamburg Nr. 11. Hamburg, 1958.

Heraud, John A. *Shakspere: His Inner Life as Intimated in His Works.* 1865.

Herford, C[harles] H. "Shakespeare's Treatment of Love and Marriage." *Shakespeare's Treatment of Love & Marriage and Other Essays.* 1921. Pp. 1–43. (Rev. from *Edda,* Hefte 3 [1916], 92–111.)

Herndl, George C. *The High Design: English Renaissance Tragedy and the Natural Law.* Lexington, Ky., 1970.

Herr, J. G. ["Brakes of Ice."] *Shakespeariana* 2 (1885), 303–4.

Hethmon, Robert H. "The Theatrical Design of *Measure for Measure.*" *Drama Survey* (St. Paul) 1 (1962), 261–77.

Hetrick, Phyllis B. "Ironic Structure in Two Jacobean Plays." *DAI* 31 (1970), 2880A. (Bowling Green.)

Heuser, Georg. *Die aktlose Dramaturgie William Shakespeares.* Marburg, 1956. (Marburg diss.)

Heyartz, Irene. "The Endings of Shakespeare's Comedies." *DA* 25 (1964), 2490. (Bryn Mawr.)

Hicks, J. Power. " 'Measure for Measure'. " 5 *N&Q* 4 (1875), 182.

Hickson, Samuel. "On the Word 'Prenzie' in 'Measure for Measure'." 1 *N&Q* 3 (1851), 454–5.

———. "What Is the Meaning of 'Delighted', as Sometimes Used by Shakspeare." 1 *N&Q* 2 (1850), 113–14.

Highley, Mona. "Shakespeare's Poetic and Dramatic Treatment of Six Religious Characters." *DA* 26 (1965), 2213–14. (Texas.)

Hinman, Charlton. "Cast-Off Copy for the First Folio of Shakespeare." *SQ* 6 (1955), 259–73.

———. *The Printing and Proof-Reading of the First Folio of Shakespeare.* 2 vols. OUP, 1963.

———, ed. *The Norton Facsimile: The First Folio of Shakespeare.* New York, 1968.

Hirschberg, Julius. "Zwei Konjekturen zu 'Measure for Measure'." *SJ* 57 (1921), 81.

Hitchcock, Robert. *An Historical View of the Irish Stage.* 2 vols. Dublin, 1788–94.

Hodgkinson, J. L., & Rex Pogson. *The Early Manchester Theatre.* 1960.

Hofmannsthal, Hugo von. "Shakespeare's Kings and Noblemen." *Selected Prose.* Tr. Mary Hottinger & Tania & James Stern. Bollingen Ser. 33. New York, 1952. Pp. 247–67. (1st pub. in Ger., *SJ* 41 [1905], x–xxvii.)

Hogan, Charles B. *Shakespeare in the Theatre, 1701–1800: A Record of Performances in London.* 2 vols. OUP, 1952–7.

———, ed. *The London Stage, 1660–1800. Part 5 (1776–1800).* 3 vols. Carbondale, 1968.

Hogan, J[eremiah] J. [Review of Lever ed.] *Ren. Quarterly* 21 (1968), 228–30.
Holland, Norman N. " 'Do' or 'Die' in 'Measure for Measure' [335]." *N&Q* 202 (1957), 52.
_____. *"Measure for Measure:* The Duke and the Prince." *Comp. Lit.* 11 (1959), 16–20.
_____. *Psychoanalysis and Shakespeare.* New York, 1966.
_____. *The Shakespearean Imagination.* New York, 1964.
Holmes, Martin. *Shakespeare and His Players.* 1972.
_____. *Shakespeare's Public, the Touchstone of His Genius.* 1960.
Honigmann, E[rnst] A. J. *The Stability of Shakespeare's Text.* 1965.
Hooker, Elizabeth. "The Relation of Shakespeare to Montaigne." *PMLA* 17 (1902), 312–66.
Horn, Franz. *Shakspeare's Schauspiele.* 5 vols. Leipzig, 1823–31.
Horne, Herman H. *Shakespeare's Philosophy of Love.* [Raleigh, N.C.], 1945.
Horne, P[hilip] R. *The Tragedies of Giambattista Cinthio Giraldi.* OUP, 1962.
Horton, John A. "Shakespeare's Use of Law in *Measure for Measure."* Queen's Univ. diss., 1971.
Hotson, Leslie. "The Adventure of the Single Rapier." *Atlantic Monthly* 148 (1931), 26–31. (Rpt. in *Shakespeare's Sonnets Dated and Other Essays,* 1949, pp. 193–203.)
_____. *The Commonwealth and Restoration Stage.* Cambridge, Mass., 1928.
_____. *I, William Shakespeare, Do Appoint Thomas Russell, Esquire. . . .* 1937.
_____. " 'The Prenzie, Angelo?' " *TLS,* 22 Nov. 1947, p. 603.
Housman, A. E. *The Name and Nature of Poetry.* Cambridge & New York, 1933.
Howard-Hill, T[revor] H. "The Compositors of Shakespeare's Folio Comedies." *SB* 26 (1973), 61–106.
_____. "Knight, Crane, and the Copy for the Folio *Winter's Tale." N&Q* 211 (1966), 139–40.
_____. *Ralph Crane and Some Shakespeare First Folio Comedies.* Charlottesville, 1972. (Oxford diss.)
_____. "Ralph Crane's Parentheses." *N&Q* 210 (1965), 334–40.
Howarth, Herbert. "Puzzle of Flattery." *The Tiger's Heart: Eight Essays on Shakespeare.* London & New York, 1970. Pp. 120–42. (Rev. from "Shakespeare's Flattery in *Measure for Measure,"* SQ 16 [1965], 29–37.)
Hoy, Cyrus. *The Hyacinth Room.* New York, 1964.
_____. "Shakespeare and the Revenge of Art." *Renaissance Studies in Honor of Carroll Camden. Rice Univ. Stud.* 60 (1974), 71–94.
Hubbuch, Susan M. "The Anatomy of a Dramatic Character: A Study of the Intriguer Figure in Six Major Renaissance Dramas, 1603–1606." *DAI* 35 (1974), 3684A. (Oregon.)
Hudson, H[enry] N. *Lectures on Shakspeare.* 2nd ed. 2 vols. New York, 1848. (1st ed. 1848.)
_____. *Shakespeare: His Life, Art, and Characters.* 2 vols. Boston, 1872.
Hülsmann, Eduard. *Shakespeare: Sein Geist und seine Werke.* Leipzig, 1856.
Hughes, S[amuel] C. *The Pre-Victorian Drama in Dublin.* Dublin, 1904.
Hull, Thomas (d. 1808). MS notes quoted by Halliwell ed. 1854.
Hulme, Hilda M. *Explorations in Shakespeare's Language.* 1962.
Hunter, G[eorge] K. "Italian Tragicomedy on the English Stage." *Ren. Drama* NS 6 (1973), 123–48.
_____. "The Marking of *Sententiae* in Elizabethan Printed Plays, Poems, and Romances." 5 *Library* 6 (1951), 171–88.
_____. "Six Notes on *Measure for Measure." SQ* 15, No. 3 (1964), 167–72.
_____, ed. *All's Well that Ends Well.* New Arden Sh. 1959.
Hunter, Joseph. *New Illustrations of the Life, Studies, and Writings of Shakespeare.* 2 vols. 1845.

Hunter, Mark. "Act- and Scene-Division in the Plays of Shakespeare." *RES* 2 (1926), 295–310.

Hunter, Robert G. *Shakespeare and the Comedy of Forgiveness.* New York, 1965. (Rev. from Columbia diss.)

Hurd, Richard. *A Letter to Mr. Mason; On the Marks of Imitation.* Cambridge, 1757.

Hurdis, James. *Cursory Remarks upon the Arrangement of the Plays of Shakespear.* 1792.

H[utchesson], M. *"Shakespear* Illustrated." *Gentleman's Magazine* 60, pt. 1 (1790), 306–7.

Hutchinson, John. " 'Prenzie' in 'Measure for Measure'." 10 *N&Q* 1 (1904), 161–2.

Huxley, Aldous. *Ape and Essence.* 1949.

_____. "Shakespeare and Religion." *Aldous Huxley, 1894–1963: A Memorial Volume.* Ed. Julian Huxley. 1965. Pp. 165–75.

Hyman, Lawrence W. "Mariana and Shakespeare's Theme in *Measure for Measure.*" *University Review* 31 (1964), 123–7.

_____. "The Unity of *Measure for Measure.*" *MLQ* 36 (1975), 3–20.

Illies, Georg. *Das Verhältnis von Davenants "The Law against Lovers" zu Shakespeares "Measure for Measure" und "Much Ado about Nothing."* Halle a. S., 1900. (Halle diss.)

Ingleby, C[lement] M. *Complete View of the Shakspere Controversy.* 1861.

_____. *Occasional Papers on Shakespeare: Being the Second Part of Shakespeare the Man and the Book.* 1881.

_____. *Shakespeare Hermeneutics.* 1875. (Rpt. New York: Haskell, 1971.)

Ingleby, Holcombe. " 'Measure for Measure', [1526]." 7 *N&Q* 11 (1891), 283.

Iyengar, K. R. Srinivasa. *See* Srinivasa Iyengar.

Izard, Thomas C. *George Whetstone: Mid-Elizabethan Gentleman of Letters.* Columbia Univ. Stud. in Eng. & Comp. Lit. 158. New York, 1942.

Jabez. " 'Measure for Measure', [11–12]." 5 *N&Q* 2 (1874), 63.

Jackson, Zachariah. *A Few Concise Examples of Seven Hundred Errors in Shakspeare's Plays, Now Corrected and Elucidated.* 1818.

_____. *Shakspeare's Genius Justified.* 1819.

Jain, S. A. *Shakespeare's Conception of Ideal Womanhood.* Madras, 1948.

James VI and I. *The Basilicon Doron of King James VI.* Ed. James Craigie. Scottish Text Soc. 2 vols. Edinburgh & London, 1944–50.

Jameson, Anna B. *Shakspeare's Heroines: Characteristics of Women, Moral, Poetical, and Historical.* 1879. (Rpt. New York: AMS, 1967. 1st pub. as *Characteristics of Women, Moral, Poetical, and Historical.* 2 vols. 1832.)

Jamieson, Michael. "The Problem Plays, 1920–1970: A Retrospect." *ShS* 25 (1972), 1–10.

Janes, Kenneth. *"Measure for Measure:* From a Director's Notebook." *Drama Critique* (Detroit) 7 (1964), 47–50.

Janssen, Vincent F. *Die Prosa in Shaksperes Dramen. Erster Teil: Anwendung.* Strassburg, 1897. (Giessen diss.)

Jeakes, Thomas J. " 'Measure for Measure', [1526]." 7 *N&Q* 11 (1891), 283.

Jenkins, Anthony W. *See* Edwards, Anthony S. G.

Jenkins, Harold (1909–). Contributor to Lever ed.

Jente, Richard. "The Proverbs of Shakespeare with Early and Contemporary Parallels." *Washington Univ. Stud., Humanistic Ser.* 13 (1926), 391–444.

Jervis, Swynfen. *Proposed Emendations of the Text of Shakspeare's Plays.* 1860. (2nd, rev. ed. 1861.)

Jewett, Mike. "Shakespeare's Body Politic Imagery." *DAI* 33 (1973), 5180A–1A. (Missouri.)

Jewkes, Wilfred T. *Act Division in Elizabethan and Jacobean Plays, 1583–1616.* Hamden, Conn., 1958.

Johnson, Samuel. *A Dictionary of the English Language.* 2 vols. 1755. (4th, rev. ed., 2 vols., 1773.)

Joicey, George. " 'Measure for Measure', [316]." 7 *N&Q* 11 (1891), 81–2; 8 *N&Q* 1 (1892), 104–5.

———. " 'Measure for Measure', [1758]." 8 *N&Q* 6 (1894), 124.

Jones, Charles Inigo. *Memoirs of Miss O'Neill.* 1816.

Jones, Connie H. "Shakespeare and the Problem of Forgiveness: The Diversity between Mercy and Vain Pity in *The Two Gentlemen of Verona, Measure for Measure* and *The Tempest." DAI* 36 (1975), 903A–4A. (Alabama.)

Jones, Henry A[rthur]. "Religion and the Stage." *Nineteenth Century* 17 (1885), 154–69.

Jones, Tom. " 'Measure for Measure', [1102]: 'All-building'." 10 *N&Q* 8 (1907), 505.

Jorgensen, Paul A. *Redeeming Shakespeare's Words.* Berkeley & Los Angeles, 1962.

Joseph, Sr. Miriam. *See* Miriam Joseph, Sr.

Joyce, James. *A Portrait of the Artist as a Young Man.* 1916.

Jump, J. D., ed. *Rollo Duke of Normandy or The Bloody Brother.* 1948.

Jung, Hugo. *Das Verhältnis Thomas Middleton's zu Shakspere.* Münchener Beiträge zur romanischen und englischen Philologie 29. Leipzig, 1904.

K., H. C. "On Three Passages in 'Measure for Measure'." 1 *N&Q* 8 (1853), 194–5.

K., L. L. " 'The King of Hungary's peace' in Shakespeare." 11 *N&Q* 12 (1915), 98–9.

———. "The Plot of 'Measure for Measure'." 8 *N&Q* 4 (1893), 83–4.

Kapp, Julius. *Richard Wagner.* Berlin, 1910.

Kaufman, Helen A. *"Trappolin Supposed a Prince* and *Measure for Measure." MLQ* 18 (1957), 113–24.

Kaufmann, R[alph] J. "Bond Slaves and Counterfeits: Shakespeare's Measure for Measure." *ShakS* 3 (1967), 85–97.

Kaufmann, Walter. *From Shakespeare to Existentialism.* Boston, 1959. (2nd ed. 1960.)

Kaula, David. *Shakespeare and the Archpriest Controversy: A Study of Some New Sources.* Stud. in Eng. Lit. 85. The Hague & Paris, 1975. (Absorbs *"Measure for Measure* and John Mush's *Dialogue," ShakS* 6 [1970], 185–95.)

Keeton, G[eorge] W. *Shakespeare's Legal and Political Background.* 1967. (1st pub. as *Shakespeare and His Legal Problems.* 1930.)

Keightley, Thomas. "Are Critics Logicians?" 2 *N&Q* 10 (1860), 65–6.

———. " 'The Merchant of Venice'." 3 *N&Q* 4 (1863), 262–4.

———. *The Shakespeare-Expositor: An Aid to the Perfect Understanding of Shakespeare's Plays.* 1867. (Rpt. New York: AMS, 1973.)

———. "Three Passages in 'Measure for Measure'." 1 *N&Q* 8 (1853), 361–2.

Keller, Wolfgang. "Shakespeare und sein König." *SJ* 54 (1918), xiii–xxxiii.

Kelliher, Hilton. "A Shakespeare Allusion of 1605 and Its Author." *British Lib. Jour.* 3 (1977), 7–12.

Kellner, Leon. *Erläuterungen und Textverbesserungen zu vierzehn Dramen Shakespeares.* Ed. Walther Ebisch. Leipzig, 1931.

———. *Restoring Shakespeare: A Critical Analysis of the Misreadings in Shakespeare's Works.* 1925. (Rpt. New York: Biblo, 1969.)

Kemp, T[homas] C., & J[ohn] C. Trewin. *The Stratford Festival: A History of the Shakespeare Memorial Theatre.* Birmingham, 1953.

Kennedy, B. H. "Shakspeare's Use of the Word 'Delighted'." 1 *N&Q* 2 (1850), 139.

Kenrick, W[illiam]. *A Review of Doctor Johnson's New Edition of Shakespeare.* 1765. (Rpt. New York: AMS, 1974.)

Kerr, Barlyn B. "A Study of Selected Prompt Books for Productions of *Measure for Measure* between 1773 and 1846." M.A. thesis, Ohio State Univ., 1962.

Kilbourne, Frederick W. *Alterations and Adaptations of Shakespeare.* Boston, 1906. (Rev. from Yale diss.)

Kinnear, Benjamin G. *Cruces Shakespearianæ: Difficult Passages in the Works of Shakespeare.* 1883.

Kirchheim, Astrid. *Tragik und Komik in Shakespeares* Troilus and Cressida, Measure for Measure *und* All's Well that Ends Well. Neue Beiträge zur Anglistik und Amerikanistik 8. Frankfurt, 1971. (Rev. from Saarland diss.)

Kirsch, Arthur C. "The Integrity of 'Measure for Measure'." *ShS* 28 (1975), 89–105.

Kirschbaum, Leo. *Character and Characterization in Shakespeare.* Detroit, 1962.

Klein, J[ulius] L. *Geschichte des Drama's.* 13 vols. Leipzig, 1865–76.

Kleinschmit von Lengefeld, [Wilhelm,] Freiherr. "Der Manierismus in der Dichtung Shakespeares." *SJ* 97 (1961), 63–99.

Klene, Mary J. "Shakespeare's Use of the Renaissance Concept of Honor." *DAI* 32 (1971), 3256A–7A. (Toronto.)

Knight, Charles. *Studies of Shakspere.* 1849. (1st pub. in ed. 1842. Rpt. New York: AMS, 1972.)

Knight, G[eorge] Wilson. " 'Measure for Measure' and the Gospels." *The Wheel of Fire.* 4th, rev. ed. 1949. (1st ed. 1930; essay 1st pub. in *London Quarterly Review* 151 [1929], 172–85. Rpt. in Geckle, ed., 1970, pp. 27–49.)

Knight, Joseph. *Theatrical Notes.* 1893. (Rev. from *Athenæum.*)

Knight, W. Nicholas. "Equity and Mercy in English Law and Drama (1405–1641)." *CompD* 6 (1972), 51–67.

Knights, L[ionel] C. "The Ambiguity of 'Measure for Measure'." *Scrutiny* 10 (1942), 222–33. (Rpt. in *The Importance of Scrutiny,* ed. Eric Bentley, New York, 1948, pp. 141–50.)

Kökeritz, Helge. "Punning Names in Shakespeare." *MLN* 65 (1950), 240–3.

———. "Shakespeare's Language." *Shakespeare: Of an Age and for All Time.* Ed. C. T. Prouty. Hamden, Conn., 1954.

———. *Shakespeare's Pronunciation.* New Haven, 1953.

König, Goswin. *Der Vers in Shaksperes Dramen.* Quellen und Forschungen 61. Strassburg, 1888.

König, Wilhelm. *Shakespeare als Dichter, Weltweiser und Christ.* Berlin & Leipzig, [1873].

———. "Shakespeare und Dante." *SJ* 7 (1872), 170–213.

———. "Shakespeare und Giordano Bruno." *SJ* 11 (1876), 97–139.

———. "Ueber den Gang von Shakespeare's dichterischer Entwickelung und die Reihenfolge seiner Dramen nach demselben." *SJ* 10 (1875), 193–258.

Kohler, Josef. *Shakespeare vor dem Forum der Jurisprudenz.* 2nd ed. Berlin, 1919. (1st ed. 1883–4.)

Kolb, Catherine S. "Frustrated Expectation in Shakespeare's Problem Plays." *DAI* 36 (1976), 5319A. (Indiana.)

Koppel, Richard. "Scenen-Eintheilungen und Orts-Angaben in den Shakespeare'-schen Dramen." *SJ* 9 (1874), 269–94.

Koszul, A[ndré]. "La Technique dramatique de Shakespeare étudiée dans le premier acte de 'Measure for Measure'." *Revue de l'Enseignement des Langues Vivantes* 44 (1927), 145–52.

Krehayn, Joachim. "Problem und Komödie in Shakespeares 'Mass für Mass'." *Sinn und Form* 10 (1958), 904–16.

Kreider, Paul V. *Repetition in Shakespeare's Plays.* Princeton, 1941.

Kreyssig, Fr[iedrich]. *Vorlesungen über Shakespeare, seine Zeit und seine Werke.* 2 vols. 3rd ed. Berlin, 1877. (1st ed. 1858–60.)

Krieger, Murray. *"Measure for Measure* and Elizabethan Comedy." *PMLA* 66 (1951), 775–84. (Rpt. in Soellner & Bertsche, eds., 1966, pp. 91–9.)

Krumpelmann, John T. "Kleist's *Krug* and Shakespeare's *Measure for Measure." GR* 26 (1951), 13–21.

Kuckhoff, Armin-G. "Das Drama William Shakespeares." *Schriften zur Theaterwissen-*

schaft. Schriftenreihe der Theaterhochschule Leipzig. Ed. Rolf Rohmer. Band 3, I. Berlin, 1964.

Kussmaul, Paul. *Bertolt Brecht und das englische Drama der Renaissance.* Bern & Frankfurt, 1974.

Lacy, Margaret S. "The Jacobean Problem Play: A Study of Shakespeare's *Measure for Measure* and *Troilus and Cressida* in Relation to Selected Plays of Chapman, Dekker, and Marston." *DA* 16 (1956), 1899–1900. (Wisconsin.)

Lambrechts, Guy. "Proposed New Readings in Shakespeare: The Comedies (1)." *Hommage à Shakespeare: Bull. de la Faculté des Lettres de Strasbourg* 43 (May–June 1965), 945–58.

Lancaster, H. C[arrington]. "A Classic French Tragedy Based on an Anecdote Told of Charles the Bold." *Studies in Honor of A. Marshall Elliott.* 2 vols. Baltimore, 1911. 1:159–74.

Landauer, Gustav. *Shakespeare: Dargestellt in Vorträgen.* 2 vols. Frankfurt am Main, 1920.

Lang, Andrew. "The Comedies of Shakespeare: VI. Measure for Measure." *Harper's Magazine* 84 (1891), 62–77.

Langbaine, Gerard. *An Account of the English Dramatick Poets.* 1691. (Rpt. Menston: Scolar, 1971; New York: Garland, 1973.)

Lascelles, Gerald. "Falconry." *Shakespeare's England.* 2 vols. OUP, 1916. 2:351–66.

Lascelles, Mary. " 'Glassie Essence', *Measure for Measure,* [877]." *RES* NS 2 (1951), 140–2.

———. "Shakespeare's Comic Insight." *PBA* 48 (1962), 171–86. (Rpt. in *Notions and Facts: Collected Criticism and Research,* OUP, 1972, pp. 47–64.)

———. *Shakespeare's* Measure for Measure. 1953. (Rpt. New York: AMS, 1970.)

Latham, Grace. "The Petty Constable: His Duties and Difficulties in Shakspere's Day." *SJ* 32 (1896), 133–48.

———. "Some of Shakespeare's Metaphors, and His Use of Them in the Comedies." *N.S.S. Trans. 1887–92,* pp. 397–427.

Lavin, J. A. *"Measure for Measure." Stratford Papers, 1968–69.* Ed. B. A. W. Jackson. Hamilton, Ont., & Shannon, Ireland, 1972. Pp. 97–113.

Law, Ernest. "Shakespeare's Christmas, St. Stephen's Day, 1604." *The Times* (London), 26 Dec. 1910, p. 10.

———. *Some Supposed Shakespeare Forgeries.* 1911.

Law, Robert Adger. "On Certain Proper Names in Shakespeare." *Univ. of Texas Stud. in Eng.* 30 (1951), 61–5.

Lawlor, John. *The Tragic Sense in Shakespeare.* 1960.

Lawrence, W[illiam] J. *Shakespeare's Workshop.* Boston & New York, 1928. (Rpt. New York: Haskell, 1966.)

Lawrence, William W. *"Measure for Measure* and Lucio." *SQ* 9 (1958), 443–53. (Rpt. in Soellner & Bertsche, eds., 1966, pp. 151–61.)

———. *Shakespeare's Problem Comedies.* New York, 1931. (2nd ed. 1960.)

Lawson, Reginald. "Lucio, in *Measure for Measure." English Studies* 19 (1937), 259–64.

Lea, K[athleen] M. *Italian Popular Comedy.* 2 vols. OUP, 1934.

Leavis, F[rank] R. " 'Measure for Measure'." *The Common Pursuit.* 1952. Pp. 160–72. (1st pub. as "The Greatness of *Measure for Measure,"Scrutiny* 10 [1942], 234–47; rpt. in *The Importance of Scrutiny,* ed. Eric Bentley, New York, 1948, pp. 150–62.)

Lederbogen, Fritz. *Die inneren Beziehungen von Shakespeare's 'Measure for Measure' mit den übrigen Dramen der Hamlet-Periode.* Halle a. S., 1912. (Halle diss.)

Lee, Sidney. *A Life of William Shakespeare.* 1898. (Rev. in 1916 and 1925.)

Leech, Clifford. "The 'Meaning' of *Measure for Measure." ShS* 3 (1950), 66–73.

———. " 'More than our brother is our chastity'." *CritQ* 12 (1970), 73–4.

———. "Shakespeare's Comic Dukes." *Review of Eng. Lit.* 5 (1964), 101–14.

———. "Shakespeare's Songs and the Double Response." In *The Triple Bond.* Ed. Joseph G. Price. University Park, Pa., & London, 1975. Pp. 73–91.

Lefranc, Abel. *À la découverte de Shakespeare.* 2 vols. Paris, 1945–50.

Leges. "Note upon a Passage in 'Measure for Measure'." 1 *N&Q* 3 (1851), 401–2.

Legouis, Emile. "Le Théâtre de Shakespeare: 'Mesure pour Mesure'." *RCC* 18 (1909–10), 267–79, 298–309.

———, & Louis Cazamian. *A History of English Literature.* Tr. Helen D. Irvine & W. D. MacInnes. 1929. (1st Fr. ed. 1924.)

Leighton, J. M. *"Measure for Measure:* The Last Stage in the Transition." *ESA* 12 (1969), 31–9.

[Lennox, Charlotte Ramsay.] *Shakespear Illustrated.* 3 vols. 1753–4. (Rpt. New York: AMS, 1973.)

Leo, F[riedrich] A. "Besprechung über Verbesserungs-Vorschläge zu Shakespeare." *SJ* 15 (1880), 164–72.

———. "Emendationen." *SJ* 23 (1888), 282–9.

———. "Passage in 'Measure for Measure'." 2 *N&Q* 8 (1859), 527.

———. *Shakespeare-Notes.* 1885. (1st pub. as "Emendationen," *SJ* 19[1884], 265–70.)

Lettsom, William N. (1796–1865). Contributor to Dyce ed. 1864–7. Ed. W. S. Walker, *Shakespeare's Versification,* 1854, and *A Critical Examination of the Text of Shakespeare,* 1860.

———. "New Readings in Shakespeare." *Blackwood's Edinburgh Magazine* 74 (Aug. 1853), 181–202.

———. "Shakspeare Correspondence." 1 *N&Q* 7 (1853), 377–8.

Lever, J[ulius] W. "The Date of *Measure for Measure.*" *SQ* 10 (1959), 381–8.

Lever, Katherine. "Proverbs and *Sententiae* in the Plays of Shakspere." *ShAB* 13 (1938), 173–83, 224–39.

Levi, A[ngelo] R. *Storia della letteratura inglese.* 2 vols. Palermo, 1898–1901.

———. *Studi su Shakspeare.* Treviso, 1875.

Levin, Harry. "Shakespeare's Nomenclature." *Essays on Shakespeare.* Ed. Gerald W. Chapman. Princeton, 1965. Pp. 59–90.

Levin, Richard. "The King James Version of *Measure for Measure.*" *Clio* (Univ. of Wisconsin) 3 (1974), 129–63.

———. "On Fluellen's Figures, Christ Figures, and James Figures." *PMLA* 89 (1974), 302–11.

———. "Refuting Shakespeare's Endings." *MP* 72 (1975), 337–49, and 75 (1977), 132–58.

Levison, William S. "Restoration Adaptations of Shakespeare as Baroque Literature." *DAI* 34 (1973), 730A. (Illinois.)

Lewes, Louis. *The Women of Shakespeare.* Tr. Helen Zimmern. New York & London, 1895. (1st Ger. ed. 1893.)

Lewis, Edward T. "Images of Social Order: A Study of Shakespeare's Changing Concept of Society." *DAI* 34 (1973), 279A. (Denver.)

Liebrecht, Felix, ed. *John Dunlop's Geschichte der Prosadichtungen,* tr., augmented & corrected. Berlin, 1851.

Lings, Martin. *Shakespeare in the Light of Sacred Art.* 1966.

Linthicum, M[arie] Channing. *Costume in the Drama of Shakespeare and His Contemporaries.* OUP, 1936.

Lirondelle, André. *Shakespeare en Russie, 1748–1840.* Paris, 1912. (Paris thesis.)

Livermore, Ann. "Shakespeare and St. Augustine." *Quarterly Review* 303 (1965), 181–93.

Lloyd, Julius (1830–92). Contributor to Clark, Glover, & Wright ed. 1863–6.

Lloyd, W[illiam] Watkiss. " 'Measure for Measure', [1526]." 7 *N&Q* 12 (1891), 204.

_____. "Shakspeare Notes." *Athenæum* No. 2597 (4 Aug. 1877), 143.

_____. "Shakspeare Notes. 'Measure for Measure'." *Athenæum* No. 2899 (19 May 1883), 636–7; No. 2954 (7 June 1884), 727–8.

Long, John H. *Shakespeare's Use of Music: The Final Comedies.* Gainesville, Fla., 1961.

Long, Michael. *The Unnatural Scene: A Study in Shakespearean Tragedy.* 1976.

Longo, Joseph A. "Shakespeare's 'Dark Period' Reviewed in the Light of Mid-Twentieth Century Criticism." *DA* 24 (1964), 2892–3. (Rutgers.)

Lucas, F[rank] L., ed. *The Complete Works of John Webster.* 4 vols. 1927.

Lucius. "Critical Remarks on the Late Editions of Shakspeare's Plays." *Edinburgh Magazine* 4 (1786), 354–61.

Lüthi, Max. *Shakespeares Dramen.* Berlin, 1957.

Lynch, Barbara F. "Shakespeare's Comic Plots and the Nature of Man: A Study of the Relationship between the Romantic and the Low Life Plots in Light of Man's Unique Position in the Great Chain of Being." *DAI* 32 (1972), 4619A. (Pennsylvania.)

Lyons, Charles R. *Shakespeare and the Ambiguity of Love's Triumph.* Stud. in Eng. Lit. 68. The Hague, 1971.

_____. "'Use' in *Measure for Measure.*" *Filologia Moderna* 35 (Apr.–Aug. 1969), 173–84.

Lyons, Clifford. "Stage Imagery in Shakespeare's Plays." *Essays on Shakespeare and Elizabethan Drama in Honor of Hardin Craig.* Ed. Richard Hosley. Columbia, Mo., 1962. Pp. 261–74.

M., W. G. "Prenzie." 1 *N&Q* 3 (1851), 522.

McBride, Tom. "*Measure for Measure* and the Unreconciled Virtues." *CompD* 8 (1974), 264–74.

McCanles, Michael. *Dialectical Criticism and Renaissance Literature.* Berkeley & Los Angeles, 1975.

McCord, Howard. "Law and Equity in *Measure for Measure.*" *Research Studs., Washington State Univ.* 30 (1962), 63–70.

McGinn, Donald J. "The Precise Angelo." *Joseph Quincy Adams Memorial Studies.* Ed. James G. McManaway, Giles E. Dawson, & Edwin E. Willoughby. Washington, 1948. Pp. 129–39.

McIntosh, Angus. "*Measure for Measure:* 'Prenzie' and Some Other Problems." *Studies in Language, Literature, and Culture of the Middle Ages and Later.* Ed. E. B. Atwood & A. A. Hill. Austin, Tex., 1969. Pp. 352–6.

Mackail, J[ohn] W. *The Approach to Shakespeare.* OUP, 1930.

Mackay, Eileen. "*Measure for Measure.*" *SQ* 14 (1963), 109–13. (Rpt. in Soellner & Bertsche, eds., 1966, pp. 161–6.)

Mackenzie, Agnes Mure. *The Women in Shakespeare's Plays.* 1924.

MacKinnon, Alan. *The Oxford Amateurs.* 1910.

McManaway, James G. "Additional Prompt-Books of Shakespeare from the Smock Alley Theatre." *MLR* 45 (1950), 64–5.

McPeek, James A. S. *The Black Book of Knaves and Unthrifts in Shakespeare and Other Renaissance Authors.* Storrs, Conn., 1969.

MacPhedran, John D. "The Effect of Shakespearean Criticism on Shakespearean Production: A Case Study." *DAI* 34 (1974), 5111A. (Bowling Green.)

Madden, D[odgson] H. *The Diary of Master William Silence.* 1897. (Rpt. New York: Greenwood, 1969. 2nd ed. 1907.)

Maginn, William. "Dr. Farmer's Essay on the Learning of Shakspeare Considered." *Fraser's Magazine* 20 (1839), 254–73, 476–90, 648–66. (Rpt. in *Miscellaneous Writings,* vol. 3: *The Shakespeare Papers,* New York, 1856, pp. 223–346.)

Mahood, M[olly] M. *Shakespeare's Wordplay.* 1957.

_____. "Unblotted Lines: Shakespeare at Work." *PBA* 58 (1972), 163–76.

Mainusch, Herbert. "Gnade und Gerechtigkeit in Shakespeares 'Measure for Measure'." *NS* n.F. 8 (1959), 407–17.

Malina, Arnold H. "Tragicomedy and the Struggle between Common Law and Equity in the Reign of James I." *DAI* 35 (1975), 7872A. (Colorado.)

Malone, Edmond. "An Attempt to Ascertain the Order in Which the Plays Attributed to Shakspeare Were Written." In Johnson & Steevens ed. 1778. 1: < 269–346 > .

———. *A Second Appendix to Mr. Malone's Supplement to the Last Edition of the Plays of Shakspeare.* 1783.

———. *Supplement to the Edition of Shakspeare's Plays Published in 1778.* 2 vols. 1780.

Mansell, Darrel, Jr. " 'Seemers' in *Measure for Measure.*" *MLQ* 27 (1966), 270–84.

M[arder], L[ouis]. "Will Isabella Marry the Duke?" *ShN* 21 (1971), 16.

Markels, Julian. "Melville's Markings in Shakespeare's Plays." *Am. Lit.* 49 (1977), 34–48.

Marsh, Derick R. C. "The Mood of *Measure for Measure.*" *SQ* 14 (1963), 31–8.

———. *Passion Lends Them Power: A Study of Shakespeare's Love Tragedies.* Sydney, Manchester, & New York, 1976.

Martin, L[eonard] C. "Shakespeare, Lucretius, and the Commonplaces." *RES* 21 (1945), 174–82.

Martin, Walther. "Re Angelo. Zur Beurteilung von Angelos Charakter in *Measure for Measure.*" *SJW* 102 (1966), 227–44.

Masefield, John. *William Shakespeare.* Home Univ. Lib. [1911.]

Mason, John Monck. *Comments on the Last Edition of Shakespeare's Plays.* 1785. (Rpt. of Dublin ed. New York: AMS, 1973.)

———. *Comments on the Plays of Beaumont and Fletcher: With an Appendix containing Some Further Observations on Shakespeare.* 1797–8. (Rpt. of *Appendix* New York: Garland, 1972.)

Masson, David. *Shakespeare Personally.* Ed. Rosaline Masson. 1914. (Lectures delivered 1865–95.)

Matheson, Belle S. *The Invented Personages in Shakespeare's Plays.* Philadelphia, 1932. (Pennsylvania diss.)

Mathew, Frank. *An Image of Shakespeare.* [1922.]

Matthews, Bache. *A History of the Birmingham Repertory Theatre.* 1924.

Matthews, Brander. *Molière: His Life and His Works.* New York, 1910.

———. *Shakspere as a Playwright.* New York, 1913.

Matthews, Honor. *Character & Symbol in Shakespeare's Plays.* Cambridge, 1962.

Matturro, Richard C. "Shakespeare and Sex: A Comprehensive Study of Shakespeare's Attitude toward Sex as Reflected in His Works." *DAI* 34 (1973), 1863A–4A. (State Univ. of New York at Albany.)

Maxwell, J[ames] C. " 'At once' in Shakespeare." *MLR* 49 (1954), 464–6.

———. "Correspondence." *SQ* 23 (1972), 461.

———. "Creon and Angelo: A Parallel Study." *Greece & Rome* 18 (1949), 32–6.

———. "Keats as a Guide to Shakespeare." *N&Q* 197 (1952), 126.

———. "*Measure for Measure:* A Footnote to Recent Criticism." *Downside Review* 65 (1947), 45–59.

———. "*Measure for Measure:* The Play and the Themes." *PBA* 60 (1974), 199–218.

———. "*Measure for Measure:* 'Vain Pity' and 'Compelled Sins'." *EIC* 16 (1966), 253–5.

———. " 'Measure for Measure', [1241–4]." *N&Q* 213 (1968), 141.

———. "Shakespeare: The Middle Plays." *The Pelican Guide to English Literature.* Ed. Boris Ford. Vol. 2: *The Age of Shakespeare.* London & Baltimore, 1955. Pp. 201–27.

Meader, William G. *Courtship in Shakespeare: Its Relation to the Tradition of Courtly Love.* New York, 1954. (Columbia diss.)

Mehl, Dieter. "Versucher und Versuchte im Drama Shakespeares und einiger Zeitgenossen." *SJH* (1966), pp. 146–72.

Mendl, R. W. S. *Revelation in Shakespeare.* 1964.

Merchant, W. Moelwyn. *Shakespeare and the Artist.* 1959.

Meredith, E[dmund] A. *Some New Emendations in Shakespeare.* Read before the Canadian Institute, 1883.

Messiaen, Pierre. "Les Comédies de Shakespeare." *RCC* 38 (1937), 244–51, 421–9.

Mézières, A[lfred]. *Shakspeare, ses œuvres et ses critiques.* 2nd ed. Paris, 1865. (1st ed. 1860.)

Mikkelsen, Robert S. "To Catch a Saint: Angelo in *Measure for Measure.*" *Western Humanities Review* 12 (1958), 261–75.

Miles, Rosalind. *The Problem of Measure for Measure: A Historical Investigation.* London & New York, 1976. (Rev. from Birmingham diss.)

Millet, Stanton. "The Structure of *Measure for Measure.*" *Boston Univ. Stud. in Eng.* 2 (1956), 207–17.

Milunas, Joseph G. "Shakespeare and the Christian View of Man." *DA* 14 (1954), 526–7. (Stanford.)

Mincoff, Marco. "Measure for Measure: A Question of Approach." *ShakS* 2 (1966), 141–52.

Minor, Jakob. "Zum deutschen Drama des 17. Jahrhunderts. I. Die englischen Komödianten und Shakespeares Mass für Mass." *VLit* 1 (1888), 277–80.

Miriam Joseph, Sr. *Shakespeare's Use of the Arts of Language.* Columbia Univ. Stud. in Eng. & Comp. Lit. 165. New York, 1947. (Columbia diss.)

[Mitford, John.] "Conjectural Emendations on the Text of Shakspere, with Observations on the Notes of the Commentators." *Gentleman's Magazine* NS 22 (1844), 115–36.

Mittenzwei, Werner. *Bertolt Brecht: Von der "Massnahme" zu "Leben des Galilei".* Berlin, 1962.

Montaigne, Michel de. *Essays.* Tr. John Florio. 3 vols. Everyman's Lib. London & New York, 1910.

Montague, C[harles] E. *Dramatic Values.* 1911.

──────. "Miss Wallis in *Measure for Measure.*" *The Manchester Stage, 1880–1900, Criticisms Reprinted from "The Guardian."* [?1900.] Pp. 70–5.

Moor, Edward. *Suffolk Words and Phrases.* Woodbridge, 1823.

Moore, Daniel. "The Obeli of the Globe Edition in 'Measure for Measure'." 7 *N&Q* 6 (1888), 303–4.

Moore, Edward M. "William Poel." *SQ* 23 (1972), 21–36.

More, Arthur. "Shaksperian Coincidencies." *Theatrical Inquisitor,* Oct. 1815, pp. 290–6.

Morgan, Shirley V. "The Regal Figures in Two Jacobean Dramas." *DAI* 32 (1972), 5799A. (Denver.)

Morley, Henry. *English Writers: An Attempt towards a History of English Literature.* 11 vols. 1887–95.

Morris, Harry C. "Nineteenth and Twentieth Century Criticism of Shakespeare's Problem Comedies." *DA* 17 (1957), 1546–7. (Minnesota.)

Moulton, Richard G. *Shakespeare as a Dramatic Thinker.* 1907. (1st pub. as *The Moral System of Shakespeare,* 1903.)

Muir, Kenneth. "The Duke's Soliloquies in 'Measure for Measure'." *N&Q* 211 (1966), 135–6.

──────. "A Reconsideration of *Edward III.*" *ShS* 6 (1953), 39–48. (Rev. in *Shakespeare as Collaborator,* 1960, pp. 10–30.)

──────. [Review of Sisson ed.] *London Magazine* 1, No. 11 (Dec. 1954), 102–8.

──────. "Shakespeare and Erasmus." *N&Q* 201 (1956), 424–5.

──────. "Shakespeare and Rhetoric." *SJ* 90 (1954), 49–68.

_____. *Shakespeare's Sources. I: Comedies and Tragedies.* 1957.

_____. *The Sources of Shakespeare's Plays.* 1977.

Mukherji, Asoke Kumar. "Shakespeare's Temptation Scenes: A Study of Some of the Lesser Ones." *Shakespeare Commemoration Volume.* Ed. Taraknath Sen. Calcutta, 1966. Pp. 138–58.

Murphy, Arthur. "The Theatre." *London Chronicle,* 1 Mar. 1757, p. 215; 12–14 Oct. 1758, p. 367. (Rpt. in *Shakespeare: The Critical Heritage,* ed. Brian Vickers, 1976, 4:284–5, 346–8.)

Murray, Patrick. *The Shakespearian Scene: Some Twentieth-Century Perspectives.* 1969.

Murry, John Middleton. *Shakespeare.* 1936.

_____. "Shakespeare and Love." *Countries of the Mind.* 1922. Pp. 9–28.

Musgrove, S[tephen]. "Some Composite Scenes in *Measure for Measure.*" *SQ* 15, No. 1 (1964), 67–74.

Mutschmann, H[einrich], & K[arl] Wentersdorf. *Shakespeare and Catholicism.* New York, 1952. (1st Ger. ed. 1950.)

Naef, Irene. *Die Lieder in Shakespeares Komödien: Gehalt und Funktion.* Schweizer Anglistische Arbeiten 86. Bern, 1976.

Nagarajan, Sankalapuram. "The Heroines of Shakespeare's Problem Comedies." Harvard diss., 1962.

_____. "*Measure for Measure* and Elizabethan Betrothals." *SQ* 14 (1963), 115–19.

_____. "A Note on the Duke in *Measure for Measure.*" *Half Yearly Journal of the Mysore Univ.* 13 (1953), 1–9.

Nares, Robert. *A Glossary; or, Collection of Words, Phrases, Names, and Allusions . . . in the Works of English Authors, Particularly Shakespeare and His Contemporaries.* 1822.

Nathan, Norman. "The Marriage of Duke Vincentio and Isabella." *SQ* 7 (1956), 43–5.

_____. "Nineteen Zodiacs: *Measure for Measure* [261]." *SQ* 20 (1969), 83–4

Nelson, Raymond S. "*Measure for Measure* as Satiric Comedy." *Iowa State Jour. of Research* 47 (1973), 253–63.

Ness, Frederic W. *The Use of Rhyme in Shakespeare's Plays.* Yale Stud. in Eng. 95. New Haven, 1941.

A New English Dictionary. See The Oxford English Dictionary.

New York Theatre Critics' Reviews. 38 vols. New York, 1940–77.

The New York Times Theater Reviews, 1870–1919. 6 vols. New York, 1975.

The New York Times Theater Reviews, 1920–1970. 10 vols. New York, 1971.

Newbolt, Henry. "The Poet and His Audience." *EngRev* 25 (1917), 198–214.

Newcomer, Alphonso G., ed. *Much Ado About Nothing. Parallel Passage Edition.* Stanford Univ. Pubs., Univ. Ser., Lang. and Lit. 1, No. 2. Stanford, 1929.

Newman, Ernest. *The Life of Richard Wagner.* 4 vols. New York, 1933–46.

Nichols, John. *Illustrations of the Literary History of the Eighteenth Century.* 8 vols. 1817–58.

_____. *The Progresses, Processions, and Magnificent Festivities, of King James the First.* 4 vols. 1828.

_____. *See* Theobald, Lewis, and Steevens, George,

Nicholson, B[rinsley]. " 'Measure for Measure'." 3 *N&Q* 10 (1866), 368.

_____. " 'Measure for Measure', [300]." 6 *N&Q* 12 (1885), 25.

_____. " 'Measure for Measure', [1309 and 1312]." 6 N&Q 7 (1883), 464.

_____. " 'Measure for Measure', [1526]." 7 *N&Q* 11 (1891), 464.

_____. "Shakespeare and the Bible." 3 *N&Q* 9 (1866), 55–6.

Nicoll, Allardyce. *A History of Restoration Drama, 1660–1700.* Cambridge, 1923.

_____. *Shakespeare.* 1952.

Nigra, Costantino. *Canti popolari del Piemonte.* Torino, 1888.

Noble, Richmond. *Shakespeare's Biblical Knowledge and Use of the Book of Common Prayer.* 1935.

————. *Shakespeare's Use of Song: With the Text of the Principal Songs.* OUP, 1923.

Nosworthy, J[ames] M. *Shakespeare's Occasional Plays: Their Origin and Transmission.* 1965.

Nowottny, Winifred. *See* Dodds, W. M. T.

————. "Shakespeare and *The Orator.*" *Hommage à Shakespeare: Bull. de la Faculté des Lettres de Strasbourg* 43 (May–June 1965), 813–33.

Nutt, Sarah M. "The Arctic Voyages of William Barents in Probable Relation to Certain of Shakespeare's Plays." *SP* 39 (1942), 241–64.

Nuttall, A[nthony] D. "Measure for Measure: Quid pro Quo?" *ShakS* 4 (1968), 231–51.

————. " 'Measure for Measure': The Bed-trick." *ShS* 28 (1975), 51–6.

O'Brien, Constance. "Shakspere Talks with Uncritical People. XXV. Measure for Measure." *Monthly Packet* 16 (1888), 264–77.

O'Brien, Edward J., ed. *Elizabethan Tales.* 1937.

O'Connor, Frank [O'Donovan, Michael]. *Shakespeare's Progress.* Cleveland, 1960. (Rev. ed. of *The Road to Stratford,* 1948.)

O'Connor, John Sylvester. "Compositors D and F of the Shakespeare First Folio." *DAI* 35 (1974), 3002A. (Virginia.)

————. "Compositors D and F of the Shakespeare First Folio." *SB* 28 (1975), 81–117.

Odell, George C. D. *Annals of the New York Stage.* 15 vols. New York, 1927–49.

————. *Shakespeare from Betterton to Irving.* 2 vols. New York, 1920.

Odinga, Theodor. "Christian Zyrls Salomon." *VLit* 2 (1889), 228–46.

Oesterley, Hermann, ed. *Wendunmuth von Hans Wilhelm Kirchhof.* Bibliothek des Litterarischen Vereins in Stuttgart 95–9. 5 vols. Tübingen, 1869.

O'Keefe, Sr. Frances St. Anne. "The Dramatic Function of Lucio in *Measure for Measure.*" *Kiyo; Stud. in Eng. Lit.* (Okayama, Japan), Winter 1966, pp. 23–9.

Omega. "Original Observations on *Shakspeare.*" *Gentleman's Magazine* 54 (1784), 407.

Onions, C[harles] T. *A Shakespeare Glossary.* OUP, 1911. (2nd, rev. ed. with enl. addenda 1953.)

Oppel, Horst. *Shakespeare: Studien zum Werk und zur Welt des Dichters.* Heidelberg, 1963.

Orger, J[ohn] G. *Critical Notes on Shakspere's Comedies.* [1890.]

Ornstein, Robert. *The Moral Vision of Jacobean Tragedy.* Madison, 1960.

————, ed. *Discussions of Shakespeare's Problem Comedies.* Boston, 1961.

Orr, David. *Italian Renaissance Drama in England before 1625: The Influence of Erudita Tragedy, Comedy, and Pastoral on Elizabethan and Jacobean Drama.* Univ. of North Carolina Stud. in Comp. Lit. 49. Chapel Hill, 1970.

Osztoya, A. H. v. "Zur Quelle von Shakespeares 'Mass für Mass'." *ZVL* n.F. 7 (1894), 223–6.

Owen, Lucy. "Mode and Character in *Measure for Measure.*" *SQ* 25 (1974), 17–32.

————. "The Representation of Forgiveness in Shakespeare and Medieval Drama." *DAI* 36 (1976), 4516A–17A. (Virginia.)

The Oxford English Dictionary. Ed. James A. H. Murray et al. 12 vols. & suppl. OUP, 1933. (Orig. pub. as *A New English Dictionary on Historical Principles,* 10 vols., 1884–1928.)

Oxford Shakespeare Concordances: Measure for Measure. Ed. T. H. Howard-Hill. OUP, 1969.

Pace, Caroline J. "The Anatomy of Justice in Shakespeare's Plays." North Carolina diss., 1949.

Pache, Walter. "*Measure for Measure* und *Die Rundköpfe und die Spitzköpfe:* Zur Shakespeare Rezeption Bertolt Brechts." *Canadian Review of Comp. Lit.* 3 (1976), 173–96.

———. "Shakespeares *Measure for Measure* und Richard Wagners Jugendwerk *Das Liebesverbot.*" *Arcadia* 12 (1977), 1–16.

Palmer, John [Leslie]. *Comedy.* [1914.]

Parker, John, ed. *Who's Who in the Theatre.* 4th ed. London & Boston, 1922; 9th ed. London & New York, 1939.

Parker, M[arion] D. H. *The Slave of Life: A Study of Shakespeare and the Idea of Justice.* 1955. (B.Litt. thesis Oxford.)

Parrott, Thomas M. *Shakespearean Comedy.* New York: OUP, 1949. (Rpt. New York: Russell, 1962.)

Partee, Morriss H. "The Comic Unity of *Measure for Measure.*" *Genre* 6 (1973), 274–97.

Partridge, A[stley] C. *Orthography in Shakespeare and Elizabethan Drama: A Study of Colloquial Contractions, Elision, Prosody and Punctuation.* 1964.

Partridge, Eric. *Shakespeare's Bawdy: A Literary & Psychological Essay and a Comprehensive Glossary.* 1947. (3rd ed. 1969.)

Pater, Walter. "Measure for Measure." *Appreciations, with an Essay on Style.* 1889. Pp. 170–84. (Rev. from "A Fragment on *Measure for Measure,*" *Fortnightly Review* NS 16 [1874], 652–8.)

Patrick, Julian W. O. "The Place of Free-Standing Characters in Three Plays of Shakespeare: *Henry IV, Part One; Hamlet;* and *Measure for Measure.*" *DAI* 36 (1976), 8078A. (Yale.)

Patterson, Robert. *Natural History of the Insects Mentioned in Shakspeare's Plays.* 1842. (1st ed. 1838.)

Payne, Ben Iden. *A Life in a Wooden O: Memoirs of the Theatre.* New Haven & London, 1977.

Payne, Francis John. "Brakes of Ice." *Academy* 72 (1907), 276, 373.

Payne, Rhoda. "Shakespeare on Stage: A Study in the Criticism and Production of Five Plays." *DAI* 32 (1971), 1682A–3A. (Case Western Reserve.)

Pearce, Howard D. "Hawthorne's Old Moodie: 'The Blithedale Romance' and 'Measure for Measure'." *South Atlantic Bull.* 38, No. 4 (Nov. 1973), 11–15.

Pearlman, E. "Shakespeare, Freud, and the Two Usuries, or, Money's a Meddler." *ELR* 2 (1972), 217–36.

Pendleton, Thomas A. "The Reciprocal Relationship between Shakespeare and John Marston." *DAI* 34 (1974), 5117A–18A. (Fordham.)

Pérez Gállego, Candido. *Shakespeare y la politica: Las comedias de Shakespeare alegoria politica.* Madrid, 1971.

Perott, Joseph de. "Spanische Einflüsse bei Shakespeare." *ESn* 40 (1909), 153–5.

Perring, Philip. " 'Brakes of Ice'." *Academy* 72 (1907), 298.

———. *Hard Knots in Shakespeare.* 1885.

———. " 'Measure for Measure', [1102]: 'All-building'." 10 *N&Q* 8 (1907), 163.

Peterson, Douglas L. " 'Measure for Measure' and the Anglican Doctrine of Contrition." *N&Q* 209 (1964), 135–7.

Pettet, E[rnest] C. *Shakespeare and the Romance Tradition.* London & New York, 1949. (Rev. from B.Litt. thesis Trinity College, Dublin.)

Phelps, W. May, & John Forbes-Robertson. *The Life and Life-Work of Samuel Phelps.* 1886.

Philips, Carl. *Lokalfärbung in Shakespeares Dramen.* 2 vols. Köln, 1888–90.

Phillips, O[wen] Hood. *Shakespeare and the Lawyers.* 1972.

Platt, Isaac Hull. " 'His glassy essence', 'Measure for Measure' [877]." 10 *N&Q* 5 (1906), 465–6.

Poel, William. *Shakespeare in the Theatre.* 1913.

———. "Was Isabella a Novice?" *TLS*, 16 July 1931, p. 564.

Pogson, Beryl. *In the East My Pleasure Lies: An Esoteric Interpretation of Some Plays of Shakespeare.* 1950. (Rpt. New York: Haskell, 1974.)

Pope, Elizabeth M. "The Renaissance Background of *Measure for Measure.*" *ShS* 2 (1949), 66–82. (Rpt. in Geckle, ed., 1970, pp. 50–72.)

———. "Shakespeare on Hell." *SQ* 1 (1950), 162–4.

Porson, Richard (1759–1808). Contributor to Malone 1780.

Potts, Abbie F. *Shakespeare and the Faerie Queene.* Ithaca, 1958.

Pourtalès, Guy de. "Préface à une lecture de Shakespeare: *Mesure pour Mesure.*" *De Hamlet à Swann.* Paris, 1924. Pp. 19–46.

Powell, Jocelyn. "Theatrical *Trompe l'oeil* in *Measure for Measure.*" *Shakespearian Comedy.* Stratford-upon-Avon Stud. 14. 1972. Pp. 181–209.

Prager, Leonard. "The Language of Shakespeare's Low Characters: An Introductory Study." *DA* 27 (1966), 751A. (Yale, 1957.)

Praz, Mario. " 'All-Bridling Law'." *TLS,* 13 Feb. 1937, p. 111.

———. *Il dramma elisabettiano.* Roma, 1944.

———. *La poesia metafisica inglese del seicento: John Donne.* Roma, 1945.

Price, Hereward T. "Mirror-scenes in Shakespeare." *Joseph Quincy Adams Memorial Studies.* Ed. James G. McManaway, Giles E. Dawson, & Edwin E. Willoughby. Washington, 1948. Pp. 101–13.

Price, Jonathan R. *"Measure for Measure* and the Critics: Towards a New Approach." *SQ* 20 (1969), 179–204.

Price, Thomas. *The Wisdom and Genius of Shakspeare.* Philadelphia, 1839. (1st ed. 1838; 2nd, enl. ed. 1853.)

Prouty, Charles T. "George Whetstone and the Sources of *Measure for Measure.*" *SQ* 15, No. 2 (1964), 131–45.

Pushkin, A[lexander] S. "Notes on Shylock, Angelo and Falstaff." Tr. Albert Siegel. *ShAB* 16 (1941), 120–1. (1st pub. in Russian 1837; also tr. in *The Critical Prose of Alexander Pushkin,* ed. Carl R. Proffer, Bloomington, Ind., 1969, pp. 240–1, and in *Pushkin on Literature,* ed. Tatiana Wolff, 1971, pp. 464–5.)

Pye, Henry James. *Comments on the Commentators on Shakespear.* 1807.

[Quincy, Josiah P.] *Manuscript Corrections from a Copy of the Fourth Folio of Shakspeare's Plays.* Boston, 1854.

R., W. "Remarks on *Shakspeare.*" *Gentleman's Magazine* 50 (1780), 518–20.

Rabkin, Norman. *Shakespeare and the Common Understanding.* New York & London, 1967.

Radbruch, Gustav. *Gestalten und Gedanken: Acht Studien.* Leipzig, 1944.

Raleigh, Walter. *Shakespeare.* Eng. Men of Letters. 1907.

Rank, Otto. *Das Inzest-Motiv in Dichtung und Sage.* 2nd, rev. ed. Leipzig, 1926. (1st ed. 1912.)

Rankin, Michael H. *The Philosophy of Shakspere.* 1841.

Rapin, René. "Mesure pour mesure." *RAA,* Oct. 1930, pp. 42–51.

Ray, John. *A Collection of English Proverbs.* Cambridge, 1670. (2nd ed. 1678.)

Reddington, John P. "Repetition and Development in Shakespeare's Plot-Situations." *DA* 26 (1965), 3307–8. (Pennsylvania.)

Redman, David N. "Shakespeare and the Unfinished Work: Four Essays." *DAI* 34 (1974), 7202A. (Yale.)

Reed, Isaac (1742–1807). Contributor to v1785, v1793.

Rees, James. *Shakespeare and the Bible.* Philadelphia, 1876. (Rpt. New York: AMS, 1972.)

Rees, Joan. *Shakespeare and the Story: Aspects of Creation.* 1978.

Reichelt, Kurt. *Richard Wagner und die englische Literatur.* Leipzig, 1912.

Reid, Sidney W., Jr. "The Spellings of Jaggard's Compositor B in Certain Plays in the First Folio of Shakespeare." *DAI* 33 (1973), 3667A. (Virginia.)

Reid, Stephen A. "A Psychoanalytic Reading of 'Troilus and Cressida' and 'Measure for Measure'." *Psychoanalytic Review* 57 (1970), 263–82.

Reimer, Christian J. *Der Begriff der Gnade in Shakespeares "Measure for Measure."* Marburg, 1937. (Marburg diss.)

Rentoul, Gervais. *This Is My Case.* 1944.

Rhodes, R[aymond] Crompton. *Shakespeare's First Folio.* OUP, 1923.

Richardson, Charles, ed. *A New Dictionary of the English Language.* 2 vols. 1836–7.

Richardson, William. *Essays on Shakespeare's Dramatic Character of Sir John Falstaff, and on His Imitation of Female Characters.* 1789. (1st ed. 1788.)

Richmond, Hugh M. *Shakespeare's Sexual Comedy: A Mirror for Lovers.* Indianapolis, 1971.

––––––. " 'Take, Oh Take Those Lips Away'." *Boston Univ. Stud. in Eng.* 4 (1960), 214–22.

Richter, Helene. "Der Humor bei Shakespeare." *SJ* 45 (1909), 1–50.

––––––. "Shakespeare's Gestalten." *NS,* Beiheft nr. 18 (1930).

Ridley, M[aurice] R. *Keats' Craftsmanship: A Study in Poetic Development.* OUP, 1933. (Rpt. Lincoln: Univ. of Nebraska, 1963.)

––––––. *Shakespeare's Plays: A Commentary.* 1937.

Righter, Anne. *Shakespeare and the Idea of the Play.* 1962. (Rev. from Cambridge diss.)

––––––. *See* Barton, Anne.

Rimbault, Edward F. *Who Was "Jack Wilson," the Singer of Shakespeare's Stage?* 1846.

Ringler, William A., ed. *The Poems of Sir Philip Sidney.* OUP, 1962.

Ritson, Joseph (1752–1803). Contributor to v1793.

––––––. *Remarks, Critical and Illustrative, on the Text and Notes of the Last Edition of Shakspeare.* 1783. (Rpt. London: Cass, 1967.)

Roberts, Jeanne A. "Laughter and the Law: Shakespeare's Comic Constables." *The Police in Society.* Ed. Emilio C. Viano & Jeffrey H. Reiman. Lexington, Mass., 1975. Pp. 131–7.

Roberts, William Hayward (1734–91). Contributor to v1773, v1821.

Robertson, John M. *Montaigne and Shakspere.* 1897. (2nd, rev. ed. 1909. Rpt. New York: Haskell, 1968.)

––––––. *The Shakespeare Canon, Part II.* 1923.

Robinson, Edwin Arlington. *Untriangulated Stars: Letters of Edwin Arlington Robinson to Harry De Forest Smith, 1890–1905.* Ed. Denham Sutcliffe. Cambridge, Mass., 1947.

Robson, William. *The Old Play-Goer.* 1846. (Rpt. Fontwell, Sussex, 1969.)

Robson, W[illiam] W. "All Difficulties Are but Easy . . . ?" *Cambridge Quarterly* 1 (1965–6), 90–6.

Rogers, Robert. *A Psychoanalytic Study of the Double in Literature.* Detroit, 1970.

Rolfe, W[illiam] J. "Measure for Measure, [331–2]." *Literary World* 12 (1881), 352.

Roscelli, William J. "Isabella, Sin, and Civil Law." *Univ. of Kansas City Review* 28 (1962), 215–27.

Rose, Brian. "Friar-Duke and Scholar-King." *ESA* 9 (1966), 72–82.

Rosebury, Theodor. *Microbes and Morals: The Strange Story of Venereal Disease.* New York, 1973. (1st ed. 1971.)

Rosenbaum, David. "Shakespeare's *Measure for Measure,* I ii." *Expl* 33 (1975), item 57.

Rosenberg, Marvin. "Shakespeare's Fantastic Trick: *Measure for Measure.*" *SR* 80 (1972), 51–72.

Rosenfeld, Sybil. *Strolling Players & Drama in the Provinces, 1660–1765.* Cambridge, 1939.

Rosenheim, Judith. "Philosophical and Religious Backgrounds to the Dramatic Oppositions of Shakespeare's *Measure for Measure.*" *DAI* 37 (1976), 1569A. (City Univ. of New York.)

Rossiter, Arthur P. (d. 1957). Contributor to Winny ed. 1959.

―――. *English Drama from Early Times to the Elizabethans.* 1950.

―――. "The Problem Plays." *Angel with Horns and Other Shakespeare Lectures.* Ed. Graham Storey. 1961. (Lecture delivered 1952.)

Rothe, Hans. *Shakespeare als Provokation.* München, 1961.

Ruegg, August. *Shakespeare: Eine Einführung in seine Dramen.* Bern, 1951.

Rushton, William L. *Shakespeare Illustrated by Old Authors.* 2 parts. 1867–8.

―――. *Shakespeare's Legal Maxims.* Liverpool, 1907.

―――. " 'Tongue far from Heart'." 4 *N&Q* 10 (1872), 183.

Ruskin, John. *Proserpina.* Vol. 2. 1882. *Works,* ed. E. T. Cook & Alexander Wedderburn, 39 vols., 1903–12.

―――. *Sesame and Lilies.* 1864.

Rylands, George. "Shakespeare's Poetic Energy." *PBA* 37 (1951), 99–119.

―――. *Words and Poetry.* London & New York, 1928. (Rpt. New York: AMS, 1972.)

S., M. "Various Passages in *Measure for Measure* Illustrated by Correspondent Passages from a Book of More Antient Date than Those Which His Commentators Seem Principally to Have Consulted." *Gentleman's Magazine* 65, pt. 2 (1795), 644–7.

S., N. "*Remarks* on the *Tragedy* of the *Orphan.*" *Gentleman's Magazine* 18 (1748), 502–6, 551–3. (Part rpt. in *Shakespeare: The Critical Heritage,* ed. Brian Vickers, 1975, 3:328–33.)

Sachs, Hanns. "The Measure in *Measure for Measure.*" *The Creative Unconscious.* Cambridge, Mass., 1942. 2nd, rev. ed., New York, 1951. (Rpt. in *The Design Within: Psychoanalytic Approaches to Shakespeare,* ed. M. D. Faber, New York, 1970, pp. 481–97.)

Saintsbury, George. *A History of English Prosody.* 3 vols. 1906–10. (Rpt. New York: Russell, 1961.)

―――. "Shakespeare: Life and Plays." *Cambridge History of English Literature.* 1910. 5:186–249. (Rpt. as *Shakespeare,* Cambridge & New York, 1934.)

―――. *A Short History of English Literature.* 1898.

Sale, Roger. "The Comic Mode of *Measure for Measure.*" *SQ* 19 (1968), 55–61.

Salgãdo, Gãmini. *Eyewitnesses of Shakespeare: First Hand Accounts of Performances, 1590–1890.* London & New York, 1975.

Salingar, Leo. *Shakespeare and the Traditions of Comedy.* Cambridge, 1974.

Sandmann, Paul. "Shakespeares Measure for Measure und Whetstones Historie of Promos and Cassandra." *Archiv* 68 (1882), 263–94.

Sarrazin, Gregor. "Herzog Vincentio in 'Mass für Mass' und sein Urbild, Herzog Vincenzio Gonzaga." *SJ* 31 (1895), 165–9.

―――. "Wortechos bei Shakespeare." *SJ* 34 (1898), 119–69.

―――. *See* Schmidt, Alexander.

Schäfer, Jurgen. *Shakespeares Stil: Germanisches und romanisches Vokabular.* Frankfurt am Main, 1973. (Rev. from Münster diss.)

Schanzer, Ernest. "The Marriage-Contracts in *Measure for Measure.*" *ShS* 13 (1960), 81–9.

―――. *The Problem Plays of Shakespeare: A Study of* Julius Caesar, Measure for Measure, Antony and Cleopatra. 1963.

Schelling, Felix E. *Elizabethan Playwrights.* New York, 1925.

Schieder, Theodor. "Shakespeare und Machiavelli." *Archiv für Kulturgeschichte* 33 (1951), 131–73. (Rpt. in *Begegnungen mit der Geschichte,* Göttingen, 1962, pp. 9–55.)

Schilling, Kurt. *Shakespeare: Die Idee des Menschseins in seine Werken.* München & Basel, 1953.

Schlegel, August W. von. *Course of Lectures on Dramatic Art and Literature.* Tr. John Black, rev. by A. J. W. Morrison. 1846. (Delivered in 1808; 1st Ger. ed., 2 vols., 1809–11; tr. John Black, 2 vols., 1815; rpt. of 1846 ed. New York: AMS, 1965.)

Schlösser, Anselm. "Implizierte Satire in *Mass für Mass.*" *SJW* 106 (1970), 100–26.

Schmidt, Alexander. *Shakespeare-Lexicon.* 2 vols. Berlin, 1874–5. (3rd ed., enl. by Gregor Sarrazin, 1902. Rpt. New York: Dover, 1971.)

Schröder, Rudolf Alexander. "Shakespeares Mass für Mass, 1949." *Gesammelte Werke.* Berlin, 1952. 2:334–7.

Schücking, Levin L. *Character Problems in Shakespeare's Plays.* London & New York, 1922. (1st Ger. ed. 1919.)

———. *Shakespeare und der Tragödienstil seiner Zeit.* Bern, 1947.

Schwartz, Jill H. "The Compassionate Playwright: A Study of Shakespeare's *All's Well that Ends Well* and *Measure for Measure.*" *DA* 28 (1967), 203A. (Cornell.)

Schwarze, Hans-Wilhelm. *Justice, Law and Revenge.* Studien zur englischen Literatur 6. Bonn, 1971.

Schweikart, Patsy. "A Feminist Critique of 'Measure for Measure'." *Univ. of Michigan Papers in Women's Studies* 1, No. 3 (1974), 147–57.

Scott, J. W. " 'Measure for Measure' and Castiglione." *N&Q* 217 (1972), 128.

Scott, William O. *The God of Arts: Ruling Ideas in Shakespeare's Comedies.* Univ. of Kansas Pub., Humanistic Stud. 48. Lawrence, Kans., 1977.

Scouten, Arthur H. "An Historical Approach to *Measure for Measure.*" *PQ* 54 (1975), 68–84.

———, ed. *The London Stage, 1660–1800. Part 3 (1729–47).* 2 vols. Carbondale, 1961.

Sears, Lloyd C. *Shakespeare's Philosophy of Evil.* North Quincy, Mass., 1974.

Seaton, Ethel. *Literary Relations of England and Scandinavia in the Seventeenth Century.* OUP, 1935.

Sehrt, Ernst T. *Vergebung und Gnade bei Shakespeare.* Stuttgart, [1952].

———. *Wandlungen der Shakespeareschen Komödie.* Göttingen, 1961. (Rev. from *SJ* 95 [1959], 10–46.)

Sen Gupta, S[ubodh] C. *Shakespearian Comedy.* Calcutta: OUP, 1950.

———. *The Whirligig of Time: The Problem of Duration in Shakespeare's Plays.* Calcutta, 1961.

Seng, Peter J. *The Vocal Songs in the Plays of Shakespeare: A Critical History.* Cambridge, Mass., 1967.

Sequeira, Isaac. "Is *Measure for Measure* a Problem Play?" *Osmania Jour. of Eng. Stud.* (Hyderabad) 4 (1964), 115–24.

Sewell, Arthur. *Character and Society in Shakespeare.* OUP, 1951. (Rpt. of pp. 64–72 in Ornstein, ed., 1961, pp. 97–100.)

Seymour, E. H. *Remarks, Critical, Conjectural, and Explanatory, upon the Plays of Shakespeare.* 2 vols. 1805.

Shalvi, Alice. *The Relationship of Renaissance Concepts of Honour to Shakespeare's Problem Plays.* Salzburg Stud. in Eng. Lit., Jacobean Drama Stud. 7. Salzburg, 1972.

———. " 'Reputation' in *Measure for Measure.*" In *Further Studies in English Language and Literature.* Ed. A. A. Mendilow. Scripta Hierosolymitana 25. 1973. Pp. 19–35.

———. "Shakespeare's 'Problem' Plays." In A. A. Mendilow & Alice Shalvi. *The World & Art of Shakespeare.* New York & Jerusalem. 1967. Pp. 190–202.

Shanker, Sidney. *Shakespeare and the Uses of Ideology.* Stud. in Eng. Lit. 105. The Hague & Paris, 1975.

Shattuck, Charles H., ed. *John Philip Kemble Promptbooks.* 11 vols. Charlottesville, 1974. (Vol. 6. *Measure for Measure.* 1803.)

_____. *The Shakespeare Promptbooks: A Descriptive Catalogue.* Urbana, 1965.

Shaw, [George] Bernard. *Plays; Pleasant and Unpleasant.* 2 vols. 1898.

_____. *Shaw on Shakespeare: An Anthology of Bernard Shaw's Writings on the Plays and Production of Shakespeare.* Ed. Edwin Wilson. New York, 1961.

Shedd, Robert G. "The *Measure for Measure* of Shakespeare's 1604 Audience." *DA* 13 (1953), 801. (Michigan.)

Sheldon, Esther K. *Thomas Sheridan of Smock-Alley.* Princeton, 1967.

Sheldon, W. L. "The Antigone of Sophocles and Shakespeare's Isabel." *Poet-lore* 4 (1892), 609–12.

Shklanka, Diana, ed. "A Critical Edition of George Whetstone's *An Heptameron of Civill Discourses* (1582)." *DAI* 38 (1977), 2817A. (British Columbia.)

Shugg, Wallace. "Prostitution in Shakespeare's London." *ShakS* 10 (1977), 291–313.

Siegel, Paul N. "Angelo's Precise Guards." *PQ* 29 (1950), 442–3.

_____. "Measure for Measure: The Significance of the Title." *SQ* 4 (1953), 317–20.

_____. *Shakespeare in His Time and Ours.* Notre Dame, Ind., 1968.

Siemon, James E. "The Canker Within: Some Observations on the Role of the Villain in Three Shakespearean Comedies." *SQ* 23 (1972), 435–43.

_____. "Disguise in Marston and Shakespeare." *Huntington Lib. Quarterly* 38 (1975), 105–23.

Simmons, Ernest J. "La Littérature anglaise et Pouchkine." *RLC* 17 (1937), 79–107.

Simpson, Lucie. "The Sex Bias of Measure for Measure." *The Secondary Heroes of Shakespeare and Other Essays.* 1950. (1st pub. in *Fortnightly Review* NS 115 [1924], 519–28.)

Simpson, Percy. *Shakespearian Punctuation.* OUP, 1911.

Simpson, Richard. *See* Bowden, Henry S.

Simrock, Karl. *The Remarks of M. Karl Simrock, on the Plots of Shakespeare's Plays.* With Notes and Additions by J. O. Halliwell. Sh. Soc. Pubs. 43. 1850. (1st pub. in Ger. 1831. 2nd ed. as *Die Quellen des Shakspeare in Novellen Märchen und Sagen.* 2 parts. Bonn, 1870.)

Sims, James H. *Dramatic Uses of Biblical Allusions in Marlowe and Shakespeare.* Univ. of Florida Monographs, Humanities 24. Gainesville, Fla., 1966.

Singer, Samuel W. " 'Anywhen' and 'Seldom-When': Unobserved Instances of Shakspeare's Use of the Latter." 1 *N&Q* 7 (1853), 335.

_____. "On a Passage in 'Measure for Measure'." 1 *N&Q* 3 (1851), 456.

_____. "On a Passage in 'Measure for Measure', Act I. Sc. 1." 1 *N&Q* 5 (1852), 435–6.

_____. *The Text of Shakespeare Vindicated from the Interpolations and Corruptions Advocated by John Payne Collier Esq. in His Notes and Emendations.* 1853.

Sisson, C[harles] J. "The Mythical Sorrows of Shakespeare." *PBA* 20 (1934), 45–70. (Rpt. in *Studies in Shakespeare: British Academy Lectures,* ed. Peter Alexander, OUP, 1964, pp. 9–32.)

_____. *New Readings in Shakespeare.* Shakespeare Problems 8. 2 vols. Cambridge, 1956.

Sitwell, Edith. *A Notebook on William Shakespeare.* 1948.

Sjögren, Gunnar. "The Setting in Measure for Measure." *RLC* 35 (1961), 25–39.

Skeat, Walter W. "The 'Prenzie' Angelo." *Academy* 49 (1896), 285.

_____. "Shakespeare, 'Measure for Measure', [493]." *MLR* 5 (1910), 197–8.

Skottowe, Augustine. *The Life of Shakspeare; Enquiries into the Originality of His Dramatic Plots and Characters; and Essays on the Ancient Theatres and Theatrical Usages.* 2 vols. 1824.

Skulsky, Harold. "Pain, Law, and Conscience in *Measure for Measure.*" *Spirits Finely*

Touched: The Testing of Value and Integrity in Four Shakespearean Plays. Athens, Ga., 1976. Pp. 87–119. (Rev. from *Jour. of the History of Ideas* 25 [1964], 147–68.)

Slack, Robert C. "The Realms of Gold and the Dark Comedies." In *"Starre of Poets": Discussions of Shakespeare.* Carnegie Ser. in Eng. 10. Pittsburgh, 1966. Pp. 49–64.

———. "Shakespeare's *Measure for Measure.*" In *Shakespeare: Lectures on Five Plays.* Carnegie Ser. in Eng. 4. Pittsburgh, 1958. Pp. 19–35.

Sleeth, Charles R. "Shakespeare's Counsellors of State." *RAA* 13 (1935), 97–113.

Smeaton, Oliphant. *Shakespeare, His Life and Work.* Everyman's Lib. London & New York, [1911].

Smirnov, A[leksander] A. *Shakespeare: A Marxist Interpretation.* Tr. Sonia Volochova. New York, 1936. (1st Russian ed. 1934.)

Smith, C. Alphonso. "The Short Circuit in English Syntax." *MLN* 19 (1904), 113–21.

Smith, Charles G. *Shakespeare's Proverb Lore: His Use of the* Sententiae *of Leonard Culman and Publilius Syrus.* Cambridge, Mass., 1963.

Smith, Donald George. "Studies in Shakespeare's *Measure for Measure.*" Duke diss., 1956.

Smith, Gordon Ross. "Isabella and Elbow in Varying Contexts of Interpretation." *Jour. of General Education* 17 (1965), 63–78.

Smith, James. *Shakespearian and Other Essays.* Cambridge, 1974.

Smith, John Hazel. "Charles the Bold and the German Background of the 'Monstrous Ransom' Story." *PQ* 51 (1972), 380–93.

Smith, Marion Bodwell. *Dualities in Shakespeare.* Toronto, 1966.

———. "Shakespeare and the Polarity of Love." *Humanities Assn. Bull.,* Spring 1965, pp. 7–18.

Smith, Robert M. "Interpretations of *Measure for Measure.*" *SQ* 1 (1950), 208–18.

Smith, Warren D. "More Light on *Measure for Measure.*" *MLQ* 23 (1962), 309–22.

Smith, William (1690–1767). Contributor to Grey 1754.

Smith, William George, ed. *The Oxford Dictionary of English Proverbs.* OUP, 1935. (3rd ed. rev. by F. P. Wilson, 1970.)

Smith, Winifred. "Two *Commedie dell'Arte* on the *Measure for Measure* Story." *RR* 13 (1922), 263–75.

Smithers, G[eoffrey] V. "Guide-Lines for Interpreting the Uses of the Suffix '*-ed*' in Shakespeare's English." *ShS* 23 (1970), 27–37.

Snider, Denton J. "Shakespeare's 'Measure for Measure'." *Jour. of Speculative Philosophy* 9 (1875), 312–25.

———. *System of Shakespeare's Dramas.* 2 vols. St. Louis, 1877.

Soellner, Rolf. *Shakespeare's Patterns of Self-Knowledge.* Columbus, Ohio, 1972.

———, & Samuel Bertsche, eds. Measure for Measure: *Text, Source, and Criticism.* Houghton Mifflin Research Ser. 11. Boston, 1966.

Sonnenschein, E. A. "Shakspere and Stoicism." *University Review* 1 (1905), 23–41.

Southall, Raymond. "*Measure for Measure* and the Protestant Ethic." *EIC* 11 (1961), 10–33.

Spalding, K[enneth] J. *The Philosophy of Shakespeare.* New York: OUP, 1953.

Speaight, Robert. *Christian Theatre.* Twentieth Century Encyclopaedia of Catholicism 124. New York, 1960.

———. *Shakespeare on the Stage: An Illustrated History of Shakespearian Performance.* 1973.

———. *Shakespeare: The Man and His Achievement.* New York, 1977.

———. *William Poel and the Elizabethan Revival.* 1954.

Spedding, James (1808–81). Contributor to Clark, Glover, & Wright ed. 1863–6.

Spence, R. M. "The Obeli of the Globe Edition in 'Measure for Measure'." 7 *N&Q* 5 (1888), 442–4.

Spencer, Christopher. "Lucio and the Friar's Hood." *ELN* 3 (1965), 17–21.

Spencer, Hazelton. *The Art and Life of William Shakespeare.* New York, 1940.
———. *Shakespeare Improved.* Cambridge, Mass., 1927.
Spencer, Jamieson. "Innovative Dramaturgy: Shakespeare's 'Middle Period'." *DAI* 33 (1972), 1181A–2A. (Washington Univ.)
Spencer, T[erence] J. B., ed. *Elizabethan Love Stories.* 1968.
———. "Shakespeare's Careless Art." *Shakespeare's Art: Seven Essays.* Ed. Milton Crane. Chicago & London, 1973. Pp. 115–35.
Spencer, Theodore. *Death and Elizabethan Tragedy.* Cambridge, Mass., 1936.
Sprague, Arthur Colby. "Shakespeare and William Poel." *UTQ* 17 (1947–8), 29–37.
———. *Shakespearian Players and Performances.* 1953.
Sproat, Kezia B. V. "A Reappraisal of Shakespeare's View of Women." *DAI* 36 (1975), 3664A. (Ohio State.)
Spurgeon, Caroline F. E. *Keats's Shakespeare.* 1928.
———. *Shakespeare's Imagery and What It Tells Us.* Cambridge, 1935.
Srinivasa Iyengar, K. R. *Shakespeare, His World and His Art.* Bombay & New York, 1964.
Stamp, A[lfred] E. *The Disputed Revels Accounts.* Reproduced in collotype facsimile, with a paper read before the Shakespeare Association. 1930.
Stanley, Emily B. "Seeing and Perceiving: A Study of the Use of Disguised Persons and Wise Fools in Shakespeare." *DA* 21 (1961), 2279. (Florida.)
Stauffer, Donald A. *Shakespeare's World of Images: The Development of His Moral Ideas.* New York, 1949.
Staunton, Howard. "Unsuspected Corruptions of Shakspeare's Text." *Athenæum* No. 2352 (23 Nov. 1872), 666–7; No. 2355 (14 Dec. 1872), 769–70; No. 2357 (28 Dec. 1872), 867.
Stead, C[hristian] K., ed. *Shakespeare:* Measure for Measure, *A Casebook.* 1971.
Steevens, George (1736–1800). Contributor to Malone 1780, v1803.
———, & John Nichols, eds. *Six Old Plays, on Which Shakespeare Founded His Measure for Measure, etc.* 2 vols. 1779.
Stege, John J. "Communication Therapy, Paradox, and Change in *The Merchant of Venice, Measure for Measure,* and *The Tempest.*" *DAI* 35 (1975), 6112A. (New Mexico.)
Sternfeld, F[rederick] W. *Music in Shakespearean Tragedy.* 1963.
———. "Take, o take those lips away." Appendix II in Lever ed. 1965. Pp. 201–3.
Stevenson, David L. *The Achievement of Shakespeare's* Measure for Measure. Ithaca, 1966.
———. "Design and Structure in *Measure for Measure:* A New Appraisal." *ELH* 23 (1956), 256–78.
———. "On Restoring Two Folio Readings in *Measure for Measure.*" *SQ* 7 (1956), 450–3.
———. "The Role of James I in Shakespeare's *Measure for Measure.*" *ELH* 26 (1959), 188–208.
Stewart, J[ohn] I. M. *Character and Motive in Shakespeare.* 1949.
Stockholder, Katherine S. "In Depth and Breadth: Shakespeare's Fusion of Comedy and Tragedy." *DA* 25 (1965), 5263–4. (Univ. of Washington.)
Stoessl, Otto. *Geist und Gestalt.* Wien, 1935.
Stoffel, C. *See* Van Dam, B. A. P.
Stokes, Henry P. *An Attempt to Determine the Chronological Order of Shakespeare's Plays.* The Harness Essay, 1877. 1878.
Stoll, Elmer E. *From Shakespeare to Joyce.* New York, 1944.
———. "Molière and Shakespeare." *RR* 35 (1944), 1–18.
Stone, George Winchester, ed. *The London Stage, 1660–1800. Part 4 (1747–76).* 3 vols. Carbondale, 1962.

Stone, W. G. "Notes on the Textual Difficulties in *Measure for Measure.*" *N.S.S. Trans. 1880–6.* [1886.] Pp. 112*–17*.

———. "Shakespeare, Cicero, and Dante." 5 *N&Q* 11 (1879), 286–7.

Stopes, Marie C. " 'Prenzie Gardes'." *TLS,* 6 Dec. 1947, p. 629.

Strachey, Lytton. "Shakespeare's Final Period." *Books and Characters French and English.* 1922. (1st pub. in *Independent Review* 3 [1904], 405–18.)

Stroup, Thomas B. *"Promos and Cassandra* and *The Law against Lovers." RES* 8 (1932), 309–10.

Styan, J[ohn] L. *Drama, Stage and Audience.* 1975.

———. *The Shakespeare Revolution: Criticism and Performance in the Twentieth Century.* Cambridge, 1977.

———. *Shakespeare's Stagecraft.* Cambridge, 1967.

Suddard, S[arah] J. Mary. *"Measure for Measure* as a Clue to Shakespeare's Attitude towards Puritanism." *Keats, Shelley and Shakespeare.* Cambridge, 1912. Pp. 136–52. (1st pub. as "The Poet and the Puritan," *Contemporary Review* 96 [1909], 712–21.)

Sullivan, Edward. " 'Measure for Measure', [1309–12]." *TLS,* 12 Aug. 1926, p. 537.

Swadley, Don R. "Clerical Characters in Shakespeare's Plays." *DAI* 33 (1972), 2345A. (Louisiana State.)

Swinburne, Algernon C. *Shakespeare.* OUP, 1909. (Written in 1905.)

———. *A Study of Shakespeare.* 1880.

Swinden, Patrick. *An Introduction to Shakespeare's Comedies.* 1973.

Symington, Rodney T. K. *Brecht und Shakespeare.* Studien zur Germanistik, Anglistik und Komparatistik 2. Bonn, 1970.

Symons, Arthur. "Measure for Measure." *Studies in the Elizabethan Drama.* 1920. Pp. 44–52. (Rpt. New York: AMS, 1972; 1st pub. in Irving & Marshall ed., 5 [1889], 170–2.)

Sympson, Mr., of Gainsborough. Contributor to *The Works of Mr. Francis Beaumont, and Mr. John Fletcher.* 10 vols. 1750.

Sypher, Wylie. *The Ethic of Time.* New York, 1976.

———. "Shakespeare as Casuist: *Measure for Measure." SR* 58 (1950), 262–80.

Tannenbaum, Samuel A. *Shakspere Forgeries in the Revels Accounts.* New York, 1928.

———. *Shaksperian Scraps and Other Elizabethan Fragments.* New York, 1933.

———. "Some Emendations of Shakspere's Text." *ShAB* 6 (1931), 105–10.

Tarsitano, Marie A. "Sweet Disaster: Development of Shakespearean Tragicomedy." *DAI* 36 (1975), 1540A. (State Univ. of New York at Binghamton.)

Taylor, Geoffrey. "The Beetle and the Giant." *TLS,* 20 Oct. 1945, p. 499.

Taylor, George Coffin. *Shakspere's Debt to Montaigne.* Cambridge, Mass., 1925.

Taylor, John. "On the Word 'Prenzie' in 'Measure for Measure'." 1 *N&Q* 3 (1851), 499–500.

Temple, William. *Mens Creatrix: An Essay.* 1917.

ten Brink. *See* Brink.

T[errell], H[ull]. *Was Shakespeare a Lawyer?* 2nd ed. 1871.

Terry, Francis E. " 'Measure for Measure'." *TLS,* 30 Oct. 1924, p. 686.

Teslar, Joseph A. *Shakespeare's Worthy Counsellor.* Rzym, 1960.

Thaler, Alwin. " 'The Devil's Crest' in *Measure for Measure." SP* 50 (1953), 188–94.

———. *Shakspere's Silences.* Cambridge, Mass., 1929.

Theobald, Lewis. [Letters to Warburton; originals in Folger Library.] In John Nichols. *Illustrations of the Literary History of the Eighteenth Century.* 8 vols. 1817–58. 2:204–655.

———. *Shakespeare Restored.* 1726. (Rpt. London: Cass, 1969.)

Theobald, William. *The Classical Element in the Shakespeare Plays.* 1909.

Thiselton, Alfred E. *Notulae Criticae.* 5 pts. 1904–8.

———. *Some Textual Notes on Measure, for Measure.* 1901.

Thompson, Edward Maunde (1840–1929). Contributor to Wilson ed. 1922.

Thompson, James Westfall. "Shakespere and Puritanism." *North American Review* 212 (1920), 228–37.

Thompson, Karl F. *Modesty and Cunning: Shakespeare's Use of Literary Tradition.* Ann Arbor, 1971.

Thümmel, Julius. "Der Liebhaber bei Shakespeare." *SJ* 19 (1884), 42–85.

―――. *Shakespeare-Charaktere.* 2 vols. 2nd ed. Halle, 1887. (1st ed. 1881.)

―――. "Shakespeare's Greise." *SJ* 18 (1883), 127–55.

Tieck, Ludwig. *Das Buch über Shakespeare* [c. 1794]. Aus seinem Nachlass herausgegeben von Henry Lüdeke. Neudrucke deutscher Literaturwerke des 18. und 19. Jahrhunderts Nr. 1. Halle a. S., 1920.

Tiessen, Ed[uard]. "Beiträge zur Feststellung und Erklärung des Shakspearetextes." *ESn* 2 (1879), 185–204, 440–75.

Tilley, Morris P. *A Dictionary of the Proverbs in England in the Sixteenth and Seventeenth Centuries.* Ann Arbor, 1950.

―――. "Recurrent Types of Confusion in Shakespeare's Clownish Dialogue." *ShAB* 5 (1930), 104–22.

Tillyard, E[ustace] M. W. *Shakespeare's Problem Plays.* Toronto, 1949.

Todd, Henry J., ed. *A Dictionary of the English Language:* by Samuel Johnson. With numerous corrections, and with the addition of several thousand words. 3 vols. 2nd ed. 1827. (1st ed., 4 vols., 1818.)

―――, ed. *The Poetical Works of John Milton.* 6 vols. 1801. 2nd ed. 7 vols. 1809.

Tollet, George (1725–79). Contributor to v1778.

Toole, William B. "Character Juxtaposition and the Motif of Place in *Measure for Measure.*" *Arlington Quarterly* 3 (Winter 1970–1), 21–37.

―――. *Shakespeare's Problem Plays: Studies in Form and Meaning.* Stud. in Eng. Lit. 19. The Hague, 1966.

Toscano, Paul J. "*Measure for Measure:* Tragedy and Redemption." *Brigham Young Univ. Stud.* 16 (1976), 277–89.

Townley, Richard. *A Journal Kept in the Isle of Man.* 2 vols. Whitehaven, 1791.

Towse, John R. *Sixty Years of the Theatre: An Old Critic's Memories.* New York & London, 1916.

Trautmann, Karl. "Englische Komödianten in Rothenburg ob der Tauber." *ZVL* n.F. 7 (1894), 60–7.

Traversi, Derek A. *An Approach to Shakespeare.* 3rd, rev. enl. ed. New York, 1969. ("Measure for Measure" first pub. in *Scrutiny* 11 [1942], 40–58.)

Trewin, J[ohn] C. *The Birmingham Repertory Theatre, 1913–1963.* 1963.

―――. *John Neville.* 1961.

―――. *Peter Brook.* 1971.

―――. *A Play To-night.* 1952.

―――. *See* Kemp, T[homas] C.

Trombetta, James. "Versions of Dying in *Measure for Measure.*" *ELR* 6 (1976), 60–76.

Turnbull, Andrew D. "Motifs of Bedmate Substitution and Their Reconciliatory Functions in Shakespearean and Jacobean Drama." *DAI* 38 (1977), 2148A. (Indiana.)

Tynan, Kenneth. *He That Plays the King.* 1950.

Tyrwhitt, Thomas (1730–86). Contributor to v1773, v1778, v1785.

―――. *Observations and Conjectures upon Some Passages of Shakespeare.* Oxford, 1766. (Rpt. London: Cass, 1969.)

Ulrici, Hermann. *Shakspeare's Dramatic Art.* Tr. A. J. W. M[orrison]. 1846. (1st Ger. ed. 1839.) Tr. L. Dora Schmitz. 2 vols. 1876 (from 3rd, rev. Ger. ed., 3 pts., 1868–9.)

Underhill, Arthur. "Law." *Shakespeare's England.* 2 vols. OUP, 1916. 1:381–412.

Upham, Alfred H. *The French Influence in English Literature.* Columbia Univ. Stud. in Comp. Lit. New York, 1908.

Upton, John. *Critical Observations on Shakespeare.* 1746. 2nd ed. 1748. (Rpt. of 1748 ed. New York: AMS, 1973.)

Ure, Peter. *William Shakespeare: The Problem Plays.* Writers and Their Work 140. 1961. (Rpt. in *Shakespeare: The Writer and His Work,* 1964.)

Urnow, Dmitrij M. "Puschkin und Shakespeares *Mass für Mass.*" *SJW* 105 (1969), 140–57.

Van Dam, B[astiaan] A. P., & C. Stoffel. *William Shakespeare, Prosody and Text.* Leyden, 1900.

Van Doren, Mark. *Shakespeare.* New York, 1939.

van Kaam, Adrian, & Kathleen Healy. "Angelo in Shakespeare's *Measure for Measure.*" *The Demon and the Dove: Personality Growth through Literature.* Pittsburgh, 1967. Pp. 139–67.

Van Laan, Thomas F. *Role-Playing in Shakespeare.* Toronto, 1978.

Van Lennep, William, ed. *The London Stage, 1660–1800. Part 1 (1660–1700).* Carbondale, 1965.

Vehse, Eduard. *Shakespeare als Protestant, Politiker, Psycholog und Dichter.* 2 vols. Hamburg, 1851.

Velie, Alan R. *Shakespeare's Repentance Plays: The Search for an Adequate Form.* Rutherford, N.J., 1972. (Stanford diss.)

Velz, John W. "The Grotesque and the Comedic in Shakespeare." *ShN* 26, No. 5 (1976), p. 33 [41].

———. *Shakespeare and the Classical Tradition: A Critical Guide to Commentary, 1660–1960.* Minneapolis, 1968.

———. "Shakespeare's Vienna as a Modern World." *English* 21 (1972), 89–91.

Velz, Sarah C. "Man's Need and God's Plan in 'Measure for Measure' and Mark iv." *ShS* 25 (1972), 37–44.

Venezky, Alice S. *Pageantry on the Shakespearean Stage.* New York, 1951. (Rpt. as by Alice V. Griffin, New Haven, 1962. Columbia diss.)

Vessie, P. R. "Psychiatry Catches up with Shakespeare." *Medical Record* 144 (1936), 141–5.

Vickers, Brian. *The Artistry of Shakespeare's Prose.* 1968.

Vincent, Jeffrey S. "Jacobean Intrigue Comedy." *DAI* 35 (1975), 6685A–6A. (Rutgers.)

Vroonland, Jewell K. "Mannerism and Shakespeare's 'Problem Plays': An Argument for Revaluation." *DAI* 30 (1969), 2502A–3A. (Kansas State.)

Vyvyan, John. *Shakespeare and the Rose of Love.* London & New York, 1960.

———. *The Shakespearean Ethic.* 1959.

Wagner, Hugh K. *"Measure for Measure": A Review.* Belleville, Ill., 1934.

Wagner, Richard. *Das Liebesverbot. The Ban on Love. La Défense d'Aimer.* Ed. Otto Singer, Eng. tr. Edward Dent, French tr. Amédée et Frieda Boutarel. Sämtlichen Musikdramen 12. Leipzig, 1922.

Wahl, M. C. "Das parömiologische Sprachgut bei Shakespeare." *SJ* 22 (1887), 45–130; 23 (1888), 21–98.

Wain, John. *The Living World of Shakespeare: A Playgoer's Guide.* 1964.

Walker, William Sidney. *A Critical Examination of the Text of Shakespeare.* [Ed. W. N. Lettsom.] 3 vols. 1860.

———. *Shakespeare's Versification.* [Ed. W. N. Lettsom]. 1854.

Walkley, A[rthur] B. *Drama and Life.* 1907.

Walters, C. Flamstead. "Italian Influence on Shakespeare." *Gentleman's Magazine* 279 (1895), 571–84.

Warburton, William. MS notes in Johnson ed. 1765 at Folger Library.

———. *See* Bennet, Norman.

Ward, A[dolphus] W. *A History of English Dramatic Literature to the Death of Queen Anne.* Rev. ed. 3 vols. 1899. (1st ed., 2 vols., 1875.)

Warren, Clyde T. *See* Clarkson, Paul S.

Wasson, John. "*Measure for Measure:* A Play of Incontinence." *ELH* 27 (1960), 262–75.

_____. "*Measure for Measure:* A Text for Court Performance?" *SQ* 21 (1970), 17–24.

Watkins, W[alter] B. C. *Shakespeare & Spenser.* Princeton, 1950.

Watson, Curtis B. *Shakespeare and the Renaissance Concept of Honor.* Princeton, 1960.

_____. "Shakspere's Dukes." *ShAB* 16 (1941), 33–41.

[Watson, Frederick B.] *Religious and Moral Sentences Culled from the Works of Shakespeare, Compared with Sacred Passages Drawn from Holy Writ.* 1843.

Weber, Elisabeth. *Das Oxymoron bei Shakespeare.* Hamburg, 1963.

Webster, Margaret. *Don't Put Your Daughter on the Stage.* New York, 1972.

_____. *Shakespeare Today.* 1957. (1st pub. as *Shakespeare without Tears,* New York, 1942.)

Weil, Herbert S., Jr. "Form and Contexts in *Measure for Measure.*" *CritQ* 12 (1970), 55–72.

_____. "The Options of the Audience: Theory and Practice in Peter Brook's 'Measure for Measure'." *ShS* 25 (1972), 27–35.

_____. "Shakespeare's Comic Control in *Measure for Measure:* Sub-plot as Key to Dramatic Design." *DA* 25 (1965), 5289. (Stanford.)

Weilgart, Wolfgang J. *Shakespeare Psychognostic: Character Evolution and Transformation.* Tokyo, 1952. (Rpt. New York: AMS, 1972.)

Weinthal, Ada. "Shakespeare's Ironic Use of Sources in Five Comedies." *DAI* 37 (1977), 6520A. (Toronto.)

Weiser, David K. "The Ironic Hierarchy in *Measure for Measure.*" *Texas Stud. in Lit. and Lang.* 19 (1977), 323–47.

Weisstein, Ulrich. "Two Measures for One: Brecht's *Die Rundköpfe und die Spitzköpfe* and Its Shakespearean Model." *GR* 43 (1968), 24–39.

Wellesley, Henry. *Stray Notes on the Text of Shakespeare.* 1865.

Wells, Stanley. "Happy Endings in Shakespeare." *SJH,* 1966, pp. 103–23.

Wendell, Barrett. *William Shakspere: A Study in Elizabethan Literature.* New York, 1894. (Rpt. Folcroft, Pa., 1973.)

Wentersdorf, Karl. "Shakespearean Chronology and the Metrical Tests." *Shakespeare-Studien. Festschrift für Heinrich Mutschmann.* Ed. Walther Fischer & Karl Wentersdorf. Marburg, 1951. Pp. 161–93.

_____. *See* Mutschmann, Heinrich.

West, E[dward] J. "Dramatist at the Crossroads (A Suggestion concerning *Measure for Measure*)." *ShAB* 22 (1947), 136–41.

West, Rebecca. *The Court and the Castle.* New Haven, 1957.

Whalley, Peter (1722–91). Contributor to v1785.

_____. *An Enquiry into the Learning of Shakespeare.* 1748. (Rpt. London: Cass, 1967.)

Wheatley, Henry B. "*Measure for Measure.* Act III., sc. 1." *Antiquary* 8 (1883), 200–1.

Whetstone, George. *An Heptameron of Ciuill Discourses.* 1582.

_____. *Promos and Cassandra.* 1578.

Whitaker, Virgil K. "Philosophy and Romance in Shakespeare's 'Problem' Comedies." In *The Seventeenth Century.* Ed. R. F. Jones. Stanford, 1951. Pp. 339–54.

_____. *Shakespeare's Use of Learning.* San Marino, Calif., 1953.

White, Edward J. *Commentaries on the Law in Shakespeare.* St. Louis, 1911.

White, Eric. "Early Theatrical Performances of Purcell's Operas." *ThN* 13 (1959), 43–65.

White, R. S., Jr. MS notes dated 1799 in Folger Library copy 2 of Malone ed. 1790.

White, Richard Grant. *Shakespeare's Scholar.* New York, 1854.

_____. *Studies in Shakespeare.* Boston, 1885. (Rpt. of 1887 ed. New York: AMS, 1973.)

White, Thomas (1771–?, of Pembroke Hall, Cambridge). "More Notes on Shakespeare!!! Written in the year 1793." MS at Birmingham Public Library. (Printed inaccurately in *The Shakespeare Repository,* ed. James H. Fennell, 1853, pp. 14–15, 20–1, 29–31; rpt. New York: AMS, 1974.)

White, Thomas Holt (1763–1841). Contributor to v1793.

_____. "Parallel Passages and Remarks on *Shakspeare.*" *Gentleman's Magazine* 55 (1785), 277–8.

Whiter, Walter. *A Specimen of a Commentary on Shakspeare.* 1794. (Rpt. Menston: Scolar, 1972. 2nd, rev. enl. ed., ed. Alan Over & Mary Bell, 1967.)

Whiting, B[artlett] J., & Helen W. Whiting. *Proverbs, Sentences, and Proverbial Phrases: From English Writings Mainly Before 1500.* Cambridge, Mass., 1968.

Whittaker, Herbert. "Introduction." *The Stratford Festival, 1953–1957: A Record in Pictures and Text of the Shakespearean Festival in Canada.* Toronto, 1958.

Wiles, R[oy] M. "*Measure for Measure:* Failure in the Study, Triumph on the Stage." *Proc. and Trans. of the Royal Soc. of Canada,* 4th ser., 2 (1964), 181–93.

Wilkes, George. *Shakespeare, from an American Point of View.* 3rd, rev. ed. New York, 1882. (1st ed. London, 1876.)

Willcock, J[ohn]. "Shakespeariana: 'Measure for Measure', [2671–2]." 11 *N&Q* 11 (1915), 27–8.

Williams, Charles. *The English Poetic Mind.* OUP, 1932. (Rpt. New York: Russell, 1963.)

_____. *He Came Down from Heaven,* and *The Forgiveness of Sins.* 1950. (*The Forgiveness of Sins* 1st pub. 1942.)

Williams, Harcourt. *Old Vic Saga.* 1949.

Williams, Haydn M. "Metaphysical Elements in Two Problem Comedies: *All's Well & Measure for Measure.*" *Shakespeare: A Book of Homage.* Jadavpur Univ., Calcutta, 1965. Pp. 21–49.

Williams, J. M., ed. *The Dramatic Censor: or, Critical and Biographical Illustration of the British Stage. For the Year 1811.* [1812.]

Williams, J[ohn] D. E. *Sir William Davenant's Relation to Shakespeare.* Liverpool, 1905. (Strassburg diss.)

Williams, W. W. Contributor to Collier ed. 1858.

_____. "Notes on 'Measure for Measure'." *The Parthenon* 1 (1862), 442.

Williamson, Audrey. *Old Vic Drama.* 1948.

_____. *Theatre of Two Decades.* 1951.

Williamson, Jane. "The Duke and Isabella on the Modern Stage." In *The Triple Bond.* Ed. Joseph G. Price. University Park, Pa., & London, 1975. Pp. 149–69.

Williamson, Marilyn L. "Oedipal Fantasies in *Measure for Measure.*" *Michigan Academician* 9 (1976), 173–84.

Wilson, A[lbert] E. *Edwardian Theatre.* 1950.

Wilson, F[rank] P. *Elizabethan and Jacobean.* OUP, 1945.

_____. "Ralph Crane, Scrivener to the King's Players." 4 *Library* 7 (1926), 194–215.

_____, ed. *The Oxford Dictionary of English Proverbs.* 3rd ed. OUP, 1970.

Wilson, Harold S. "Action and Symbol in *Measure for Measure* and *The Tempest.*" *SQ* 4 (1953), 375–84. (Rpt. in *Shakespeare: Modern Essays in Criticism,* ed. Leonard Dean, New York: OUP, 1957, pp. 267–81.)

Wilson, J[ohn] Dover. *The Essential Shakespeare.* Cambridge, 1932.

Wilson, Robert H. "The Mariana Plot of *Measure for Measure.*" *PQ* 9 (1930), 341–50.

Winny, James. "A Shakespeare Emendation." *TLS,* 18 Apr. 1958, p. 209.

Winstanley, Lilian. *Hamlet and the Scottish Succession.* 1921.

Winter, William. *The Wallet of Time.* 2 vols. New York, 1913.

Witting, Clifford. *Measure for Murder.* New York & London, 1976. (1st ed. 1941.)

Wolf, Adolf. "Volkslieder aus Venetien." *Sitzungsberichte der Philosophisch-Historischen Classe der Kaiserlichen Akademie der Wissenschaften* (Wien) 46 (1864), 257–379.

Wolf, William D. " 'Dark Deeds Darkly Answered': Romantic Comedy and Measure for Measure." *ShN* 26, No. 4 (1976), 33.

Wolff, Max J. *Shakespeare: Der Dichter und sein Werk.* 2 vols. München, 1907.

————. "Shakespeare und die Commedia dell' arte." *SJ* 46 (1910), 1–20.

Wolff, Tatiana A. "Shakespeare's Influence on Pushkin's Dramatic Work." *ShS* 5 (1952), 93–105.

Wordsworth, Charles. *Shakspeare's Knowledge and Use of the Bible.* 2nd, enl. ed. 1864; 3rd, rev. enl. ed. 1880. (1st ed. 1864. Rpt. of 1880 ed. New York: AMS, 1973.)

Worsley, T[homas] C. *The Fugitive Art: Dramatic Commentaries, 1947–1951.* 1952.

Wurth, Leopold. *Das Wortspiel bei Shakspere.* Wiener Beiträge 1. Wien & Leipzig, 1895.

Yeats, W. B., ed. *Samhain, An Occasional Review, Edited by W. B. Yeats, Containing Notes by the Editor.* Dublin & London, 1901–8. (Rpt. 1970, Eng. Little Magazines 14, and rpt. of note in *Uncollected Prose,* ed. John P. Frayne & Colton Johnson, New York, 1970–6, 2:374.)

Young, George. *An English Prosody on Inductive Lines.* Cambridge, 1928.

Yuckman, Paul A. "A Pretie Parcell of Popery: Studies in the Problem Plays." *DAI* 36 (1975), 1542A. (Ohio Univ.)

Zeeveld, W. Gordon. *The Temper of Shakespeare's Thought.* New Haven, 1974.

Ziino, Giuseppe. *Shakespeare e la scienza moderna: Studio medico-psicologico e giuridico.* Palermo, 1897.

INDEX

INDEX

Compiled by Vivian Foss and Mark Eccles

SIGLA AND SYMBOLS
IN THE TEXTUAL NOTES

The following list will help to identify editors and to locate sigla in their chronological sequence. Sigla in parentheses refer to works only occasionally consulted; they are listed on the opposite page below the list of editions collated. For full descriptions of the works, see pp. xii ff.

ALEX	Alexander, 1951	KTLY	Keightley, 1864
ARD	ARD1 & ARD2	MAL	Malone, 1790
ARD1	Hart, 1905	(mF2FL)	Anon., –1733
ARD2	Lever, 1965	(mSTAU)	Staunton, –1874
(BLAIR)	Blair, 1753	(mTHEO)	Theobald, 1723–33
BUL	Bullen, 1904	(mTBY1, 2, 3)	Thirlby, 1723–33,
CAM	CAM1, CAM2, & CAM3		1733–47, 1747–53
CAM1	Clark, Glover, & Wright,	(N&H)	Neilson-Hill, 1942
	1863	NLSN	Neilson, 1906
CAM2	Wright, 1891	(OXF1)	Craig, [1891]
CAM3	Wilson, 1922	PEL1	Bald, 1956
CAP	Capell, 1767	PEN2	Nosworthy, 1969
(CAPN)	Capell, 1779–83	POPE	POPE1 & POPE2
(CLN2)	Houghton, 1970	POPE1, 2	Pope, 1723, 1728
COL	COL1, (COL2), COL3, &	RANN	Rann, 1786
	COL4	(RID)	Ridley, 1935
COL1, (2), 3,	Collier, 1842, 1853, 1858,	(RLF1)	Rolfe, 1882
4	1875	(RLTR)	Chambers, 1906
(COLNE)	Collier, 1853	ROWE	ROWE1, ROWE2, &
(COT)	Cotgrave, 1655		ROWE3
(DAV)	Davenant, 1673	ROWE1, 2, 3	Rowe, 1709, 1709, 1714
DEL4	Delius, 1872	SING	SING1 & SING2
DYCE	DYCE1, DYCE2, & DYCE3	SING1, 2	Singer, 1826, 1856
DYCE1, 2, 3	Dyce, 1857, 1864, 1875	SIS	Sisson, 1954
(EV1)	Herford, 1899	STAU	Staunton, 1859
EVNS	Evans, 1974	THEO	THEO1, THEO2, & THEO4
Ff	F1, F2, F3, & F4	THEO1, 2, 4	Theobald, 1733, 1740,
F1, 2, 3, 4	Folios, 1623, 1632,		1757
	1663–4, 1685	(TIECK)	Tieck, 1831
(GIL)	Gildon, 1700	v1773,	Johnson & Steevens,
GLO	Clark & Wright, 1864	v1778	1773, 1778
HAL	Halliwell, 1854	v1785	Johnson, Steevens, &
HAN1, (2)	Hanmer, 1743, 1745		Reed, 1785
(HARN)	Harness, 1825	v1793	Steevens & Reed, 1793
(HENL)	Henley, 1901	v1803,	Reed, 1803, 1813
HUD(1), 2	Hudson, 1851, 1880	v1813	
IRV	Irving & Marshall, 1889	v1821	Boswell, 1821
JOHN	JOHN1 & JOHN2	(VERP)	Verplanck, 1847
JOHN1, 2	Johnson, 1765, 1765	WARB	Warburton, 1747
KIT1	Kittredge, 1936	WH	WH1 & WH2
KNT	KNT1, KNT2, & KNT3	WH1, 2	White, 1857, 1883
KNT1, 2, 3	Knight, 1840, 1842, 1867		

Symbols used in the textual notes:

^	punctuation missing or omitted
~	verbal form of lemma unchanged (while punctuation varies)
-	(between sigla) all fully collated eds. between and including those indicated by the two sigla
+	(after a siglum) and all succeeding fully collated eds.
(−)	all sigla following the minus sign within parentheses indicate eds. that agree, not with the variant, but with the Variorum text (i.e., with F1)